Adobe® Creative Suite® 5 Design Premium
ALL-IN-ONE
FOR DUMMIES®

by Jennifer Smith, Christopher Smith, and Fred Gerantabee

WILEY

Wiley Publishing, Inc.

Adobe® Creative Suite® 5 Design Premium All-in-One For Dummies®

Published by
Wiley Publishing, Inc.
111 River Street
Hoboken, NJ 07030-5774
www.wiley.com

Copyright © 2010 by Wiley Publishing, Inc., Indianapolis, Indiana

Published by Wiley Publishing, Inc., Indianapolis, Indiana

Published simultaneously in Canada

For general information on our other products and services, please contact our Customer Care Department within the U.S. at 877-762-2974, outside the U.S. at 317-572-3993, or fax 317-572-4002.

For technical support, please visit www.wiley.com/techsupport.

Wiley also publishes its books in a variety of electronic formats. Some content that appears in print may not be available in electronic books.

Library of Congress Control Number: 2010928474

ISBN: 978-0-470-60746-6

Manufactured in the United States of America

10 9 8 7 6 5 4 3 2 1

WILEY

About the Authors

Jennifer Smith is the co-founder and Vice President of Aquent Graphics Institute (AGI). She has authored numerous books on Adobe's software products, including development of many of the Adobe *Classroom in a Book* titles. She regularly speaks at conferences and seminars, including the CRE8 Conference. Jennifer has worked in all aspects of graphic design and production, including as an art director of an advertising agency. Jennifer combines her practical experience and technical expertise as an educator. She has developed training programs for Adobe Systems and for all types of designers involved in creating print, Web, and interactive solutions, along with designers creating fashion and apparel. Her teaching and writing style show the clear direction of a practiced designer with in-depth knowledge of the Adobe Creative Suite applications. When she's not speaking or teaching, she can be found in suburban Boston, Massachusetts, with her husband and five children. You can read about Jennifer's seminar and conference appearances at www.agitraining.com.

Christopher Smith is president of the American Graphics Institute. He is the author of more than ten books on Web, interactive, and print publishing technology, including many of Adobe's official training guides. Christopher is also the creator and editor of the *Digital Classroom* series of books, published by Wiley, which are widely used by schools that teach creative software tools. Learn more about American Graphics Institute's training programs at www.agitraining.com or follow them on Twitter @agitraining. You can follow Christopher on Twitter @cgsmith or read his blog posts at www.agitraining.com/blogs.

Fred Gerantabee is an Emmy award–winning interactive designer, Web developer, and author based in New York City. Fred has been involved in Web design and development since 1996, and has authored/coauthored over a dozen books and videos on Web design and development, including the *Flash CS5 Professional Digital Classroom* from Wiley. Widely considered a "go to" expert on Flash ActionScript, Dreamweaver, and HTML/CSS, Fred continues to explore new technologies in the field, as well as speak at industry conferences and events. Fred lives by the beach in New York with his wife, Samantha, dog Q, and several guitars that have yet to been named. Drop him a line at www.fgerantabee.com.

Authors' Acknowledgments

Jennifer Smith: Thanks to all our friends and colleagues at Adobe Systems for their support and the many product team members who responded to our questions throughout the writing process. Extra thanks to Ron Friedman and Lori Defurio of Adobe Systems for their inspiration and encouragement.

To the highly professional instructional staff at Aquent Graphics Institute (AGI), we appreciate your great insight into the best ways to help others discover creative software applications.

Thanks to all at Wiley Publishing and to our technical editor Cathy Auclair for her great insight.

Grant, Elizabeth, and Edward — thanks for putting up with our long hours in front of the keyboard night after night.

Thanks to all of Kelly and Alex's friends for permission to use their photos.

Christopher Smith: Thanks to my many colleagues at AGI and Avlade who assisted in making this and so many of our other books possible. Especially Greg and Jeremy for assistance with technical details and reader inquiries, Chris for making us always sound and look good, to Jaime and Andrea for making sure our clients receive the best care possible, and Peter for making certain we all get paid. A special thank you to my two co-authors, Jennifer and Fred, it's a pleasure and honor to work with such talented and articulate individuals. Merci beaucoup to Mademoiselle Nathalie for her expert guidance as we bring our work to a wider audience internationally.

Fred Gerantabee: Fred would like to thank Amy Fandrei, Kim Darosett, Becky Whitney, and the excellent team at Wiley publishing. Thank you to Christopher and Jennifer Smith and the AGI team; Robin Rusch, James Wu, and my colleagues at BrandWizard Technologies & Interbrand in New York. Carisa Gasser of Jambone Creative; the brothers of APD; my mom Francine Gray, Cindy and Michael Urich, my wife Samantha for her love and support. In loving memory of Michael Gueran.

Publisher's Acknowledgments

We're proud of this book; please send us your comments at http://dummies.custhelp.com. For other comments, please contact our Customer Care Department within the U.S. at 877-762-2974, outside the U.S. at 317-572-3993, or fax 317-572-4002.

Some of the people who helped bring this book to market include the following:

Acquisitions and Editorial

Project Editor: Kim Darosett

Acquisitions Editor: Amy Fandrei

Copy Editor: Rebecca Whitney

Technical Editor: Cathy Auclair

Editorial Manager: Leah Cameron

Editorial Assistant: Amanda Graham

Sr. Editorial Assistant: Cherie Case

Cartoons: Rich Tennant
(www.the5thwave.com)

Composition Services

Project Coordinator: Katherine Crocker

Layout and Graphics: Claudia Bell, Ashley Chamberlain, Joyce Haughey

Proofreaders: John Greenough, Evelyn Wellborn

Indexer: BIM Indexing & Proofreading Services

Contribution: *Flash Professional CS5 & Flash Catalyst CS5 For Dummies,* Ellen Finkelstein and Gurdy Leete. Copyright © 2010 by Wiley Publishing Inc., Indianapolis, Indiana

Reproduced with permission of John Wiley & Sons, Inc.

Publishing and Editorial for Technology Dummies

    Richard Swadley, Vice President and Executive Group Publisher

    Andy Cummings, Vice President and Publisher

    Mary Bednarek, Executive Acquisitions Director

    Mary C. Corder, Editorial Director

Publishing for Consumer Dummies

    Diane Graves Steele, Vice President and Publisher

Composition Services

    Debbie Stailey, Director of Composition Services

Contents at a Glance

Table of Contents

Introduction

Adobe software has always been highly respected for creative design and development. Adobe creates programs that allow you to produce amazing designs and creations with ease. The Adobe Creative Suite 5 (CS5) Design Premium is the company's latest release of sophisticated and professional-level software that bundles many separate programs as a suite. Each program in the suite works individually, or you can integrate the programs by using *Version Cue*, the Adobe work management software that helps keep track of revisions and edits, and *Adobe Bridge*, an independent program that helps you control file management with thumbnails and metadata and other organizational tools.

You can use the Adobe CS5 Design Premium programs to create a wide range of products, from illustrations, page layouts, and professional documents to Web sites and photographic manipulations. Integrating the CS5 programs extends the possibilities for you as a designer. Don't worry about the programs being too difficult to figure out — just come up with your ideas and start creating!

About This Book

Adobe Creative Suite 5 Design Premium All-in-One For Dummies is written in a thorough and fun way to show you the basic steps of how to use each program included in the suite. You find out how to use each program individually and how to work with the programs together, letting you extend your projects even further. You find out just how easy it is to use the programs by following simple steps so that you can discover the power of the Adobe software. You'll be up and running in no time!

Here are some things you can do with this book:

✦ Create page layouts using text, drawings, and images in InDesign.

✦ Make illustrations using drawing tools with Illustrator.

✦ Manipulate photographs using filters and drawing or color correction tools with Photoshop.

✦ Create PDF (Portable Document Format) documents with Adobe Acrobat or other programs.

✦ Create Web pages and put them online with Dreamweaver.

✦ Create animations and videos with Flash.

✦ Create Web images, rollovers, image maps, and slices with Fireworks.

You discover the basics of how to create all these different kinds of things throughout the chapters in this book in fun, hands-on examples and clear explanations, getting you up to speed quickly!

Foolish Assumptions

You don't need to know much before picking up this book and getting started with the Design Premium suite. All you have to know is how to use a computer in a very basic way. If you can turn on the computer and use a mouse, you're ready for this book. A bit of knowledge about basic computer operations and using software helps, but it isn't necessary. We show you how to open, save, create, and manipulate files using the CS5 programs so that you can start working with the programs quickly. The most important ingredient to have is your imagination and creativity — we show you how to get started with the rest.

Conventions Used in This Book

Adobe CS5 Design Premium is available for both Windows and the Macintosh. We cover both platforms in this book. Where the keys you need to press or the menu choice you need to make differs between Windows and the Mac, we let you know by including instructions for both platforms. For example:

✦ Press the Alt (Windows) or Option (Mac) key.

✦ Choose Edit⇨Preferences⇨General (Windows) or InDesign⇨ Preferences⇨General (Mac).

The programs in Design Premium Suite often require you to press and hold down a key (or keys) on the keyboard and then click or drag with the mouse. For brevity's sake, we shorten this action by naming the key you need to hold down and adding a click or drag, like this:

✦ Shift-click to select multiple files.

✦ Move the object by Ctrl-dragging (Windows) or ⌘-dragging (Mac).

Here are the formatting conventions used in this book:

✦ **Bold:** We use **bold** to indicate when you should type something or to highlight an action in a step list. For example, the action required to open a dialog box would appear in bold in a step list.

✦ `Code font:` We use this computerese font to show you Web addresses (URLs), e-mail addresses, and bits of HTML code. For example, you type a URL into a browser window to access a Web page, such as `www.google.com`.

✦ *Italics:* We use *italics* to highlight a new term, which we then define. For example, *filters* may be a new term to you. The word itself is italicized and is followed by a definition to explain what the word means.

What You Don't Have to Read

This book is pretty thick; you may wonder whether you have to read it from cover to cover. You don't have to read every page of this book to discover how to use the programs in the Design Premium Suite. Luckily, you can choose bits and pieces that mean the most to you and will help you finish a project you may be working on. Perhaps you're interested in creating a technical drawing and putting it online. You can choose to read a couple chapters in Book III on Illustrator and then skip ahead to Book VI on Dreamweaver and just read the relevant chapters or sections on each subject. Later, you may want to place some associated PDF documents online, so read a few chapters in Book V on Acrobat or Book II on exporting InDesign documents. Find out how to create animations for the Web and video in Book VII covering Flash.

You don't have to read everything on each page, either. You can treat many of the icons in this book as bonus material. Icons supplement the material in each chapter with additional information that may interest or help you with your work. The Technical Stuff icons are helpful if you want to find out a bit more about technical aspects of using the program or your computer, but don't feel that you need to read these icon paragraphs if technicalities don't interest you.

How This Book Is Organized

Adobe Creative Suite 5 Design Premium All-in-One For Dummies is split into eight quick-reference guides, or minibooks. You don't have to read these minibooks sequentially, and you don't even have to read all the sections in any particular chapter. You can use the table of contents and the index to find the information you need and quickly get your answer. In this section, we briefly describe what you find in each minibook.

Book I: Adobe Creative Suite 5 Basics

Book I shows you how to use the features in Design Premium programs that are similar across all the programs described in this book. You discover the menus, panels, and tools that are similar or work the same way in most of the CS5 programs. You also find out how to import and export and use common commands in each program. If you're wondering about what short-cuts and common tools you can use in the programs to speed up your work-flow, this part has tips and tricks you'll find quite useful. The similarities in all the programs are helpful because they make using the programs that much easier.

Book II: InDesign CS5

Book II describes how to use InDesign CS5 to create simple page layouts with text, images, and drawings. Hands-on steps show you how to use the drawing tools in InDesign to create illustrations and also use other menus and tools to add text and pictures. Importing stories and illustrations into InDesign is an important part of the process, so you find out how this task is done effectively as well. Book II shows you how easily you can create effec-tive page layouts with this powerful and professional design program.

Book III: Illustrator CS5

Book III starts with the fundamentals of Adobe Illustrator CS5 to help you create useful and interesting illustrations. Check out this minibook to dis-cover how to take advantage of features that have been around for many versions of Illustrator, such as the Pen tool, as well as new and exciting fea-tures, such as vector tracing. See how to take advantage of the Appearance panel and save time by creating graphical styles, templates, and symbols. Pick up hard-to-find keyboard shortcuts that can help reduce the time you spend mousing around for menu items and tools.

Book IV: Photoshop CS5

Book IV on Photoshop CS5 is aimed to help you achieve good imagery, start-ing with basics that even advanced users may have missed along the way. In this minibook, you find out how to color correct images like a pro and use tools to keep images at the right resolution and size, no matter whether the image is intended for print or the Web.

This minibook also shows you how to integrate new features in Photoshop, such as the new Adjustments panel and Masks panel, as well as inform you of the new 3D tools. By the time you're finished with this minibook, you'll feel like you can perform magic on just about any image.

Book V: Acrobat 9.0

Adobe Acrobat 9.0 is a powerful viewing and editing program that allows you to share documents with colleagues, clients, and production personnel, such as printers and Web-page designers. Book V shows you how you can save time and money previously spent on couriers and overnight shipping by taking advantage of annotation capabilities. Discover features that even advanced users may have missed along the way and see how you can feel comfortable about using PDF as a file format of choice.

Book VI: Dreamweaver CS5

Book VI shows you how creating a Web site in Dreamweaver CS5 can be easy and fun. Take advantage of the tools and features in Dreamweaver to make and maintain quite a clean and usable site. Discover how to take advantage of improved Cascading Style Sheets (CSS) capabilities as well as exciting roll-over and action features that add interactivity to your site. In the past, these functions required lots of hand-coding and tape on the glasses, but now you can be a designer and create interactivity easily in Dreamweaver — no hand-coding or pocket protectors required.

Book VII: Flash Professional CS5

Find out how to create interactive animations for the Web and video with Flash CS5. Start with the basics, such as creating simple animations with tweening, all the way up to animations that allow for user interaction. This Timeline-based program may be different from anything you've ever worked with, but Flash is sure to be an exciting program to discover.

Book VIII: Fireworks CS5

As the newest addition to the suite, Fireworks CS5 offers you the capabilities you need to create virtually any sort of Web graphic. By using Fireworks, you can optimize (prepare for the Web) images and graphics as well as create cool rollover effects and sliced graphics. Find out in Book VIII how to spice up your Web site with buttons, image maps, and more!

Icons Used in This Book

What's a *For Dummies* book without icons pointing you in the direction of truly helpful information that's sure to help you along your way? In this section, we briefly describe each icon we use in this book.

The Tip icon points out helpful information that's likely to make your job easier.

 This icon marks a generally interesting and useful fact — something you may want to remember for later use.

 The Warning icon highlights lurking danger. When we use this icon, we're telling you to pay attention and proceed with caution.

 When you see this icon, you know that there's techie-type material nearby. If you're not feeling technical-minded, you can skip this information.

Where to Go from Here

Adobe Creative Suite 5 Design Premium All-in-One For Dummies is designed so that you can read a chapter or section out of order, depending on what subjects you're most interested in. Where you go from here is entirely up to you!

Book I is a great place to start reading if you've never used Adobe products or if you're new to design-based software. Discovering the common terminology, menus, and panels can be quite helpful for later chapters that use the terms and commands regularly!

Book I

Adobe Creative Suite 5 Basics

Contents at a Glance

Chapter 1: Introducing Adobe Creative Suite 5

In This Chapter

✔ Looking over InDesign CS5

✔ Drawing with Illustrator CS5

✔ Introducing Photoshop CS5

✔ Getting started with Acrobat 9.0

✔ Creating Web sites with Dreamweaver CS5

✔ Getting into Flash Professional CS5 and Flash Catalyst CS5

✔ Getting fired up with Fireworks CS5

✔ Putting Adobe Bridge into your workflow

✔ Integrating the programs in Adobe CS5

*W*ith the Adobe Creative Suite 5 (CS5) Design Premium release, you get not only the tools you need to be creative for print and the Web but also Adobe Fireworks, to make Web sites more attractive than ever.

The diverse software in Adobe CS5 Design Premium enables you to create everything from an interactive e-commerce Web site to a printed book. Each piece of software in the Adobe Creative Suite works on its own as a robust tool. Combine all the applications, including Adobe Bridge, and you have a dynamic workflow that just can't be matched.

In this minibook, you see the many features that are consistent among the applications in the suite. You find consistencies in color, file formats, and text editing as well as general preferences for rulers and guides throughout all applications in CS5. This minibook also shows you where to find the new features and how to save time by taking advantage of them.

In this chapter, you meet each of the components in Adobe CS5 Design Premium and discover what you can create with each of these powerful tools.

Introducing InDesign CS5

InDesign is a diverse and feature-rich page layout program. With InDesign, you can create beautifully laid-out page designs. You can also execute complete control over your images and export them to interactive documents, such as Acrobat PDF. You can use InDesign to

✦ Use images, text, and even rich media to create unique layouts and designs.

✦ Import native files from Photoshop and Illustrator to help build rich layouts in InDesign that take advantage of transparency and blending modes.

✦ Export your work as an entire book, including chapters, sections, automatically numbered pages, and more.

✦ Create interactive PDF documents.

✦ Create drawings with the basic drawing tools included in the software.

InDesign caters to the layout professional, but it's easy enough for even beginners to use. You can import text from word processing programs (such as Microsoft Word, Notepad, or Adobe InCopy) as well as tables (say, from Microsoft Excel) into your documents and place them alongside existing artwork and images to create a layout. In a nutshell, importing, arranging, and exporting work is a common process when working with InDesign. Throughout this entire process, you have a large amount of control over your work, whether you're working on a simple one-page brochure or an entire book of 800-plus pages.

If you're already using InDesign, read Book II, Chapter 1 to find out about some of the new features in CS5. InDesign CS5 has new features for creating Web pages and interactive documents. Interactive documents that used to be created only in Flash or Web pages that used to be created only by using Dreamweaver can now be developed using InDesign.

Using Illustrator CS5

Adobe Illustrator is the industry's leading vector-based graphics software. Aimed at everyone from graphics professionals to Web users, Illustrator allows you to design layouts, logos for print, or vector-based images that can be imported into other programs, such as Photoshop, InDesign, or even Flash. Adobe also enables you to easily and quickly create files by saving Illustrator documents as templates (so that you can efficiently reuse designs) and using a predefined library and document size.

Illustrator also integrates with the other products in the Adobe Creative Suite by allowing you to create PDF documents easily within Illustrator. In addition, you can use Illustrator files in Photoshop, InDesign, and the Adobe special effects program After Effects. Illustrator allows you to beef up your rich interactive documents by introducing Flash features that give you the tools you need to build exciting interactive designs in Flash.

Here are some of the things you can create and do in Illustrator:

✦ Create technical drawings (floor plans or architectural sketches, for example), logos, illustrations, posters, packaging, and Web graphics.

✦ Add effects, such as drop shadows and Gaussian blurs, to vector images.

✦ Enhance artwork by creating your own, custom brushes.

✦ Align text along a path so that it bends in an interesting way.

✦ Lay out text into multicolumn brochures — text automatically flows from one column to the next.

✦ Create charts and graphs using graphing tools.

✦ Create gradients that can be imported and edited into other programs, such as InDesign.

✦ Create documents quickly and easily using existing templates and included stock graphics in Illustrator.

✦ Save a drawing in almost any graphic format, including Adobe's PDF, PSD, EPS, TIFF, GIF, JPEG, and SVG formats.

✦ Save your Illustrator files for the Web by using the Save for Web & Devices dialog box, which allows you to output GIF, HTML, and JPEG files.

✦ Save Illustrator files as secure PDF files with 128-bit encryption.

✦ Export assets as symbols to Flash.

Illustrator has many new features for you to investigate, many of them integrated in the chapters in Book III. Find out about new tools, including the new perspective grid, stroke, and gradient mesh enhancements as well as the new Shape Builder tool. Find additional features by reading Book III, Chapter 1.

Getting Started with Photoshop CS5

Photoshop is the industry standard software for Web designers, video professionals, and photographers who need to manipulate bitmap images. Using Photoshop, you can manage and edit images by correcting color, editing photos by hand, and even combining several photos to create interesting and unique effects. Alternatively, you can use Photoshop as a painting program, where you can artistically create images and graphics. Photoshop even includes a file browser that lets you easily manage your images by assigning keywords or allowing you to search the images based on metadata.

Photoshop allows you to create complex text layouts by placing text along a path or within shapes. You can edit the text after it has been placed along a path; you can even edit the text in other programs, such as Illustrator CS5. Join text and images into unique designs or page layouts.

Sharing images from Photoshop is easy to do. You can share multiple images in a PDF file, create an attractive photo gallery for the Web with a few clicks of the mouse, or upload images to an online photo service. You can preview multiple filters (effects) at once without having to apply each filter separately. Photoshop CS5 also supports various artistic brush styles, such as wet and dry brush type effects and charcoal and pastel effects. Photoshop also has some great features for scanning. You can scan multiple images at a time, and Photoshop can straighten each photo and save it as an individual file.

It's hard to believe that Photoshop can be improved on, but Adobe has done it again in Adobe Photoshop CS5. Book IV shows you the diverse capabilities of Photoshop. From drawing and painting to image color correction, Photoshop has many uses for print and Web design alike. Read Book IV, Chapter 1 to discover all the new features in Photoshop CS5, including new and improved adjustment layers and new 3D tools and features.

Working with Acrobat 9.0

Acrobat 9.0 Professional is aimed at both business and creative professionals and provides an incredibly useful way of sharing, securing, and reviewing the documents you create in your Design Premium Suite applications.

Portable Document Format (PDF) is the file format used by Adobe Acrobat. It's used primarily as an independent method for sharing files. This format allows users who create files on either Macintosh or PC systems to share files with each other, and with users of handheld devices or Unix computers. PDF files generally start out as other documents — whether from a word processor or a sophisticated page layout and design program.

Although PDF files can be read on many different computer systems using the free Adobe Reader, users with the Professional or Standard version of Adobe Acrobat can do much more with PDF files. With your version of Acrobat, you can create PDF documents, add security to them, use review and commenting tools, edit documents, and build PDF forms.

Use Acrobat to perform any of the following tasks:

✦ Create interactive forms that can be filled out online.

✦ Allow users to embed comments within the PDF files to provide feed-back. Comments can then be compiled from multiple reviewers and viewed in a single summary.

✦ Create PDF files that can include MP3 audio, video, SWF, and even 3D files.

✦ Combine multiple files into a single PDF and include headers and footers as well as watermarks.

✦ Create secure documents with encryption.

✦ Take advantage of a new, intuitive user interface. You can now complete tasks more quickly with a streamlined user interface, new customizable toolbars, and a Getting Started page to visually direct you to commonly used features. In other words, you get an interface more in line with what you may see in the rest of the Creative Suite products.

✦ Combine multiple files into a searchable, sortable PDF package that maintains the individual security settings and digital signatures of each included PDF document.

✦ Use auto-recognize to automatically locate form fields in static PDF documents and convert them to interactive fields that can be filled electronically by anyone using Adobe Reader software (Windows only).

✦ Manage shared reviews — without IT assistance — to allow review participants to see one another's comments and track the status of the review. Shared reviews are possible through Acrobat Connect, formerly Breeze.

✦ Enable advanced features in Adobe Reader to enable anyone using free Adobe Reader software to participate in document reviews, fill and save electronic forms offline, and digitally sign documents.

✦ Permanently remove metadata, hidden layers, and other concealed information and use redaction tools to permanently delete sensitive text, illustrations, or other content.

✦ Save your PDF to Microsoft Word. This feature is a treasure! You can now take advantage of improved functionality for saving Adobe PDF files as Microsoft Word documents, retaining the layout, fonts, formatting, and tables.

✦ Enjoy improved performance and support for AutoCAD. Using AutoCAD, you can now more rapidly convert AutoCAD drawing files into compact, accurate PDF documents, without the need for the native desktop application.

Want to discover other great Acrobat improvements? Read Book V to find out all about Acrobat and PDF creation.

Introducing Dreamweaver CS5

Dreamweaver CS5 is used to create professional Web sites quickly and efficiently, without the need to know or understand HTML (HyperText Markup Language). You can work with a visual authoring workspace (commonly known as *Design view*), or you can work in an environment where you work with the code. Dreamweaver enables you to set up entire Web sites of multiple pages on your hard drive, test them, and then upload them to a Web server. With Dreamweaver's integration capabilities, you can create pages easily that contain imagery from Adobe Illustrator, Photoshop, and Flash.

Dreamweaver also has built-in support for *CSS (Cascading Style Sheets),* a language that allows you to format your Web pages and control text attributes, such as color, size, and style of text. CSS gives you control over the layout of the elements on your Web pages.

Go to Book VI to find out how to use Dreamweaver CS5 to create exciting Web sites that include text, images, and multimedia. Read Book VI, Chapter 1 to discover all the new features in Dreamweaver, including a better interface, faster CSS integration, and improved Spry widget features.

Moving into Flash Professional CS5 and Flash Catalyst CS5

Flash combines stunning motion graphics, visual effects, and interactivity that have made it the industry standard for creating Web sites, CD-ROM presentations, and interactive learning tools.

Create graphics and type in Flash with its comprehensive set of drawing tools and then put them in motion with timeline-based animation, movie clips, and interactive buttons. Add photos, sound, and video for an even richer experience or use Flash's built-in scripting language, *ActionScript,* to create complex interactive environments that stand out.

The most recent versions of Flash have continued to revolutionize the way Web sites, presentations, and rich Internet applications are built. With improved drawing tools, advanced video features, effects filters, and further improvements on ActionScript, Flash CS5 promises to continue its place as the "king of all media."

Flash Catalyst enables you to create a working Web site using your Photoshop or Illustrator files and allows designers of large desktop applications to create prototypes of their applications within Flash Catalyst.

Turn to Book VII to discover how to use Flash to create drawings and animations, to use ActionScript to create interactive Web pages, and more. See Book VII, Chapter 10 for more on Flash Catalyst.

Welcoming You to Fireworks CS5

In the Design Premium suite, you have a tool for creating Web graphics. Fireworks is a much needed tool in the Creative Suite package because it offers features that were available in ImageReady in the CS2 suite.

You may wonder why Fireworks is included in the Design Premium suite when it already includes two other image editing programs, Photoshop and Illustrator. Among other things, Fireworks is useful for mocking up Web page designs, making it quick and easy to design a Web page layout and Web applications. Fireworks also enables you to edit both bitmap and vector images.

Use Fireworks to

✦ Compare file formats before exporting Web graphics.

✦ Create animations, rollovers, and pop-up windows.

✦ Create sliced images that use HTML tables or CSS (Cascading Style Sheets).

✦ Make wireframes, or mock up a Web site using the template and pages features.

Find out more in Book VIII about the helpful Web creation tools in Fireworks.

Crossing the Adobe Bridge

Adobe Bridge is truly an incredible application, especially with the CS5 release, because the processing speed is greatly improved and new features are available, including the ability to take advantage of the new Mini Bridge in several of the CS5 applications such as Photoshop and InDesign.

Bridge CS5 is a separate application you can access from the Creative Suite applications. It allows you to quickly access and manage multiple documents (such as images, text files, and Adobe stock photos), which you can use in all the CS5 applications.

Mini Bridge works much like the full launch of Adobe Bridge, but stays present like a panel, allowing you to quickly and easily access your files at any time.

You can find out more about Adobe Bridge and Mini Bridge in Chapter 5 of this minibook.

Integrating Software

With so many great pieces of software in a single package, it's only natural that you'll want to start using the programs together to build exciting projects. You may want to design a book using InDesign (with photos edited in Photoshop and drawings created in Illustrator) and then create a Web site for that content in Dreamweaver. Similarly, you may want to take a complex PDF file and make it into something that everyone can view online. Or you might create a symbol or Flash text in Illustrator and complete the animation in Flash. All tools in the Adobe Creative Suite are built to work together, and achieving these tasks suddenly becomes much easier to do because the products are integrated.

Integrating software is typically advantageous to anyone. Integration allows you to streamline the workflow among programs and sometimes team members. Tools exist that let you drop native images into Dreamweaver, InDesign, Illustrator, and Flash. With Adobe Bridge, you can view files and investigate specific information about them, such as color mode and file size, before selecting them for placement.

Chapter 2: Using Common Menus and Commands

In This Chapter

✔ Discovering common menus and dialog boxes

✔ Addressing CS5 alerts

✔ Working with common menu options

✔ Understanding contextual menus

✔ Speeding up your workflow with shortcuts

✔ Changing preferences

*W*hen you work with Adobe Creative Suite 5 Design Premium, you may notice that many menus, commands, and options are similar among its various programs. Discovering how to use menus and dialog boxes is essential to using the programs in the Creative Suite.

You may already be familiar with using dialog boxes and menus from other software packages. The way you use these elements is much the same for any program. Some specific keyboard shortcuts are the same across programs, even ones made by different software companies. This consistency makes finding out how to use the commands and options easy. This chapter provides an overview of some of the common menus, dialog boxes, options, commands, and preferences that exist in most or all of the programs in Adobe CS5 Design Premium.

Discovering Common Menus

When you work with programs in Adobe CS5 Design Premium, you probably notice that many of the menus on the main menu bar are the same. And then you probably see that these menus often contain many of the same commands across each program. These menus are somewhat similar to other graphics programs you may have used. Similar functionality makes finding certain commands easy, even when you're completely new to the software you're using.

Menus contain options and commands that control particular parts or functions of each program. You may have the option of opening a dialog box, which is used to enter settings or preferences or to add something to a document. A menu may also contain commands that perform a particular action. For example, you may save the file as a result of selecting a particular command in a menu. Menus that commonly appear in the CS5 programs are described in this list:

✦ **File:** Contains many commands that control the overall document, such as creating, opening, saving, printing, and setting general properties for the document. The File menu may also include options for importing or exporting data into or from the current document.

✦ **Edit:** Contains options and commands for editing the current document. Commands include copying, pasting, and selecting as well as options for opening preferences and setting dialog boxes that are used to control parts of the document. Commands for spell-checking and transforming objects are also common parts of the Edit menu.

✦ **View:** Contains options for changing the level of magnification of the document. The View menu also sometimes includes options for viewing the workspace in different ways, showing rules, grids, or guides, and turning snapping on and off.

✦ **Window:** Contains options primarily used to open or close whatever panels are available in the program. You can also choose how to view the workspace and save a favorite arrangement of the workspace.

✦ **Help:** Contains the option to open the Help documentation that's included with the program. This menu may also include information about updating the software, registration, and tutorials.

Adobe Design Premium on the Mac has an additional menu that bears the name of the program itself. This menu includes options for showing or hiding the program on the screen, setting preferences, and opening documents that provide information about the software.

Figure 2-1 shows a menu in Photoshop that contains many common options to control the program.

Notice that more menus are available in the programs than are in the previous list. Each program has additional, program-specific menus determined by the specific needs of whichever software you're using. For example, you can use the Photoshop Image menu to resize the image or document, rotate the canvas, and duplicate the image, among other functions. InDesign has a Layout menu you can use to navigate the document, edit page numbering, and access controls for creating and editing the document's table of contents. Which additional menus exist in each program is determined by what the software is designed to do; we discuss these menus where appropriate throughout this book.

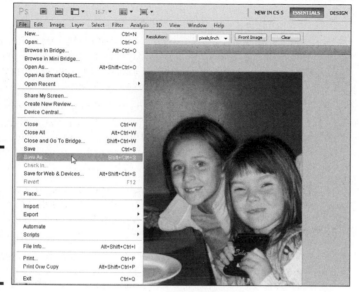

Figure 2-1: Menus in Photoshop let you choose and control different options.

Using Dialog Boxes

A *dialog box* is a window that contains a combination of options formatted as drop-down lists, panes, text fields, option buttons, check boxes, and buttons that enable you to make settings and enter information or data as necessary. You use dialog boxes to control the software or your document in various ways. For example, when you open a new file, you typically use the Open dialog box to select a file to open. When you save a file, you use the Save As dialog box to select a location for saving the file, to name the file, and to execute the Save command.

Some dialog boxes also include tabs. These dialog boxes may need to contain many settings of different types that are organized into several sections by using tabs. A dialog box typically has a button that executes the particular command and one that cancels and closes the dialog box without doing anything. Figure 2-2 shows a common dialog box.

A dialog box in Windows is a lot like a dialog box you find on the Mac. Dialog boxes perform similar tasks and include the same elements to enter or select information. For example, here are some tasks you perform by using dialog boxes:

✦ Save a new version of a file.

✦ Specify printing or page-setup options.

✦ Set up preferences for the software you're using.

✦ Check the spelling of text in a document.

✦ Open a new document.

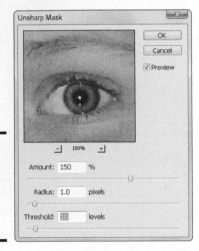

Figure 2-2:
Using a dialog box to change filter settings.

 You can't use the program you're working with until the dialog box is closed. When you have a dialog box open in the program you're using, the window pops up on the screen. Before you can begin working with the program again, you have to close the dialog box. You can close it by either making your choices and clicking a button (such as Save or OK) when you're finished or clicking the Cancel button to close it without making any changes.

Encountering Alerts

Alerts, which are common on any operating system and in most programs, are similar to dialog boxes in that they're small windows that contain information. However, alerts are different from dialog boxes because you can't edit the information in them. Alerts are designed simply to tell you something and give you one or more options that you select by clicking a button. For example, an alert may indicate that you can't select a particular option. Usually you see an OK button to click to acknowledge and close the alert. You may see on the alert another button to cancel what you were doing or one that opens a dialog box. Figure 2-3 shows a typical alert.

Figure 2-3:
A simple
choice: OK
or cancel.

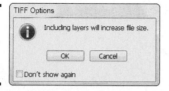

You can sometimes use an alert to confirm an action before executing it. Sometimes an alert window also offers the option (typically in the form of a check box) of not showing the alert or warning again. You may want to select this option if you repeatedly perform an action that shows the warning and you don't need to see the warning every time.

Getting to Know Common Menu Options

Various menu options are typically available in each of the CS5 Design Premium programs. However, within each of these menus, several other options are available. Some of them open dialog boxes — this type of option is typically indicated by an ellipsis that follows the menu option, as shown in Figure 2-4.

Figure 2-4:
Choosing
a menu
option with
an ellipsis
opens a
dialog box.

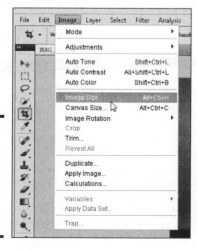

The following menu options are found in several CS5 programs, and these commands either perform similar (or the same) functions or they open similar dialog boxes:

✦ **New:** Creates a brand-new document in the native file format. For example, in InDesign, a new *INDD* (the extension for InDesign documents) file is created by choosing File⇨New⇨Document. You can sometimes choose the type of new file you want to create.

✦ **Open:** Opens a dialog box where you can choose a (supported) file to open on your hard drive or a disk.

✦ **Close:** Closes the current document. If it has unsaved changes, you're prompted to save those changes first.

✦ **Save:** Saves the changes you've made to the current document.

✦ **Save As:** Saves a new copy of the current document.

✦ **Import:** Imports a file, such as an image or sound file, into the current document.

✦ **Export:** Exports the current data to a specified file format. You can sometimes select several different kinds of file formats to save the current data in.

✦ **Copy:** Copies the selected data to the computer's Clipboard.

✦ **Paste:** Pastes the data from the Clipboard into the current document.

✦ **Undo:** Undoes the most recent task you performed in the program. For example, if you just created a rectangle, the rectangle is removed from the document.

✦ **Redo:** Repeats the steps you applied the Undo command to. For example, if you removed that rectangle you created, the Redo command adds it back to the document.

✦ **Zoom In:** Magnifies the document so that you can view and edit its contents closely.

✦ **Zoom Out:** Scales the view smaller so that you can see more of the document at a time.

✦ **Help:** Opens the Help documentation for the current program.

About Contextual Menus

The contextual menu is an incredibly useful, quick way to make selections or issue commands, and it's available in all kinds of programs. Contextual menus include some of the most useful commands you may find yourself choosing repeatedly.

A *contextual menu* is similar to the menu types we describe in the previous sections; however, it's context-sensitive and opens when you right-click (Windows) or Control-click (Mac) something in the program. *Contextual* means that which options appear on the menu depends on which object or item you right-click (Windows) or Control-click (Mac).

For example, if you open a contextual menu when the cursor is over an image, commands involving the image are listed on the menu. However, if you right-click (Windows) or Control-click (Mac) the document's background, you typically see options that affect the entire document instead of just a particular element within it. You can therefore select common commands specifically for the item you've selected. Figure 2-5 shows a contextual menu that appears when you right-click (Windows) or Control-click (Mac) an object in Photoshop.

Figure 2-5: Open a contextual menu in Windows by right-clicking an image or object.

The tool you select in the Tools panel may affect which contextual menus you can access in a document. You may have to select the Selection tool first to access certain menus. If you want to open a contextual menu for a particular item in the document, make sure that the object is selected before you right-click (Windows) or Control-click (Mac).

If you're using a Mac, you can right-click to open a contextual menu if you have a two-button mouse hooked up to your Mac. Otherwise, you press Control-click to open a contextual menu.

Using Common Keyboard Shortcuts

Shortcuts are key combinations that enable you to quickly and efficiently execute commands, such as save or open files or copy and paste objects. Many of these shortcuts are listed on the menus discussed in previous sections. If the menu option has a key combination listed next to it, you can press that combination to access the command rather than use the menu to select it. Figure 2-6 shows shortcuts associated with a menu item.

View	Window	Help	
Proof Setup		▶
Proof Colors		Ctrl+Y
Gamut Warning		Shift+Ctrl+Y
Pixel Aspect Ratio		▶
Pixel Aspect Ratio Correction		
32-bit Preview Options...		
Zoom In		Ctrl++
Zoom Out		Ctrl+-
Fit on Screen		Ctrl+0
Actual Pixels		Ctrl+1
Print Size		
Screen Mode		▶
✓ Extras		Ctrl+H
Show		▶
Rulers		Ctrl+R
✓ Snap		Shift+Ctrl+;
Snap To		▶
Lock Guides		Alt+Ctrl+;
Clear Guides		
New Guide...		
Lock Slices		
Clear Slices		

Figure 2-6: Shortcuts are shown next to their associated commands.

For example, if you open the File menu, next to the Save option is Ctrl+S (Windows) or ⌘+S (Mac). Rather than choose File➪Save, you can press the shortcut keys to save your file. It's a quick way to execute a particular command.

Some commonly used shortcuts in the Adobe Creative Suite 5 Design Premium programs are listed in Table 2-1.

Table 2-1	Common Keyboard Shortcuts	
Command	*Windows Shortcut*	*Mac Shortcut*
New	Ctrl+N	⌘+N
Open	Ctrl+O	⌘+O
Save	Ctrl+S	⌘+S
Undo	Ctrl+Z	⌘+Z
Redo	Shift+Ctrl+Z	Shift+⌘+Z
Copy	Ctrl+C	⌘+C
Paste	Ctrl+V	⌘+V
Print	Ctrl+P	⌘+P
Preferences (General)	Ctrl+K	⌘+K
Help	F1 or sometimes Ctrl+?	F1 or sometimes ⌘+?

Many additional shortcuts are available in each program in the CS5 programs, and not all are listed on menus. You can find these shortcuts throughout the documentation provided with each program. Memorizing the shortcuts can take some time, but the time you save in the long run is worth it.

Changing Your Preferences

Setting your preferences is important when you're working with new software. Understanding what your preferences can do for you gives you a good idea about what the software does. All programs in the Design Premium Suite have different preferences; however, the way the Preferences dialog box works in each program is the same.

You can open the Preferences dialog box in each program by choosing Edit➪Preferences (Windows) or *Program Name*➪Preferences➪General (Mac). The Preferences dialog box opens, as shown in Figure 2-7. Click an item in the list on the left side of the dialog box to navigate from one topic to the next.

The Preferences dialog box contains a great number of settings you can control by entering values into text fields using drop-down lists, buttons, check boxes, sliders, and other, similar controls. Preferences can be quite detailed. However, you don't have to know what each preference does or even change any of them: Most dialog boxes containing preferences are quite detailed in outlining which features the preferences control and are therefore intuitive to use. Adobe also sometimes includes a Description area near the bottom of the dialog box. When you hover the mouse over a particular control, a description of that control appears in the Description area.

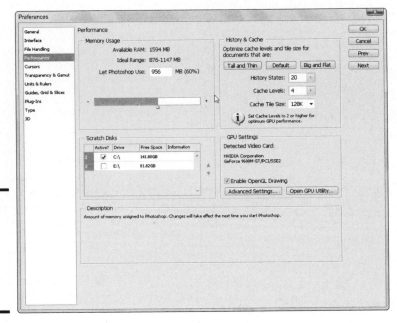

Figure 2-7:
Click an item on the left to navigate among topics.

In some Preferences dialog boxes, a list box on the left side of the dialog box contains the different categories of preferences you can change. When you finish changing the settings in that topic, select a new topic from the list and change the settings for another topic.

In some programs, not all settings you can modify are in the Preferences dialog box. For example, in Illustrator, you can change the color settings by choosing Edit⇨Color Settings to open the Color Settings dialog box. When you hover the mouse over a particular drop-down list or button, a description of that control appears at the bottom of this extremely useful dialog box.

By launching Adobe Bridge (described in Chapter 5 of this minibook) and choosing Edit⇨Creative Suite Color Settings, you can change your color preferences across all Design Premium programs at one time, as shown in Figure 2-8.

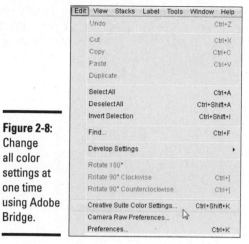

Figure 2-8:
Change
all color
settings at
one time
using Adobe
Bridge.

In many CS5 programs, you have the option to specify your main preferences for the overall document, such as setting up page dimensions, number of pages in the document, or page orientation (landscape or portrait). These kinds of options are available by choosing the following command in each program:

✦ **File➪New:** Dreamweaver

✦ **File➪Document Setup:** Illustrator and InDesign

✦ **Image➪Image Size:** Photoshop

Figure 2-9 shows the Image Size dialog box.

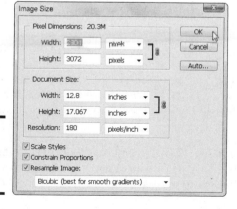

Figure 2-9:
The Image
Size dialog
box.

Chapter 3: Exploring Common Panels

In This Chapter

✔ **Exploring the synchronized workspace**

✔ **Manipulating panels in the workspace**

✔ **Discovering different kinds of panels**

✔ **Getting to know the common panels in Adobe CS5**

The panel is an integral part of working with most of the programs in Adobe Creative Suite 5 (CS5) because it contains many of the controls and tools you use when you're creating or editing a document.

The basic functionality of panels is quite similar across the programs in Adobe Creative Suite, and the purpose of all panels is the same. Panels offer a great deal of flexibility in how you organize the workspace and the parts of it you use. The task you use each program for and the level of expertise you have may affect which panels you have open at a given moment. This chapter gives you an overview of how to work with the panels you find in Adobe CS5.

Understanding the Synchronized Workspace

One thing you immediately notice when opening applications in the Creative Suite is the synchronized workspace. All the applications look similar and have the same set of features to help you organize your workspace.

The tools in InDesign, Illustrator, and Photoshop appear on a space-saving, single-column toolbar, and panels (described in detail in the next section) are arranged in convenient, self-adjusting docks that can be widened to full size or narrowed so that the panels are collapsed to icons.

Here are some pointers to help you navigate the workspace in the Creative Suite applications:

✦ **To expand tools to two columns:** Click the right-facing double arrows on the gray bar on top of the tools.

✦ **To collapse tools to a single column:** Click the left-facing double arrows on the gray bar on top of the Tools panel.

✦ **To expand a docked panel:** Simply click the icon in the docking area, as shown in Figure 3-1. The panel you selected expands but goes away when you select a different panel.

If you have difficulty identifying the panel, you can choose the panel you want from the Window menu.

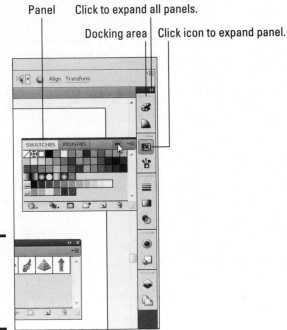

Figure 3-1: Click an icon to expand the panel.

✦ **To expand all docked panels:** Click the left-facing double-arrow icon at the top of the docking area; put away the panels by clicking the right-facing double-arrow icon in the gray bar above them.

✦ **To undock a panel:** Simply click the tab (where the panel name is located) and drag it out of the docking area. You can re-dock the panel by dragging the panel back into the docking area.

Using Panels in the Workspace

Panels are small windows in a program that contain controls, such as sliders, menus, buttons, and text fields, that you can use to change the settings or attributes of a selection or an entire document. Panels may also include information about a section or about the document itself. You can use this information or change the settings in a panel to modify the selected object or the document you're working on.

Whether you're working on a Windows machine or on a Mac, panels are similar in the way they look and work. Here are the basic instructions for working with panels:

✦ **Open a panel:** Open a panel in a Creative Suite program by using the Window menu: Choose Window and then select the name of a panel. For example, to open the Swatches panel (which is similar in many programs in the suite), choose Window⇨Swatches.

✦ **Close a panel:** If you need to open or close a panel's tab or panel altogether, just choose Window⇨*Panel's Tab Name*. Sometimes a panel contains a close button (an X button in Windows or the red button on a Mac), which you can click to close the panel.

✦ **Organize the workspace:** All Creative Suite programs now offer options for workspace organization. You can return to the default workspace, which restores panels to their original locations, by choosing Window⇨Workspace⇨Default. You can also open frequently used panels, position them where you want, and save a customized workspace by choosing Window⇨Workspace⇨Save (or New) Workspace. Name the workspace and click OK; the saved workspace is now a menu item that you can open by choosing Window⇨Workspace⇨*Your Saved Workspace's Name*.

You can also choose from a wide range of included presets designed for a variety of specialized tasks.

✦ **Access the panel menu:** Panels have a panel menu, which opens when you click the arrow in the upper-right corner of the panel, as shown in Figure 3-2. The panel menu contains a bunch of options you can select that relate to the selected tab when you click the panel menu. When you select an option from the panel menu, it may execute an action or open a dialog box. Sometimes a panel menu has few options, but particular panels may have a bunch of related functionality and therefore many options on the panel menu.

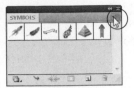

Figure 3-2:
Displaying
the panel
menu.

✦ **Minimize/maximize:** All you need to do to minimize a selected panel is
  click the Collapse to Icons double-arrow button on the title bar of the
  panel (if it's available). If the panel is undocked, you can also double-
  click the tab itself (of an undocked panel) in the panel. This action either
  partially or fully minimizes the panel. If it only partially minimizes, double-
  clicking the tab again fully minimizes it. Double-clicking the active tab
  when it's minimized maximizes the panel again.

  Panels that partially minimize give you the opportunity to work with
  panels that have differing amounts of information, which simplifies the
  workspace while maximizing your screen real estate.

Most panels contain tabs, which help organize information and controls in a
program into groupings. Panel tabs contain a particular kind of information
about a part of the program; a single panel may contain several tabs. The
name on the tab usually gives you a hint about the type of function it controls or displays information about, and it's located at the top of the panel
(refer to Figure 3-2). Inactive tabs are dimmed.

Moving panels

You can move panels all around the workspace, and you can add or remove
single tabs from a panel. Each panel snaps to other panels, which makes
it easier to arrange panels alongside each other. Panels can overlap each
other as well. To snap panels to each other, drag the panel to a new location
onscreen, as shown in Figure 3-3; you see the top bar of the panel become
shaded, indicating that it's becoming part of another panel's group.

Figure 3-3:
To move a
panel, drag
it by its tab.

Group similar tabs by moving them into a single grouped panel. Accessing different functions in your document becomes a lot easier because then you have less searching to do to find related functions for a task. If you want to return to the original workspace, you can choose Reset Workspace from the Window menu in the Workspace category.

You can hide all panels by pressing the Tab key. Press it again to reveal all panels you've hidden.

Looking at common panels

Many panels are similar across programs in the Creative Suite. Although not every panel has exactly the same content in every program it's in, many have extremely similar content. You use these panels in similar ways, no matter which program or operating system you're using.

Acrobat doesn't contain numerous panels, like other programs in the Creative Suite. Instead, Acrobat relies mainly (but not entirely) on a system of menus and toolbars filled with buttons and drop-down lists. In Acrobat, you can open dialog boxes that contain a bunch of settings you can enter for your documents.

The following panels are available in most, but not all, Creative Suite programs. This list describes what you can do with each one:

✦ **Color:** Select or mix colors for use in the document you're working on. You can use different color modes and several ways of mixing or choosing colors in the Colors panel.

✦ **Info:** See information about the document itself or a particular selection you've made. The Info panel includes information on the size, positioning, and rotation of selected objects. You can't enter data into the Info panel: It only displays, not accepts, information, so you have to use the Transform panel (described in this list) to make these modifications, if necessary.

✦ **Swatches:** Create a swatch library, which can be saved and imported into other documents or other programs. You can store on the Swatches panel any colors and gradients you use repeatedly (refer to Figure 3-1).

✦ **Tools:** You use this important panel, sometimes called the *toolbox* (and not available in all Creative Suite programs), to select tools — such as the Pencil, Brush, or Pen — to use in creating objects in a document.

✦ **Layers:** Display and select layers, change the layer order, and select items on a particular layer.

✦ **Align:** Align selected objects to each other or align them in relation to the document itself so that you can arrange objects precisely.

✦ **Stroke:** Select strokes and change their attributes, such as color, width/weight, style, and cap. The program you're using determines which attributes you can change.

✦ **Transform:** Display and change the *shear* (skew), rotation, position, and size of a selected object in the document. You can enter new values for each transformation.

✦ **Character:** Select fonts, font size, character spacing, and other settings related to using type in your documents.

Chapter 4: Using Common Extensions and Filters

In This Chapter

✔ Discovering the real purpose of filters and extensions

✔ Using common extensions and filters in Adobe CS5

*E*xtensions, also known as *plug-ins,* are pieces of software installed or saved on your computer that work as add-ons to existing programs. For example, you may be able to use an extension to integrate with a different program, help add usefulness to a program (such as the ability to create 3D text), change the appearance of an object in your software, or add a 3D effect to a video file. Filters are used to change parts of a document. Even if you haven't used Photoshop, you're probably already familiar with some popular Photoshop filters, such as Watercolor and Emboss, used for artistic effects. This chapter shows you common plug-ins, extensions, and filters, as well as how to use them in the Creative Suite.

Looking at Common Extensions and Filters

Extensions are sometimes used for similar tasks in several programs and are designed to enhance a program's existing capabilities. Extensions and filters can also dramatically speed up the creative process. At the mere click of a button, you can add to your project an amazing effect that may have taken many hours to accomplish without the plug-in.

Additional filters and plug-ins for the programs are available or linked from the Adobe Web site. You can also easily find plug-ins for downloading from the Web. A search yields many results for these packages. A good place to start is at the Adobe Marketplace & Exchange: www.adobe.com/cfusion/exchange. You can then download and install a wealth of tools for all Creative Suite applications.

The Photoshop filter is probably the most common type of add-on you find online. Some filters you have to purchase before downloading and using them; however, some are free.

Installing extensions

Extensions can be installed in a few different ways. Sometimes you use an executable file: Double-click the file on your hard drive and it automatically installs the software. This process is a lot like installing any other program on your computer, such as the programs in the Creative Suite itself.

Sometimes individual files need to be placed in a folder first. In that case, you need to find the Plug-Ins folder on your computer in the install directory of the program the plug-in or filter works with. For example, if your plug-in works with InDesign on Windows, you have to find the directory `C:\Program Files\Adobe\ InDesign CS5\Plug-Ins`. You then copy and paste or move the files you downloaded into this directory on your hard drive. If your plug-in works with Photoshop on the Mac, find this folder on your hard drive: `Applications\ Adobe Photoshop CS5\Plug-Ins`.

Then copy and paste or move the files into the folder.

You can also take advantage of the Adobe Extension Manager CS5 application, installed automatically with the default CS5 installation. Locate Extension Manager in your Programs (Windows) or Applications (Mac) folder and double-click to launch it. Select the application for which you want to install the extension, click the Install button to locate the extension you want to install, and click the Select button — you're on your way!

If you're unsure how to install a plug-in, locate instructions for the software that explain how to install the plug-in on your computer. You can find instructions on the manufacturer's Web site or bundled with the plug-in file in a text file (usually named `readme.txt`).

Plugging into InDesign

There are many plug-ins available in InDesign that allow you to extend the feature set that already exists. Here are some of the things you can do with additional plug-ins in InDesign:

✦ Lay out spreads correctly for a printer.

✦ Create sophisticated indexes and tables of contents.

✦ Create advanced cross-references within your documents.

✦ Create page previews and thumbnails of your documents.

Other filters created for InDesign can help import certain content, such as text. You often find that text formatting is lost when you import content into InDesign. Filters can help you retain this original formatting when you're importing text. These plug-ins and filters are just a small sample of what's available for InDesign. In all likelihood, many more plug-ins will be created for the software.

Adding on to Photoshop

Photoshop has many preinstalled plug-ins and filters that increase the program's functionality. You can find additional filters and also plug-ins to add new features that inevitably add interesting effects to your documents. One plug-in, for example, installs a number of filters in Photoshop. By using the filters and plug-ins you find for Photoshop, you can

✦ Remove blemishes and scratches from photos using special tools.

✦ Create 3D text, objects, and effects by using several different plug-ins. Effects include more realistic drop shadows, bevels, and embossments than the ones already available in Photoshop.

✦ Use special masking tools to create amazing selections of difficult items such as fur and hair.

✦ Use one of thousands of special effects (made by many companies) to enhance and modify images.

✦ Add a frame from a library to place around favorite images.

This list describes only some of the tasks you can perform using the available Photoshop plug-ins, which commonly comprise a set of numerous bundled filters.

Many plug-ins have custom interfaces you can use to specify settings, including sliders, text fields, and buttons and usually a thumbnail preview of how the filter is affecting the image. These interfaces vary greatly in style and number of features but are usually fairly intuitive and easy to use.

Using Illustrator plug-ins

You can find many tools to extend the capabilities of Illustrator. Plug-ins are available that enable you to take 3D illustration further than standard 3D features allow. You can create forms from drawings and also turn 3D files into line drawings. Other plug-ins, ranging from simple to quite complex, let you

✦ Create multipage documents.

✦ Organize font sets.

✦ Add common symbols, such as road signage, to use in documents. Symbols are organized into libraries that you can use directly in the Illustrator workspace.

✦ Import computer-aided design (CAD) files into documents.

✦ Create interactive documents.

✦ Handle patterns geared toward creating textures and backgrounds.

You can enhance Illustrator capabilities after you download and install a few plug-ins. Simple projects become much more interesting or complex when you merely enter a value and click a button.

A fun item to download and install into Illustrator is a custom brush. You can then have a wider array of brushes available to work with when you create drawings and illustrations. Styles, usually obtained for free, can also be installed in Illustrator. You can even download and install custom brushes for Photoshop.

Adding capabilities to Acrobat

Several Acrobat plug-ins help speed and diversify project workflow. Some available plug-ins are designed to help you

✦ Add new stamps to documents.

✦ Add features such as page numbering and watermarks.

✦ Streamline productivity by offering solutions for batch processing.

✦ Convert file formats to diversify the kinds of documents you can create in Acrobat.

✦ Work with and fix — quickly and efficiently — the Portable Document Format (PDF) in prepress.

Many plug-ins available for Acrobat enable you to batch-process (all at one time) the pages in a document. Many plug-ins for Acrobat help save lots of time when you're creating PDF files. Plug-ins are usually designed to be easy to use and can thus save you from having to perform a tedious and repetitive task.

Plug-ins for Acrobat are available from the Adobe Web site and from numerous third-party Web sites.

Extending Dreamweaver

Dreamweaver offers you a quick and easy way to make Web pages, but you can add more tools to Dreamweaver to diversify the types of tasks the program can do. These extensions (essentially, plug-ins) also speed the process of creating Web sites. Some available Dreamweaver plug-ins let you

✦ Add e-commerce modules to a Web site automatically.

✦ Create professional DHTML (Dynamic HTML) and CSS (Cascading Style Sheets)-based vertical and horizontal menus.

✦ Add a calendar pop-up.

✦ Add PayPal to your Web site.

For additional interactivity or interest, Dreamweaver lets you add *behaviors* (premade JavaScript scripts) to your Web site, along with premade templates. Many are available at www.adobe.com/cfusion/exchange.

Using Filters and Plug-Ins

You can install plug-ins and filters in your Creative Suite programs. For example, a filter can enhance an existing photo in an exciting way. After you install into Photoshop or Illustrator a plug-in that includes a bunch of additional filters, check out what the filter can do to your photos.

Install some filters for Photoshop (or Illustrator or any other program in the suite). After you complete the installation and restart your computer, if necessary, open Photoshop and locate the Filter menu option. (New filters are available on this menu.)

To use a filter or plug-in after installing it, follow these steps:

1. **Open a file in the appropriate program so that you can try your new filter or plug-in.**

   For example, if you downloaded a Photoshop plug-in that added a new filter, open an interesting photo that you want to apply an effect to in Photoshop. Choose a photo that has many colors or a lot of contrast to work with.

2. **Choose a filter from the Filter menu.**

   Select a filter that you installed from the Filter menu. You may also find that a plug-in created a new menu item in the program — in that case, use the new menu item to apply the effect.

3. **Modify the filter's (or plug-in's) settings, if necessary, and click OK to apply the effect.**

   Sometimes you see a thumbnail preview to assess how the filter changes the image. For some filters and plug-ins, you even use a custom interface to manipulate the document. You can then change the settings accordingly until you're happy with the modifications to be applied.

4. **Look at the image or document after you choose and apply the filter or plug-in.**

   Your image or file is updated immediately. If you're unhappy with the results, you can either undo your changes by choosing Edit⇨Undo or reapply the filter or plug-in.

Though filters add a great deal of interest and variety to documents, you can easily suffer from filter overload when using them. You can use filters in many different ways in the Design Premium suite, and some ways (and even the filters themselves) are considered better than others. Experiment freely with filters — just make sure that you don't use too many on one part of an image when you're creating a final project. For example, if you bevel and emboss a particular letter in a few different ways, that character can become illegible. Similarly, adding a huge drop shadow can distract the eye from other parts of the text.

Know what you intend to accomplish with your document before you start creating it. If you set out to create a project with a particular design in mind, you can sometimes achieve better results. Try drawing your ideas on paper first, writing down notes about the effect you want to achieve, and thinking about the plug-ins you want to use to create it. Use one filter at a time, and make sure that you like the results before moving on. The alternative is to continue adding filters to achieve a particular result when you aren't quite sure which effect you're after or how to create it.

Chapter 5: Importing and Exporting

In This Chapter

✔ Integrating Adobe Bridge into your workflow

✔ Importing content

✔ Moving files from one CS5 application to another

✔ Exporting content out of your documents

✔ Exporting content from CS5 programs

*I*mporting and exporting content are important tasks for much of the creative process you experience while using programs in the Creative Suite. You commonly import content to work on within your documents: You might import text composed by a designated writer into an InDesign document so that you can include the content in a page layout, or you might import a 3D design into an Illustrator document so that you can use the image in a design. Importing is necessary in all kinds of circumstances during a typical workflow.

Exporting content from each program is sometimes necessary when you want to save the document as a different file format. You may want to do this for compatibility reasons: Your audiences, or the people you're working with, need a different file format in order to open your work; or you may need to export to a different file format in order to import the work into a different program.

Discovering the Adobe Bridge Application

In this version of the Creative Suite, Adobe has dramatically enhanced the Adobe Bridge application and even included a mini panel version for Photoshop CS5 named, appropriately, Mini Bridge. The *Adobe Bridge* application helps you organize and manage your assets, such as pictures, text, and movie and audio files, as well as non-Adobe applications such as Word or Excel files. Adobe Bridge acts like a hub for the Creative Suite; for example, by choosing to open files using the Bridge interface, you can browse directories quickly and see thumbnail previews of files, as shown in Figure 5-1. You can even use the Filter panel to help find files and view metadata to your file, including important information such as keywords and copyright information.

Figure 5-1:
The Adobe Bridge workspace.

Bridge not only makes a great deal of information accessible, but it can also be used as a central resource for all your Help needs.

Not all Adobe Bridges are the same. If you installed the Adobe programs separately (not using the Creative Suite installer), the program on your machine may be lacking some features. If you notice that you don't have access to features mentioned in this chapter, check to see whether all the CS5 applications are installed or run the CS5 installer again.

Accessing the Bridge software

Knowing where to locate the Adobe Bridge application is helpful. Bridge should already be in your system if you completed a standard installation of any product in the entire suite. If you don't find Bridge installed, go back and choose to install it using your original installation media. After you install the Bridge software, you can open it in one of three ways:

✦ **Access the Bridge software with the directory system of your computer.** Navigate to `C:\Programs\Adobe\Adobe Bridge\Bridge` (Windows) or `Hard Drive\Applications\Adobe Bridge\Bridge` (Mac).

✦ **Click the Launch Bridge button on the Application bar,** as shown in Figure 5-2. If you don't see the Launch Bridge icon, you can choose File➪Browse in Bridge. Launch into Bridge from any of the applications included in the Creative Suite.

✦ **In Photoshop, you can click the MB (Mini Bridge) on the Application bar** to open a panel with a miniature version of Bridge, as shown in Figure 5-3.

Figure 5-2:
To open
Bridge, click
the Launch
Bridge
button.

Figure 5-3:
Open the
Mini Bridge
application.

Navigating in Adobe Bridge

To navigate Bridge, simply use the Folders panel in the upper-left corner to
choose the folder you want to view. Watch in amazement as previews are
created and automatically replace the standard file format icon.

Adobe Bridge may take a fair amount of time to build the preview the first
time you use it, so be patient. Either choose Tools⇨Cache⇨Build and Export
Cache to save this data or choose Tools⇨Cache⇨Purge Cache to free up file
space.

Select an individual file by clicking it once (twice opens it) or select multiple
files by Ctrl-clicking (Windows) or ⌘-clicking (Mac).

With one or more files selected, you can

✦ Relocate the files to another location by dragging them to a folder in the Folders panel in the upper-left corner. Use Bridge as a central filing system. Using the commands on the File menu, you can create new folders and delete or move files or groups of files.

✦ Read metadata in the Metadata panel in the lower-right corner. The metadata includes important information such as Camera, Flash, and F-stop. See Figure 5-4.

Figure 5-4:
Use the Metadata panel to find important information about your selected image.

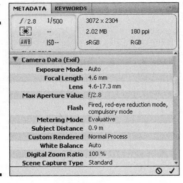

✦ Enter your own metadata for any item listed by clicking the pencil icon to the right.

✦ Use the Keywords panel, shown in Figure 5-5, to enter your own keywords to help you find your images later.

Figure 5-5:
The Keywords panel can help you locate images.

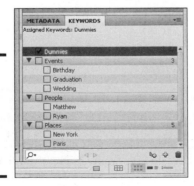

✦ Choose Edit⇨Find or use the Filter panel to locate your files within the Bridge by entering criteria, such as Keywords, Description, Date Created, and more.

✦ Create image stacks. You can select many files in Bridge by holding down the Ctrl key (Windows) or ⌘ key (Mac) and clicking multiple files. You can then choose Stacks➪Group as Stack or use the keyboard shortcut Ctrl+G (Windows) or ⌘+G (Mac). It stacks the images into one compact thumbnail, as shown in Figure 5-6.

The number of images in the stack is shown in the upper-left corner of the image stack. To reopen the stack, click the stack number; to close the stack, click the stack number again. If you no longer want the stack, you can choose Stacks➪Ungroup from Stack or use the keyboard shortcut Ctrl+Shift+G (Windows) or ⌘+Shift+G (Mac).

✦ Check under the Tools menu for application-specific tools, such as *Photomerge* (merging panoramic images), *Live Trace* (tracing images as vector images), and PDF Presentation.

Number of images in stack

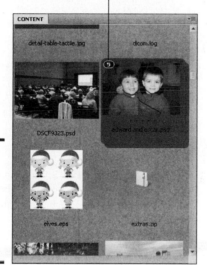

Figure 5-6:
Stack
similar
images
to help
keep files
organized.

Managing color

Using Bridge for color management is a timesaver and a production boost! Color settings can be set across the board in all Creative Suite applications right in Adobe Bridge. Create consistent color choices in all Creative Suite applications by using the synchronized color-management controls that Adobe Bridge offers.

Choose Edit➪Creative Suite Color Settings to choose a color management setting that remains consistent throughout all Creative Suite applications, as shown in Figure 5-7. Read more about color correction in Book IV, Chapter 7.

The setting for Joe's Press, shown in Figure 5-7, was created in Adobe Photoshop. If your printer can send you the Joe's Press color settings, you can load them using the Suite Color Settings dialog box in Photoshop and then make them accessible to all your CS5 applications by selecting the settings in Adobe Bridge.

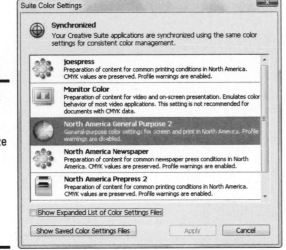

Figure 5-7: Use color settings to synchronize color management policies in Adobe Bridge.

Importing Files into a Document

Importing files works similarly, no matter which program you're working with. Importing content is more important in some programs than others. A program like InDesign relies on importing content into a document that's then incorporated into a page layout. However, in programs like Photoshop, importing content is much less important because you frequently start out editing an image you *open* in Photoshop. In this section, we take a look at importing content into each program.

Placing content in InDesign

Placing content in InDesign is a familiar task when you're creating a new layout. You need to import images and text for many of your layouts. When you choose File⇨Place, you can then select text or image files from your hard drive or network. You can also choose sound and video files that you can use when you're creating PDF documents for electronic distribution. After you choose a file to import, a new cursor icon appears, with a thumbnail preview of your image, when you place it over the page or pasteboard.

To place the imported content, click the page where you want the upper-left corner to be placed.

When you import different kinds of images, you see the Place dialog box, in which you can select a variety of options for importing selected content. However, to access additional settings, you must select the Show Import Options check box in the Place dialog box. In Figure 5-8, you see the additional options that appear when an image is placed.

Figure 5-8: When importing text and graphics, you can see additional options.

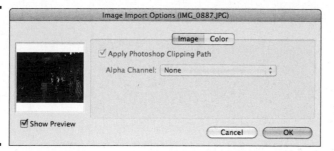

Select a file and click the Open button. Another dialog box opens with options specific to the type of file you're importing. For example, if you're importing a bitmap image (say, a JPEG), you can choose how you want the bitmap to appear, whether it contains a background or color management information, and other, similar options.

When you import text information, you may lose some text formatting that was made in the original file. Anything that InDesign doesn't understand isn't imported into the document. Column information, as well as margins, also typically isn't retained when you import text. However, some plug-ins are available that help remedy the situation to some extent.

You can use the Launch Bridge button in the center of the Application bar in InDesign to open Adobe Bridge. Then simply drag and drop the images you want to use directly from Bridge.

Adding content to a Photoshop file

In Photoshop, you can choose to open an image to work with or import content into a document that's open already. Choose File⇨Place to import AI, EPS, PDP, or PDF files. These files import into a new layer in the document, and you can then use tools to manipulate the imported content, as shown in Figure 5-9.

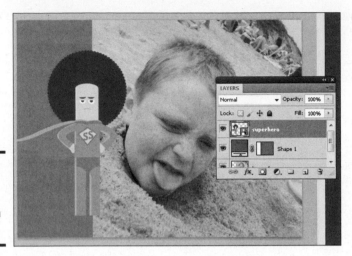

Figure 5-9:
Imported
content is
placed on a
new layer.

 Your placed Illustrator file is embedded, as a default, into the Photoshop file. You can read about the Smart Object feature in Book IV, Chapter 9. Double-click the placed artwork layer to open and edit the embedded Illustrator file. After the file has been saved, the changes are immediately reflected in Photoshop. Note that your original file isn't changed.

If you want to import images from your digital camera directly into Adobe Bridge, choose File⇨Get Photos from Camera.

Placing files into Illustrator

Illustrator lets you place images and other forms of data in a new document. You can import Photoshop, PDF, image, and vector files by choosing File⇨Place. The Place dialog box opens and you can choose a file to import. Click Place to import the file. An Import dialog box may appear at this point, depending on the type of file you're importing. This dialog box offers several options for choosing a way to import the content into Illustrator. For example, you can sometimes choose between flattening layers or retaining layers when you import a document containing layers.

Encapsulated PostScript (EPS) is a commonly used file format for saving vector drawings (although it can be used for other file types as well). Because this file format is used in many programs, you may find other people giving you these files to work with. To import an EPS document, you also choose File⇨Place; after you import an EPS document into Illustrator, the file is converted to Illustrator objects but isn't editable. To edit the EPS object, choose File➪Open to open the file, or double-click the image name in the Links panel.

You can also import text files into Illustrator. Microsoft Word, TXT (text only), RTF (Rich Text Format), and Unicode, among other text documents, are all supported by Illustrator, and you can import them by choosing File➪Place. When you import the text file, you're prompted to choose the character set used for the text.

You can not only use the Place command for importing files but also copy and paste from other programs. You can select part of an image in Photoshop and copy it to the Clipboard by pressing Ctrl+C (Windows) or ⌘+C (Mac) and then pasting it into the Illustrator document.

Use the Place command whenever possible to avoid losing quality in the content you're importing. Also, transparency isn't supported from one application to another when you copy and paste, but it is when Place is used.

When you have particular plug-ins installed, you can import additional file types, such as CAD files, into Illustrator.

Adding to Acrobat

Adobe Acrobat is primarily a tool for sharing completed documents — you'll complete most document construction and editing in other programs, such as InDesign or Illustrator. However, you can import several kinds of data into PDF documents, and you can do some creative things when you place data into PDF files as well:

✦ **Comments:** The most useful and common items to import into an Adobe PDF file are comments made using the review and markup tools provided by Adobe Acrobat. By importing comments into a PDF file, you can consolidate suggestions and input from several *reviewers* (people editing a document) into a single document. This feature helps consolidate the reviewing process when many people are working on a single document. To import someone's comments into a PDF, choose Comments➪Import Comments. If you're reviewing a document, you can also export only the comments rather than send the document owner the entire PDF file.

✦ **Form data:** You can import form data into a PDF document by choosing Forms➪Manage Form Data➪Import Data. The data you import can be generated by exporting the form data from another PDF form, or it can come from a delimited text file. You can then share form data between forms or from a database.

✦ **Trusted identities:** If you share digitally signed files or secured files with another Acrobat user, you can import the public version of that person's signature file into your list of trusted users with whom you share files. To import the identity of a user, choose Advanced⇨Manage Trusted Identities, and in the Manage Trusted Identities dialog box that appears, click the Add Contacts button.

✦ **Multimedia files:** If you've ever had the urge to add a movie or sound file to your PDF documents, you're in luck. By using the Sound tool or Movie tool, you can identify the location on the page where you want the file to appear and then choose whether to embed the multimedia file (compatible with Acrobat 6 or later) or create a link to the file (compatible with Acrobat 5 and earlier).

✦ **Buttons:** Creating buttons to turn pages, print a document, or go to a Web site makes your PDF files easier to use. Adding custom button images, such as pictures of arrows or a printer icon, makes your document unique. Use the Button tool to create the location of the button and then select the graphic file to be used as the image on the button. The image file you use must first be converted to a PDF graphic.

✦ **Preflight information:** If you're creating a PDF file to be sent to a commercial printer for reproduction, you may want to preflight the file to ensure that it meets the specifications and needs of the printer and has all the necessary assets (such as fonts and images) that it needs to print correctly. If your printer has supplied a preflight profile for Acrobat, you can import the profile to ensure that Acrobat checks for the elements your printer has requested, such as certain font types or color specifications. Import a preflight profile by choosing Advanced⇨Print Production⇨Preflight, and in the Preflight window that opens, choose Options⇨Import Preflight Profile.

Importing into Dreamweaver

In Dreamweaver, you can import several different kinds of files into a site you're creating:

✦ Insert images and other media such as Flash, FlashPaper, and Flash Video by using the Insert menu item.

✦ Import XML files and XHTML documents exported from InDesign.

✦ Cut and paste a layered file in Photoshop. Simply choose Edit⇨Copy Merged and paste the file directly into Dreamweaver. An Image Preview window opens (see Figure 5-10), and you can then optimize the image for the Web. Choose your settings and click OK. (You can read about the best settings for Web imagery in Book IV, Chapter 10.)

Figure 5-10:
The Image
Preview
window
opens when
a native
PSD file is
pasted into
a Dream-
weaver
page.

Exporting Your Documents

Exporting content from Adobe Creative Suite documents is important if you're importing the content into another program, placing the document where it's publicly available and where it needs to be interpreted on other computers. Similarly, you may be working with a team of individuals who need your document to be readable on their machines when it's imported into other programs. Exporting a document in a different file format helps solve these issues, and Adobe Creative Suite offers you the flexibility of allowing you to export a document as many different file formats.

Other programs sometimes accept native Adobe documents as files you can import. For example, Adobe Flash CS5 can import Illustrator AI files, Photoshop PSD files, and PDF documents.

Exporting from InDesign

In InDesign, you can export pages or a book as several file types. Most notably, you can export layouts as PDF documents, which anyone who has the free Adobe Reader installed can view. InDesign can also export to other image and vector formats, such as EPS and JPEG. An InDesign document can also export to SVG (Scalable Vector Graphics) and XML (Extensible Markup Language), which is useful when you export documents for the Web. InDesign has a handy feature to package your work for Dreamweaver: By choosing File⇨Export for Dreamweaver, you can export a project you're working on and have it ready for page creation in Dreamweaver.

Exporting content from Photoshop

Because Photoshop can export paths in a document to Illustrator (in an AI file), your work in Photoshop is easy to manipulate after you open it with Illustrator.

You have another option, though: Export your Photoshop file by using the Zoomify feature. This useful feature can export a large file to a smaller, more compact SWF file. This file can be easily sent by e-mail and opened using the free Flash Player, which almost everyone already has installed.

To use Zoomify, follow these steps:

1. **Choose File⇨Export⇨Zoomify.**

2. **Click Folder in the Output Location section of the Zoomify dialog box and choose a folder location for your SWF file.**

3. **Choose the quality and size and then click OK.**

   The Zoomify Preview window appears (see Figure 5-11). Use this window to zoom in to see detail.

   You can then retrieve the files that were created in your destination folder and post them online or attach them to an e-mail message.

Figure 5-11: The image before it rebuilds after zooming in, and the image after it rebuilds.

Exporting Illustrator files

Illustrator supports exporting to many different file formats. You can export files in a long list of image formats. Choose File⇨Export, and the Export dialog box opens. Click the Save As Type (Windows) or Format (Mac) drop-down list to view the exportable file formats.

After you choose a file type to export to, a second dialog box may appear, allowing you to enter a bunch of settings for the exported file.

Try choosing the Flash SWF file format when you export a file. A second dialog box opens that includes many settings, such as options to generate an HTML page, save each layer as a separate SWF document, and preserve editability (when possible). The options that are available when you export a document depend on the type of file format to which you're exporting.

Exporting Acrobat content

Acrobat lets you export certain parts of a PDF document you're working on. For example, you may be using *form data* — the data that's filled into a form made of text fields and so on — in one of your files. You can export this data from Acrobat and then send it online, which is helpful because PDF documents tend to be rather large for the Web. Therefore, only a small amount of formatted data is sent online, not a huge PDF file.

You can also export parts of an Acrobat document to use in other programs. You can export comments in a PDF to a Microsoft Word file that was used to create the PDF by choosing Comments⇨Export Comments to Word. You can also export comments to an AutoCAD file (assuming that it was used to create the PDF). In both cases, you need the original document that was used to generate the PDF file in order to successfully import the comments.

Similarly, you can export all comments from a PDF file by choosing Comments⇨Export Comments to Data File and then import them into another version of the same document. You can use this option to consolidate comments from multiple reviewers or overlay comments from a draft with a final version to confirm that all edits were completed.

Exporting Dreamweaver content

In Dreamweaver, you can export your sites so that they're prepared for publishing and ready to be placed on a live Web site. The site you're working on in Dreamweaver is exported to your hard drive before you put it somewhere on a server. The HTML styles used in a site you're working on can be exported and saved as an XML document, which in turn can be reused if necessary. These files can then be imported into another Dreamweaver project you're working on.

Chapter 6: Handling Graphics, Paths, Text, and Fonts

In This Chapter

✔ Livening up your documents with graphics

✔ Getting control of paths and strokes

✔ Getting the scoop on text and font fundamentals

✔ Creating a layout

Graphics, paths, text, and fonts are all integral parts of creating documents with Adobe Creative Suite. You must know how to handle each element in your documents and how to make these elements successfully work together. Discovering the different ways you can work with images, text, and drawings is the fun part!

Whether you're designing Web sites or creating a brochure layout, you can use these elements on their own or together, and you'll likely find out something new every time you work with them. A layout can include text, images, and drawings but sometimes includes more. If you're creating documents for the Web or creating PDF (Portable Document Format) files with multimedia elements, you may be working with sound, animation, and video alongside text, images, and illustrations.

Using Graphics in Your Documents

A *graphic* can be an image, a drawing, or a vector object. You can create graphics manually by making marks on a page or create them electronically using software. Graphics can be displayed in many formats, such as on a computer screen, projected on a wall, or printed in a magazine or book.

Computer graphics come in many forms, grouped by the way they're created electronically. Bitmap and vector graphics are formed in different ways to achieve the result you use in your documents.

Working with bitmap images

Bitmap images are pictures made up of many tiny squares, or *bits,* on an invisible grid. When these dots are next to each other, the picture is formed, depending on where and how the colors are arranged on the grid. If you zoom in far enough, you can even see the blocky dots, or *pixels,* that make up the image. At 400 percent zoom, notice how the image in Figure 6-1 is made of large squares. However, when you look at most bitmap images at their true sizes, you don't even see pixels.

Figure 6-1:
A bitmap image is created from pixels.

The bitmap is a useful way to display photographs and apply effects to text. When you paint or create detailed graphics, you frequently use bitmaps. However, remember that images can lose quality if you *scale* them (change their size). Resizing pixels causes the image to lose definition and quality. Most problems occur when an image is enlarged. Common kinds of bitmap files are BMP, GIF, JPEG, PICT, and TIFF. You can read more about bitmaps in Book IV.

Discovering vector graphics

A vector image (or graphic or drawing) is quite different from a bitmap image. A *vector image* is created by a series of mathematical calculations or code that describes how the image should be formed. These calculations tell the computer how the lines should display and render on the page.

Vector images are usually smaller files than bitmap graphics because the mathematical information required to make the calculations to create the vector image is usually smaller in file size than the information that it takes to make up each pixel of a bitmap. Compression can lessen a bitmap's file size, but they're usually larger and slower to display.

For this reason and because vectors are helpful in scaling an image, as shown in Figure 6-2, these graphics are well suited for the Web.

Figure 6-2:
A vector image is smooth at any zoom level.

Scaling is easy to do when you're using vectors because the program needs to modify the calculations only slightly to make the image larger or smaller. This means the file size won't change, and the scaling is very quick. You can scale the image on a Web page to fill the browser window, whatever size it is, or make the image huge for a large banner. The quality doesn't degrade, and the file size remains the same.

Vectors aren't always perfect for the Web. A bitmap is frequently the best way to display a photograph because if you change a bitmap image into a vector drawing (which is possible by using tools), you lose too much of the photograph's detail for many purposes. Also, certain effects, such as the drop shadow, are best displayed as bitmap images.

Working with Paths and Strokes

Paths are the vector lines and outlines you create in a document. You can use paths to outline an image, separate areas of text, or be part of an illustration you create. You typically make paths using a Line tool or a Pen tool or the shape tools. You can use these tools to create paths of different shapes and sizes. You also can use tools to modify the color and size of *strokes* (the actual line that makes up a path).

You can use paths to create clipping paths and paths for text. *Clipping paths* are used to mask (or *hide*) elements on a page. You define that mask with paths to create a shape for the area you need to hide. Clipping paths can even be saved in a file and imported into a different design pattern. A common workflow is to create an image in Photoshop CS5 with a clipping path and import the image into InDesign. Because InDesign can *interpret* the clipping path, you can automatically remove the area you want to mask.

When you want to create text that flows along a path, begin by creating a new path and then use the Type On a Path tool to type text directly on that path. For example, in Illustrator, you create a path with the Pen tool and then select the Type On a Path tool in the Tools panel. If you click the tool on the path you created, you can type new text along that path.

If you have an existing path, you can select the Pen tool and cross over the select path. The Type tool cursor changes to indicate that it is loaded as a Type On a Path tool as you see in Figure 6-3. Click on the path, and the type is attached to the path.

Figure 6-3:
The Type tool cursor changes when you cross over an active path.

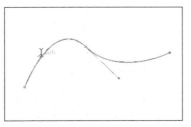

A *stroke* is the color, width, and style of the line that makes up the path you create. You might draw a line with the Pen tool, and the line making up that path is the stroke. However, that path can also have no stroke (represented as a diagonal line in the Tools panel), which means that you don't see the path itself. However, you may see a color or pattern filling that stroke (the *fill*), as shown in Figure 6-4.

You can change the color, width, style (or *type*), and shape of a stroke using controls and tools in the Tools panel and the Stroke panel in Illustrator and InDesign. You can also therefore create dashed or solid strokes of different patterns that are wide or narrow. Some strokes are shown in Figure 6-5.

Figure 6-4:
This path
has a fill but
no stroke
applied to it.

Figure 6-5:
Paths
that have
different
strokes
can add a
creative
flair.

Adding Text

You may add text to your projects for different reasons. Text is frequently used to educate and inform people who read it, and this kind of document is a lot different from ones that use text for artistic purposes only. For example, if you're creating an article, you may place the text in columns on the page under a large title at the top. At other times, you may use text as a creative element or even as an object instead of a letter. Alternatively, you may be laying out a Web page and use the text for both a creative element in an animation and the content on pages that make up the Web site.

You can add text to a document by using the Text tool or by importing the text from another source, such as Microsoft Word. You can create a single line of text in a text field or large blocks of text with or without columns. Text fields can be rotated and resized, and you can change the color, font face, orientation, and character size of the text.

Text can also be placed on a path, as we mention briefly in the earlier section "Working with Paths and Strokes." You can then add text to your documents in a different way because you can draw a path and have the text follow it. Paths are particularly useful for headings on a page, footers, and artistic works that use text as one of their elements.

Using fonts

A *font* refers to the typeface of a set of characters. You can set the font to be a number of sizes, such as the miniscule size 2 or the gargantuan size 200. Fonts are given names, such as Times New Roman or Comic Sans.

You may also hear about the *glyph,* which is an actual character. For example, S is a glyph. A set of glyphs make up a font. You can view glyphs in the Glyph panel in Illustrator (choose Window⇔Type⇔Glyphs), which is especially useful when you're using fonts such as Wingdings that are made of pictures instead of letters and numbers.

The fonts you use can make a huge difference to the look, feel, and style of your documents. Whether you're working on a layout for a magazine article or creating a digital piece of art, the kinds of fonts you use help the feel of the work.

Two major groupings for fonts exist, as illustrated in Figure 6-6:

✦ **Serif:** Each character has a small line that intersects the end of each line, such as the feet on the letters *rif* in *serif.*

✦ **Sans serif:** A character has no small, intersecting line at the end of a line.

Figure 6-6: Serif and sans serif fonts.

Serif **Sans-serif**

Sometimes sans serif fonts feel more modern, whereas serif sometimes looks more historical, formal, or literary. (This topic is, of course, all a matter of opinion.) Take a moment to look at how text is used around the Web and in books, magazines, advertisements, and even the newspaper. How text is commonly used greatly affects how other people view your work and find the overall *feel* of it. Finding an appropriate font is sometimes a challenging design task, but it can also be fun.

Discovering types of fonts

Although you can find a gazillion fonts for free on the Internet, be concerned about the quality of your finished product. Typically, people in the professional graphics industry use PostScript fonts, and preferably OpenType fonts, which are more reliable when printing, as compared to TrueType fonts, which may reflow when printing to different resolutions.

✦ **TrueType:** Like other digital typefaces, the *TrueType* font file contains information, such as outlines, hinting instructions, and character mappings (which characters are included in the font). Available for both the Mac and Windows formats, the TrueType fonts designed for each operating system have slight differences; therefore, Mac and Windows users can't share TrueType fonts.

✦ **PostScript (Type 1):** The scalable *PostScript* font system is compatible with PostScript printers; users can see fonts on the screen the same way the fonts would be printed. Type 1 font files consist of two files — a screen font with bitmap information for onscreen display and a file with outline information for printing. For high-end printing, both parts of the Type 1 font files (Printer and Screen fonts) must be included with the file. Because of differences in their structure, Mac and Windows PostScript Type 1 fonts aren't cross-platform compatible.

✦ **OpenType:** The *OpenType* font technology was created in a joint effort between Adobe and Microsoft and is an extension of the TrueType font format that can also contain PostScript data. OpenType fonts are *cross-platform* — the same font file works under both Macintosh and Windows operating systems. This digital type format offers extended character sets and more advanced typographic controls. As with TrueType, a single file contains all the outline, metric, and bitmap data for an OpenType font. Although any program that supports TrueType fonts can use OpenType fonts, not all non-Adobe programs can access the full features of the OpenType font format. You can find the symbols on the Font menus of many of the CS5 programs representing the type of font.

Using text and fonts on the Web

Using text and fonts on the Web is a difficult task at times. When you use fonts in a Web page, system fonts are used to display text. You usually specify a font or a group of fonts to use on each page, and the fonts that are installed on the visitor's computer are used to display the text. The problem arises if you use (or want to use) fonts that aren't installed on the visitor's computer. For example, if you use the Papyrus font and the visitor doesn't have that font, a different font is substituted and the page looks completely different as a result.

When you're using Dreamweaver to create Web sites, you can set up a set of fonts that you want to use on each page. These fonts are similar in how they look, and if one of the fonts isn't available, the next font is used instead. Among the fonts in the set, at least one of them should be installed on the visitor's computer, to ensure that your pages will look similar to your original layout.

You can use Photoshop and Illustrator to create an image using any font installed on your computer and then save that image for the Web (choose File⇨Save for Web & Devices). Then you can place that image in your Web page with Dreamweaver. This option is best used for small amounts of text — say, for buttons on a navigation bar, headings to separate areas of text, or a customized banner at the top of a Web page.

The Fundamentals of Page Layout

Page layout incorporates the many elements we discuss earlier in this chapter, mainly text and images (and sometimes other forms of multimedia), to create a design on a page. When you're creating a page design, you must consider how people view a layout, such as how the eye moves across the page to take in the flow of information. Also consider how the elements are arranged and how much empty space surrounds them.

Two main kinds of page layout are discussed in this book: print and Web layouts. Both formats require you to work with many of the same elements.

Deciding which Creative Suite programs to use

Many differences exist between preparing a layout for the Web and preparing it for print; however, you'll find that you use many of the same tools for both, and a great deal of information crosses over between the two mediums.

Image manipulation for the Web is frequently done in Photoshop. It's also the standard program for manipulating and correcting images intended for print. You can even design a page for print and also put it online by using the Export XHTML/Dreamweaver command in InDesign.

However, you have to make certain considerations when you post information online. Navigation, usability, file size, dimensions, and computer capabilities are considerations for the Web that aren't a concern when you're working for print. However, resolution, colors, and cropping (to name a few) are considerations of someone designing a piece for print, which aren't concerns for the Web.

Another option for creating Web page layout is to use Adobe Fireworks, included in the Creative Suite. Fireworks not only helps you create Web graphics but also provides excellent prototyping tools for the Web. Using

Fireworks, you can establish styles, build a master page, and even apply interactivity to your pages. Building multiple page prototypes with hyperlinks is a synch using Fireworks.

Designing a layout for print

When you design a page layout for print, you have to factor in the size and type of paper that will be used. Sometimes, you create letterhead with certain elements on the page that remain the same, whereas other elements (the main content) differ from page to page. You can also create page layouts that serve as templates for a book and use particular elements (such as bullets or sidebars) repeatedly in varying ways throughout the pages. Page size, font size, and image resolution are all important considerations in print.

Onscreen image resolution is measured in *pixels per inch (ppi),* which refers to the number of pixels that are within 1 inch onscreen. The printed resolution of an image is measured in *dots per inch (dpi)* — a dot of ink is printed for each pixel. A higher dpi means that the image is clearer and has finer detail, which is extremely important for print. Printed images almost always use a higher resolution than onscreen images, so you may find that an image that measures 4 x 4 inches onscreen (at 72 ppi) prints at less than 1 x 1 inch (at 300 dpi). Read more about resolution in Book IV, Chapter 6.

Templates are available for page layouts that factor in common dimensions of paper and help you lay out content into defined areas. Many different kinds of templates are available online, and you can download them sometimes for free; others are available for a small or modest fee depending on the template. For example, if you're creating a brochure, you may have to think about where the page will be folded and how to orient images and text so that they're facing the correct way when someone reads the brochure.

Here are a few issues to think about when you're laying out a page:

✦ **Use a grid and snapping-to-align elements whenever possible.** If certain elements on your page aren't aligned, you should have a good reason.

✦ **The eye travels in the direction of the elements on the page.** For example, if a picture of a person is facing away from the center of a spread, the eye travels in that direction. Make sure that the eye travels to the important elements on the page.

✦ **Follow the rule of thirds and divide pages into thirds.** Parts of your layout should fall into these three areas.

Choosing a Web page layout

Layout for the Web is quite different from layout for print. However, many of the same issues arise in both print and Web layout, such as keeping text legible and flowing across the page (or screen) in an intelligent way. In Web layouts, navigation and usability open a few doors for issues you should consider when planning a Web page:

✦ **Usability:** A usable site is accessible to most, if not all, of your visitors. Visitors must be able to access your content easily because the text is legible, the file formats work on their computers, and they can find content on your site. Also, visitors who have physical challenges, such as sight or reading problems, can use software on their computers so that the site is read or described aloud to them.

✦ **Size:** File size should always be kept to a minimum, which may mean changing the size of your layout. If many parts of your design require large images, you may need to change the design completely to reduce file size. Also, you need to design the page with monitors in mind. If a visitor's monitor is set to a resolution of 800 x 600, your site scrolls horizontally if it's designed any larger than 780 pixels wide. Most Web surfers dislike this horizontal scrolling effect, so you must consider the dimensions of visitors' displays when designing sites.

✦ **Navigation:** Users have to navigate between pages on your site. To help them do so, you need to create links to those pages by using buttons, text links, menus, and other screen elements. Making navigational controls easy to find and use takes some forethought and planning. Be sure that navigation is a big part of the plan when designing the layout of your site.

You have to think not only about usability and navigation but also the different kinds of computers accessing the page and how people from all over the world may try to access your page. If you need your page to be universal, you may need to translate it into different languages and use different character sets. (This statement applies to print also, if you're designing a page that requires a special character set other than the ones you regularly use.)

Because you may be using multimedia (such as images and animation) alongside text, you're constrained to the dimensions and color limitations of a computer monitor and have to think about both file size and scrolling.

Chapter 7: Using Color

In This Chapter

✓ Discovering color modes

✓ Finding out about swatches

✓ Using color for print

✓ Using color on the Web

*U*sing color in documents is one of the most important considerations in creating your projects. The colors you use, the mode you use them in, and even the way you select colors make a difference in the way you create a document and the final output of that document. Even though you can create a document that looks the same on a monitor in different color modes, how that file prints on paper is a different matter. Color is quite a broad subject, and in this chapter you find out the basic facts about how color affects the projects you work on.

Figuring out the kinds of colors you're using is important, and this decision is greatly determined by the kind of output you've planned for the document. Different color modes are appropriate for work for the Web and work you're having professionally printed. Monitors and printers have different modes for color, so you need to work with your files in different color modes (although you can change the mode after you start working on a file, if necessary).

You may also be in situations where particular colors are required in your work. You may be working with specific colors that a company needs in order to match its logo or creating an image that replicates how a building should be painted with specific colors of paint. You may need to use particular Pantone colors or color mixes — if not for the printing process, then for the purpose of matching a client's needs.

In this chapter, we introduce you to color modes and how to use them. You discover new terminology and how to find, mix, and add colors to your documents in the Creative Suite.

Looking at Color Modes and Channels

Several different color modes are available for use in Creative Suite applications. When you start a new document in Photoshop and Illustrator, you can choose the color mode you want to work in. In fact, both Photoshop and Illustrator help you by letting you choose a color mode in the New Document dialog box. The choice you make affects how colors are created. You can change the color mode later by choosing File⇨Document Color Mode in Illustrator or Image⇨Mode in Photoshop.

If you're working with print, generally you use CMYK mode. If you're working on files to be displayed on a monitor, RGB is the right choice.

Using RGB

RGB (Red, Green, Blue) is the color mode used for onscreen presentation, such as an image displayed on the Web or a broadcast design for TV. Each color displayed onscreen has a certain level (between 0 and 100 percent) of red, green, and blue to create the color. In a Color panel, you can either use sliders to set the level in values, as shown in Figure 7-1, or enter a percentage into a text field (such as in CMYK Color mode).

Figure 7-1:
Creating colors with the sliders in RGB mode.

Note the exclamation point on the Color panel, which indicates that this color wouldn't reproduce correctly in CMYK mode. You can click the CMYK warning exclamation point to convert to a color that's suitable for the CMYK gamut. Color is discussed in Book IV, Chapter 3, including more details about how you can adjust the Color Settings dialog box.

When you create a Web page, the color is represented as a *hexadecimal* number, which starts with a pound sign (#) followed by three pairs of letters and numbers (A through F and 0 through 9) — the first pair for red, the second pair for green, and the last pair for blue. The lowest value (the least amount of the color) in a hexadecimal number is 0 (zero), and the highest value (the greatest amount of the color) is F. For example, #000000 is black, #FFFFFF is white, #FF0000 is red, and #CCCCCC is light gray. To see what a particular hexadecimal color looks like, go to Webmonkey at www.web monkey.com/reference/Color_Charts.

Working with CMYK

RGB (Red, Green, Blue) color mode is the color standard for monitors and the Web, and CMYK — Cyan, Magenta, Yellow, and Key (or Black) — is the standard color mode for print media, particularly in commercial printing such as what a service provider does.

The CMYK color scheme is based on *pigment* (a substance used as coloring) color separation, and it describes how light reflects off pigments. When you work with this color mode, you create black by adding the maximum values of cyan, magenta, and yellow all at one time. You can create different levels of gray by combining equal, but not maximum, amounts of cyan, magenta, and yellow. White is simply the absence of all color. Many color printers now work by using the CMYK color model and can simulate almost any color by printing two colors very close to each other; however, some at-home desktop printer models made by Epson, Hewlett-Packard (HP), and Canon use their own color systems to print your work.

Saving in grayscale

You've seen a lot of *grayscale* images (color images displayed or printed in black-and-white) because the pictures in this book were printed in grayscale. Grayscale refers to the different shades of gray that can be used when printing using only black ink on a white page. Halftone patterns are used to help simulate different color values, by adding dots to simulate shadows and gradients between colors. *Halftone* patterns are created when an image uses dots of varying diameter or when an image uses many small dots in the same area to simulate different shades of gray.

Looking at color channels

When you work with an image in Photoshop, the image has at least one (but typically more) color channels. A *color channel* stores information about a particular color in a selected image. For example, an RGB image has three color channels: one that handles the reds (R), one for handling green information (G), and the last for information about the blues (B). See Figure 7-2.

You can have, in addition to the three color channels, an *alpha channel,* which can hold the transparency information about a particular image. If you're working with a file format that supports transparency, you can add and use the alpha channel to save alpha information.

You can also use an alpha channel to save a selection. By choosing Select⇨ Save Selection in Photoshop, you create an alpha channel with your selection saved to it. You can choose Select⇨Load Selection and choose the channel to reload your selection at any time.

In Photoshop, you can access the channels in your image by choosing Windows⇨Channels. When the Channels panel opens, you can toggle the visibility of each icon by clicking the eye icon next to each channel (refer to Figure 7-2).

Figure 7-2:
This RGB file is created from a Red, Green, and Blue channel.

Choosing Colors

When you create a document, you may have to consider which colors you use, or you may have the freedom to use an unlimited number of colors. If you print your documents, you can choose a specific set of colors to use. You may be restricted to only the two colors in a company logo, or you may have to print in grayscale. Finding the colors you need to use in each program is important — and then figuring out how to access those colors repeatedly in a document saves you a great deal of time.

Using swatches

A swatch is a good way to choose a color, particularly when you intend to print a document. The Swatches panel in Creative Suite programs contains colors and sometimes gradients. (The Swatches panel, shown in Figure 7-3, is from Illustrator.) You can create libraries of swatches that contain colors you can use repeatedly across several documents.

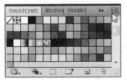

Figure 7-3:
Swatches panels are similar in most CS5 applications.

You can choose libraries of swatches from the panel menu or load and save swatch libraries. You can customize a swatch library by adding or deleting colors.

Mixing colors

A color mixer, found in the Color panel, helps you choose colors. You can use the Eyedropper tool to choose a color or, if you prefer, enter values for each hue or percentage. You can use one of several different color modes in the programs you use, which offers you a lot of flexibility for all your projects.

Follow these steps to choose a color in a specified color mode:

1. **In a program that has a Color panel, choose Window➪Color to open the Color panel (if it's not open already).**

The Color panel is available in Illustrator, InDesign, and Photoshop.

2. **Click the Color panel menu to choose a new color mode.**

Open this menu by clicking the arrow button in the upper-right corner of the Color panel.

3. **Choose the RGB color mode from the panel menu that opens.**

The panel switches to RGB color mode.

4. **In the Color panel, click either the Fill box (solid square) or the Stroke box (hollow square) to choose the color you want to change.**

If you click the Fill box, you can modify the color of a *fill* (the color inside a shape). If you click the Stroke box, you can modify the color of a *stroke* (the outline of a shape or a line).

5. **Use the sliders in the Color panel to change the color values.**

You can also change the percentage values to the right of each slider.

6. **After you choose a color you're happy with, return to your document and create a new shape that uses the color.**

Hold down the Shift key when adjusting any one-color slider and the other color sliders adjust proportionally to provide you with various tints from your original.

Using Color on the Web

In the past, you had to consciously choose which colors you used on the Web. Some computer monitors were limited in the number of colors they could display. Nowadays, color monitors are much more advanced and can handle a full range of colors, so images on the Web are much more likely to be properly displayed.

Though this statement doesn't have to do with color, Macintosh and Windows computers usually display your work differently because of gamma differences on these machines. Generally speaking, colors on a Mac appear lighter, and colors on a PC look darker.

Even though most computers can handle a full range of colors, you may have to consider color limitations. If you're designing a site specifically targeted at old computers or a certain user base, you may have to limit colors to the 256 Web-safe colors, which means that any other colors used are approximated, which can look poor. If your site will likely be viewed by users with older computers, consider these suggestions:

✦ **Use a Web-safe palette of 216 colors to design Web sites so that you specifically design with those older displays in mind and know what the pages will look like.** This number is 216 instead of 256 because the lower number is compatible with both Mac and Windows computers. You can access this panel, usually known as *Web-Safe Palette* or *Web-Safe RGB,* from the Swatches panel menu in Illustrator and Photoshop.

✦ **Avoid using gradients, if possible.** They use a wide range of colors (many unsupported in a limited Web panel).

✦ **Avoid dithering if you can.** A color that's approximated because it can't be handled by someone's computer *is dithered* — the computer tries to use two or more colors to achieve the one you specified, causing a typically displeasing granular appearance. So a limited number of colors can have a negative effect on an image; notice the granular appearance on what should be the shape of a face in Figure 7-4.

If you keep the preceding suggestion list in mind, you're ready to start designing for the Web! Remember also that you don't have to worry about using the Web-safe palette of colors if you're designing primarily for more up-to-date computers.

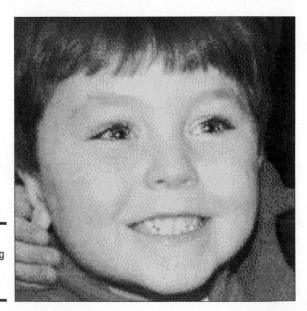

Figure 7-4:
The shading in the face is dithered.

Chapter 8: Printing Documents

You can print documents in many ways in Adobe Creative Suite 5. Similarly, you can print many different kinds of documents. You can create anything from a CD-ROM sticker to a 300-page book to a T-shirt iron-on transfer using the programs you find in the Creative Suite. Whatever you're working on, knowing the options that are available for printing your work is a good idea. Knowing the kinds of printers you can work with, what to buy (and from where) in order to use them, and how to save your work help improve the quality of the print job when you've finished your work.

Choosing Printers

When it comes to printers, you encounter hundreds of options at a great variety of prices. Printers can differ greatly in the areas of quality, cost of maintenance, and the speed at which the printer can print. Some inkjet printers excel at printing full-color photos but don't print text well; a low-end or medium-end laser printer may print black-and-white documents at good speed and quality but can't print in color.

Using consumer printers

The most common type of consumer (home) printer is now an *inkjet printer,* which works by spraying ink stored in cartridges onto a sheet of paper while it passes through the printer. This type of printer is common in households because it's the least expensive type of color printer. It's also versatile. You can walk into virtually any computer store and buy a color inkjet printer (which can print résumés, photos, and brochures) for a low price.

The lone drawback of inkjets is that they can be expensive to maintain in the long run. Depending on how much you print, you may need to replace the black or color cartridges often, which can get costly and quickly exceed the cost of the printer itself.

Looking at professional printers

Professional printers typically have a more rounded feature set compared to consumer printers. Professional printers can either be inkjet or laser printers and can even perform multiple functions within the office. Not surprisingly, printers that have several roles within the office are often referred to as *multifunction* or *all-in-one* printers and typically also include scanning, photocopying, or faxing capabilities in addition to printing. These all-in-one units are useful in small offices and home offices because they save the consumer some money while providing access to a variety of useful tools.

Laser printers have several benefits: They typically produce a higher quality printout and print pages faster than inkjet printers, as well as produce a clean, professional-looking document. You can also print more pages per ink cartridge, saving you money in consumable items.

Buying a Printer

Some common features to look for when purchasing a printer (either consumer or professional) are

+ **Speed:** Printers are rated in *pages per minute (PPM)*. Low-end inkjet printers typically print about 12 or fewer PPM when printing black-and-white pages. When you're printing color documents, the number of pages printed per minute is less.

+ **Color:** Almost all inkjet printers can print in color, but most print only in black and white. Color printers can be expensive to maintain because most inkjet printers have one cartridge for black ink and a second cartridge for colored inks. When one color runs out, you're forced to replace the entire cartridge or else none of the colors will look right when you print the document. Color laser printers are available, although they're usually very expensive.

+ **Resolution:** Similar to monitors, a printer's quality can be rated in resolution. Higher resolution means images and text appear crisper. Low-end or older inkjet printers may print only a maximum of 600 dpi (dots per inch), which is more than fine for text but may be low if you want to print high-quality photographs.

+ **Connectivity:** You can connect a printer to your computer in three ways. Older printers typically connect to your system using a parallel (36-pin) port, whereas newer printers often offer both parallel and USB (Universal Serial Bus) connections. The third way of connecting to a printer is by connecting a printer to your network, although this option is usually seen only on professional printers.

✦ **Duplexing:** Another feature to consider is *Duplexing,* the ability to print on both sides of a sheet of paper without having to manually flip the piece of paper and place it back in the paper tray.

Printing Your Work

When it comes to printing, countless options and settings can affect the final result of your document. Whether you're printing banners, business cards, T-shirt iron-on transfers, or lost-cat posters, you must be aware of several factors, such as paper quality, printer quality, and ink usage. You also have to decide whether to print to documents yourself at home or take them to a professional printing business to get the work done.

Although RGB (Red, Green, Blue) is the color standard for the Web, CMYK (Cyan, Magenta, Yellow, and Key [or Black]) is the standard in print. For information about using the RGB and CMYK color modes in the Creative Suite, see Chapter 7 of this minibook.

Choosing where and how to print

You can choose from several options when it comes to printing your files. You can take your digital files to a *printing service provider,* which is an establishment that prints electronic documents (such as FedEx Kinko's), or even print the files yourself at home on your inkjet or laser printer. Each option has several advantages and disadvantages. Depending on how many copies and the number of colors, having files printed professionally can be cost prohibitive. Having files printed by a professional print house, however, almost always means that the print quality will be much better than if the document were printed on a low-end inkjet printer.

Naturally, if you're only printing flyers to distribute around the neighborhood, you may not need high-quality output, and a home inkjet or laser printer would be more than adequate. However, printing documents professionally may be cheaper than printing them at home if you're going to use up large amounts of black ink or perhaps one or two cartridges of toner.

If you're using an inkjet printer, often you can get an average of 400 to 600 pages of black text before you need to replace a cartridge; a laser printer prints around 2,500 to 4,000 pages before you need to purchase new toner. Simply using a laser printer can save hundreds of dollars a year, depending on the number of pages you need to print and whether you need to print in color. If you need to print in color, many color laser printers are available (although they can be expensive). Entry-level color laser printers can cost around $500; some high-end color laser printers can cost more than $10,000. In comparison, black-and-white laser printers can cost as little as $100. So unless you plan to print lots of documents, outsourcing your printing to a service provider may be the best solution.

The kind of printer you use (such as a commercial or PostScript printer or a low-cost household inkjet) makes a great difference in the quality of output. Some illustrations or layouts will look a lot better when printed commercially depending on what's in your document.

Looking at paper

Before printing your documents, consider the type of paper that's best for the job. If you're printing on glossy paper, make sure that the paper works with your printer type. Although most glossy paper works fine in inkjet or laser printers, some brands or types of paper may not.

Always double-check paper when purchasing it to make sure that it won't damage your printer. The kinds of printers supported by the type of paper are listed on the paper's packaging.

One benefit to using glossy paper is that it has a finish similar to photo paper finish, which can make your printouts appear to have a higher quality.

Using good paper can result in photos that have richer colors and show more detail. When purchasing printer paper, here are some important characteristics to look for:

✦ **Brightness:** Refers to how bright the paper is. Higher numbers mean the paper looks brighter and cleaner.

✦ **Weight:** Refers to how heavy the paper is. Higher weights mean a thicker, more durable piece of paper.

✦ **Opacity:** Refers to how translucent, or transparent, the paper is. If the paper is too thin, too much light can pass through it; also, you may be able to see the ink through the other side of the page (which can be a problem if you want to print on both sides of the sheet). Opacity relates to weight, in that a heavier sheet of paper would be thicker and allow less light to pass through it.

✦ **Texture:** Refers to the smoothness or roughness of the surface of the paper. Texture can provide dramatic differences between inkjet and laser printers. Inkjet printers spray ink onto a page, so having a slightly textured surface to print on can be beneficial because the texture allows ink to dry somewhat faster and bleed a little less, making the finished product look a little sharper. When you're using a laser printer, the opposite is true. Having a smooth, flat surface for the toner to transfer onto produces better results.

Remember that you may not always print on 8½-x-11-inch paper (also referred to as Letter or A4). Many printers also allow you to print on envelopes, labels, stickers, business cards, and even iron-on transfers. You can use iron-on transfers to create your own T-shirts with your company logo or shirts with your face on the front. Some newer printers even allow you to print directly onto the surface of a CD-ROM. You can even purchase small printers designed solely to print standard-size photographs.

Another important note is the difference in paper sizes globally. Whereas the United States and Canada use inches to measure paper, the rest of the globe uses a metric system based on an ISO (International Organization for Standardization) standard.

The North American Letter format may be replaced by the ISO A4 format. The other differences between the U.S. and Canadian systems from the ISO is that the ISO paper sizes always follow a set ratio, whereas the U.S. and Canadian systems uses two different aspect ratios.

Saving files for a service provider

When working with a professional print service provider, make sure to find out which file formats it accepts. Almost all print service providers accept files created using an Adobe program (Illustrator, Photoshop, InDesign, or Acrobat, for example) as well as files created using QuarkXPress, CorelDRAW, or other professional-level programs. Also confirm which version and operating system the service provider accepts because you may be required to save your files so that they're compatible with whichever version of software the service provider uses.

You may want to export your work as a different file format, such as PDF (Portable Document Format), if your service provider doesn't accept native InDesign or QuarkXPress files. In fact, exporting as a PDF is an intelligent choice. When you create a PDF (with the correct settings), you essentially package up all you need to print your file correctly.

To create a PDF of your document, choose File⇨Print and select Postscript File from the Printer drop-down list, as shown in Figure 8-1.

After you save a Postscript file, you can launch Adobe Distiller (which is in the Adobe Acrobat application folder installed with the Creative Suite) and choose File⇨Open to open your PostScript file. Distiller automatically converts the file to a PDF, based on your present settings. Read more about PDF options in Book V, Chapter 2.

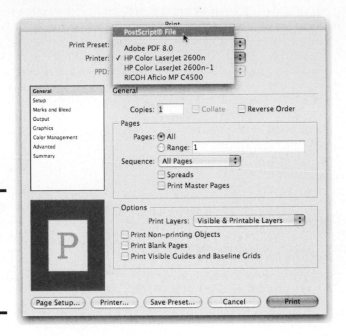

Figure 8-1:
Print to a
PostScript
file and
then open
in Adobe
Distiller.

Printing at home

When you're ready to print your documents, you can open the Print dialog box and then specify a number of settings depending on which kind of printer you've installed. For this example, Adobe Distiller is used.

Though you can simply save a Photoshop PDF from the regular Save menu, we walk you through the steps of creating a PDF file from the Photoshop Print dialog box. Using the Print dialog box, you can take advantage of additional options that aren't available on the Save menu, such as the ability to preview printed documents, scale images, and apply color settings.

To print a file as a PDF from Photoshop CS5, follow these steps:

1. **Choose File➪Print.**

The Print dialog box opens, as shown in Figure 8-2.

The Print dialog box differs, depending on which program you're using. In this dialog box, Photoshop allows you to change the scale of the image by entering a value in the Scale text box or selecting and dragging a handle on the preview image on the left side.

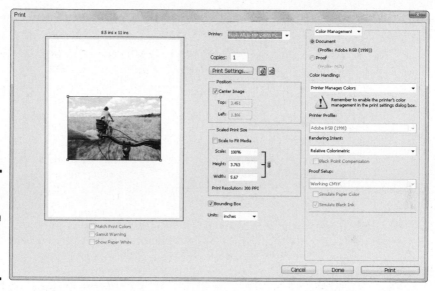

Figure 8-2:
The Print
dialog box in
Photoshop
CS5 for
Windows.

2. **From the Printer drop-down list, choose Adobe PDF.**

   If you want to choose the settings for an installed printer, you can also
   select it here.

3. **If necessary, scale the image to fit the paper and then click the Print
   Settings button.**

   A second Print dialog box appears, as shown in Figure 8-3.

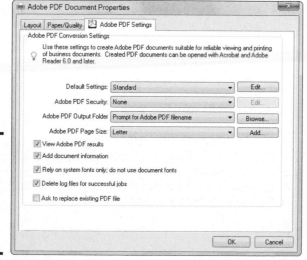

Figure 8-3:
The
secondary
Print dialog
box in
Photoshop
CS5.

4. **Choose the quality of PDF that you want to create from the Default Settings drop-down list.**

5. **(Optional) If you want to see your PDF file right after it's created, choose View Adobe PDF Results and then click OK.**

   You return to the Print dialog box.

6. **Click Print.**

   The Save PDF File As dialog box appears.

7. **Enter a name for the PDF, navigate to the location where you want to save the file, and click Save.**

   The document is saved as a PDF file.

Because most printers have custom interfaces for defining settings, you may need to consult your printer's documentation for detailed information on using the printer's features.

Book II

InDesign CS5

Contents at a Glance

Chapter 1: What's New in InDesign CS5

In This Chapter

✔ Creating content for print or Web

✔ Creating interactive documents

✔ Using multiple page sizes in the same document

✔ Tracking changes to an InDesign document

✔ Working with layers

✔ Taking a look at minor productivity enhancements

*B*efore the CS5 version existed, InDesign was used almost exclusively for print publishing. But in InDesign CS5, Adobe has added all sorts of new features for creating Web pages and interactive documents. Interactive documents that used to be created only in Flash, or Web pages that used to be created using only Dreamweaver, can now be developed using InDesign. Of course, you can still create print documents, but one big change between CS4 and CS5 is the addition of new types of files you can create.

If you're new to InDesign, you should know that your initial designs for any type of project can be created using InDesign. Because Adobe is just starting to add Web and interactive design tools to InDesign, you're better off using Dreamweaver to create Web pages or Flash to build most interactive projects. Interactive documents are just starting to get used, and because the iPad does not support the Flash format to which InDesign exports, you'll be limited primarily to PDF as the export option.

In this chapter, you'll discover some new features added to InDesign CS5 and references to chapters within this minibook where you can find more details. We haven't included every single new feature so that this chapter doesn't become a laundry list. Instead, we picked out the biggest changes and describe them here, and you'll find references to smaller changes in relevant chapters throughout this minibook.

Creating Web Content

The first time you create a new document, you see that InDesign lets you create more than print documents. In the New Document dialog box, shown in Figure 1-1, you specify whether you're creating content for Web or print and, if you're creating for the Web, you can specify measurements in pixels (the measurement used on computer displays) rather than inches or centimeters, which you might use in print.

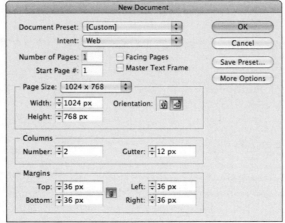

Figure 1-1: The New Document dialog box now lets you specify whether you're creating for print or the Web.

If you plan to create for the Web, you can have InDesign create Cascading Style Sheets (CSS) when you export to XHTML.

Creating Interactive Documents

InDesign CS5 provides three new panels you can use to create and work with interactive documents:

✦ **Media panel:** When you create interactive documents, you want to be able to include movies, so Adobe now lets you import FLV and MP3 files into an InDesign layout. After you import the movies, you can use the new Media panel to specify which frame from the video is displayed as the placeholder — the *poster* — and you can set options, such as whether the video plays only one time or should loop continuously.

✦ **Animation panel:** You can use the new Animation panel, shown in Figure 1-2, to create animations, or if you want to animate an object in your layout using a preset option, you can take advantage of the new motion presets. You can also animate objects along a path by creating a motion path.

✦ **Timing panel:** The new Timing panel lets you set the time when objects play, and the States panel lets you create buttons that look different when the mouse rolls over them or when they're clicked.

Figure 1-2: Animate an object along a path or use motion presets.

Export selected items on a page to Adobe Flash Player, and when exporting to Flash, choose more options such as resolution and background color.

Choosing from Multiple Page Sizes

Before this version of InDesign, all page sizes within a document had to be the same. It didn't matter if you needed a smaller size for a document such as a fold-out panel of a brochure, you could select and use only one size.

But Adobe has decided to trust you with more than one size in your documents. Using the Pages panel, you can select specific pages and change the page size, as shown in Figure 1-3. Master pages, which act as templates for document pages, can be of varying sizes as well.

As a designer, you might want to create a business card, letterhead, and envelope all in the same file — even though they're different sizes. Or, brochures and publications may have a gatefold that allows for a page to fold out from a design.

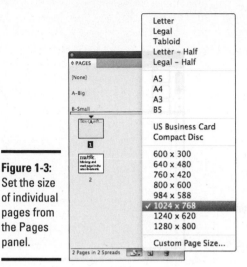

Figure 1-3:
Set the size
of individual
pages from
the Pages
panel.

Tracking Changes to Your Documents

When several people are working on the same document, determining what they have modified can be difficult. Adobe, borrowing an idea from Microsoft Word, now lets you track the changes made to the text of an InDesign document by each user. Change to Story Editor view to look at your text and you can see any proposed edits, such as deleting, moving, or inserting text, as shown in Figure 1-4. You can then accept or reject proposed edits by using the Track Changes panel.

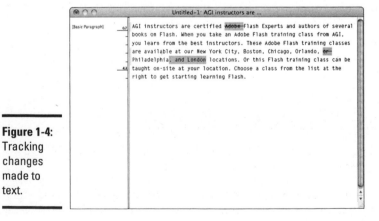

Figure 1-4:
Tracking
changes
made to
text.

Working with Layers

The Layers panel has been updated in InDesign CS5, making it similar to the one used in Illustrator. Here are some of the ways you can use this panel:

✦ View the stacking order of documents on a layer by clicking the triangle next to the layer name in the Layers panel, shown in Figure 1-5.

Figure 1-5:
The Layers panel in InDesign CS5 lets you work with individual objects within a layer.

✦ Expand groups, buttons, and multistate objects to see the stacking order of objects and select them.

✦ If you don't like the default names of the program's more generic objects, such as the shape type or text frames, which are named by the first few words within the frame, you can rename the objects.

✦ Just as with layers, you can move objects vertically within a layer to change their stacking order so that one object can appear on top of or below another object.

✦ You can change the visibility of individual items on a page and lock or unlock them. Locked objects cannot be edited without first unlocking them.

Exploring Minor Productivity Changes

Adobe changed or added many smaller features in InDesign CS5. Some of the more noteworthy changes include:

✦ **Color swatches have been added to the Control panel.** You can still access from the Swatches panel any color swatch used in a document.

✦ **Pouring content into your layouts is easier.** If you frequently place many objects at a single time, merely select several items to place — either text or graphics — and put them on the page.

✦ **You can now more easily access the metadata and have it used as captions in documents.** You can print lots of images and use their metadata as captions, such as the photographer name, product name, caption, or copyright information.

✦ **Mini Bridge makes it possible to locate and place images into documents without leaving InDesign.** Mini Bridge provides a small panel in which you can navigate your computer or network, locate items you might want to use in the layout, and place them into your document. The window is rather small, and you might still find it easier to simply click and drag items from your operating system, or you can use the Place command.

✦ **Adobe has added new review and commenting features.** You can share your designs across the Internet so that other people can provide feedback and input if you initiate them by using the new Review panel.

Chapter 2: Introducing InDesign CS5

*I*nDesign is a sophisticated page layout program. You can use it to create professional-looking documents, including newsletters, books, and magazines. You can also use it to create HTML pages and PDF documents that include interactivity or videos. InDesign has become a tool that lets you publish just about anywhere. For example, you can create a document that includes hyperlinks and video and export it to PDF, or you can export XML (Extensible Markup Language) from InDesign. You can even export XHTML and then import it into Dreamweaver to create Web pages.

As powerful an application as InDesign is, you'd think it would be difficult to use, but it isn't. This minibook shows you how to use InDesign to make creative page layouts. In this chapter, you discover the InDesign interface and start your first publication.

Getting Started with InDesign CS5

InDesign is used for creating page layouts that include type, graphics (such as fills and strokes), and images. The InDesign document you see in Figure 2-1 includes elements from Adobe Illustrator (logos) and Photoshop (images). If this file were to be exported as a PDF or HTML file, it could include video and even Flash files.

In the following sections, you get familiar with creating and opening documents in InDesign. In Chapters 3 through 9 in this minibook, you see how to add various elements to your pages.

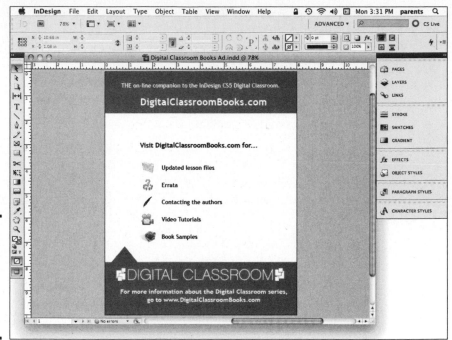

Figure 2-1:
A sample
page layout
created
using
InDesign
CS5.

Creating a new publication

After you launch InDesign, you can create a new InDesign document. Just follow these steps to create a new publication:

1. **Choose File⇨New⇨Document.**

The New Document dialog box opens, as shown in Figure 2-2.

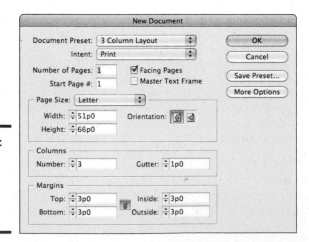

Figure 2-2:
Setting
up a new
document
with
InDesign.

2. **Select whether you're designing for Print or Web from the Intent drop-down menu.**

3. **Enter a value in the Number of Pages text field for the number of pages in the document.**

   This value can be between 1 and 9999. If you want a text frame on the master page, select the Master Text Frame check box.

   You can discover more about text frames in Chapter 3 of this minibook.

4. **For this example, select the Facing Pages check box to have the pages arranged as spreads with left and right pages.**

   With this option selected, pages in your document are arranged in pairs, so you have *spreads,* which are facing or adjacent pages in a layout. For example, you select this option if you're creating a publication that will be arranged like a book or magazine. If you deselect this option, pages are arranged individually, which is a good choice for a single-page flyer or a flyer with only a front and back side.

5. **Choose a page size for the document from the Page Size drop-down list.**

   The page size should be set to the size of paper you intend to print on or the size at which the content will be displayed. The Width and Height values below this drop-down list change, depending on the size you choose.

   You can also enter your own settings to create a custom size. The Orientation setting changes from Portrait (tall) to Landscape (wide) based on the settings you enter in the Width and Height fields of the Page Size section.

   The Page Size drop-down list also includes resolution sizes such as 1024 x 768, which is helpful if you're creating a Web page or an interactive PDF.

   You can enter page sizes using most common forms of measurement or just use the appropriate abbreviation. For example, you enter **8 in.** for 8 inches or **15 cm** for 15 centimeters. You can use most forms of measurement in all InDesign dialog boxes and panels; just make sure to specify the form of measurement you want to use.

6. **Choose a number for the columns on the page.**

   This step sets nonprinting guides for columns, which helps you organize your page. You can also enter a value in the Gutter field, which specifies the space between each of the columns. For more information about using columns in page layout, see Chapter 5 of this minibook.

7. **Choose values for the page margins.**

   Notice the Make All Settings the Same button, which is a chain icon, in the middle of the four text fields where you enter margin values. Click this button to set all margins to the same value.

If you see Top, Bottom, Inside, and Outside, you're specifying margins for a page layout that has facing pages, which you specified earlier. If you see Top, Bottom, Left, and Right, you're creating a page layout without facing pages. The *inside* margins refer to the margins at the middle of the spread, and the *outside* margins refer to the outer left and right margins of a book or magazine. You can set the Inside setting to accommodate the binding of a book, which may need wider margins than the outside.

If you use the same settings repeatedly, saving those settings as a preset is a good idea. Get your settings the way you want them and then click the Save Preset button in the New Document dialog box before you click OK. Enter a name for the preset and then click OK. After you save your settings, you can select settings from the Document Preset drop-down list (refer to the top of Figure 2-2) whenever you create a new document.

8. **When you're finished, click OK.**

   After you click OK in the New Document dialog box, the new document is created with the settings you just specified.

Margins, columns, orientation, and page size are discussed in more detail in Chapter 5 of this minibook.

Opening an existing publication

You may have InDesign files on your hard drive that you created or have saved from another source. To open existing InDesign documents (files that end with .indd), follow these steps:

1. **Choose File⇨Open.**

   The Open dialog box appears.

2. **Browse your hard drive and select a file to open.**

   Select a file by clicking the document's title. To select more than one document, press Ctrl (⌘ on the Mac) while you click the filenames.

3. **Click the Open button to open the file.**

   The file opens in the workspace.

Looking at the document setup

If you need to change the size of your pages or the number of pages in a document that's already open in the workspace, you can make those changes in the Document Setup dialog box. To access and modify settings in the Document Setup dialog box, follow these steps:

1. **Choose File⇨Document Setup.**

   The Document Setup dialog box opens.

Note: You can change the value in the Number of Pages text field if you need the number of pages in your document to be greater than or less than the current value.

The number of pages in your document updates after you close this dialog box. You can also change this number later by choosing Layout⇨Pages⇨Insert Pages or by using the Pages panel.

2. **Select a new option from the Page Size drop-down list or manually enter values into the Width and Height text fields to change the page size.**

   You can also click the up and down arrows in the Width and Height text fields to choose a new value.

3. **Click the Portrait or Landscape button to change the page orientation.**

   The page orientation updates in the workspace after you close this dialog box.

4. **Click OK when you finish changing your document setup.**

   The modifications are applied to the open document.

If you make changes to the Document Setup dialog box when you have no documents open, the changes become the default settings for all new documents you create.

Touring the Workspace

Just like the other applications in the CS5 Suite, InDesign has a standardized layout. Using panels that can be docked and a single-row Tools panel, you can keep much more space open in your work area.

The InDesign workspace, or *user interface,* is designed to be intuitive and efficient. You'll use several panels over and over again, so keep them accessible. Many of these panels are already docked to the right in the default user workspace. Figure 2-3 shows how the InDesign workspace layout looks on a Macintosh. The Windows workspace is slightly different from the Macintosh version. You'll notice a difference in the main menu bar.

Here are the elements that create the InDesign workspace:

✦ **Page:** The main area of the InDesign workspace is a page. It's the area that's printed or exported when you finish making a layout.

✦ **Master page:** You can define how certain text elements and graphics appear in an entire document (or just portions of it) by using a master page. It's much like a template for your document because you can reuse elements throughout the pages. For example, if you have an element you want on each page (such as page numbering), you can create it on the master page. If you need to change an element on the master page, you can change it at any time and your changes are reflected on every page that the master page is applied to. You find out more about master pages in Chapter 5 of this minibook.

✦ **Spread:** A spread refers to a set of two or more pages that will be printed side-by-side. You usually see spreads in magazines and books when you open them — just like the book you're holding now.

✦ **Pasteboard:** The pasteboard is the area around the edge of a page. You can use the pasteboard to store objects until you're ready to put them into your layout. Pasteboards aren't shared between pages or spreads. For example, if you have certain elements placed on a pasteboard for pages 4 and 5, you can't access these elements when you're working on pages 8 and 9 — so each page or spread has its own pasteboard.

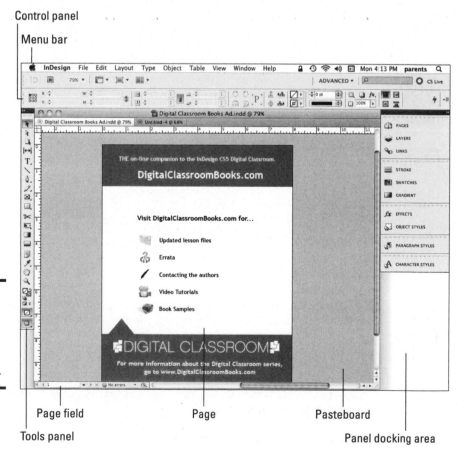

Control panel

Menu bar

Figure 2-3:
The
InDesign
Windows
default
workspace.

Page field

Tools panel

Page

Pasteboard

Panel docking area

Tools

The Tools panel is where you find tools to edit, manipulate, or select elements in your document. Simply use the cursor and click a tool to select it. See Figure 2-4 for the default Tools panel layout.

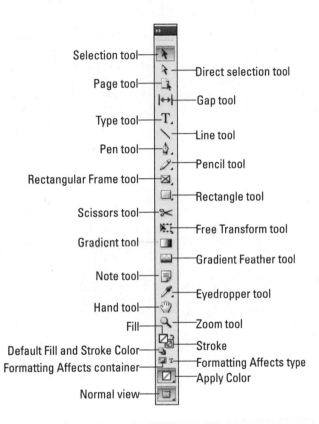

Selection tool
Direct selection tool
Page tool
Gap tool
Type tool
Line tool
Pen tool
Pencil tool
Rectangular Frame tool
Rectangle tool
Scissors tool
Free Transform tool
Gradient tool
Gradient Feather tool
Note tool
Eyedropper tool
Hand tool
Fill
Zoom tool
Stroke
Default Fill and Stroke Color
Formatting Affects container
Formatting Affects type
Apply Color
Normal view

Figure 2-4:
The Tools panel contains tools needed to create, select, and edit elements.

**Book II
Chapter 2**

Introducing
InDesign CS5

TIP

If you decide that a single row of tools just isn't for you, you can go back to an older version's Tools panel by clicking the two arrows in the gray bar at the top of the Tools panel. If you want to relocate the tools, click the silver bar at the top of the tools and drag to a new location.

You can find out more about these tools and how to use them in the related chapters of this minibook. For example, we discuss the drawing tools in Chapter 4 of this minibook.

With the tools in the Tools panel, you can

✦ Create stunning new content on a page using drawing, frame, and text tools.

 ✦ Select existing content on a page to move or edit.

 ✦ View the page in different ways by moving (panning) and magnifying the page or spread.

 ✦ Edit existing objects, such as shapes, lines, and text. Use the Selection tool to select existing objects so that you can change them.

When a tool has a small arrow next to the button's icon, more tools are hiding behind it. When you click the tool and hold down the mouse button, a menu opens that shows you other available tools. While pressing the mouse, move the cursor to the tool you want and release the mouse button after it's highlighted.

Menus

The menus on the main menu bar are used to access some of the main commands and control the user interface of InDesign. They also allow you to open and close panels used to edit and make settings for the publication.

InDesign menu commands such as New, Open, and Save are similar to most other applications you're probably familiar with. The InDesign menus also include commands that are especially used for page layout, such as Insert with Placeholder Text. For more information on using menus, see Book I, Chapter 2. Remember to refer to the common commands and shortcuts that are also detailed in that chapter.

The InDesign main menu has the following options:

 ✦ **File:** This menu includes some of the basic commands to create, open, and save documents. It also includes the Place command to import new content and many options to control document settings, exporting documents, and printing.

 ✦ **Edit:** You can access many commands for editing and controlling selections in this menu — such as copying and keyboard shortcuts. The dictionary and spell checker are on this menu, too.

 ✦ **Layout:** Use this menu to create guides. These options help you lay elements on the page accurately and properly align them. Use the menu to navigate the document's pages and spreads.

 ✦ **Type:** From this menu, you can select fonts and control characters in the layout. You can access the many settings related to text from this menu, which opens the associated panel where you make the changes.

 ✦ **Object:** You can modify the look and placement of objects on the page with this menu. Which options are available on this menu depends on which element you've selected in the workspace, such as a text field or an image.

+ **Table:** Use this menu to create, set up, modify, and control tables on the page.

+ **View:** You can modify the view of the page from this menu, including zooming in and out, as well as work with guides, rulers, or grids to help you lay out elements.

+ **Window:** Use this menu to open and close panels or switch between open documents.

+ **Help:** This menu is where you can access the Help documents for InDesign and configure any plug-ins you have installed.

Panels

In the default layout, you see a large area for the document, typically referred to as the page. To the right of the page are several *panels* that snap (are *docked*) to the edge of the workspace. Panels are used to control the publication and edit elements on pages. *Docked* panels are panels attached to the edge of the user interface. Panels can be maximized and minimized away from the main work area, moved around, or closed altogether.

To expand a panel, you can simply click the panel name and it automatically expands. The magic of this improved panel system is that the panels you expand are automatically collapsed again when a different panel is selected.

If you'd rather work with all panels expanded, simply click the left-facing double arrows on the gray bar above the panels. You can collapse all the panels again by clicking the right-facing double arrows on the gray bar above the expanded panels.

Even though some InDesign panels perform different functions, similar panels are grouped together depending on what they're used for. You can change the groupings by clicking and dragging a panel's tab into another grouping.

Some panels work intelligently when you're manipulating content on an InDesign page. If you work with a particular element, for example, the associated panel is activated. Throughout Chapters 3 through 9 of this minibook, you discover these specific panels as you create layouts. For now, we briefly show you two general InDesign panels: Control and Pages.

Control panel

The Control panel is used to edit just about any element in InDesign, as shown for the Type tool in Figure 2-5. This panel is *context sensitive,* so it changes depending on which element you've selected on a page. For example, if you have selected text on the page, the Control panel displays options allowing you to edit the text. If you have a shape selected, the panel displays options allowing you to modify the shape.

Figure 2-5:
The Control panel, when the Type tool is active.

Figure 2-6 shows the Control panel when a frame is selected using the Selection tool. The Control panel menu allows you to select options for the frame.

Figure 2-6:
The Control panel, when a frame is selected using the Selection tool.

Pages panel

You can control pages by using the Pages panel, as shown in Figure 2-7. This panel allows you to arrange, add, and delete pages in your document. You can also navigate among pages with this panel, which we discuss further in Chapter 5 of this minibook.

You can also add and delete pages by choosing Layout⇨Pages, and even use a keyboard shortcut to add pages, Ctrl+Shift+P (Windows) or ⌘+Shift+P (Mac).

You can hide all open panels (including the Control panel) by pressing the Tab key; press Tab for them to return to view. In InDesign CS5, you can leave tools and panels hidden and access them when you want by moving the cursor to the left or right side of the work area. Pause when you see a tinted vertical gray bar appear, and the tools or panels (depending on which side of the workspace you're in) reappear! By the way, they go away again after you leave the area.

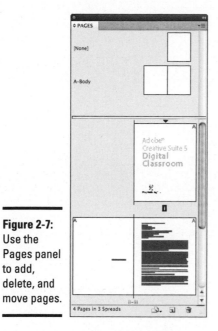

Figure 2-7: Use the Pages panel to add, delete, and move pages.

You can navigate the document's pages by using the left and right arrow buttons on either side of the page number in the lower left corner of the document window. You can also move to a specific page by entering a page number into the page field and pressing Enter or by selecting the page from the drop-down list in the lower left corner of the document window.

Contextual menus

Contextual menus (or context menus) are menus that pop up when you right-click (Windows) or Control-click (Mac) the mouse. Contextual menus change depending on which element you click and which tool you're using. If you have no elements selected, the contextual menu opens for the overall InDesign document, allowing you to select options such as Zoom, Paste, Rulers, and Guides. If you have an element selected, your options include transforming, modifying, and editing the object.

Contextual menus are context sensitive (hence the name!). Remember to select an element on the page before you right-click to open the contextual menu. If you don't select the object first, the menu is for the document instead of for the object.

You can find out more about editing and transforming elements in Chapters 3 and 4 of this minibook.

Setting Up the Workspace

Workspace settings are important because they help you quickly create the type of layout you need. Overall document settings control elements such as grids or guides that help you align elements on the page. Grids and guidelines are pretty much the same thing, except that grids are designed to repeat across the page and be a specified distance apart. Neither guides nor grids print when you print your document.

Showing and hiding grids and guides

Use grids when you need to align elements across a document. You can have objects on a page snap to the grid, which helps you to align or space several objects accurately. Guides are only slightly different, because they're often created individually, but they're also nonprinting lines. Guides can be placed anywhere on the page (or pasteboard) and are used to accurately position objects in a layout. Objects can snap to guides just like they can snap to a grid. Grids differ from guides in that grids aren't freely placed anywhere on the page.

The *document grid* is used for aligning elements on the page, and the *baseline grid* is used for aligning the bottom of text across multiple columns.

✦ To show or hide the document grid, choose View➪Grids & Guides➪ Show (or hide) Document Grid.

✦ To show or hide the baseline grid, choose View➪Grids & Guides➪ Show (or hide) Baseline Grid.

You can immediately see the difference between these two kinds of grids.

To snap objects in your page layout to a guide or the document grid, you must have snapping enabled. To enable snapping, choose View➪Grids & Guides➪Snap to Guides or View➪Grids & Guides➪Snap to Document Grid. If these options are already selected, clicking them will turn them off.

To create a guide and show or hide guides, follow these steps:

1. **Make sure that rulers are visible by choosing View➪Show Rulers.**

Rulers appear in the workspace. If you already have rulers visible, the option View➪Hide Rulers is on the View menu. Do not hide the rulers.

2. **Move the cursor to a horizontal or vertical ruler.**

Make sure that the cursor is over a ruler.

3. **Click the ruler and drag the mouse toward the page.**

A *ruler guide* shows on the page as a line.

4. **Release the mouse where you want the guide.**

   You just created a ruler guide!

5. **To hide the guide, choose View⇨Grids & Guides⇨Hide Guides.**

   This step hides the guide you created but doesn't delete it. You can make the guide reappear easily in the next step.

6. **To see the guide again, choose View⇨Grids & Guides⇨Show Guides.**

   The guide you created is shown on the page again.

You can edit the color of the ruler guide you created by positioning the mouse over it, clicking once to select it, and then right-clicking (Windows) or ctrl-clicking it (Mac) and selecting a new color from the Ruler Guides option.

You can find out more about the different kinds of guides and how to use them in page layout in Chapter 5 of this minibook.

You can also control the color of the guides and grid in your preferences. Access them by choosing Edit⇨Preferences⇨Grids (Windows) or InDesign⇨Preferences⇨Grids (Mac). When the Preferences dialog box opens, you can change the color and spacing of the lines. Click Guides & Pasteboards in the list on the left to change the color settings for guides.

Snapping to a grid or a guide

You can have elements on the page snap to a grid or a guide. Grid or guide snapping is useful so that you don't have to eyeball the alignment of several elements to one another, because they're precisely aligned to a grid or guide. In fact, grids and guides are fairly useless unless you have elements snap to them! To make sure that this setting is enabled, choose View⇨Grids & Guides⇨Snap to Document Grid or View⇨Grids & Guides⇨Snap to Guides.

Using smart guides

Give yourself an added hand when aligning objects on the InDesign page with Smart Guides. Illustrator and Photoshop users may be familiar with these interactive guides, but if you're not, read on to discover how you can take advantage of them.

You can experiment with this new feature by creating two objects in an InDesign document. It doesn't matter which object or shape — any will do!

With the Selection tool, click and drag one object in a circular motion around the other. You'll notice guides appear and disappear, indicating when the objects are aligned either on the top, center, or bottom of the other object, as shown in Figure 2-8.

Figure 2-8:
Click and drag one shape around another to see the interaction with Smart Guides.

As a default, pink guides appear when you align an object with the center of the page, as shown in Figure 2-9.

Figure 2-9:
Know when your object is at the exact center of the page when a guide crosshair appears.

You can see a print preview of your document by clicking the Preview Mode button at the bottom of the Tools panel. When you click this button, all object bounding boxes, guides, and the grid disappear.

Saving a custom workspace

You've seen that InDesign has a number of panels. If you find that you're using some panels more than others, you can have InDesign remember the grouping of panels you use most frequently — InDesign calls it a workspace. The next time you want a certain group of panels open together, you can return to the workspace you previously saved. The workspace isn't attached to a particular document, so you can have one workspace for editing text and another for working with a layout.

To save a custom workspace, follow these steps:

1. **Have the InDesign workspace configured in the way you want to save it — with any panels open that you might want to access together.**

   The open panels are saved as a custom workspace.

2. **Choose Window⇨Workspace⇨New Workspace.**

   The New Workspace dialog box opens.

3. **Type a new name for the workspace in the Name text field.**

   When you finish, this name is displayed on the Workspaces menu. Save it using a name that reflects the type of work you do in that workspace, such as text editing or layout.

4. **Click OK.**

   The custom workspace is saved.

To access your workspace, choose Window⇨Workspace⇨*Your Workspace* (where *Your Workspace* is the name you gave the workspace in Step 3).

You can delete the workspace if you no longer want it saved. Simply choose Window⇨Workspace⇨Delete Workspace.

Working with Documents

After you're comfortable getting around the InDesign workspace, you're ready to begin working with a new document. After you've started working on a document, you should find out how to import content from other programs and to save that document on your hard drive. A lot of the content you use when creating layouts with InDesign is imported from other programs. You use InDesign to organize, modify, and integrate text and graphics into a layout. To begin, we show you the steps needed to import content and save new files.

We show you how to open new and existing documents earlier in this chapter, in the sections "Creating a new publication" and "Opening an existing publication."

You may also be working with a *template,* which is a layout you reuse by applying it to a document that requires a particular predesigned format. For example, a company may use a template for its official letterhead because every new letter requires the same page format and design. InDesign templates use the .indt file extension.

Importing new content

You can use many different kinds of content in an InDesign document because you can import many supported file types. You can import text, formatted tables, and graphics that help you create an effective layout. This capability makes integration with many different programs easy.

Follow these steps to import an image file into InDesign (in this example, we import a bitmap graphic file):

1. **Choose File⇨New⇨Document.**

The New Document dialog box appears.

2. **Review the settings and click the OK button.**

A new document opens. Feel free to alter the settings to change the number of pages or page size before clicking the OK button.

3. **Choose File⇨Place.**

The Place dialog box opens, enabling you to browse the contents of your hard drive for supported files. If you were to select the Show Import Options check box, another dialog box opens before the file imports. Leave this option deselected for now.

4. **Click the file you want to import and then click the Open button.**

Certain files, such as bitmap photo, graphic, and PDF files, show a thumbnail preview at the bottom of the dialog box.

When you click the Open button, the Place dialog box closes and the cursor becomes an upside-down L.

5. **Click the location on the page where you want the upper left corner of the imported file (for example, an image) to appear.**

The imported file is placed on the page.

Click and drag to place the file into a specific frame size, or if you have created an empty frame on the page, clicking on top of the frame causes the object being imported — whether it's text or an image — to be placed inside the frame.

You can Ctrl-click (Windows) or ⌘-click (Mac) to place multiple files. After you select the images and click OK, each click places an image on the page, or you can hold down the Shift+Ctrl (Windows) or Shift+⌘ (Mac) while dragging a rectangle to have all selected images placed, spaced evenly, in a grid.

Note that when you're placing multiple images, you can see a thumbnail of each image before it's placed. You can also scroll through the loaded images by pressing the arrow keys on your keyboard.

For general information about importing and exporting using the Adobe Creative Suite, check out Book I, Chapter 5. For more information on importing different kinds of file formats, such as text, images, spreadsheets, and PDFs, see Chapters 3 and 5 in this minibook.

Viewing content

You can view elements in several different ways on your document's pages. For example, sometimes you need to see objects on a page close up so that you can make precise edits. InDesign offers several ways to navigate documents:

✦ **Scroll bars:** You can use the scroll bars to move pages around. The scroll bars are located below and to the right of the pasteboard. Click a scroll bar handle and drag it left and right or up and down.

✦ **Zoom:** Zoom in or out from the document to increase or decrease the display of your document. Select the Zoom tool (the magnifying glass icon) from the Tools panel and click anywhere on the page to zoom in. Press the Alt (Windows) or Option (Mac) key and click to zoom out.

✦ **Hand tool:** Use the Hand tool to move the page around. This tool is perhaps the best and quickest way to move pages around and navigate documents. Select the Hand tool by pressing the spacebar and then click and drag to move around the pasteboard.

✦ **Keyboard:** Press Ctrl++ (plus sign) or ⌘++ (plus sign) to zoom in using the keyboard; replace the plus sign with the minus sign to zoom out.

Saving your publication

Even the best computers and applications fail from time to time, so you don't want to lose your hard work unnecessarily. Saving a publication often is important so that you don't lose any work if your computer or software crashes or the power goes out.

To save a file, choose File⇨Save or press Ctrl+S (Windows) or ⌘+S (Mac).

Some people save different versions of their files. You may want to do this in case you want to revert to an earlier version of the file. For example, you may decide to make a radical change to the page layout but keep an earlier version in case the radical change just doesn't work out. You do this by using the Save As command, which makes it easy to create different versions of documents.

Choose File⇨Save before proceeding if you want the current document to save the revisions you've made since you last saved the file. All new additions to the document are made in the new version of the file.

To save a new version of the current document and then continue working on the new document, follow these steps:

1. **Choose File⇨Save As.**

The Save As dialog box opens.

2. **Choose the directory you want to save the file in.**

3. **In the File Name text field, enter a new name for the document.**

This step saves a new version of the file. Consider a naming scheme at this point. If your file is `myLayout.indd`, you might call it `myLayout02.indd` to signify the second version of the file. Future files can then increase the number for each new version.

4. **Click the Save button when you're finished.**

This step saves the document in the chosen directory with a new name.

The File⇨Save As command is also used for other means. You may want to save your design as a template. After you create the template, choose File⇨Save As and then choose InDesign CS5 Template from the Save As Type (Windows) or Format (Mac) drop-down list.

You can also choose File⇨Save a Copy. This command saves with a new name a copy of the current state of the document you're working on, but you then continue working on the original document. Both commands are useful for saving incremental versions of a project you're working on.

To find out more about working with files, go to Chapter 9 of this minibook.

Chapter 3: Working with Text and Text Frames

In This Chapter

✔ Understanding text and frames in a publication

✔ Adding and importing text

✔ Exploring text frame options

✔ Changing paragraph settings

✔ Editing with text editors and spell checking

✔ Working with tables

✔ Creating and editing text on a path

Most of the documents you create contain text, so it's important to know how to format, style, and control text in your layouts. Text is made up of characters, and the characters are styled in specific fonts. If you want to find out more about fonts, check out Book I, Chapter 6, where we explain more about fonts and type faces.

This chapter explains how to create, edit, and style text using InDesign. You get started by editing and manipulating text placed inside *text frames* — containers on the page that hold text content. The most important concepts you can take away from this chapter are how to add text to documents and then change the text so that it looks the way you want on the page. In Chapter 5 of this minibook, find out how to create effective layouts that contain both text and graphics so that your audience is encouraged to read everything you create.

Understanding Text, Font, and Frames

Text is usually integral to a publication because it contains specific information you want or need to convey to an audience. Understanding the terminology that appears in the following pages is important: *Text* and *font* are quite different from each other:

✦ **Text:** The letters, words, sentences, and paragraphs making up content in the text frames in your publication.

✦ **Font:** The particular design forming a set of characters used to style text. You can find thousands of styles of fonts from many manufacturers, and many are included in the Creative Suite 5 when you install it on your computer.

Frames resemble containers that are used to hold content. You can use two kinds of frames in a publication:

✦ **Text:** Contains text on the page in your InDesign document. You can link text frames so that text flows from one text frame to another, and you can have text wrap around graphic frames.

✦ **Graphic:** Holds an image that you place in your publication.

When you create frames using InDesign, they can contain either text or graphics — so the methods for creating both types of frames are identical. InDesign automatically changes frames to adapt to content, so you can use both the frame and shape tools for designing your layout and creating frames that will contain text or graphics.

Creating and Using Text Frames

Text frames contain any text you add to a publication. You can create a new text frame in many different ways. In InDesign, you can add text to creative shapes you draw, thereby changing them into text frames. Creating and using text frames in a publication is important because you typically use a lot of text. Throughout the following subsections, we show you how to create text frames in different but important ways using three different tools. If you need a guide to the tools, check out Chapter 2 of this minibook.

Text frames are sometimes automatically created when you import text into a publication. You find out how to do this in the "Importing text" section, later in this chapter.

Creating text frames with the Type tool

You can use the Type tool to create a text frame. If you use the Type tool and click the page, nothing happens unless you've first created a frame to hold the text. Here's how to create a text frame by using the Type tool:

1. **Select the Type tool in the Tools panel and place the tool over the page.**

   The Type tool cursor is an I-bar. Move the cursor to the spot where you want to place the upper left corner of the text frame.

2. **Drag diagonally to create a text frame.**

   When you click, the mouse has a cross-like appearance. When you drag, an outline of the text frame appears, giving you a reference to its dimensions, as shown in Figure 3-1.

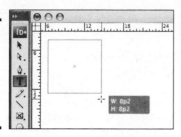

Figure 3-1:
Using the
Type tool,
drag to
create a
text frame.

3. **Release the mouse button when the frame is the correct size.**

   The text frame is created and an insertion point is placed in the upper left corner of the frame. You can start typing on the keyboard to enter text or to import text from another source (see the later section "Importing text").

Creating text frames with the Frame tool

You can use the Frame tool to create frames that are rectangular, oval, or polygonal. Then, after you've placed the frame on the page, you can turn it into a text frame or use it as a graphic frame or simply a design object on the page. To create a new text frame with the Frame tool, follow these steps:

1. **Choose the Frame tool from the Tools panel and drag diagonally to create a new frame.**

   A new frame is created on the page.

2. **Select the Type tool and click inside the frame.**

   The X across the frame disappears, and the frame is now a text frame instead of a graphic frame.

3. **Choose the Selection tool and use it to move the text frame.**

   You can move the text frame if you click within the frame using the Selection tool and drag it to a new location.

Creating text frames from a shape

If you have an interesting shape that you've created with the drawing tools or copied and pasted from Illustrator, you can easily change the shape into a text frame so that it can be filled with text. Just follow these steps:

1. **Use the Pen tool or Pencil tool or a Shape tool to create a shape with a stroke color and no fill. Or, copy and paste artwork from Illustrator.**

   A shape is created on the page that doesn't have a solid color for the fill.

2. **Select the Type tool from the Tools panel.**

   The Type tool becomes active.

3. **Click inside the shape you created in Step 1 and enter some text or import text (see the section "Importing text," later in this chapter).**

   This step changes the shape into a text frame. Notice how the text is confined within the shape as you type.

Adding Text to Your Publication

In the previous section's step lists, you find out how to add text by simply clicking in the text frame and typing new content, but you can also add text to publications in other ways. Doing so is particularly useful when you use other applications to create and edit documents containing text.

Importing text

You can import text you've created or edited using other software, such as Adobe InCopy or Microsoft Word or Excel. Importing edited text is a typical workflow activity when creating a publication, because dedicated text-editing software is often used to edit manuscripts before layout.

To import text into InDesign, follow these steps:

1. **Choose File➪Place.**

   The Place dialog box opens. Choose an importable file (such as a Word document, an InCopy story, or a plain text file) by browsing your hard drive.

2. **Select a document to import and click the Open button.**

   The Place Text icon, the cursor arrow, and a thumbnail image of the text appear. Move the cursor around the page to the spot where you want the upper left corner of the text frame to be created when the document is imported.

3. **Click to place the imported text.**

   This step creates a text frame and imports the text.

If you select a text frame *before* importing text, the text is automatically placed inside the text frame — so, in this case, you wouldn't have to use the cursor to place the text. You can move the text frame anywhere on the page after the text is added or resize the frame, if necessary.

Controlling text flow

Control the flow of the text by using these simple modifier keys while placing text:

✦ Choose File⇨Place, select the file you want to import, and click Open. Hold down the Shift key, and when the loaded cursor turns into a curvy arrow, click the document. The text is imported and automatically flows from one column to another or from page to page until it runs out. InDesign even creates pages, if needed.

✦ Choose File⇨Place, select the file you want to import, and click Open. Hold down the Alt (Windows) or Option (Mac) key. Then click and drag a text area. (Do not release the Alt key or Option key!) As you continue clicking and dragging additional text frames, your text flows from one text frame to another until you run out of copy.

If you check the Show Import Options check box in the Place window, a second window appears in which you can choose to remove styles and formatting from text and tables. This action brings in clean, unformatted text to edit.

Adding placeholder text

Suppose that you're creating a publication but the text you need to import into it isn't ready to import into InDesign. (Perhaps the text is still being created or edited.) Rather than wait for the final text, you can use placeholder text and continue to create your publication's layout. *Placeholder text* is commonly used to temporarily fill a document with text. The text looks a lot like normal blocks of text, which is more natural than trying to paste the same few words repeatedly to fill up a text frame. However, placeholder text isn't in any particular language, because it's just being used as filler.

InDesign can add placeholder text into a text frame automatically. Here's how:

1. **Create a frame on the page by selecting the Type tool and dragging diagonally to create a text frame.**

2. **Choose Type⇨Fill with Placeholder Text.**

   The text frame is automatically filled with characters and words, similar to the one shown in Figure 3-2.

Copying and pasting text

You can move text from one application into a publication by copying and pasting the text directly into InDesign. If you select and copy text in another program, you can paste it directly into InDesign from your computer's Clipboard. Here's how:

1. **Highlight the text you want to use in your publication and press Ctrl+C (Windows) or ⌘+C (Mac) to copy the text.**

   When you copy text, it sits on the Clipboard (until it's replaced by something new) and you can transfer this information into InDesign.

Figure 3-2:
The text
frame,
filled with
placeholder
text.

2. **Open InDesign and press Ctrl+V (Windows) or ⌘+V (Mac) to create a new text frame and paste the text into it.**

   A new text frame appears centered on the page with your selected text inside it.

   You can also click in a text frame and press Ctrl+V (Windows) or ⌘+V (Mac) to paste text from the Clipboard directly into an existing frame. You can do the same thing with an image.

   All you need to do is double-click a text frame if you want to access or edit some text or type or paste it into the frame.

Looking at Text Frame Options

In the previous sections of this chapter, we show you how to create text frames and enter text into them. In this section, we show you how to organize text frames in your publication and achieve the results you need. Controlling text frames so that they do what you need them to do is a matter of knowing how they work after you put text in them.

InDesign gives you a lot of control over the text in your publications. Changing text frame options allows you to change the way text is placed inside a frame. Changing these kinds of settings is sometimes important when you're working with particular kinds of fonts. (To read more about fonts, check out Book I, Chapter 6.)

The text frame contextual menu contains many options for working with the text frame. You use this menu to perform basic commands, such as copy and paste, fill the text frame with placeholder text, make transformations, add or modify strokes, and change the frame type. Access the text frame contextual menu by right-clicking (Windows) or Control-clicking (Mac) a text frame. You can also find most of these options on the Type and Object menus.

Changing text frame options

To change text frame options that control the look of the text within the frame, follow these steps:

1. **Create a rectangular text frame on the page, select the frame, and choose Object⇨Text Frame Options.**

   You can also press Ctrl+B (Windows) or ⌘+B (Mac) or use the text frame's contextual menu to open the Text Frame Options dialog box.

   You can tell that a text frame is selected when it has handles around its bounding box.

   The Text Frame Options dialog box appears, showing you the current settings for the selected text frame.

2. **Select the Preview check box to automatically view updates.**

   Now any changes you make in the dialog box are instantly updated on the page, so you can make changes and see how they'll look before you apply them.

3. **In the Inset Spacing area of the dialog box, change the Top, Bottom, Left, and Right values.**

   These values are used to inset text from the edges of the text frame. The text is pushed inside the frame edge by the value you set.

   You can also indent text, which we discuss in the section "Indenting your text," later in this chapter. You can choose in this dialog box how to align the text vertically (Top, Center, Bottom, or Justify). You can align the text to the top or bottom of the text frame, center it vertically in the frame, or evenly space the lines in the frame from top to bottom (Justify).

4. **When you finish making changes in this dialog box, click OK.**

   The changes you made are applied to the text frame.

Using and modifying columns

You can specify that the document contain a certain number of columns on the page when you create a new publication. Using columns allows you to snap new text frames to columns so that they're properly spaced on the page. You can even modify the size of the *gutter*, which is the spacing between columns.

You can also create columns within a single text frame by using the Text Frame Options dialog box. You can add as many as 40 columns in a single text frame. If you already have text in a frame, it's automatically divided among the columns you add. The following steps show you how to add columns to a text frame on a page:

1. **Create a rectangular text frame on the page.**

    Use the Text or Frame tool to create the text frame. You can create columns in text frames that are rectangular, oval, or even freehand shapes drawn on the page.

2. **Select the text frame and enter some text.**

    You can type some text, paste text copied from another document, or add placeholder text by choosing Type⇨Fill with Placeholder Text.

3. **With the text frame still selected, choose Object⇨Text Frame Options.**

    The Text Frame Options dialog box opens. Be sure to select the Preview check box in the dialog box, which enables you to immediately view the changes your settings make to the frame on the page.

4. **In the Columns section, change the value in the Number text field.**

    In this example, we entered **2** in the Number text field. The selected text frame divides the text in the frame into two columns.

5. **Change the width of the columns by entering a new value in the Width text field.**

    The width of the columns is automatically set, depending on the width of the text frame you created. We entered **10** (picas) in the Width text field for this example. The text frame changes size depending on the width you set in this column. When you click in a different text field in the dialog box, the text frame updates on the page to reflect the new value setting.

6. **Change the value in the Gutter text field.**

    The gutter value controls the amount of space between columns. If the gutter is too wide, change the value in the Gutter text field to a lower number. We entered **0p5** in the Gutter text field for this example to change the gutter width to half a point.

7. **When you finish, click OK to apply the changes.**

    The changes are applied to the text frame you modified.

After you create columns in a text frame, you can resize the frame by using the handles on its bounding box, detailed in the later section "Resizing and moving the text frame." The columns resize as necessary to divide the text frame into the number of columns you specified in the Text Frame Options dialog box. If you select the Fixed Column Width check box in the Text Frame Options dialog box, your text frames are always the width you specify, no matter how you resize the text frame. When you resize the text frame, the frame snaps to the designated fixed width.

Modifying and Connecting Text Frames on a Page

Making modifications to text frames and then connecting them to other text frames in a publication so that the story can continue on a separate page is vital in most publications. You typically work with stories of many paragraphs that need to continue on different pages in the document.

When you have a text frame on the page, you need to be able to change the size, position, and linking of the frame. You need to link the frame to other frames on the page so that the text can flow between them — which is important if you're creating a layout that contains a lot of text.

If you paste more text content than is visible in the text frame, the text still exists beyond the boundaries of the text frame — so if you have a text frame that's 20 lines tall but you paste in 50 lines of text, the last 30 lines are cropped off. You need to resize the text frame or have the text flow to another frame in order to see the rest of the text you pasted. You can tell that the frame has more content when you see a small plus sign (+) in a special handle in the text frame's bounding box.

Resizing and moving the text frame

When creating layouts, you regularly resize text frames and move them around the document while you figure out how you want the page layout to look. You can resize and move a text frame by following these steps:

1. **Use the Selection tool to select a text frame on the page.**

   A bounding box with handles appears on the page. If the text frame has more text than it can show at the current size, a small handle with a red box appears on the bounding box. Therefore, you can't use this handle to resize the text frame.

2. **Drag one of the handles to resize the text frame.**

   The frame updates automatically on the page while you drag the handles, as shown in Figure 3-3. Change the width or height by dragging the handles at the center of each side of the frame, or change the height and the width at the same time by dragging a corner handle.

   Shift-drag a corner handle to scale the text frame proportionally.

Figure 3-3:
Resize a text
frame by
dragging its
handles.

3. **When you're finished resizing the text frame, click the middle of a selected frame and move it around the page.**

If you click within the frame once and drag it, you move the frame around the page. An outline of the frame follows the cursor and represents the spot where the frame is placed if you release the mouse button. Simply release the frame when you finish moving it.

If you're using guides or grids on the page, the text frame snaps to them. Also, if you opened a document with columns, the text frame snaps to the columns when you drag the frame close to the column guidelines. You can find out about guides, grids, and snapping in Chapter 5 of this minibook.

You can also use the Transform panel to change the location and dimensions of a text frame. If the Transform panel isn't already open, choose Window⇨Object and Layout⇨Transform to open it. Then follow these steps:

1. **Change the values in the X and Y text fields.**

Enter **1** in both the X and Y text fields to move the text frame to the upper left corner of the page.

The X and Y coordinates (location) of the text frame update to 1,1. The small square in the middle or along the edge of the text is the *reference point* of the text frame: The X and Y coordinates you set match the position of this point.

Change the reference point by clicking any point in the reference point indicator in the upper left corner of the control panel.

2. **Change the values in the W and H text fields.**

For this example, we entered **35** (picas) in the W and H text fields. The text frame's width and height changes to the dimensions you specify. Using the Transform panel to change the width and height is ideal if you need to set an exact measurement for the frame.

You can not only resize and move text frames but also change their shapes. Select a text frame and choose the Direct Selection tool from the Tools panel. You can then select the corners on the text frame and move them to reshape the text frame.

Threading text frames

Understanding how to thread text frames together is important if you plan to build page layouts with a lot of text. *Threading* occurs when text frames are arranged so that the text in one frame continues in a second text frame. Threading is useful for most layouts because you can't always include all text in a single frame.

First, take a look at some of the related terminology because Adobe has given some special names to text frames that are linked. Figure 3-4 shows some of the icons we refer to in the following list:

+ **Flowing:** Describes text starting in one frame and continuing in a second frame.

+ **Threading:** Describes two text frames that have text flowing from the first frame to the second.

+ **Story:** The name of a group of sentences and paragraphs in threaded text frames.

Book II
Chapter 3

Working with Text
and Text Frames

An out port with text flowing into another frame

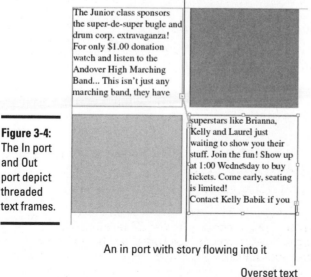

The Junior class sponsors the super-de-super bugle and drum corp. extravaganza! For only $1.00 donation watch and listen to the Andover High Marching Band... This isn't just any marching band, they have

superstars like Brianna, Kelly and Laurel just waiting to show you their stuff. Join the fun! Show up at 1:00 Wednesday to buy tickets. Come early, seating is limited!
Contact Kelly Babik if you

Figure 3-4:
The In port and Out port depict threaded text frames.

An in port with story flowing into it

Overset text

✦ **In port:** An icon on the upper left side of a text frame's bounding box indicating that a frame is the first one in a story or has text flowing in from another frame. An In port icon has a story flowing into it if it contains a small arrow; otherwise, the in port icon is empty.

✦ **Out port:** An icon on the lower right side of the text frame's bounding box indicating that a frame has text flowing out of it. The Out port icon contains a small arrow if the frame is threaded to another frame; an empty Out port icon signifies that the frame isn't connected to another text frame.

If a text frame isn't connected to another frame and has *overset text* (more text than can be displayed in a text frame), the Out port shows a small red plus sign (+) icon.

Find a block of text that you want to thread (for best results, use one that has formed sentences as opposed to placeholder text) and then follow these steps:

1. **Copy some text on the Clipboard, such as from the InDesign Help files, a page loaded in a Web browser window, or a Word, Notepad, or SimpleText document.**

   The type of content you're pasting doesn't matter. You only need to make sure the text is at least a few paragraphs long so that you have enough text to flow between frames.

   In Figure 3-4, you can see the text thread represented by a line connecting one text frame to another. InDesign shows you text threads if you choose View➪Extras➪Show Text Threads.

2. **Use the Type tool to create two text frames on a page.**

   The text frames can be above or beside one another, similar to the layout shown in Figure 3-5.

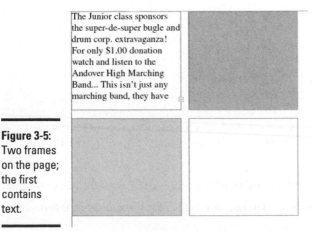

Figure 3-5:
Two frames on the page; the first contains text.

The Junior class sponsors the super-de-super bugle and drum corp. extravaganza! For only $1.00 donation watch and listen to the Andover High Marching Band... This isn't just any marching band, they have

3. **Using the Text tool, click in the first text frame, which is above or to the left of the second text frame.**

   The blinking insertion point that appears in the first text frame lets you know that you can enter or paste text into the frame.

4. **Press Ctrl+V (Windows) or ⌘+V (Mac) to paste the text into the text frame.**

   The text you've copied to the Clipboard enters into the frame. If you've pasted enough text, you see the overset text icon (a red plus sign) on the lower right side of the text frame (refer to Figure 3-5). If you don't see the overset text icon, use the Paste command a second time so that more text is entered into the frame.

5. **Click the overset text icon with the Selection tool.**

   The cursor changes to the loaded text icon so that you can select or create another text frame to thread the story.

6. **Move the cursor over the second text frame and click.**

   The cursor changes to the thread text icon when it hovers over the second text frame. When you click the second text frame, the two frames are threaded because the text continues in the second frame.

You can continue creating frames and threading them. You can thread them on the same page or on subsequent pages.

You can *unthread* text as well, which means that you're breaking the link between two text frames. You can rearrange the frames used to thread text, such as changing the page the story continues on when it's threaded to a second text frame. Break the connection by double-clicking the In port icon or the Out port icon of the text frame that you want to unthread. The frame is then unthreaded (but no text is deleted).

If your document doesn't have multiple pages in, choose File➪Document Setup. Change the value in the Number of Pages text field to 2 or greater and click OK when you're finished. Now you can click through the pages using the Page Field control at the bottom of the workspace.

Adding a page jump number

If your document has multiple pages, you can add a *page jump number* (text that indicates where the story continues if it jumps to a text frame on another page) to an existing file. Before you start, make sure that a story threads between text frames on two different pages and then follow these steps:

1. **Create a new text frame on the first page and type** continued on page.

2. **Use the Selection tool to select the text frame you just created.**

3. Move the text frame so that it slightly overlaps the text frame containing the story.

Let InDesign know what text frame it's tracking the story from or to. Overlap the two text frames (and keep them overlapped), as shown in Figure 3-6, so that InDesign knows to associate these text frames (the continued-notice text frame and the story text frame) with each other.

Figure 3-6: Slightly overlap the two text frames so that the story can be tracked.

You can then *group* these two text frames (they move together). Choose Object⊅Group with both text frames selected. (Shift-click with the Selection tool to select both text frames.)

4. Double-click the new text frame, which contains the text *continued on page*, to place the insertion point at the spot where you want the page number to be inserted.

The page number is inserted at the insertion point, so make sure that a space appears after the preceding character.

5. Choose Type⊅Insert Special Character⊅Markers⊅Next Page Number.

A number is added into the text frame. The number is sensitive to the location of the next threaded text frame, so if you move the second text frame, the page number updates automatically.

You can repeat these steps at the spot where the story is continued *from* — just choose Type⊅Insert Special Character⊅Markers⊅Previous Page Number in Step 5 instead.

Understanding Paragraph Settings

You can change the settings for an entire text frame or a single paragraph in a text frame in several ways. You can use the Paragraph panel to make adjustments to a single paragraph or to an entire text frame's indentation, justification, and alignment. Open the Paragraph panel by choosing Window⇨ Type & Tables⇨Paragraph.

If you want changes in the Paragraph panel to span across all text frames you create, don't select any paragraph or text frame before making the changes; instead, first select the entire text frame or frames on the page. Then the selections you make in the Paragraph panel affect all paragraphs in the selected text frames, not just one paragraph. If you want the selections you make in the Paragraph panel to affect just one paragraph within a text frame, select that paragraph first by using the Type tool, and then make your changes.

Indenting your text

You can indent a paragraph in a story by using the Paragraph panel. Indentation moves the paragraph away from the edges of the text frame's bounding box. Here's how to modify indentation:

1. **Create a text frame on the page and fill it with text.**

   You can fill the text frame by typing text, copying and pasting text, or inserting placeholder text by choosing Text⇨Fill with Placeholder Text.

2. **Make sure that the insertion point is blinking in the text frame in the paragraph you want to change or use the Selection tool to select the text frame.**

3. **Choose Window⇨Type & Tables⇨Paragraph to open the Paragraph panel.**

   The Paragraph panel opens, showing the text frame's current settings. See Figure 3-7 to find out the name of each setting control.

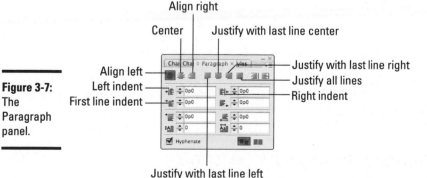

Figure 3-7:
The
Paragraph
panel.

4. **Change the value in the Left Indent text field and press Enter.**

The larger the number, the greater the indent. You can specify the unit of measurement as you enter the text by entering *in* for inches or *pt* for points, using any forms of measurement InDesign supports.

5. **Change the value in the First Line Left Indent text field and press Enter.**

To change all paragraphs in a story, click the insertion point in a paragraph and choose Edit➪Select All before changing settings.

Text alignment and justification

You can use the alignment and justification buttons in the Paragraph panel to format text frames:

✦ **Align** helps you left-, center-, or right-align text with the edges of the text frames.

✦ **Justification** lets you space text in relation to the edges of the text frame, and it lets you justify the final line of text in the paragraph.

To align or justify a block of text, click the Align or Justify button, respectively. (Refer to Figure 3-7 to see the Align and Justify buttons in the Paragraph panel.)

Saving a paragraph style

Do you ever go to all the trouble of finding just the right indent, font, or spacing to use in your copy, just to find that you have to apply those attributes a hundred times to complete your project? Or, have you ever decided that the indent is too much? Wouldn't it be nice to change one indent text box and have it update all other occurrences? You can do this using paragraph styles in InDesign.

To create a paragraph style, follow these steps:

1. **Create a text frame, add text, and apply a first-line indent of any size you want.**

Select some text — you don't have to select it all.

2. **Choose Window➪Type & Tables➪Paragraph Styles.**

The Paragraph Styles panel opens.

3. **From the Paragraph Styles panel menu, choose New Paragraph Style.**

The New Paragraph Style dialog box opens. Note that every attribute, font, size, and indent is already recorded in this unnamed style. You don't have to do anything at this point other than name the style.

4. **Change the name from Paragraph Style 1 to something more appropriate, such as** BodyCopy, **and click OK.**

   Your style is created! After you click OK, the dialog box closes and the new style is added to the Paragraph Styles panel list. You can modify the settings by double-clicking the style name in the Paragraph Styles panel. You can apply the style to other text frames by selecting the frame and clicking the style in the Paragraph Styles panel.

   If you want to change an existing style, the New Paragraph Style dialog box has several different areas in a large list on the left side. Select an item in the list to view and change its associated paragraph properties on the right side of the dialog box to update all instances of that paragraph style.

   You can import paragraph styles from other documents or from a file on your hard drive, which is particularly useful when you need to use a particular set of styles for a template. To import paragraph styles, choose Load Paragraph Styles from the Paragraph Styles panel menu. A dialog box prompts you to browse your hard drive for a file. Select the file to load and click OK.

Editing Stories

Your documents likely contain all sorts of text, and some of that text may need to be edited. InDesign has a built-in story editor for editing text. This feature can be useful when it's inconvenient or impossible to open another text editor to make changes.

InDesign also integrates with another Adobe product: InCopy. It's a text editor that is similar to Microsoft Word but has integration capabilities with InDesign for streamlined page layout. If you have some users who only write and others who only handle layout, you might want to have a look at InCopy as a possible text editor.

Using the story editor

The InDesign story editor lets you view a story outside tiny columns and format the text as necessary. To open the story editor to edit a piece of text, follow these steps:

1. **Find a piece of text that you want to edit and select the text frame with the Selection tool.**

   A bounding box with handles appears around the text frame.

2. **Choose Edit⇨Edit in Story Editor or use the keyboard shortcut Ctrl+Y (Windows) or ⌘+Y (Mac).**

   The story editor opens in a new window directly in the InDesign workspace.

3. **Edit the story in the window as necessary and click the Close button when you finish.**

Your story appears in one block of text. Any paragraph styles you apply to the text in the story editor are noted in an Information pane on the left side of the workspace.

Notice in Figure 3-8 that you can now see tables in the story editor. Click the small table icon to collapse and expand the table in the story editor.

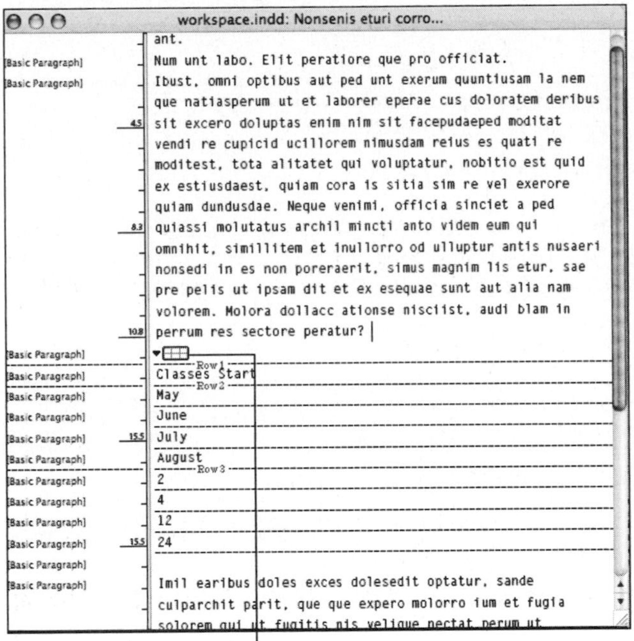

Figure 3-8:
You can
see text and
tables in the
story editor.

Table icon

Checking for correct spelling

Typos and spelling errors are easy to make. Therefore, you must check for incorrect spelling in a document before you print or export it to a PDF. Here's how to check for spelling in InDesign:

1. **Choose Edit⇨Spelling⇨Check Spelling.**

2. **In the Check Spelling dialog box that appears, choose a selection to search from the Search drop-down list and then click the Start button.**

The spell check automatically starts searching the story or document.

3. **Choose from three options:**

   - Click the Skip button to ignore a misspelled word.

   - Select a suggested spelling correction from the list in the Suggested Corrections pane and click the Change button.

   - Click Ignore All to ignore any more instances of that word.

   The spelling is corrected in the text frame and moves to the next spelling error.

4. **Click the Done button to stop the spell check; otherwise, click OK when InDesign alerts you that the spell check is done.**

Using custom spelling dictionaries

You can easily add words, such as proper nouns, to your dictionary by clicking the Add button.

You can create a user dictionary or add user dictionaries from previous InDesign versions, from files that others have sent you, or from a server. The dictionary you add is used for all your InDesign documents.

Follow these steps to create your own, custom dictionary:

1. **Choose Edit↪Preferences↪Dictionary (Windows) or InDesign↪ Preferences↪Dictionary (Mac).**

   The Preferences dialog box appears with the Dictionary section visible.

2. **From the Language drop-down list, choose the language of your dictionary.**

3. **Click the New User Dictionary button below the Language drop-down list.**

4. **Specify the name and location of the user dictionary and then click OK.**

If you want to see when a spelling error occurs without opening the Check Spelling dialog box, choose Edit↪Spelling↪Dynamic Spelling. Unknown words are then highlighted. To correct the spelling, right-click (Windows) or ⌘-click (Mac) and select the correct spelling from the contextual menu or add the word to your dictionary.

Using Tables

A *table* is made of columns and rows, which divides a table into cells. You see tables every day on television, in books and magazines, and all over the Web. In fact, a calendar is a table: All the days in a month are shown down a column, every week is a row, and each day is a cell. You can use tables for many different tasks, such as listing products, employees, or events.

The following list describes the components of a table and how to modify them in InDesign:

✦ **Rows:** Extend horizontally across a table. You can modify the height of a row.

✦ **Columns:** Are vertical in a table. You can modify the width of a column.

✦ **Cells:** A text frame. You can enter information into this frame and format it like any other text frame in InDesign.

Creating tables

The easiest way to create a table is to have data ready to go. (Mind you, this isn't the only way.) But flowing in existing data is the most dynamic way of seeing what InDesign can do with tables.

Follow these steps to experiment with the table feature:

1. **Create a text area and insert tabbed copy into it.**

The example use dates for an event:

Summer Events

June	July	August
1	2	3
4	5	6

Notice that the text was simply keyed in by pressing the Tab key between every new entry. The text doesn't even need to be lined up.

2. **Select the text and choose Table➪Convert Text to Table.**

The Convert Text to Table Options dialog box appears. You can select columns there or let the tabs in your text determine columns. You can find out more about table styles in the later section "Creating table styles."

You can assign a table style at the same time you convert text to a table.

3. **Click OK to accept the default settings.**

4. **Hold down the Shift key and use your mouse to click and grab the outside right border to stretch the table in or out.**

The cells proportionally accommodate the new table size.

5. **Click and drag across the cells and then choose Table➪Merge Cells to merge the top three cells.**

To create a new table without existing text, follow these steps:

1. **Create a new text frame with the Type tool.**

    The insertion point should be blinking in the new text frame you create. If it isn't blinking, or if you created a new frame another way, double-click the text frame so that the insertion point (I-bar) is active. You can't create a table unless the insertion point is active in the text frame.

2. **Choose Table⇨Insert Table.**

3. **In the Insert Table dialog box that opens, enter the number of rows and columns you want to add to the table in the Rows and Columns text fields and then click OK.**

    For example, we created a table with six rows and three columns.

Editing table settings

You can control many settings for tables. InDesign lets you change the text, fill, and stroke properties for each cell or for the table itself. Because of this flexibility, you can create fully customized tables to display information in an intuitive and creative way. In this section, we show you some basic options for editing tables.

To start editing table settings, follow these steps:

1. **Select the table you want to make changes to by clicking in a cell.**

2. **Choose Table⇨Table Options⇨Table Setup.**

    The Table Options dialog box opens with the Table Setup tab selected. The dialog box contains several tabs that contain settings you can change for different parts of the table.

    From the Table Setup tab, you edit the columns and rows, border, and spacing and specify how column or row strokes are rendered in relation to each other. For example, we changed the number of rows and columns and changed the table border weight to a 3-point stroke.

3. **Select the Preview check box at the bottom of the dialog box.**

    The Preview opens so that you can view the changes you made on the page while you're using the dialog box.

4. **Click the Row Strokes tab and change the options.**

    For this example, we selected Every Second Row from the Alternating Pattern drop-down list, changed the Table Border Weight option to 2, and changed the Color property for the first row to C=15, M=100 Y=100, K=0 (the CMYK equivalent of red).

This step causes every second row to have a red, 2-point stroke. You can also click the Column Strokes tab to change the properties for column strokes. The two tabs work the same way.

5. **Click the Fills tab and change the options.**

   For this example, we chose Every Other Column from the Alternating Pattern drop-down list, changed the Color property to the same CMYK equivalent of red, and left the Tint at the default of 20 percent. This step changes the first row to a red tint.

6. **Click OK.**

   The changes you made in the Table Options dialog box are applied to the table.

7. **Click a table cell so that the insertion point is blinking.**

   The table cell is selected.

8. **Find an image you can copy to the Clipboard and then press Ctrl+C (Windows) or ⌘+C (Mac) to copy the image.**

9. **Return to InDesign and paste the image into the table cell by pressing Ctrl+V (Windows) or ⌘+V (Mac).**

   The image appears in the table cell, and the height or width (or both) of the cell changes based on the dimensions of the image. Make sure that the insertion point is active in the cell if you have problems pasting the image.

You can not only change the table itself but also customize the cells within it. Choose Table⇨Cell Options⇨Text to open the Cell Options dialog box. You can also make changes to each cell by using the Paragraph panel. Similarly, you can change the number of rows and columns and their widths and heights from the Tables panel. Open the Tables panel by choosing Window⇨Type & Tables⇨Table.

InDesign lets you import tables from other programs, such as Excel. If you want to import a spreadsheet, choose File⇨Place. The spreadsheet is imported into InDesign as a table that you can further edit as necessary.

Creating table styles

If you've spent time customizing strokes, fills, and spacing for your table, you certainly want to save it as a style. Creating a table style lets you reuse your table setup for future tables. To create a table style, follow these steps:

1. **Make a table look the way you want.**

   The easiest way to create a table style is to complete the table setup and make a table look the way you want it at completion.

2. **Select the table.**

   Click and drag to select it with the text tool.

3. **Choose Window⇨Type & Tables⇨Table Styles.**

   The Table Styles panel appears.

4. **Hold down the Alt (Windows) or Option (Mac) key and click the Create New Style button at the bottom of the Table Styles panel.**

   The New Table Style dialog box appears.

5. **Name the style and click OK.**

   Your table attributes are saved as a style.

If you want to edit table style attributes, you can simply double-click the named style in the Table Styles panel. (Make sure nothing is selected.)

Looking at Text on a Path

You can create some interesting effects with text on a path. Using the Type On a Path tool, you can have text curve along a line or shape. This feature is particularly useful when you want to create interesting titling effects on a page.

To create text on a path, follow these steps:

1. **Use the Pen tool to create a path on the page.**

   Create at least one curve on the path after you create it. (See Chapter 4 of this minibook to find out how to wield the Pen tool with confidence).

2. **Click and hold the Type tool to select the Type On a Path tool.**

3. **Move the cursor near the path you created.**

   When you move the cursor near a path, a plus sign (+) symbol appears next to the cursor, and you can click and start typing on the path.

4. **Click when you see the + icon and type some text on the path.**

   An insertion point appears at the beginning of the path after you click, and you can then add text along the path. You select type on a path as you would normally select other text — by dragging over the text to highlight it.

To change properties for type on a path, you can use the Type On a Path Options dialog box, which you open by choosing Type⇨Type On a Path⇨ Options. In the Type On a Path Options dialog box, you can use effects to modify the way each character is placed on the path. You can also flip the text, change character spacing, and change character alignment to the path in the Align drop-down list or to the stroke of the path in the To Path drop-down list. Play with the settings to see how they affect your type. Click OK to apply changes; to undo anything you don't like, press Ctrl+Z or ⌘+Z.

To hide the path while keeping the text visible, set the stroke weight for the path to 0 pt.

Chapter 4: Drawing in InDesign

Many of the tools you find in the InDesign Tools panel are used for drawing lines and shapes on a page, so you have several different ways of creating interesting drawings for your publications. You can create anything from basic shapes to intricate drawings inside InDesign, instead of having to use a drawing program such as Illustrator. Even though InDesign doesn't replace Illustrator (see Book III), which has many more versatile drawing tools and options for creating intricate drawings, InDesign is adequate for simple drawing tasks. In this chapter, you discover how to use the most popular InDesign drawing tools and how to add colorful fills to illustrations.

Getting Started with Drawing

When you're creating a document, you may want drawn shapes and paths to be a part of the layout. For example, you may want to have a star shape for a yearbook page about a talent show or to run text along a path. Whatever it is you need to do, you can draw shapes and paths to get the job done.

Paths and shapes

Paths can take a few different formats. They can either be open or closed and with or without a stroke:

✦ **Path:** The outline of a shape or object. Paths can be closed and have no gaps, or they can be open like a line on the page. You can draw freeform paths, such as squiggles on a page, freely by hand.

✦ **Stroke:** A line style and thickness that you apply to a path. A stroke can look like a line or like an outline of a shape.

Figure 4-1 shows the different kinds of paths and strokes you can create.

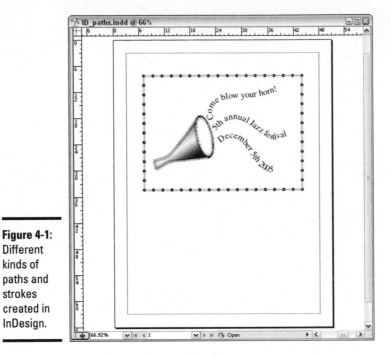

Figure 4-1:
Different kinds of paths and strokes created in InDesign.

Paths contain points where the direction of the path can change. (You can find out more about points in the later section "Points and segments.") You can make paths by using freeform drawing tools, such as the Pen or Pencil tools, or by using the basic shape tools, such as Ellipse, Rectangle, Polygon, or Line.

The shape tools create paths in a predefined way so that you can make basic geometric shapes, such as a star or ellipse. All you need to do is select the shape tool and drag the cursor on the page, and the shape is automatically drawn. Creating shapes this way is a lot easier than trying to create them manually using the Pen or Pencil tool. Figure 4-2 shows shapes drawn with the shape tools found in the Tools panel.

You can change shapes into freeform paths, like those drawn with the Pencil or Pen tools. Similarly, you can make freeform paths into basic shapes. Therefore, you don't need to worry about which tool you initially choose.

We created the stars and starburst shown in Figure 4-2 by double-clicking the Polygon tool and changing the options. Read more about the Polygon tool in the "Drawing Shapes" section, later in this chapter.

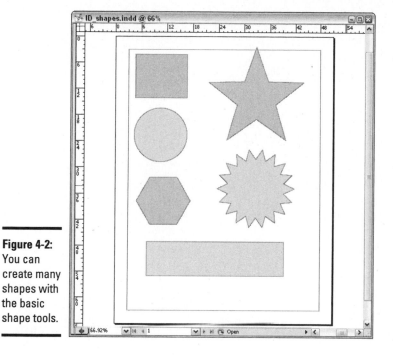

Book II
Chapter 4

Drawing in InDesign

Figure 4-2:
You can
create many
shapes with
the basic
shape tools.

Points and segments

Paths are made up of points and segments:

✦ **Point:** Where the path changes somehow, such as a change in direction. Many points along a path can be joined with segments. Points are sometimes called *anchor points.* You can create two kinds of points:

• *Corner points:* Have a straight line between them. Shapes such as squares and stars have corner points.

• *Curve points:* Occur along a curved path. Circles or snaking paths have lots of curve points.

✦ **Segment:** A line or curve connecting two points — similar to connect-the-dots.

Figure 4-3 shows corner points and curve points joined by segments.

Getting to Know the Tools of the Trade

The following subsections introduce you to tools that you'll probably use most often when creating drawings in your publications. When you draw with these tools, you're using strokes and fills to make designs. The following subsections show you what these common tools can do to help you create basic or complex illustrations in InDesign.

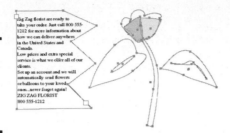

Figure 4-3:
Points
are joined
by line
segments.

The Pencil tool

The Pencil tool is used to draw simple or complex shapes on a page. Because the Pencil tool is a freeform tool, you can freely drag it all over the page and create lines or shapes, instead of having them automatically made for you, such as when you use basic shape tools. The Pencil tool is an intuitive and easy tool to use. You find out how to use it in the later section "Drawing Freeform Paths."

The Pen tool

The Pen tool is used to create complex shapes on the page. The Pen tool works with other tools, such as the Add, Remove, and Convert Point tools. The Pen tool works by adding and editing points along a path, thereby manipulating the segments that join them.

Drawing with the Pen tool isn't easy at first. In fact, it takes many people a considerable amount of time to use this tool well. Don't become frustrated if you don't get used to it right away — the Pen tool can take some practice to get it to do what you want. You find out how to use the Pen tool in the "Drawing Freeform Paths" section, later in this chapter.

Basic shapes and frame shapes

Basic shapes are preformed shapes that you can add to a document by using tools in the Tools panel. The basic shape tools include the Line, Rectangle, Ellipse, and Polygon tools.

You can also draw these shapes and turn them into *frames* (containers that hold content in a document). You can use a frame as a text frame or as a graphic frame used to hold pictures and text. Draw a basic shape and then convert it to a graphic or text frame by choosing Object⇨Content⇨Text or Object⇨Content⇨Graphic. We discuss graphic frames and text frames in more detail in Chapter 3 of this minibook.

The frame and shape tools look the same and can even act the same. Both can hold text and images, but look out! By default, shapes created with the shape tools have a 1-point black stroke around them. Many folks don't see these strokes on the screen but later discover them surrounding their text boxes when they print. Stick with the frame tools, and you'll be fine.

Drawing Shapes

InDesign allows you to create basic shapes in a document. You can easily create a basic shape by following these steps:

1. **Create a new document by choosing File⇨New.**

2. **When the New Document dialog box appears, click OK.**

A new document opens.

3. **Select the Rectangle tool in the Tools panel.**

4. **Click anywhere in the page and drag the mouse diagonally.**

When the rectangle is the dimension you want, release the mouse button. You've created a rectangle.

Book II
Chapter 4

Drawing in InDesign

That's all you need to do to create a basic shape. You can also use these steps with the other basic shape tools (the Line, Ellipse, and Polygon tools) to create other basic shapes. To access the other basic shapes from the Tools panel, follow these steps:

 1. **Click the Rectangle tool and hold down the mouse button.**

A menu that contains all the basic shapes opens.

2. **Release the mouse button.**

The menu remains open, and you can mouse over the menu items. Each menu item becomes highlighted when the mouse pointer is placed over it.

3. **Select a basic shape tool by clicking a highlighted menu item.**

The new basic shape tool is now active. Follow the preceding set of steps to create basic shapes using any of these tools.

 To draw a square shape, use the Rectangle tool and press the Shift key while you drag the mouse on the page. The sides of the shape are all drawn at the same length, so you create a perfect square. You can also use the Shift key with the Ellipse tool if you want a perfect circle — just hold down Shift while you're using the Ellipse tool. Release the mouse before the Shift key to ensure that this constrain shape trick works!

Creating a shape with exact dimensions

Dragging on the page to create a shape is easy, but making a shape with precise dimensions using this method requires a few more steps. If you want to make a shape that's a specific size, follow these steps:

1. **Select the Rectangle tool or the Ellipse tool.**

   The tool is highlighted in the Tools panel.

2. **Click anywhere on the page, but don't drag the cursor.**

   This point becomes the upper right corner of the Rectangle or Ellipse *bounding box* (the rectangle that defines the object's vertical and horizontal dimensions). After you click to place a corner, the Rectangle or Ellipse dialog box appears.

3. **In the Width and Height text fields, enter the dimensions for creating the shape.**

4. **Click OK.**

   The shape is created on the page, with the upper right corner at the place where you initially clicked the page.

Using the Polygon tool

A *polygon* is a shape that has many sides. For example, a square is a polygon with four sides, but the Polygon tool enables you to choose the number of sides you want for the polygon you create. When you're using the Polygon tool, you may not want to create a shape with the default number of sides. You can change these settings before you start drawing the shape.

To customize the shape of a polygon, follow these steps:

1. **Select the Polygon tool in the Tools panel by selecting the Rectangle tool and holding down the mouse button until the menu pops up.**

2. **Double-click the Polygon tool in the Tools panel.**

   The Polygon dialog box opens, as shown at the bottom of Figure 4-4.

3. **In the Number of Sides text field, enter the number of sides you want the new polygon to have.**

   To create a star instead of a polygon, enter a number in the Star Inset text field for the percentage of the star inset you want the new shape to have.

   A higher percentage means that the sides are inset farther toward the center of the polygon, creating a star. If you want a regular polygon and not a star, enter **0** in the Star Inset text field. If you want a star, enter **50%**; for a starburst, enter **25%**.

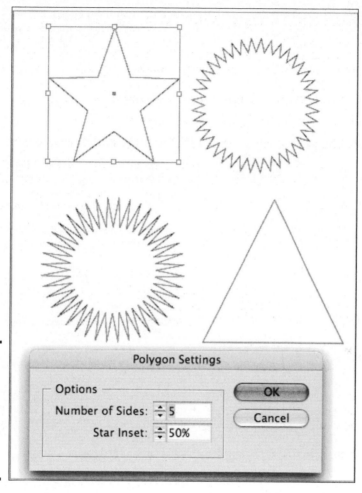

Figure 4-4:
Change the
star inset
percentage
to create
different
kinds of
shapes.

4. **Click OK.**

5. **Move the cursor to the page and click and drag to create a new polygon or star.**

   Your new polygon or star appears on the page.

Figure 4-4 shows what a few different polygons and stars with different settings look like.

Editing Basic Shapes

You can edit basic shapes using several panels in InDesign and therefore create original shapes and craft exactly the kind of design you require in a page layout. You aren't stuck with predetermined shapes, such as a square or an oval. You can make these forms take on much more complicated or original shapes.

You can edit basic shapes in InDesign in only a few ways. You can edit shapes and manipulate their appearance in other ways. We cover some of these ways, such as editing fills, in the later section "Using Fills."

Changing the size with the Transform panel

You can change the size of a shape by using the Transform panel. Here's how:

1. **With the Selection tool (the tool that's used to select objects), select the shape you want to resize.**

   When the shape is selected, a bounding box appears around it. You can see a selected shape in Figure 4-5.

Bounding box

Selected object

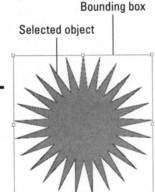

Figure 4-5:
A selected shape with the bounding box visible.

2. **Open the Transform panel by choosing Window⇨Object and Layout⇨Transform.**

3. **In the Transform panel that appears, enter different number values in the W and H fields to change the size of the shape.**

   The shape automatically changes size on the page to the new size dimensions you specify in the Transform panel.

Changing the size with the Free Transform tool

Easily resize objects in InDesign by using the Free Transform tool.

To resize a selected object with the Free Transform tool, follow these steps:

1. **Make sure that *only* the object you want to resize is selected.**

   Group multiple objects if you want to resize several objects simultaneously. To group objects, select one object and Shift-click to add it to the selection, and then press Ctrl+G (Windows) or ⌘+G (Mac).

2. **Select the Free Transform tool.**

   A bounding box appears around the selected objects.

3. **Click any corner point and drag to resize the object.**

   Hold down the Shift key while dragging to keep the objects constrained proportionally as you resize.

Changing the stroke of a shape

You can change the stroke of shapes you've created. The *stroke* is the outline that appears around the edge of the shape. The stroke can range from no stroke to a very thick stroke, and it's measured in point sizes. Even if a shape has a stroke set to 0 points, it still has a stroke — you just can't see it.

Follow these steps to edit the stroke of your shapes:

1. **Select a shape on the page.**

   A bounding box appears around the selected shape.

2. **Select a new width for the Stroke by using the Stroke Weight drop-down list in the Control panel.**

   As soon as a value is selected, the stroke automatically changes on the page. This number is measured in points. You use some of the other options in the following step list.

You can click in the Stroke text field and manually enter a numerical value for the stroke width. The higher the number you enter, the thicker the stroke. You can also change the style of the stroke from the Stroke panel by following these steps:

1. **With a basic shape selected, select the stroke type from the drop-down list in the Control panel and select a new line.**

   As soon as a value is selected, the stroke automatically changes.

2. **Choose a new line weight from the Stroke Weight drop-down list.**

   For example, we chose 10 points. The shape updates automatically on the page.

If you want to create custom dashes, you can see more options by choosing Window➪Stroke. Select a dashed stroke and notice, at the bottom of the Stroke panel, that you can define the dash and gap size. Enter one value for an even dash or several numbers for custom dashes for maps, diagrams, fold marks, and more!

Add special ends to the lines with the Start and End drop-down lists. For example, you can add an arrowhead or a large circle to the beginning or end of the stroke. The Cap and Join buttons allow you to choose the shape of the line ends and how they join with other paths when you're working with complex paths or shapes. For more information on creating and editing lines and strokes, see Book I, Chapter 6.

Changing the shear value

You can change the shear of a shape by using the Transform panel. *Skew* and *shear* mean the same thing: The shape is slanted, so you create the appearance of some form of perspective for the skewed or sheared element. This transformation is useful if you want to create the illusion of depth on a page.

Follow these simple steps to skew a shape:

1. **With a basic shape selected, choose Window➪Object and Layout➪Transform.**

2. **Select a value from the Shear drop-down list in the lower right corner of the Transform panel.**

   After you select a new value, the shape skews (or shears), depending on what value you select. Manually entering a numerical value into this field also skews the shape.

Rotating a shape

You can change the rotation of a shape by using the Transform panel. The process of rotating a shape is similar to skewing a shape (see the preceding section):

1. **With a basic shape selected, choose Window➪Object and Layout➪Transform.**

   The Transform panel opens.

2. **Select a value from the Rotation drop-down list.**

   After you select a new value, the shape rotates automatically, based on the rotation angle you specified. You can also manually enter a value into the text field.

Drawing Freeform Paths

You can use different tools to draw paths. For example, you can use the Pencil tool to draw freeform paths. These kinds of paths typically look like lines, and you can use the Pencil and Pen tools to create simple or complex paths.

Using the Pencil tool

The Pencil tool is perhaps the easiest tool to use when drawing freeform paths (see Figure 4-6).

Figure 4-6: This freeform drawing was created with the Pencil tool.

Follow these steps to get started:

1. **To create a new document, choose File⇨New and then click OK in the New Document dialog box that appears.**

2. **Select the Pencil tool in the Tools panel.**

3. **Drag the cursor around the page.**

   You've created a new path by using the Pencil tool.

Using the Pen tool

Using the Pen tool is different from using the Pencil tool. When you start out, the Pen tool may seem a bit complicated — but after you get the hang of it, using it isn't hard after all. The Pen tool uses points to create a particular path. You can edit these points to change the segments between them. Gaining control of these points can take a bit of practice.

To create points and segments on a page, follow these steps:

1. **Close any existing documents and create a new document by choosing File⇨New Document.**

2. **Click OK in the New Document dialog box that appears.**

   A new document opens with the default settings.

 3. **Select the Pen tool in the Tools panel.**

4. **Click anywhere on the page and then click a second location.**

   You've created a new path with two points and one segment joining them.

5. **Ctrl-click (Windows) or ⌘-click (Mac) an empty part of the page to deselect the current path.**

   After you deselect the path, you can create a new path or add new points to the path you just created.

6. **Add a new point to a selected segment by hovering the mouse over the line and clicking.**

   A small plus (+) icon appears next to the Pen tool cursor. You can also do the same thing by selecting the Add Anchor Point tool (located on the menu that flies out when you click and hold the Pen icon in the Tools panel).

7. **Repeat Step 6, but this time click a new location on a line segment and drag away from the line.**

   This step creates a curved path. The segments change and curve depending on where the points are located along the path. The point you created is a *curve* point.

For more information about working with the Pen tool, check out Book III, Chapter 5.

Editing Freeform Paths

Even the best artists sometimes need to make changes or delete parts of their work. If you've made mistakes or change your mind about a drawing, follow the steps in this section to make changes.

To change a path segment, select a point with the Direct Selection tool. When a point is selected, it appears solid; unselected points appear hollow.

Select the Direct Selection tool by pressing the A key.

All you need to do to select a point is use the cursor to click the point itself. Then you can use the handles that appear when the point is selected to modify the segments. Follow these steps:

1. **Select the Direct Selection tool from the Tools panel and then click a point.**

   The selected point appears solid. If you select a curve point, handles extend from it.

   A curved point and a corner point edit differently when you select and drag them. Curve points have handles that extend from the point, but corner points don't.

2. **Drag the point where you want it; to edit a curve point, click a handle end and drag the handle left or right.**

   The path changes, depending on how you drag the handles.

Suppose that you want to make a corner point a curve point. You can do just that with the Convert Direction Point tool. To understand how the Convert Direction Point tool works best, you should have a path that contains both straight and curved segments. Follow these steps to change a corner point into a curved point and vice versa:

1. **Select the Convert Direction Point tool.**

   This tool resides on a menu under the Pen tool in the Tools panel. Hold down the mouse button over the Pen tool icon until a menu appears; select the Convert Direction Point tool from the menu.

2. **Click a curved point with the Convert Direction Point tool.**

   The point you click changes into a corner point, which changes the path's appearance.

3. **Click and drag a corner point with the Convert Direction Point tool.**

   The point is modified as a curved point. This step changes the appearance of the path again.

This tool is handy when you need to alter the way a path changes direction. If you need to manipulate a point in a different way, you may need to change its type by using the Convert Direction Point tool.

Book II
Chapter 4

Drawing in InDesign

Modifying Frame Corners

You can use corner effects on basic shapes to customize the shape's look. Corner effects are useful for adding an interesting look to borders. You can be quite creative with some of the shapes you apply effects to or by applying more than one effect to a single shape. Here's how to create a corner effect on a rectangle:

1. **Select the Rectangle tool and create a new rectangle anywhere on the page.**

Hold the Shift key when using the Rectangle tool if you want to create a square.

2. **With the Selection tool, select the shape and then choose Object⇨ Corner Options.**

The Corner Options dialog box opens.

3. **Choose an effect from the Effects drop-down list and enter a value into the Size text field.**

For example, choose the Drop Shadow option to create a soft shadow behind an object or choose Bevel and Emboss to give an object a 3D effect.

4. **Click OK.**

The corner option is applied to the shape.

Using Fills

A fill is located inside a path. You can fill paths and shapes with several different kinds of colors, transparent colors, or even gradients. Fills can help you achieve artistic effects and illusions of depth or add interest to a page design.

You may have already created a fill. The Tools panel contains two swatches: one for the stroke (a hollow square) and one for the fill (a solid box). (Refer to Figure 2-4 in Chapter 2 of this minibook to locate the Fill and Stroke boxes.) If the Fill box contains a color, your shape has a fill when it's created. If the Fill box has a red line through it, the shape is created without a fill.

Creating basic fills

You can create a basic fill in several different ways. One of the most common ways is to specify a color in the Fill swatch before you create a new shape. To create a shape with a fill, follow these steps:

1. **Make sure that the Fill box is selected so that you aren't adding color to the stroke instead.**

2. **Open the Color panel by choosing Window⇨Color⇨Color.**

3. **Select a color in the Color panel.**

   You can enter values into the CMYK (Cyan, Magenta, Yellow, Black) fields manually or by using the sliders. Alternatively, you can use the Eyedropper tool to select a color from the color ramp at the bottom of the Color panel. For more information on color modes, such as CMYK and RGB, see Book I, Chapter 7.

   Use the Color panel menu to select different color modes if CMYK isn't already selected. Click and hold the arrow button and select CMYK from the Color panel menu.

   The Fill box in the Tools panel is updated with the new color you've selected in the Color panel.

4. **Create a new shape on the page.**

   Select a shape tool and drag on the page to create a shape. The shape is filled with the fill color you chose.

As in the other Creative Suite 5 applications, you can create tints of a color built with CMYK by holding down the Shift key while dragging any color's slider. All color sliders then move proportionally.

You can also choose to use color swatches to select a fill color by using the Swatches panel (choose Window⇨Color ⇨Swatches to open the Swatches panel). Create a new color swatch (of the present color) by clicking the New Swatch button at the bottom of the panel. Double-click the new swatch to add new color properties by using sliders to set CMYK color values or by entering numbers into each text field.

Perhaps you already have a shape without a fill and you want to add a fill to it, or maybe you want to change the color of an existing fill. Select the shape and, with the Fill box in the Tools panel selected, select a color from the Color or Swatches panel. A new fill color is applied to the shape.

You can drag and drop a swatch color to fill a shape on a page, even if that shape isn't selected. Open the Swatches panel by choosing Window⇨Color⇨ Swatches and then drag the color swatch over to the shape. Release the mouse button, and the fill color is applied automatically to the shape.

Making transparent fills

Fills that are partially transparent can create some interesting effects for the layout of your document. You can set transparency to more than one element on the page and layer those elements to create the illusion of depth and stacking.

Follow these steps to apply transparency to an element on the page:

1. **Using the Selection tool, select a shape on the page.**

   A bounding box appears around the selected shape.

2. **Open the Effects panel by choosing Window⇨Effects.**

3. **Use the Opacity slider to specify how transparent the shape appears.**

   Click the arrow to open the slider or click in the text field to manually enter a value using the keyboard. The effect is immediately applied to the selected shape.

4. **Select Stroke or Fill in the Effects panel to apply a separate opacity to each one.**

Looking at gradients

A *gradient* is the color transition from one color (or no color) to a different color. Gradients can have two or more colors in the transition.

Gradients can add interesting effects to shapes, including 3D effects. Sometimes you can use a gradient to achieve glowing effects or the effect of light hitting a surface. The two kinds of gradients available in InDesign are radial and linear, as shown in Figure 4-7 and described in this list:

✦ **Radial:** A transition of colors in a circular fashion from a center point radiating outward

✦ **Linear:** A transition of colors along a straight path

You can apply a gradient to a stroke or a fill or even to text. To apply a gradient to a stroke, simply select the stroke instead of the fill.

Even though you can apply a gradient to the stroke of live text, you'll create a printing nightmare — use these features sparingly!

Here's how to add a gradient fill to a shape:

1. **With the Selection tool, select the object you want to apply a gradient to and then choose Window⇨Color⇨Swatches.**

   The Swatches panel opens.

2. **Choose New Gradient Swatch from the Swatches panel menu.**

   The New Gradient Swatch dialog box opens (see Figure 4-8).

3. **Type a new name for the swatch in the Swatch Name field.**

   Sometimes, giving the swatch a descriptive name, such as one indicating what the swatch is being used for, is helpful.

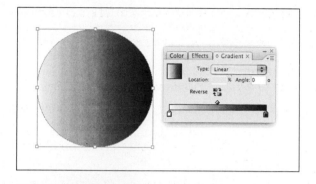

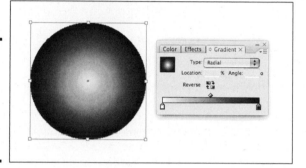

Figure 4-7:
A linear
gradient
(top) and
radial
gradient
(bottom).

Figure 4-8:
The New
Gradient
Swatch
dialog box.

4. **Choose Linear or Radial from the Type drop-down list.**

   This option determines the type of gradient the swatch creates every time you use it. We chose Radial from the drop-down list (refer to Figure 4-8).

5. **Manipulate the gradient stops below the Gradient Ramp to position each color in the gradient.**

Gradient stops are the color chips located below the Gradient Ramp. You can move the diamond shape above the Gradient Ramp to determine the center point of the gradient. You can select each gradient stop to change the color and move them around to edit the gradient. When the gradient stops are selected, you can change the color values in the Stop Color area by using sliders or entering values in each CMYK text field.

You can add a new color to the gradient by clicking the area between gradient stops. Then you can edit the new stop, just like you edit the others. To remove the gradient stop, drag the stop away from the Gradient Ramp.

6. **Click OK.**

   The gradient swatch is created and applied to the selected object.

To edit a gradient, double-click the gradient's swatch. This step opens the Gradient Options dialog box, where you can modify the settings made in the New Gradient Swatch dialog box.

Removing fills

Removing fills is even easier than creating them. Follow these steps:

1. **Select the shape with the Selection tool.**

   A bounding box appears around the shape.

2. **Click the Fill box in the Tools panel.**

3. **Click the Apply None button, located below the Fill box.**

   The button is white with a red line through it. The fill is removed from the selected shape and the Fill box changes to No Fill. You also see the None fill on the Swatches and Color panels.

   If you're using a single-row Tools panel, you don't see the Apply None button unless you click and hold down the Apply Gradient (or Apply Color) button because the button is hidden beneath it.

Adding Layers

Layers are like transparent sheets stacked on top of one another. If you add layers to a drawing, you can create the appearance that graphics are stacked on top of one another. The Layers panel allows you to create new layers, delete layers you don't need, or even rearrange layers to change the stacking order. Use layers to create alternative versions of InDesign files, or just to replace logos.

Here's how to work with layers in InDesign:

1. **Open the Layers panel by choosing Window⇨Layers.**

   This panel allows you to create, delete, and arrange layers.

2. **Draw a shape on the page using a shape tool.**

   Create the shape anywhere on the page, and make it large enough so that you can easily stack another shape on top of part of it.

3. **Click the Create New Layer button in the Layers panel to create a new layer.**

   A new layer is stacked on top of the selected layer and becomes the active layer.

   Double-click a layer to give it an appropriate name or, even better, hold down the Alt (Windows) or Option (Mac) key and click the New Layer button to open the Layer Options dialog box before the layer is created.

   Make sure that the layer you want to create content on is selected before you start modifying the layer. You can tell which layer is selected because it's always highlighted in the Layers panel. You can easily but accidentally add content to the incorrect layer if you don't check this panel frequently. (If you add an item to the wrong layer, you can always cut and paste items to the correct layer.)

4. **Make sure that a shape tool is still selected, and then create a shape on the new layer by dragging the cursor so that part of the new shape covers the shape you created in Step 2.**

   The new shape is stacked on top of the shape you created in Step 2.

For more information about working with layers, refer to Book III, Chapter 8.

Chapter 5: Understanding Page Layout

In This Chapter

✔ Working with and importing image files

✔ Selecting images on the page

✔ Knowing page layout settings

✔ Using text and graphics in your layouts

✔ Working with pages

✔ Using master pages and spreads

*T*his chapter shows you how to put graphics and text together so that you can start creating page layouts. Interesting and creative page layouts help draw interest to the pictures and words contained within the publication. An interesting layout motivates more members of the audience to read the text you place on a page.

Importing Images

You can add several kinds of image files to an InDesign document. Some of the most common are GIF, JPEG, AI, PSD, and TIF. Images are imported into graphic frames. You can create the frames before importing, or if you don't have a frame, InDesign creates one for you instantly when you add the image to the page.

When you import an image into your InDesign layout, the original image is still needed when you print or export the final document. You use special controls to keep track of the linked image and to work on specific settings, such as those that modify the quality and color. You also find additional settings at the time you import an image, which you access using the Image Import Options dialog box. In the "Importing other InDesign documents" section, later in this chapter, you find out how to change various import options.

For now, follow these steps to import an image into your InDesign layout:

1. **Make sure that nothing on the page is selected.**

If an object on the page is selected, click an empty area so that everything is deselected before you proceed.

2. **Choose File⇨Place.**

   The Place dialog box opens, where you can browse your hard drive for image files to import. You can use this dialog box to import various kinds of files into InDesign, not just images.

3. **Select the image you want to import and click Open.**

   The Place dialog box closes and the cursor displays a thumbnail of the image you selected.

   You can import multiple images at a time into an InDesign layout. Simply hold down the Ctrl (Windows) or ⌘ (Mac) key and select multiple files in the Place dialog box.

4. **Move the cursor to wherever you want the upper left corner of the first image to be placed on the page and then click the mouse.**

   If you've selected multiple images, you can use the left and right arrow keys to navigate the thumbnail images in your loaded cursor before clicking on the page. After you click on the page, the next image is placed, until there are no more images to place.

   Images are imported and placed into the publication inside a graphic frame. You can resize, move, and modify the image using the Selection or Direct Selection tool or modify the frame and image together using the Selection tool.

Don't worry if the image is imported and is too large for the layout or needs to be cropped. For more information about selecting graphic frames and modifying them, check out Chapter 3 of this minibook. To find out about importing and working with text and stories, also see Chapter 3 of this minibook.

It's sometimes easier to create an empty graphic frame and then add an image to it than to import the image and create the frame at the same time. You can create an empty frame and even set fitting properties before you import an image — so that the image fits correctly at the time you import it. To set the fitting properties in a blank frame, choose Object⇨Fitting⇨Frame Fitting Options.

Importing PDFs

You can import PDF files to place them as images in InDesign layouts. When importing, you can preview and crop the pages by using the Place PDF dialog box (choose File⇨Place, select the Show Import Options check box, and then click Open). You import one page at a time, so you need to use the Forward and Back buttons displayed under the preview to select a page to place. Also, you can't import any video, sound, or buttons, and you can't edit the PDF after it's imported into InDesign — so it is more like importing a static image such as a JPEG file.

The Place PDF dialog box offers the following options:

✦ **Crop To:** You can crop the page you're importing using this drop-down list. Some options may be unavailable because they depend on what's in the PDF you're importing. The hatched outline in the preview shows you the crop marks.

✦ **Transparent Background:** Selecting this check box makes the PDF background transparent so that elements on the InDesign page show through. The PDF background is imported as solid white if this option isn't selected.

Importing other InDesign documents

You can place one InDesign document inside another. This feature might sound a bit odd, but it has many uses. For example, if you have a page from a book that you want to promote in a catalog, you can import an image of the book page to place into a catalog — all without converting the book page into some type of image format. This strategy not only removes a step but also creates a higher-quality version of the image being placed into InDesign.

Here's how to take advantage of this feature:

1. **With a document open, choose File⇨Place or use the keyboard short-cut Ctrl+D (Windows) or ⌘+D (Mac).**

   The Place dialog box appears.

2. **Select the Show Import Options check box at the bottom of the Place dialog box.**

3. **Navigate to an InDesign file and double-click to open it.**

   The Place InDesign Document dialog box appears, as shown in Figure 5-1, offering you the opportunity to choose which page or pages you want to place.

4. **Click OK.**

5. **Click the page to place the document.**

   If you're placing a document with multiple pages, click again to place each additional page.

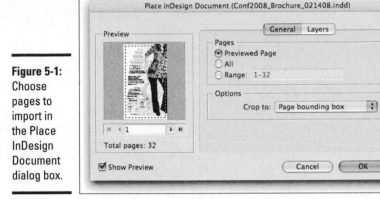

Figure 5-1:
Choose pages to import in the Place InDesign Document dialog box.

Linking and Embedding Images

You can have images that you import either linked to your document or embedded in your document. Here's the difference between linking and embedding:

✦ **Linking:** The image that appears in the InDesign document is a preview of the image stored somewhere else on your computer or network. If the file you linked to your InDesign document is changed, it must be updated.

✦ **Embedding:** The image is copied into and saved within the InDesign document itself. It doesn't matter where the original file is located or whether you alter the file, because an embedded image is copied and saved directly within the InDesign document.

When you print or export a document, InDesign uses the linked images to generate the information necessary to create a high-quality printed document, a PDF file, or an image for posting on the Web. InDesign keeps track of linked files and alerts you if any of them is moved or changed. You can update links for an image by selecting the image in the Links panel and choosing Update Link or Relink from the Links panel menu. You're prompted to find that file on your hard drive so that the file can be linked to the new location. And, if you send your InDesign file to someone else, make sure to also send its linked files along with the document.

If you choose to embed images rather than link to images, your publication's file size increases because of the extra data that's being stored within it.

To find out which files are embedded or linked, look at the Links panel. Choose Window⇨Links to open the panel and see whether any linked or embedded images are listed in the panel.

You can choose to embed a file by using the Links panel menu. Click the triangle in the upper right corner to access the panel menu and select Embed Link if you want a linked file to be embedded within the document. Alternatively, choose Unembed Link from the Link panel menu to link a file rather than have it embedded in the document. We recommend linking to all images so that your files don't become too large and because it provides you with flexibility to manipulate the image files separately.

Setting Image Quality and Display

You can select quality settings that determine how images are displayed when they're part of an InDesign layout. These settings may help speed up your work if your computer is older or slower, or if you have many images. Displaying images at a higher resolution can give you a better idea of the finished print project and may avoid the need to print the project several times for proofing. These settings are applicable only to how you see the images while using InDesign to create a document —they don't impact the final printed or exported product.

To change the image display quality, choose Edit⇨Preferences⇨Display Performance (Windows) or InDesign⇨Preferences⇨Display Performance (Mac). You can then select one of the following settings from the Default View drop-down list:

✦ **Fast:** To optimize performance, the entire image or graphic is grayed out.

✦ **Typical (Default):** This setting tends to make bitmaps look a little blocky, particularly if you zoom in. The speed of zooming in and out is increased if you select this option. InDesign uses a preview that it created (or that was already imported with the file) to display the image on the screen.

✦ **High Quality:** The original image is used to display onscreen. You can preview an accurate depiction of the final layout, but you may find that InDesign runs slowly when you use this option.

Notice the difference among these settings in Figure 5-2.

Figure 5-2:
From left to right: Fast Display, Typical Display, and High Quality Display.

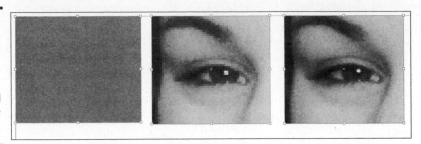

To change the display for an individual image, select the graphic frame and choose View➪Display Performance. Then choose one of the three options from the submenu.

Selecting Images

After you import an image into a document, you can select images in several different ways with the Selection or Direct Selection tools. It is useful to use the different methods depending upon whether you want to select and edit just the graphic frame or just the image inside it.

To select and then edit an image on the page, follow these steps:

1. **Place an image on a page by importing it or pasting it into InDesign.**

   The image is placed within a graphic frame.

2. **With the Selection tool, drag one of the corner handles on the graphic frame in towards the center of the frame.**

   The graphic frame is resized but not the image. The image appears to be cropped because you resized the graphic frame — though the image remains the same size within the frame, as shown in the center of Figure 5-3.

3. **Choose Edit➪Undo or press Ctrl+Z (Windows) or ⌘+Z (Mac) to undo changes to the image.**

   The image returns to its original appearance on the page.

4. **Continue to use the Selection tool to click the center of the picture where a circle appears and move the picture within the frame.**

   The frame remains the same size, but its content is relocated. You can also use the Selection tool to move the frame and contents together by clicking anywhere within the frame; however, it is good practice to click on the center section, because this works with both the Selection and Direct Selection tools.

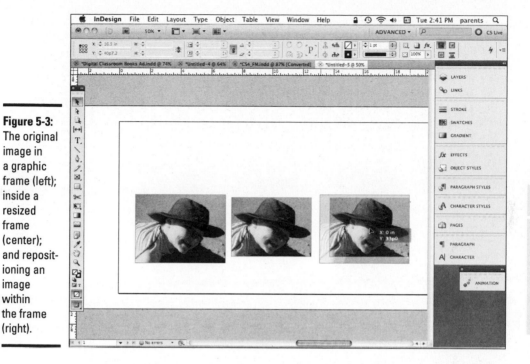

Figure 5-3:
The original image in a graphic frame (left); inside a resized frame (center); and repositioning an image within the frame (right).

5. Switch to the Direct Selection tool and then click within the image and drag to move the image within the graphic frame-bounding box.

A hand appears when you move the cursor over the graphic; when you move the image just past the edge of the graphic frame boundaries, that part of the image is no longer visible — it doesn't print and doesn't show when exported.

When you reposition a graphic within a frame, the entire image appears. Areas outside the frame appear ghosted, as shown in the image on the right in Figure 5-3. Seeing the dimmed image allows you to crop more effectively.

You can set the frame or image to resize by choosing Object⇨Fitting and selecting an option. You can even set this fitting before you place an image, which is especially helpful when creating templates. Resize before an image is placed by choosing Object⇨Fitting⇨Frame Fitting Options.

The Links panel can help you find images within documents, open images so that you can edit them, and view important information about selected images. Figure 5-4 can help you navigate the Links panel and work with your images more effectively.

Update Link

Go to Link   Edit Original

Relink

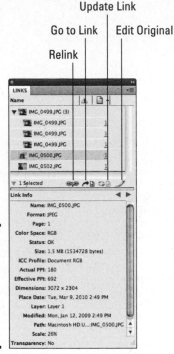

Figure 5-4:
The Links
panel keeps
track of
all images
used in your
documents.

Manipulating Text and Graphics in a Layout

InDesign offers many tools that help you work with text and graphics
together in a layout. From the tools in the Tools panel to commands to panel
options, InDesign offers you an immense amount of control over the manipulation of graphics and text in a spread.

Page orientation and size

When you create a new document, you can set its page orientation and size.
If you ever need to change your settings after you've created a document,
choose File➪Document Setup and change the following options, which affect
all pages in your document:

✦ **Page Orientation:** Select either Landscape or Portrait. One of the first
things you decide on when you create a new document is how to orient
the pages. A *landscape* page is wider than it is tall; a *portrait* orientation
is taller than it is wide.

✦ **Page Size:** Choose from many standardized preset sizes, such as Letter,
Legal, and Tabloid. Alternatively, you can set a custom page size for the
document. Make sure to properly set the page size so that it fits the kind
of paper you need to print on.

You can also use the pages panel to adjust the size of individual pages and make some pages a different size. This topic is covered later in this chapter, in the section "Working with Pages and the Pages Panel."

Margins, columns, and gutters

Margins, columns, and gutters help divide a page for layout and confine its dimensions:

✦ **Margin:** The area between the edge of the page and the main printed area. Together, the four margins (top, bottom, left, and right) look like a rectangle around the page's perimeter. Margins don't print when you print or export the publication.

✦ **Column:** Divide a page into sections used for laying out text and graphics on a page. A page has at least one column when you start, which is between the margins. You can add column guides, represented by a pair of lines separated by a *gutter* area. Column guides aren't printed when you print or export the publication.

✦ **Gutter:** The space between two columns on the page. A gutter prevents columns from running together. You can define the gutter's width by choosing Object⇨Text Frame Options; see Chapter 3 of this minibook for more information.

You can set margins and columns when you create a new document, which we discuss in Chapter 2 of this minibook. However, you can also modify margins and columns after the document has been created and specify different values for each page. You can modify the *gutter,* which is the width of the space between each column.

You can change margins and columns by setting new values in the Margins and Columns dialog box. Choose Layout⇨Margins and Columns and then modify each individual page.

Margins and columns are useful for placing and aligning elements on a page. These guides can have objects snap to them, enabling you to accurately align multiple objects on a page.

Using guides and snapping

Using guides when you're creating page layouts is a good idea because guides help you more precisely align elements on a page and position objects in the layout. Aligning objects by eyeballing them is difficult because you often can't tell whether an object is out of alignment by a small amount unless you zoom in to a large percentage.

Make sure that snapping is enabled by choosing View⇨Grids and Guides⇨ Snap to Guides. *Snapping* makes guides and grids useful. When you drag the object close to the grid, the object attaches to the guideline like it's a magnet. Aligning an object to a guide is easy after you create a guide, and you'll notice that InDesign displays temporary guides when you move an object near another object or near a guide.

Because guides are useful in creating a layout, check out the following kinds, available in InDesign (see Figure 5-5):

Ruler guide

Margin guide Column guides Margin guide

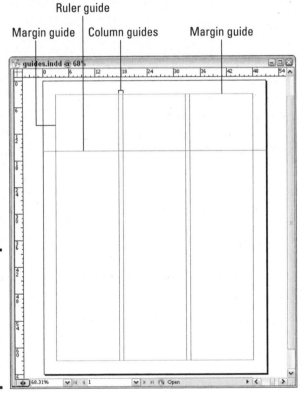

Figure 5-5:
Column guides, margin guides, and ruler guides help create a layout.

✦ **Column guides:** Evenly distribute a page into columns and can be used to align text frames in a document. These guides are set when you open a new document in InDesign that contains more than one column. Column guides evenly distribute the page into columns and can be used to align text frames in a document.

✦ **Margin guides:** Define the area between the edge of the page and the main printable area. (We discuss these guides in the previous section.)

✦ **Ruler guides:** Manually defined and can be used to align graphics, measure objects, or specify the location of a particular asset you want to lay out. See Chapter 2 of this minibook for details about adding ruler guides to the workspace.

✦ **Smart guides:** As previously mentioned, smart guides offer the ability to align objects on an InDesign page to other objects or even to the page. Smart Object alignment allows for easy snapping to page item centers or edges or page centers. In addition to snapping, Smart Guides give feedback to the user indicating the object to which you are snapping.

To find out how to show and hide grids and guides, see Chapter 2 of this minibook.

**Book II
Chapter 5**

**Understanding
Page Layout**

Don't forget that in InDesign CS5 you delete all guides at once by right-clicking the ruler (Windows) or Control-clicking the ruler (Mac) and selecting Delete All Guides from the contextual menu.

Locking objects and guides

You can lock in place elements such as objects and guides. This feature is particularly useful after you've carefully aligned elements on a page. Locking objects or guides prevents you from accidentally moving them from that position.

To lock an element, follow these steps:

1. Use a drawing tool to create an object on a page and then select the object with the Selection tool.

A bounding box with handles appears when the object is selected.

2. Choose Object⇨Lock.

The object is locked in position. Now when you try to use the Selection or Direct Selection tools to move the object, it doesn't move from its current position.

To lock guides in place, follow these steps:

1. Drag a couple of ruler guides to the page by clicking within a ruler and dragging toward the page.

A line appears on the page. (If rulers aren't visible around the pasteboard, choose View⇨Rulers.)

2. Drag a ruler guide to a new location, if needed; when you're happy with the ruler guides' placements, choose View⇨Grids and Guides⇨Lock Guides.

All guides in the workspace are locked. If you try selecting a guide and moving it, the guide remains in its present position. If you have any column guides on the page, they're locked as well.

Use layers in your publications for organization. Layers are a lot like transparencies that lie on top of each other, so they can be used for stacking elements on a page. For example, you may want to stack graphics or arrange similar items (such as images or text) on the same layer. Each layer has its own bounding box color, which helps you determine which item is on which corresponding layer. For more information on layers in general, see Book III, Chapter 8.

Merging Text and Graphics

When you have text and graphics together on a page, they should flow and work with each other to create an aesthetic layout. Luckily, you can work with text wrap to achieve a visual flow between text and graphics. In this section, you find out how to wrap text around images and graphics in your publications.

Wrapping objects with text

Images can have text wrapped around them, as shown in Figure 5-6. Wrapping is a typical feature of page layout in print and on the Web. You can choose different text wrap options by using the Text Wrap panel, which you open by choosing Window➪Text Wrap. Use the five buttons at the top of the panel to specify which kind of text wrapping to use for the selected object. Below the buttons are text fields where you can enter offset values for the text wrap. The fields are grayed out if the option isn't available.

You use the drop-down list at the bottom of the Text Wrap panel to choose from various contour options. The following list describes what happens when you click one of these buttons to wrap text around an object's shape:

✦ **No Text Wrap:** Use the default setting or to remove any text wrapping from the selected object.

✦ **Wrap around Bounding Box:** Wrap text around all sides of the bounding box of the object.

✦ **Offset:** Enter an amount to offset the text from wrapping around the object.

✦ **Wrap around Object Shape:** Wrap text around the edges of an object.

✦ **Contour Options:** Select a contour from this drop-down list, which tells InDesign how the edges of the image are determined. You can choose from various vector paths or the edges to be detected around an object or image with transparency.

(a) No text wrap

(d) Jump object

(b) Wrap around bounding box

(e) Jump to next column

Figure 5-6:
You can
wrap text
around
images in
InDesign
in several
ways.

(c) Wrap around object shape

✦ **Top Offset:** Enter a value for the top offset modifier to offset the text wrapping around the object.

✦ **Jump Object:** Make the text wrapping around the image jump from above the image to below it, with no text wrapping to the left or right of the object in the column.

✦ **Jump to Next Column:** Make text end above the image and then jump to the next column. No text is wrapped to the left or right of the image.

✦ **Offset:** Enter offset values for text wrapping on all sides of the object.

To add text wrapping to an object (a drawing or an image), follow these steps:

1. **Create a text frame on the page.**

Add text to the text frame by typing text, pasting text from elsewhere, or filling the frame with placeholder text. This text wraps around the image, so make sure that the text frame is slightly larger than the graphic frame you'll use.

2. **Use the Selection tool to select a graphic frame on the page and move it over the text frame.**

   Bounding box handles appear around the edges of the image or graphic.

3. **Choose Window⇨Text Wrap to open the Text Wrap panel.**

   The Text Wrap panel opens.

4. **With the graphic frame still selected, click the Wrap around Object Shape button.**

   The text wraps around the image instead of hiding behind it.

5. **If you're working with an image that has a transparent background, choose Detect Edges or Alpha Channel from the Contour Options drop-down list.**

   The text wraps around the edges of the image — refer to the (c) Wrap around Object Shape example in Figure 5-6.

Modifying a text wrap

If you've applied a text wrap around an object (as we show you how to do in the preceding section), you can then modify that text wrap. If you have an image with a transparent background around which you've wrapped text, InDesign created a path around the edge of the image; if you have a shape you created with the drawing tools, InDesign automatically uses those paths to wrap text around.

Before proceeding with the following steps, be sure that the object uses the Wrap around Object Shape text wrap. (If not, open the Text Wrap panel and click the Wrap around Object Shape button to apply text wrapping.) Remember to choose Detect Edges if you're using an image with a transparent background.

To modify the path around an image with text wrapping, using the Direct Selection tool, follow these steps:

1. **Select the object by using the Direct Selection tool.**

   The image is selected and you can see the path around the object.

2. **Drag one of the anchor points on the path by using the Direct Selection tool.**

   The path is modified according to how you move the point. (For more about manipulating paths, take a look at Chapter 4 of this minibook.) The text wrapping immediately changes, based on the modifications you make to the path around the object.

3. **Select the Delete Anchor Point tool from the Tools panel and delete an anchor point.**

The path changes again, and the text wrapping modifies around the object accordingly.

You can also use the Offset values in the Text Wrap panel to determine the distance between the wrapping text and the edge of the object. Just increase the values to move the text farther from the object's edge.

Working with Pages and the Pages Panel

The *page* is the central part of any publication — it's where the visible part of your publication is created. Navigating and controlling pages is a large part of what you do in InDesign. The Pages panel allows you to select, move, and navigate pages in a publication. When you use default settings, pages are created as *facing pages,* which means that they're laid out as two-page spreads. Otherwise, pages are laid out individually. This option is reflected in, and can be changed in, the Pages panel.

The Pages panel, which you open by choosing Window⇨Pages, also lets you add new pages to the document, duplicate pages, delete a page, or change the size of a page. The pages panel, shown in Figure 5-7, contains two main areas: the master pages (upper) section and the (lower) section containing the document's pages.

To discover more about master pages and how they differ from regular pages in your document, see the "Using Master Spreads in Page Layout" section, later in this chapter.

Selecting and moving pages

Use the Pages panel to select a page or spread in your publication. Select a page by clicking the page. If you Ctrl-click (Windows) or ⌘-click (Mac) pages, you can select more than one page at a time. The Pages panel also lets you move pages to a new position in the document: Select a page in the document pages area of the panel and then drag it wherever you want to move the page. A small line and changed cursor indicate where the page will be moved. You can move a page so that it's between two pages in a spread; a hollow line indicates where you're moving the page. If you move a page after a spread, a solid line appears. Release the mouse button to move the page to the new location.

Master pages

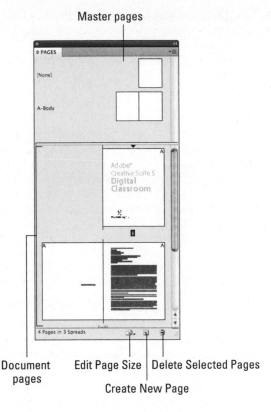

Figure 5-7:
The Pages
panel
with page
previews.

Document pages   Edit Page Size | Delete Selected Pages

Create New Page

Adding and deleting pages

You can also add new pages to the publication by using the Pages panel. To add a new page, follow these steps:

1. **Choose Window⇨Pages to open the Pages panel.**

The Pages panel opens.

2. **Click the Create New Page button.**

A new page is added to the document.

Alt-click (Windows) or Options-click (Mac OS) the Create New Page button and you can then specify the exact number of pages to add and the location of these new pages.

3. **Select a page in the Pages panel.**

The selected page is highlighted in the Pages panel.

4. **Click the Create New Page button again.**

A new page is added following the selected page.

To delete a page, select it in the Pages panel and click the Delete Selected Pages button. The selected page is removed from the document.

You can also add, delete, and move pages and more without the Pages panel by choosing Layout⇨Pages.

Numbering your pages

When you're working with longer documents, adding page numbers before you print or export the publication is a good idea. You don't have to add them manually: A special InDesign tool lets you number pages automatically. This tool is particularly useful when you move pages around the document. You don't have to keep track of updating the numbering when you make these kinds of edits.

To number pages, follow these steps:

1. **Using the Type tool, create a text frame on the page where you want the page number to be added.**

2. **Choose Type⇨Insert Special Character⇨Markers⇨Current Page Number.**

   The current page number appears in the text frame you selected. If you added the page number to a master page, the master pages' letter appears in the field instead.

If you want page numbers to appear on all pages in the document, add the text frame to a master page. Remember that page numbers are added only to the pages in your document that are associated with that master page. If you want to add page numbers to the left and right sides of a book or magazine, you need to repeat this process on the left and right sides of the master pages. Remember that if you add the page only on a document page — and not on a master — the page number is added to only that single page.

To modify automatic-numbering settings, choose Layout⇨Numbering and Section Options. You can choose to have numbering start from a specific number or use a different style, such as Roman numerals.

Using Master Spreads in Page Layout

Master pages are a lot like templates you use to format page layouts. The settings, such as margins and columns, are applied to each layout that the master page is applied to. If you put a page number on a master page, the number also appears on every page that uses the layout. You can have more than one master page in a single publication, and you can choose which pages use a particular master page.

A master page or spread typically contains parts of a layout that are applied to many pages. The master page has elements that are used on many pages, such as page numbering, text frames to enter text into, background images, or a heading that's used on every page. You can't edit the items you have on a master page on the pages assigned to it — you can edit those items only on the master page.

Master pages are lettered. The first master page is the A-Master by default. If you create a second master page, it's the B-Master by default. When you create a new publication, the A-Master is applied to all pages you initially open in the document. You can add pages at the end that don't have a master page applied to them.

Creating master pages and applying them to your publication enables you to create a reusable format for it, which can dramatically speed your workflow when you put together documents with InDesign.

Creating a master spread

You may need more than one master page or master spread for a document. You may have another series of pages that need a unique format. In this situation, you need to create a second master page. You can create a master page or a master spread from any other page in the publication, or you can create a new one with the Pages panel.

To create a master page using a page in the publication, do one of the following:

✦ Choose New Master from the Page panel's menu and then click OK. A blank master page is created.

✦ Drag a page from the pages section of the panel into the master page section of the Pages panel. The document page turns into a master page.

If the page you're trying to drag into the master pages section is part of a spread, select *both pages in the spread* before you drag it into the master pages section. You can drag individual pages into the master page section only if they're *not* part of a spread.

Applying, removing, and deleting master pages

After you create a master page, you can apply it to a page. You can also remove a page from a master page layout and delete a master page altogether:

✦ **To add master page formatting to a page or spread in a publication:** In the Pages panel, drag the master page you want to use from the master page section on top of the page you want to format in the document pages section. When you drag the master page on top of the page, it has a thick outline around it. Release the mouse button when you see this outline, and the formatting is applied to the page.

✦ **To remove any master page applied to a document page:** In the Pages panel, drag the None page from the master area in the Pages panel to that document page. You may need to use the scroll bar in the master pages area of the Pages panel to find the None page.

✦ **To delete a master page:** In the Pages panel, select the unwanted master page and then choose Delete Master Spread from the panel menu.

This action *permanently* deletes the master page — you can't get it back — so think carefully before deleting a master page.

Changing individual page sizes

Using the Pages panel, you can change the size of individual pages in a document, which is useful if you have one page that folds out and is larger than others. Or, maybe you want to create a single document that includes a business card, an envelope, and a letterhead.

To change the size of individual pages using the Pages panel, follow these steps:

1. **In the Pages panel, click to select the page you want to modify.**

2. **Click the Edit Page Size button at the bottom of the Pages panel and select the new size.**

3. **Repeat the process to adjust the size for any pages you want to modify.**

When you're done editing the size of the pages, continue to work on their design and layout like you would work on any other pages. The only difference is that some pages in your document may be a different size.

Chapter 6: Clipping Paths, Alignment, and Object Transformation

In This Chapter

✔ Transforming objects with the Transform panel

✔ Transforming objects with the Free Transform tool

✔ Rotating and scaling objects

✔ Shearing and reflecting objects

✔ Adding a clipping path

✔ Aligning and distributing objects in a layout

In this chapter, you discover several different ways to manipulate and arrange objects on a page. You find out how to use the Transform panel and other tools in the Tools panel to transform objects on page layouts. You can make the same transformation in many different ways in InDesign, so for each way you can transform an object, we show you a couple different ways to do the same job.

Aligning and distributing objects and images helps you organize elements logically on a page. In this chapter, you find out how to align objects by using the Align panel. In Chapter 5 of this minibook, we touch on vector paths. This chapter provides more information about clipping paths. We show you how to create a new path to use as a clipping path for an image in your document.

Working with Transformations

Chapter 4 of this minibook shows you how to transform graphic objects by skewing them. You can manipulate objects in InDesign in many other ways. You can transform an object by selecting an individual object and choosing Object⇨Transform, by using the Transform panel (choose Window⇨Object & Layout⇨Transform), or by using the Free Transform tool to visually adjust objects.

Looking at the Transform panel

The Transform panel, shown in Figure 6-1, is extremely useful for changing the way an image or graphic looks and also for changing the scale, rotation, or skew of selected objects. You can choose from a range of values for some of these modifiers or manually set your own by typing them.

Figure 6-1: The Transform panel makes it easy to resize, rotate, and reposition selected objects.

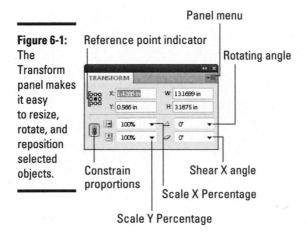

Panel menu

Reference point indicator

Rotating angle

Constrain proportions

Shear X angle

Scale X Percentage

Scale Y Percentage

The Transform panel offers the following information and functionality:

✦ **Reference point:** Indicates which handle is the reference for any transformations you make. For example, if you reset the X and Y coordinates, the reference point is set to this position. In Figure 6-1, the reference point is in the center, as indicated by the solid square.

✦ **Position:** Change these values to reset the X and Y coordinate position of the selected object.

✦ **Size:** The W and H text fields are used to change the current dimensions of the object.

✦ **Scale:** Enter or choose a percentage from the Scale X Percentage and Scale Y Percentage drop-down lists to scale (resize) the object on either of these axes.

✦ **Constraining proportions:** Click the Constrain Proportions button to maintain the current proportions of the object being scaled.

✦ **Shearing:** Enter or choose a negative or positive number to modify the shearing angle (skew) of the selected object.

✦ **Rotation angle:** Set a negative value to rotate the object clockwise; a positive value rotates the object counterclockwise.

When you're scaling, shearing, or rotating an object in your layout, it transforms based on the reference point in the Transform panel. For example, when you rotate an object, InDesign considers the reference point to be the center point of the rotation.

Click a new reference point square in the Transform panel to change the reference point of the graphic to the equivalent bounding box handle of the selected object.

You can open dialog boxes for each kind of transformation by choosing Object➪Transform. These dialog boxes have similar functionality to the Transform panel.

Using the Free Transform tool

 The multipurpose Free Transform tool lets you transform objects in different ways. Using the Free Transform tool, you can move, rotate, shear, reflect, and scale objects.

The functions of the Free Transform Tool are represented in InDesign by different cursors, as shown in Figure 6-2.

Figure 6-2:
Different cursors indicate options for using the Transform tool.

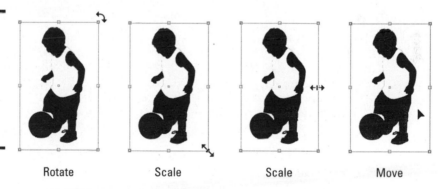

Rotate   Scale   Scale   Move

To move an object using the Free Transform tool, follow these steps:

1. Use the Selection tool to select an object on the page.

You can use an object that's already on the page or create a new shape by using the drawing tools. When the object is selected, you see handles around its edges.

2. Select the Free Transform tool from the Tools panel.

The cursor changes to the Free Transform tool.

3. **Move the cursor over the middle of the selected object.**

   The cursor changes its appearance to indicate that you can drag to move the object (refer to Figure 6-2). If you move the cursor outside the edges of the object, the cursor changes when other tools, such as rotate, scale, and shear, become active.

4. **Drag the object to a different location.**

   The object is moved to a new location on the page.

Rotating objects

You can rotate an object by using the Free Transform tool or the Transform panel. Use the panel to enter a specific degree that you want the object to rotate. The Free Transform tool lets you visually manipulate the object on the page.

To rotate an image by using the Free Transform tool, follow these steps:

1. **Select an object on the page with the Selection tool.**

   Handles appear around the edges of the object. You can rotate any object on the page.

2. **Select the Free Transform tool in the Tools panel and move it near the handle of an object outside the bounding box.**

   The cursor changes when you move it close to the handle of an object. For rotation, you must keep the cursor just outside the object.

3. **When the cursor changes to the rotate cursor, drag to rotate the object.**

   Drag the cursor until the object is rotated the correct amount.

Alternatively, you can use the Rotate tool to spin an object by following these steps:

1. **With the object selected, select the Rotate tool in the Tools panel and move the cursor near the object.**

   The cursor looks similar to a cross hair.

2. **Click the cursor anywhere on the page near the object.**

   The point that the object rotates around is set on the page.

3. **Drag the cursor outside the object.**

   The object rotates around the reference point you set on the page. Hold the Shift key if you want to rotate in 45-degree increments.

You can also rotate objects by using the Transform panel. Here's how:

1. **Select an object on the page with the Selection tool.**

   The bounding box with handles appears around the selected object.

2. **If the Transform panel isn't open, choose Window⇨Object & Layout⇨ Transform.**

   The Transform panel appears.

3. **Select a value from the Rotation Angle drop-down list or click the text field and enter a percentage.**

   The object rotates to the degree you set in the Transform panel. Negative angles (in degrees) rotate the image clockwise, and positive angles (in degrees) rotate the image counterclockwise.

Scaling objects

You can scale objects by using the Transform panel (refer to Figure 6-1), the Scale tool, or the Free Transform tool. Use the Transform panel to set exact width and height dimensions that you want to scale the object to, just as you can set exact percentages for rotating.

To scale an object by using the Free Transform tool or the Scale tool, follow these steps:

1. **Select an object on the page.**

   A bounding box appears around the object.

2. **Select the Free Transform tool or the Scale tool from the Tools panel.**

3. **Move the cursor directly over a corner handle.**

   The cursor changes into a double-ended arrow (refer to Figure 6-2).

4. **Drag outward to increase the size of the object; drag inward to decrease the size of the object.**

   If you want to scale the image proportionally, hold down the Shift key while you drag.

5. **Release the mouse button when the object is scaled to the correct size.**

To resize an object using the Transform panel, select the object and enter new values into the W and H text fields in the panel. The object then resizes to those exact dimensions.

Shearing objects

Shearing an object means that you're skewing it horizontally, slanting it to the left or right. A sheared object may appear to have perspective or depth because of this modification. You use the Shear tool to create a shearing effect, as shown in Figure 6-3.

Figure 6-3:
The original image is on the left, and the sheared image is on the right.

Follow these steps to shear an object:

1. **Select an object on the page.**

The bounding box appears around the object that's selected.

 2. **Choose the Shear tool in the Tools panel by clicking and holding the Free Transform tool.**

The cursor changes so that it looks similar to a cross hair. Click the corner of the object that you want to shear from, and a cross hair appears, as shown in Figure 6-3.

3. **Click anywhere above or below the object and drag.**

The selected object shears depending on which direction you drag. Press the Shift key while you drag to shear an object in 45-degree increments.

 To shear objects with the Free Transform tool, begin dragging a handle and then hold down Ctrl+Alt (Windows) or ⌘+Option (Mac) while dragging.

You can also enter an exact value into the Transform panel to shear an object. Select the object and then enter a positive or negative value in the panel representing the amount of slant you want to apply to the object.

 You can apply shear by choosing Object⇨Transform⇨Shear to display the Shear dialog box.

Reflecting objects

You can reflect objects to create mirror images by using the Transform panel menu. The menu provides several additional options for manipulating objects.

Follow these steps to reflect an object:

1. **Select an object on the page and then press F9 to open the Transform panel or open it from the Window menu.**

    The object's bounding box and handles appear. The Transform panel shows the current values of the selected object.

2. **Click the panel menu in the Transform panel.**

    The menu opens, revealing many options available for manipulating the object.

3. **Select Flip Horizontal from the Transform panel menu.**

    The object on the page flips on its horizontal axis. You can repeat this step with other reflection options in the menu, such as Flip Vertical.

You can also reflect objects with the Free Transform tool by dragging a corner handle past the opposite end of the object. The object reflects on its axis.

Understanding Clipping Paths

Clipping paths allow you to create a path that crops a part of an image based on the path, such as removing the background area of an image. This shape can be one you create using InDesign, or you can import an image that already has a clipping path. InDesign can also use an existing alpha or mask layer, such as one created using Photoshop or Fireworks, and treat it like a clipping path. Clipping paths are useful when you want to block out areas of an image and have text wrap around the leftover image.

You can create a clipping path directly in InDesign by using a drawing tool, such as the Pen tool. You use the tool to create a shape and then paste an image into this shape on the page. Here's how:

1. **Choose File⇨Place and browse to locate an image.**

2. **With the Pen tool, create a path right on top of the image.**

    The path should be created so that it can contain the image.

3. **With the Selection tool, click to select the image and then choose File⇨Cut.**

4. **Select the shape you created in Step 1 and choose Edit⇨Paste Into.**

The image is pasted into the selected shape you drew with the Pen tool.

Arranging Objects on the Page

In other chapters of this minibook, we show you how to arrange objects on the page. However, you can arrange text or objects in a few other ways. This section covers the additional ways you can arrange objects, which gives you more control over the placement of elements in your document.

Aligning objects

In CS5, you can align visually without the need for any extra tools or panels. If you keep Smart Guides activated (they're on by default), when you use the Selection tool to select and move objects around a page, guides appear automatically. These guides appear when the selected object is aligned with other objects on the page or with the page itself. If viewing these pesky guides starts to bother you, choose Edit⇨Preferences⇨Guides & Pasteboard (Windows) or InDesign⇨Guides & Pasteboard (Mac) and turn off the four options underneath the Smart Guide Options heading.

You can also align objects on a page by using the Align panel: Choose Window⇨Object & Layout⇨Align. This panel gives you control over the way elements align to one another or to the overall page. The Align panel has many buttons to control selected objects. Mouse over a button to see its tooltip describe how that button aligns elements.

If you're not sure what each button does after reading the associated tooltip, look at the icon on the button. The icon is sometimes helpful in depicting what the Align button does to selected objects.

Here's how to align elements on the page:

1. **Select several objects on the page with the Selection tool.**

Hold the Shift key while clicking each object to select several objects.

Each object is selected when you click it on the page. If you don't have a few objects on a page, quickly create a couple new objects by using the drawing tools.

2. **Choose Window➪Object & Layout➪Align.**

The Align panel opens.

3. **Select the kind of alignment you want to apply to the selected objects.**

Try clicking the Align Vertical Centers button. Each selected object aligns to the vertical center point on the page.

Distributing objects

In the preceding step list, we show you how to align a few objects on a page, which is easy enough. However, what if the objects you're aligning aren't distributed evenly? Maybe their centers are lined up but there's a large gap between two of the images and a narrow gap between the other ones. In that case, you need to *distribute* objects and align them. Distribute objects on the page to space them relative to the page or to each other in different ways. Here's how:

1. **Select objects on a page that are neither aligned nor evenly distributed, by using the Selection tool while holding the Shift key.**

The objects are selected when you click each one. All objects you select will be aligned to each other on the page.

2. **If the Align panel isn't open, choose Window➪Object & Layout➪Align.**

The Align panel opens.

3. **Click the Distribute Horizontal Centers button and then click the Align Vertical Centers button directly above it on the Align panel.**

The selected objects are distributed evenly and aligned horizontally on the page.

Don't forget about the cool Multiple Place feature: It lets you distribute and align on the fly! Try this handy option to place several images at one time:

1. **Choose File➪Place.**

2. **Press Ctrl (Windows) or ⌘ (Mac), select multiple images, and then click the Open button.**

3. **Before clicking to place the images, hold down Ctrl+Shift (Windows) or ⌘+Shift (Mac).**

The cursor appears as a grid, as shown in Figure 6-4.

Figure 6-4:
Place multiple images by holding down Ctrl+Shift (Windows) or ⌘+Shift (Mac) and dragging.

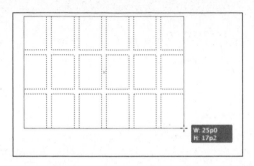

4. **Click and drag to create the rectangle that you want your images aligned to and distributed within.**

   The images are aligned and distributed automatically, as shown in Figure 6-5.

Figure 6-5:
Images are aligned and distributed automatically when placed.

Chapter 7: Understanding Color and Printing

In This Chapter

✔ Using color in page layout

✔ Looking at color controls and models

✔ Discovering swatches and swatch libraries

✔ Understanding bleeding and trapping

✔ Looking at printing and preferences

Color is an important part of your layouts. It impacts the design and must be printed correctly. Advertisements often rely on color to relay brands or effective messages — think of the package delivery company based on brown or the purple-and-orange company known for overnight shipments. Similarly, the success of a printed piece greatly depends on *how* color is used in the layout. Color, used correctly, can enhance your message and, used consistently, helps create a brand identity. In this chapter, you find out some of the fundamental aspects of working with color and the basic instructions on how to prepare documents for printing.

For more information on general subjects about color, see Book I, Chapters 7 and 8, which cover subjects such as color modes, inks, and printers, and basic color correction across the programs in the Adobe Creative Suite.

Selecting Color with Color Controls

You have several different color modes and options to choose when working in InDesign. Because the use of color in print media can be quite a science, you must have control over how your documents print on the page. In Chapter 4 of this minibook, we show you how to add color to drawings with the Color panel. In this section, we cover using the Color panel to choose colors and apply them to the elements on your page.

You should use swatches whenever possible because they use named colors that a service provider can match exactly. A swatch can have exactly the same appearance as any color you choose that's unnamed, but a swatch establishes a link between the color on the page and the name of a color, such as a Pantone color number. Discover more about these kinds of color in the later section "Using Color Swatches and Libraries."

You can use these color controls for choosing colors for selections in a document:

✦ **Stroke color:** Choose colors for strokes and paths in InDesign. A hollow box represents the Stroke color control.

✦ **Fill color:** Choose colors for filling shapes. A solid square box represents the Fill color control.

You can toggle between the Fill and Stroke color controls by clicking them. Alternatively, you can press X on the keyboard to toggle between selected controls.

✦ **Text color:** When you're working with text, a different color control becomes active. The Text color control is visible and displays the selected text color. Text can have both the stroke and fill colored.

To apply colors to selections, you can click the Apply color button below the color controls in the Tools panel. Alternatively, you can select and click a color swatch.

The default colors in InDesign are a black stroke and no fill color. Restore the default colors at any time by pressing D. This shortcut works while using any tool except the Type tool.

Understanding Color Models

You can use any of three kinds of color models in InDesign: CMYK (Cyan, Magenta, Yellow, Black), RGB (Red, Green, Blue), and LAB colors (*lightness* and *A* and *B* for the *color*-opponent dimensions of the color space). A *color model* is a system used for representing each color as a set of numbers or letters (or both). The best color model to use depends on how you plan to print or display your document:

✦ If you're creating a PDF that will be distributed electronically and probably not printed, use the RGB color model. RGB is how colors are displayed on a computer monitor.

✦ You must use the CMYK color model if you're working with *process color:* Instead of having inks that match specified colors, you have four ink colors layered to simulate a particular color. Note that the colors on the monitor may differ from the ones that are printed. Sample swatch books and numbers can help you determine which colors you need to use in a document to match colors printed in the end.

✦ If you know that the document needs to be printed by professionals who determine what each color is before it's printed, it doesn't matter whether you use RGB, PMS (Pantone Matching System), or LAB colors. Make sure to use named colors (predetermined swatches are a good idea) so that the service provider knows which color should be printed. In this case, you're using *spot colors,* which are mixed inks that match the colors you specify in InDesign.

For more information on color models, check out Book I, Chapter 7. This chapter explains how colors are determined in the different color modes.

Using Color Swatches and Libraries

The Swatches panel and swatch libraries help you choose colors. Swatch libraries help you use colors for specific publishing purposes. The colors you use in a document can vary greatly depending on what you're creating the document for. For example, one publication you make with InDesign may be for a catalog that has only two colors; another may be for the Web, where many colors are available to you.

The Swatches panel

You can create, apply, and edit colors from the Swatches panel. In addition to using this panel to create and edit tints and gradients and then apply them to objects on a page, you can also create and save solid colors. Choose Window⇨Swatches to open or expand the Swatches panel.

To create a new color swatch to use in a document, follow these steps:

1. **Click the arrow in the upper right corner to open the Swatches panel menu; choose New Color Swatch.**

   The New Color Swatch dialog box opens.

2. **Type a new name for the color swatch or leave the color named by color values.**

   (The colors in the Swatches panel appear this way as a default.)

   This name is displayed next to the color swatch when it's entered into the panel.

3. **Choose the color type from the Color Type drop-down list.**

   Are you using a spot color (Pantone, for example) or CMYK (Cyan, Magenta, Yellow, Black)?

4. **Choose the color mode.**

   From the Color Mode drop-down list, select a color mode. For this example, we use CMYK. Many of the other choices you see are prebuilt color libraries for various systems.

5. **Create the color by using the color sliders.**

   Note that if you start with Black, you have to adjust that slider to the left to see the other colors.

6. **Click OK or Add.**

   Click Add if you want to continue adding colors to the Swatches panel or click OK if this color is the only one you're adding. The color or colors are added to the Swatches panel.

You can make changes to the swatch by selecting it in the Swatches panel and then choosing Swatch Options from the panel menu.

Swatch libraries

Swatch libraries, also known as color libraries, are standardized sets of named colors that help you because they're the most commonly and frequently used sets of color swatches. You can avoid trying to mix your own colors, which can be a difficult or tedious process to get right. For example, InDesign includes a swatch library for Pantone spot colors and a different library for Pantone process colors. These libraries are quite useful if you're working with either color set. (See the earlier section "Understanding Color Models," where we explain the difference between spot and process colors.)

To choose a swatch from a swatch library, follow these steps:

1. **Choose New Color Swatch from the Swatches panel menu.**

   The New Color Swatch dialog box opens.

2. **Choose the color type you want to work with from the Color Type drop-down list.**

   Choose from Process or Spot Color types.

3. **Select a color library from the Color Mode drop-down list.**

   The drop-down list contains a list of color swatch libraries to choose from, such as Pantone Process Coated or TRUMATCH. After choosing a swatch set, the library opens and appears in the dialog box. For this example, we chose standard, solid-coated Pantone. If you're looking for the standard numbered Pantone colors, this set is the easiest to choose from. The Pantone solid-coated library of swatches loads.

4. **Pick a swatch from the library.**

   Type a Pantone number, if you have one, in the Pantone text box. Most companies have set Pantone colors that they use for consistency. You can also scroll and click a swatch in the library's list of colors, shown in Figure 7-1.

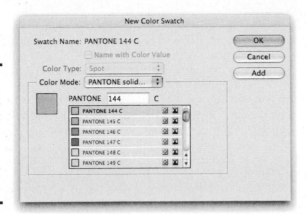

Figure 7-1:
Choose a color from the swatch library to add it to the Swatches panel.

Picking Pantone colors this way is rarely accurate. Spending money on the Pantone Color Bridge Set is a wise investment. Get more details about this guide at www.pantone.com and search for *Color Bridge*.

5. **Click the Add button.**

   This step adds the swatch to your list of color swatches in the Swatches panel. You can add as many color swatches as you like.

6. **When you finish adding swatches, click the Done button.**

   After you add a new color, the swatch is added to the list of swatches in the swatches panel and is ready to use in your project. Look in the swatches panel to see the newly added colors.

Printing Your Work

You can print your work from an InDesign document in many different ways, with many kinds of printers and processes. You can either use a printer at home or in your office, which are of varying levels of quality and design, or you can take your work into a professional establishment to print. Printing establishments (or service providers) also vary in the quality of production they can offer you.

The following subsections look at the different ways you can set up a document for printing and the kinds of issues you may encounter during this process.

What's a bleed?

If you want an image or span of color to go to the edge of a page, without any margins, you bleed it off the edge of the document. *Bleeding* extends the print area slightly beyond the edge of the page into the area that will be cut as usual during the printing process. When you print your work, you can turn on crop and bleed marks to show where the page needs to be trimmed and to make sure that the image bleeds properly. We cover this topic at the end of this chapter, in "Doing it yourself: Printing at home or in the office."

About trapping

When you print documents, the printer is seldom absolutely perfect when creating a printed page with multiple inks. The *registration* (which determines the alignment of the separate colors when printed) will most surely be off. This discrepancy can potentially cause a gap between two colors on a page so that unprinted paper shows through between them. To solve this problem, use *trapping,* which overlaps elements on the page slightly so that the gap doesn't appear between elements. The basic principle of trapping is to spread the lighter of the colors into the other. See Figure 7-2 for an example.

Figure 7-2:
Text as it appears in InDesign (left). Text (right) as it appears when printed with trapping applied.

InDesign has built-in software for trapping. The settings you specify are applied to the entire page. You choose settings in the Trap Presets panel. You can use the default settings, customize the trapping settings, or decide not to use trapping. To modify the default settings and then apply the customized settings, follow these steps:

1. **Choose Window⇨Output⇨Trap Presets.**

The Trap Presets panel opens. The trapping presets in InDesign are document-wide, but you can assign individual trappings by using the Attributes panel (choose Window⇨Attributes) to overprint strokes on selected art only.

2. **Double-click [Default] in the panel's list.**

The Modify Trap Preset Options dialog box opens, as shown in Figure 7-3. The default settings are perfectly adequate for many printing jobs.

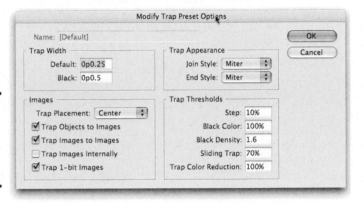

Figure 7-3:
The Modify
Trap Preset
Options
dialog box.

3. **Change the trap preset options, if you know what's necessary, and then click OK to close the dialog box.**

If you don't know what to change, investigate the options for a better understanding of how they work. You can also request settings from your print provider.

4. **In the Trap Presets panel, choose New Preset from the panel menu.**

The New Trap Preset dialog box opens.

5. **Type an appropriate name for the new trap preset.**

You see this name in the list of trap presets in the Trap Presets panel when it's opened. You might create a name for a printer that has different settings from another.

6. **Review and make any changes to the new preset in the dialog box.**

You can change the presets by using these options:

- *Trap Width:* The default value specifies the width of the trap for any ink, except black, that you use in the document. Enter the value for black in the Black text field.

- *Images:* Control how InDesign handles trapping between elements on the document page and any imported graphics on it. Use the Trap Placement drop-down list to define how images trap to objects on the page. When bitmap images are next to each other, select the Trap Images to Images check box.

- *Trap Appearance:* Do some fine-tuning and change how the corner points appear in trapping. Select the way corner points appear by using the Join Style drop-down list; select how end points appear (overlapped or separated) by using the End Style drop-down list.

- *Trap Thresholds:* Control how InDesign traps the areas between two colors in a document. You can control whether InDesign traps two objects of similar colors (for example, how different the colors have to be before InDesign starts trapping).

7. **Click OK to create the trap preset.**

   The New Trap Preset dialog box closes and the customized preset is added to the panel.

To assign a trap preset to a number of pages (or all of them), click the arrow in the upper right corner of the Trap Preset panel and choose Assign Trap Preset from the panel menu. in the dialog box that opens, choose a trapping style and assign it to all pages or a range of pages. Click the Assign button to assign the preset before clicking the Done button.

You have other ways to apply trapping to a document manually. This process goes beyond the scope of this book but is worthwhile to look into if you want to fully realize what trapping is all about. See *InDesign CS5 Bible* by Galen Gruman (Wiley) for more information on trapping.

Taking your files to a service provider

If you're taking a file to a professional print service (service provider), you may have to save the .indd document in a different format. Even though all service providers should (in our opinion) have InDesign, not all of them do.

The two major groups of printers are PostScript and non-PostScript. PostScript printers read files written in the PostScript language. PostScript files describe the contents of each page and how they should look when printed. Most printers you find in a home or office aren't PostScript printers.

If you're giving a file to someone to print, you can pass on your work in a few different ways. You can give the person printing the document your original InDesign document. Of course, he (or the business) must have a copy of InDesign on hand to open the file. Or, you can send a PostScript file or PDF file to print. Sometimes, you have to ask about the preferred file type for opening and printing the document. You probably should send the original InDesign file (if you can) or a PDF file. When you create a PDF, your documents should print accurately.

The *Package* feature is used to check for quality in documents and tells you information about the document you're printing (such as listing its fonts, print settings, and inks). Using Preflight can help you determine whether

your InDesign document has unlinked images or missing fonts before printing it. Choose File⇨Package to open the Package dialog box.

You can determine whether any elements associated with the file are missing and then package it into a single folder to take the document to a service
provider. Here's how:

1. **Choose File⇨Package.**

    The Package dialog box opens. The Summary screen is open to begin
    with, and it shows you all current images and fonts in the document.
    Essentially, the summary is based on an analysis of the document.

2. **Click Fonts in the list on the left side of the dialog box.**

    Any fonts in your document are listed on this screen. Select fonts from
    this list and click the Find Font button to discover where they're located.
    These fonts are saved directly into the package folder when you finish.

3. **Click Links and Images in the list on the left side of the dialog box.**

    The Links and Images screen lists the images within your document.
    Find the image, update it, and repair links before packing the file. If any
    images aren't properly linked, your document is incomplete and prints
    with pictures missing. Also, make sure that if you're sending your work
    to a professional printer, you've properly converted your images to
    CMYK mode. For your desktop printer, RGB mode is fine.

4. **When you're finished, click the Package button at the bottom of the
    dialog box.**

    Your document and all its associated files are saved into a folder. You're
    given the opportunity to name the folder and specify a location on your
    hard drive.

Doing it yourself: Printing at home or in the office

You've probably printed documents in the past, and perhaps you've even
played with the printer settings. These settings depend on which kind of
printer you're using and which associated printer drivers are installed on
your system. Whichever operating system you work with and whichever
printer you use, you have settings that control the printer's output. This section deals only with the more basic and common kinds of printing you may
perform at home or in the office.

Choose File⇨Print to open the Print dialog box. Many printing options are
available in the list on the left side of the Print dialog box. Click an item
and the dialog box changes to display the settings you can change for the
selected item.

This list describes the options you're most likely to use when printing InDesign documents:

✦ **General:** Set the number of copies of the document you want to print and the range of pages to print. You can select the Reverse Order check box to print from the last to first page. Select an option from the Sequence drop-down list to print only even or odd pages instead of all pages. If you're working with spreads that need to be printed on a single page, select the Spreads check box.

✦ **Setup:** Define the paper size, orientation (portrait or landscape), and scale. You can scale a page so that it's as much as 1,000 percent of its original size or as little as 1 percent. You can (optionally) constrain the scale of the width and height so that the page remains at the same ratio. The Page Position drop-down list is useful when you're using paper that's larger than the document you've created. This option helps you center the document on larger paper.

✦ **Marks and Bleed:** Turn on or off many of the printing marks in the document, such as crop, bleed, and registration marks. For example, you may want to show these marks if a bleed extends past the boundaries of the page and you need to show where to crop each page. You see a preview of what the page looks like when printed, and you can select options to print page information (such as filename and date) on each page.

✦ **Output:** Choose how to print pages — for example, as a separation or a composite, using which inks (if you're using separations), or with or without trapping. InDesign can separate and print documents as plates (which are used in commercial printing) from settings you specify.

✦ **Graphics:** Control how graphics and fonts in the document are printed. The Send Data drop-down list controls bitmap images and specifies how much of the data from these images is sent to the printer. Here are some other options available when printing:

  • *All:* Sends all bitmap data

  • *Optimized Subsampling:* Sends as much image data as the printer can handle

  • *Proxy:* Prints lower-quality images mostly to preview them

  • *None:* Prints placeholder boxes with an X through them

✦ **Color Management:** Choose how you want color handled when it's output. If you have profiles loaded in your system for your output devices, you can select the profiles here.

✦ **Advanced:** Determine how you want images to be sent to the printer. If you don't have a clue about Open Prepress Interface (OPI), you can leave this setting at the default. Also known as image-swapping technology, the *OPI* process allows low-resolution images inserted into InDesign to be swapped with the high-resolution version for output.

Flattening needs to be addressed if you use a drop shadow, feather an object in InDesign, or apply transparency to any objects, even if they were created in Photoshop or Illustrator.

Use the preset Medium Resolution for desktop printers and High Resolution for professional press output.

✦ **Summary:** You can't make modifications but you can see a good overview of all your print settings.

After you finish your settings, click the Save Preset button if you want to save the changes you've made. If you think you may print other documents with these settings repeatedly, using the Save Preset feature can be a great timesaver.

After you click the Save Preset button, the Save Preset dialog box opens, where you can enter a new name to save the settings. The next time you print a document, you can select the saved preset from the Print Preset drop-down list in the Print dialog box.

Click the Print button at the bottom of the Print dialog box when you're ready to print the document.

**Book II
Chapter 7**

**Understanding
Color and Printing**

Chapter 8: Integrating InDesign with Other Creative Suite Applications

In This Chapter

✔ **Creating interactive PDF files for Acrobat**

✔ **Creating multimedia Flash files**

✔ **Working with Illustrator and Photoshop files in InDesign**

✔ **Using InDesign to create Web pages for Dreamweaver**

The Adobe Creative Suite and InDesign offer you many ways to create projects that meet your needs in print and online. When you *integrate* products, you work on a single project using more than one piece of software. Because the Adobe software products are built as a suite, the products work together.

Creating Interactive PDF Files Using InDesign

You can import PDF files into an InDesign layout as well as you can export InDesign files to PDF format. After exporting to PDF, you can manipulate these files using Adobe Acrobat (as described in Book V) or add certain features using InDesign, such as multimedia elements that appear when viewing the PDF file. In this section, we look at some other ways you can control PDF attributes within InDesign.

InDesign is a helpful tool for designing and creating PDF documents. With InDesign, you can add features and interactivity to a PDF by setting up page transitions and adding these elements:

✦ Clickable elements, such as hyperlinks and bookmarks

✦ Links that perform actions

✦ Movies such as Flash SWF files or WMV and sound files

Creating a PDF hyperlink using InDesign

You can add hyperlinks to link to another piece of text, a page, or a URL (a Web site address) within an InDesign document. After you create hyperlinks, they're visible to users who work with PDF files you have exported. To create a URL hyperlink in a PDF with InDesign, follow these steps:

1. **Open a new document that includes some text in a text frame.**

   Choose a document that you want to add a hyperlink to.

2. **Choose Window➪Interactive➪Hyperlinks to open the Hyperlinks panel.**

   The Hyperlinks panel opens. Notice that its menu contains several options, and you can use buttons along the bottom of the panel to add or delete links from the panel.

3. **Use the Text tool to select some text.**

   Select the text that you want to make into a hyperlink.

4. **Click the Create New Hyperlink button at the bottom of the Hyperlinks panel.**

   The New Hyperlink dialog box opens, as shown in Figure 8-1. Make sure that URL is selected in the Type drop-down list.

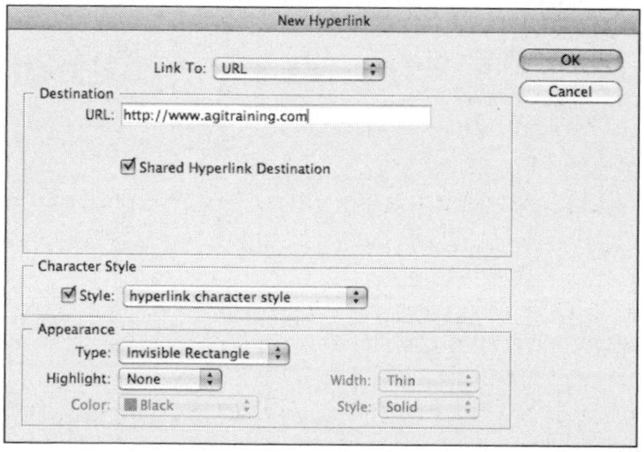

Figure 8-1:
The New
Hyperlink
dialog box.

5. **Type a URL in the URL text field, if necessary.**

   The type you enter is the Web page the URL links to. Make sure that it's a complete URL, such as `http://www.`*`yourdomain`*`.com`. This field also accepts `mailto:` actions if you want to create an e-mail link. Simply enter an e-mail address, such as `mailto:`*`you@yourdomain`*`.com`, in the URL text field.

6. **Choose an appearance for the clickable text.**

   In the Appearance section, you can choose to have a visible or invisible rectangle (whether you want a rectangle to appear around the link). Then you can choose the highlight, color, width, and style of the link.

7. **Click OK.**

   The dialog box closes. When you export the document as a PDF, this text becomes a clickable hyperlink. Clicking the text opens a browser window to the Web page you entered in the URL text field. Make sure that the Hyperlinks check box is selected in the Export PDF dialog box when you create the PDF file. Exporting to PDF is explained in more detail in Chapter 9 of this minibook.

You can also create a hyperlink by selecting a URL that exists in the text frame. To do so, select the URL and right-click (Windows) or Control-click (Mac) the selected text. Choose Interactive⇨New Hyperlink Destination, and the dialog box opens so that you can edit the link. Click OK and a hyperlink is created.

Adding multimedia files and interactive page transitions to PDF files

In this section, we show you how to add some basic interactivity to a PDF file by adding a movie file. You can add an SWF file or an MOV file, depending on which one you have available. These media files don't play while you're using InDesign. However, the files play if you export the document to PDF or XML format. To view a movie in a PDF file, double-click the movie icon.

Viewers need at least Acrobat Reader 6 to view the PDF file and play the media files.

You can add the following movie files to a PDF: AVI, MOV, MPEG, and SWF. You can add these types of audio files: AIF, AU, and WAV.

To add a media file or an interactive page transition to a PDF document, follow these steps in InDesign:

1. **Choose File⇨Place.**

   The Place dialog box opens, where you can choose a media file to import.

2. **Choose an AVI, MOV, MPEG, or SWF file to import.**

3. **Click within the document window to place the media file on the page.**

The Place cursor appears after you select a file to import into the document. Click where you want the upper left corner to be located on the page.

4. **Using the Pages panel, add at least two more pages.**

   For information about using the Pages panel, see Chapter 5 in this minibook.

5. **Add some content to the other pages.**

   For example, add text, images, or more interactive objects such as movies or SWF Flash files.

6. **Using the Pages panel, select any page (except the last page) in the document and choose Page Transitions from the Pages panel menu in the upper right corner of the panel.**

7. **Select the desired transition for when this page appears.**

8. **To export to an interactive PDF file, choose File⇨Export and choose Adobe PDF (Interactive) from the Save As Type (Windows) or the Format (Mac) drop-down list.**

9. **Select a location, enter a name for the file, and then click Save.**

   The Export to Interactive PDF dialog box appears.

10. **Choose All from the Pages section, select View after Exporting, and choose From Document from the Page Transitions drop-down list to use the transitions you just applied.**

11. **In the Presentation section, choose Open in Full Screen Mode and, in the Buttons and Multimedia section, select Include All.**

12. **Click OK to create the interactive PDF.**

    Your file should open in Adobe Acrobat. If you're working on a Mac and your PDF viewer is set to Preview, you may need to launch Acrobat and then view the file by choosing File⇨Open from within Acrobat.

    The page transitions you created appear as you navigate from one page to the next.

Creating Multimedia Flash Files from InDesign

You can export InDesign documents into Flash so that they can be either viewed using Flash Player or edited using Flash Professional. The page transitions you find out how to apply to your document in the previous section can be used, and you can also use an interactive page flip, not available within Acrobat.

When you export a file to the Flash format and then open the file in a Web browser, you can move from page to page by grabbing a corner of the page and flipping it, as shown in Figure 8-2. As you turn from page to page, you see your page transitions at work.

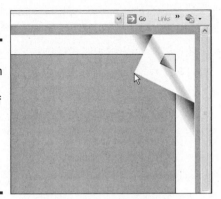

Figure 8-2: Readers can flip through the pages of a document when you publish it in Flash SWF format.

To export your InDesign document to Flash, follow these steps:

1. **Choose File➪Export and select Flash Player (SWF) from the Format drop-down menu.**

2. **In the dialog box that appears, enter a name for the file, select a location to save it, and then click Save.**

   The Export SWF dialog box appears.

3. **In the General section, make sure that the Generate HTML File and View SWF after Exporting options are both selected and then click OK.**

   The file is exported to an SWF file, and an HTML container for the file is created and displayed within your Web browser. Use the mouse to click and drag the page corners to turn the pages, or use the left and right arrow keys to navigate forward and backward in the Flash document.

You can further refine your InDesign multimedia project using Flash Professional. Rather than export to Flash SWF, choose the Flash Professional option when exporting and then open the file using Flash Professional and make your edits.

Integrating InDesign with Photoshop

You can create designs in Photoshop (which we discuss thoroughly in Book IV) and then import the native PSD files from Photoshop directly into InDesign. InDesign provides you with additional control over the designs after an image is imported into a layout.

Using InDesign, you can import a layered Photoshop file, turn layers on and off, or even layer comps to be placed. Follow these steps:

1. **Have a layered Photoshop file ready to place.**

2. **Using InDesign, choose File⇨Place.**

3. **Browse to the location of a layered image file, select the file you want to import, select the Show Import Options check box, and then click Open.**

   A dialog box similar to the one shown in Figure 8-3 appears.

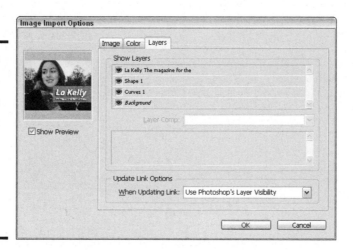

Figure 8-3: Choose which Photoshop layers you want to use when placing a PSD file into your InDesign layout.

4. **Click the Layers tab and turn off and on the visibility of the layers you want to change or select a saved layer comp from the Layer Comp drop-down list.**

5. **Click OK to close the Image Import Options dialog box.**

Transparency support and clipping paths

Many Photoshop files use transparency. The transparency in the PSD files is imported and interpreted by InDesign. This feature is particularly useful when you have an established background or want to have interesting text wrap around an image you import from Photoshop. Basically, you can use the transparency as a clipping path in InDesign. A *clipping path* resembles a hard-edged mask that hides parts of an image, such as a background, that you don't want visible around a certain part of the image. (See Book IV, Chapter 5 for more about Photoshop clipping paths.)

You can use alpha channels, paths, and masks that you create in Photoshop in InDesign. InDesign recognizes these parts of the PSD file, so you can use them when you're wrapping text around the image or when you want to create a clipping path. Alternatively, you can also use these parts to remove a background from the image. For example, if you have an image with one of these assets, you can use the Detect Edges feature in InDesign to detect the edges and wrap text around the image. (We explain text wrapping in Chapter 3 of this minibook.)

Photoshop spot colors in InDesign

If you're using spot colors in an image you import from Photoshop, those colors show up in the Swatches panel in InDesign. There is a chance that a color from your spot colors channel won't be recognized. If that's the case, the color is shown as gray instead. You can find more information on spot and process colors in Chapter 7 of this minibook.

You can use the swatches imported with the Photoshop file with other parts of your file. Simply use the swatches as you would any other swatch in InDesign. You can't delete these swatches unless you remove the Photoshop file that you imported into InDesign. For more information about using the Swatches panel in InDesign, see Chapter 7 of this minibook.

Book II
Chapter 8

Integrating InDesign
with Other Creative
Suite Applications

Integrating InDesign with Illustrator

Illustrator, which we discuss at great length in Book III, is a tremendous drawing program that enables you to create complex drawings. Therefore, it's a helpful tool to use for creating illustrations bound for InDesign page layouts. Luckily, you have several ways to control your Illustrator artwork directly in InDesign. You can import Illustrator 5.5 (and later) files into InDesign and maintain the editability of the objects from the AI (Illustrator) file within InDesign if you copy and paste (rather than import). (This means that you can edit the objects further after they're imported.) Also, because any transparency in the AI file is preserved when you import it, you can wrap text around the drawings you create.

You can also copy and paste graphics from Illustrator to InDesign and then edit them directly in InDesign. Simply select an object in your Illustrator project, choose Edit⇨Copy, and then move into your InDesign project and choose Edit⇨Paste.

Integrating InDesign with InCopy

The Adobe *InCopy* text-editing software enables writers to write and edit documents while layout is prepared separately. InCopy is similar to Microsoft Word in that you can make notes and comments, track changes, and use other similar editing features.

Your computer may not have InCopy installed because it isn't part of the Adobe Creative Suite and must be purchased separately. If you work in a newspaper or magazine environment with other writers, you may want to investigate this option. You can integrate InCopy with InDesign in several important ways that you shouldn't overlook. If you're extensively editing stories, you may want to consider using InCopy for writing text and importing and editing it further with InDesign.

Using InCopy with InDesign enables you to use a particular workflow because you can tell whether a file needs to be updated or whether it's being edited, by a series of icons that appear on the page in InDesign. The following sections describe some of the ways you can directly manipulate InCopy stories with InDesign.

Importing InCopy stories

Follow these steps to import stories from InCopy:

1. **In InCopy, create and save a text file.**

   If you don't have a copy of InCopy, you can download a 30-day trial version from www.adobe.com.

2. **Return to InDesign, create a text frame, and keep it selected.**

3. **Choose File⇨Place.**

4. **Browse to locate your InCopy file.**

   (InCopy files end with the file extension .incx.)

   The InCopy story is placed into the text frame and in the Links panel, just like a graphic.

If you've decided to try the cloud-based word processing software Buzzword from Adobe, you can also place files directly from Buzzword. You need to log in to your CS Live account and then choose File⇨Place from Buzzword. From there, you can place any Buzzword documents right into your InDesign layout.

Updating InCopy stories

When a file is out of date, you need to update that story so that the most recent revisions are available to you for editing.

When you see the warning icon in the Links panel, follow these steps to update the InCopy story in InDesign:

1. **Choose the story listed in the Links panel.**

2. **Click the Update Link button at the bottom of the Links panel.**

   The story is updated and the warning icon disappears. You can now work with the up-to-date version of the story in InDesign.

Creating for the Web: Exporting to Dreamweaver

Exporting an InDesign document to Dreamweaver allows you to bring your pages into Dreamweaver so that they can be prepared for use on the Web. Documents coming from InDesign typically require a fair amount of editing and styling before they can be put on the Web, so be sure to read Book VI for the lowdown on using Dreamweaver.

To export an InDesign document for Dreamweaver, follow these steps:

1. **With an InDesign document open, choose File⇨Export For⇨Dreamweaver.**

   The Save As window appears.

2. **Find a location on your hard drive for the package and enter a name for the html file in the Save As text field.**

3. **Click the Save button.**

   The XHTML Export Options dialog box appears. In this dialog box, you can determine whether you're exporting only the selection (if you had something selected) or the entire document. You can also map how to handle bullets.

4. **Select Images in the left column to see options for saving optimized images.**

5. **Leave the Image Conversion drop-down list set to Automatic to let InDesign decide whether an image is best saved as a GIF or JPEG file or to specify in which format you prefer to save all images.**

6. **Click the Advanced option to determine how Cascading Style Sheets (CSS) are handled, whether you want to use them, or whether you want them to reference an external CSS style it will link to.**

7. **After you complete the options, click the Export button.**

   You can now open and edit the XHTML file directly in Dreamweaver.

Chapter 9: Exporting Documents for Printing and as Graphics

In This Chapter

✔ Understanding file formats

✔ Exporting to different file formats

*Y*ou can export publications into several different kinds of file formats from InDesign, just as you can import various kinds of file formats. In this chapter, we take a closer look at the different kinds of files you can create electronically from an InDesign document. If you need to export an interactive document as either a PDF or Flash file, see Chapter 8 of this minibook.

Understanding File Formats

The kind of file you decide to create by exporting depends on your needs. The first thing to determine is where you'll use the exported file. For example, you might need to

✦ Put an image of your InDesign document or page on the Web

✦ Send an entire document to someone who doesn't have InDesign but wants to receive it by e-mail

✦ Import the content into a different program, such as Macromedia Flash or Adobe Illustrator

✦ Take a particular kind of file somewhere else to print it

Exporting InDesign documents lets you make them "portable" so that they can be used in different ways — such as on the Web or in another program. You can choose from the many file formats InDesign supports, and you can control many settings related to the files you create.

Some of the file formats you can create from InDesign are listed in Table 9-1.

Table 9-1	File Formats
File Format	*Description*
JPEG (Joint Photographic Experts Group)	A commonly used format for compressed images and a good choice for creating a picture of an InDesign page to post on a Web site.
EPS (Encapsulated PostScript)	A self-contained image file that contains high-resolution printing information about all the text and graphics used on a page. This format is commonly used for high-quality printing when you need to have an image of an InDesign page used within another document — such as a picture of a book cover created with InDesign that needs to appear in a promotional catalog — so that you can use an EPS of the book cover in your layout.
XML (Extensible Markup Language)	Lets you separate the content from the layout so that all the content on a page can be repurposed and used in different ways — online or in print.
SVG (Scalable Vector Graphics)	An alternative to EPS for describing a page. This graphic file format has never truly caught on. You can export files in SVG format, which combines XML and CSS to display files. The SVG vector-based format is also used for displaying content online using the oversized SVG Viewer plug-in. You can download it for the Mac or Windows from `www.adobe.com/svg/ viewer/install/main.html`.
PDF (Portable Document Format)	Used to exchange documents with users on different computer systems and operating systems. This format is used extensively for distributing files such as e-books and brochures. You may need to distribute the file to a wide audience or to a service provider for printing. Anyone who has installed Adobe Reader (also known as Acrobat Reader) on a computer can view your document. PDF is also used for importing as an image or text into other programs, such as Flash.
Rich or Plain text (text files)	Can include formatting (Rich) or plain text only (Plain). A text file is a simple way to export content. If you need the text from your document only to incorporate or send elsewhere, you can export it as plain (Text Only), tagged, or rich text. If you need to send a document to someone who doesn't have InDesign, exporting it as text may be a good option.

JPEG and EPS files can be exported from InDesign and then imported into other software programs. You can export these images for use in print after they're imported into a different graphics program, or you can use the images on the Web. It all depends on how you set up the document for export and the settings you use.

After determining in which file format to export your file, take a look at how to export these files and the different kinds of settings you can control when doing so. The rest of this chapter shows you how to export different file types from InDesign.

Exporting Publications

You can export publications from the Export dialog box. After you open it by choosing File➪Export, you can choose the file format, name, and location. After specifying a name and location and a format to export to, click Save. A new dialog box opens, where you can make settings specific to the file format you picked. We discuss in the following sections some of the most common file formats you're likely to use for export.

Exporting PDF documents for printing

Use InDesign to export a PDF file of your document or book. If you choose to export a PDF document, you have many options to customize the document you're exporting. You can control the amount of compression in the document, the marks and bleeds it has in InDesign, and its security settings. Here's how to export to PDF:

1. **Choose File➪Export.**

The Export dialog box opens.

2. **Choose a location in which to save the file and then enter a new filename.**

Browse to a location on your hard drive using the Save In drop-down list (if you're using Windows) and name the file in the File Name text field. If you are using a Mac, name the file in the Save As text field and choose a location using the Where drop-down list.

3. **Select Adobe PDF Print from the Save As Type (Windows) or Format (Mac) drop-down list.**

4. **Click Save.**

The Export PDF dialog box appears with the General options screen open.

5. **Choose a preset from the Preset drop-down list.**

These presets are easy to use. If you're familiar with Adobe Acrobat and the Adobe Distiller functions, they're the same. (For more detailed information about what each setting does, see Book V.)

The presets on the Preset drop-down list automatically change the export settings of a document. For example, you can select Smallest File Size from the list if you're displaying your work online or select High Quality Print if you plan for the PDF to be printed on home printers. Select Press Quality if you intend to have the PDF professionally printed.

6. Leave the Standard drop-down list at None.

Leave it at None unless, of course, you know about PDF/X and know which form of it to select. The details of PDF/X are explained in Book V.

7. Select a range of pages to export by typing the start page (and then a hyphen) and the end page in the Range text box.

You can also print nonconsecutive pages by separating the page numbers with a comma.

You can choose to export all pages or a range of pages.

8. Choose a compatibility setting for the PDF from the Compatibility drop-down list.

Compatibility settings determine which kind of reader is required in order to view the document. Setting compatibility to Acrobat 5 (PDF 1.4) ensures that a wide audience can view your PDF files. Some older PDF readers may not be able to interpret certain features in your document if you choose compatibility for a higher version.

9. Choose whether to embed thumbnails and whether to optimize the document, and then choose which kinds of elements to include in the file by selecting the check box to the left of the options in the Include section.

Other settings specify including bookmarks, links, and other elements in the file. Unless you've added any of these elements, you don't need to worry about selecting these options. You may want to embed thumbnail previews, but an Acrobat user can create thumbnails when the file is open as well.

Click Security in the list on the left of the Export PDF dialog box to open the Security screen, where you can specify passwords to open the document. You can also choose a password that's required to print or modify the PDF file.

10. Click the Export button to export the file.

The file is saved to the location you specified in Step 2.

Exporting EPS files

From InDesign, you can export EPS files, which are useful for importing into other programs. EPS files are single-page graphics files, which means that each exported InDesign page is saved as a separate EPS file. Here's how to export EPS files:

1. Choose File➪Export.

The Export dialog box opens.

2. **Select a location on your hard drive to save the EPS files, enter a new filename, and select EPS from the Save As Type (Windows) or Format (Mac) drop-down list; click Save.**

   The Export EPS dialog box opens.

3. **Choose a page or range of pages to export.**

   Select the All Pages option to export all pages or select the Ranges option and enter a range of pages. If you want spreads to export as one file, select the Spreads check box.

   If you're creating more than one EPS file (for example, exporting more than one page of your InDesign document), the file is saved with the filename, an underscore, and then the page number. For example, page 7 of a `cats.indd` file would be saved as `cats_7.eps` in the designated location.

   You have no need to export an EPS file to place an InDesign file into another InDesign file! If you're creating classified pages or any page that contains other InDesign pages, you can save yourself a few steps by simply choosing File⇨Place and selecting the InDesign file.

4. **From the Color drop-down list, select a color mode; from the Embed Fonts drop-down list, select how to embed fonts.**

   From the Color drop-down list, select Leave Unchanged to retain the color mode you're using for the InDesign document. You can also change the color mode to CMYK (Cyan, Magenta, Yellow, Black), Gray (grayscale), or RGB (Red, Green, Blue). For more information on color modes, flip back to Chapter 7 of this minibook.

   From the Embed Fonts drop-down list, select Subset to embed only the characters used in the file. If you select Complete, all fonts in the file are loaded when you print the file. Selecting None means that a reference to where the font is located is written into the file.

5. **Choose whether you want a preview to be generated for the file by choosing from the Preview drop-down list.**

   A *preview* (a small thumbnail image) is useful if an EPS file can't be displayed. For example, if you're browsing a library of images, you see a small thumbnail image of the EPS file; so whether or not you use the image or open it on your computer, you can see what the file looks like. From the Preview drop-down list, you can select TIFF to generate a preview; select None if you don't want a preview to be created.

6. **Click the Export button to export the files.**

   The files are saved to the location you designated in Step 2.

Book II
Chapter 9

Exporting Documents
for Printing and as
Graphics

Exporting JPEG files

You can export JPEG files from an InDesign document. You can export a single object on the selected page or export entire pages and spreads as a JPEG image. JPEG files allow you to effectively compress full color or black-and-white images, which is useful if you need a picture of an InDesign page to appear on the Web.

To export a JPEG image, follow these steps:

1. **Select an object on a page or make sure that no object is selected if you want to export a page or spread.**

2. **Choose File⇨Export.**

   The Export dialog box opens.

3. **Type a filename, locate the spot where you want to save the file on your hard drive, and select JPEG from the Save As Type (Windows) or Format (Mac) drop-down list; click Save.**

   The Export JPEG dialog box opens.

4. **If you want to export a page, select the Page option and enter the page number; if you want to export the selected object, make sure that the Selection option is selected.**

   The Selection option is available only if a selection was made in Step 1.

5. **Choose an image quality and format to export by choosing from the Image Quality and Format Method drop-down lists.**

   The Image Quality drop-down list controls the amount of compression that's used when you export a JPEG file. Choose from these two options:

   - *Maximum:* Creates an image with the largest file size and highest quality

   - *Low:* Creates a smaller file of lesser quality because it includes less image information

   If you choose the Baseline format from the Format Method drop-down list, the entire image has to be downloaded before it's displayed in a Web browser. Select Progressive to show the image in a progressively complete display as it downloads in a Web browser.

6. **Click the Export button.**

   The file is exported and saved to the location you specified in Step 3.

Exporting to Flash

Using InDesign CS5, you can export an InDesign document as a Flash Professional file. This process creates an SWF (Shockwave Flash file). To export, follow these steps:

1. **Choose File⇨Export.**

   The Export dialog box appears.

2. **Choose a location to save the files, enter a new filename, and choose Flash CS5 Professional (FLA) from the Save As Type (Windows) or Format (Mac) drop-down list.**

   If you need to include video, audio, animation, and complex interactivity, export the file in Flash CS5 Professional format because you can then use Flash Professional to modify and edit the file until it meets your exact needs.

   In the Export SWF dialog box, shown in Figure 9-1, you can set the output size, specify pages to include, and make various conversion and compression choices.

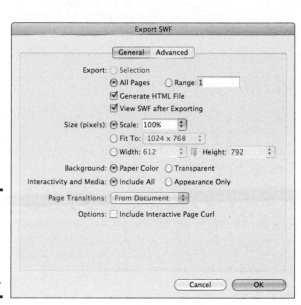

Figure 9-1:
Choose
the export
options to
export a file
SWF format.

3. **Choose the size you want for the exported file.**

   Select the Scale option and leave the drop-down list at 100% if you don't want to change the size of the exported file. Otherwise, select the Fit To option and choose from the drop-down list or select the Width option and enter your own dimensions in the Width and Height drop-down lists.

4. **Select which page or pages you want to export.**

   Select the All option to export the entire document; select Range and enter a page number if you want to export only a specific page or pages. Select the Spreads check box to export page spreads.

5. **From the Text drop-down list, select how to export text.**

   When you're exporting to Adobe Flash your InDesign objects remain as vectors unless transparency is applied, and you have the option to export InDesign text as editable Flash text, vectors, or pixels.

   If you choose InDesign Text to Flash Text, note that the text is laid out in Flash with each line becoming a separate text object, so try to do all editing inside InDesign because editing the text within Flash is difficult.

6. **Select the Interactivity options you want by choosing whether you want to include all interactive options or only those that affect appearance.**

7. **Choose the image compression, JPEG quality, and curve quality you want from the Image Compression, JPEG Quality, and Curve Quality drop-down lists. If a small file size is important to you, select a reduce quality.**

8. **Click OK to export your InDesign document as a Flash file.**

Exporting text files

You can extract text from an InDesign document so that it can be edited or used elsewhere. The text formats vary slightly depending on the text in your document.

To export text, follow these steps:

1. **Select the Text tool from the toolbox and select some text within a text frame in your document, or place the cursor within a text frame where you want to export all the text.**

   The cursor must be in a text frame in order to export text.

2. **Choose File⇨Export.**

   The Export dialog box opens.

3. **Enter a filename, select a location to save the file in, and select Text Only from the Save As Type (Windows) or Format (Mac) drop-down list; click Save.**

   The Text Export Options dialog box opens.

4. Choose a platform and encoding for the export.

Select either PC or Macintosh from the Platform drop-down list to set the PC or Mac operating system compatibility. Select an encoding method for the platform you choose from the Encoding drop-down list; you can choose either Default Platform or Unicode.

The universal character-encoding standard *Unicode* is compatible with major operating systems. *Encoding,* which refers to how characters are represented in a digital format, is essentially a set of rules that determines how the character set is represented by associating each character with a particular code sequence.

5. Click the Export button.

The file is exported and saved to the location you specified in Step 3.

Book III

Illustrator CS5

The 5th Wave   By Rich Tennant

"Ooo—look! Sgt. Rodriguez has the felon's head floating in a teacup!"

Contents at a Glance

Chapter 1: What's New in Illustrator CS5

In This Chapter

✔ Working with multiple artboards

✔ Creating unique brush strokes with the Bristle Brush tool

✔ Building shapes with the Shape Builder tool

✔ Using the perspective grid

*I*llustrator only gets better and better, and you can discover the latest and greatest new features in this chapter. Many of these features are discussed in detail in the rest of the chapters in this minibook.

Managing Multiple Artboards with the New Artboard Panel

If you've ever dreamed of producing multiple-page documents in Illustrator, your dream has come true: CS4 introduced multiple artboards. Before then, you added pages by using a rather convoluted method of making a large artboard and then tiling its pages. But now you can create multiple artboards (as many as 100!) as soon as you open the New Document dialog box.

What makes the artboard feature enhanced in CS5? For one thing, artboards now have a dedicated panel. Use this panel to easily locate and select an artboard. Using the Artboard panel, you can also reorder, delete, and even copy artboards.

Creating a document with multiple artboards

To create a document with multiple artboards, follow these steps:

1. **Launch Adobe Illustrator CS5 and choose File⇨New.**

   The New Document dialog box appears, as shown in Figure 1-1.

2. **Specify the number of artboards to start with by entering a number in the Number of Artboards text box.**

   In our example, we added four artboards.

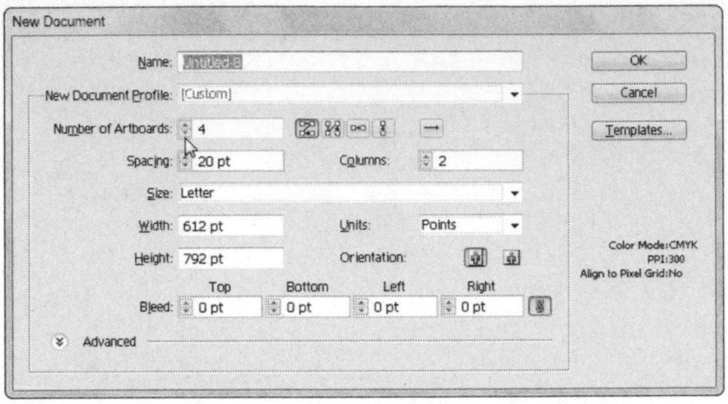

Figure 1-1:
Add multiple
artboards
right from
the start.

3. **To specify how to arrange the artboard, click a grid or row arrangement icon to the right of the Number of Artboards text box, as shown in Figure 1-2.**

Figure 1-2:
Choose
how you
want the
artboards
arranged.

Using these grid boxes, you can

- Specify how many rows and columns to use.
- Change the direction of the layout from left to right or right to left.

4. **Enter an amount in the Spacing text box to determine the distance between artboards.**

Enter **0** (zero) if you want the artboards to butt against each other, or a higher value if you want some space between them.

5. **Click OK to create your new document.**

The example, showing four artboards, looks like the ones you see in Figure 1-3.

Exploring enhanced artboard features

After you create multiple artboards, choose Window➪Artboards to see a panel with artboards listed individually, as shown in Figure 1-4.

Here are some swell things you can do to artboards from the Artboard panel:

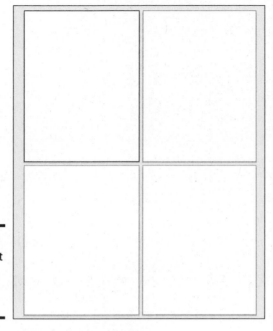

Figure 1-3:
A document created using four artboards.

Figure 1-4:
The new Artboard panel, keeping your project organized.

New Artboard

✦ **Navigate to a specific artboard:** Just double-click the artboard's name.

✦ **Rearrange artboards:** Drag the artboards inside the Artboard panel to reorganize their stacking order.

✦ **Delete an artboard:** Drag it to the trashcan icon.

✦ **Copy an existing artboard:** Drag it to the New Artboard icon.

✦ **Create a new artboard:** Click the New Artboard icon.

✦ **Rename an artboard:** From the panel menu, choose Artboard Options to open the Artboard Options dialog box, shown in Figure 1-5. Then you can rename artboards or make additional changes to them.

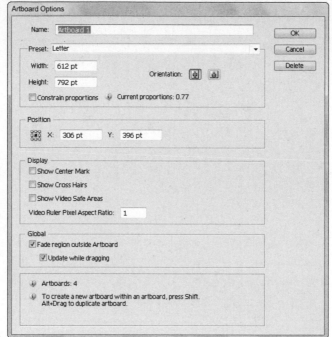

Figure 1-5:
Edit existing artboards by using the Artboard Options dialog box.

Printing a document with multiple artboards

Pay close attention before you print a document with multiple artboards, or else you may print needless pages. To control which artboards are printed, follow these steps:

1. **Choose File➪Print.**

   The Print dialog box appears, as shown in Figure 1-6.

2. **Below the Preview box, in the lower left corner, click the arrows to preview the artboards.**

3. **After you decide which artboards to print, enter them into the Range text box.**

   To print all artboards, make sure that the All radio button is selected; otherwise, enter a consecutive range such as **1–3** in the Range text box. You can also print nonconsecutive pages by separating them with commas — enter **1, 3, 4** to print only artboards 1, 3 and 4.

4. **Click the Print button to print selected artboards.**

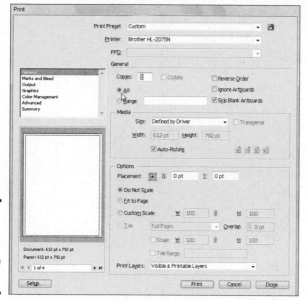

Figure 1-6:
Printing a
document
with multiple
artboards.

Having Fun with the New Bristle Brush

If you've been looking for the perfect method to mimic ink or watercolor on paper, you'll love the new Bristle Brush in Adobe Illustrator CS5. To take advantage of this fantastic tool, you need to first create a new brush. Follow these steps for a quick introduction to finding the Bristle Brush and using all the options that come with it:

1. **If the Brushes panel isn't visible, choose Window⇨Brushes.**

2. **Click the panel menu and choose New Brush.**

   The New Brush dialog box appears.

3. **Choose Bristle Brush, shown in Figure 1-7, and then click OK.**

Figure 1-7:
Finding the
new Bristle
Brush.

When you select Bristle Brush, the Bristle Brush Options dialog box opens, as shown in Figure 1-8, where you can choose the brush shape and other fun-to-explore options.

4. **Specify options for the Bristle Brush and then click OK to close the dialog box.**

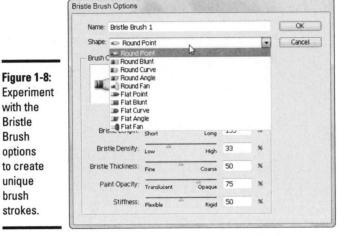

Figure 1-8: Experiment with the Bristle Brush options to create unique brush strokes.

Making Drawing Easier by Using Drawing Modes

Using the new drawing modes users have increased control when adding new objects to the artboard. If your Tools panel is not expanded to two columns, click the arrows at the top of the Tools panel (see Figure 1-9) to see all three drawing tools.

Figure 1-9: Expand your Tools panel.

Take a look at the bottom of the Tools panel to see the new Drawing Mode icons (see Figure 1-10); the modes are described in the following list:

✦ **Draw Normal:** Place newly drawn objects on top of other objects in the artboard or selected layer.

✦ **Draw Behind:** Make newly created objects fall behind the existing objects on the artboard or selected layer.

✦ **Draw Inside:** Draw inside another shape only when you have a selected object.

Draw Normal Mode

    Draw Behind Mode

        Draw Inside Mode

Figure 1-10:
The new
Drawing
modes.

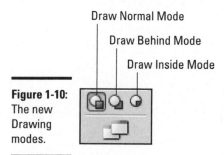

To see what each mode looks like while you're drawing new objects, check out Figure 1-11.

Normal Mode   Draw Behind Mode

Draw Inside Mode

Figure 1-11:
Drawing
modes in
action.

Book III
Chapter 1

What's New in
Illustrator CS5

You can also use Draw Inside mode to create a quick clipping path: Simply choose the mode and copy the objects you want to *clip* (mask inside another shape), select the object you want to clip into, and choose Edit➪Paste. The selected object becomes the mask, as shown in Figure 1-12.

Figure 1-12:
Use Draw
Inside
mode to
create quick
and easy
clipping
paths.

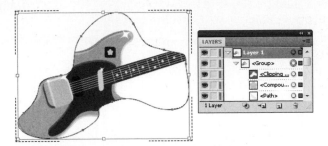

Transparency in Meshes

The Gradient Mesh tool helps you to create incredible photo-realistic illustrations using meshes you build on vector objects. If you have already discovered the Gradient Mesh tool, you know how useful this tool is. Add in the transparency feature, and the number of ways you can use it skyrockets.

Follow these simple steps to try out the new transparency feature:

1. **Choose a solid color for your fill and no stroke.**

2. **Create a shape.**

    In our example, we created a circle.

3. **Choose Object➪Create Gradient Mesh, leave it at the default of 4 Rows and 4 Columns, Appearance, Flat, as shown in Figure 1-13, and click OK.**

Figure 1-13:
Choose
how many
rows and
columns you
want to start
your mesh
with.

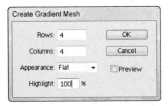

A gradient mesh appears in your shape with multiple mesh nodes.

4. **Using the Direct Selection tool, click an individual node, as shown in Figure 1-14.**

Figure 1-14:
Selecting an
individual
node in the
Gradient
Mesh.

5. **Either choose another color to create a blending effect from one color to another or choose Window⇨Transparency and decrease the value of the transparency slider.**

    The individual node becomes transparent based on the value you select.

Building Custom Shapes with the Shape Builder Tool

 The new Shape Builder tool will make many designers happy by making it easier than ever to make custom shapes. Follow these steps to use this useful tool:

1. **Create several overlapping shapes and then select them all.**

2. **Choose the Shape Builder tool from the Tools panel.**

3. **Click and drag over the closed edges of the shapes to unite them into one shape, as shown in Figure 1-15.**

Figure 1-15:
Click and
drag over
closed
edges by
using the
Shape
Builder tool.

4. **Hold down the Alt (Windows) or Opt (Mac) key to erase a segment of a shape, as shown in Figure 1-16.**

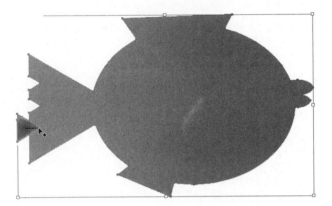

Figure 1-16:
Hold down the Alt/ Opt key to delete a shape from a closed shape.

Working with the Perspective Grid

Believe it or not, not everyone using Adobe Illustrator has suffered through a perspective drawing class. And luckily for them (and those of us who still didn't grasp the concept), Illustrator has a new Perspective Grid tool. You can use the Perspective Grid feature to build illustrations that have the illusion of space and distance.

Choose View➪Perspective Grid➪Show to display an adjustable perspective grid appears on your page, as shown in Figure 1-17.

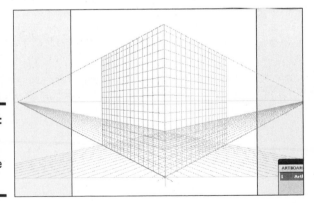

Figure 1-17:
Setting up the initial perspective grid.

Here's how you can take advantage of this feature:

✦ **Create an object:** Notice that as you click and drag a shape, it follows the perspective plane. As you reposition the object or create new objects, they follow the perspective grid.

✦ **Clone an object:** When you use the Selection tool and Alt+drag (Windows) or Opt-drag (Mac) objects to other locations, notice that the perspective plane is followed.

✦ **Customize the grid:** Experiment with the Perspective Grid tool.

✦ **Edit your shape:** Click and hold on the Perspective Grid tool to select the Perspective Selection tool, as shown in Figure 1-18.

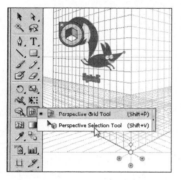

Figure 1-18: Use the Perspective Selection tool to edit an object that has perspective applied to it.

Little Enhancements Make a Big Difference

Illustrator has many little improvements in this version, and you can find them mixed into later chapters in this minibook. Don't miss these two:

✦ **Ruler origin:** If rulers have confused you (yes, the zero point was located in the lower left corner), you'll be thrilled to know that the origin point (zero) is now where you would expect, in the upper left corner.

✦ **Joining paths:** Easily join two or more open paths by pressing Ctrl+J (Windows) or ⌘+J (Mac). In the past, you had to painstakingly select just the endpoints in order to join paths.

Chapter 2: Discovering Illustrator CS5

In This Chapter

↙ **Knowing when to use Illustrator**

↙ **Opening and creating documents**

↙ **Looking around the Document window**

↙ **Checking out the tools and panels**

↙ **Changing your view**

↙ **Zooming in and out**

Adobe Illustrator goes hand in hand with other Adobe products but serves its own, unique purpose. Although Illustrator can create multiple-page artwork (with artboards), it isn't meant to create lengthy documents with repeated headers, footers, and page numbers. Those types of files are more appropriate for applications such as InDesign. Typically, you wouldn't create artwork from Illustrator that's made from pixels, such as images edited or created in Photoshop. Illustrator is generally used to create vector logos, illustrations, maps, packages, labels, signage, Web art, and more. (See the nearby "Vector graphics" sidebar for more information.)

This chapter gets you started with Illustrator and helps you understand when Illustrator is the tool best suited for creating your art.

Deciding When to Use Illustrator CS5

How do you draw a line in the sand and decide to create graphics in Illustrator rather than in Photoshop? By using Illustrator, you gain these benefits:

✦ **Illustrator can save and export graphics into most file formats.** By choosing to save or export, you can create a file that can be used in most other applications. For instance, Illustrator files can be saved as `.bmp`, `.jpg`, `.pdf`, `.svg`, `.tiff`, and even `.swf` (Flash) files, to name a few.

Vector graphics

Vector graphics are made up of lines and curves defined by mathematical objects called *vectors*. Because the *paths* (the lines and curves) are defined mathematically, you can move, resize, or change the color of vector objects without losing quality in the graphic.

Vector graphics are *resolution-independent:* They can be scaled to any size and printed at any resolution without losing detail. On the other hand, a predetermined number of pixels create bitmap graphics, so you can't *scale* (resize) them easily — if you scale them smaller, you throw out pixels; if you scale them larger, you end up with a blocky, jagged picture.

The following figure shows the differences between an enlarged vector graphic (top; notice the smooth edges) and an enlarged bitmap graphic (bottom; note the jagged edges). Many company logos were created as vectors to avoid problems with scaling: A vector graphic logo maintains its high-quality appearance at any size.

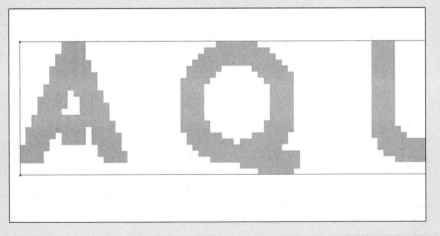

✦ **Illustrator files are easily integrated into other Adobe applications.** You can save Illustrator files in their native format and open or place them in other Adobe applications such as Dreamweaver, Fireworks, Flash, InDesign, and Photoshop. You can also save Illustrator artwork in the `.pdf` (Portable Document Format) format. It lets anyone using the free Acrobat Reader software open and view the file but maintain editing capabilities when the file is opened later in Illustrator.

✦ **Illustrator artwork is reusable because the resolution of vector artwork isn't determined until output.** In other words, if you print to a 600 dpi (dots per inch) printer, the artwork is printed at 600 dpi; print to a 2,400 dpi printer and the artwork prints at 2,400 dpi. Illustrator graphics are quite different from the bitmap images you create or edit in Photoshop, where resolution is determined as soon as you scan, take a picture, or create a new bitmap (created from pixels) document.

✦ **Illustrator has limitless scalability.** You can create vector artwork in Illustrator and scale it to the size of your thumb or to the size of a barn, and either way, it still looks good. See the nearby sidebar "Vector graphics" for more information.

Opening an Existing Document

It is a good idea to familiarize yourself with the workspace before starting to work in Adobe Illustrator. In this section, you jump right in by opening an existing document. If you haven't already created an Illustrator file, you can open a sample file packaged with the Illustrator application, such as `Loyal Order of Wormword` in the Sample Art folder. The path to the file is `C:\Programs\Adobe\Adobe Illustrator CS5\Cool Extras\Sample Files\Sample Art` (Windows) or `Applications\Adobe Illustrator CS5\Cool Extras\Sample Files\Sample Art` (Mac)

When you launch Illustrator CS5 for the first time, a Welcome screen appears, giving you various options. Click the Open icon and then browse to locate a file to open. (*Note:* You can select the Don't Show Again check box if you don't want to see the Welcome screen at launch.)

If your preferences have been changed from the original defaults, the Welcome screen may not appear. To open a file in that case, choose File⇨ Open and select the file in the Open dialog box. This dialog box is used to open existing Adobe Illustrator files or even files from other Adobe applications.

TIP

Choose File⇨Open to open PDF files in Illustrator and in many other file formats.

**Book III
Chapter 2**

Discovering
Illustrator CS5

Creating a New Document

To create a new document in Illustrator, follow these steps:

1. **Choose File⇨New.**

   The New Document dialog box appears, as shown in Figure 2-1. You use it to determine the new document's profile, size, measurement unit, color mode, and page orientation as well as the number of artboards (pages) you want in the document.

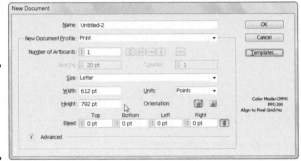

Figure 2-1:
Creating
a new
document in
Illustrator.

2. **Enter a name for your new file in the Name text field.**

   You can determine the name of the file now or later when you save the document.

3. **Choose a profile from the New Document Profile drop-down list.**

   Selecting the correct profile sets up preferences, such as resolution and colors, correctly. Click the Advanced down arrow (in the lower left corner of the New Document dialog box) to see which settings are selected for each profile and to change them if necessary.

4. **In the Number of Artboards text box, enter the number of artboards you want in the document.**

   If you want a single page document, leave this setting at 1.

5. **Enter in the Spacing text box the amount of space to leave between artboards.**

   If you want pages to abut, enter **0** (zero), or enter additional values if you want a little space between each artboard. If you're adding artboards, you can enter in the Columns text box the number of columns of artboards you want arranged in the document.

6. **Choose from the Size drop-down list or type measurements in the Width and Height text fields to set the size of the document page.**

You can choose from several standard sizes in the Size drop-down list or enter your own measurements in the Width and Height text fields. Note that several Web sizes are listed first, followed by other typical paper sizes.

7. **Choose from the Units drop-down list to select the type of measurement you're most comfortable with.**

   Your selection sets all measurement boxes and rulers to the increments you choose: points, picas, inches, millimeters, centimeters, or pixels.

8. **Pick the orientation for the artboard.**

   The *artboard* is your canvas for creating artwork in Illustrator. You can choose between *Portrait* (the short sides of the artboard on the top and bottom) and *Landscape* (the long sides of the artboard on the top and bottom).

9. **Add values in the Bleed text boxes, if necessary.**

   A *bleed value* is the amount of image area that extends beyond the artboard. To print from edge to edge, enter a value for the bleed. Keep in mind that most desktop printers need a grip area that forces any image area near the edge of a page to not print. Bleeds are typically used in jobs to be printed from a press.

10. **When you're finished making selections, click OK.**

    One or more Illustrator artboards appear.

The document size and color mode may need to be changed later. You can change them by choosing File➪Document Setup and making changes in the Document Setup dialog box.

Need a design boost? Try a template

In the New Document dialog box, click the Templates button to get a jump-start with professional designs precreated as Illustrator templates. Start with a simple template for a CD cover, as shown in Figure 2-2, or start your brochure, business cards, or flyers with a template that includes imagery, text, and professional layouts.

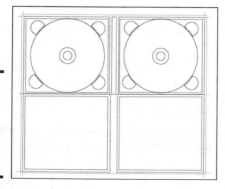

Figure 2-2: Precreated templates lead to successful designs.

Taking a Look at the Document Window

To investigate the work area (shown in Figure 2-3) and become truly familiar with Illustrator, open a new document and take a look around. In the
Illustrator work area, a total of 227 inches in width and height help create
your artwork (and all artboards). That's helpful, but it also leaves enough
space to lose objects! The following list explains the tools you work with as
you create artwork in Illustrator:

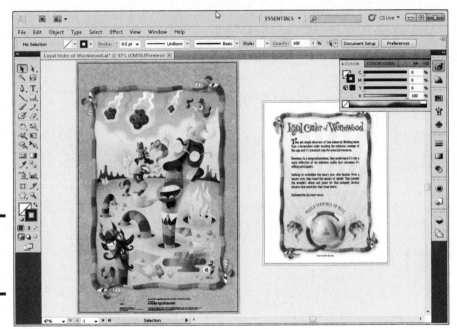

Figure 2-3:
The
Illustrator
work area.

✦ **Imageable area:** The space inside the innermost dotted lines, which
marks the printing area on the page. Many printers can't print all the
way to the edges of the paper, so the imageable area is determined by
the printer you set in the Print dialog box. As a default, the print tiling
dotted line is not visible. To turn this dotted border on or off, choose
View➪Hide/Show Print Tiling.

You can move the imageable area around on your page by using the
Print Tiling tool. See the nearby sidebar, "The Print Tiling tool," for more
on this tool.

✦ **Edge of the page:** The page's edge is marked by the outermost set of
dotted lines.

The Print Tiling tool

Use the Print Tiling tool to move the printable area of your page to a different location. For example, if your printer can print only on paper that's 8.5 x 11 inches or smaller but the page size is 11 x 17, you can use the Print Tiling tool (a hidden tool accessed by holding down the mouse button on the Hand tool) to indicate which part of the page you want to print. Follow these steps to use the Print Tiling tool:

1. **When adjusting page boundaries, choose View⇨Fit in Window so that you can see all your artwork.**

2. **Hold down the Hand tool to select the hidden Print Tiling tool.**

The pointer becomes a dotted cross when you move it to the active window.

3. **Position the mouse over the artboard and click and drag the page to a new location.**

While you drag, the Print Tiling tool acts as though you're moving the page from its lower left corner. Two gray rectangles are displayed. The outer rectangle represents the page size, and the inner rectangle represents the printable area of a page. You can move the page anywhere on the artboard; just remember that any part of a page that extends past the printable area boundary doesn't print.

✦ **Nonimageable area:** Choose View⇨Show Print Tiling to see the imageable area based on the selected print driver. The space on the outside of the dotted lines represents the imageable area and the edge of the page. The nonimageable area is the margin of the page that can't be printed on.

✦ **Artboard:** This area, bounded by solid lines, represents the entire region that can contain printable artwork. By default, the artboard is the same size as the page, but it can be enlarged or reduced. The U.S. default artboard size is 8.5 x 11 inches, but it can be set as large as 227 x 227 inches. You can hide the artboard boundaries by choosing View⇨Hide Artboard.

✦ **Scratch area:** This area outside the artboards extends to the edge of the 227-inch square window. The scratch area represents a space on which you can create, edit, and store elements of artwork before moving them onto the artboard. Objects placed onto the scratch area are visible on-screen, but they don't print. However, objects in the scratch area appear if the document is saved and placed as an image in other applications.

Basically, the rules regarding the work area are simple: If you're printing directly from Illustrator, make sure that you choose the proper paper size and printer in the Print dialog box. Open the Print dialog box by choosing File⇨Print.

Becoming Familiar with the Tools

As you begin using Illustrator, you'll find it helpful to be familiar with its tools. Tools are used to create, select, and manipulate objects in Illustrator. The tools should be visible as a default, but if not, you can access them by choosing Window➪Tools.

Table 2-1 lists the tools that we show you how to use throughout this minibook. Hover the cursor over the tool in the Tools panel to see the name of the tool in a ToolTip. In parentheses on the ToolTip (and noted in Column 2 of Table 2-1) is the keyboard command you can use to access that tool. When you see a small triangle at the lower right corner of the tool icon, it contains additional, hidden tools. Select the tool and hold the mouse button to see them.

Table 2-1	**Illustrator CS5 Tools**		
Icon	*Tool or Keyboard Command*	*Task*	*See Minibook Chapter*
	Selection (V)	Activate objects	3
	Direct Selection (A)	Activate individual points or paths	3
	Group Selection (A)	Select grouped items	3
	Magic Wand (Y)	Select based on similarity	3
	Lasso (Q)	Select freehand	3
	Pen (P)	Create paths	5
	Type (T)	Create text	6
	Line Segment (/)	Draw line segments	5
	Shape (M)	Create shape objects	4

Icon	Tool or Keyboard Command	Task	See Minibook Chapter
	Paint Brush (B)	Create paths	5
	Pencil (N)	Create paths	5
	Blob Brush (Shift+B)	Create freeform brush paths	5
	Eraser (Shift+E)	Erase vector paths	2
	Rotate (R)	Rotate objects	10
	Scale (S)	Enlarge or reduce objects	10
	Width tool (Shift+W)	Draw strokes of variable widths	10
	Free Transform (E)	Transform objects	10
	Shape Builder (Shift+M)	Combine, edit, and fill shapes	4
	Perspective Grid (Shift+P)	Provide perspective plane	11
	Mesh (U)	Create a gradient mesh	11
	Gradient (G)	Modify gradients	11
	Eyedropper (I)	Copy and apply attributes	9
	Blend (W)	Create transitional blends	11
	Symbol Sprayer (Shift+S)	Spray symbols	11
	Column Graph (J)	Create graphs	NA

Book III
Chapter 2

Discovering
Illustrator CS5

(continued)

Table 2-1		Illustrator CS5 Tools	
Icon	*Tool or Keyboard Command*	*Task*	*See Minibook Chapter*
	Artboard tool (Shift+O)	Adds or edit artboards	1
	Slice (Shift+K)	Create HTML slices	2
	Print Tiling	Tile print output	2
	Zoom (Z)	Increase and decrease the onscreen view	2

Checking Out the Panels

The standardized interface in Adobe Creative Suite is a useful boost for users because the Illustrator panel system is similar to all other products in the suite. This consistency makes working and finding tools and features easier.

When you first open Illustrator, notice that some panels have been reduced to icons on the right. To select a panel, click the appropriate icon and the panel appears.

If all you see is an icon, how do you know which icon brings up which panel? Good question. If you're hunting around for the appropriate panels, you can

✦ Choose Window➪*Name of Panel*.

✦ Position your mouse on the left side of the icons and when you see the double-arrow icon, click and drag to the left. The panel names appear.

✦ Click the Expand Panels button on the gray bar at the top of the icons, as shown in Figure 2-4. The panels expand so that you can see their contents and names.

Figure 2-4: Expand the panels to see more options.

The panels you see as a default are docked together. To *dock* a panel means that, for organizational purposes, the panel is attached in the docking area.

You can arrange panels to make them more helpful for production. You may choose to have only certain panels visible while working. Here's the low-down on using Illustrator panels:

✦ To see additional options for each panel (because some options are hidden), click the panel menu in the upper right corner of the panel (see Figure 2-5).

Figure 2-5: Some panels have additional menu options.

✦ To move a panel group, click and drag above the tabbed panel name.

✦ To rearrange or separate a panel from its group, drag the panel's tab. Dragging a tab outside the docking area creates a new, separate panel.

✦ To move a tab to another panel, drag the tab to that panel.

Look out for those panels — they can take over your screen! Some panels, but not all, can be resized. A panel that you can resize has an active lower right corner (denoted by three small lines). To change the size of a panel, drag its lower right corner (Windows) or drag the size box in the lower right corner of the panel (Mac).

As you become more efficient, you may find it helpful to reduce the clutter on your screen by hiding all panels except the ones necessary for your work. You can save your own panel configuration by choosing Window➪Workspace➪Save Workspace. Choose Window➪Workspace➪ Essentials to return to the default workspace.

Changing Views

When you're working in Illustrator, precision is important, but you also want to see how the artwork looks. Whether for the Web or print, Illustrator offers several ways in which to view your artwork:

✦ **Preview and Outline views:** By default, Illustrator shows Preview view, where you see colors, stroke widths, images, and patterns as they should appear when printed or completed for onscreen presentation.

Sometimes this view can become a nuisance, especially if you're trying to create a corner point by connecting two thick lines. At times like this, or whenever you want the strokes and fills reduced to the underlying structure, choose View➪Outline. You now see the outline of the illustration, shown in Figure 2-6.

Figure 2-6:
Preview
mode (left)
and Outline
mode (right).

✦ **Pixel view:** If you don't want to be surprised when your artwork appears in your Web browser, use Pixel view. This view, shown in Figure 2-7, maintains the vectors of your artwork but shows how the pixels will appear when the image is viewed on-screen, as though it's on the Web.

Figure 2-7:
See how
your
artwork
translates
into pixels in
Pixel view.

Pixel view is helpful for previewing the look of text onscreen — some fonts just don't look good as pixels, especially if the text is small. In Pixel view, you can review several different fonts until you find one that's easily readable as pixels.

✦ **Overprint view:** For people in print production, the Overprint preview can be a real timesaver. Choose Window⇨Attributes to bring up the Attributes panel, which you can use to set the fill and stroke colors to overprint. This view creates additional colors when printing and aids printers when trapping abutting colors.

Trapping is the slight overprint of a lighter color into a darker color to correct for press *misregistration.* When several colors are printed on one piece, the likelihood of perfectly alignment is slim! Setting a stroke to Overprint on the Window⇨Attributes panel is one solution. With Overprint selected, the stroke is overprinted on the nearby colors. This mixing of color produces an additional color, but is less obvious to the viewer than a white space created by misregistration. Select Overprint to see the result of overprinting in Overprint view, as shown in Figure 2-8.

Figure 2-8: Overprint view.

Book III Chapter 2

Discovering Illustrator CS5

Navigating the Work Area with Zoom Controls

You can navigate the work area efficiently by using the Hand tool and the various zoom controls. You can change the magnification of the artboard in several ways, including using menu items, the Zoom tool, and keyboard commands. Choose the method you feel most comfortable with:

✦ **Hand tool:** Scroll around the Document window by using the scrollbars or the Hand tool. The Hand tool lets you scroll by dragging. You can imagine that you're pushing a piece of paper around on your desk when you use the Hand tool.

Hold down the spacebar to temporarily access the Hand tool while any tool (except the Type tool) is selected. Holding down the spacebar while the Type tool is selected gives you only spaces!

✦ **View menu:** Using the View menu, you can easily select the magnification you want by using Zoom In, Zoom Out, Fit in Window (especially useful when you're lost in the scratch area), and Actual Size (provides a 100 percent view of your artwork).

✦ **Zoom tool:** Using the Zoom tool, you can click the Document window to zoom in; to zoom out, Alt-click (Windows) or Option-click (Mac). Double-click with the Zoom tool to quickly resize the Document window to 100 percent. Control which elements are visible when using the Zoom tool by clicking and dragging over the area you want zoomed into.

✦ **Keyboard shortcuts:** If you aren't the type of person who likes to use keyboard shortcuts, you may change your mind about using them for magnification. They make sense and are easy to use and remember. Table 2-2 lists the most popular keyboard shortcuts to change magnification.

The shortcuts in Table 2-2 require a little coordination to use, but they give you more control in your zoom. While holding down the keys, drag from the upper left corner to the lower right corner of the area you want to zoom to. A marquee appears while you're dragging; when you release the mouse button, the selected area zooms to the size of your window. The Zoom Out command doesn't give you much control; it simply zooms back out, much like the commands in Table 2-3.

Table 2-2	Magnification Keyboard Shortcuts	
Command	*Windows Shortcut*	*Mac Shortcut*
Actual Size	Ctrl+1	⌘+1
Fit in Window	Ctrl+0 (zero)	⌘+0 (zero)
Zoom In	Ctrl++ (plus)	⌘++ (plus)
Zoom Out	Ctrl+– (minus)	⌘+– (minus)
Hand tool	Spacebar	Spacebar

Table 2-3	Zoom Keyboard Shortcuts	
Command	*Windows Shortcut*	*Mac Shortcut*
Zoom In to Selected Area	Ctrl+spacebar+drag	⌘+spacebar+drag
Zoom Out	Ctrl+Alt+spacebar	⌘+Option+spacebar

Chapter 3: Using the Selection Tools

In This Chapter

✔ Knowing the anchor points, bounding boxes, and selection tools

✔ Working with a selection

✔ Grouping and ungrouping selections

✔ Constraining movement and cloning objects

If someone has been coaching you in using Adobe Illustrator, you may have heard the old line "You have to select it to affect it." It means that if you want to apply a change to an object in Illustrator, you must have that object selected or else Illustrator doesn't know what to change. You sit there repeatedly clicking a color swatch and nothing happens. Although making selections may sound simple, it can become tricky when you're working on complicated artwork.

Getting to Know the Selection Tools

Before delving into the world of selecting objects in Illustrator, you must know what the selection tools are. In this section, we take you on a quick tour of the anchor points (integral to the world of selections), the bounding box, and, of course, the selection tools. (Yes, Illustrator has several selection tools.)

Anchor points

To understand selections, you must first understand how Illustrator works with *anchor points,* which act like handles and can be individually selected and moved to other locations. You essentially use the anchor points to drag objects or parts of objects around the workspace. After you place anchor points on an object, you can create strokes or paths from the anchor points.

You can select several anchor points at the same time, as shown in Figure 3-1, or only one, as shown in Figure 3-2. Selecting all anchor points in an object lets you move the entire object without changing the anchor points in relationship to one another. You can tell which anchor points are selected and active because they appear as solid boxes.

Figure 3-1:
Multiple anchor points are selected.

Figure 3-2:
One anchor point is selected.

Bounding boxes

As a default, Illustrator shows a bounding box when an object is selected with the Selection tool. (A bounding box is shown in Figure 3-1.) This feature can be helpful if you understand its function but confusing if you don't know how to use it.

By dragging on the handles, you can use the bounding box for quick transforms, such as scaling and rotating. To rotate, you pass the mouse cursor (without clicking) outside a handle until you see a rotate symbol and then drag.

If the bounding box bothers you, you can turn off the feature by choosing View⇨Hide Bounding Box.

Selection tools

Illustrator CS5 offers five selection tools:

✦ **Selection:** Selects entire objects or groups. This tool activates all anchor points in an object or group at the same time, allowing you to move an object without changing its shape.

✦ **Direct Selection:** Selects individual points.

✦ **Group Selection:** Hidden in the Direct Selection tool in the Tools panel and used to select items within a group. This tool adds grouped items as you click objects in the order in which they were grouped. This selection tool becomes more useful to you as you find out about grouping objects in Illustrator.

✦ **Magic Wand:** Use the Magic Wand tool to select objects with like values, such as fill and stroke colors, based on a tolerance and stroke weight. Change the options of this tool by double-clicking it.

✦ **Lasso:** Use the Lasso tool to click and drag around anchor points you want to select.

You can select an object with the Selection tool by using one of three main methods:

✦ Click the object's path.

✦ Click an anchor point of the object.

✦ Drag a marquee around part or all of the object's path. (In the later section "Using a marquee to select an object," we discuss using the marquee method.)

Working with Selections

After you have an understanding about the basics of selections, you'll probably be eager to try out some techniques. In this section, you see the basics: Make a selection, work with anchor points and the marquee, make multiple selections, and of course, save your work.

Smart guides, turned on by default in Illustrator CS5, can help you make accurate selections. These guides are visible as you're drawing, they display names such as anchor point and path, and they highlight paths when you're lined up with endpoints or center points. You can come to love these helpful aids, but if you don't want to see them, simply choose View⇨Smart Guides or press the keyboard shortcut Ctrl+U (Windows) or ⌘+U (Mac) to toggle the smart guides off and on.

Creating a selection

To work with selections, you need to have something on the page in Illustrator. Follow these steps to make a selection:

1. **Create a new page in Adobe Illustrator. (Any size or profile is okay.)**

Alternatively, you can open an existing illustration; see Chapter 2 of this minibook for instructions. Skip to Step 3 if you're working with an existing illustration.

2. **If you're starting from a new page, create an object to work with.**

For example, click and hold down the Rectangle tool to select the Star tool. Then click and drag from the upper left to the lower right to create a star shape.

Exact size doesn't matter, but make it large enough that you can see it. To start over, choose Edit⇨Undo or press Ctrl+Z (Windows) or ⌘+Z (Mac).

As a default, all shapes start with a black stroke and a white fill (see Figure 3-3). If yours isn't black and white, press D, which changes the selected object to the default colors.

You can see the width and height of your object while you click and drag. If you don't want those values to display, choose Edit⇨Preferences⇨Smart Guides (Windows) or Illustrator⇨Preferences⇨Smart Guides (Mac) and deselect the Measurements Labels check box.

3. **Using the Selection tool, click the object to make sure it's active.**

All anchor points are solid, indicating that they're all active (refer to Figure 3-3). You see, as a default, many additional points you can use to transform your selected object.

Figure 3-3:
A shape created by a selection tool.

4. **Click and drag the shape to another location.**

   All anchor points travel together.

5. **When you are finished relocating your selection, press Ctrl+D (Windows) or ⌘+D (Mac) to, deactivate your selection.**

   You can use one of these three methods:

   - Choose Select⇨Deselect.
   - Ctrl+click (Windows) or ⌘-click (Mac) anywhere on the page.
   - Use the key command Ctrl+Shift+A (Windows) or ⌘+Shift+A (Mac).

Selecting an anchor point

When you have a selection to work with (see the numbered list), you can deselect all active anchor points and then make just one anchor point active. Follow these steps:

1. **Choose Select⇨Deselect to make sure the object isn't selected.**

2. **Select the Direct Selection tool (the white arrow) from the Tools panel.**

3. **Click one anchor point.**

   Only one anchor point (the one you clicked) is solid, and the others are hollow, as shown in Figure 3-4.

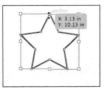

Figure 3-4:
Select only one anchor point.

4. **Click and drag that solid anchor point with the Direct Selection tool.**

   Only that solid anchor point moves.

Note that an anchor point enlarges when you cross over it with the Direct Selection tool. This enlargement is a big break for people who typically have to squint to see where the anchor points are positioned.

Using a marquee to select an object

Sometimes you can more easily surround the object you want to select by dragging the mouse to create a marquee. Follow these steps to select an object by creating a marquee:

1. **Choose the Selection tool.**

2. **Click outside the object and drag over a small part of it, as shown in Figure 3-5.**

   The entire object becomes selected.

Figure 3-5: Select an entire object.

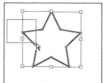

You can also select only one anchor point in an object by using the marquee method:

1. **Choose Select⇨Deselect to make sure the object isn't selected and then choose the Direct Selection tool.**

2. **Click outside a corner of the object and drag over only the anchor point you want to select.**

   Notice that only that anchor point is active, which can be a sight-saver when you're trying to select individual points (see Figure 3-6).

Figure 3-6: Select individual anchor points.

You can use this method to cross over just the two top points or side anchor points to activate multiple anchor points as well.

Selecting multiple objects

If you have multiple items on a page, you can select them by using one of these methods:

✦ **Select one object or anchor point and then hold down the Shift key and click another object or anchor point.** Depending on which selection tool you're using, you either select all anchor points on an object (Selection tool) or additional anchor points only (Direct Selection tool).

 You can use the Shift key to deactivate an object as well. Shift+click a selected object to deselect it.

✦ **Choose Select⇨All or press Ctrl+A (Windows) or ⌘+A (Mac).**

✦ **Use the marquee selection technique and drag outside and over the objects.** When you use this technique with the Selection tool, all anchor points in the objects are selected; when using the Direct Selection tool, only the points you drag over are selected.

Saving a selection

Spending way too much time trying to make your selections? Illustrator comes to the rescue with the Save Selection feature. After you have a selection that you may need again, choose Select⇨Save Selection and name the selection. The selection now appears at the bottom of the Select menu. To change the name or delete the saved selection, choose Select⇨Edit Selection. This selection is saved with the document.

New in Illustrator CS5, you can use the same Select-behind keyboard shortcut that has existed in InDesign for several versions. To select an object behind another, simply place the cursor over the area where you know that the object (to be selected) is located and press Ctrl+click (Windows) or ⌘+click for Mac OS.

Grouping and Ungrouping

Keep objects together by grouping them. The Group function is handy when you're creating something from multiple objects, such as a logo. Using the Group function, you can ensure that all objects that make up the logo stay together when you move, rotate, scale, or copy it.

Creating a group

Follow these steps to create a group:

1. **If you aren't already working with an illustration that contains a bunch of objects, create several objects on a new page — anywhere, any size.**

   For example, select the Rectangle tool and click and drag the page several times to create additional rectangles.

2. **Select the first object with the Selection tool and then hold down the Shift key and click a second object.**

3. **Choose Object➪Group or press Ctrl+G (Windows) or ⌘+G (Mac).**

4. **Choose Select➪Deselect and then click one of the objects with the Selection tool.**

   Both objects become selected.

5. **While the first two objects are still selected, Shift+click a third object.**

6. **With all three objects selected, choose Object➪Group again.**

   Illustrator remembers the grouping order. To prove it, choose Select➪Deselect to deselect the group and switch to the Group Selection tool. (Hold down the mouse button on the Direct Selection tool to access the Group Selection tool.)

7. **With the Group Selection tool, click the first object; all anchor points become active. Click the first object again; the second object becomes selected. Click the first object again and the third object becomes selected.**

   This tool activates the objects in the order you grouped them. After you group the objects, you can treat them as a single object.

To ungroup objects, choose Object➪Ungroup or use the key command Ctrl+Shift+G (Windows) or ⌘+Shift+G (Mac). In a situation where you group objects twice (because you added an object to the group, for example), you have to choose Ungroup twice.

Using Isolation mode

When you use *Isolation mode* in Illustrator, you can easily select and edit objects in a group without disturbing other parts of your artwork. Simply double-click a group and it opens in a separate Isolation mode, where all objects outside the group are dimmed and inactive. Do the work you need to do on the group and exit from Isolation mode by clicking the arrow to the left of Group in the upper-left corner of the window, shown in Figure 3-7.

 Click the Isolate Selected Object button in the Control panel to quickly access the Isolation mode.

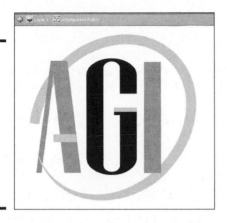

Figure 3-7:
In Isolation mode, you can edit group contents without disturbing other artwork.

Manipulating Selected Objects

In the following list, you discover a few other cool things you can do with selected objects:

✦ **Move selected objects:** When an object is selected, you can drag it to any location on the page, but what if you only want to nudge it a bit? To nudge an item one pixel at a time, select it with the Selection tool and press the left-, right-, up-, or down-arrow key to reposition the object. Hold down the Shift key as you press an arrow key to move an object by ten pixels at a time.

✦ **Constrain movement:** Want to move an object over to the other side of the page without changing its alignment? Constrain something by selecting an object with the Selection tool and dragging the item and then holding down the Shift key before you release the mouse button. By pressing the Shift key mid-drag, you constrain the movement to 45-, 90-, or 180-degree angles!

✦ **Clone selected objects:** Use the Selection tool to easily *clone* (duplicate) an item and move it to a new location. To clone an item, simply select it with the Selection tool and then hold down the Alt key (Windows) or Option key (Mac). Look for the cursor to change to two arrows (see Figure 3-8) and then drag the item to another location on the page. Notice that the original object is left intact and that a copy of the object has been created and moved.

✦ **Constrain the clone:** By Alt+dragging (Windows) or Option+dragging (Mac) an item and then pressing Shift, you can clone the item and keep it aligned with the original.

Don't hold down the Shift key until you're in the process of dragging the item; otherwise, pressing Shift deselects the original object.

**Book III
Chapter 3**

**Using the
Selection Tools**

Figure 3-8:
Drag the double arrow to clone an object.

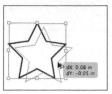

After you clone an object to a new location, try this neat trick to create multiple objects the same distance apart from each other by using the Transform Again command: Choose Object➪Transform➪Transform Again or press Ctrl+D (Windows) or ⌘+D (Mac) to have another object cloned the exact distance as the first cloned object (see Figure 3-9). We discuss transforms in more detail in Chapter 10 of this minibook.

Figure 3-9:
Using the Transform Again command.

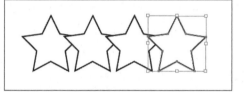

✦ **Use the Select menu:** By using the Select menu, you can gain additional selection controls, such as choosing Select➪Inverse, which allows you to select one object and then turn your selection inside out. Also, choosing the Select➪Same option lets you select one object and then select additional objects on the page based on similarities in color, fill, stroke, and other special attributes.

Take advantage of the Select Similar button on the Control panel to easily access that feature. Notice that in Figure 3-10 you can hold down the arrow to the right of the Select Similar button to choose which similarities should be considered to make the selection.

Figure 3-10:
Define the similarities you want your selections based on.

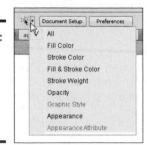

Chapter 4: Creating Basic Shapes

In This Chapter

✓ **Introducing rectangles, ellipses, stars, and polygons**

✓ **Resizing shapes after creation**

✓ **Creating shapes**

Shapes, shapes, shapes — they're everywhere in Illustrator. Basic shapes, such as squares, circles, polygons, and stars, are used in all types of illustrations. With the right know-how and the right shape tools, you can easily create these shapes exactly the way you want. In this chapter, you find out how to use these tools to control a shape's outcome, create shapes based on precise measurements, and change the number of points a star has.

The Basic Shape Tools

The only visible shape tool in the Tools panel is, as a default, the Rectangle tool. Click and hold down that tool and you have access to the Rounded Rectangle, Ellipse, Polygon, and Star tools, shown in Figure 4-1. (Although you see the Flare tool, it isn't a basic shape.)

Figure 4-1:
Basic shape
tools.

You can tear off this tool set so that you don't have to find the hidden shapes later. Click and hold the Rectangle tool and drag to the arrow on the far right side. Wait until you see the pop-up hint (Tearoff) and then release the mouse button. These tools are now on a free-floating toolbar that you can drag to another location.

Creating rectangles and ellipses

Rectangles and ellipses are the most fundamental shapes you can create (see Figure 4-2). To create a rectangle shape freehand, select the Rectangle tool and simply click the page where you want the shape to appear. Then drag diagonally toward the opposite side, drag your mouse the distance you want the shape to be in size, and release the mouse button. You can drag up or down. You do the same to create an ellipse by using the Ellipse tool.

Figure 4-2: Click and drag diagonally to create a shape.

After you create the shape, adjust its size and position by using the Selection tool. Reposition the shape by clicking the selected object and dragging. Resize the object by grabbing a handle and adjusting in or out. To adjust two sides together, grab a corner handle. To resize a shape proportionally, Shift+drag a corner handle.

Using the Rounded Rectangle tool

You can create a rounded rectangle by using one of two methods:

+ Click and drag freehand to create the rounded rectangle shape.

+ Click the artboard once to open the Rounded Rectangle dialog box, where you can enter values to define the shape.

The difference between these two methods is that when you open the Rounded Rectangle dialog box (see Figure 4-3), you can enter a value in the Corner Radius text field, which determines how much rounding is applied to the corners of the shape.

Figure 4-3: Customize the size of a rounded rectangle.

Rounded Rectangle	
Options	
Width: 5 pt	OK
Height: 4	Cancel
Corner Radius: 9 pt	

Change the rounded corner visually by pressing the up and down keys on your keyboard *while* you're dragging out the Rounded Rectangle shape on the artboard.

The smaller the value, the less rounded the corners; the higher the value, the more rounded the corners. Be careful: You can round a rectangle's corners so much that it becomes an ellipse!

Using the Polygon tool

You create stars and polygons in much the same way as you create rectangles and ellipses. Select the Polygon tool and click and drag from one corner to another to create the default six-sided polygon shape. You can also select the Polygon tool and click once on the artboard to change the Polygon tool options in the Polygon dialog box.

You can change the polygon shape by entering new values in the Radius and Sides text fields, as shown in Figure 4-4. The radius is determined from the center to the edge of the polygon. The value for the number of sides can range from 3 (making triangles a breeze to create) to 1,000. Whoa — a polygon with 1,000 sides would look like a circle unless it was the size of Texas!

Figure 4-4:
Creating
a polygon
shape.

Using the Star tool

To create a star shape, select the Star tool from the Tools panel. (Remember that it may hide under other shape tools.) If you click the artboard once to open the Star dialog box, you see three text fields in which you can enter values to customize your star shape:

✦ **Radius 1:** Distance from the outer points to the center of the star

✦ **Radius 2:** Distance from the inner points to the center of the star

✦ **Points:** Number of points that comprise the star

The closer together the Radius 1 and Radius 2 values are to each other, the shorter the points on your star. In other words, you can go from a starburst to a seal of approval by entering values that are close in the Radius 1 and Radius 2 text fields, as shown in Figure 4-5.

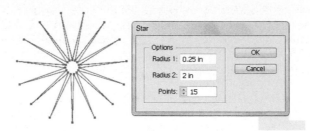

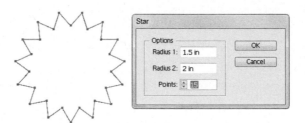

Figure 4-5:
Radius 1
and Radius
2 are closer
to each
other in the
star on the
bottom.

Resizing Shapes

You often need a shape to be an exact size (for example, 2 x 3 inches). After
you create a shape, the best way to resize it to exact measurements is to use
the Transform panel, shown in Figure 4-6. Have the object selected and then
choose Window➪Transform to open the Transform panel. Note that on this
panel you can enter values to place an object in the X and Y fields as well
as enter values in the width (W) and height (H) text fields to determine the
exact size of an object.

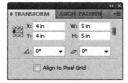

Figure 4-6:
Precisely
set the size
of a shape.

In many Adobe Illustrator panels, you may see measurement increments
consisting of points, picas, millimeters, centimeters, or inches, which can be
confusing and maybe even intimidating. But you can control which measurement increments to use.

Show rulers by choosing View➪Rulers➪Show Rulers or press Ctrl+R (Windows) or ⌘+R (Mac). Then right-click (Windows) or Control-click (Mac) the ruler to change the measurement increment to an increment you're more familiar with. Using the contextual menu that appears, you can change the measurement increment directly on the document.

Alternatively, you can simply type the number followed by a measurement extension into the width and height text fields in the Transform panel (refer to Figure 4-6) and the measurement converts properly for you. Table 4-1 lists the extensions you can use.

Table 4-1	Measurement Extensions
Extension	*Measurement Unit*
in (or ")	Inch
Pt	Point
mm	Millimeter
pp	Pica

If you don't want to bother creating a freehand shape and then changing its size, select the Shape tool and click the artboard. The Options dialog box specific to the shape you're creating appears, in which you can type values into the width and height text fields.

If you accidentally click and drag, you end up with a tiny shape on your page. Don't fret. Simply get rid of the small shape by selecting it and pressing the Delete key, and then try again.

Tips for Creating Shapes

The following simple tips can improve your skills at creating basic shapes in Illustrator:

✦ Press and hold the Shift key while dragging with the Rectangle or Ellipse tool to create a perfect square or circle. This trick is also helpful when you're using the Polygon and Star tools — holding down the Shift key constrains them so that they're straight (see Figure 4-7).

✦ Create a shape from the center out by holding down the Alt (Windows) or Option (Mac) key while dragging. Hold down Alt+Shift (Windows) or Option+Shift (Mac) to pull a constrained shape out from the center.

Figure 4-7:
Use the
Shift key to
constrain
a shape
while you
create it.

✦ When entering values in a shape dialog box, you can click either the Width or Height text to match the other value. In Figure 4-8, we entered the value 4 in the Height text box and then clicked the word *Width* to make the values match.

Figure 4-8:
Match
values
easily.

✦ When creating a star or polygon shape by clicking and dragging, if you keep the mouse button down, you can then press the up- or down-arrow key to interactively add points or sides to your shape.

Creating advanced shapes

At times, it may be wise to use advanced tools in Illustrator to create unique shapes. The Pathfinder panel is an incredible tool you can use to combine, knock out (eliminate one shape from another), and even create shapes from other intersected shapes.

You use the Pathfinder panel, shown in Figure 4-9, to combine objects into new shapes. To use the Pathfinder panel, choose Window➪Pathfinder.

Figure 4-9:
Combine
objects into
new shapes.

Across the top row of the Pathfinder panel are the Shape modes, which let
you control the interaction between selected shapes. You can choose from
the Shape modes listed in Table 4-2.

Table 4-2		Shape Modes
Button	*Mode*	*What You Can Do with It*
⬚	Add to Shape Area	Unite the selected shape into one.
⬚	Subtract from Shape Area	Cut out the topmost shape from the underlying shape.
⬚	Intersect Shape Areas	Use the area of the topmost shape to clip the underlying shape as a mask would.
⬚	Exclude Overlapping Shape Areas	Use the area of the shape to invert the underlying shape, turning filled regions into holes and vice versa.

 If you like the result from using Exclude Overlapping Shapes mode, you
can also create a similar effect by selecting several shapes and choosing
Object➪Compound Path➪Make. This command "punches" the topmost
shapes from the bottom shape.

 The shapes remain separate so that you can still adjust them, which is helpful if you like to tweak your artwork (but it drives some people crazy). You
can turn the result of using the Shape Mode buttons into one shape by either
clicking the Expand button after selecting Shape mode or holding down the
Alt key (Windows) or Option key (Mac) when clicking a Shape Mode button.

**Book III
Chapter 4**

**Creating Basic
Shapes**

Using the Pathfinders

Pathfinders are the buttons at the bottom of the Pathfinder panel that let you create new shapes from overlapping objects. Table 4-3 summarizes what each Pathfinder does.

Table 4-3		The Pathfinders
Button	*Mode*	*What You Can Do with It*
	Divide	Divide all shapes into their own, individual shapes. This tool is quite useful tool when you're trying to create custom shapes.
	Trim	Remove the part of a filled object that's hidden.
	Merge	Remove the part of a filled object that's hidden. Also, remove any strokes and merge any adjoining or overlapping objects filled with the same color.
	Crop	Delete all parts of the artwork that fall outside the boundary of the topmost object. You can also remove any strokes. If you want strokes to remain when using this feature, select them and choose Object⇨Path⇨Outline Stroke.
	Outline	Divide an object into its shape's line segments, or edges, useful for preparing artwork that needs a trap for overprinting objects.
	Minus Back	Delete an object that's in the back of frontmost object.

Using the Shape Builder tool

New in Illustrator CS5, you can intuitively combine, edit, and fill shapes on your artboard. Follow these steps to create your own unique shape using the Shape Builder tool:

1. **Create several overlapping shapes.**

2. **Select the shapes that you want to combine.**

 3. **Select the Shape Builder tool and then click and drag across the selected shapes, as shown on the left in Figure 4-10.**

   The selected shapes are combined into one shape, as shown on the right in Figure 4-10.

Figure 4-10:
Create several shapes in order to use the Shape Builder tool.

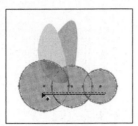

The Shape Builder tool also enables merging objects, breaking overlapping shapes, subtracting areas, and more.

4. **Create another shape that overlaps your new combined shape.**

5. **Using the Selection tool, select both shapes.**

6. **Select the Shape Builder tool again.**

7. **Hold down the Alt (Windows) or Option (Mac) key and click and drag across the newly added shape, as shown in Figure 4-11.**

   It is subtracted from the underlying shape.

Figure 4-11:
Use the Shape Builder tool to subtract from another shape.

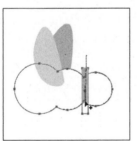

 Coloring fills and strokes is easier now, too. When you're finished making your shape, you can use the hidden Live Paint Bucket tool to intuitively fill your shape with color.

Chapter 5: Using the Pen Tool and Placing Images

In This Chapter

✔ Familiarizing yourself with the Pen tool

✔ Creating paths, closed shapes, and curves

✔ Using the hidden Pen tools

✔ Tracing some artwork

✔ Placing images in Illustrator CS5

✔ Working with Layer Comps

You've seen illustrations that you know are made from paths, but how do you make your own? In this chapter, we show you how to use the Pen tool to create paths and closed shapes.

Using the Pen tool requires a little more coordination than do other Illustrator tools. Fortunately, Adobe Illustrator CS5 includes new features to help make using the Pen tool a little easier. After you master the Pen tool, the possibilities for creating illustrations are unlimited. Read this chapter to build your skills using the most popular feature in graphical software: the Bézier curve.

Pen Tool Fundamentals

You can use the Pen tool to create all sorts of elements, such as straight lines, curves, and closed shapes, which you can then incorporate into illustrations:

✦ **Bézier curve:** Originally developed by Pierre Bézier in the 1970s for CAD/CAM operations, the Bézier curve (shown in Figure 5-1) became the underpinnings of the entire Adobe PostScript drawing model. A *Bézier curve* is one that you can control the depth and size of by using direction lines.

✦ **Anchor point:** You can use anchor points to control the shape of a path or object. Anchor points are created automatically when using shape tools. You can manually create anchor points by clicking from point to point with the Pen tool.

Figure 5-1:
Bézier
curves are
controlled
by direction
lines.

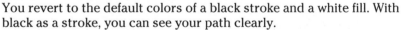

✦ **Direction line:** These lines are essentially the handles you use on curved points to adjust the depth and angle of curved paths.

✦ **Closed shape:** When a path is created, it becomes a closed shape when the start point joins the endpoint.

✦ **Simple path:** A *path* consists of one or more straight or curved segments. Anchor points mark the endpoints of the path segments.

In the next section, we show you how to control the anchor points.

Creating a straight line

A basic function of the Pen tool is to create a simple path. You can create a simple, straight line with the Pen tool by following these steps:

1. **Press D or click the small black-and-white color swatches at the bottom of the Tools panel.**

You revert to the default colors of a black stroke and a white fill. With black as a stroke, you can see your path clearly.

The trick of pressing D to change the foreground and background colors to the default of black and white also works in Photoshop and InDesign.

2. **Click the Fill swatch, at the bottom of the Tools panel, to ensure that the Fill swatch is in front of the Stroke swatch, and then press the forward slash (/) key to change the fill to None.**

3. **Open a new blank page and select the Pen tool.**

Notice that when you move the mouse over the artboard, the Pen cursor appears with an X beside it, indicating that you're creating the first anchor point of a path.

4. **Click the artboard to create the first anchor point of a line.**

The X disappears.

Avoid dragging the mouse or you'll end up creating a curve rather than a straight segment.

5. **Click anywhere else on the document to create the ending anchor point of the line.**

Illustrator creates a path between the two anchor points. Essentially, the path looks like a line segment with an anchor point at each end (see Figure 5-2).

Figure 5-2:
A path connected by two anchor points.

To make a correction to a line you created with the Pen tool (as described in the preceding step list), follow these steps:

1. **Choose Select⇨Deselect to make sure that no objects are selected.**

2. **Select the Direct Selection tool from the Tools panel.**

Notice the helpful feature that enlarges the anchor point when you pass over it with the Direct Selection tool.

3. **Click an anchor to select one point on the line.**

Notice that the selected anchor point is solid and the other is hollow. *Solid* indicates that the anchor point you clicked is active whereas *hollow* is inactive.

4. **Click and drag the anchor point with the Direct Selection tool.**

The selected anchor point moves, changing the direction of the path while not affecting the other anchor point.

Use the Direct Selection tool (press A to use the keyboard shortcut to select the Direct Selection tool) to make corrections to paths.

Make sure that only the anchor point you want to change is active. If the entire path is selected, all anchor points are solid. If only one anchor point is selected, all but that one point will be hollow.

Creating a constrained straight line

In this section, we show you how to create a real straight line — one that's on multiples of a 45-degree angle. Illustrator makes it easy; just follow these steps:

1. **Select the Pen tool and click the artboard anywhere to place an anchor point.**

2. **Hold down the Shift key and click another location to place the ending anchor point.**

   Notice that when you're holding down the Shift key, the line snaps to a multiple of 45 degrees.

Release the mouse button before you release the Shift key or else the line pops out of alignment.

Creating a curve

In this section, you see how to use the Bézier path to create a curved segment. We don't guarantee that you'll love this process — not at first, anyway. But after you know how to use a Bézier path, you'll likely find it useful. To create a Bézier path, follow these steps:

1. **Starting with a blank artboard, select the Pen tool and click the artboard anywhere to place the first anchor point.**

2. **Click someplace else to place the ending anchor point — don't let go of the mouse button — and then drag the cursor until a direction line appears.**

   If you look closely, you see that anchor points are square and that direction lines have circles at the end, as shown in Figure 5-3.

Figure 5-3:
Click and
drag with
the Pen tool
to create a
curved path.

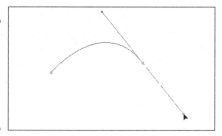

3. **Drag the direction line closer to the anchor point to flatten the curve; drag farther away from the anchor point to increase the curve, as shown in Figure 5-4.**

4. **When you're happy with the curve, release the mouse button.**

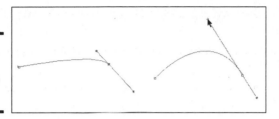

Figure 5-4:
Adding
curve to the
curve.

You've created an *open path,* or a path that doesn't form a closed shape. We show you in the next section how to reconnect to the starting point of the path to make a closed shape.

To alter a curved segment after you create it, follow these steps:

1. **Choose Select⇨Deselect to ensure that no objects are selected.**

2. **Choose the Direct Selection tool and click the last anchor point created.**

    If the direction lines aren't already visible, they appear.

    If you have difficulty selecting the anchor point, drag a marquee around it with the Direct Selection tool.

3. **Click precisely at the end of one of the direction lines; drag the direction line to change the curve.**

Reconnecting to an existing path

Creating one segment is fine if you want just a line or an arch. But if you want to create a shape, you need to add more anchor points to the original segment. If you want to fill your shape with a color or a gradient, you need to close it, which means that you need to eventually return to the starting anchor point.

To add segments to your path and create a closed shape, follow these steps:

1. **Create a segment (straight or curved).**

    We show you how in the preceding sections of this chapter.

    You can continue from this point, clicking and adding anchor points until you eventually close the shape. For this example, you deselect the path so that you can discover how to continue adding to paths that have already been created. Knowing how to edit existing paths is extremely helpful when you need to make adjustments to artwork.

2. **With the Pen tool selected, move the cursor over an end anchor point on the deselected path.**

3. **Click when you see the Pen icon with a forward slash to connect your next segment.**

   The forward slash indicates that you're connecting to this path.

4. **Click someplace else to create the next anchor point in the path; drag the mouse if you want to create a curved segment.**

5. **Click to place additional anchor points, dragging as needed to curve those segments.**

   Remember that you want to close this shape, so place the anchor points so that you can eventually come back to the first anchor point.

   The shape shown in Figure 5-5 is a result of adding several linked anchor points.

Figure 5-5:
Adding
anchor
points to
create a
shape.

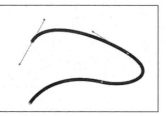

6. **When you return to the first anchor point, move the cursor over it and click when the close icon (a small, hollow circle) appears, as shown in Figure 5-6.**

   The shape now has no end points.

Figure 5-6:
Click when
the close
path icon
appears.

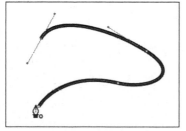

Controlling curves

After you feel comfortable creating curves and paths, take control of those curves so that you can create them with a greater degree of precision. The following steps walk you through the manual method for changing the direction of anchor points and reveal helpful keyboard commands to make controlling paths a little more fluid. At the end of this section, we introduce new tools that you may also want to take advantage of to help you get control of the Pen tool.

To control a curve, follow these steps:

1. **Create a new document and then choose View➪Show Grid to show a series of horizontal and vertical rules that act as guides.**

If it helps, use the Zoom tool to zoom in to the document.

2. **With the Pen tool, click an intersection of any of these lines in the middle area of the page to place the initial anchor point and drag upward.**

Let go but don't click when the direction line has extended to the horizontal grid line above it, as shown in Figure 5-7a.

3. **Click to place the second anchor point on the intersection of the grid directly to the right of your initial point; drag the direction line to the grid line directly below it, as shown in Figure 5-7b.**

If you have difficulty keeping the direction line straight, hold down the Shift key to constrain it.

Figure 5-7:
Creating a
controlled
Bézier
curve.

  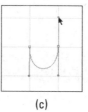

(a)   (b)   (c)

4. **Choose Select➪Deselect to deselect your curve.**

Congratulations! You've created a controlled curve. In these steps, we created an arch that's going up, so we first clicked and dragged up. Likewise, to create a downward arch, you must click and drag down. Using the grid, try to create a downward arch like the one shown in Figure 5-7c.

Creating a corner point

To change the direction of a path from being a curve to a corner, you have to create a *corner point,* shown on the right in Figure 5-8. A corner point has no direction lines and allows for a sharp directional change in a path.

Figure 5-8:
Smooth
versus
corner
points.

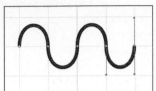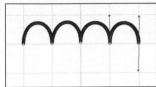

You can switch from the Pen tool to the Convert Anchor Point tool to change a smooth anchor point into a corner point, but that process is time-consuming. An easier way is to press the Alt (Windows) or Option (Mac) key — the Pen tool temporarily changes into the Convert Anchor Point tool — while clicking the anchor point.

To change a smooth anchor point into a corner point by using the shortcut method, follow these steps:

1. **Create an upward arch.**

We show you how in the preceding section "Controlling the curves" (refer to Figure 5-7b).

2. **Hold down the Alt (Windows) or Option (Mac) key and position the cursor over the last anchor point (the last point that you created with the Pen tool).**

3. **When the cursor changes to a caret (that's the Convert Anchor Point tool), click and drag until the direction line is up to the grid line above, as shown on the left in Figure 5-9.**

Figure 5-9:
Converting
from smooth
to corner.

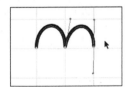

4. **Release the Alt (Windows) or Option (Mac) key and the mouse button, move the cursor to the grid line to the right, and click and drag down.**

The Hidden Pen Tools

Hold down the Pen tool icon in the Tools panel to access additional tools: the Add Anchor Point, Delete Anchor Point, and Convert Anchor Point tools, shown in Table 5-1. In the preceding section, we show you how to create a corner point by using the shortcut method, by pressing the Alt (Windows) or Option (Mac) key to access the Convert Anchor Point tool. You may feel more comfortable switching to that tool when you need to convert a point, but switching tools can be more time-consuming.

Table 5-1	The Hidden Pen Tools
Icon	*Tool*
	Pen
	Add Anchor Point
	Delete Anchor Point
	Convert Anchor Point

Even though you can use a hidden tool to delete and add anchor points, Illustrator automatically does this as a default when you're using the Pen tool. When you move the cursor over an anchor point by using the Pen tool, a minus icon appears. To delete that anchor point, simply click. Likewise, when you move the cursor over a part of the path that doesn't contain anchor points, a plus icon appears. Simply click to add an anchor point.

If you prefer to use the tools dedicated to adding and deleting anchor points, choose Edit⇨Preferences⇨General (Windows) or Illustrator⇨Preferences⇨General (Mac); in the Preferences dialog box that appears, select the Disable Auto Add/Delete check box. Then, when you want to add or delete an anchor point, select the appropriate tool and click the path.

Adding tools to help make paths

Some Pen tool modifiers are available in the Control panel in Illustrator CS5. You can take advantage of them for many Pen tool uses, but using keyboard shortcuts to switch the Pen tool to its various options is probably still faster. If you're resistant to contorting your fingers while trying to create a path, you should appreciate these tools.

 To see the Control panel tools, select the Pen tool and start creating a path. Notice that the Control panel has a series of buttons available, shown in Figure 5-10.

Figure 5-10:
Control
panel tools
for easy
editing.

Hide Handles for Multiple
Selected Anchor Points

Convert Selected
Anchor Points to Smooth

Connect Selected End Points

Cut Path at Selected Anchor Points

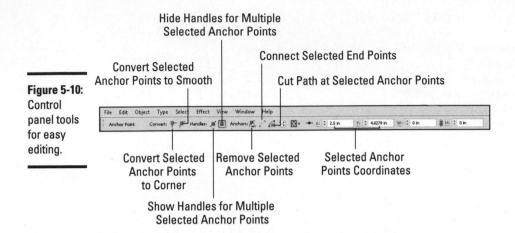

Convert Selected
Anchor Points
to Corner

Remove Selected
Anchor Points

Selected Anchor
Points Coordinates

Show Handles for Multiple
Selected Anchor Points

Using the Eraser tool

The Eraser tool is a tool that all users will love! You can use it to quickly remove areas of artwork as easily as you erase pixels in Photoshop by stroking with your mouse over any shape or set of shapes.

New paths are automatically created along the edges of the erasure, even preserving its smoothness, as shown in Figure 5-11.

Figure 5-11:
The Eraser
tool deletes
sections of
a path.

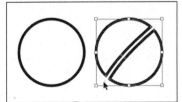

By double-clicking the Eraser tool, you can define the diameter, angle, and roundness of your eraser (see Figure 5-12). If you're using a drawing tablet, you can even set Wacom tablet interaction parameters, such as Pressure and Tilt.

If you want to erase more than a single selected object, use Isolation mode to segregate grouped objects for editing. Remember that in order to enter this mode, you simply double-click a group of items. You can then use the eraser on all objects in that group at one time without disturbing the rest of your design.

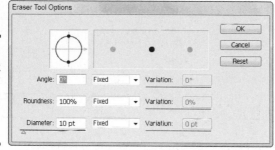

Figure 5-12:
Double-click
the Eraser
tool to set
various tool
options.

Tracing Artwork

You can use a template layer to trace an image manually. A *template layer* is
a locked, dimmed layer you can use to draw over placed images with the Pen
tool, much like you would do with a piece of onion skin paper over the top of
an image.

Creating a template layer

Just follow these steps to create a template layer:

1. **Take a scanned image or logo and save it in a format that Illustrator
   can import from your image-editing program, such as Photoshop.**

   Typically, you save the image as an `.eps`, a `.tif`, or a native `.psd`
   (Photoshop) file.

2. **Choose File⇨Place to open the Place dialog box.**

3. **In the Place dialog box, locate the saved image; then select the
   Template check box and click Place.**

   Note that the Template check box may be in a different location depending
   on your platform, but it's always located at the bottom of the dialog box.

   Selecting the Template check box tells Illustrator to lock down the scanned
   image on a layer. Essentially, you can't reposition or edit your image.

   After you click Place, a template layer is automatically created for you,
   and another layer is waiting for you to create your path. The newly created top layer resembles a piece of tracing paper that has been placed
   on top of the scanned image.

4. **Re-create the image by tracing over it with the Pen tool.**

5. **When you're done, turn off the visibility of the placed image by clicking the Visibility icon to the left of the template layer.**

You now have a path you can use in place of the image, which is useful if you're creating an illustration of an image or are digitally re-creating a logo.

For more about layers, check out Chapter 8 of this minibook.

Keep practicing to become more comfortable with clicking and dragging, flowing with the direction line pointing the way you want the path to be created; everything will fall into place.

Using Live Trace

Use the Live Trace feature to automatically trace raster images into vector paths. This feature works well in many instances but definitely isn't a "magic pill" for re-creating images as vectors. For example, a logo with many precise curves and straight lines isn't a good candidate for this feature, but a hand-drawn illustration, clip art, or other drawing works well.

Here are the steps you follow to use Live Trace:

1. **Choose File⇨Place and place a scan or raster illustration that you want to convert to vector paths.**

Immediately after placing, you see that the Control panel now has additional buttons available, as shown in Figure 5-13.

Figure 5-13:
Live Trace
Control
panel
features.

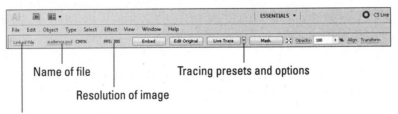

Name of file

Tracing presets and options

Resolution of image

File is linked, not embedded

2. **You can either click the Live Trace button to automatically trace based on default settings or, better, click and hold on the Tracing Options arrow and choose a more appropriate setting.**

Choose Tracing Options from the bottom of the Tracing Options drop-down list to customize settings.

3. **After you select settings you're happy with, you can either use the Live Paint features to color in the work or click the Expand button in the Control panel to expand the trace object to vector paths that can be edited.**

See Chapter 9 of this minibook for more information on painting fills and strokes.

Other Things You Should Know about Placing Images

In the preceding section, you discover how to place an image as a template. But what if you want to place an image to be used in an illustration file? Simply choose File⇨Place.

Click an image once to see its Link check box. If you keep the check box selected, the image is linked to the original file, which is helpful if you plan to reference the file several times in the illustration (it saves file space) or edit the original and have it update the placed image in Illustrator. This option is usually selected by people in the prepress industry who want to have access to the original image file. Just remember to send the image with the Illustrator file if it's to be printed or used someplace other than on your computer.

If you deselect the Link check box, the image is embedded into the Illustrator file. This option keeps the filing system cleaner but doesn't leave much room to edit the original image later. In certain instances, such as when you want an image to become a symbol (see Chapter 11 of this mini-book), the image will have to be embedded, but most functions work with both linked and unlinked files.

Using Photoshop Layer Comps

Book III
Chapter 5

Using the Pen Tool and Placing Images

The *Layer Comps* feature in Photoshop lets you set the visibility, appearance, and position of layers. You can take advantage of this useful organizational tool in other Adobe products. Read more about Photoshop in Book IV.

You can place in Illustrator a .psd (Photoshop) image that has saved Layer Comps and choose which layer comp set you want visible.

Chapter 6: Using Type in Illustrator

In This Chapter

✔ Introducing the Type tools

✔ Getting to know text areas

✔ Manipulating text along paths and within shapes

✔ Assigning font styles

✔ Discovering the Character, Control, and Paragraph panels

✔ Saving time with text utilities

*O*ne of Illustrator's strongest areas is manipulating text. Whether you're using Illustrator to create logos, business cards, or type to be used on the Web, you have everything you need to create professional-looking text.

In this chapter, you meet the Type tools and discover a few basic (and more advanced) text-editing tricks that you can take advantage of. You then find out about other text tools, such as the Character and Paragraph panels. At the end of this chapter, you get the quick-and-dirty lowdown on the Illustrator text utilities. These utilities can save you loads of time, so don't skip this section.

Working with Type

You can do all sorts of cool things with type, from the simplest tasks of creating a line of text and dealing with text overflow to more complicated tricks such as placing text along paths and wrapping text around objects.

Figure 6-1 shows the Type tools with an example of what you can do with each one. Click and hold the Type tool to see the hidden tools. The different tools give you the ability to be creative and also accommodate foreign languages.

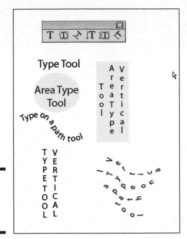

Figure 6-1:
The Type
tools.

Creating text areas

A *text area* is a region that you define. Text, when inserted in this region, is constrained within the shape. To create a text area, click and drag with the Type tool.

As you create and finish typing in a text area, you may want to quickly click and drag to create a new text area elsewhere on your artboard. Unfortunately, Illustrator doesn't allow you to do that. You do have two options that will help you to create multiple textboxes quickly on your artboard:

✦ Choose Select⇨Deselect and then create another area.

✦ Hold down the Ctrl (Windows) or ⌘ (Mac) key, and click anywhere on the artboard outside of the active text area. By clicking, you deactivate the current text box so that you can click and drag out a new text area.

Creating a line of text

To create a simple line of text, select the Type tool and click the artboard. A blinking insertion point appears. You can now start typing. With this method, the line of type goes on forever (even beyond the end of the Scratch area) until you press Enter (Windows) or Return (Mac) to start a new line of text. This excess length is fine if you just need short lines of text for callouts or captions, for example, but it doesn't work well if you're creating a label or anything else that has large amounts of copy.

Many new users click and drag an ever-so-small text area that doesn't allow room for even one letter. If you accidentally do this, switch to the Selection tool, delete the active type area, and then click to create a new text insertion point.

Flowing text into an area

Select the Type tool and then drag on the artboard to create a text area. The cursor appears in the text area; text you type flows automatically to the next line when it reaches the edge of the text area. You can also switch to the Selection tool and adjust the width and height of the text area with the handles.

Need an exact size for a text area? With the Type tool selected, drag to create a text area of any size. Then choose Window⇨Transform to view the Transform panel. Type an exact width measurement in the W text field and an exact height measurement in the H text field.

Dealing with text overflow

Watch out for excess text! If you create a text area that's too small to hold all the text you want to put into it, a red plus sign appears in the lower right corner, as shown in Figure 6-2.

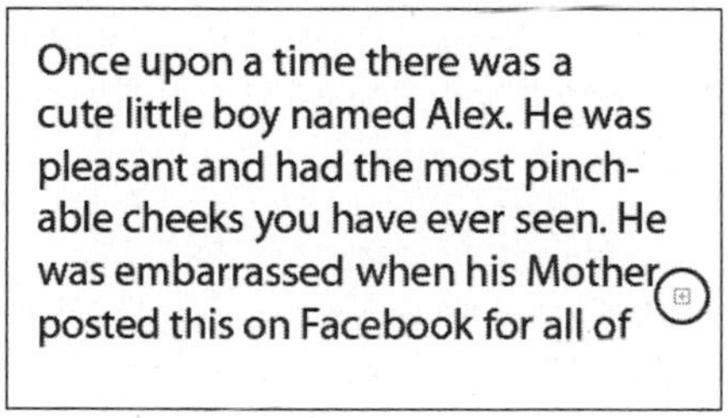

Figure 6-2:
The plus icon indicates that text is overflowing.

> Once upon a time there was a cute little boy named Alex. He was pleasant and had the most pinchable cheeks you have ever seen. He was embarrassed when his Mother posted this on Facebook for all of

Book III Chapter 6

Using Type in Illustrator

When Illustrator indicates that you have too much text for the text area, you have several options:

✦ Make the text area larger by switching to the Selection tool and dragging the handles.

✦ Make the text smaller until you no longer see the overflow indicator.

✦ *Thread* this text area (link it to another), which is a topic covered later in this chapter, in the "Threading text into shapes" section.

Creating columns of text with the Area Type tool

The easiest and most practical way to create rows and columns of text is to use the area type options in Adobe Illustrator. This feature lets you create rows and columns from any text area. You can have only rows or have only columns (much like columns of text in a newspaper) or even both.

1. **Select the Type tool and drag on the artboard to create a text area.**

2. **Choose Type⇨Area Type Options.**

   The Area Type Options dialog box appears, as shown in Figure 6-3. At the end of this section, a list explains all options in the Area Type Options dialog box.

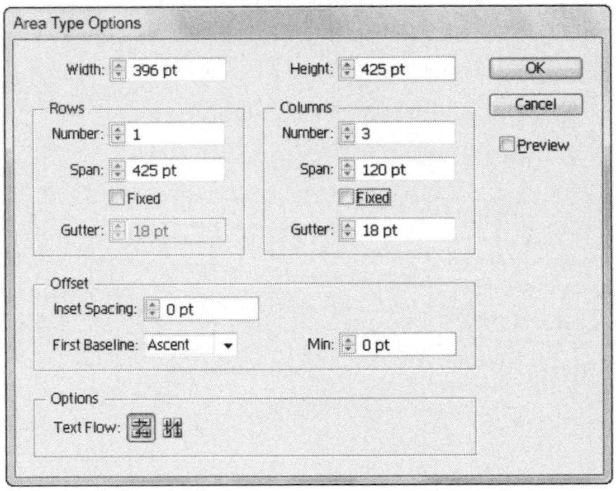

Figure 6-3: The Area Type Options dialog box lets you create columns of text.

3. **In the Area Type Options dialog box, enter a width and height in the Width and Height text fields.**

   The Width and Height text fields contain the height and width of your entire text area. In Figure 6-3, 396 pt is in the Width text field and 425 pt is in the Height text field.

4. **In the Columns area, enter the number of columns you want to create in the Number text field, the span distance in the Span text field, and the gutter space in the Gutter text field.**

   The *span* specifies the height of individual rows and the width of individual columns. The *gutter* is the space between columns and is automatically set for you, but you can change it to any value you like.

5. **Click OK.**

When you create two or more columns of text from the Area Type Options dialog box, text flows to the next column when you reach the end of the previous column, as shown in Figure 6-4.

Figure 6-4:
One column of text flows into the next.

> **Overview of integration with WPF:** VideoRendererElement rendering a webcam. Screenshot showing the example program running the VideoRendererElement. In debug mode you can do a "Connect to Remote Graph..." in GraphEdit to look at the DirectShow graph it builds internally.
>
> DirectShow is part of the Windows Platform SDK. As far as install base, Directshow comes with all versions of windows since probably windows 98.
>
> **Introduction to DirectShow**
>
> Microsoft® DirectShow® is an architecture for streaming media on the Microsoft Windows® platform. DirectShow provides for high-quality capture and playback of multimedia streams. It supports a wide variety of formats, including Advanced Systems Format (ASF), Motion Picture Experts Group (MPEG), Audio-Video Interleaved (AVI), MPEG Audio Layer-3 (MP3), and WAV sound files. It supports capture from digital and analog devices based on the Windows Driver Model (WDM) or Video for Windows. It automatically detects and uses video and audio acceleration hardware when available, but also supports systems without acceleration hardware.
>
> DirectShow is based on the Component Object Model (COM). To write a DirectShow application or component, you must understand COM client programming. For most applications, you do not need to implement your own COM objects. DirectShow provides the components you need. If you want to extend DirectShow by writing your own components, however, you must implement them as COM objects. DirectShow is designed for C++. Microsoft does not provide a managed API Provides

The following list breaks down the other options available in the Area Type Options dialog box (refer to Figure 6-3):

+ **Width and Height:** The present width and height of the entire text area.

+ **Number:** The number of rows and/or columns that you want the text area to contain.

+ **Span:** The height of individual rows and the width of individual columns.

+ **Fixed:** Determines what happens to the span of rows and columns if you resize the type area. When this check box is selected, resizing the area can change the number of rows and columns but not their width. Leave this option deselected if you want to resize the entire text area and have the columns automatically resize with it.

+ **Gutter:** The empty space between rows or columns.

+ **Inset Spacing:** The distance from the edges of the text area.

+ **First Baseline:** Where you want the first line of text to appear. The default Ascent option starts your text normally at the top. If you want to put in a fixed size, such as 50 points from the top, select Fixed from the drop-down list, and enter 50 pt in the Min text field.

+ **Text Flow:** The direction in which you read the text as it flows to another row or column. You can choose to have the text flow horizontally (across rows) or vertically (down columns).

Threading text into shapes

Create custom columns of text that are in different shapes and sizes by threading closed shapes together. This technique works with rectangles, circles, stars, or any other closed shape and can lead to some creative text areas.

Follow these steps to thread text into shapes:

1. **Create any shape, any size.**

For this example, we've created a circle.

2. **Create another shape (it can be any shape) someplace else on the page.**

3. **With the Selection tool, select one shape and Shift-click the other to make just those two shapes active.**

4. **Choose Type⇨Threaded Text⇨Create.**

A threading line appears, as shown in Figure 6-5, indicating the direction of the threaded text.

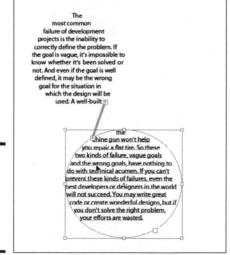

Figure 6-5:
Threaded
text areas
flow from
one area to
another.

5. **Select the Type tool, click the top of the first shape to start the threading, and start typing.**

Continue typing until the text flows over into the other shape.

If you no longer want the text to be threaded, choose Type⇨Threaded Text⇨Remove Threading, which eliminates all threading from the text shapes. To remove one or more, but not all, shapes from the threading, select the shape you want to remove from the threading and choose Type⇨Threaded Text⇨Release Selection.

Wrapping text

Wrapping text isn't quite the same as wrapping a present — it's easier! A *text wrap* forces text to wrap around a graphic, as shown in Figure 6-6. This feature can add a bit of creativity to any piece.

Figure 6-6: The graphic is forcing the text to wrap around it.

First, create a text area and either enter text or paste text into it. Then place an image that you can wrap the text around. Follow these steps to wrap text around another object or group of objects.

1. **Select the wrap object.**

   This object is the one you want the text to wrap around.

2. **Make sure that the wrap object is on top of the text you want to wrap around it by choosing Object⇨Arrange⇨Bring to Front.**

   If you're working in layers (which we discuss in Chapter 8 of this mini-book), make sure that the wrap object is on the top layer.

3. **Choose Object⇨Text Wrap⇨Make.**

   An outline of the wrap area is visible.

4. **Adjust the wrap area by choosing Object⇨Text Wrap⇨Text Wrap Options.**

   The Text Wrap Options dialog box appears, as shown in Figure 6-7.

Figure 6-7: Adjust the distance of the text wrap from the object.

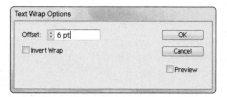

You have these options:

- *Offset:* Specifies the amount of space between the text and the wrap object. You can enter a positive or negative value.

- *Invert Wrap:* Wraps the text on the inside of the wrap object instead of around it.

5. **When you finish making selections, click OK.**

If you want to change the text wrap at a later point, select the object and choose Object⇨Text Wrap⇨Text Wrap Options. Make your changes and click OK.

If you want to unwrap text from an object, select the wrap object and choose Object⇨Text Wrap⇨Release.

Outlining text

Illustrator gives you the opportunity to change text into outlines or artwork. Basically, you change the text into an object, so you can no longer edit that text by typing. The plus side is that it saves you the trouble of sending fonts to everyone who wants to use the file. Turning text into outlines makes it appear as though your text was created with the Pen tool. You want to use this tool when creating logos that will be used frequently by other people or artwork that you may not have control over.

To turn text into an outline, follow these steps:

1. **Type some text on your page.**

   For this example, just type a word (say, your name) and make sure that the font size is at least 36 points. You want to have it large enough to see the effect of outlining it.

2. **Switch to the Selection tool and choose Type➪Create Outlines.**

   You can also use the keyboard command Ctrl+Shift+O (Windows) or ⌘+Shift+O (Mac).

   The text is now grouped together in outline form.

3. **If you're being creative, or just particular, and want to move individual letters, use the Group Select tool or choose Object➪Ungroup to separate the letters, as shown in Figure 6-8.**

Figure 6-8:
Letters converted to outlines.

When you convert type to outlines, the type loses its *hints,* which are the instructions built into fonts to adjust their shape so that your system displays or prints them in the best way based on their size. Without hints, letters such as lowercase *e* or *a* might fill in as the letter forms are reduced in size. Make sure that the text is the approximate size it might be used at before creating outlines. Because the text loses the hints, try not to create outlines on text smaller than 10 points.

Putting text on a path, in a closed shape, or on the path of a shape

Wow — that's some heading, huh? You've probably seen text following a swirly path or inside a shape. Maybe you think that accomplishing such a task is too intimidating to even attempt. In this section, we show you just how easy these tasks are! Some Type tools are dedicated to putting type on a path or a shape (refer to Figure 6-1), but we think you'll find that the key modifiers we show you in this section are easier to use.

Creating text on a path

Follow these steps to put type on a path:

1. **Create a path with the Pen, Line, or Pencil tool.**

   Don't worry if it has a stroke or fill applied.

2. **Select the Type tool and simply cross over the start of the path.**

3. **Look for an I-bar with a squiggle to appear (which indicates that the text will run along the path) and click.**

   The stroke and fill of the path immediately change to None.

4. **Start typing, and the text runs on the path.**

5. **Choose Window⇨Type⇨Paragraph and change the alignment in the Paragraph panel to reposition where the text falls on the path.**

   Alternatively, switch to the Selection tool and drag the first of the three I-bars that appears, as shown in Figure 6-9. This allows you to freely move the text on that path. The path in Figure 6-9 was created with the Pen tool.

Flip the text to the other side of a path by clicking and dragging the I-bar under or over the path.

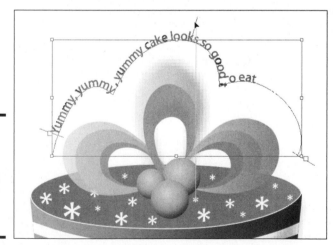

Figure 6-9: Use the Selection tool to drag the I-bar to adjust the text.

Creating text in a closed shape

Putting text inside a shape can add spunk to a layout. This feature allows you to custom-create a closed shape with the shape tools or the Pen tool and flow text into it. Follow these steps to add text inside a shape:

1. Create a closed shape — a circle or oval, for example.

2. Select the Type tool and cross over the path of the closed shape.

3. When you see the I-bar swell or become rounded, click inside the shape.

4. Start typing, and the text is contained inside the shape.

Text on the path of a closed shape

Perhaps you want text to run around the edge of a shape instead of inside it. Follow these steps to have text created on the path of a closed shape:

1. Create a closed shape, such as a circle.

2. Select the Type tool and cross over the path of the circle.

3. Don't click when you see the I-bar swell up; hold down the Alt (Windows) or Option (Mac) key instead.

   The icon changes into the squiggle I-bar you see when creating text on a path.

4. When the squiggle line appears, click.

5. Start typing, and the text flows around the path of the shape, as shown in Figure 6-10.

Figure 6-10:
Holding down the Alt or Option key flows text around a closed shape.

To change the origin of the text or move it around, use the alignment options in the Paragraph panel or switch to the Selection tool and drag the I-bar to a new location on the path.

You can drag the I-bar in and out of the shape to flip the text so that it appears on the outside or inside of the path.

Assigning Font Styles

After you have text on your page, you'll often want to change it to be more interesting than the typical 12-point Times font. Formatting text in Illustrator isn't only simple, but you can also do it multiple ways. In the following list, we name and define some basic type components (see Figure 6-11):

Figure 6-11: Components of type.

✦ **Font:** A complete set of characters, letters, and symbols of a particular typeface design.

✦ **X height:** The height of type, based on the height of the small *x* in that type family.

✦ **Kerning:** The space between two letters. Often used for letters in larger type that need to be pulled closer together, such as *W i*. Kern a little to slide the *i* in a little closer to the *W,* maybe even moving into the space occupied by the *W,* as shown in Figure 6-12. Kerning doesn't distort the text; it only increases or decreases the space between two letters.

✦ **Leading:** Space between the lines of text.

Figure 6-12: Before kerning (left) and after (right).

Wi Wi

✦ **Tracking:** The space between multiple letters. Designers like to use this technique to spread out words by increasing the space between letters. Adjusting the tracking doesn't distort text; it increases or decreases the space between the letters, as shown in Figure 6-13.

Figure 6-13:
Tracking
set at 0 (top)
and 300
(bottom).

AGI TRAINING

AGI TRAINING

Pretty good tracking and kerning has already been determined in most fonts. You don't need to bother with these settings unless you're tweaking text for a more customized look.

+ **Baseline:** The line that type sits on. The baseline doesn't include *descenders,* type that extends down, like lowercase *y* and *g.* You adjust the baseline for trademark signs or mathematical formulas, as shown in Figure 6-14.

Figure 6-14:
Adjust the
baseline for
superscript.

$$AGI \ TRAINING^{TM}$$

$$E = MC^2$$

**Book III
Chapter 6**

**Using Type
in Illustrator**

The keyboard shortcuts for type shown in Table 6-1 work with Adobe Illustrator, InDesign, and Photoshop.

Table 6-1	Keyboard Shortcuts for Type	
Command	*Windows*	*Mac*
Align left, right, or center	Shift+Ctrl+L, R, or C	Shift+⌘+L, R, or C
Justify	Shift+Ctrl+J	Shift+⌘+J
Insert soft return	Shift+Enter	Shift+Return
Reset horizontal scale to 100 percent	Shift+Ctrl+X	Shift+⌘+X
Increase or decrease point size	Shift+Ctrl+> or <	Shift+⌘+> or <
Increase or decrease leading	Alt+↑ or ↓	Option+↑ or ↓

(continued)

Command	Windows	Mac
Set leading to the font size	Double-click the leading icon in the Character panel	Double-click the leading icon in the Character panel
Reset tracking or kerning to 0	Alt+Ctrl+Q	Option+⌘+Q
Add or remove space *(kerning)* between two characters	Alt+→ or ←	Option+→ or ←
Add or remove space *(kerning)* between characters by 5 times the increment value	Alt+Ctrl+→ or ←	Option+⌘+→ or ←
Add or remove space *(kerning)* between selected words	Alt+← or →	Option+← or →
Add or remove space *(kerning)* between words by 5 times the increment value	Shift+Alt+Ctrl+\ or Backspace	Shift+Option+⌘+\ or Backspace
Increase or decrease baseline shift	Alt+Shift+↑ or ↓	Option+Shift+↑ or ↓

Using the Character Panel

To visualize changes you're making to text and to see characteristics that are already selected, choose Window➪Type➪Character or press Ctrl+T (Windows) or ⌘+T (Mac), which opens the Character panel. Click the triangle in the upper right corner to see a panel menu of additional options. Choose Show Options, and additional type attributes appear, such as baseline shift, underline, and strikethrough.

Pressing Ctrl+T (Windows) or ⌘+T (Mac) is a toggle switch to either show or hide the Character panel. If you don't see the Character panel appear at first, you may have hidden it by pressing the keyboard shortcut. Just try it again.

The following list explains the options in the Character panel (see Figure 6-15):

✦ **Font:** Pick the font you want to use from this drop-down list.

In the Windows version, you can click and drag across the font name in the Character panel or Control panel, and press the up- or down-arrow key to automatically switch to the next font above or below on the font list. Do this while you have text selected to see the text change live!

Figure 6-15:
The Character panel shows additional options.

+ Set font style: Pick the style (for example, Bold, Italic, or Bold Italic) from this drop-down list. The choices here are limited by the fonts you have loaded. In other words, if you have only Times regular loaded in your system, you don't have the choice to bold or italicize it.

+ Type size: Choose the size of the type in this combo box. Average readable type is 12-point; headlines can vary from 18 points and up.

+ Leading: Select how much space you want between the lines of text in this combo box. Illustrator uses the professional typesetting method of including the type size in the total leading. In other words, if you have 12-point and want it double-spaced, set the leading at 24 points.

+ Kerning: Use this combo box by placing the cursor between two letters. Increase the amount by clicking the up arrow or by typing a value to push the letters farther apart from each other; decrease the spacing between the letters by typing a lower value, even negative numbers, or by clicking the down arrow.

+ Tracking: Use the Tracking combo box by selecting multiple letters and increasing or decreasing the space between them all at once by clicking the up or down arrows or by typing a positive or negative value.

+ Horizontal scale: Distort selected text by stretching it horizontally. Enter a positive number to increase the size of the letters; enter a negative number to decrease the size.

+ Vertical scale: Distort selected text vertically. Enter a positive number to increase the size of the letters; enter a negative number to decrease the size.

Using horizontal or vertical scaling to make text look like condensed type often doesn't give good results. When you distort text, the nice thick and thin characteristics of the typeface also become distorted and can produce weird effects.

+ Baseline shift: Use baseline shift for trademark signs and mathematical formulas that require selected characters to be moved above or below the baseline.

+ Character rotation: Rotate just the selected text by entering an angle in this text field or by clicking the up or down arrows.

**Book III
Chapter 6**

**Using Type
in Illustrator**

✦ **Rotate:** Choose to rotate selected text on any angle.

✦ **Underline and strikethrough:** These simple text attributes underline and strikethrough selected text.

✦ **Language:** Choose a language from this drop-down list. *Note:* The language you specify here is used by Illustrator's spell checker and hyphenation feature. We discuss these features in the later section "Text Utilities: Your Key to Efficiency."

Using the Control Panel

Use the Control panel to quickly access your Type tools and Type panels. Note in Figure 6-16 that when you have active text, hyperlinked text buttons allow you to quickly access panels, such as the Character and Paragraph panels. You can also use this Control panel as a quick and easy way to select the font, size, alignment, color, and transparency.

Figure 6-16: Control panel type functions.

Using the Paragraph Panel

Access the Paragraph panel quickly by clicking the Paragraph hyperlink in the Control panel or by choosing Window➪Type➪Paragraph. This panel, shown in Figure 6-17, has all the attributes that apply to an entire paragraph (such as alignment and indents, which we discuss in the next two sections, and hyphenation, which we discuss later in this chapter). For example, you can't flush left one word in a paragraph — when you click the Flush Left button, the entire paragraph flushes left. To see additional options in the Paragraph panel, click the triangle in the upper right corner of the panel (the panel menu) and choose Show Options.

Figure 6-17: Use this panel to open typographic controls that apply to paragraphs.

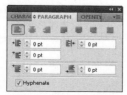

Alignment

You can choose any of the following alignment methods by clicking the appropriate button on the Paragraph panel:

✦ **Flush Left:** All text is flush to the left with a ragged edge on the right. This is the most common way to align text.

✦ **Center:** All text is centered.

✦ **Flush Right:** All text is flush to the right and ragged on the left.

✦ **Justify with the Last Line Aligned Left:** Right and left edges are both straight, with the last line left-aligned.

✦ **Justify with the Last Line Aligned Center:** Right and left edges are both straight, with the last line centered.

✦ **Justify with the Last Line Aligned Right:** Right and left edges are both straight, with the last line right-aligned.

✦ **Justify All Lines:** In this *forced justification* method, the last line is stretched the entire column width, no matter how short it is. This alignment is used in many publications, but it can create some awful results.

Indentation

You can choose from the following methods of indentation:

✦ **First Line Indent:** Indents the first line of every paragraph. In other words, every time you press the Enter (Windows) or Return (Mac) key, this spacing is created.

To avoid first-line indents and space after from occurring — if you just want to break a line in a specific place, for example — create a line break or a soft return by pressing Shift+Enter (Windows) or Shift+Return (Mac).

✦ **Right Indent:** Indents from the right side of the column of text.

✦ **Left Indent:** Indents from the left side of the column of text.

Use the Eyedropper tool to copy the character, paragraph, fill, and stroke attributes. Select the text you want, select the Eyedropper tool, and click the text once with the attributes you want to apply to the selected text.

By default, the Eyedropper affects all attributes of a type selection, including appearance attributes. To customize the attributes affected by these tools, double-click the Eyedropper tool to open the Eyedropper dialog box.

Text Utilities: Your Key to Efficiency

After you have text in an Illustrator document, you may need to perform various tasks within that text, such as search for a word to replace with another word, check your spelling and grammar, save and create your own styles, or change the case of a block of text. You're in luck because Illustrator provides various text utilities that enable you to easily and efficiently perform all these otherwise tedious tasks. In the following sections, we give you a quick tour of these utilities.

Find and Replace

Generally, artwork created in Illustrator isn't text heavy, but the fact that Illustrator has a Find and Replace feature can be a huge help. Use the Find and Replace dialog box (choose Edit⇨Find and Replace) to search for words that need to be changed, such as changing Smyth to Smith, or to locate items that may be difficult to find otherwise. This feature works much like all other search-and-replace methods.

Spell checker

Can you believe there was a time when Illustrator didn't have a spell checker? Thankfully, it does now — and its simple design makes it easy to use.

To use the spell checker, choose Edit⇨Check Spelling and then click the Start button in the dialog box that appears. The spell checker works much like the spell checker in Microsoft Word or other popular applications: When a misspelled word is found, you're offered a list of replacements. You can choose to fix that instance, fix all instances, ignore the misspelling, or add the word to the dictionary.

If you click the arrow to the left of Options, you can set other specifications, such as whether you want to look for letter case issues or have the spell checker note repeated words.

Note: The spell checker uses whatever language you specify in the Character panel. We discuss this panel in the earlier section "Using the Character Panel."

If you work in a specialized industry that uses loads of custom words, save yourself time by choosing Edit⇨Edit Custom Dictionary and then adding your own words. We recommend that you do so before you're ready to spell check a document so that the spell checker doesn't flag the custom words later (which slows you down).

The Hyphenation feature

Nothing is worse than trying to read severely hyphenated copy. Most designers either use hyphenation as little as possible or avoid it altogether by turning off the Hyphenation feature.

Here are a few things you should know about customizing your hyphenation settings if you decide to use this feature:

✦ **Turning the Hyphenation feature on or off:** Activate or deactivate the feature in the Hyphenation dialog box (see Figure 6-18); open this dialog box by choosing Window⇨Type⇨Paragraph, clicking the arrow in the upper right corner of the Paragraph panel to access the panel menu, and then choosing Hyphenation from the list of options that appears. If you won't use the Hyphenation feature, turn it off by deselecting the Hyphenation check box at the top of the Hyphenation dialog box.

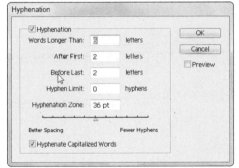

Figure 6-18: Customizing hyphenation settings.

You can also simply click the Paragraph hyperlink in the Control panel to access the Paragraph panel.

✦ **Setting specifications in the Hyphenation dialog box:** Set specifications in the dialog box that determine the length of words to hyphenate, the number of hyphens to be used in a single document, whether to hyphenate capitalized words, and how words should be hyphenated. The Before Last setting is useful, for example, if you don't want to have a word, such as *liquidated* hyphenated as *liquidat-ed.* Type **3** in the Before Last text field and Illustrator won't hyphenate words if it leaves only two letters on the next line.

✦ **Setting the Hyphenation Limit and Hyphenation Zone:** They're not diets or worlds in another dimension — the Hyphenation Limit setting enables you to limit the number of hyphens in a row. For example, type **2** in the Hyphenation Limit text field so that you never see more than two hyphenated words in a row. The Hyphenation Zone text field enables you to set up an area of hyphenation based on a measurement. For example, you can specify 1 inch to allow for only one hyphenation every inch. You can also use the slider to determine whether you want better spacing or fewer hyphens. This slider works only with the Single-Line Composer (the default).

The Find Font feature

If you work in production, you'll love the Find Font feature, which enables you to list all fonts in a file that contains text and then search for and replace fonts (including the font's type style) by name. You do so from the Find Font dialog box (see Figure 6-19), opened by choosing Type⇨Find Font. Select the font you want to replace from the Fonts in Document list. Next, select a font from the Replace with Font From list. Note that the font must already appear in the document. Click the Change button to replace the font (or click the Change All button to replace all instances of the font) and then click OK. That's it!

Figure 6-19: Use the Find Font dialog box to find and replace typefaces.

This cool feature enables you to replace fonts with fonts from the current working document or from your entire system. Select System from the Replace with Font From drop-down list to choose from all fonts loaded in your system.

The Change Case feature

Doesn't it drive you crazy when you type an entire paragraph before discovering that you somehow pressed the Caps Lock key? Fix it fast by selecting the text, choosing Type➪Change Case, and then choosing one of these options:

✦ **Uppercase:** Makes the selected text all uppercase

✦ **Lowercase:** Makes the selected text all lowercase

✦ **Title Case:** Capitalizes the first letter in each word

✦ **Sentence Case:** Capitalizes just the first letter in selected sentences

In Illustrator CS5, you use the same type engine used by InDesign for high-quality text control. You're working, as a default, in what's referred to as Single-Line Composer. Select Single or Every Line composer from the Paragraph panel menu.

The options include

✦ **Single-Line Composer:** Useful if you prefer to have manual control over how lines break. In fact, this method had been in place in the past. The Single-Line Composer option doesn't take the entire paragraph into consideration when expanding letter space and word spacing, so justified text can sometimes look odd in its entire form (see Figure 6-19).

✦ **Every-Line Composer:** A professional way of setting text; many factors are taken into account as far as spacing is concerned, and spacing is based on the entire paragraph. With this method, you see few spacing issues that create strange effects, such as the ones on the left in Figure 6-20.

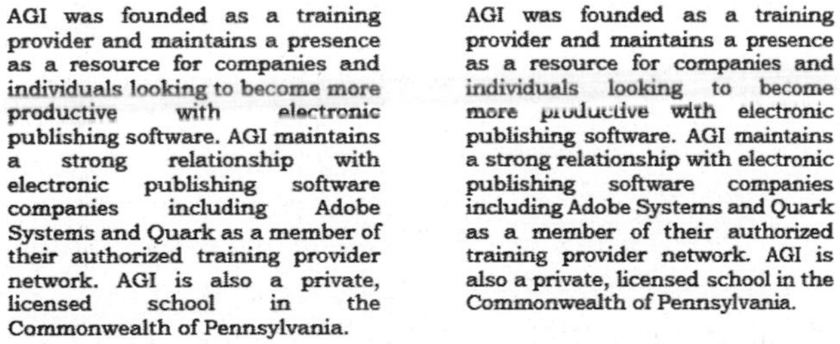

Figure 6-20:
Single-Line
Composer
(left) and
Every-Line
Composer
(right).

AGI was founded as a training provider and maintains a presence as a resource for companies and individuals looking to become more productive with electronic publishing software. AGI maintains a strong relationship with electronic publishing software companies including Adobe Systems and Quark as a member of their authorized training provider network. AGI is also a private, licensed school in the Commonwealth of Pennsylvania.

AGI was founded as a training provider and maintains a presence as a resource for companies and individuals looking to become more productive with electronic publishing software. AGI maintains a strong relationship with electronic publishing software companies including Adobe Systems and Quark as a member of their authorized training provider network. AGI is also a private, licensed school in the Commonwealth of Pennsylvania.

Text styles

A *text style* is a saved set of text attributes, such as font and size. Creating text styles keeps you consistent and saves you time by enabling you to efficiently implement changes in one step rather than have to select the text attributes for each instance of that style of text (say, a heading or caption).

So when you're finally happy with the way your headlines appear and how the body copy looks or when your boss asks whether the body copy can be a smidgen smaller (hmm, how much is a smidgen?), you can confidently answer, "Sure!"

If you've created styles, changing a text attribute is simple. What's more, the change is applied at once to all text using that style. Otherwise, you would have to make the attribute change to every occurrence of body text, which could take a long time if your text is spread out.

Illustrator offers two types of text styles:

✦ **Character:** Saves attributes for individual selected text. If you want just the word *New* in a line of text to be red, 20-point Arial, you can save it as a character style. Then, when you apply it, the attributes apply to only the selected text (and not to the entire line or paragraph).

✦ **Paragraph:** Saves attributes for an entire paragraph. A span of text is considered a paragraph until it reaches a hard return or paragraph break. Note that pressing Shift+Enter (Windows) or Shift+Return (Mac) is considered a soft return, and paragraph styles continue to apply beyond the soft return.

You can create character and paragraph styles in many ways, but we show you the easiest and most direct methods in the following subsections.

Creating character styles

Create a character style when you want individual sections of text to be treated differently from other text in the paragraph. So rather than repeatedly apply a style manually, you create and implement a character style. To do so, open a document containing text and follow these steps:

1. **Set up text with the text attributes you want included in the character style in the Character and Paragraph panels and then choose Window⇨Type⇨Character Styles.**

The Character Styles panel opens.

2. **Select the text from Step 1 and Alt-click (Windows) or Option-click (Mac) the New Style button (the dog-eared page icon) at the bottom of the Character Styles panel.**

3. **In the Character Styles Options dialog box that appears, name your style and click OK.**

Illustrator records which attributes have been applied already to the selected text and builds a style from them.

4. **Create another text area by choosing Select⇨Deselect and using the Type tool to drag out a new text area.**

   We discuss using the Type tool in the earlier section "Creating text areas."

5. **Change the font and size to dramatically different choices from your saved style and type some text.**

6. **Select some (not all) of the new text and then Alt-click (Windows) or Option-click (Mac) the style name in the Character Styles panel.**

   Alt-click (Windows) or Option-click (Mac) to eliminate any attributes that weren't part of the saved style. The attributes of the saved character style are applied to the selected text.

When you create a new panel item (any panel) in Adobe Illustrator, InDesign, or Photoshop, we recommend that you get in the habit of Alt-clicking (Windows) or Option-clicking (Mac) the New Style button. This habit allows you to name the item (style, layer, or swatch, for example) while adding it to the panel.

Creating paragraph styles

Paragraph styles include attributes that are applied to an entire paragraph. What constitutes a paragraph is all text that falls before a hard return (you create a hard return when you press Enter in Windows or Return on the Mac), so this could be one line of text for a headline or ten lines in a body text paragraph.

To create a paragraph style, open a document that contains text or open a new document and add text to it; then follow these steps:

1. **Choose Window⇨Type⇨Paragraph Styles to open the Paragraph Styles panel.**

2. **Find a paragraph of text that has the same text attributes throughout it and put your cursor anywhere in that paragraph.**

   You don't even have to select the whole paragraph!

3. **Alt-click (Windows) or Option-click (Mac) the Create New Style button (the dog-eared icon at the bottom of the Paragraph panel) to create a new paragraph style; give your new style a name.**

   Your new style now appears in the Paragraph Styles panel list of styles.

4. **Create a paragraph of text elsewhere in your document and make its attributes different from the text in Step 2.**

Book III
Chapter 6

Using Type
in Illustrator

5. Put your cursor anywhere in the new paragraph and Alt-click (Windows) or Option-click (Mac) your named style in the Paragraph Styles panel.

The attributes from the style are applied to the entire paragraph.

Updating styles

When you use existing text to build styles, reselect the text and assign the style. In other words, if you put the cursor in the original text whose attributes were saved as a style, it doesn't have a style assigned to it in the Styles panel. Assign the style by selecting the text or paragraph and clicking the appropriate style listed in the Styles panel. By doing so, you ensure that any future updates to that style apply to that original text and to all other instances.

To update a style, simply select its name in either the Character or Paragraph Styles panel. Choose Options from the panel menu, which you access by clicking the arrow in the upper right corner of the panel. In the resulting dialog box (see Figure 6-21), make changes by clicking the main attribute on the left and then updating the choices on the right. After you do so, all tagged styles are updated.

Figure 6-21: Updating a paragraph style.

 Documents created in older versions of Adobe Illustrator (Version 10 or earlier) contain *legacy text,* which is text using the older text engine. When these files are opened, you see a warning dialog box. If you click the Update button, any text on the document will most likely reflow, causing line breaks, leading, and other types of spacing to change.

Click the OK button to update the file after it's opened to lock down the text. If necessary, you can use the Type tool to click a selected text area to update only the contained text. Another Warning dialog box appears that gives you the opportunity to update selected text, copy the text object, or cancel the text tool selection. This method is the best way to see which changes are occurring so that you can catch any spacing issues right off the bat. See Figure 6-22 for samples of the three options in the warning dialog box.

Figure 6-22:
Original text (left), updated text (middle), and text object copied (right).

tia della minestrone, i ravioli, e la farinata.
    La città all'ovest della Liguria é San
Remo, che é accanto al Monaco. San
Remo é famosa per il museo di pasta e la festa di musica. La città
all'est della Liguria é La
Spezia, che é conosciu-
ta per una base
navale. La Spezia é
vicino à Carrara, il
posto   dové
Michelangelo prese
la sua marma.
    Da Genova si
andrà in barca alle
Cinque Terre, una zona
che non é possibile rag-

noce, e il pesce. E anche la regione nattia
della minestrone, i ravioli, e la farinata.
    La città all'ovest della Liguria é San
Remo, che é accanto al Monaco. San
Remo é famosa per il museo di pasta e la
festa di musica. La città all'est della Liguria é La Spezia, che é conosciuta
per una base navale. La
Spezia é vicino à Carrara, il
posto dové Michelan-
gelo prese la sua
marma.
    Da Genova si andrà
in barca alle Cinque
Terre, una zona che non
é possibile raggiungere in
machina; si deve andare o in
barca o in treno. Le Cinque Terre

noce, e il pesce. E anche la regione nattia
della minestrone, i ravioli, e la farinata.
    La città all'ovest della Liguria é San
Remo, che é accanto al Monaco. San
Remo é famosa per il museo di pasta e la
festa di musica. La città all'est della Liguria é La Spezia, che é conosciuta
per una base navale. La
Spezia é vicino à Carrara, il
posto dové Michelan-
gelo prese la sua
marma.   dové
Vi Da Genova si andrà
in barca alle Cinque
Terre, una zona che non
é possibile raggiungere in
machina; si deve andare o in
barca o in treno. Le Cinque Terre

If you click Copy the Text Object, you can use the underlying locked copy to adjust the new text flow to match the old. Throw away the legacy text layer by clicking and dragging it to the trash icon in the Layers panel, or click the visibility eye icon to the left of the Legacy Text layer to hide it when you're finished.

Chapter 7: Organizing Your Illustrations

In This Chapter

✔ Using rulers

✔ Using ruler and custom guides

✔ Working with the Transform panel for placement

✔ Changing ruler origin

✔ Rearranging, hiding, and locking objects

✔ Masking objects

*Y*ou can know about all the neat special effects in Illustrator, but if you have no strong organization skills, you can become exasperated when things just don't work as you expect them to. In this chapter, we focus on a few organizational tricks of the trade.

Setting Ruler Increments

Using rulers to help accurately place objects in an illustration sounds simple (and it is), but not knowing how to effectively use the rulers in Illustrator can drive you over the edge.

To view rulers in Illustrator, choose View➪Rulers➪Show Rulers or press Ctrl+R (Windows) or ⌘+R (Mac). When the rulers appear, their default measurement setting is the point (or whichever measurement increment was last set up in the preferences).

To change the ruler increment to the measurement system you prefer, use one of these methods:

✦ Create a new document and select a measurement unit in the New Document dialog box.

✦ Right-click (Windows) or Control-click (Mac) the horizontal or vertical ruler and pick a measurement increment.

✦ Choose Edit➪Preferences➪Units (Windows) or Illustrator➪Preferences➪ Units and Display Performance (Mac) to open the Preferences dialog box.

Change the ruler unit only by using the General drop-down list in the Preferences dialog box. If you change the measurement unit on the Stroke and Type tabs, you can end up with 12-*inch* type rather than that dainty 12-*point* type you were expecting.

Setting general preferences changes them in all future documents.

✦ Choose File➪Document Setup to change the measurement unit for only the document you're working on.

Using Guides

Guides can help you create more accurate illustrations. After a guide is created, you can turn its visibility off or one quickly with the View menu. You can use two kinds of guides in Illustrator:

✦ **Ruler guides:** These straight-line guides are created by clicking the ruler and dragging out to the artboard.

✦ **Custom guides:** These guides, created from Illustrator objects such as shapes or paths, are helpful for replicating the exact angle of a path, as shown in Figure 7-1.

Figure 7-1:
Turn selected paths and shapes into custom guides.

Creating a ruler guide

A ruler guide is the easiest guide to create: Click the vertical or horizontal ruler anywhere and drag it to the artboard, as shown in Figure 7-2. By default, the horizontal ruler creates horizontal guides (no kidding), and the vertical ruler creates vertical guides. You can press Alt+drag (Windows) or Option+drag (Mac) to change the orientation of the guide. The vertical ruler then creates a horizontal guide, and the horizontal ruler then creates a vertical guide.

Figure 7-2:
Click the
ruler and
drag out a
guide.

Creating a custom guide

Create a custom guide by selecting a path or a shape and choosing View⇨
Guides⇨Make Guides. The selected object turns into a nonprinting guide.
Changing a path into a guide isn't a permanent change. Choose View⇨
Guides⇨Release Guides to turn guides back into paths.

Using the Transform Panel for Placement

Placing shapes and paths precisely where you want them can be difficult
even if you have steady hands. Save yourself some aggravation by using
the Transform panel to perform such tasks as scaling and rotating objects.
On a more practical note, however, you can type x, y coordinates on the
Transform panel and then position objects exactly where you want them.

In Adobe Illustrator and InDesign, the Reference Point Indicator icon is on
the left side of the Transform panel. Click the handle of the icon to change
the point of reference. To measure from the upper left corner, click the indicator on the handle there. If you want to know the exact center of an object,
click the center point in the indicator. The point of reference is the spot on
the object that falls at the x, y coordinates, which specify the placement of
the selected object:

> ✦ **x coordinate:** From left to right
>
> ✦ **y coordinate:** From top to bottom

**Book III
Chapter 7**

**Organizing Your
Illustrations**

Changing the Ruler Origin

In Adobe Illustrator, InDesign, and Photoshop, you can change the *ruler
origin,* which defines the start of a printing area of an image.

To change the ruler origin, follow these steps:

1. **Move the pointer to the upper left corner of the rulers where the
rulers intersect, as shown in Figure 7-3.**

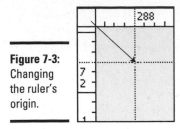

Figure 7-3:
Changing
the ruler's
origin.

2. **Drag the pointer to the spot where you want the new ruler origin.**

   While you drag, a cross hair in the window and in the rulers indicates
   where the new ruler origin will be placed.

   You can restore the original ruler origin by double-clicking the ruler
   intersection.

Thinking about Object Arrangement

Just like the stacks of paper on your desk, new objects in Illustrator are
placed on top of existing objects. Change their order by choosing the
Object⇨Arrange menu options.

The easiest choices are to bring an object to the front or send it to the back.
The results of sending forward or backward can be unnerving if you don't
know the exact order in which objects were created. The illustration in
Figure 7-4 shows that we rearranged objects by using four available
choices. Figure 7-5 shows the result of each choice.

Figure 7-4:
Objects in
their original
positions.

To change the stacking order, select the object (or objects) whose placement you want to change and then choose one of these commands:

✦ **Object⇨Arrange⇨Bring to Front:** Moves the selected object to the top
   of the painting order. In Figure 7-5a, the square is brought in front by
   using the Bring to Front command.

✦ **Object⇨Arrange⇨Bring Forward:** Moves a selected object in front of the object created just before it or one level closer to the front. In Figure 7-5b, the circle is moved in front of the square by using the Bring Forward command.

✦ **Object⇨Arrange⇨Send Backward:** Moves a selected object so that it falls under the object created just before it or one level back. In Figure 7-5c, the triangle is sent backward so that it's just under the circle.

✦ **Object⇨Arrange⇨Send to Back:** Moves a selected object to the bottom of the painting order. In Figure 7-5d, the triangle is placed on the bottom by using the Send to Back command.

Figure 7-5:
Rearranging
objects.

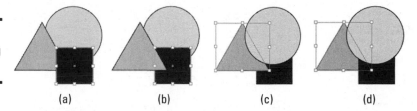

(a)   (b)   (c)   (d)

Hiding Objects

Seasoned Illustrator users love the Hide command. Use it when the object you want to select is stuck behind something else or when you need to select one object and another repeatedly activates instead.

A good opportunity to use the Hide command is when you're creating text inside a shape. In Chapter 6 of this minibook, we show you that as soon as you turn a shape into a text area, the fill and stroke attributes turn into None. Follow these steps to hide a shape:

1. **Create a shape.**

For this example, we created an ellipse.

2. **Click the Fill color box at the bottom of the Illustrator Tools panel and then choose Window⇨Swatches.**

The Swatches panel appears.

3. **In the Swatches panel, choose a color for the fill.**

In this example, yellow is selected. The stroke doesn't matter; this one is set to None.

Clicking a shape with the Type tool converts the shape to a text area and converts the fill and stroke to None. To have a colored shape remain, you must hide a copy.

4. **After selecting a colored shape, choose Edit⇨Copy; alternatively, you can press Ctrl+C (Windows) or ⌘+C (Mac).**

   This step makes a copy of your shape.

5. **Choose Edit⇨Paste in Back or press Ctrl+B (Windows) or ⌘+B (Mac).**

   This step puts a copy of your shape exactly in back of the original.

6. **Choose Object⇨Hide or press Ctrl+3 (Windows) or ⌘+3 (Mac).**

   The copy of the shape is now hidden; what you see is your original shape.

7. **Switch to the Type tool by selecting it in the Tools panel or pressing T.**

8. **Use the cursor to cross over the edge of the shape and change it to the Area Type tool.**

   You use the Area Type tool to type text in a shape.

9. **When you see the type insertion cursor swell up, as shown in Figure 7-6, click the edge of the shape.**

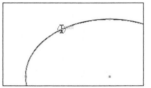

Figure 7-6:
The type insertion cursor on the edge of a shape.

The insertion point is now blinking inside the shape, and the fill and stroke attributes of the shape have been changed to None.

10. **Type some text, as shown in Figure 7-7.**

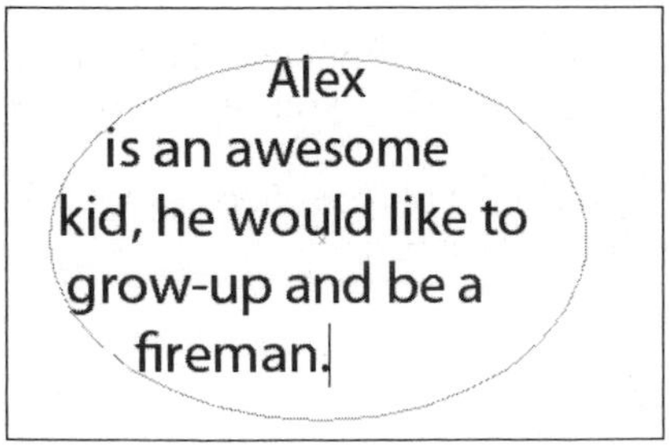

Alex
is an awesome
kid, he would like to
grow-up and be a
fireman.

Figure 7-7:
Type directly in the shape.

11. **When you finish entering text, choose Object⇨Show All or press Ctrl+Alt+3 (Windows) or ⌘+Option+3 (Mac).**

The colored shape reappears with the text in the middle of it, as shown in Figure 7-8.

Alex
is an **awesome
kid**, he would like to
grow-up and be a
fireman.

Use the Hide command anytime you want to tuck away objects for later use. We promise: Nothing hidden in Illustrator will be lost. Just use the Show All command and any hidden objects are revealed, exactly where you left them. (Too bad the Show All command can't reveal where you left your car keys!)

Locking Objects

Being able to lock items is handy when you're building an illustration. The Lock command not only locks down objects you don't want to change but also drives anyone crazy who tries to edit your files. In fact, we mention locking mainly to help preserve your sanity. Sometimes you need to make simple adjustments to another designer's artwork and can't, unless the objects are first unlocked. Follow these instructions:

✦ **To lock an object:** Choose Object⇨Lock or press Ctrl+2 (Windows) or ⌘+2 (Mac) to lock an object so that you can't select it, move it, or change its attributes.

✦ **To unlock an object:** Choose Object⇨Unlock All or press Ctrl+Alt+2 (Windows) or ⌘+Option+2 (Mac). Then you can make changes to it.

You can also lock and hide objects with layers. See Chapter 8 in this mini-book for more information about using layers.

Creating a Clipping Mask

Creating a clipping mask may sound complex, but it's easy and highlights some topics in this chapter, such as arranging objects. Similar to peering through a hole in a piece of paper to the objects underneath it, a *clipping mask* allows a topmost object to define the selected shapes underneath it; with a clipping mask, however, the area around the defining shape is transparent, as shown in Figure 7-9.

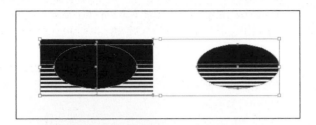

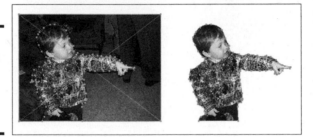

Figure 7-9:
Some items
using the
clipping
mask
feature.

You may recall what a film mask looks like — it's black to block out the picture and clear where you want to view an image, as shown in Figure 7-10.

Figure 7-10:
A conven-
tional film
mask.

The clipping mask feature uses the same principle as the conventional film mask. It hides the area outside the mask area. To create a clipping mask, follow these steps:

1. **Choose File⇨Place to place an image.**

Masks work with objects created in Illustrator and with objects placed (scanned or otherwise imported) there.

2. **Create the item you want to use as a mask by using the Pen tool to create a shape or a closed path.**

   For example, in Figure 7-11, the circle is the mask. (The photo underneath it is the placed image from Step 1.) The circle is placed where the mask will be created. The shape's color, fill, and stroke values don't matter because they automatically change to None when you create a mask.

   Note: When creating a clipping mask, make sure that the object to be used as a mask is a closed shape and is at the top of the stacking order.

Figure 7-11: Position the mask shape over the object.

3. **Use the Selection tool to select the placed image and the shape.**

   Shift-click to add an object to the selection.

4. **Choose Object➪Clipping Mask➪Make.**

   Alternatively, you can use the keyboard shortcut Ctrl+7 (Windows) or ⌘+7 (Mac) to create the clipping mask.

   Ta-da! You created the clipping mask. Masked items are grouped, but you can use the Direct Selection tool to move the image or mask individually.

5. **To turn off the clipping mask, choose Object➪Clipping Mask➪Release.**

You can also use text as a clipping mask: Type a word and ensure that it's positioned over an image or another Illustrator object (or objects). Then select both the text and the object and choose Object➪Clipping Mask➪Make.

Creating a Clipping Path Using the New Draw Inside Button

You can use the Draw Inside button, new in Illustrator CS5, to create a clipping path. The button is at the bottom of the Tools panel. Just follow these steps:

1. Select your artwork and choose Edit➪Copy or Cut.

In Figure 7-12, the artwork to the right has been cut to fit into the star image.

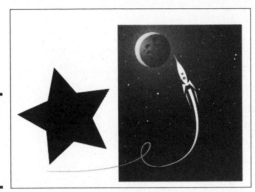

Figure 7-12: Select artwork and copy or paste it.

2. Select the artwork that you want to "paste into" existing artwork and then click the Draw Inside button.

3. Choose Edit➪Paste.

The artwork is pasted inside the shape, as shown in Figure 7-13.

After you have pasted your artwork, you can use the Direct Selection tool to reposition it.

Figure 7-13: Create a clipping path by using the Draw Inside button at the bottom of the Tools panel.

Chapter 8: Using Layers

In This Chapter

✔ **Working with layers**

✔ **Using layers for a selection**

✔ **Changing the stacking order of a layer**

✔ **Moving and cloning objects to another layer**

✔ **Hiding and locking layers**

This chapter shows you just how simple it is to use layers and how help-ful layers can be when you're producing complex artwork. Layers are similar to clear pages stacked on top of your artwork: You can place content (text, shapes, and other objects) on a layer, lift up a layer, remove a layer, hide and show layers, or lock a layer so that you can't edit its content. The incredible Layer feature can help you

✦ Organize the painting (stacking) order of objects.

✦ Activate objects that would otherwise be difficult to select by using either the Selection or Direct Selection tool.

✦ Lock items that you don't want to reposition or change.

✦ Hide items until you need them.

✦ Repurpose objects for artwork variations. For example, a company's business cards use the same logo and company address, but the name and contact information changes for each person. In this case, placing the logo and company address on one layer and the person's name and contact information on another layer lets you easily create a new busi-ness card by just changing the person's name.

Many Illustrator users don't take advantage of layers. Maybe these people don't understand the basic functions of layers or they think that layers are much more complicated than they are. After reading this chapter, you'll be able to take advantage of layers in Illustrator.

Unlike in Photoshop, layers in Illustrator don't unreasonably increase file size.

Creating New Layers

When you create a new Illustrator document, you automatically have one layer to start with. To understand how layers work, create a new file and then follow these steps to create new layers and put objects on them:

1. **If the Layers panel isn't already visible, choose Window⇨Layers.**

   The Layers panel appears. In Illustrator CS5, you see layer color bars to help identify selected objects and the layer they're on, as shown in Figure 8-1.

Figure 8-1:
The Layers panel.

In Figure 8-2, the Notes layer name is in italic because the creator double-clicked that layer (to open the Layer Options dialog box) and deselected the Print check box.

Figure 8-2:
You can double-click a layer to change its options.

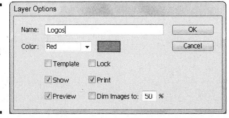

2. **Create a shape anywhere on the artboard.**

   The size of the shape doesn't matter, but make sure that it has a colored fill so that you can see it easily. For example, create a square.

3. **Click the Fill button in the Control panel and select any color for the shape from the Color Picker that appears, as shown in Figure 8-3.**

   The Fill button is the swatch with an arrow on the left side of the Control panel.

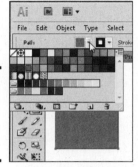

Figure 8-3: Select any color from the Fill Color Picker.

The blue handle color that appears on the active shape matches the blue color bar you see in the Layers panel on the left side of the layer name and the small selection square to the right of the radio button. The small selection square on the right disappears if you choose Select⊳ Deselect. You use that square to see which layer a selected object is on.

Notice in Figure 8-4 that you've added a shape to this layer, so an arrow appears to the left of the layer name. This arrow indicates that you now have a *sublayer,* which is essentially a layer within a layer. Click the arrow to expand the layer and show any sublayers nested underneath it; sublayers are automatically created when you add objects, which helps when you're making difficult selections.

Figure 8-4: Adding objects to a layer automatically creates sublayers.

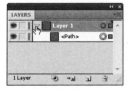

4. **Alt-click (Windows) or Option-click (Mac) the Create New Layer button at the bottom of the Layers panel to create a new layer.**

The Layer Options dialog box appears (see Figure 8-5), and you can use it to name a layer and change the selection color. You don't have to hold down the Alt or Option key when making a new layer, but if you don't, you don't have the opportunity to name the layer when you create it.

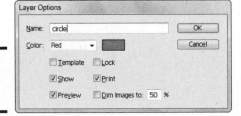

Figure 8-5: Creating a new layer.

5. **Enter a name for the new layer in the Name text box and click OK.**

   In Figure 8-5, we entered **circle** because it's the shape we add in Step 6.

   If you want to stay organized, you can name the original layer **square**, by double-clicking Layer 1. Just make sure that you click the circle layer again to make it the active layer.

   A new layer is added to the top of the stack in the Layers panel.

6. **Make a shape on the new layer and overlap the shape you created in Step 2 (see Figure 8-6).**

   We created a circle, shown in Figure 8-6.

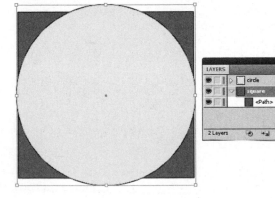

Figure 8-6: A circle on the new layer overlaps the square on its underlying layer.

7. **Change the fill color for your new shape.**

   Check out the selection handles: They change to a different color, indicating that you're on a different layer. The different handle colors are for organizational purposes only and aren't printed.

8. **Just to be different this time, choose New Layer from the panel menu.**

   The Layer Options dialog box appears.

9. **(Optional) In the Layer Options dialog box, change the color of the selection handles by selecting an option from the Color drop-down list.**

   You can also hide or lock the contents of the layer.

10. **Enter a name for this new layer in the Name text field, click OK, and then create a shape on it.**

    For the example shown in Figure 8-7, we entered **star** into the Name text box and used the Star tool to create a star on the new layer.

Figure 8-7:
Create a
new layer
using the
panel menu.

11. **Again, change the fill color of your newest shape so that it's different from the other shapes.**

12. **Use the Selection tool to move the new shape so that it overlaps the others slightly.**

You can open the Options dialog box for any existing layer by choosing Options for Layer (Named Layer) from the panel menu in the Layers panel, or by double-clicking on a layer in the Layers panel.

You've created new layers and now have a file that you can use to practice working with layers.

Using Layers for Selections

When you have a selected object on a layer, a color selection square appears to the right of the named layer. If you click the radio button directly to the right of the layer's name in the Layers panel, as shown in Figure 8-8, all objects are selected on that layer.

Figure 8-8:
Selecting
the entire
contents of
a layer.

Sublayers have their own radio buttons. If sublayers are visible, you can use the same technique to select objects that may be buried behind others.

If you think you'll be selecting sublayers frequently, double-click the default name and type a more descriptive name for that layer.

Changing the Layer Stacking Order

In Chapter 7 of this minibook, we tell you about the Object⇨Arrange feature in Illustrator; with layers, this process becomes slightly more complicated. Each layer has its own *painting order,* the order in which you see the layers. To move a layer (and thereby change the stacking order of the layers), click and drag that layer until you see the black insertion line where you want the layer to be moved.

As you add shapes to a layer, a sublayer is created, and it has its own little stacking order that's separate from other layers. In other words, if you choose to send an object to the back and it's on the top layer, it goes only to the back of that layer and is still in front of any objects on layers beneath it.

Understanding how the stacking order affects the illustration is probably the most confusing part about layers. Just remember that in order for an object to appear behind everything else, it has to be on the bottom layer (and at the bottom of all objects on that bottom layer); for an object to appear in front of everything else, it has to be on the topmost layer.

Moving and Cloning Objects

To move a selected object from one layer to another, click the small color-selection square (shown in Figure 8-9) to the right of the layer's radio button in the Layers panel, drag the object to the target layer, and release. That's all there is to moving an object from one layer to another.

Figure 8-9:
Drag the small square icon to move the selected object to another layer.

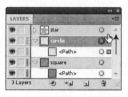

You can also *clone* an item, or make a copy of it while you move the copy to another layer. Clone an object by Alt+dragging (Windows) or Option+dragging (Mac) the color selection square to another layer. A plus sign appears while you drag (so you know that you're making a clone of the object). Release when you reach the cloned object's target layer.

Choose Paste Remembers Layers from the Layers panel to have Illustrator automatically remember which layer you copied an object from. No matter which layer is active, Illustrator always pastes the object back on the original layer it was copied from.

Hiding Layers

To the left of each layer in the Layers panel is an eye icon — a visibility toggle button. Simply clicking the eye icon hides the layer (the eye disappears, denoting that this layer is hidden). Click the empty square (where the eye icon was) to show the layer again.

Alt-click (Windows) or Option-click (Mac) an eye icon to hide all layers except the one you click; Alt-click (Windows) or Option-click (Mac) the eye icon to show all layers again.

**Book III
Chapter 8**

Using Layers

Ctrl-click (Windows) or ⌘-click (Mac) the eye icon to turn just the selected layer into Outline view. In Outline view, all you see are the outlines of the artwork with no stroke widths or fill colors. The rest of your artwork remains in Preview mode, with strokes and fills visible. This tricky technique is helpful when you're looking for stray points or need to close paths. Ctrl-click (Windows) or ⌘-click (Mac) the eye icon again to return the layer to Preview mode.

Locking Layers

Lock layers by clicking the empty square to the right of the Visibility (eye) icon. A padlock icon appears so that you know the layer is now locked. Locking a layer prevents you from making changes to the objects on that layer. Click the padlock to unlock the layer.

Chapter 9: Livening Up Illustrations with Color

In This Chapter

✔ Choosing a color mode

✔ Using the Swatches and Color panels

✔ Working with strokes and fills

✔ Changing the stroke width and type

✔ Saving and editing colors

✔ Discovering patterns

✔ Employing gradients and copying color attributes

✔ Exploring the Live Trace and Live Paint features

This chapter is all about making your brilliant illustrations come alive with color. We show you how to create new and edit existing colors, save custom colors that you create, create and use patterns and gradients, and even apply color attributes to many different shapes.

Choosing a Color Mode

Every time you create a new file, you choose a profile. This profile determines, among other things, in which color mode to create your document. Typically, anything related to Web, mobile, or video is in RGB mode, and the print profile is in CMYK. You can also simply choose Basic CMYK or Basic RGB. Here are the differences between the color modes:

✦ **Basic CMYK (Cyan, Magenta, Yellow, and Black):** Use this mode if you're taking your illustration to a professional printer and the files will be separated into cyan, magenta, yellow, and black plates for printing.

✦ **Basic RGB (Red, Green, Blue):** Use this mode if your final destination is the Web, a mobile device, a video player, a color copier or desktop printer, or a screen presentation.

The decision you make affects the premade swatches, brushes, and styles and a slew of other choices in Adobe Illustrator.

You can change the color mode at any time without losing information by choosing File➪Document Color Mode.

Using the Swatches Panel

Accessing color from the Control panel is probably the easiest way to make color choices: You can use the Fill and Stroke drop-down lists to quickly access the Swatches panel, shown in Figure 9-1, and at the same time ensure that the color is applied to either the fill or stroke. How many times have you mixed up colors and assigned the stroke color to the fill or vice versa?

Figure 9-1: Use these buttons to quickly access color options.

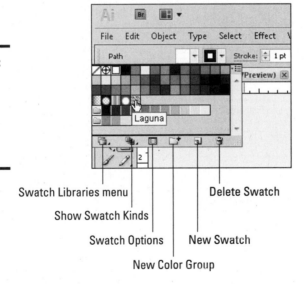

Swatch Libraries menu

Show Swatch Kinds

Swatch Options

New Color Group

Delete Swatch

New Swatch

You can also access the Swatches panel, which you open by choosing Window➪Swatches. Although limited in choice, its basic colors, patterns, and gradients are ready to go. You can use the buttons at the bottom of the Swatches panel (refer to Figure 9-1) to quickly open color libraries, select kinds of colors to view, access swatch options, create color groups, add new swatches, and delete selected swatches.

You may notice some odd color swatches — for example, the cross hair and the diagonal line.

The cross hair represents the Registration color. Use this swatch only when creating custom crop marks or printer marks. The Registration color looks black, but it's created from 100 percent of all colors. This way, when artwork is separated, the crop mark appears on all color separations.

 The diagonal line represents None. Use this option if you want no fill or stroke.

Applying Color to the Fill and Stroke

Illustrator objects are created from *fills* (the inside) and *strokes* (border or path). Look at the bottom of the Tools panel for the Fill and Stroke color boxes. If you're applying color to the fill, the Fill color box must be forward in the Tools panel. If you're applying color to the stroke, the Stroke color box must be forward.

Table 9-1 lists keyboard shortcuts that can be a tremendous help to you when applying colors to fills and strokes.

Table 9-1	Color Keyboard Shortcuts
Function	*Keyboard Shortcut*
Switch the Fill or Stroke color box position	X
Inverse the Fill and the Stroke color boxes	Shift+X
Default (black stroke, white fill)	D
None	/
Last color used	<
Last gradient used	>
Color Picker	Double-click the Fill or Stroke color box

**Book III
Chapter 9**

**Livening Up
Illustrations
with Color**

 Try this trick: Drag a color from the Swatches panel to the Fill or Stroke color box. This action applies the color to the color box that you dragged to. It doesn't matter which is forward!

To apply a fill color to an existing shape, drag the swatch directly to the shape. Select a swatch, hold down Alt+Shift+Ctrl (Windows) or Option+Shift+⌘ (Mac), and drag a color to a shape to apply that color to the stroke.

Changing the Width and Type of a Stroke

Access the Stroke panel by clicking the Stroke hyperlink in the Control panel. In the Stroke panel, shown in Figure 9-2, you can choose *caps* (the end of a line), *joins* (the end points of a path or dash), and the *miter limit* (the length of a point). The Stroke panel also enables you to turn a path into a dashed line.

Figure 9-2:
The Align Stroke options.

In the Stroke panel options, you can choose to align the stroke on the center (default) of a path, the inside of a path, and the outside of a path. Figure 9-3 shows the results.

Figure 9-3:
The Align Stroke options affect the placement of the stroke.

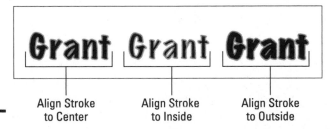

| Align Stroke
to Center | Align Stroke
to Inside | Align Stroke
to Outside |

This feature is especially helpful when stroking outlined text. Refer to Figure 9-3 to compare text with the traditional centered stroke, as compared to the new option for aligning the stroke outside of a path.

You can't adjust the alignment of a stroke on text unless you change the text to outlines first. Select the Selection tool and choose Type⇨Create Outlines to enable the Align Stroke options.

You can also customize the following aspects of a stroke from the Stroke panel by clicking the buttons we describe:

✦ **Cap Options:** The endpoints of a path or dash

- *Butt Cap:* Makes the ends of stroked lines square
- *Round Cap:* Makes the ends of stroked lines semicircular
- *Projecting Cap:* Makes the ends of stroked lines square and extends half the line width beyond the end of the line

✦ **Join Options:** How corner points appear

- *Miter Join:* Makes stroked lines with pointed corners
- *Round Join:* Makes stroked lines with rounded corners
- *Bevel Join:* Makes stroked lines with squared corners

✦ **Dashed Lines:** Regularly spaced lines, based on values you set

To create a dashed line, specify a dash sequence by entering the lengths of dashes and the gaps between them in the Dash Pattern text fields (see Figure 9-4). The numbers entered are repeated in sequence so that after you set up the pattern, you don't need to fill in all the text fields. In other words, if you want an evenly spaced dashed stroke, just type the same number in the first and second text fields and all dashes and spaces will be the same length (say, 12 points). Change that number to 12 in the first text field and 24 in the next to create a larger space between dashes.

**Book III
Chapter 9**

Livening Up
Illustrations
with Color

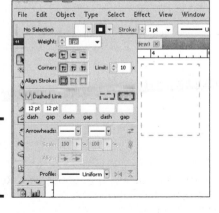

Figure 9-4:
Setting up
a dashed
stroke.

✦ **Arrowhead:** Arrowheads have been surprisingly difficult for new users to locate and use in previous versions of Illustrator. In CS5, you can just open the Stroke dialog box, shown in Figure 9-5, and use simple drop-down menus to set start and end times to your arrowhead as well as the scale.

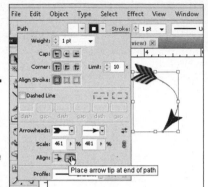

Figure 9-5: Arrowheads are easy to find and use in the Stroke dialog box.

Using the Color Panel

The Color panel (choose Window➪Color) offers another method for choosing color. You must custom-pick a color using values on the color ramp. You see as a default only the *color ramp* — the large color well spanning the panel. If you don't see all color options, choose Show Options from the Color panel's panel menu (click the triangle in the upper-right corner to access the panel menu).

If you ever want to create tints of a CMYK color but aren't quite sure how to adjust individual color sliders, just hold down the Shift key while adjusting the color slider of any color. Then watch as all colors move to a relative position at the same time!

As shown in Figure 9-6, the panel menu offers many other choices. Even though you may be in RGB or CMYK color mode, you can still choose to build colors in Grayscale, RGB, HSB (Hue, Saturation, Brightness), CMYK, or Web Safe RGB. Choosing Invert or Complement from the panel menu reverses the color of the selected object or changes it to a complementary color, respectively. You can also choose the Fill and Stroke color boxes in the upper left corner of the Color panel.

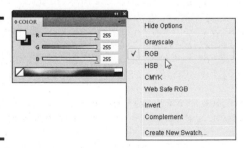

Figure 9-6: Different color models are available in the Color panel.

You see the infamous cube-and-exclamation-point in the Color panels in most Adobe software. The cube warns you that the color you've selected isn't one of the 216 nondithering, Web-safe colors, and the exclamation point warns you that your color isn't within the CMYK print gamut. In other words, if you see the exclamation point in the Color panel, don't expect the cool electric blue you see onscreen to print correctly — it may print as dark purple!

Click the cube or exclamation point symbols when you see them to select the closet color in the Web safe or CMYK color gamut.

Saving Colors

Saving colors not only keeps you consistent but also makes edits and changes to colors easier in the future. Any time you build a color, drag it from the Color panel to the Swatches panel to save it as a color swatch for future use. You can also select an object that uses the color and click the New Swatch button at the bottom of the Swatches panel (refer to Figure 9-1 to see this button). To save a color and name it at the same time, Alt-click (Windows) or Option-click (Mac) the New Swatch icon. The New Swatch dialog box opens, where you can name and edit the color, if you want. By double-clicking a swatch in the Swatches panel, you can access the options at any time.

A color in the Swatches panel is available only in the document in which it was created. Read the next section on custom libraries to see how to import swatches from saved documents.

Building and using custom libraries

When you save a color in the Swatches panel, you're essentially saving it to your own, custom library. You import the Swatches panel from one document into another by using the Libraries feature.

Retrieve colors saved in a document's Swatches panel by selecting the Swatch Libraries menu button at the bottom of the Swatches panel and dragging down to Other Library. You can also access swatch libraries, including those in other documents, by choosing Window⇨Swatch Libraries⇨Other Library. Locate the saved document and click Open. A panel appears with the document name, as shown in Figure 9-7. You can't edit the colors in this panel, but you can use the colors in this panel by double-clicking a swatch (to edit the color) or dragging it to the current document's Swatches panel.

You can also click the Swatch Libraries button to access color libraries for Pantone colors, Web colors, and some neat creative colors, such as jewel tones and metals.

Figure 9-7:
An imported
custom
swatch
library.

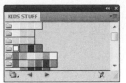

Using the Color Guide and color groups

Perhaps you failed at color selection in art class or just don't feel that you're one of those people who picks colors that look good together. Fortunately, you can use the Color Guide to find colors and save them to organized color groups in your Swatches panel. You can create color schemes based on 23 classic color-harmony rules, such as the Complementary, Analogous, Monochromatic, and Triad options, or you can create custom harmony rules.

Sounds complicated, doesn't it? Fortunately, all you have to do is choose a base color and then see which variations you come up with according to rules you choose. Give it a try:

1. **Choose Window⇨Color Guide.**

The Color Guide appears, as shown in Figure 9-8.

Figure 9-8:
The Color
Guide panel
identifies
related
colors.

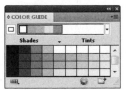

2. **Select a color from the Swatches panel. If it isn't visible, choose Window⇨Swatches.**

Immediately, the Color Guide panel kicks in to provide you with colors related to your original swatch.

3. **Change the harmony rules by clicking the Edit Colors button at the bottom of the Color Guide panel.**

The Edit Colors dialog box, shown in Figure 9-9, appears.

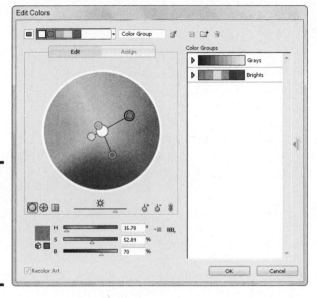

Figure 9-9:
Choose and save color groups in the Edit Colors dialog box.

You can spend days experimenting in the Edit Colors dialog box; for the scope of this book, however, you dive into changing simple harmony rules. To do this, click the Harmony Rules arrow to the right of the color bar. A drop-down list appears with many choices for selecting colors, as shown in Figure 9-10. Choose a color harmony.

**Book III
Chapter 9**

Livening Up
Illustrations
with Color

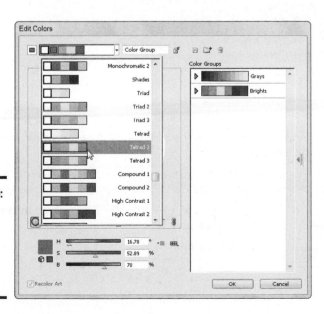

Figure 9-10:
Make a selection from the Harmony Rule drop-down list.

4. **Save your color selection as a color group by clicking the New Color Group icon.**

   If you like, you can rename the color group by double-clicking the group name in the Color Group section of the Live Color window.

5. **Click OK.**

   The color group is added to the Swatches panel.

You don't have to use the Edit Colors dialog box to save a group of colors. You can Ctrl-click (Windows) or ⌘-click (Mac) to select multiple colors and then click the New Color Group button at the bottom of the Swatches panel.

Adding Pantone colors

If you're looking for the typical swatches numbered in the Pantone Matching System (PMS), click the Swatch Libraries menu button at the bottom of the Swatches panel. From the drop-down list, choose Color Books and then Pantone Solid Coated or whatever Pantone library you want to access.

Colors in the Pantone numbering system are often referred to as PMS 485 or PMS 201 or whatever number the color has been designated. You can locate the numbered swatch by typing the number into the Find text field of the Pantone panel, as shown in Figure 9-11. When that number's corresponding color is highlighted in the panel, click it to add it to your Swatches panel. Many users find it easier to see colored swatches by using List view. Choose Small List View or Large List View from the panel menu.

Figure 9-11: Use the Find text box to locate Pantone colors.

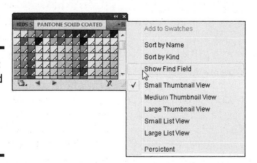

Editing Colors

Edit colors in the Swatches panel by using the Swatch Options dialog box (shown in Figure 9-12), which you access by double-clicking the color or choosing Swatch Options from the Swatches panel menu.

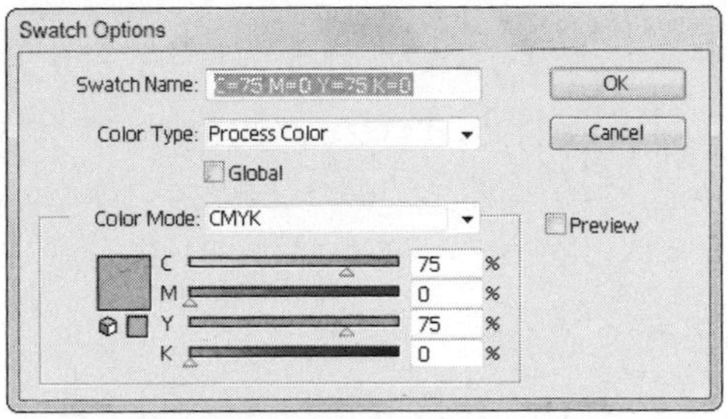

Figure 9-12: Edit a color swatch in the Swatch Options dialog box.

Use the Swatch Options dialog box to

✦ **Change color values:** Change the values in a color by using the sliders or typing values in the color text fields. Being able to enter exact color values is especially helpful if you're given a color build to match. Select the Preview check box to see results as you make the changes.

✦ **Use global colors:** If you plan to use a color frequently, select the Global check box. If it's selected and you use the swatch throughout the artwork, you have to change the swatch options only one time and then all instances of that color are updated.

One important option to note in the Swatch Options dialog box is the Color Type drop-down list. You have two choices: spot color and process color. What's the difference?

✦ **Spot color:** A color that isn't broken down into the CMYK values. Spot colors are used for 1 or 2 color print runs or when precise color matching is important.

Suppose that you're printing 20,000 catalogs and decide to run only 2 colors: red and black. If you pick spot colors, the catalogs have to be run through the press only two times: once for black and once for red. If red were a process color, however, it would be created from a combination of cyan, magenta, yellow, and black inks, and the catalogs would need to be run through the press four times in order to build that color. Plus, if you went to a print service and asked for red, what color would you get — fire engine red, maroon, or a light and delicate pinkish red? But if the red you pick is PMS 485, your printer in Kutztown, Pennsylvania, can then print the same color of red on your brochure as the printer making your business cards in Woburn, Massachusetts.

✦ **Process color:** A color that's built from four colors (cyan, magenta, yellow, and black); used for multicolor jobs.

Book III Chapter 9

Livening Up Illustrations with Color

For example, you would use process colors to send an ad to a 4-color magazine. Its printers certainly want to use the same inks they're already running, and using a spot color would require another run through the presses in addition to the runs for the cyan, magenta, yellow, and black plates. In this case, you convert to process colors any spot colors created in corporate logos or similar projects.

Choose the Spot Colors option from the Swatches panel menu to choose whether you want spot colors changed to Lab or CMYK values:

✦ Choose **Lab** to produce the best possible CMYK conversion for the actual spot color when using a color-calibrated workflow.

✦ Choose **CMYK** (the default) to see the manufacturer's standard recommended conversion of spot colors to process. Results can vary depending on printing conditions.

Building and Editing Patterns

Using patterns can be as simple or as complicated as you want. If you become familiar with the basic concepts, you can take off in all sorts of creative directions. To build a simple pattern, start by creating the artwork you want to use as a pattern on your artboard — polka dots, smiley faces, wavy lines or whatever. Then select all components of the pattern and drag them to the Swatches panel. That's it — you made a pattern! Use the pattern by selecting it as the fill or stroke of an object.

You can't use patterns in artwork that will then be saved as a pattern. If you have a pattern in your artwork and try to drag it into the Swatches panel, Illustrator kicks it back out with no error message. On a good note, you can drag text directly into the Swatches panel to become a pattern.

You can update patterns you created or patterns that already reside in the Swatches panel. To edit an existing pattern, follow these steps:

1. **Click the pattern swatch in the Swatches panel and drag it to the artboard.**

2. **Deselect the pattern and use the Direct Selection tool to change its colors or shapes or whatever.**

   Keep making changes until you're happy with the result.

3. **To update the pattern with your new edited version, use the Selection tool to select all pattern elements and Alt+drag (Windows) or Option+drag (Mac) the new pattern over the existing pattern swatch in the Swatches panel.**

4. **When a black border appears around the existing pattern, release the mouse button.**

All instances of the pattern in your illustration are updated.

To add some space between tiles, as shown in Figure 9-13, create a bounding box using a rectangle shape with no fill or stroke (representing the repeat you want to create). Send the box behind the other objects in the pattern and drag all objects, including the bounding box, to the Swatches panel.

Figure 9-13: A pattern with a transparent bounding box.

We cover transformations in detail in Chapter 10 of this minibook, but some specific transform features apply to patterns. To scale a pattern, but not the object it's filling, double-click the Scale tool, shown in the margin. In the Scale dialog box that appears, type the value that you want to scale and deselect all options except Patterns, as shown in Figure 9-14. This method works for the Rotate tool as well.

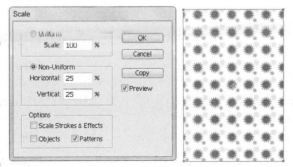

Figure 9-14: Choose to scale or rotate only the pattern, not the object.

Working with Gradients

Create gradients for smooth metallic effects or just to add dimension to illustrations. If you're not sure which swatches are considered gradients, choose Gradient from the Show Swatch Kinds button at the bottom of the Swatches panel (refer to Figure 9-1).

After the Gradient panel (shown in Figure 9-15) is applied, you can access it by choosing Window⇨Gradient. If the Gradient options are not visible, choose Show Options from the Gradient panel menu to see more options.

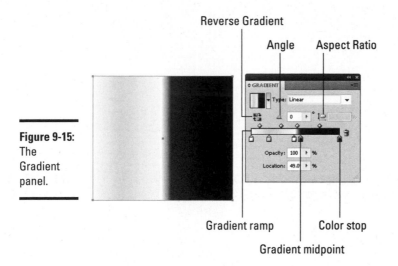

Figure 9-15:
The
Gradient
panel.

On the Gradient panel, use the Type drop-down list to choose a *Radial* gradient (one that radiates from the center point) or a *Linear* gradient (one that follows a linear path).

Use the Gradient tool to change the direction and distance of a gradient blend:

1. **Select an object and apply any existing gradient from the Swatches panel to its fill.**

2. **Choose the Gradient tool (press G) and drag in the direction you want the gradient to go.**

   Drag a long path for a smooth, long gradient. Drag a short path for a short, more defined gradient.

Before following the next steps, it would be a good idea to undock your Color panel. Click the Color tab on the Color panel and drag it out to the artboard, essentially separating it from the rest of the panel group.

To create a new gradient, follow these steps:

1. **Click the Fade to Black swatch in the Swatches panel, as shown in Figure 9-16, to reach a good base point.**

Figure 9-16: Select the Fade to Black swatch from the Swatches panel.

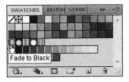

2. **Notice the Gradient slider that appears at the bottom of the Gradient panel. On the left and right side of the slider, you see color stops. Click on the left color stop on the Gradient Slider to see that this black color stop is set to 100% opacity, as shown in Figure 9-17.**

Figure 9-17: Click on the color stop to activate it.

3. **Click on the right black color stop to see that it is set to 0% opacity.**

When a color stop is active, the triangle on top turns solid.

4. **Choose Window⇨Color to access the Color panel. If the ramp on the Color panel is transitioning from black to white, click the triangle in the upper right corner to open the panel menu; choose RGB or CMYK colors.**

This provides you with a color ramp.

5. **Click the gradient ramp (across the bottom) in the Color panel to pick a random color (or enter values in the text fields to select a specific color) for the active color stop in the Gradient panel.**

6. **In the Gradient panel, click the right color stop and change the Opacity to 100%, as shown in Figure 9-18.**

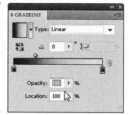

7. **With the right color stop still selected, click another color in the color ramp in the Colors panel.**

To add color stops, click beneath the gradient ramp and then choose a color from the Color panel. You can also drag a swatch from the Swatches panel to add a new color to the gradient. To remove a color stop, drag it off the Gradient panel.

You can click the gradient ramp to add colors and also to change the opacity of that location of the ramp by entering values in the Opacity text box. This technique is a helpful way to create stripes and other reflective gradients.

Copying Color Attributes

Wouldn't it be helpful if you had tools that could record all the fill and stroke attributes and apply them to other shapes? You're in luck — the Eyedropper tool can do just that. Copy the fill and stroke of an object and apply it to another object by using the Eyedropper tool:

1. **Create several shapes with different fill and stroke attributes, or open an existing file that contains several different objects.**

2. **Select the Eyedropper tool and click a shape that has attributes you want to copy.**

3. **Alt-click (Windows) or Option-click (Mac) another object to apply those attributes.**

Not only is this technique simple but you can also change which attributes the Eyedropper applies. Do so by double-clicking the Eyedropper tool; in the dialog box that appears, select only the attributes you want to copy.

The Live Trace Feature

If you're looking for good source art to use to experiment with color, look no further than your own sketches and scanned images. You can automatically trace bitmap images by using a variety of settings that range from black-and-white line art to vector art with multitudes of color that can be extracted from your image.

To use the Live Trace feature, follow these steps:

1. **Choose File⇨Place and select an image that you want to trace.**

   The file you place can be a logo, a sketch, or even a photo. Notice that after you place the image, the Control panel offers additional options.

2. **Click the arrow to the right of the Live Trace button.**

   This drop-down list provides Live Trace presets that may help you better trace your image.

3. **Scroll to the bottom and choose Tracing Options.**

   The Tracing Options dialog box appears, as shown in Figure 9-19.

Figure 9-19:
When converting bitmap images to vector objects, you can experiment with different tracing options.

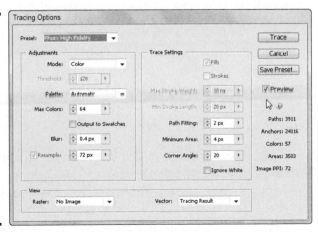

4. **Select the Preview check box and experiment with the various settings, as shown in Figure 9-20.**

5. **When you find the setting that works best for your image, click the Trace button.**

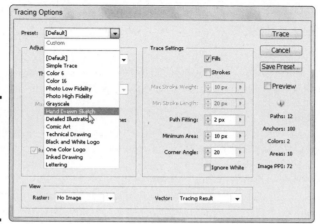

Figure 9-20: Turn bitmap artwork into vector with the Live Trace feature.

You can return to the Tracing Options dialog box and change settings repeatedly until you find the best one.

Painting Made Easy: The Live Paint Feature

 Don't worry about filling closed shapes or letting fills escape from objects with gaps into unwanted areas. Using the Live Paint feature, you can create the image you want and fill in regions with color. The Live Paint bucket automatically detects regions composed of independent intersecting paths and fills them accordingly. The paint within a given region remains live and flows automatically if any paths are moved.

If you want to give it a try, follow these steps to put together an example to experiment with:

1. **Use the Ellipse tool to create a circle on your page.**

   Make the circle large enough to accommodate two or three inner circles.

2. **Press D (and nothing else).**

   As long as you aren't on the Type tool, you revert to the default colors of a black stroke and a white fill.

3. **Double-click the Scale tool and enter 75% in the Uniform Scale text box.**

4. **Press the Copy button and then click OK.**

   You see a smaller circle inside the original.

5. **Press Ctrl+D (Windows) or ⌘+D (Mac) to duplicate the transformation and create another circle inside the last one.**

6. **Choose Select⇨All or press Ctrl+A (Windows) or ⌘+A (Mac) to activate the circles you just created.**

7. **Make sure that the Fill swatch is forward.**

   The Fill swatch is at the bottom of the Tools panel.

8. **Use the Swatches or Color panel and choose any fill color.**

9. **Select the Live Paint Bucket tool, which is hidden under the Shape Builder tool, and move the cursor over the various regions of the circles.**

   See how the different regions become highlighted?

10. **Click when the region you want to fill is activated.**

    Now try it with other fill colors in different regions, as shown in Figure 9-21.

**Book III
Chapter 9**

Livening Up
Illustrations
with Color

Figure 9-21:
Painting
objects
with the
Live Paint
feature.

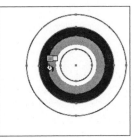

A companion feature to the Live Paint Bucket is support for gap detection. With this feature in its arsenal, Illustrator automatically and dynamically detects and closes small to large gaps that may be part of the artwork. You can determine whether you want paint to flow across region gap boundaries by using the Gap Options dialog box, accessible by choosing Object⇨Live Paint⇨Gap Options.

Before you save a file for an older version of Illustrator that uses the Live Paint feature, first select the occurrences of Live Paint and choose Object⇨Expand. When the Expand dialog box appears, leave the options at their defaults and click OK. This setting breaks down the Live Paint objects to individual shapes, which older versions of Illustrator can understand.

Chapter 10: Using the Transform and Distortions Tools

In This Chapter

✔ **Discovering transformation methods**

✔ **Putting the Transform tools to work**

✔ **Becoming familiar with the Liquify tools**

✔ **Distorting, warping, and otherwise reshaping objects**

T ransformations you can give to objects in Illustrator include scaling, rotating, skewing, and distorting. In this chapter, we show you how to use the general Transform tools as well as some of the neat Liquify and Envelope Distort features available in Illustrator.

Working with Transformations

Using just the Selection tool, you can scale and rotate a selected object. Drag the bounding box handles to resize the object, shown in Figure 10-1, or move outside a handle and then, when the cursor changes to a flippy arrow (a curved arrow with arrowheads on both ends), drag to rotate the object.

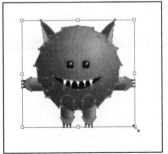

Figure 10-1: Use the bounding box to resize or rotate a selected object.

If you want to scale proportionally, hold down the Shift key while you drag to resize. To rotate an object at 45 degree increments, hold down the Shift key while you're rotating.

When you use the bounding box to rotate a selection, the bounding box rotates with the object, but its handles show the object's original orientation, as shown in Figure 10-2. The orientation can help you keep track of the original placement but can also interfere when you're building additional artwork. To reset the bounding box so that it's straight at the new orientation, choose Object➪Transform➪Reset Bounding Box.

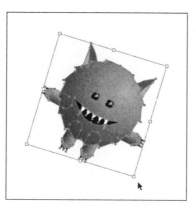

Figure 10-2: The bounding box in its original position and after it has been reset.

When you scale, rotate, or use any other type of transformation in Illustrator, the final location becomes the *zero point.* In other applications, such as InDesign, you can rotate an object by any number of degrees (45 degrees, for example) and later enter 0 for the rotation angle in the Transform panel or in the Rotate dialog box to return the object to its original position. In Illustrator, if you enter **0** for the rotation angle to return a rotated object to its original position, the object doesn't change its position. To return the object to the previous position in Illustrator, you have to enter the negative of the number you originally entered to rotate the object, so you would enter **–45** for the degree of rotation in this example.

Transforming an object

The Rotate, Reflect, Scale, and Shear tools all use the same basic steps to perform transformations. Read on for those basic steps, and then follow some individual examples of the most often used Transform tools. The following sections show five ways to transform an object: one for an arbitrary transformation and four others for exact transformations based on a numeric amount you enter.

Arbitrary transformation method

Because this transformation method is arbitrary, you're eyeballing the transformation of an object — in other words, you don't have an exact percentage or angle in mind, and you want to freely transform the object until it looks right. Just follow these steps:

1. **Select an object and then choose a Transform tool (Rotate, Reflect, Scale, or Shear).**

2. **Click the artboard once.**

   Be careful where you click because the click determines the point of reference, or *axis point,* for the transformation. In Figure 10-3, the click put the axis point above the right ear. The image is rotated on the axis created at that point.

Point of reference

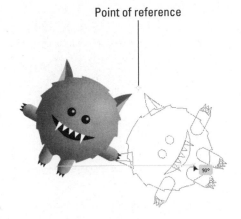

Figure 10-3:
The first mouse click creates the axis point.

3. **Drag in one smooth movement.**

   Just drag until you create the transformation you want.

Hold down the Alt (Windows) or Option (Mac) key when dragging to clone a newly transformed item while keeping the original object intact. This trick is especially helpful when you're using the Reflect tool.

Exact transformation methods

In the methods in this section, we show you how to perform transformations using specific numeric information:

Exact transformation method 1 — using the tool's dialog box:

1. **Select an object and then choose the Rotate, Reflect, Scale, or Shear tool.**

2. **Double-click the Transform tool in the Tools panel.**

   A dialog box specific to your chosen tool appears, as shown in Figure 10-4. In this example, we selected and then double-clicked the Rotate tool to open the Rotate dialog box.

Figure 10-4:
Double-click
a Transform
tool to open
its dialog
box.

3. **Type an angle, a scaled amount, or a percentage in the appropriate text field.**

4. **Select the Preview check box to see the effect of the transformation before you click OK; click the Copy button instead of OK to keep the original object intact and transform a copy.**

Exact transformation method 2 — using the reference point:

1. **Select an object and then choose the Rotate, Reflect, Scale, or Shear tool.**

2. **Alt-click (Windows) or Option-click (Mac) wherever you want to place the reference point.**

3. **In the appropriate Transform tool dialog box that appears, enter values and click OK or click the Copy button to apply the transformation.**

    This method is the best one to use if you need to rotate an object an exact amount on a defined axis.

Exact transformation method 3 — using the Transform menu:

1. **Select an object and then choose a transform option from the Object⇨Transform menu.**

    The appropriate transform dialog box appears.

2. **Enter some values and click OK or the Copy button.**

Exact transformation method 4 — using the Transform panel:

1. **Select an object and choose Window⇨Transform to access the Transform panel, shown in Figure 10-5.**

2. **Set your options.**

Though using the Transform panel is probably the easiest way to go, it doesn't give you the option of specifying an exact reference point (by clicking your mouse) or other options that apply to the individual Transform tools.

Figure 10-5:
Enter values on the Transform panel.

Using the Transform tools

In this section, we show you how to use some of the most popular Transform tools to create transformations.

The Reflect tool

Nothing is symmetrical, right? Maybe not, but objects not created symmetrically in Illustrator can look off-kilter. Using the Reflect tool, you can reflect an object to create an exact mirrored shape of it; just follow these steps:

1. **Open a new document in Illustrator and type some text or create an object.**

   If you want to reflect text, make sure that you use at least 60-point type so that you can easily see it.

2. **Select the Reflect tool (hidden under the Rotate tool) and click the object; if you're using text, click in the middle of the text baseline.**

   This step sets the reference point for the reflection.

3. **Alt+Shift+drag (Windows) or Option+Shift+drag (Mac) and release when the object or text is reflecting itself, as shown in Figure 10-6.**

   This step not only clones the reflected object or text but also snaps it to 45 degree angles.

Figure 10-6:
The completed reflection.

The Scale tool

Using the Scale tool, you can scale an object proportionally or non-uniformly. Most people like to be scaled non-uniformly — maybe a little taller, a little thinner — but on with the topic. Follow these steps to see the Scale tool in action:

1. **Create a shape and give it no fill and a 5-point black stroke.**

   For this example, we created a circle. See Chapter 4 of this minibook if you need a reminder on how to do it.

2. **Select the shape and double-click the Scale tool.**

   The Scale dialog box appears.

3. **Type a number in the Scale text field (in the Uniform section) and click the Copy button.**

   We entered 125 in the Scale text field to increase the size of the object by 125 percent.

4. **Press Ctrl+D (Windows) or ⌘+D (Mac) to repeat the transformation as many times as you want.**

   Every time you press Ctrl+D (Windows) or ⌘+D (Mac), the shape is copied and sized by the percentage you entered in the Scale text field. This trick, especially handy with circles, creates an instant bull's-eye!

To experiment with the Scale tool, create different shapes in Step 1 and enter different values in Step 3. Remember that if you type 50% in the Scale text field, the object is made smaller; surpass 100 percent — say, to 150 percent — to make the object larger. Leaving the Scale text field at 100 percent has no effect on the object.

The Shear tool

The Shear tool lets you shear an object by selecting an axis and dragging to set a shear angle, as shown in Figure 10-7.

Figure 10-7:
Create perspective with the Shear tool.

The axis is always the center of the object unless you use method 1 or 2 from the earlier section "Exact transformation methods." Use the Shear tool in combination with the Rotate tool to give an object perspective.

The Reshape tool

The Reshape tool lets you select anchor points and sections of paths and adjust them in one direction. You determine that direction by dragging an anchor point with the Reshape tool selected.

 The Reshape tool works differently from the other Transform tools. To use it, follow these steps:

1. **Select just the anchor points on the paths that you want to reshape. Deselect any points that you want to remain in place.**

2. **Select the Reshape tool (hidden under the Scale tool) and position the cursor over the anchor point you want to modify; click the anchor point.**

   If you click a path segment, a highlighted anchor point with a square around it is added to the path.

3. **Shift-click more anchor points or path segments to act as selection points.**

   You can highlight an unlimited number of anchor points or path segments.

4. **Drag the highlighted anchor points to adjust the path.**

The Free Transform tool

 You use the Free Transform tool in much the same way as you use the bounding box. (See the earlier section "Working with Transformations.") This tool is necessary only if you choose View➪Hide Bounding Box but want free transform capabilities.

Creating Distortions

You can bend objects — make them wavy, gooey, or spiky — by creating simple to complex distortions with the Liquify tools and the Envelope Distort features.

The Liquify tools

The Liquify tools can accomplish all sorts of creative or wacky (depending on how you look at it) distortions to your objects. You can choose from eight Liquify tools. Even though we define them for you in Table 10-1, you should experiment with these tools to understand their full capabilities. Here are some tips:

✦ A variety of Liquify tools are available by holding down the mouse button on the default selection, the Width tool. If you use the tools frequently, drag to the arrow at the end of the tools and release when you see the tooltip for Tearoff. You can then position the tools anywhere in your work area.

✦ Double-click any Liquify tool to open a dialog box specific to the selected tool.

✦ When a Liquify tool is selected, the brush size appears. Adjust the diameter and shape of the Liquify tool by holding down the Alt (Windows) or Option (Mac) key while dragging the brush shape smaller or larger. Press the Shift key to constrain the shape to a circle.

 New in CS5 is the Width tool. Using the Width tool, cross over a selected path. When a hollow square appears, click and drag outward (or inward), and the stroke width at that location is adjusted. See Figure 10-8.

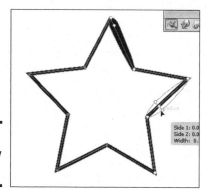

Figure 10-8:
Use the new
Width tool.

If you want a little more accuracy, you can double-click the stroke by using the Width tool and create, modify, or delete the width point by using the Width Point Edit dialog box, shown in Figure 10-9.

Figure 10-9:
Customize
the Width
tool in this
dialog box.

Width Point Edit		
Width Options		OK
Side 1: 0.5 pt		Cancel
Side 2: 0.5 pt		Delete
Total Width:		
☐ Adjust Adjoining Width Points		

Table 10-1		The Liquify Tools
Icon	*Tool Name*	*What It Does to an Object*
	Width	Increases the stroke width or height when you click and drag a path.
	Warp	Molds it with the movement of the cursor. (Pretend that you're pushing through dough with this tool.)
	Twirl	Creates swirling distortions within it.
	Pucker	Deflates it.
	Bloat	Inflates it.
	Scallop	Adds curved details to its outline. (Think of a seashell with scalloped edges.)
	Crystallize	Adds many spiked details to the outline of an object, such as crystals on a rock.
	Wrinkle	Adds wrinkle-like details to the outline of an object.

Using the Envelope Distort command

Use the Envelope Distort command to arch text and apply other creative distortions to an Illustrator object. To use the Envelope Distort command, you can use a preset warp (the easiest method), a grid, or a top object to determine the amount and type of distortion. In this section, we discuss all three methods.

Using the preset warps

Experimenting with warp presets is a little more interesting if you have a word or an object selected before trying them out. To warp an object or some text to a preset style, follow these steps:

1. **Select the text or object that you want to distort and then choose Object⇨Envelope Distort⇨Make with Warp.**

   The Warp Options dialog box appears.

2. **Choose a warp style from the Style drop-down list and then specify any other options you want.**

3. **Click OK to apply the distortion.**

If you want to experiment with warping but also want to revert to the original at any time, choose Effect⇨Warp. You later change or delete the warp effect by double-clicking it in the Appearance panel or by dragging the effect to the trash can in the Appearance panel. Find out more in Chapter 12 of this minibook about exciting effects you can apply to objects.

Reshaping with a mesh grid

You can assign a grid to an object so that you can drag different points and create your own, custom distortion, as shown in Figure 10-10.

Figure 10-10:
Custom
distortion
using a
mesh grid.

Follow these steps to apply a mesh grid:

1. **Using the Select tool, select the text or object that you want to distort and then choose Object⇨Envelope Distort⇨Make with Mesh.**

   The Envelope Mesh dialog box appears.

2. **Specify the number of rows and columns you want the mesh to contain and then click OK.**

3. **Drag any anchor point on the mesh grid with the Direct Selection tool to reshape the object.**

To delete anchor points on the mesh grid, select an anchor point by using the Direct Selection tool and press the Delete key.

 You can also use the Mesh tool to edit and delete points when using a mesh grid on objects.

Reshaping an object with a different object

To form letters into the shape of an oval or to distort selected objects into another object, use this technique:

1. **Create text that you want to distort.**

2. **Create the object you want to use as the** *envelope* **(the object to be used to define the distortion).**

3. **Choose Object⊳Arrange to ensure that the envelope object is on top, as shown in Figure 10-11.**

Figure 10-11: Position the shape over the text.

4. **Select the text and Shift-click to select the envelope object.**

5. **Choose Object⊳Envelope Distort⊳Make with Top Object.**

The underlying object is distorted to fit the shape of the top (envelope) object.

 Choose Effect⊳Distort and Transform⊳Free Distort to take advantage of the Free Distort dialog box, shown in Figure 10-12. Effects can be edited or undone at any time by clicking or deleting the Free Distort effect from the Appearance menu.

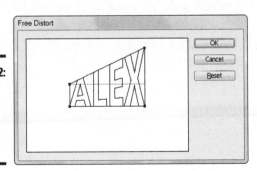

Figure 10-12: Distort an object from the Free Distort dialog box.

Chapter 11: Working with Transparency and Special Effects Tools

In This Chapter

✔ **Adding dimension with the Mesh tool**

✔ **Getting to know the Blend tool**

✔ **Using the Symbol Sprayer tool**

✔ **Discovering transparency, blend modes, and opacity masks**

This chapter is full of neat things you can do using some of the more advanced features in Adobe Illustrator. These special effects tools can help you create art that makes an impact: Discover how to make your art look like a painting with the Gradient Mesh tool, create morph-like blends with the Blend tool, become a graffiti artist by trying out the Symbol Sprayer tool, and see what's underneath objects by using transparency.

The Mesh Tool

If you're creating art in Illustrator that requires solid colors or continuous patterns, you can achieve those results quite easily. But if you're working on an element that requires continuous tones, such as a person's face, you turn to the handy Mesh tool to create smooth tonal variations in your illustration. Choose to blend one color into another and then use the Mesh tool to adjust your blend. Now in Illustrator CS5, you can apply varying levels of transparency to these mesh points.

The Mesh tool can be as complex or simple as you want. Create intense illustrations that look like they were created by an airbrush or just use the tool to give dimension to an object, as in the illustration shown in Figure 11-1.

We show you how to create a gradient mesh in two different ways: Clicking gives you a little more freedom to put mesh points where you want them, and manually setting the number of rows and columns in the mesh is more precise.

Figure 11-1:
Mesh tool
illustrations
can be
complex or
simple.

You can change the color in mesh points by choosing the Direct Selection tool and either clicking a mesh point and picking a fill color or clicking in the center of a mesh area and choosing a fill. Whether you select the mesh point (see the left side of Figure 11-2) or the area between the mesh points (see the right side of Figure 11-2), it changes the painting result. To add a mesh point without changing to the current fill color, Shift-click anywhere in a filled vector object.

Figure 11-2:
The mesh
point
changes
the painting
result.

To create a gradient mesh by clicking, follow these steps:

1. **Create any shape by using the shape tools. Make sure the shape has a solid color; any color will do.**

2. **Deselect all objects by choosing Select⇨Deselect.**

3. **Select a fill color that you want to apply as a mesh point to an object.**

   For example, if you want to add a shaded white spot to a red circle, choose white for the fill color.

 4. **Select the Mesh tool (the keyboard shortcut is U) and click anywhere in a filled vector object.**

   The object is converted to a mesh object.

5. **Click the object as many times as you want to add additional mesh points.**

To create a gradient mesh by setting the number of rows and columns, follow these steps:

1. **Select an object.**

2. **Choose Object⇨Create Gradient Mesh.**

   The Create Gradient Mesh dialog box appears.

3. **Set the number of rows and columns of mesh lines to create on the object by entering numbers in the Rows and Columns text fields.**

4. **Choose the direction of the highlight from the Appearance drop-down list.**

   The direction of the highlight determines which way the gradient flows (see Figure 11-3); you have these choices:

   - *Flat:* Applies the object's original color evenly across the surface, resulting in no highlight

   - *To Center:* Creates a highlight in the center of the object

   - *To Edge:* Creates a highlight on the edges of the object

5. **Enter a percentage of white highlight to apply to the mesh object in the Highlight text field.**

6. **Click OK to apply the gradient mesh to the object.**

Book III
Chapter 11

**Working with
Transparency and
Special Effects Tools**

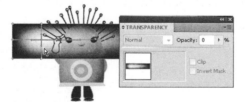

Figure 11-3:
Choose a
highlight
direction.

Using a new feature in CS5, you can select individual or multiple mesh points
and apply varying levels of transparency to them. Follow these steps to
apply transparency to a gradient mesh:

1. **Select a shape tool and click and drag to the artboard to add the
   shape to your document.**

2. **Give the shape a solid fill (any color) and no stroke.**

3. **Choose the Mesh tool and click anywhere in the object.**

   This step adds a mesh point to your object.

4. **Choose Window⇨Transparency and drag the slider from 100 percent
   to 0 or any other value you want.**

   As you can see in Figure 11-4, an illustration was sent behind the object
   to demonstrate transparency in the object.

Figure 11-4:
Mesh points
in CS5 —
the trans-
parency
varies.

The Blend Tool

Use the Blend tool (located in the main Illustrator Tools panel) to transform
one object to another to create interesting morphed artwork or to create
shaded objects. Using the Blend tool, you can give illustrations a rendered
look by blending from one color to another or create an even number of

shapes from one point to another. Figure 11-5 shows examples of what you can do with this tool.

Figure 11-5:
Some
objects
using the
Blend tool.

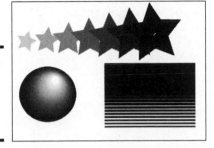

Creating a blend

Creating a blend isn't difficult, and as you get used to it you can take the process even further, to create incredibly realistic effects. Follow these steps to create a simple blend from one rectangle size to another, creating an algorithmic stripe pattern (a rectangle of one height blended to a rectangle of another height):

1. **Create a rectangle.**

   Size doesn't matter in this example; just be sure that you can see a difference in shapes when you blend. We're using a rectangle that measures roughly 4 x 1 inches.

2. **Give your shape a fill and assign None to the stroke.**

   You can use other settings, but we recommend keeping it simple if you're still new to working with blends.

3. **Using the Selection tool, click the rectangle and Alt+drag (Windows) or Option+drag (Mac) toward the bottom of the artboard to clone your shape; press the Shift key before you release the mouse button to make sure that the cloned shape stays perfectly aligned with the original shape.**

4. **Reduce the cloned shape to about half its original height by using the Transform panel.**

   If the Transform panel isn't visible, choose Window➪Transform.

   Alternatively, you can hold down the Shift key and drag the lower-middle bounding box handle, shown in Figure 11-6.

**Book III
Chapter 11**

**Working with
Transparency and
Special Effects Tools**

5. **In the swatches panel (choose Window⇨Swatches), change the cloned shape's fill to a different color but keep the stroke set to None.**

   Changing the color just helps you see the blend effect a little better.

6. **Using the Blend tool, click the original shape and then click the cloned shape.**

Figure 11-6:
Reduce
the size of
the cloned
shape.

As a default action, the Blend tool creates a smooth blend that transitions from one color to another, as shown in Figure 11-7. To change the blend effect, experiment with the Blend Options dialog box.

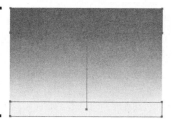

Figure 11-7:
Creating
a smooth
transition
between
rectangles.

Setting Blend options

You can change the way a blend appears by using the Blend Options dialog box: Choose Object⇨Blend⇨Blend Options. From the Spacing drop-down list, change the blend to one of these options:

✦ **Smooth Color:** Blend steps are calculated to provide the optimum number of steps for a smooth transition.

✦ **Specified Steps:** Determine the number of steps in a blend by typing a number in the text field to the right of the drop-down list.

✦ **Specified Distance:** Control the distance between steps in the blend by typing a number in the text field to the right of the drop-down list.

You can also choose between two orientation options:

✦ **Align to Page:** Orients the blend perpendicular to the x-axis of the page.

✦ **Align to Path:** Orients the blend perpendicular to the path. You probably won't see a difference when changing orientation unless you've edited the blend path.

You can easily access the Blend tool options by selecting a blended object and double-clicking the Blend tool in the Tools panel.

If you're feeling adventurous, try changing a smooth blend (such as the one you create in the preceding step list) into a logarithmic blend. In the Blend Options dialog box, choose Specified Steps from the Spacing drop-down list and change the value to 5. This change creates the blend in 5 steps rather than in the more than 200 steps that may have been necessary to create the smooth blend.

Here are a few more tips to help you become more comfortable using blends. You can

✦ Blend between an unlimited number of objects, colors, opacities, or gradients.

✦ Edit blends directly with tools, such as Selection, Rotate, or Scale.

✦ Switch to the Direct Selection tool and edit the blend path by dragging anchor points. A straight path is created between blended objects when the blend is first applied.

✦ Edit blends that you created by moving, resizing, deleting, or adding objects. After you make editing changes, the artwork is blended again automatically.

The Symbol Sprayer Tool

The super Symbol Sprayer tool is one you must experiment with in order to understand its full potential. In a nutshell, it works like a can of spray paint that sprays, rather than paints, *symbols* — objects that, in Illustrator, can be either vector- or pixel-based. Each symbol is an *instance*.

Exploring the symbol tools

Illustrator comes with a library of symbols ready for use in the symbols panel. (If the symbols panel isn't visible, choose Window➪Symbols.) Use this panel as a storage bin or library to save repeatedly used artwork or to create your own symbols to apply as instances in your artwork, like blades of grass or stars in the sky. You can then use the symbolism tools, described in Table 11-1, to adjust and change the appearance of the symbol instances.

Book III Chapter 11

Working with Transparency and Special Effects Tools

Table 11-1		The Symbol Tools
Icon	*Tool Name*	*What You Can Do with It*
	Symbol Sprayer	Create a set of symbol instances.
	Symbol Shifter	Move symbol instances around; can also change the relative paint order of symbol instances.
	Symbol Scruncher	Pull apart, or put together, symbol instances.
	Symbol Sizer	Increase or decrease the size of symbol instances.
	Symbol Spinner	Orient the symbol instances in a set. Symbol instances located near the cursor spin in the direction you move the cursor.
	Symbol Stainer	Colorize symbol instances.
	Symbol Screener	Increase or decrease the transparency of the symbol instances in a set.
	Symbol Styler	Apply or remove a graphic style from a symbol instance.

Press the Alt (Windows) or Option (Mac) key to reduce the effect of the symbolism tools. In other words, if you're using the Symbol Sizer tool, you click and hold to make the symbol instances larger; hold down the Alt (Windows) or Option (Mac) key to make the symbol instances smaller.

You can also selectively choose the symbols you want to effect with the Symbolism tools by activating them in the Symbols panel. Ctrl-click (Windows) or ⌘-click (Mac) multiple symbols to change them at the same time.

Just about anything can be a symbol, including placed objects and objects with patterns and gradients. If you're going to use placed images as symbols, however, choose File➪Place and deselect the Linked check box in the Place dialog box.

Creating and spraying symbols on the artboard

To create a symbol, select the object and drag it to the Symbols panel or click the New Symbol button at the bottom of the Symbols panel. Yes, it's that easy. Then use the Symbol Sprayer tool to apply the symbol instance on the artboard by following these steps:

1. **Select the symbol instance in the Symbols panel.**

   Either create your own symbol or use one of the default symbols supplied in the panel.

2. **Drag with the Symbol Sprayer tool, spraying the symbol on the artboard (see Figure 11-8).**

   That's it. You can increase or reduce the area affected by the Symbol Sprayer tool by pressing the bracket keys. Press] repeatedly to enlarge the application area for the symbol or press [to make it smaller.

Figure 11-8:
Using the Symbol Sprayer tool to create fish.

**Book III
Chapter 11**

**Working with
Transparency and
Special Effects Tools**

Note that you can access all sorts of symbol libraries from the Symbols panel menu. Find 3D, nature, map, flower, and even hair and fur symbol collections by selecting Open Symbol Library.

If you want to store artwork that you frequently need to access, simply drag selected objects to the Symbols panel or Alt-click (Windows) or Option-click (Mac) the New Symbol button to name and store the artwork. Retrieve the artwork later by dragging it from the Symbols panel to the artboard. In fact, you can drag any symbol out to your artboard to change or use it in your own artwork. To release the symbol back into its basic elements, choose Object⇨Expand. In the Expand dialog box, click OK to restore the defaults.

Transparency

Using transparency can add a new level to your illustrations. The transparency feature does exactly what its name implies — changes an object to make it transparent so that what's underneath that object is visible to varying degrees. You can use the Transparency panel for simple applications of transparency to show through to underlying objects or for more complex artwork using *opacity masks,* which can control the visibility of selected objects.

Choosing Window⇨Transparency opens the Transparency panel, where you can apply different levels of transparency to objects. To do so, create an arrangement of objects that intersect, select the topmost object, and then change the transparency level of the object in the Transparency panel, by either moving the Opacity slider or entering a value of less than 100 in the Opacity text field.

Blend modes

A *blending mode* determines how the resulting transparency will look. To achieve different blending effects, you choose different blend modes from the Blend Mode drop-down list in the Transparency panel.

Truly, the best way to find out what all these modes do is to create two overlapping shapes and start experimenting. Give the shapes differently colored fills (but note that many blending modes don't work with black-and-white fills). Then select the topmost object and change the blending mode by selecting an option from the Blend Mode drop-down list in the Transparency panel. You see all sorts of neat effects and might even pick a few favorites.

We define each blend mode in the following list, but we'll say it again: The best way to see what each mode does is to apply them — so start experimenting.

✦ **Normal:** Creates no interaction with underlying colors.

✦ **Darken:** Replaces only the areas that are lighter than the blend color. Areas darker than the blend color don't change.

✦ **Multiply:** Creates an effect similar to drawing on the page with magic markers, or like the colored film you see on theater lights.

✦ **Color Burn:** Darkens the base color to reflect the blend color. If you're using white, no change occurs.

✦ **Lighten:** Replaces only the areas that are darker than the blend color. Areas lighter than the blend color don't change.

✦ **Screen:** Multiplies the inverse of the underlying colors. The resulting color is always a lighter color.

✦ **Color Dodge:** Brightens the underlying color to reflect the blend color. If you're using black, there's no change.

✦ **Overlay:** Multiplies or screens the colors, depending on the base color.

✦ **Soft Light:** Darkens or lightens colors, depending on the blend color. The effect is similar to shining a diffused spotlight on the artwork.

✦ **Hard Light:** Multiplies or screens colors, depending on the blend color. The effect is similar to shining a harsh spotlight on the artwork.

✦ **Difference:** Subtracts either the blend color from the base color or the base color from the blend color, depending on which has the greater brightness value. The effect is similar to a color negative.

✦ **Exclusion:** Creates an effect similar to, but with less contrast than, Difference mode.

✦ **Hue:** Applies the *hue* (color) of the blend object to underlying objects but keeps the underlying shading, or luminosity.

✦ **Saturation:** Applies the saturation of the blend color but uses the luminance and hue of the base color.

✦ **Color:** Applies the blend object's color to the underlying objects but preserves the gray levels in the artwork; works well for tinting objects or changing their color.

✦ **Luminosity:** Creates a resulting color with the hue and saturation of the base color and the luminance of the blend color. This mode is essentially the opposite of Color mode.

Opacity masks

Just like in Photoshop, you can use masks to make more interesting artwork in Illustrator. Create an opacity mask from the topmost object in a selection of objects or by drawing a mask on a single object. The mask uses the grayscale of the selected object as its opacity mask. Black areas are transparent; shades of gray are semitransparent, depending on the amount of gray; white areas are opaque. Figure 11-9 shows the effect of using an opacity mask.

To create an opacity mask, follow these steps:

1. **Open the Transparency panel menu.**

Also, be sure that the Blend Mode drop-down list is set to Normal.

2. **Create a shape anywhere on the artboard or open a document that has artwork on it.**

We're using a circle, but the shape doesn't matter. Make sure that the artwork has a fill. A solid color helps you see the effect.

Figure 11-9:
An opacity
mask
converts
the topmost
object into
a mask that
then masks
out the
underlying
objects.

3. **Open the Symbols panel (choose Window⇨Symbols Panel) and drag a symbol to the artboard.**

   In this example, we're using the drums symbol.

4. **Using the Selection tool, enlarge your symbol so that it fills the shape (see the image on the left in Figure 11-10).**

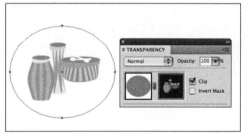

Figure 11-10:
Creating
an opacity
mask.

5. **Select both the symbol and the shape and then choose Make Opacity Mask from the Transparency panel menu (see the image on the right in Figure 11-10).**

   The symbol turns into a mask, showing varying levels of the underlying box of the newly created mask, depending on the original color value. To delete an opacity mask, choose Release Opacity Mask from the Transparency panel menu.

Click the right thumbnail (which represents the mask) in the Transparency panel and a black border appears around it, indicating that it's active. You can move the items on the mask or even create items to be added to the mask. The mask works just like the regular artboard, except that anything done on the mask side is used only as an opacity mask. To work on the regular artboard, click the left thumbnail.

Chapter 12: Using Filters and Effects

In This Chapter

✔ Applying effects

✔ Getting to know the Appearance panel

✔ Discovering graphic styles

✔ Making artwork 3D

✔ Playing with additional fills and strokes

✔ Creating the illusion of space and distance with the Perspective Grid

Effects give you the opportunity to make jazzy changes to your Illustrator objects, such as add drop shadows and squiggling artwork. You can even use Photoshop filters directly in Illustrator. In this chapter, you find out how to apply, save, and edit effects; you also take a quick tour of the Appearance panel (your trusty sidekick when performing these tasks).

Working with Effects

If you're an Adobe Illustrator user from any version before CS4, you might be wondering where the Filter menu is. (If you're just starting to use Illustrator, you don't need to know about, or even care about, this major change.) All items that appeared on the Filter menu are now on the Effects menu.

Filters apply permanent changes to artwork, referred to as *destructive* changes, because after you save and close the file, you can't undo the results for the filter. On the other hand, effects are quite different: They're connected dynamically to objects. You can apply, change, and even remove effects at any time from the Appearance panel (choose Window➪ Appearance).

Understanding the Appearance panel

You can apply multiple effects to one object and even copy them to multiple objects, which is when a good working knowledge of the Appearance panel is necessary. If it isn't visible, choose Window➪Appearance to open the

Appearance panel, shown in Figure 12-1, alongside an object with several effects applied to it.

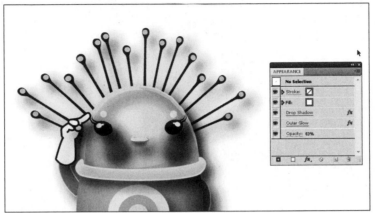

Figure 12-1:
Discover
how
useful the
Appearance
panel
can be.

If you have no effects applied, you see as a default only a fill and a stroke listed in the Appearance panel. As you create effects, they're added to this list. You can even add more strokes and fills to the list. Why would you do that? Because you can do incredible things with additional fills and strokes (which we show you in the next section). See Figure 12-2 for a breakdown of the features on the Appearance panel.

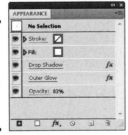

Figure 12-2:
Use the
icons in the
Appearance
panel for
effects.

Applying an effect

In this section, you see how to apply an effect. You can choose from many effects, and they're all applied in much the same manner. In this example, we apply the Arrowhead effect.

Follow these steps to apply an effect:

1. **Create a new document, choose any color mode, and draw a line in your document.**

You can use either the Line tool or the Pen tool to create a straight line. For this example, make the path at least 3 inches long and positioned horizontally on the page, as you see in Figure 12-3.

Figure 12-3:
Creating a horizontal line.

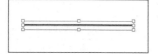

2. **In the Control panel at the top of the Illustrator document, change the stroke to 3 pt and make sure that the fill is set to None.**

   Using a 3-point stroke enables you to see the stroke a little better.

3. **Choose Effect⟹Distort and Transform⟹Zig Zag.**

   Choose the settings that work well to make your straight line appear as a zigzag. In Figure 12-4, we selected Smooth to round out the points of the zigzag effect.

Figure 12-4:
Convert a straight path into a zigzag using the Zig Zag effect.

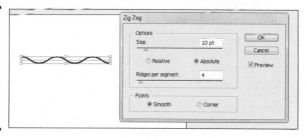

**Book III
Chapter 12**

Using Filters and Effects

Effects are linked dynamically to the object they're applied to. They can be scaled, modified, and even deleted with no harm done to the original object.

Adding a Drop Shadow effect

Creating a drop shadow is a quick and easy way to add dimension and a bit of sophistication to your artwork. The interaction between the object with the drop shadow and the underlying objects can create an interesting look. To add the Drop Shadow effect to an illustration, follow these steps:

1. **Select the object (or objects) to apply the drop shadow to.**

2. **Choose Effect⟹Stylize⟹Drop Shadow.**

3. **In the Drop Shadow dialog box that appears, as shown in Figure 12-5, select the Preview check box in the upper-right corner.**

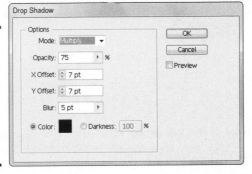

Figure 12-5: The Drop Shadow dialog box gives the effect's options and preview.

You now see the drop shadow applied as you make changes.

4. **Choose from the following options in the dialog box:**

   - *Mode:* Select a blending mode from this drop-down list to choose how you want the selected object to interact with the objects underneath it. The default is Multiply, which works well — the effect is similar to coloring with a magic marker.

   - *Opacity:* Enter a value or use the drop-down list to determine how opaque or transparent the drop shadow should be. If it's too strong, choose a lower amount.

   - *Offset:* Enter a value to determine how close the shadow is to the object. If you're working with text or small artwork, smaller values (and shorter shadows) look best. Otherwise, the drop shadow may look like one big, indefinable glob.

     The X Offset shifts the shadow from left to right, and the Y Offset shifts it up or down. You can enter negative or positive numbers.

   - *Blur:* Use Blur to control how fuzzy the edges of the shadow are. A lower value makes the edge of the shadow more defined.

   - *Color and Darkness:* Select the Color radio button to choose a custom color for the drop shadow. Select the Darkness radio button to add more black to the drop shadow. Zero percent is the lowest amount of black, and 100 percent is the highest.

     As a default, the color of the shadow is based on the color of your object, sort of — the Darkness option also has a play in this task. As a default, the shadow is made up of the color in the object if it's solid. Multicolored objects have a gray shadow.

5. **When you're finished, click OK to close the dialog box.**

Saving Graphic Styles

A *graphic style* is a combination of all settings you choose for a particular filter or effect in the Appearance panel. By saving this information in a graphic style, you store these attributes so that you can quickly and easily apply them to other objects later.

Choose Window➪Graphic Styles; in the panel that appears are thumbnails of many different styles that Adobe provides to you as a default. Create a new shape, such as a simple rectangle or an ellipse, and click any graphic style to apply it to an active object. Look at the Appearance panel while you click different styles to see that you're applying combinations of attributes, including effects, fills, and strokes (see Figure 12-6).

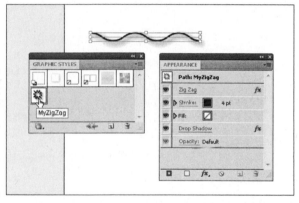

Figure 12-6: The Graphic Styles panel stores effects and other attributes.

**Book III
Chapter 12**

**Using Filters
and Effects**

Find more styles by choosing the Graphic Styles panel menu (click the arrow in the upper-right corner of the panel) and selecting Open Graphic Style Library.

You can store attributes as a graphic style in several ways; we show you two easy methods. If you already applied a combination of attributes to an object, store them by completing one of these tasks:

✦ With the object selected, Alt-click (Windows) or Option-click (Mac) the New Graphic Style button at the bottom of the Graphic Styles panel. Alt-click (Windows) or Option-click (Mac) to name the style when it's added.

✦ Drag the selected object directly into the Graphic Styles panel. The panel stores its attributes, but you have to double-click the new style to name it.

After you store a graphic style, simply select the object you want to apply the style to and then click the saved style in the Graphic Styles panel.

Creating 3D Artwork

All Illustrator effects are excellent, but the 3D feature is even better. You can not only add dimension by using the 3D effect but also *map artwork* (wrap artwork around a 3D object) and apply lighting to the 3D object. You can then design a label for a jelly jar, for example, and adhere it to the jar to show a client.

Here are the three choices for the 3D effect:

✦ **Extrude & Bevel:** Uses the z-axis to extrude an object. For example, a square becomes a cube.

✦ **Revolve:** Uses the z-axis and revolves a shape around it. You can use this option to change an arc into a ball.

✦ **Rotate:** Rotates a 3D object created using the Extrude & Bevel or Revolve effects or rotates a 2D object in 3D space. You can also adjust the perspective of a 3D or 2D object.

To apply a 3D effect, you need to create an object appropriate for the 3D effect. The Extrude & Bevel feature works well with shapes and text. If you want to edit an object that already has a 3D effect applied to it, double-click the 3D effect in the Appearance panel.

To apply a 3D effect, follow these steps:

1. **Select the object you want to apply the 3D effect to.**

2. **Choose Effect⇨3D⇨Extrude & Bevel.**

   Options for your chosen 3D effect appear. To see the 3D Extrude & Bevel Options dialog box, see Figure 12-7.

3. **Select the Preview check box so that you can see results as you experiment with these settings.**

4. **Click the Preview pane (which shows a cube in Figure 12-7) and drag to rotate the object in space.**

   It makes selecting the proper angle (or *positioning the object in space*) fun to do, or you can choose the angle from the Position drop-down list above the preview.

   Never use the Rotate tool to rotate a 3D object, unless you want some funky results; use the Preview pane in the Extrude & Bevel Options dialog box instead.

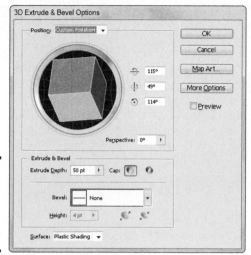

Figure 12-7:
The Extrude
& Bevel
Options
dialog box.

5. **(Optional) Use the Perspective drop-down list to add perspective to your object.**

6. **In the Extrude & Bevel section of the dialog box, choose a depth for your object and a cap.**

   The cap determines whether your shape has a solid cap on it or is hollow, as shown in Figure 12-8.

Figure 12-8:
Cap on
(left), cap off
(right).

7. **Choose a bevel (edge shape) from the Bevel drop-down list and set the height using the Height drop-down list.**

   You have a choice of two ways to apply the bevel:

   - *Bevel Extent Out:* The bevel is added to the object.

   - *Bevel Extent In:* The bevel is subtracted from the object.

8. **Choose a rendering style from the Surface drop-down list or click the More Options button for in-depth lighting options, such as changing the direction or adding lighting.**

9. **Click the Map Art button.**

The Map Art dialog box opens, as shown at the top of Figure 12-9. Use this dialog box to apply artwork to a 3D object.

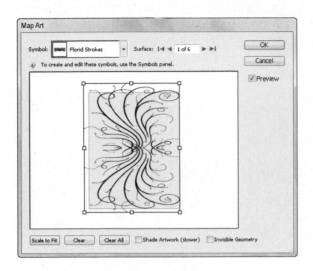

Figure 12-9: In the Map Art dialog box, you can select a surface and apply a symbol to it.

10. **Using the Surface arrow buttons, select the surface you want the artwork applied to and then choose a symbol from the Symbol drop-down list.**

    The result is shown at the bottom in Figure 12-9.

11. **Click OK to close the dialog box.**

Keep these points in mind when mapping artwork:

✦ An object must be a symbol to be used as mapped artwork. You simply need to select and drag to the Symbols panel the artwork you want mapped, to make it a selectable item in the Map Art dialog box.

✦ The light gray areas in the Preview pane are the visible areas based on the object's present position. Drag and scale the artwork in this pane to place the artwork where you want it.

✦ Shaded artwork (enabled by selecting the Shaded Artwork check box at the bottom of the Map Art dialog box) looks good but can take a long time to render.

Note: All 3D effects are rendered at 72 dpi (dots per inch; low resolution) so as not to slow down the processing speed. You can determine the resolution by either choosing Effect⇨Document Raster Effects Settings or saving or exporting the file. You can also select the object and choose Object⇨Rasterize. After the object is rasterized, you can no longer use it as an Illustrator 3D object, so save the original!

Adding Multiple Fills and Strokes

Using the panel menu in the Appearance panel, you can add more fills and strokes. You can use this feature to put differently colored fills on top of each other and individually apply effects to each one, creating truly interesting and creative results.

Just for fun, follow along to see what you can do to a single object from the Appearance panel:

1. **Create a star shape.**

Neither the size of the shape nor its number of points matters — just make the shape large enough to work with.

2. **Use the Swatches panel (choose Window⇨Swatches) to fill the shape with yellow and give it a black stroke.**

3. **Choose Window⇨Stroke to use the stroke panel to make the stroke 1 point; alternatively, choose 1 from the Stroke drop-down list in the Control panel.**

Notice that the present fill and stroke are listed in the Appearance panel. Even in its simplest form, the Appearance panel helps track basic attributes. You can easily take advantage of the tracking to apply effects to just a fill or a stroke.

4. **Click Stroke in the Appearance panel.**

If the Appearance panel isn't visible, choose Window⇨Appearance.

5. Choose Effect⇨Path⇨Offset Path.

6. In the Offset Path dialog box that appears, enter –5pt in the Offset text box and select the Preview check box.

   Notice that the stroke moves into the fill rather than on the edge.

7. Change the offset to a number that works with your star shape and click OK.

   Depending on the size of your star, you may want to adjust the amount of offset up or down.

8. From the panel menu of the Appearance panel, add a fill to the star shape. Click the arrow next to the new fill to open the Swatches panel and change the new fill to a different color, as shown in Figure 12-10.

Figure 12-10:
Change the new fill to a different color right in the Appearance panel.

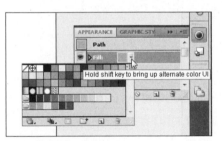

This step may seem ridiculous, but you can create some super effects with multiple fills.

9. Click Fill in the Appearance panel (the top one) and choose Effect⇨Distort and Transform⇨Twist.

10. In the Twist dialog box that appears, type 45 in the Angle text field and select the Preview check box.

    Notice how only the second fill is twisted. Neat, right?

11. Click OK to close the Twist dialog box.

12. Select the top fill from the Appearance panel again.

    Always be sure to select the fill or stroke you want before doing anything meant to change just that specific fill or stroke.

13. In the Transparency panel (choose Window⇨Transparency), choose 50% from the Opacity slider or simply type 50% in the Opacity text field.

    Now you can see your original shape through the new fill.

14. **With the top fill still selected, change the color or choose a pattern in the Swatches panel for a truly different appearance.**

Continue playing with combinations of fills and strokes for hours, if you want. We hope that this process "clicks" and that you can take it further on your own.

Using the New Perspective Grid

You can create and edit artwork based on a new CS5 feature — the perspective grid, shown in Figure 12-11. The grid is a huge help in creating successful perspective illustrations.

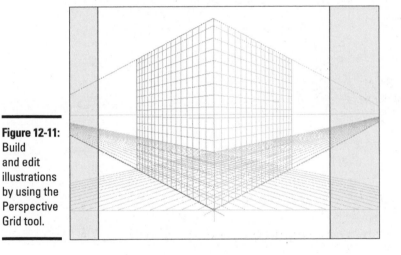

Figure 12-11: Build and edit illustrations by using the Perspective Grid tool.

To show or hide the default perspective grid, press Ctrl+Shift+I (Windows) or ⌘+Shift+I (Mac).

 You can use the Perspective Grid tool on the toolbar to fine-tune the grid.

Here are some simple instructions to help you start using the perspective grid:

1. **Create a new document and turn on the perspective grid by pressing Ctrl+Shift+I (Windows) or ⌘+Shift+I (Mac).**

2. **Select a shape tool, such as the Ellipse, and click and drag it to create the shape on the perspective grid.**

Notice that the shape's perspective is controlled by the grid.

3. **Select the Perspective Selection tool.**

It's the hidden tool in the Perspective Grid tool.

4. **Using the Perspective Selection tool, click and drag the shape to see that it's adjusted in position and location using the perspective grid.**

   Figure 12-12 shows the result of dragging an ellipse with the Perspective Selection tool.

   Note that you can also select and drag the grid itself by using the Perspective Selection tool.

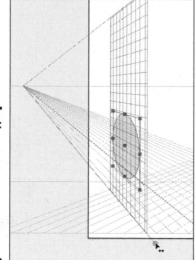

Figure 12-12: Click and drag to change the perspective using the Perspective Selection tool.

5. **Choose View➪Perspective Grid, as shown in Figure 12-13, and then select the type of perspective to apply.**

   In this step, you further customize your grid and choose other options to make your illustrations more precise.

Figure 12-13: Customize settings for the perspective grid by using the View menu.

Chapter 13: Using Your Illustrator Images

In This Chapter

✔ Saving Illustrator files

✔ Exporting files for use in other applications

✔ Preparing art for the Web

✔ Exporting to Flash

✔ Flattening your transparency

✔ Printing in Illustrator

So you have beautiful artwork but aren't sure how to remove it from your screen. You could have a party and invite all interested clients to stand around your monitor and admire it or share or sell your artwork by posting it on the Internet or printing it.

In this chapter, we show you how to use your illustrations in a variety of workflows, from using Illustrator files in page layout programs to exporting files for Photoshop (and other programs) and the Web. This chapter can help you use your artwork effectively and understand the saving and flattening choices available in Adobe Illustrator.

Saving and Exporting Illustrator Files

In this section, we show you how general choices differ in the Save As dialog box (choose File➪Save As) and describe their benefits.

When you choose File➪Save or File➪Save As, you save your file in one of these formats: Adobe Illustrator, EPS, FXG (a vector-based file format that describes graphical elements), PDF, SVG, SVG Compressed, or Template. We discuss all these formats throughout this chapter.

 If you need a file format not listed in the regular Save As dialog box, choose File➪Export to see additional choices. Using the File Export command, you can choose to save your files in any format listed in Table 13-1.

Table 13-1	Available File Formats
File Format	*Extension*
AutoCAD Drawing	.dwg
AutoCAD Interchange File	.dxf
BMP	.bmp
Enhanced Metafile	.emf
Flash	.swf
JPEG	.jpg
Macintosh PICT	.pct
Photoshop	.psd
PNG	.png
Targa	.tga
Text Format	.txt
TIFF	.tif
Windows Metafile	.wmf

Many formats *rasterize* artwork, so they no longer maintain vector paths and the benefits of being vector. Scalability isn't limited, for example. If you think that you may want to edit your image again later, be sure to save a copy of the file and keep the original in the .ai format.

The native Adobe Illustrator file format

If you're working with the programs in the Creative Suite, the best way to save a file is as a native Illustrator .ai file. For instance, the .ai format works with Adobe applications such as Adobe InDesign for page layout, Adobe Dreamweaver for Web page creation, Adobe Photoshop for photo retouching, and Adobe Acrobat for cross-platform documents.

Understanding when it's best to use the .ai format is important. Saving your Illustration as an .ai file ensures that it's editable; it also ensures that any transparency is retained, even if you use the file in another application.

To save and use a file in native Illustrator format, follow these steps:

1. **Make an illustration with transparency (50 percent transparent, for example) in Adobe Illustrator and choose File⇨Save As.**

2. **Select Adobe Illustrator Document (`.ai`) from the Save As Type drop-down list, give the file a name, and click Save.**

3. **Leave the Illustrator Native options at their defaults and click OK.**

After you follow the preceding step list to prepare your Illustrator file, you can use the illustration in other Adobe applications:

✦ **Adobe Acrobat:** Open the Acrobat application and choose File⇨Open. Locate the `.ai` file. The native Illustrator file opens within the Acrobat application.

✦ **Adobe InDesign:** Choose File⇨Place. This method supports transparency created in Adobe Illustrator, as shown in Figure 13-1. (However, copying and pasting from Illustrator to InDesign do *not* support transparency.)

Figure 13-1:
InDesign supports transparency, even over text.

**Book III
Chapter 13**

Using Your
Illustrator Images

✦ **Adobe Photoshop:** Choose File⇨Place. By placing an Illustrator file into Adobe Photoshop, you automatically create a Photoshop smart object. You can scale, rotate, and even apply effects to the Illustrator file and return to the original illustration at any time. Read more about smart objects in Photoshop in Book IV, Chapter 9.

If you want to go crazy with an Illustrator file in Photoshop, when you save the file in Illustrator, choose File⇨Export and select the Photoshop (`.psd`) format from the Save As Type drop-down list. Choose a resolution from the Options window. If you used layers, leave the Write Layers option selected.

In Photoshop, choose File⇨Open, select the file you just saved in Illustrator in `.psd` format, and click Open. The file opens in Photoshop with its layers intact.

✦ **Adobe Flash:** Use the integration features built into Adobe Illustrator to cut and paste directly into Adobe Flash. If you choose Edit⇨Copy from Adobe Illustrator, you can then switch to Adobe Flash and choose Edit⇨Paste. The Paste dialog box appears.

You can also choose File⇨Import in Flash for additional import choices. When a native Illustrator file was selected to import to the Stage, the Import to Stage dialog box appears (directly in Flash!) so that you can import only certain layers or sublayers and respond to warning messages about incompatible objects.

✦ **Adobe Dreamweaver:** By choosing File⇨Save for Web & Devices, you can choose to save your Illustrator document in .gif, .jpg, .png, .svg, .swf, or .wbmp format. You can then insert images in those file formats into Dreamweaver by choosing Insert⇨Image in Adobe Dreamweaver.

Click the Image button in the Insert panel in Dreamweaver. When the Select Image Source dialog box appears, navigate to the location where you saved your optimized file. Select it and click OK. If your file is located out of the root folder for the site you're working on, an alert window appears, offering the opportunity to save the file with your other site assets. See Book VI, Chapter 4 for more information about importing images in Dreamweaver.

Saving Illustrator files back to previous versions

When saving an .ai or .eps file, you can choose File⇨Save As, choose an Illustrator format, and then click OK.

When the Illustrator Options dialog box appears, choose a version from the Version drop-down list. Keep in mind that any features specific to newer versions of Illustrator aren't supported in older file formats, so make sure that you save a copy and keep the original file intact. Adobe helps you understand the risk of saving back to older versions by putting a warning sign next to the Version drop-down list and showing you specific issues with the version you selected in the Warnings window.

The EPS file format

Encapsulated PostScript File (EPS) is the file format that most text editing and page layout applications accept; EPS supports vector data and is completely scalable. Because the Illustrator .eps format is based on PostScript, you can reopen an EPS file and edit it in Illustrator at any time.

To save a file in Illustrator as an EPS, follow these steps:

1. **Choose File⇨Save As and select EPS from the Save As Type drop-down list.**

2. **From the Version drop-down list, choose the Illustrator version you're saving to.**

3. **In the EPS Options dialog box that appears (shown in Figure 13-2), choose the preview from the Format drop-down list:**

- *(8-Bit Color):* A color preview for either Mac or PC

- *(Black & White):* A low-resolution, black-and-white preview

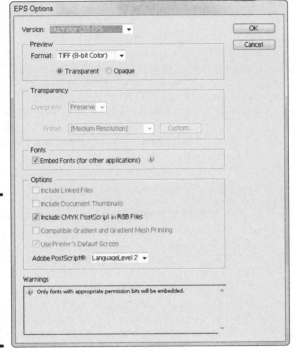

Figure 13-2:
Choose a
preview
and other
important
settings
in the EPS
Options
dialog box.

4. **Select either the Transparent or Opaque radio button, depending on whether you want the non-image areas in your artwork to be transparent or opaque.**

5. **Specify your transparency settings.**

These settings are grayed out if you haven't used transparency in the file. (See the "Flattening Transparency" section, later in this chapter, for more about this setting.)

6. **Leave the Embed Fonts (for Other Applications) check box selected to leave fonts you used embedded in the EPS file format.**

7. **In the Options section, leave the Include CMYK PostScript in RGB Files check box selected.**

   If you don't know which Adobe Postscript level you want to save to, leave it at the default.

8. **Click OK to save your file in EPS format.**

The PDF file format

If you want to save your file in a format that supports more than a dozen platforms and requires only Acrobat Reader, available as a free download at www.adobe.com, choose to save your file as a PDF (Portable Document Format) file.

If you can open an Illustrator file in Acrobat, why would you need to save a file in PDF format? For one thing, you can compress a PDF to a smaller size; also, the receiver can double-click the file and then Acrobat or Acrobat Reader launches automatically.

Depending on how you save the PDF, you can allow some level of editability in Adobe Illustrator. To save a file as a PDF, follow these steps:

1. **Choose File⇨Save As, choose Illustrator PDF (.pdf) from the Save As Type drop-down list, and then click Save.**

2. **In the Adobe PDF Options dialog box that appears, choose one of these options from the Preset drop-down list:**

   - *Illustrator Default:* Creates a PDF file in which all Illustrator data is preserved. PDF files created using this preset can be reopened in Illustrator with no loss of data.

   - *High Quality Print:* Creates PDF files for desktop printers and proofers.

   - *PDF/X-1a:2001:* The least flexible, but quite powerful, delivery method for PDF content data; requires that the color of all objects be CMYK (Cyan, Magenta, Yellow, Black) or spot colors. Elements in RGB (Red, Green Blue) or Lab color spaces or tagged with International Color Consortium (ICC) profiles are prohibited. All fonts used in the job must be embedded in the supplied PDF file.

   - *PDF/X-3:2002:* Has slightly more flexibility than the X-1a:2001 method (see preceding bullet) in that color managed workflows are supported elements in Lab and attached ICC source profiles may also be used.

   - *PDF/X-4:2008:* Based on PDF 1.4, which includes support for live transparency and has the same color management and ICC color specifications as PDF/X-3. You can open PDF files created for PDF/X-4 compliance in Acrobat 7.0 and Reader 7.0 and later.

- *Press Quality:* Creates a PDF file that can be printed to a high-resolution output device. The file will be large but maintain all information that a commercial printer or service provider needs in order to print files correctly. This option automatically converts the color mode to CMYK, embeds all fonts used in the file, prints at a higher resolution, and uses other settings to preserve the maximum amount of information contained in the original document.

  Before creating an Adobe PDF file by using the Press Quality preset, check with your commercial printer to determine the output resolution and other settings.

- *Smallest File Size:* Creates a low-resolution PDF suitable for posting on the Internet or sending by e-mail.

- *Standard:* Lets you select, from the Standard drop-down list, the type of PDF/X file you want to create. Avoid picking a PDF/X standard unless you have a specific need or are filling a request.

- *Compatibility:* Makes different features available for different versions, such as the ability to support layers in Version 6 or higher. For the most compatible file type, choose Acrobat 5 (PDF 1.4). To take advantage of layers or to preserve spot colors, you must choose Acrobat 6 or higher.

3. **Click Save PDF to save your file in PDF format.**

   If you want to be able to reopen the PDF file and edit it in Illustrator, make sure that you leave the Preserve Illustrator Editing Capabilities check box selected in the Adobe PDF Options dialog box.

In the Adobe PDF Options dialog box, to the left of the preset choices, are options you can change to customize your settings. Skim the options to see how to change resolution settings and even add printer's marks. Take a look at Book V to find out more about the additional Acrobat PDF options.

Want a press-quality PDF but don't want to convert all your colors to CMYK? Choose the Press setting and then click the Output options. In the Color Conversion drop-down list, select No Conversion.

Saving Your Artwork for the Web

If you need to save artwork for the Web, no feature is better than Save for Web & Devices. This dialog box opens a preview pane where you can test different file formats before you save the file.

To save an Illustrator file that you intend to use in a Web page, just follow these steps:

1. Choose File⇨Save for Web & Devices.

The Save for Web & Devices dialog box appears, showing your artwork on the Optimized tab. (See Figure 13-3.)

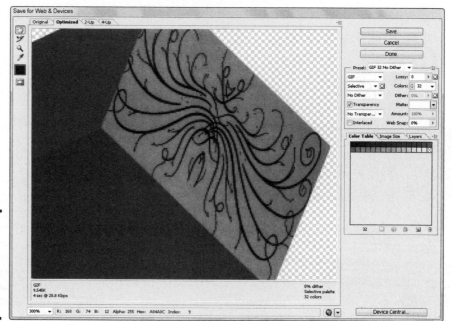

Figure 13-3:
Use Save for the Web to optimize your images for the Web.

2. Choose a tabbed view: Original, Optimized, 2-Up, or 4-Up.

You see as a default the artwork in Optimized view, which previews the artwork as it will appear based on the settings to the right. The best choice is 2-Up view because it shows your original image versus the optimized version.

3. Choose a setting for your file from the options on the right.

If you want to make it easy on yourself, choose a preset from the Preset drop-down list. Keep these points in mind:

- *Graphics Interchange Format (GIF) is generally used for artwork with spans of solid color.* GIF isn't a lossy format. You can make your artwork smaller by reducing the number of colors in the image — hence the choices, such as GIF 64 No Dither (64 colors). The lower the number of colors, the smaller the file size. You can also increase or decrease the number of colors in the file by changing the preset values in the Color text field or by clicking the arrows to the left of the Color text field.

- *Dithering tries to make your artwork look like it has more colors by creating a pattern in the colors.* It looks like a checkerboard pattern up close and even far away, as shown in Figure 13-4. It also makes a larger file size, so why use it? Most designers don't like the effect and choose the No Dither option.

Figure 13-4:
Dithering.

- *Joint Photographic Experts Group (JPEG) is used for artwork that has subtle gradations from one shade to another.* Photographs are often saved in this format. If you have drop shadows or blends in your artwork, select this format. JPEG is a *lossy* file format — it reduces an image to a lesser quality and can create odd artifacts in your artwork. You have choices, such as High, Medium, and Low in the Settings drop-down list — make sure to choose wisely. You can also use the Quality slider to tweak the compression.

- *PNG-8 is quite similar to the GIF file format.* Unless you have a certain reason for saving as PNG-8, stick with the GIF file format.

- *PNG-24 supports the best of two formats (GIF and JPEG).* The Portable Network Graphics (PNG) format supports not only the nice gradients from one tonal value to another (such as JPEGs) but also transparency (such as GIFs). It isn't just any old transparency: If you make an object 50 percent transparent in Adobe Illustrator and then save it by selecting Save for Web & Devices as a PNG-24 file with the Transparency check box selected, the image shows through to any other objects underneath it on its destination page.

- *The Shockwave Flash (SWF) graphics file format is a version of the Adobe Flash Player vector-based graphics format.* Because a SWF file is vector based, its graphics are scalable and play back smoothly on any screen size and across multiple platforms. From the Save for Web & Devices dialog box, you can save your image directly to SWF from Adobe Illustrator. Using the SWF choice, you can preview and make decisions about how you want to export to the file and make decisions about how to export layers.

- *Scalable Vector Graphics (SVG) is an emerging Web standard for two-dimensional graphics.* SVG is written in plain text and rendered by the browser, except that in this case it isn't just text that's rendered but also shapes and images, which can be animated and made interactive. SVG is written in XML (Extensible Markup Language). You can choose to save Scalable Vector Graphics out of Adobe Illustrator from the Save for Web & Devices dialog box.

- *Use the Wireless Application Protocol Bitmap Format (WBMP) format for bitmap images for mobile devices.* This format produces a black-and-white image that is not necessarily attractive, but necessary for some mobile devices.

4. **When you're satisfied with your chosen settings, click Save.**

When saving illustrations for the Web, keep these points in mind — they make the whole process much easier for you and anyone who uses your illustrations:

✦ **Keep file sizes small.** Don't forget that if you're saving illustrations for a Web page, many other elements will also be on that page. Try to conserve on file size to make downloading the page quicker for viewers with dial-up connections. Most visitors don't wait more than ten seconds for a page to download before giving up and moving to another Web site.

When you make your choices, keep an eye on the file size and the optimized artwork in the lower left corner of the preview window. A GIF should be around 10K on average, and a JPEG around 15K. (Though these rules aren't written in stone, *please* don't try to slap a 100K JPEG on a Web page.)

You can change the download time by clicking the panel menu in the upper right corner of the Save for Web & Devices dialog box and choosing Optimize to File Size. Then you can enter a final file size and have Illustrator create your settings in the Save for Web & Devices dialog box.

✦ **Preview the file before saving it.** If you want to see the artwork in a Web browser before saving it, click the Preview in Default Browser button at the bottom of the Save for Web & Devices dialog box. The browser of choice appears with your artwork in the quality level and size in which it will appear. If no browser is selected, click and hold down the Preview in Default Browser button to choose Other and then browse to locate a browser you want to use for previewing. Close the browser to return to the Save for Web & Devices dialog box.

✦ **Change the size.** Many misconceptions abound about the size of Web artwork. Most people generally view their browser windows in an area measuring approximately 700 x 500 pixels. Depending on the screen resolution, this setting may cover the entire screen on a 14-inch monitor. Even viewers with 21-inch, high-resolution monitors often don't want to have their entire screens covered by a browser window, however, so their areas still measure approximately 700 x 500 pixels. When choosing a size for your artwork, choose one with proportions similar to these. For example, if you want an illustration to occupy about a quarter of the browser window's width, make your image about 175 pixels wide (700÷4 = 175). If you notice that the height of your image is more than 500 pixels, whittle the height in size as well or else viewers have to scroll to see the whole image (and it will probably take too long to download).

Use the Image Size tab to enter new sizes. As long as the Constrain Proportions check box is selected, both the height and width of the image change proportionally. Click the Apply button to change the size, but don't close the Save for Web & Devices dialog box.

✦ **Finish the save.** If you aren't finished with the artwork but want to save your settings, hold down the Alt (Windows) or Option (Mac) key and click the Remember button. (When you aren't holding down the Alt or Option key, the Remember button is the Done button.) When you're finished, click the Save button and save your file in the appropriate location.

Flattening Transparency

You may find that all those cool effects you added to your illustration don't print correctly. When you print a file that has effects, such as drop shadows, cool gradient blends, and feathering, Illustrator *flattens* them, by turning into pixels any transparent areas that overlap other objects and leaving what it can as vectors.

To understand flattening, look at Figure 13-5 to see the difference between the original artwork (on the left) and the flattened artwork (on the right). Notice that in the figure, when the artwork was flattened, some areas turned into pixels. But at what resolution? Flattening helps you determine the quality of art — before receiving an unpleasant surprise at the outcome.

**Book III
Chapter 13**

**Using Your
Illustrator Images**

Figure 13-5:
Artwork before and after flattening is applied.

Flattening a file

If you've taken advantage of transparency, or effects using transparency (which we discuss in Chapter 11 of this minibook), follow these steps to produce the highest-quality artwork in your file:

1. **Make sure that the artwork you created is in CMYK mode.**

You can change the document's color mode by choosing File➪Document Color Mode.

2. **Choose Effects➪Document Raster Effects Settings.**

The Document Raster Effects Settings dialog box appears, as shown in Figure 13-6.

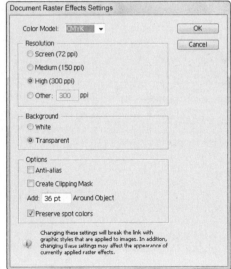

Figure 13-6: Choosing the quality of rasterized artwork.

3. **Choose the resolution you want to use by selecting an option in the Resolution area.**

Select the Screen (72 ppi) option for Web graphics, Medium (150 ppi) for desktop printers and copiers, and High (300 ppi) for graphics to be printed on a press.

4. **Choose whether you want a white or transparent background.**

If you select the Transparent option, you create an alpha channel that's retained if the artwork is exported into Photoshop.

5. **You can generally leave the items in the Options section deselected:**

   - *The Anti-Alias check box* applies antialiasing to reduce the appearance of jagged edges in the rasterized image. Deselect this option to maintain the crispness of fine lines and small text.

   - *The Create Clipping Mask check box* creates a mask that makes the background of the rasterized image appear transparent. You don't need to create a clipping mask if you select the Transparent option for your background.

   - *The Add around Object text field* adds the specified number of pixels around the rasterized image.

   - *The Preserve Spot Colors check box* keeps any spot colors you have defined intact. Leave this checked.

6. **Click OK.**

   The next step is to set the transparency options in the Document Setup dialog box.

7. **Choose File⇨Document Setup.**

   From the Transparency section in the middle of the dialog box, click the Preset drop-down list and select the Low, Medium, High, or Custom option. Select the Low option for onscreen viewing, the Medium option for printers and copiers, or the High option for press quality. To control more settings, click the Custom button to the right of the drop-down list.

8. **Click OK.**

If you customize settings regularly, choose Edit⇨Transparency Flattener Presets to create and store your own presets.

You can apply the flattening in several ways. Here are three simple methods:

- ✦ Select the objects that require flattening and choose Object⇨Flatten Transparency. Choose a default setting or a custom preset (that you created) from the Preset drop-down list and click OK.

- ✦ Choose File⇨Print and select Advanced from the list of print options on the left. Choose a preset from the Overprint and Transparency Flattener options. If you used the Attributes panel to create overprints (for trapping used in high-end printing), make sure to preserve the overprints.

  Overprints aren't preserved in areas that use transparency.

- ✦ Choose File⇨Save As and choose Illustrator EPS. In the Transparency section of the EPS Options dialog box, choose a flattening setting from the Preset drop-down list. If your transparency options are grayed out, your file has no transparency.

Using the Flattener Preview panel

If you want to preview your flattening, open the Flattener Preview panel by choosing Window➪Flattener Preview.

The Flattener Preview panel doesn't apply flattening, but it shows you a preview based on your settings. Click the Refresh button and choose Show Options from the panel menu. Test various settings without flattening the file. Experiment with different settings and then save your presets by selecting Save Transparency Flattener Preset from the panel menu. The saved settings can be accessed in the Preset drop-down list in the Options dialog boxes that appear when you save a file in EPS format or in the Document Setup dialog box.

To update the preview, click the Refresh button after making changes.

Zoom in on artwork by clicking in the Preview pane. Scroll the artwork in the Preview pane by holding down the spacebar and dragging. Zoom out by Alt-clicking (Windows) or Option-clicking (Mac).

Printing from Illustrator

Printing from Illustrator gives you lots of capabilities, such as printing composites to separations and adding printer's marks.

To print your illustration, follow these steps:

1. **Choose File➪Print.**

2. **In the Print dialog box that appears, select a printer if one isn't already selected.**

3. **If the PPD isn't selected, choose one from the PPD drop-down list.**

A *PPD* is a printer description file. Illustrator needs one in order to determine the specifics of the PostScript printer you're sending your file to. This setting lets Illustrator know whether the printer can print in color, the paper size it can handle, and its resolution, as well as many other important details.

4. **Choose from other options.**

For example, use the General options section to pick pages to print. In the Media area, select the size of the media you're printing to. In the Options area, choose whether you want layers to print and any options specific to printing layers.

5. **Click the Print button to print your illustration.**

That's it. Although printing illustrations can be quite simple, the following list highlights some basic points to keep in mind as you prepare one for printing:

✦ **Print a composite:** A *composite* is a full-color image, where all inks are applied to the page (and not separated out onto individual pages — one apiece for cyan, magenta, yellow, and black). To ensure that your settings are correct, click Output in the print options pane on the left side of the Print dialog box and select Composite from the Mode drop-down list.

✦ **Print separations:** To separate colors, click Output in the print options pane on the left side of the Print dialog box; from the Mode drop-down list, choose the Separations (Host-Based) option. Select the In-RIP Separations option only if your service provider or printer asks you to. Other options to select from are described in this list:

• The resolution is determined by your PPD, based on the dots per inch (dpi) in the printer description. You may have only one option available in the Printer Resolution drop-down list.

• Select the Convert Spot Colors to Process check box to make your file 4-color.

• Click the printer icons to the left of the listed colors to turn off or on the colors you want to print.

✦ **Printer's marks and bleeds:** Click Marks and Bleeds in the print options pane on the left side of the Print dialog box to turn on all printer's marks, or just select the ones that you want to appear.

Specify a bleed area if you're extending images beyond the trim area of a page. If you don't specify a bleed, the artwork stops at the edge of the page and doesn't leave a trim area for the printer.

TIP

After you create a good set of options specific to your needs, click the Save Preset button (which is the disk icon to the right of the Print Preset drop-down list). Name your presets appropriately; when you want to use a particular preset, select it from the Print Preset drop-down list at the top of the Print dialog box for future print jobs.

Book III
Chapter 13

Using Your
Illustrator Images

Book IV

Photoshop CS5

The 5th Wave   By Rich Tennant

"I'm going to assume that most of you — but
not all of you — understand that this session
on 'masking' has to do with Photoshop."

Contents at a Glance

Chapter 1: Exploring New Features in Photoshop CS5

In This Chapter

✓ Working faster with the improved workspace

✓ Creating better selections with the new features

✓ Organizing and finding files faster with the new Mini Bridge

✓ Taking advantage of the new Puppet Warp feature

✓ Exploring new and improved 3D features

*P*hotoshop CS5 includes significant improvements to its workspace, selection tools, and more. In this chapter, you take a quick tour of some of its most exciting new capabilities. The features you see depend on which version of Photoshop CS5 you have (Standard or Extended).

If you want to dive immediately into the new features, choose Window⇨ Workspace⇨New in CS5. Instantly, all new features are highlighted on the menus! (We have to say that not all highlighted features are totally new — many existed in previous versions. Perhaps you didn't notice some of these features in the last version, so highlighting them isn't a bad idea.

You will find lots more new features sprinkled throughout the rest of this minibook because most of the best improvements need to be presented in context, or else they just can't be properly appreciated.

An Improved Workspace Helps You Find the Tools You Need

You have to give it up to the Adobe Photoshop engineers: They hear the pleas of average users and are trying to help. "Help with what," you ask? Help with understanding Photoshop terminology and the unique names of the program's tools and controls. Many people who have been using Photoshop for years feel at ease with the unique terminology, but new users seem to have a more difficult time finding the tools and options they want to use.

By default, some of the panels in Photoshop are collapsed to a compact view and represented by space-saving icons. This workspace makes focusing on images easier, and the tools become a natural extension of your work.

Photoshop CS5 continues to make extensive use of panels. Here's how to work with them:

✦ To activate a panel, simply click the appropriate panel icon. If you select another one, its panel is brought to the front of the display.

✦ To return all panels to icons, click the Collapse to Icons bar at the top of the panel docking area.

✦ When you drag an icon to the work area, the panel automatically expands; when you drag the panel back into the docking area, it turns back into an icon.

✦ Showing and hiding all your tools and panels is easy: Press the Tab key. To cause them to reappear, move the cursor over the left or right side of your screen and pause when you see the vertical gray bar — the toolbar or panels then appear!

If you want them all to show again, press Tab again.

Find what you need quickly by changing to an easy-to-locate workspace choice: Essentials, Design, Painting, Photography, 3D, Motion, or New in CS5. By selecting a workspace, you can have the relevant panels visible and ready when you need them.

Many users find that they develop, over time, a unique combination of panels when working in Photoshop. Fortunately, you can click the double arrow, shown in Figure 1-1, to choose a different workspace.

Figure 1-1:
Choose a
workspace.

Improve Your Compositions with New Selection Improvements

Creating a professional selection is important when the goal is to create realistic compositions, and Photoshop CS5 has somehow managed to come up with improvements to help you do a better job.

The program has so many helpful additions to make you a selection pro that you will want to read Chapter 4 of this minibook to experience them all. Nonetheless, we take a stab at listing some of the best (which are available in the Refine Edge dialog box) to whet your appetite.

You can access the improved Refine Edge feature by activating any Selection tool (Rectangle, Marquee, and so on) and then clicking the Refine Edge button that appears in the options panel. The CS5 Refine Edge dialog box provides opportunities to take edge selection further with these new and improved features:

✦ **Edge detection and color decontamination:** Use these features to make difficult selections (like hair) easier than ever to make.

✦ **Adjust Edge:** Use the Adjust Edge functions to visually make variations on the edge of your selection. In Figure 1-2, you see that the feathering can be previewed and changed before confirming the selection edge change.

✦ **Output To:** A favorite feature has to be the opportunity to use the Output To drop-down menu, shown in Figure 1-2. Use the options on this menu to extract your newly selected content to a new layer, to a mask, or even to a new document. Now you have no excuses for helmet head!

Figure 1-2:
Use the new and improved Refine Edge dialog box to make previously difficult selections easy.

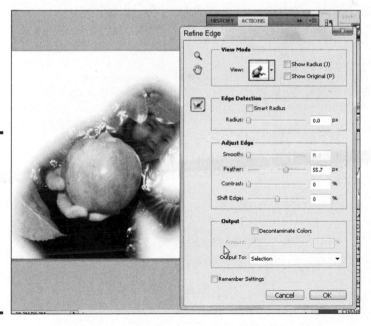

A Bridge to Better Organization

Adobe Bridge has always been a huge timesaving application, for anyone who ventured into taking advantage of it. But others found it cumbersome to have a separate application open, or else the amount of space needed was just too valuable for anyone short on monitor real estate.

Fret no more! Now Bridge fans and soon-to-be Bridge fans can take advantage of the new Mini Bridge. It exists as a panel that you can open and access at any time. Simply choose File⇨Browse in Mini Bridge to open the Mini Bridge panel, shown in Figure 1-3. The amount of real estate it occupies is reasonable, and it can be collapsed in an instant to free up space. Many of the same great features exist in Mini Bridge that are available in the Bridge application — and guess what? If you want the best of both worlds, Bridge and Mini Bridge both exist. Find out more about Bridge and Mini Bridge in Book I, Chapter 5.

Figure 1-3: The convenient Mini Bridge panel helps organize and find files.

Advanced Warping Capabilities

Who hasn't played with puppets? Using the new Puppet Warp feature, you can create custom warps from the contents of your images. By choosing Edit⇨Puppet Warp, you can add multiple pins to an image, which you can click and drag to warp independently, or you can select multiple pins to warp several locations in the image simultaneously. (See Figure 1-4.) Why the name Puppet Warp? Because the pins hinge off of each other as you make warp changes.

You have three modes from which to choose the type of warp you want, located on the Mode drop-down menu of the Options bar:

✦ **Rigid:** Considers the object being deformed as more stiff or rigid. This option is good for bending items such as body parts.

✦ **Normal:** Distorts to the grid.

✦ **Distort:** Serves as more of a creative option that you can use to manipulate large photographs. Small changes in pin positions can result in large overall deformation.

Figure 1-4: The Puppet Warp grid and multiple pins.

Content Aware Retouching

The Spot Healing tool has always been a useful tool, but now it's even better. You can select the Content Aware option from the Tool Options bar and retouch like magic. By selecting the Spot Healing tool and then checking the Content Aware option in the Options bar, you can brush over the area in the image (where you want to remove a flaw or replace an image area), and Photoshop will make its best attempt to replace the retouched area with pixels that match the surrounding area, as shown in Figure 1-5.

You can not only use the Spot Healing tool to apply content aware fill but also use the Edit⇨Fill command. Find out more about these incredible retouching tools in Chapter 8 of this minibook.

Book IV
Chapter 1

Exploring New
Features in
Photoshop CS5

Figure 1-5:
Retouch like a pro by taking advantage of the content-aware fill feature.

Step into 3D

Even if you don't typically work in the 3D environment, you now have the opportunity to get your feet wet with the new Repoussé feature. You use it to convert 2D objects into 3D by taking advantage of the same technique that metalworkers use: hammering or pressing on the reverse side of an object.

After selecting a text layer, selection, path, or mask, choose 3D⇨Repoussé. The Repoussé dialog box appears and offers the opportunity to convert that item into 3D, as shown in Figure 1-6. (You can also choose Window⇨3D to access the 3D Scene panel to convert any layer to a 3D object.) With the active layer (or path) selected, choose the shape preset you want to convert to as well as other options, such as extrude depth, material, and bevel, and then click OK.

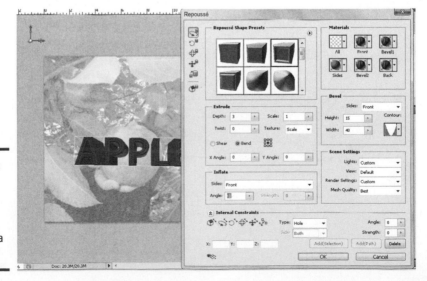

Figure 1-6:
Convert any layer, selection, path, or mask into a 3D object.

We hope that you're so intrigued by the incredible new features in Photoshop CS5 that you're inspired to read the rest of this minibook. Count on discovering more features as you progress through the chapters.

Chapter 2: Getting Into Photoshop CS5 Basics

*N*avigating the work area in Photoshop can be slightly cumbersome at first, especially if you've never worked in a program that relies so heavily on panels. In this chapter, we introduce you to the Photoshop CS5 work area, show you what the Photoshop CS5 tools are all about, and reveal how to neatly organize and hide panels. We also show you how to do basic tasks, such as open, crop, and save an image.

Getting to Know the Tools

Tools are used to create, select, and manipulate objects in Photoshop CS5. When you open Photoshop, the Tools panel appears along the left edge of the workspace (see Figure 2-1), and panels appear on the right side of the screen. (We discuss panels in the later section "Navigating the Work Area.")

In the Tools panel, look for the name of the tool to appear in a tooltip when you hover the cursor over the tool. Following the tool name is a letter in parentheses, which is the keyboard shortcut command you can use to access that tool. Simply press the Shift key along with the key command you see to access any hidden tools. In other words, pressing P activates the Pen tool, and pressing Shift+P activates the hidden tools under the Pen tool in the order they appear. When you see a small triangle at the lower right corner of the tool icon, you know that the tool contains hidden tools.

Table 2-1 lists the Photoshop tools, describes what each one is used for, and specifies in which chapter you can find more information about each one.

Tools panel

Figure 2-1:
The Photoshop CS5 workspace includes the Tools panel.

Table 2-1		Photoshop CS Tools	
Button	*Tool*	*What You Can Do with It*	*See This Chapter in Book IV*
	Move (V)	Move selections or layers	4
	Marquee (M)	Select the image area	4
	Lasso (L)	Make freehand selections	4
	Quick Selection (W)	Select similar pixels	4
	Crop (C)	Crop an image	2
	Eyedropper (I)	Create HTML slices	N/A

Button	Tool	What You Can Do with It	See This Chapter in Book IV
	Spot Healing Brush (J)	Retouch flaws	8
	Brush (B)	Paint the foreground color	8
	Clone Stamp (S)	Copy pixel data	8
	History Brush (Y)	Paint from the selected state	8
	Eraser (E)	Erase pixels	8
	Gradient (G)	Create a gradient	8
	Blur	Blur pixels	8
	Toning (O)	Dodge, burn, saturate	8
	Pen (P)	Create paths	5
	Type (T)	Create text	9
	Path Selection (A)	Select paths	5
	Vector Shape (U)	Create vector shapes	9
	3D Object Rotate (K)	Rotate 3D objects	9
	3D Camera Rotate (N)	Rotate 3D objects	9
	Hand (H)	Navigate page	9
	Zoom (Z)	Increase or decrease the view	2

Looking for the Magic Wand tool? Click and hold the Quick Selection tool in the Tools panel to access it.

Navigating the Work Area

Getting around in Photoshop isn't much different from getting around in other Adobe applications. All Adobe applications make extensive use of panels, for example. In the following sections, we cover the highlights of navigating in Photoshop.

Docking and saving panels

Panels, panels everywhere — do you really need them all? Maybe not just yet, but when you increase your skill level, you'll take advantage of most (if not all) of the Photoshop panels. They give you easy access to important functions. Book I, Chapter 3 provides a lot of basic information about using panels in the Adobe Creative Suite, so check out that chapter if you need a refresher on using panels. We add only a few topics here that are specific to using the panels in Photoshop.

When you work in Photoshop, keep in mind these two key commands:

✦ Press Tab to switch between hiding and showing the tools and panels.

✦ Press Shift+Tab to hide the panels, leaving only the Tools panel visible.

If you find that you're always using the same panels, hide the panels you don't need and arrange the others onscreen where you want them. Then follow these steps to save that panel configuration:

1. **Choose Window⇨Workspace⇨New Workspace.**

The New Workspace dialog box appears.

2. **Name your workspace and click Save.**

3. **Any time you want the panels to return to your saved locations, choose Window⇨Workspace⇨*Name of Workspace*.**

Name of Workspace is the name you supplied in Step 2.

Choose Window⇨Workspace⇨Reset Essentials to restore the panels to the order they were in after the initial installation.

Taking advantage of new workspace features

Photoshop CS5 includes many new saved workspaces that you can take advantage of to streamline workspaces and open the panels you need for specific tasks. Some of these new workspaces can be used for photography, painting, or design, for example.

Increase your work area by turning panels into icons, as shown in Figure 2-2. Do so by either right-clicking the tab of a panel and selecting Collapse to Icons or clicking the Auto Collapse gray bar at the top of the *panel drawer*. Yes, you read it correctly — the area where the panels are located is a drawer that can be adjusted in or out by crossing over the vertical pane to the left of the panels, and then dragging when the double-arrow appears.

Figure 2-2:
Turn panels
into icons.

Zooming in to get a better look

Images that look fine at one zoom level may look extremely bad at another. You'll zoom in and out quite often while working on images in Photoshop. You can find menu choices for zooming on the View menu; a quicker way to zoom is to use the keyboard commands listed in Table 2-2.

Table 2-2	Zooming and Navigation Keyboard Shortcuts	
Command	*Windows Shortcut*	*Mac Shortcut*
Actual size	Alt+Ctrl+0 (zero)	⌘+1
Fit in window	Ctrl+0 (zero)	⌘+0 (zero)
Zoom in	Ctrl++ (plus sign) or Ctrl+spacebar	⌘++ (plus sign) or ⌘+spacebar
Zoom out	Ctrl+– (minus) or Alt+spacebar	⌘+– (minus) or Option+spacebar
Hand tool	Spacebar	Spacebar

This list describes a few advantages of working with the Zoom tool to get a better look at your work:

✦ **100 percent view:** Double-clicking the Zoom tool in the Tools panel gives you a 100 percent view. Do it before using filters to see a more realistic result of making changes.

✦ **Zoom marquee:** Drag from the upper left corner to the lower right corner of the area you want to zoom to. While you drag, a marquee appears; when you release the mouse button, the marqueed area zooms to fill the image window. The Zoom marquee gives you much more control than just clicking the image with the Zoom tool. Zoom out again to see the entire image by pressing Ctrl+0 (Windows) or ⌘+0 (Mac). Doing so fits the entire image in the viewing area.

✦ **Keyboard shortcuts:** If a dialog box is open and you need to reposition or zoom to a new location on an image, you can use the keyboard commands without closing the dialog box.

✦ **A new window for a different look:** Choose Window➪Arrange➪New Window to create an additional window for the frontmost image. This technique is helpful when you want to see the entire image (say, at actual size) to see the results as a whole yet zoom in to focus on a small area of the image to do some fine-tuning. The new window is linked dynamically to the original window so that when you make changes, the original and any other new windows created from the original are immediately updated.

✦ **Cycle through images:** Press Ctrl+Tab (Windows) or ⌘+Tab (Mac) to cycle through open images.

Choosing Your Screen Mode

You have a choice of three screen modes in which to work. Most users start and stay in the default (standard screen) mode until they accidentally end up in another. The modes are accessible by clicking and holding Screen Mode, located in the Application bar, as shown in Figure 2-3.

Figure 2-3:
Change
your screen
mode.

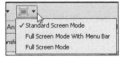

✦ **Standard Screen Mode:** In this typical view, an image window is open, but you can see your desktop and other images open behind it.

✦ **Full Screen Mode with Menu Bar:** In this view, the image is surrounded, to the edge of the work area, with neutral gray. Working in this mode prevents you not only from accidentally clicking out of an image and leaving Photoshop but also from seeing other images behind the working image.

✦ **Full Screen Mode:** A maximized document window fills all available space between docks and resizes when dock widths change.

Getting Started with Basic Tasks in Photoshop CS5

Unless you use Photoshop as a blank canvas for painting, you may rarely create a new file in Photoshop. The reason is that you usually have a source image you start with that may have been generated by a scanner, digital camera, or stock image library.

The following sections show you how to open an existing image file in Photoshop, create a new image (if you want to use Photoshop to paint, for example), crop an image, and save an edited image.

Opening an image

You can open an existing Photoshop image in one of several ways:

✦ Choose File⇨Open, select the file in the Open dialog box, and then click the Open button.

✦ Choose File⇨Browse. By selecting Browse instead of Open, you launch the Adobe Bridge application. Read more about Adobe Bridge later in this section and also in Book I, Chapter 5.

✦ Double-click an image in the Mini Bridge panel.

Photoshop can open a multitude of file formats, even if the image was created in another application, such as Illustrator or another image-editing program. However, you have to open the image in Photoshop by choosing File⇨Open or, using Adobe Bridge, by selecting an image and dragging it to the Photoshop icon on the taskbar (Windows) or Dock (Mac). If you double-click an image file (one that wasn't originally created in Photoshop, or from different versions) in a folder, the image may open only in a preview application.

If you're opening a folder of images that you want to investigate first, choose File⇨Browse to open Adobe Bridge, the control center for Adobe Creative Suite. You can use Adobe Bridge to organize, browse, and locate the assets you need to create your content. Adobe Bridge keeps available for easy access native AI, INDD, PSD, and Adobe PDF files as well as other Adobe and non-Adobe application files.

You can access the standalone Adobe Bridge application from all applications in the Creative Suite by choosing File⇨Browse or by clicking the Go to Bridge icon in the upper left corner of the application window. Use the Bridge interface to view images as thumbnails and look for metadata information. For a condensed version of Bridge, click the MB icon on the Application bar.

**Book IV
Chapter 2**

**Getting Into
Photoshop CS5
Basics**

Discover Camera Raw

If you haven't discovered the Camera Raw capabilities in Adobe Photoshop, you'll want to give them a try. The Camera Raw format is available for image capture in many cameras. Simply choose the format in your camera's settings as Raw instead of JPEG or TIFF. These Raw files are a bit larger than standard JPEG files, but you capture an enormous amount of data with the image that you can retrieve after opening. (See www.adobe.com for a complete list of cameras supporting Camera Raw.)

A Camera Raw file contains unprocessed picture data from a digital camera's image sensor, along with information about how the image was captured, such as camera and lens type, exposure settings, and white balance setting. When you open the file in Adobe Photoshop CS5, the built-in Camera Raw plug-in interprets the Raw file on your computer, making adjustments for image color and tonal scale.

When you shoot JPEG images with your camera, you're locked into the processing done by your camera, but working with Camera Raw files gives you maximum control over images, such as controlling their white balance, tonal range, contrast, color saturation, and image sharpening. Cameras that can shoot in Raw format have a setting on the camera that changes its capture mode to Raw. Rather than write a final JPEG file, a Raw data file is written, which consists of black-and-white brightness levels from each of the several million pixel sites on the imaging sensor. The actual image hasn't yet been produced, and unless you have specific software, such as the plug-in built into Adobe Photoshop, opening the file can be difficult, if not impossible.

To open a Camera Raw file, simply choose File➪Browse. Adobe Bridge opens, and you see several panels, including the Folders, Content, Preview, and Metadata panels. In the Folders panel, navigate to the location on your computer where you've saved Camera Raw images; thumbnail previews appear in the Content panel. Think of Camera Raw files as photo negatives. You can reprocess them at any time to achieve the results you want.

Right-click (Windows) or Control-click (Mac) a JPEG or TIFF file and choose Open in Camera Raw from the contextual menu. This is a great way to experiment with all the cool features available with this plug-in, but your results aren't as good as if you used an actual Raw file.

If Adobe Photoshop CS5 doesn't open your Raw file, you may need to update the Raw plug-in. (See www.adobe.com for the latest plug-in.) The plug-in should be downloaded and placed in this location in Windows: `C:\Program Files\Common Files\Adobe\Plug-Ins\CS5\File Formats`, and this location on the Macintosh: `Library\Application Support\Adobe\Plug-Ins\CS5\File Formats`.

Creating a new file

If you're creating a new file, you may be doing so to create a composite of existing files or to start with a blank canvas because you're supercreative.

For whatever reason, note that when you choose File➪New, you can choose from a multitude of basic format choices on the Preset menu. They range from basic sizes and resolutions, such as U.S. Paper or Photo, to other final output such as the Web, Mobile Devices, or Film.

Keep in mind that you're determining not only size but also resolution in the new file. If it will contain images from other files, make sure that the new file is the same resolution. Otherwise, you may see unexpected size results when cutting and pasting or dragging images into the new file. Choose Image⇨Image Size to see the document dimensions.

Cropping an image

A simple but essential task is to crop an image. *Cropping* means to eliminate all parts of the image that aren't important to its composition.

Cropping is especially important in Photoshop. Each pixel, no matter what color, takes up the same amount of information, so cropping eliminates unneeded pixels and saves on file size and processing time. For that reason, you should crop images before you start working on them.

You can crop an image in Photoshop CS5 in two ways:

- ✦ Use the Crop tool.
- ✦ Select an area with the Marquee tool and choose Image⇨Crop.

To crop an image by using the Crop tool, follow these steps:

1. **Press C to access the Crop tool and drag around the area of the image you want to crop to.**

2. **If you need to adjust the crop area, drag the handles in the crop-bounding area.**

3. **When you're satisfied with the crop-bounding area, double-click in the center of the crop area or press the Return or Enter key to crop the image.**

4. **If you want to cancel the crop, press the Esc key.**

Ever scan in an image that ends up crooked? When using the Crop tool, if you position the cursor outside any handle, a rotate symbol appears. Drag the crop-bounding area to rotate it and line it up the way you want it cropped. When you press Return or Enter, the image straightens out.

Saving images

Save an image file by choosing File⇨Save. If you're saving the file for the first time, the Save As dialog box appears. Notice in the Format drop-down list that you have plenty of choices for file formats. (File formats are discussed in more detail in Chapter 10 of this minibook.) You can always play it safe by choosing the native Photoshop (PSD) file format, which supports all Photoshop features. Choosing certain other formats may eliminate layers, channels, and other special features.

**Book IV
Chapter 2**

**Getting Into
Photoshop CS5
Basics**

Many users choose to save a native Photoshop file as a backup to any other file format. Be sure to have a backup or an original file saved as a native Photoshop (PSD) file when you start taking advantage of layers and other outstanding Photoshop elements. As a Creative Suite user, keep in mind that you can use the native file format for Photoshop in all other Creative Suite applications.

Chapter 3: Messing with Mode Matters

In This Chapter

- Editing pixels in bitmap images
- Understanding Photoshop image modes
- Working in black and white, RGB, or CMYK

*B*efore diving into Photoshop, you must know which image mode you should use and understand the importance of color settings. No matter whether you're producing a one-color newsletter, a full-color logo, or a creation halfway between, this chapter can help you create much better imagery for both the Web and print.

Working with Bitmap Images

You may have already discovered that Photoshop works a little differently from most other applications. To create those smooth gradations from one color to the next, Photoshop takes advantage of pixels. *Bitmap images* (or *raster images*) are based on a grid of pixels. The grid is smaller or larger depending on the resolution you're using. The number of pixels along the height and width of a bitmap image are the pixel dimensions of an image, measured in pixels per inch (ppi). The more pixels per inch, the more detail in the image.

Unlike *vector graphics* (mathematically created paths), bitmap images can't be scaled without losing detail. (See Figure 3-1 for an example of a bitmap image and a vector graphic.) Generally, you should use bitmap images at or close to the size you need. If you resize a bitmap image, it can become jagged on the edges of sharp objects. On the other hand, you can scale vector graphics and edit them without degrading sharp edges.

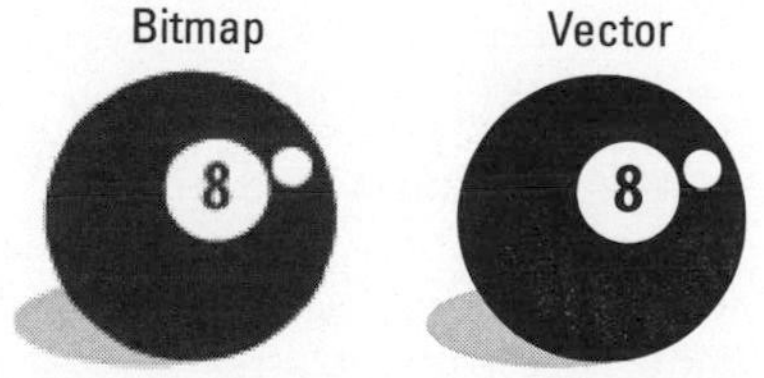

Bitmap   Vector

Figure 3-1:
Bitmap
versus
vector.

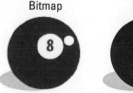

Photoshop can work on both bitmap and vector art. (See the path line around the vector shape layer and notice that the path isn't pixelated (or broken down into a step pattern created by the pixels). It gives you, as a designer, incredible opportunities when combining the two technologies.

For information on changing and adjusting image resolution, see Chapter 6 of this minibook.

Choosing the Correct Photoshop Mode

Choose Image⇨Mode to view the image mode choices you can choose from. Selecting the right one for an image is important because each mode offers different capabilities and results. For example, if you choose Bitmap mode, you can work only in black and white. That's it — no shades of color, not even gray. Most features are disabled in Bitmap mode, which is fine if you're working on art for a black-and-white logo, but not for most images. If, instead, you work in RGB (Red, Green, Blue) mode, you have full access to Photoshop's capabilities.

Read on to see which image mode is best for your needs. When you're ready to make your mode selection, open a file and choose Image⇨Mode to make a selection. You can read descriptions of each image mode in the following sections.

Along with a description of each image mode, we include a figure showing the Channels panel set to that mode. A *channel* simply contains the color information in an image. The number of default color channels in an image depends on its color mode. For example, a CMYK image has at least four channels — one each for cyan, magenta, yellow, and black information. Grayscale has one channel. If you understand the printing process, think of each channel representing a plate (color) that, when combined, creates the final image.

Bitmap

Bitmap mode offers little more than the ability to work in black and white. Many tools are unusable, and most menu options are grayed out in this mode. If you're converting an image to bitmap, you must convert it to grayscale first.

Grayscale

Use Grayscale mode, shown in Figure 3-2, if you're creating black-and-white images with tonal values, specifically for printing to one color. Grayscale mode supports 256 shades of gray in 8-bit color mode. Photoshop can work with grayscale in 16-bit mode, which provides more information, but may limit your capabilities when working in Photoshop.

Figure 3-2:
Grayscale supports 256 shades of gray.

When you choose Image⇨Mode⇨Grayscale to convert to Grayscale mode, a warning message asks you to confirm that you want to discard all color information. If you don't want to see this warning every time you convert an image to grayscale, select the option not to show the dialog box again before you click Discard.

Using the Black & White adjustment is the best way to create a good grayscale image. Simply click and hold the Create New Fill or Adjustment Layer button at the bottom of the Layers panel and choose Black & White. Set the sliders to achieve the best black-and-white image and then choose Image⇨Mode⇨Grayscale.

Duotone

Use Duotone mode when you're creating a one- to four-color image created from spot colors (solid ink, such as Pantone colors). You can also use Duotone mode to create monotones, tritones, and quadtones. If you're producing a two-color job, duotones create a beautiful solution to not having full color.

The Pantone Matching System (PMS) helps keep printing inks consistent from one job to the next. By assigning a numbered Pantone color, such as 485 for red, you eliminate the risk of one vendor (printer) using fire engine red and the next using orange-red for your company logo.

To create a duotone, follow these steps:

1. **Choose Image⇨Mode⇨Grayscale.**

2. **Choose Image⇨Mode⇨Duotone.**

3. **In the Duotone dialog box, choose Duotone from the Type drop-down list.**

   Your choices range from *monotone* (one-color) up to *quadtone* (four-color). Black is assigned automatically as the first ink, but you can change it, if you like.

4. **To assign a second ink color, click the white swatch immediately under the black swatch.**

   The Color Libraries dialog box appears, as shown in Figure 3-3.

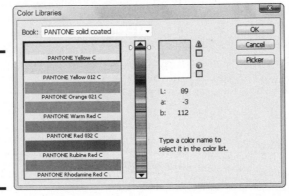

Figure 3-3:
Click the
white
swatch
to open
the Color
Libraries
dialog box.

5. **Now comes the fun part: Type (quickly!) the Pantone or PMS number you want to access and then click OK.**

   There's no text field for you to enter the number, so don't look for one. Just type the number while the Color Libraries dialog box is open.

   Try entering **300**, to select PMS 300. You can already see that you've created a tone curve.

6. **Click the Curve button to the left of the ink color to further tweak the colors.**

7. **Click and drag the curve to adjust the black in the shadow areas, perhaps to bring down the color overall. Then experiment with the results.**

8. **(Optional) If you like your duotone settings, store them by clicking the small Preset Options button to the right of the Preset text box, as shown in Figure 3-4. Type a name into the Name text box, browse to a location on your computer, and then click Save.**

   You can also use one of the presets that Adobe provides. Do this by selecting an option from the Presets drop-down menu at the top of the Duotone dialog box.

Figure 3-4:
Save your
duotone
by clicking
the Preset
Options
button.

Click the Preset Options button to find your saved presets.

Duotone images must be saved in the Photoshop Encapsulated PostScript (EPS) format in order to support the spot colors. If you choose another format, you risk the possibility of converting colors into a build of CMYK (cyan, magenta, yellow, and black).

9. Click OK when you're finished.

Index color

Even if you don't work in Index color, you probably have saved a file in this mode. Indexed Color mode (see Figure 3-5) uses a *color lookup table* (CLUT) to create the image.

Figure 3-5:
Index
color uses
a limited
number of
colors to
create an
image.

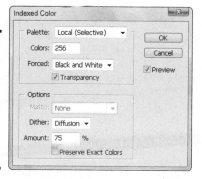

A CLUT contains all colors that make up an image, such as a box of crayons used to create artwork. If you have a box of only eight crayons that are used to color an image, you have a CLUT of only eight colors. Of course, your image would look much better if you used the 64-count box of crayons with the sharpener on the back, but those additional colors increase the size of the CLUT and the file size.

The highest number of colors that can be in Index mode is 256. When saving Web images, you often have to define a color table. We discuss the Save for Web & Devices feature (which helps you more accurately save an index color image) in Chapter 10 of this minibook.

Choose Image➪Mode➪Color Table to see the color table making up an image.

RGB

RGB (Red, Green, Blue) mode, shown in Figure 3-6, is the standard format you work in if you import images from a digital camera or scan images on a scanner. For complete access to features, RGB is probably the best color mode to work in. If you're working on images for use on the Web, color copiers, desktop color printers, and onscreen presentations, stay in RGB mode.

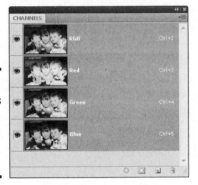

Figure 3-6: RGB creates the image from red, green, and blue.

If you're having an image printed on a press (for example, if you're having it professionally printed), it must be separated. Don't convert images to CMYK mode until you're finished the color correction and you know that your color settings are accurate. A good print service may want the RGB file so that it can complete an accurate conversion.

CMYK

CMYK (Cyan, Magenta, Yellow, Black) mode is used for final separations for the press. Use a good magnifying glass to look closely at anything printed in color and you may see the CMYK colors that created it. A typical four-color printing press has a plate for each color and runs the colors in the order of cyan, magenta, yellow, and then black.

Don't take lightly the task of converting an image into this mode. You need to make decisions when you convert an image to CMYK, such as where to print the file and on which paper stock, so that the resulting image is the best it can be. Talk to your print provider for specifications that are important when converting to CMYK mode.

LAB color

The LAB (*Lightness*, *A* channel, and *B* channel) color mode is used by many high-end color professionals use because of its wide color range. Using LAB, you can make adjustments to *luminosity* (lightness) without affecting color. In this mode, you can select and change an *L* (lightness or luminosity) channel without affecting the *A* channel (green and red) and the *B* channel (blue and yellow).

LAB mode is also good to use if you're in a color-managed environment and want to easily move from one color system to another with no loss of color.

Some professionals prefer to sharpen images in LAB mode because they can select just the Lightness channel and choose Filter⇨Sharpen⇨Unsharp Mask to sharpen only the gray matter of the image, leaving the color noise-free.

Multichannel

Multichannel is used for many things; you can end up in this mode and not know how you got there. Deleting a channel from an RGB, a CMYK, or a LAB image automatically converts the image to Multichannel mode. This mode supports multiple spot colors.

Bit depth

You have more functionality in 16-bit and even 32-bit mode. Depending on your needs, you may spend most of your time in 8-bit mode, which is more than likely all you need.

Bit depth, or *pixel depth* or *color depth,* measures how much color information is available to display or print each pixel in an image. Greater bit depth means more available colors and more accurate color representation in the digital image. In Photoshop, this increase in accuracy also limits some available features, so don't use it unless you have a specific request or need for it.

To use 16-bit or 32-bit color mode, you also must have a source to provide you with that information, such as a scanner or camera that offers a choice to scan in either mode.

Chapter 4: Creating a Selection

In This Chapter

- ✔ Discovering the selection tools
- ✔ Painting selections the easy way
- ✔ Refining your selections
- ✔ Keeping selections for later use
- ✔ Using the Vanishing Point feature

*U*sing Photoshop to create compositions that may not actually exist and retouching images to improve them is common. What you don't want is obvious retouching or a composition that looks contrived. (The exception is if you intend an image to be humorous, such as putting baby Joey's head on Daddy's body.)

That's where the selection tools come in. In this chapter, you try out several selection methods and see how to use the selection tools to make images look as though you *haven't* retouched or edited them. Even if you're an experienced Photoshop user, this chapter provides a plethora of tips and tricks that can save you time and help make your images look absolutely convincing.

Getting to Know the Selection Tools

You create selections by using selection tools. Think of *selections* as windows in which you can make changes to pixels. Areas not selected are *masked,* which means that they're unaffected by changes, much like when you tape window and door frames before painting the walls. In this section, we briefly describe the selection tools and show you how to use them. You must be familiar with these tools in order to do *anything* in Photoshop.

As with all Photoshop tools, the Options bar (viewed across the top of the Photoshop window) changes when you choose different selection tools. The keyboard commands you read about in this section exist on the tool Options bar and appear as buttons across the top.

If you move a selection with the Move tool, pixels move as you drag, leaving a blank spot in the image. To *clone* a selection (to copy and move the selection at the same time), Alt+drag (Windows) or Option+drag (Mac) the selection with the Move tool.

The Marquee tool

 The Marquee tool is the main selection tool; by that, we mean that you use it most often for creating selections. The exception, of course, is when a special situation calls for a special tool — the Lasso, Magic Wand, Quick Selection, or new Refine Radius tool (located in the Refine Edge dialog box). Throughout this section, we describe creating (and then deselecting) an active selection area; we also provide you with tips for working with selections.

The Marquee tool includes the Rectangular Marquee (for creating rectangular selections), Elliptical Marquee (for creating round or elliptical selections), and Single Row Marquee or Single Column Marquee tools (for creating a selection of a single row or column of pixels). You can access these other Marquee tools by holding down the default Rectangle Marquee tool in the Tools panel.

To create a selection, select one of the Marquee tools (remember that you can press M) and then drag anywhere on your image. When you release the mouse button, you create an active selection area. When you're working on an active selection area, whichever effects you choose are applied to the whole selection.

To deselect an area, you have three choices:

✦ Choose Select➪Deselect.

✦ Press Ctrl+D (Windows) or ⌘+D (Mac).

✦ While using a selection tool, click outside the selection area.

Creating rectangular and elliptical selections

How you make a selection is important because it determines how realistic your edits appear on the image. You can use the following tips and tricks when creating both rectangular and elliptical selections:

✦ Add to a selection by holding down the Shift key; drag to create a second selection that intersects the original selection (see the left image in Figure 4-1). The two selections become one big selection.

✦ Delete from an existing selection by holding down the Alt (Windows) or Option (Mac) key and then drag to create a second selection that intersects the original selection where you want to take away from the original selection (shown on the right in Figure 4-1).

Figure 4-1:
You can
add to and
delete from
selections.

✦ Constrain a rectangle or an ellipse to a square or circle by
Shift+dragging; make sure that you release the mouse button before
you release the Shift key. Holding down the Shift key makes a square or
circle only when there are no other selections. (Otherwise, it adds to the
selection.)

✦ Make the selection from the center by Alt+dragging (Windows) or
Option+dragging (Mac); make sure that you release the mouse button
before releasing the Alt (Windows) or Option (Mac) key.

✦ Create a square or circle from the center outward by Alt+Shift+dragging
(Windows) or Option+Shift+dragging (Mac). Again, make sure that you
always release the mouse button before releasing the modifier keys.

✦ When making a selection, hold down the spacebar before releasing the
mouse button to drag the selection to another location.

Setting a fixed size

If you've created an effect that you particularly like — say, changing a block
of color in your image — and you want to apply it multiple times throughout, you can do so. To make the same selection multiple times, follow these
steps:

1. **With the Marquee tool selected, select Fixed Size from the Style drop-
down list on the Options bar.**

You can also select Fixed Ratio from the Style drop-down list to create a
proportionally correct selection not fixed to an exact size.

2. **On the Options bar, type the Width and Height values into the appropriate text fields.**

You can change ruler increments by choosing Edit➪Preferences➪Units
and Rulers (Windows) or Photoshop➪Preferences➪Units and Rulers
(Mac).

3. **Click the image.**

A selection sized to your values appears.

**Book IV
Chapter 4**

Creating a Selection

4. **With the selection tool, drag the selection to the location you want selected.**

Shift+drag a selection to keep it aligned to a 45-degree, or 90-degree angle.

Making floating and nonfloating selections

When you're using a selection tool, such as the Marquee tool, your selections are *floating* by default, which means that you can drag them to another location without affecting the underlying pixels. You know that your selection is floating by the little rectangle that appears on the cursor (see the left image in Figure 4-2).

Figure 4-2: The Float icon is used on the left, and the Move icon is used on the right.

If you want to, however, you can move the underlying pixels. Using the selection tool of your choice, just hold down the Ctrl (Windows) or ⌘ (Mac) key to temporarily access the Move tool; the cursor changes to a pointer with scissors, denoting that your selection is nonfloating. Now, when you drag, the pixel data comes with the selection (as shown on the right in Figure 4-2).

Hold down Alt+Ctrl (Windows) or Option+⌘ (Mac) while using a selection tool and drag to clone (copy) pixels from one location to another. Add the Shift key, and the cloned copy is constrained to a straight, 45-degree, or 90-degree angle.

The Lasso tool

 Use the Lasso tool for *freeform selections* (selections of an irregular shape). To use the Lasso tool, just drag and create a path surrounding the area to be selected. If you don't return to the starting point to close the selection before you release the mouse button, Photoshop completes the path by finding the most direct route back to your starting point.

As with the Marquee tool, you can press the Shift key to add to a lasso selection and press the Alt (Windows) or Option (Mac) to delete from a lasso selection.

Hold down the Lasso tool to show the hidden Lasso tools:

✦ **Polygonal Lasso tool:** Click a start point and then click and release from point to point until you come back to close the selection.

✦ **Magnetic Lasso tool:** Click to create a starting point and then hover the cursor near an edge in your image. The Magnetic Lasso tool is magnetically attracted to edges; as you move the cursor near an edge, the Magnetic Lasso tool creates a selection along that edge. Click to manually set points in the selection; when you return to the starting point, click to close the selection.

You may find that the Polygonal Lasso and the Magnetic Lasso tools make less-than-ideal selections. Take a look at the later section "Painting with the Quick Mask tool" for tips on making finer selections.

The Quick Selection tool

The Quick Selection tool lets you quickly "paint" a selection with a round brush tip of adjustable size. Click and drag and then watch as the selection expands outward and automatically follows defined edges in the image. A Refine Edge command lets you improve the quality of the selection edges and visualize the selection in different ways for easy editing.

Follow these steps to find out how you can take advantage of this new tool:

1. **Open a file that requires a selection.**

You can find sample images in Windows at `C:\Program Files\ Adobe\Adobe Photoshop CS5\Extras\Samples` and on the Mac at `Applications\Adobe\Adobe Photoshop CS5\Samples`.

2. **Select the Quick Selection tool.**

3. **Position the cursor over the area you want to select. Notice the brush size displayed with the cursor; click and drag to start painting the selection.**

You can adjust the size of the painting selection by pressing the left bracket key ([) to make the brush size smaller or the right bracket key (]) to make the brush size larger.

By using the Add to Selection or Subtract from Selection buttons on the Options bar, you can paint more of the selection or deselect active areas (see Figure 4-3).

Figure 4-3:
Use the
Quick
Selection
tool to
paint your
selection.

The Magic Wand tool

The Magic Wand tool is particularly helpful when you're working on an image of high contrast or with a limited number of colors. This tool selects individual pixels of similar shades and colors. Select the Magic Wand tool, click anywhere on an image, and hope for the best — the Magic Wand tool isn't magic. You decide how successful this tool is. What we mean is that *you* control how closely matched each pixel must be in order for the Magic Wand tool to include it in the selection. You do so by setting the tolerance level on the Options bar.

When you select the Magic Wand tool, a Tolerance text field appears on the Options bar. As a default, the tolerance is set to 32. When you click with a setting of 32, the Magic Wand tool selects all pixels within 32 shades (steps) of the color you clicked. If it didn't select as much as you want, increase the value in the Tolerance text field (all the way up to 255). The number you enter varies with each individual selection. If you're selecting white napkins on an off-white tablecloth, you can set the number as low as 5 so that the selection doesn't leak into other areas. For colored fabric with lots of tonal values, you might increase the tolerance to 150.

Don't fret if you miss the entire selection when using the Magic Wand tool. Hold down the Shift key and click in the missed areas. If the tool selects too much, choose Edit➪Undo (step backward) or press Ctrl+Z (Windows) or ⌘+Z (Mac), reduce the value in the Tolerance text field, and try again.

Painting with the Quick Mask tool

If you have fuzzy selections (fur, hair, or leaves, for example) or you're having difficulty using the selection tools, the Quick Mask tool can be a huge help because it allows you to paint your selection uniformly in one fell swoop.

To enter Quick Mask mode, create a selection and then press Q. (Pressing Q again exits you from Quick Mask mode.) You can also click the Quick Mask button at the bottom of the Tools panel. If you have a printing background, you'll notice that the Quick Mask mode, set at its default color (red), resembles something that you may want to forget: rubylith and amberlith. (Remember slicing up those lovely films with Exacto blades before computer masking came along?) In Quick Mask mode, Photoshop shows your image as it appears through the mask. The clear part is selected; what's covered in the mask isn't selected.

 Change the default red color of the mask by double-clicking the Edit in Quick Mask Mode button (at the bottom of the Tools panel). The tooltip says Edit in Standard Mode if you're already in Quick Mask Mode. This opens the Quick Mask Options dialog box, shown in Figure 4-4.

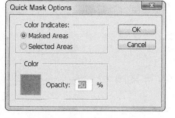

Figure 4-4:
Change the
color of the
Quick Mask.

To create and implement a quick mask, follow these steps:

1. **Press Q to enter Quick Mask mode.**

2. **Press D to change the foreground and background color boxes to the default colors of black and white.**

3. **Select the Brush tool and start painting with black in the clear area of the image in Quick Mask mode.**

   It doesn't have to be pretty; just get a stroke or two in there.

4. **Press Q to return to Selection mode.**

   You're now out of Quick Mask mode. Notice that where you painted with black (it turned red in Quick Mask mode), the pixels are no longer selected.

5. **Press Q again to reenter Quick Mask mode and then press X.**

   This step switches the foreground and background colors (giving you white in the foreground and black in the background).

**Book IV
Chapter 4**

Creating a Selection

6. **With the Brush tool, paint several white strokes in the red mask area.**

   The white strokes turn clear in Quick Mask mode.

7. **Press Q to return to Selection mode.**

   The area you painted white in Quick Mask mode is now selected.

When you're in Quick Mask mode, you can paint white over areas you want selected and black over areas you don't want selected. When painting in Quick Mask mode, increase the brush size by pressing the] key. Decrease the brush size by pressing the [key.

In Selection mode, your selection seems to have a hard edge; you can soften those hard edges by using a softer brush in Quick Mask mode. To make a brush softer, press Shift+[; to make a brush harder, press Shift+].

Because Quick Mask mode makes selections based on the mask's values, you can create a mask by selecting the Gradient tool and dragging it across the image in Quick Mask mode. When you exit Quick Mask mode, it looks as though there's a straight-line selection, but the selection transitions the same as your gradient did. Choose any filter from the Filters menu and notice how the filter transitions into the untouched part of the image to which you applied the gradient.

If you're working in Quick Mask mode, choose Window⇨Channels to see that what you're working on is a temporary alpha channel. See the later section "Saving Selections" for more about alpha channels.

Manipulating Selections with Refine Selection

After you master creating selections, you'll find that working with the selections — painting, transforming, and feathering them — can be easy and fun.

Transforming selections

Don't deselect and start over again if you can just nudge or resize a selection. You can scale, rotate, and even distort an existing selection. Follow these steps to transform a selection:

1. **Create a selection and then choose Select⇨Transform Selection.**

   You can use the bounding box to resize and rotate your selection:

   • Drag the handles to make the selection larger or smaller. Drag a corner handle to adjust width and height simultaneously. Shift+drag a corner handle to size proportionally.

- Position the cursor outside the bounding box to see the Rotate icon; drag when it appears to rotate the selection. Shift+drag to constrain to straight, 45-degree, or 90-degree angles.

- Ctrl+drag (Windows) or ⌘+drag (Mac) a corner point to distort the selection, as shown in Figure 4-5.

Figure 4-5: Distort, resize, and rotate a selection with the Transform Selection feature.

2. **Press Enter or Return or double-click in the center of the selection area to confirm the transformation; press Esc to release the transformation and return to the original selection.**

Feathering

Knowing how to retouch an image means little if you don't know how to make the retouching discreet. If you boost the color using curves to the CEO's face, do you want it to look like a pancake has been attached to his cheek? Of course not — that isn't discreet (or wise). If you *feather* a selection (blur its edges) instead, you create a natural-looking transition between the selection and the background of the image.

To feather an image, follow these steps:

1. **Create a selection.**

For the nonfeathered image shown on top in Figure 4-6, we used the Elliptical Marquee tool to make a selection. We then copied the selection, created a new, blank image, and pasted the selection into the new image.

**Book IV
Chapter 4**

Creating a Selection

To create the feathered image on the bottom in Figure 4-6, we used the Elliptical Marquee tool to select the same area on the original image and went on to Step 2.

2. **Choose Select↪Modify↪Feather.**

3. **In the Feather dialog box that appears, type a value in the Feather Radius text field and then click OK.**

For example, we entered **20** in the Feather Radius text field. (We then copied the selection, created a new image, and pasted the feathered selection into the new image to create the image on the bottom of Figure 4-6.) *Voilà!* The edges of the image are softened over a 20-pixel area, as shown on the bottom of Figure 4-6. This technique is also referred to as a *vignette* in the printing industry.

Figure 4-6:
No feathering (top); feathering applied (bottom).

The results of the feathering depend on the resolution of the image. A feather of 20 pixels in a 72ppi (pixels per inch) image is a much larger area than a feather of 20 pixels in a 300ppi image. Typical amounts for a nice vignette on an edge of an image are 20 to 50 pixels. Experiment with images to find what works best for you.

This feathering effect created a nice, soft edge to your image, but it's also useful when retouching images. Follow these steps:

1. **Using any selection method, create a selection around the part of an image you want to lighten.**

2. **Choose Select➪Modify➪Feather; in the Feather dialog box that appears, enter 25 in the Feather Radius text field and click OK.**

   If an error message, say "No pixels are more than 50% selected," click OK and create a larger selection.

3. **Choose Image➪Adjustments➪Curves.**

4. **Click in the center of the curve to add an anchor point and drag up to lighten the image.**

   This step lightens the midtones of the image.

Notice how the lightening fades out so that the correction has no definite edge. You can have more fun like this in Chapter 7 of this minibook, where we cover color correction.

Tweaking the edges of a selection with the Refine Edge feature

If you like to experiment but also want a preview of exactly what your selection changes look like, you'll love the new and improved Refine Edge feature. It's available on the Options bar across the top of the Photoshop window whenever a selection tool is active.

To use the Refine Edge feature, follow these steps:

1. **Make a selection.**

2. **With any selection tool active, click the Refine Edge button on the Options bar at the top of the Photoshop window.**

   The Refine Edge dialog box appears, as shown in Figure 4-7.

Read on to find out more about the options available in this dialog box.

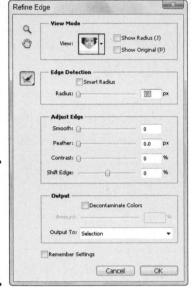

Figure 4-7:
Tweak the
edges of a
selection
with the
Refine Edge
dialog box.

Choosing a preview method

Choose a preview method by selecting the View drop-down menu at the top of the Refine Edge dialog box. On White is the default setting, and it shows your selection as it would appear on a white background. Don't worry! The rest of your image hasn't been removed; this preview helps you better see the effects of this feature.

This list describes the other selections you can choose from the View menu of the Refine Edge dialog box:

✦ *Marching Ants:* Shows the marquee selection with no image masked.

✦ *Overlay:* Shows the default, slightly transparent mask. It's typically red unless you have changed the mask color.

✦ *On Black:* Reveals black around the masked area.

✦ *Black and White:* Reveals the masked area as black and the nonmasked area as white. This option is helpful if you want to see only the mask and not the image area.

✦ *On Layers:* Bound to be the most popular view if you're creating composites. From this view, you can see the layers and how they're affected by your selection.

✦ *Reveal Layer:* Reveals the entire layer, with no indication where the selection is. Take advantage of this view if you think you might be cutting out important content.

You can cycle through views by pressing F, or disable the view by pressing X.

Making adjustments with Edge Detection

The Edge Detection section of the Refine Edge dialog box offers you the opportunity to make refinements to the selection edge. To see it in action, follow these steps:

1. **Select the Smart Radius check box, as shown in Figure 4-8.**

The Smart Radius feature automatically adjusts the radius for hard and soft edges found in the border region.

Figure 4-8: Refining the edge of a selection.

2. **Increase the radius by dragging the slider to the right.**

The Radius slider lets you precisely adjust the border area in which edge refinement occurs. Depending on the content, you will increase or decrease the radius.

In Figure 4-8, the hair selection is improved in this image by increasing the radius to a value of 3.0 pixels.

3. **If you're interested in seeing the radius, select the Show Radius check box in the upper right corner of the Refine Edge dialog box.**

Using the Refine Radius tool

To further improve the selection, click the Refine Radius tool, shown in Figure 4-9. By pressing either the right (]) or left bracket ([) key, you can increase or decrease the size of the Refine Radius tool and edit your edge selection, by painting the edge of it. If your results are a little too drastic, hold down the Alt or Option key while painting over the area with the Refine Radius tool again. This is especially helpful for creating selections of hair or fur.

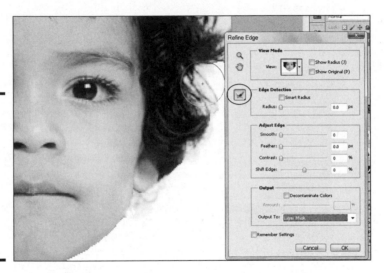

Figure 4-9: Use the Refine Radius tool to make difficult selections, like hair, easier to create.

Making additional refinements

But wait — there's more! Additional refinements can be found in the Adjust Edge section of the Refine Edge dialog box:

+ **Smooth:** Reduces irregular areas in the selection boundary.

+ **Feather:** Creates a soft-edged transition between the selection and its surrounding pixels.

+ **Contrast:** Sharpens selection edges and removes fuzzy artifacts.

+ **Shift Edge:** Contracts or expands to shrink or enlarge the selection boundary.

Selecting color decontamination

Color decontamination can create unwanted artifacts, and when this option is checked, the output option is set to create a new layer, which helps to avoid overwriting the original color pixels.

Choosing output settings

New in Photoshop CS5 is the option to choose how you want selections implemented: only selection edges, a new layer, or a layer mask, for example. If you're like most professionals, you want to make sure not to affect the original imagery, unless you're sure that you have the selection nailed down.

Here are your output options on the Output To drop-down menu:

✦ **Selection:** The typical selection of a dashed selection, referred to as *marching ants.*

✦ **Layer Mask:** Creates a mask on the active layer.

✦ **New Layer:** Duplicates the active layer and applies the refined selection to the transparency of the layer.

✦ **New Layer with Mask:** Duplicates the active layer and uses the refined selection or mask as the layer mask.

✦ **New Document:** The same as the New Layer option but creates the new layer in a new document.

✦ **New Document with Mask:** The same as the New Layer with Mask option but creates the new layer in a new document.

If you want to play it safe, select Layer Mask from the Output To drop-down menu. This option offers you the opportunity to edit the layer mask, using the painting tools just as you did with the Quick Mask tool, or to turn off the mask (by Shift-clicking the mask in the Layers panel). Read more about how to work with layer masks in Chapter 9 of this minibook.

If you worked hard to make the perfect selection, don't forget to select the Remember Settings check box so that your settings apply the next time you open the Refine Edge dialog box.

Saving Selections

The term *alpha channel* sounds complicated, but it's simply a saved selection. Depending on the mode you're in, you already have several channels to contend with. A selection is just an extra channel that you can call on at any time.

To create an alpha channel, follow these steps:

1. **Create a selection that you want to save.**

2. **Choose Select⇨Save Selection.**

3. **Name the selection and click OK.**

   An additional named channel that contains your selection appears in the Channels panel.

To load a saved selection, follow these steps:

1. **Choose Select⇨Load Selection.**

   The Load Selection dialog box appears.

2. **Select a named channel from the Channel drop-down list.**

   If you have an active selection and then choose to load a selection, you have additional options. With an active selection, you can select one of the following options:

   • *New Selection:* Eliminate the existing selection and create a new selection based on the channel you select.

   • *Add to Selection:* Add the channel to the existing selection.

   • *Subtract from Selection:* Subtract the channel from the existing selection.

   • *Intersect with Selection:* Intersect the channel with the existing selection.

3. **Click OK.**

Other Adobe applications, such as InDesign, Illustrator, Premiere, and After Effects, also recognize alpha channels.

Preserving Corrective Perspective with the Vanishing Point Feature

The incredible Vanishing Point feature lets you preserve correct perspective in edits of images that contain perspective planes, such as the sides of a building. You can do much with this feature, and we provide you with a simple introduction. Try experimenting with multiple planes and copying and pasting items into the Vanishing Point window for even more effects. Follow these steps:

1. **Open a file that you want to apply a perspective filter to.**

   If you don't have an appropriate image handy, try using a `Vanishing Point.psd` file. You can find it in Windows at `C:\Program Files\ Adobe\Adobe Photoshop CS5\Extras\Samples` and on the Mac at `Applications\Adobe\Adobe Photoshop CS5\Samples`.

2. **Create a new, blank layer by clicking the Create a New Layer button at the bottom of the Layers panel.**

   If you create a new layer every time you use Vanishing Point, the results appear on a separate layer, preserving your original image, because you can delete the result of the vanishing point filter and still retain the original layer.

3. **Choose Filter⇨Vanishing Point.**

   A separate Vanishing Point window appears. If you see an error message about an existing plane, click OK.

   If you're using a sample file from Photoshop, it will have a perspective plane already created for you. To help you understand this feature better, delete the existing plane by pressing the Delete or Backspace key.

4. **Select the Create Plane tool and define the four corner nodes of the plane surface. If necessary, press Ctrl+– (Windows) or ⌘+– (Mac) to zoom back to see the entire image.**

   Try to use objects in the image to help create the plane. In Figure 4-10, the planks of wood were used to make the perspective plane.

Figure 4-10:
Use objects in an image to build a perspective plane.

After the four corner nodes of the plane are created, the tool automatically is switched to the Edit Plane tool.

5. **Select and drag the corner nodes to make an accurate plane.**

   The plane grid should appear blue, not yellow or red, if it's accurate.

   After creating the plane, you can move, scale, or reshape the plane. Keep in mind that your results depend on how accurately the plane lines up with the perspective of the image.

   You can use your first Vanishing Point session to simply create perspective planes and then click OK. The planes appear in subsequent Vanishing Point sessions when you choose Filter➪Vanishing Point. Saving perspective planes is especially useful if you plan to copy and paste an image into Vanishing Point and need to have a ready-made plane to target.

6. **Choose the Stamp tool in the Vanishing Point window and then choose On from the Heal drop-down list on the Options bar.**

   (You'll love this one.) In the sample image Vanishing Point.psd, we simply cloned the blue broom, but it should start you thinking about all the ways you can apply this greatly improved feature.

7. **With the Stamp tool still selected, cross over part of the area or part of the image you want to clone and Alt-click (Windows) or Option-click (Mac) to define it as the source to be cloned.**

   In the image Vanishing Point.psd, we clicked the middle part of the blue broom.

8. **Without clicking, move toward the back of the perspective plane (you can even clone outside the plane) and then click and drag to reproduce the cloned part of the image.**

   Notice in Figure 4-11 that it's cloned as a smaller version, in the correct perspective for its new location.

9. **Start from Step 7 and clone any region of an image closer to the front of the perspective pane.**

   The cloned region is now cloned as a larger version of itself.

   You can use the Marquee tool options (Feather, Opacity, Heal, and Move Mode) at any time, either before or after making the selection. When you move the Marquee tool, the Stamp tool, or the Brush tool into a plane, the bounding box is highlighted, indicating that the plane is active.

10. **Click OK.**

    To preserve the perspective plane information in an image, save your document in JPEG, PSD, or TIFF format.

Figure 4-11:
Cloning in
perspective.

Chapter 5: Using the Photoshop Pen Tool

In This Chapter

✔ **Putting shape layers to work**

✔ **Working with a path as a selection**

✔ **Creating clipping paths**

The Pen tool is the ultimate method to make precise selections. You can also use it to create vector shapes and clipping paths (silhouettes). In this chapter, you see how to take advantage of this super multitasking tool. This chapter also shows you how to apply paths made with the Pen tool as shapes, selections, and clipping paths. If you're interested in the fundamental principles of creating paths with the Pen tool in Illustrator, check out Book III, Chapter 5, where we cover the Pen tool in more detail.

We recommend that you use the Pen tool as much as you can to truly master its capabilities. If you don't use it regularly, it will seem awkward, though it gets easier! Knowing how to effectively use the Pen tool puts you a grade above the average Photoshop user, and the quality of your selections will show it. Read Chapter 9 of this minibook to find out how to use the Pen tool to create layer masks and adjustment layers.

Using Shape Layers

When you start creating with the Pen tool, Photoshop automatically, as a default, creates a *path*. But you can also choose to make a vector shape or, in the rare instance that you might need it, a fill (which essentially creates pixeled, nonvector shapes and paths. Select the Pen tool and note the default setting on the left side of the Options bar. You can choose from the following options:

✦ **Shape layers:** Creates a new shape layer, a filled layer that contains the vector path.

✦ **Paths:** Creates a path only; no layer is created.

✦ **Fill pixels:** Creates pixels directly on the image. No editable path or layer is created. This option may not be useful to new users, but some existing users prefer to use this method because it's the only way to access the Line tool from earlier versions.

Shape layers can be very useful when the goal of your design is to seamlessly integrate vector shapes and pixel data. A shape layer can contain vector shapes that you can then modify with the same features of any other layer. You can adjust the opacity of the shape layer, change the blending mode, and even apply layer effects to add drop shadows and dimension. Find out how to do this in Chapter 9 of this minibook.

Create a shape layer with any of these methods:

✦ **Create a shape with the Pen tool.** With the Pen tool, you can create interesting custom shapes and even store them for future use. We show you how in the following section.

✦ **Use a Vector Shape tool, as shown in Figure 5-1.** *Vector shapes* are premade shapes (you can even create your own) that you can create by dragging the image area with a shape tool.

✦ **Import a shape from Illustrator.** Choose File➪Place and choose an .ai file; when the Options window appears, choose to place the file as a shape layer or a path. This action imports an Illustrator file as a shape layer or path into Photoshop.

Figure 5-1:
The Vector
Shape tools.

In Photoshop CS5, you can access the Vector shape and path tools directly from the Options bar, as shown in Figure 5-2, when either the Pen tool or a vector shape tool is selected.

Figure 5-2:
You can
switch to
the Vector
shape tool
with the
Options bar.

Creating and using a custom shape

Perhaps you like the wave shape (see Figure 5-3) that's been cropping up in design pieces all over the place.

Figure 5-3:
A custom wave shape integrated with an image in Photoshop.

You can copy and paste shapes directly from Illustrator CS5 into Photoshop CS5. Simply select a shape in Adobe Illustrator, choose Edit➪Copy, switch to the Photoshop application, and, with a document open, choose Edit➪Paste.

A dialog box appears, offering you the opportunity to place your path as a shape layer (vector shape), a path, or pixels.

You can create a wavy shape like that, too. With an image or blank document open, just follow these steps:

1. **Select the Pen tool, and then click the Shape Layers button on the Options bar (refer to Figure 5-2).**

2. **Click and drag with the Pen tool to create a wavy shape.**

   Don't worry about the size of the shape. The shape is vector, so you can scale it up or down to whatever size you need without worrying about making jagged edges. Just make sure to close the shape (return to the original point with the end point).

   When you create the shape, it fills in with your foreground color. Try to ignore it, if you can; the next section shows you how to change the fill color, and Chapter 8 of this minibook covers how to change it to a transparent fill.

3. **With the shape still selected, choose Edit➪Define Custom Shape, name the shape, and click OK.**

   After you save your custom shape, you can re-create it at any time. If you don't like the shape, choose Windows➪Layers to open the Layers panel and then drag the shape layer you just created to the Trash Can in the lower right corner of the panel. If you want to experiment with your custom shape now, continue with these steps.

4. **Click and hold the Rectangle tool to access the other hidden vector tools; select the last tool, the Custom Shape tool.**

   When the Custom Shape tool is selected, a Shape drop-down list appears on the Options bar at the top of the screen, as shown in Figure 5-4.

You have lots of custom shapes to choose from, including the one you've just created. If you just saved a shape, yours is in the last square; you have to scroll down to select it.

Figure 5-4:
A Shape drop-down list appears on the Options bar.

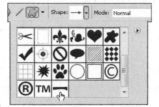

5. **Click to select your custom shape; click and drag in the image area to create your shape.**

   You can make the shape any size you want.

6. **To resize the shape, choose Edit➪Free Transform Path, press Ctrl+T (Windows) or ⌘+T (Mac), grab a bounding box handle, and drag.**

   Shift+drag a corner handle to keep the shape proportional as you resize it.

Because a shape is created on its own layer, you can experiment with different levels of transparency and blending modes in the Layers panel. Figure 5-5 shows shapes that are partially transparent. Discover lots of other features you can use with shape layers in Chapter 9 of this minibook.

Figure 5-5:
Experiment with blending modes and opacity changes on shape layers.

Changing the color of the shape

When you create a shape with a shape tool, the shape takes the color of the present foreground color. To change the color of an existing shape, open the Layers panel by choosing Window➪Layers; notice that the Vector Shape tool creates a new layer for every shape you make. Creating a new layer is a benefit when it comes to creating special effects because the shape layer is independent of the rest of your image. (Read more about using layers in Chapter 9 of this minibook.)

To change a shape's color, double-click the color thumbnail on the left in the shape layer, as shown in Figure 5-6, or click the Set Color box on the Options bar across the top of the Document window. The Color Picker appears. To select a new color, drag the Hue slider up or down or click in the large color pane to select a color with the saturation and lightness you want to use. Click OK when you're done.

Figure 5-6:
Double-click the Layer thumbnail to open the Color Picker.

With the Color Picker open, you can also move outside the picker dialog box and sample colors from other open images and objects.

Editing a shape

Like Adobe Illustrator, Photoshop provides both a Path Selection tool and a Direct Selection tool. The Direct Selection tool is hidden under the Path Selection tool. To move an entire shape on a layer, choose the Path Selection tool and drag the shape.

To edit the shape, deselect the shape. (While using the Path Selection or Direct Selection tool, click outside the shape.) Then select the Direct Selection tool. With the Direct Selection tool, click individual anchor points and handles to edit and fine-tune the shape, as shown in Figure 5-7.

Figure 5-7: Edit individual anchor points with the Direct Selection tool.

Removing a shape layer

Because the Pen tool now has multiple options, you may unexpectedly create a shape layer. Delete a shape layer by dragging the layer thumbnail to the Trash Can in the lower right corner of the Layers panel.

If you want to keep your path but throw away the shape layer, choose Window⇨Paths. Then drag the shape vector mask to the New Path icon, shown in Figure 5-8, which creates a saved path. Now you can throw away the shape layer.

Figure 5-8: Drag the shape path to the Create New Path icon.

Using a Path as a Selection

You can use the Pen tool to create precise selections that would be difficult to create using other selection methods. The Pen tool produces clean edges that print well and can be edited using the Direct Selection tool. Before using the Pen tool, make sure that you click the Paths button on the Options bar.

To use a path as a selection (which is extremely helpful when you're trying to make a precise selection), follow these steps:

1. **Open any file or create a new, blank file.**

2. **With the Pen tool (make sure that the Paths button is selected on the Options bar or else you'll create a shape layer), click to place anchor points.**

3. **Drag to create a curved path around the image area you want selected and completely close the path by returning to the start point (see Figure 5-9).**

   Use the techniques we discuss in Book III, Chapter 5 to perform this step. A circle appears before you click to close the path.

Figure 5-9: Make sure that you select the Paths button to create only the path, not a shape layer.

4. **Choose Window⇨Paths.**

   In the Paths panel, you can create new paths and activate existing paths, apply a stroke, or turn paths into selections by clicking the icons at the bottom of the panel (see Figure 5-10).

5. **Click and drag the Work Path down to the Create New Path icon at the bottom of the Paths panel.**

   The path is now named Path 1 and is saved. You can also double-click to rename the file, if you like.

6. **Click the Load Path As Selection icon.**

   The path is converted into a selection.

Use this quick and easy method for turning an existing path into a selection: Ctrl-click (Windows) or ⌘-click (Mac) the path thumbnail in the Paths panel.

Figure 5-10:
The Paths panel and its options.

Fill Path with Foreground Color

Stroke Path with Brush

Load Path as Selection

Make Work Path from Selection

Delete Current Path

Create New Path

Clipping Paths

If you want to create a beautiful silhouette that transfers well to other applications for text wrapping (see Figure 5-11), create a clipping path.

Figure 5-11:
Clipping paths allow you to create silhouettes in other applications.

Living with a teenager can be fun and trying at times. But if you have a little bit of patience... and a lot of money, you can get through this stage and see your teen blossom into a wonderful adult.

Learn more about living with teens at the Kid's Network annual seminar series. The Kid's Network has been speaking to parents for the last 10 years and creating a group of parents who seek the help of others.

For only $300.00 per person you too can learn how to be more broke and maybe meet some other parents who got suckered into paying this fee due to their desperation. Find out more about us at www.kidsnetw orkandparents.com. We don't have kids, but some of us are actors and actresses who have acted with kids on TV.

Sign up today!

Creating a clipping path is easy when you have a good path. Just follow these steps:

1. **Use the Pen tool to create a path around the image area that will become the silhouette.**

2. **In the Paths panel, choose Save Path from the panel menu (click the triangle in the upper right corner of the panel), as shown in Figure 5-12, and then name the path.**

If Save Path is not visible, your path has already been saved; skip to Step 3.

Figure 5-12:
Convert your work path to a saved path.

3. **From the same panel menu, choose Clipping Path.**

4. **In the Clipping Paths dialog box, choose your path from the drop-down list, if it's not already selected; click OK.**

   Leave the Flatness Device Pixels text field blank unless you need to change it. The flatness value determines how many device pixels are used to create your silhouette. The higher the amount, the fewer points are created, thereby allowing for faster processing time. This speed comes at a cost, though: Set the flatness value too high and you may see (if you look close) straight edges instead of curved edges.

5. **Choose File⇔Save As and, in the Format drop-down list, select Photoshop EPS; in the EPS Options dialog box that appears, accept the defaults and click OK.**

   If you see PostScript errors when printing, choose Clipping Path from the panel menu and increase the value to 2 pixels in the Flatness Device Pixels text field. Keep returning to this text field and increasing the value until the file prints, or give up and try printing your document on another printer.

   If you're placing this file in other Adobe applications, such as InDesign, you don't need to save the file as EPS; you can leave it as a Photoshop (.psd) file.

Here's an even faster method you can use to create a clipping path that can be used in other Adobe applications, such as InDesign and Illustrator:

1. **Create a path around the item you want to keep when the clipping path is created.**

   Make sure that you're working on a layer and not on the Background layer. To convert the Background to a layer, hold down the Alt key (Windows) or the Option key (Mac) and double-click the Background layer. The Background layer is now Layer 0.

2. In the Layers panel, click the Add Layer Mask button and then click the Add Layer Mask button again.

A layer vector mask is created, and everything outside the path becomes transparent, as shown in Figure 5-13.

Figure 5-13:
Creating a clipping path the easy way, with layers.

You can still edit the path by using the Direct Selection tool.

3. Save the file in the `.psd` **format.**

4. Choose File⇨Place to put the image, with its clipping path included, into other Adobe applications.

Chapter 6: Thinking about Resolution Basics

In This Chapter

✔ Understanding resolution basics

✔ Adjusting file size

✔ Applying the Unsharp Mask filter to your image

Something as important as setting the right resolution for your images deserves its own chapter, but fortunately, the topic isn't all that complex. In this chapter, you discover the necessary resolution for various uses of Photoshop imagery (from printing a high-resolution graphic to e-mailing a picture of your kids to Mom) and how to properly increase resolution and how to adjust image size.

Having the proper resolution is important to the final outcome of an image, especially if you plan to print it. Combine the information here with using the correction tools we show you in Chapter 7 of this minibook, and you should be ready to roll with great imagery.

Creating Images for Print

To see and make changes to the present size and resolution of an image in Photoshop, choose Image⇨Image Size. The Image Size dialog box appears.

The Width and Height text fields in the Pixel Dimensions area of the Image Size dialog box are used for onscreen resizing, such as for the Web and e-mail. The Width and Height text fields in the Document Size area show the size at which the image will print. The Resolution text field determines the resolution of the printed image; a higher value means a smaller, more finely detailed printed image.

Before you decide on a resolution, you should understand what some of the resolution jargon means:

✦ **dpi (dots per inch):** The resolution of an image when printed.

✦ **lpi (lines per inch):** The varying dot pattern that printers and presses use to create images (see Figure 6-1). This dot pattern is referred to as the *lines* per inch, even though it represents rows of dots. The higher the lpi, the finer the detail and the less dot pattern or line screen you see.

✦ **Dot gain:** The spread of ink as it's applied to paper. Certain types of paper spread a dot of ink farther than others. For example, newsprint has a high dot gain and typically prints at 85 lpi; a coated stock paper has a lower dot gain and can be printed at 133–150 lpi and even higher.

Human eyes typically can't detect a dot pattern in a printed image at 133 dpi or higher.

Figure 6-1:
The dot pattern used to print images is referred to as lpi (lines per inch).

Deciding the resolution or dpi of an image requires backward planning. If you want to create the best possible image, you should know where it'll print *before* deciding its resolution. Communicate with your printer service if the image is going to press. If you're sending an image to a high-speed copier, you can estimate that it will handle 100 lpi; a desktop printer handles 85 lpi to 100 lpi.

The resolution formula

When creating an image for print, keep this formula in mind:

2 x lpi = dpi (dots per inch)

This formula means that if your image is going to press using 150 lpi, have your image at 300 dpi. To save space, many people in production use 1.5 x lpi because it reduces the file size significantly and you get similar results; you can decide which one works best for you.

Changing the resolution

Using the Image Size dialog box is only one way that you can control the resolution in Photoshop. Even though you can increase the resolution, do so sparingly and avoid it, if you can. The exception is when you have an image that is large in dimension size but low in resolution, like those you typically get from a digital camera. You may have a top-of-the-line digital camera that produces 72 dpi images, but at that resolution, the pictures are 28 x 21 inches (or larger)!

To increase the resolution of an image without sacrificing quality, follow these steps:

1. **Choose Image⇨Image Size.**

The Image Size dialog box appears, as shown in Figure 6-2.

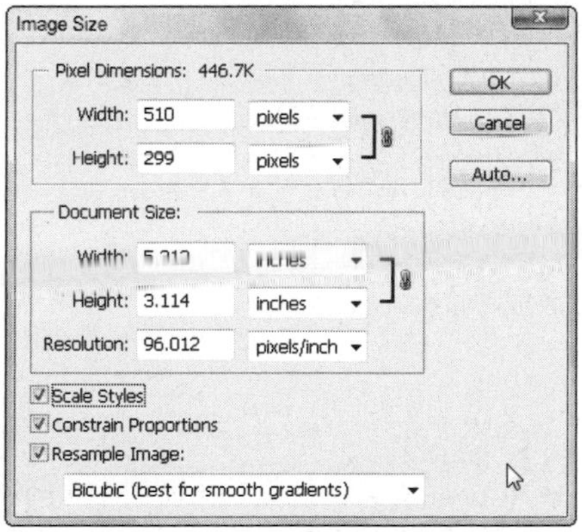

Figure 6-2:
The Image
Size dialog
box.

2. **Deselect the Resample Image check box.**

This way, Photoshop doesn't add additional pixels.

3. **Enter a resolution in the Resolution text field.**

   Photoshop keeps the *pixel size* (the size of the image onscreen) the same, but the *document size* (the size of the image when printed) decreases when you enter a higher resolution.

4. **If the image isn't the size you need, select the Resample Image check box and type the size in the Width and Height text fields in the Document Size section.**

   It's best to reduce the size of a bitmap image, such as a digital photo, rather than increase it.

   You can also deselect the Resample Image check box and essentially play a game of give-and-take to see what the resolution will be when you enter the intended size of your printed image in the Width and Height text fields in the Document Size area.

   Images can typically be scaled from 50 to 120 percent before looking jagged. (To scale by a percentage, select Percent from the drop-down lists beside the Width and Height text fields.) Keep these numbers in mind when placing and resizing images in a page layout application such as InDesign.

5. **Click OK when you're finished; double-click the Zoom tool in the Tools panel to see the image at its onscreen size.**

To increase the resolution *without* changing the image size, follow these steps. (This situation isn't perfect because pixels that don't presently exist are created by Photoshop and may not be totally accurate. Photoshop tries to give you the best image, but you may see some loss of detail.)

1. **Choose Image⇨Image Size.**

2. **When the Image Size dialog box appears, make sure that the Resample Image check box is selected.**

   Note that Bicubic is selected in the Method drop-down list. This method is the best, but slowest, way to reinterpret pixels when you resize an image. With this method, Photoshop essentially looks at all pixels and takes a good guess as how the newly created pixels should look, based on surrounding pixels.

3. **Enter the resolution you need in the Resolution text field, click OK, and then double-click the Zoom tool to see the image at its actual size.**

Determining the Resolution for Web Images

Did somebody ever e-mail you an image, and, after spending ten minutes downloading it, you discover that the image is so huge that all you can see on the monitor is your nephew's left eye? Many people are under the misconception that if an image is 72 dpi, it's ready for the Web. Actually, pixel dimension is all that matters for Web viewing of images; this section helps you make sense of this concept.

Most people view Web pages in their browser windows in an area of about 640 x 480 pixels. You can use this figure as a basis for any images you create for the Web, whether the viewer is using a 14-inch or a 21-inch monitor. (Remember that people who have large monitors set to high screen resolutions don't necessarily want a Web page taking up the whole screen.) If you're creating images for a Web page or to attach to an e-mail message, you may want to pick a standard size to design by, such as 600 x 400 pixels at 72 dpi.

To use the Image Size dialog box to determine the resolution and size for on-screen images, follow these steps:

1. **Have an image open and choose Image⇨Image Size.**

    The Image Size dialog box appears.

2. **To make the image occupy half the width of a typical browser window, type** 300 **(half of 600) in the top Width text field.**

    If a little chain link is visible to the right, the Constrain Proportions check box is selected, and Photoshop automatically determines the height from the width you entered.

3. **Click OK and double-click the Zoom tool to see the image at its actual onscreen size.**

    That's it! Whether your image is 3,000 or 30 pixels wide doesn't matter; as long as you enter the correct dimensions in the Pixel Dimension area, the image works beautifully.

Applying the Unsharp Mask Filter to an Image

When you resample an image in Photoshop, it can become blurry. A good practice is to apply the Unsharp Mask filter. You can see the difference in detail in the images shown in Figure 6-3. This feature sharpens the image based on levels of contrast while keeping smooth the areas that have no contrasting pixels. You have to set up this feature correctly to get good results.

Here's the down-and-dirty method of using the Unsharp Mask filter:

1. **Choose View⇨Actual Pixels or double-click the Zoom tool.**

    When you're using a filter, view your image at its actual size to best see the effect.

Figure 6-3:
The image without (left) and with (right) unsharp masking applied.

 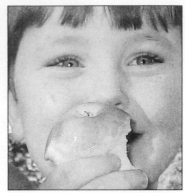

2. **Choose Filter⇨Sharpen⇨Unsharp Mask.**

   In the Unsharp Mask dialog box that appears, set these three options:

   • *Amount:* The Amount value ranges from 0 to 500. The amount you choose has a lot to do with the subject matter. Sharpening a car or appliance at 300 to 400 is fine, but do this to the CEO's 75-year-old wife and you may suffer an untimely death because every wrinkle, mole, or hair will magically become more defined. If you're not sure which amount to use, start with 150 and play around until you find an Amount value that looks good.

   • *Radius:* The Unsharp Mask filter creates a halo around the areas that have enough contrast to be considered an edge. Typically, leaving the amount between 1 and 2 is fine for print, but if you're creating a billboard or poster, increase the size.

   • *Threshold:* This option is the most important one in the Unsharp Mask dialog box. The Threshold setting determines what should be sharpened. If you leave it at zero, you see noise throughout the image, much like the grain you see in high-speed film. Increase the setting to 10 and it triggers the Unsharp Mask filter to apply only the sharpening when the pixels are ten shades or more away from each other. The amount of tolerance ranges from 1 to 255. Apply too much and no sharpening appears; apply too little and the image becomes grainy. A good number to start with is 10.

To compare the original state of the image with the preview of the Unsharp Mask filter's effect in the Preview pane of the Unsharp Mask dialog box, click and hold the image in the Preview pane; this shows the original state of the image. When you release the mouse button, the Unsharp Mask filter is previewed again.

3. **When you've made your choice, click OK.**

   The image appears to have more detail.

Once in a while, stray colored pixels may appear after you apply the Unsharp Mask filter. If you feel this is a problem with your image, choose Edit⇨Fade Unsharp Mask immediately after applying the Unsharp Mask filter. In the Fade dialog box, select the Luminosity blend mode from the Mode drop-down list and then click OK. This step applies the Unsharp Mask filter to the grays in the image only, thereby eliminating the sharpening of colored pixels.

You can also choose Filter⇨Convert for Smart Filters before you apply the Unsharp Mask filter. Smart filters let you undo all or some of any filter, including sharpening filters you apply to a layer. Find out how by reading Chapter 9 in this minibook.

Chapter 7: Creating a Good Image

In This Chapter

✓ **Understanding the histogram**

✓ **Getting ready to correct an image**

✓ **Making a good tone curve**

✓ **Editing adjustment layers**

✓ **Testing your printer**

onsidering all the incredible things you can do in Photoshop, you can easily forget the basics. Yes, you can create incredible compositions with special effects, but people who look greenish detract from the image. Get in the habit of building good, clean images before heading into the artsy filters and fun things. Color correction isn't complicated and, if it's done properly, produces magical results in your images. In this chapter, you see how to use the values you read in the Info panel and use the Curves panel to produce quality image corrections.

Reading a Histogram

Before making adjustments, look at the image's *histogram,* which displays an image's tonal values, to evaluate whether the image has sufficient detail to produce a high-quality image. In Photoshop CS5, choose Window⇨ Histogram to display the Histogram panel.

The greater the range of values in the histogram, the greater the detail. Poor images without much information can be difficult, if not impossible, to correct. The Histogram panel also displays the overall distribution of shadows, midtones, and highlights to help you determine which tonal corrections are needed.

Figure 7-1 shows a good, full histogram that indicates a smooth transition from one shade to another in the image. Figure 7-2 shows that when a histogram is spread out and has gaps in it, the image is jumping too quickly from one shade to another, producing a posterized effect. *Posterization* is an effect that reduces tonal values to a limited amount, creating a more defined range of values from one shade to another. It's great if you want it but yucky if you want a smooth tonal change from one shadow to another.

Figure 7-1:
A histogram
showing
smooth
transitions
from one
color to
another.

Figure 7-2:
A histogram
showing
a lack of
smoothness
in the
gradation of
color.

So how do you create a good histogram? If you're scanning, make sure that your scanner is set for the maximum number of colors. Scanning at 16 shades of gray gives you 16 lines in your histogram — not good.

If you have a bad histogram, we recommend that you rescan or reshoot the image. If you have a good histogram to start with, keep it that way by not messing around with multiple tone correction tools. Most professionals use the Curves feature — and that's it. Curves (choose Image➪ Adjustments➪Curves), if used properly, do all the adjusting of levels (brightness and contrast) and color balance, all in one step. You can read more about curves in the section "Creating a Good Tone Curve," later in this chapter.

Figure 7-3 shows what happens to a perfectly good histogram when someone gets too zealous and uses the entire plethora of color correction controls in Photoshop. Just because the controls are there doesn't mean that you have to use them.

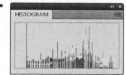

Figure 7-3:
Tonal
information
is broken up.

If a Warning icon appears while you're making adjustments, double-click anywhere on the histogram to refresh the display.

Breaking into key types

Don't panic if your histogram is smashed all the way to the left or right. The bars of the histogram represent tonal values. You can break down the types of images, based on their values, into three key types:

✦ **High key:** An extremely light-colored image, such as the image shown in Figure 7-4. Information is pushed toward the right in the histogram. Color correction has to be handled a little differently for these images to keep the light appearance to them.

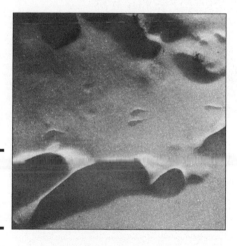

Figure 7-4:
A high key
image is a
light image.

✦ **Low key:** An extremely dark image, such as the one shown in Figure 7-5. Information is pushed to the left in the histogram. This type of image is difficult to scan on low-end scanners because the dark areas tend to blend together with little definition.

**Book IV
Chapter 7**

Creating a
Good Image

Figure 7-5:
A low key
image is a
dark image.

✦ **Mid key:** A typical image with a full range of shades, such as the image shown in Figure 7-6. These images are the most common and easiest to work with. In this chapter, we deal with images that are considered mid key.

Figure 7-6:
A typical
image with
a full range
of values is
a mid key
image.

Setting up the correction

To produce the best possible image, try to avoid correcting in CMYK (Cyan, Magenta, Yellow, Black) mode. If your images are typically in RGB (Red, Green, Blue) or LAB mode (L for lightness, and A and B for the color-opponent dimensions), keep them in that mode throughout the process. Convert them to CMYK only when you're finished manipulating the image.

Don't forget! Press Ctrl+Y (Windows) or ⌘+Y (Mac) to toggle on and off the CMYK preview so that you can see what your image will look like in CMYK mode without converting it.

Set up these items before starting any color correction:

1. **Select the Eyedropper tool (the keyboard shortcut is I); on the Options bar, change the sample size from Point Sample to 3 by 3 Average in the Sample Size drop-down list.**

   This setting gives you more accurate readings.

2. **If the Histogram panel isn't already visible, choose Window⇨ Histogram.**

3. **If the Info panel isn't already visible, choose Window⇨Info to show the Info panel so that you can check values.**

4. **Make sure that your color settings are correct.**

   If you're not sure how to check or set up color settings, see Chapter 3 of this minibook.

Creating a Good Tone Curve

A *tone curve* represents the density of an image. To produce the best image, you must first find the highlight and shadow points in it. An image created in less-than-perfect lighting conditions may be washed out or have odd color casts. See Figure 7-7 for an example of an image with no set highlight and shadow. Check out Figure 7-8 to see an image that went through the process of setting a highlight and shadow.

Figure 7-7: The image is murky before defining a highlight and shadow.

Figure 7-8:
The tonal values are opened after highlight and shadow have been set.

To make the process of creating a good tone curve more manageable, we've broken the process into four parts:

✦ Find the highlight and shadow

✦ Set the highlight and shadow values

✦ Adjust the midtone

✦ Find a neutral

Even though each part has its own set of steps, you must complete all four parts to accomplish the task of creating a good tone curve (unless you're working with grayscale images, in which case you can skip the neutral part). In this example, an adjustment layer is used for the curve adjustments. The benefit is that you can turn off the visibility of the adjustment later or double-click the adjustment layer thumbnail to make ongoing edits without destroying your image.

Finding the highlight and the shadow

In the noncomputer world, you'd spend a fair amount of time trying to locate the lightest and darkest parts of an image. Fortunately, you can cheat in Photoshop by using some features in the Curves panel. Here's how to access the panel:

1. **With an image worthy of adjustment — one that isn't perfect already — choose Window⇨Layer (if the Layers panel isn't already open).**

2. **Click and hold the Create New Fill or Adjustment Layer button at the bottom of the Layers panel and select Curves.**

   The Adjustments panel appears with the Curves panel active, as shown in Figure 7-9.

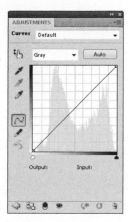

Figure 7-9:
Access the Curves panel with the Create New Fill or Adjustment Layer button.

Notice the grayed-out histogram behind the image in the Curves panel. The histogram helps you determine where you need to adjust the image's curve.

If you're correcting in RGB (as you should be), the tone curve may be the opposite of what you expect. Instead of light to dark displaying as you expect, RGB displays dark to light. Think about it: RGB is generated with light, and no RGB means that there's no light and you therefore have black. Turn on all RGB full force and you create white. Try pointing three filtered lights — one red, one green, and one blue. The three lights pointed in one direction create white.

If working with RGB confuses you, simply select Curves Display Options from the panel menu in the upper right corner of the Adjustments panel. When the Curves Display dialog box appears, as shown in Figure 7-10, select the Pigment/Ink % radio button and click OK.

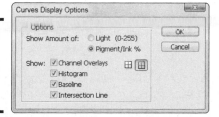

Figure 7-10:
View the curve using light or pigment.

 If you need a little more space in the Curves panel, click the Expanded View button at the bottom of the Curves panel. The panel enlarges.

Note that in the Curves panel, you see a Preset drop-down list that offers quick fixes using standard curves for certain corrections. These settings are great for quick fixes, but for the best image, create a custom curve.

The first thing you need to do in the Curves panel is determine the lightest and darkest parts of the image — referred to as *locating the highlight and shadow:*

1. **Before starting the correction, click the Set Black Point eyedropper once (labeled in Figure 7-11).**

2. **Hold down the Alt (Windows) or Option (Mac) key and click the shadow input slider (labeled in Figure 7-11).**

    If you did not change your Curve Display Options to display Pigment/Ink%, your highlight and shadow sliders will be opposite of what appears in Figure 7-11.

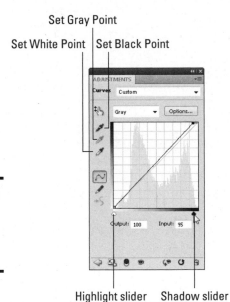

Set Gray Point

Set White Point | Set Black Point

Figure 7-11: The critical tools on the Curves panel.

Highlight slider   Shadow slider

When you Alt-click (Windows) or Option-click (Mac), the clipping preview turns on, revealing the darkest area of the image.

If you don't immediately see a dark area in the clipping preview, you can drag the shadow input slider to the left while holding down the Alt key or Option key. Note where the darkest area of the image appears.

3. **Hold down the Shift key and click directly on the image in that dark region.**

    This step drops a color sampler on the image that helps you reference that point later.

4. **Repeat Steps 1 through 3 with the highlight input slider. Select the Set White Point eyedropper (labeled in Figure 7-11) in the Curves panel.**

5. **Hold down the Alt key or Option key and click the highlight input slider.**

   Again, you can drag the slider toward the right if the lightest point doesn't immediately show up.

   When you locate the lightest point, as indicated by the lightest point in the clipping preview, you can Shift-click to drop a second color sampler, as shown in Figure 7-12.

Figure 7-12: You can Alt-click or Option+ Shift-click to drop a color sampler.

Setting the highlight and shadow values

After you determine the lightest and darkest points in an image, you can set their values. Follow these steps:

1. **To activate the eyedropper tools, select the Click and Drag button, shown in Figure 7-13.**

2. **Double-click the Set White Point eyedropper, the white eyedropper on the left side of the Curves panel.**

   When you double-click the Set White Point eyedropper, the Color Picker dialog box appears

3. **Enter a generic value for the lightest point in your image: Type 5 in the Cyan text box, type 3 in the Magenta text box, type 3 in the Yellow text box, leave the Black text box at 0 (zero), and then click OK.**

   The Black value helps to correct most images for print and online.

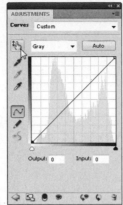

4. **When you receive an alert message asking if you want to save the new target colors as defaults, click Yes.**

5. **With the Set White Point eyedropper still selected, click the color sampler you dropped on the image, indicating the lightest point in the image.**

   Now, set the shadow point.

6. **Double-click the Set Black Point eyedropper.**

   The Color Picker dialog box appears.

7. **Type** 65 **in the Cyan text box, type** 53 **in the Magenta text box, type** 51 **in the Yellow text box, type** 95 **into the Black text box, and then click OK.**

   As with the highlight value, the Black value is a generic value that works for most print and online images.

8. **With the Set Black Point eyedropper still selected, click the color sampler you dropped on the image, indicating the darkest point in the image.**

Adjusting the midtone

You may have heard the statement, "Open up the midtones." This phrase essentially means that you're lightening the midtonal values of an image. In many cases, opening up the midtones is necessary to add contrast and bring out detail in an image.

To adjust the midtones, follow these steps:

1. **In the Curves panel, click the middle of the curve ramp to create an anchor point; drag up slightly.**

The image lightens. (If you're in Pigment/Ink % mode, drag down to lighten the image.) Move only a reasonable amount and be careful to observe what's happening in the Histogram panel (which you should always have open when making color corrections).

Because you set highlight and shadow (see the preceding section) and are now making a midtone correction, you see the bars in the histogram spreading out.

2. **To adjust the three-quarter tones (the shades around 75 percent), click halfway between the bottom of the curve ramp and the midpoint to set an anchor point.**

Use the grid in the Curves panel to find it easily. (In Pigment/Ink %, the three-quarter point is in the upper section of the color ramp.) Adjust the three-quarter area of the tone curve up or down slightly to create contrast in the image. Again, keep an eye on your histogram!

If you're working on a grayscale image, the tonal correction is done.

If you're working on a color image, keep the Curves panel open for the final steps, which are outlined in the next section.

Finding a neutral

The last steps in creating a tone curve apply only if you're working on a color image. The key to understanding color is knowing that equal amounts of color create gray. By positioning the mouse cursor over gray areas in an image and reading the values in the Info panel, you can determine which colors you need to adjust.

1. **With the Curves panel open, position it so that you can see the Info panel.**

If the Info panel is buried under another panel or a dialog box, choose Window⇨Info to bring it to the front.

2. **Position the cursor over an image and, in the Info panel, look for the RGB values in the upper left section.**

You see color values and then forward slashes and more color values. The numbers before the slash indicate the values in the image before you opened the Curves panel; the numbers after the slash show the values now that you've made changes in the Curves panel. Pay attention to the values after the slashes.

3. **Position the cursor over something gray in your image.**

It can be a shadow on a white shirt, a countertop, a road — anything that's a shade of gray. Look at the Info panel. If your image is perfectly color balanced, the RGB values following the forward slashes should all be the same.

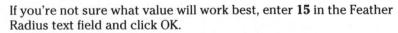

4. **If the color isn't balanced, click the Set Gray Point eyedropper in the Curves panel and click the neutral or gray area of the image.**

   The middle eyedropper (Set Gray Point) is a handy way of bringing the location you click closer together in RGB values, thereby balancing the colors.

Curves can be as complex or as simple as you make them. As you gain more confidence in using them, you can check neutrals throughout an image to ensure that all unwanted color casts are eliminated. You can even individually adjust each color's curve by selecting it from the Channel drop-down list in the Curves panel.

When you're finished with color correction, using the Unsharp Mask filter on your image is a good idea. Chapter 6 of this minibook shows you how to use this filter.

Editing an Adjustment Layer

You may make a curve adjustment only to discover that some areas of the image are still too dark or too light. Because you used an adjustment layer, you can turn off the correction or change it repeatedly with no degradation to the quality of the image.

Here are the steps to take if you still have additional adjustments to make to an image, such as lightening or darkening other parts of the image:

1. **Select the area of the image that needs adjustments.**

   See Chapter 4 of this minibook for a refresher on how to make selections in Photoshop.

2. **Choose Select⇨Modify⇨Feather to soften the selection.**

   The Feather dialog box appears.

3. **Enter a value into the Feather dialog box.**

   If you're not sure what value will work best, enter **15** in the Feather Radius text field and click OK.

   You can also click the Refine Edge button in the Options panel (when you have a selection tool active) to preview the feather amount.

4. **If the Layers panel isn't visible, choose Windows⇨Layers; click and hold the Create New Fill or Adjustment Layer icon and select Curves.**

5. **In the Curves panel, click the middle of the curve ramp to create an anchor point; drag up or down to lighten or darken the selected area.**

Notice in the Layers panel (see Figure 7-14) that the adjustment layer, Curves 2 by default, has a mask to the right of it. This mask was automatically created from your selection. The selected area is white; unselected areas are black.

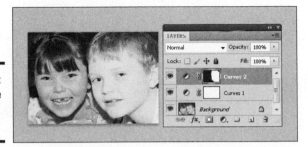

Figure 7-14: Paint on the adjustment layer mask.

6. **With the adjustment layer selected in the Layers panel, use the Brush tool to paint white to apply the correction to other areas of the image; paint with black to exclude areas from the correction.**

   You can even change the opacity with the Brush tool in the Options bar at the top to apply only some of the correction!

Testing a Printer

If you go to all the trouble of making color corrections to images and you still see printed images that look hot pink, it may not be your fault. Test your printer by following these steps:

1. **Create a neutral gray out of equal RGB values (double-click the Fill Color swatch in the Tools panel).**

2. **Create a shape, using neutral gray as the fill color.**

   For example, you can use the Ellipse tool to create a circle or oval.

3. **Choose File⇨Print and click OK to print the image from a color printer.**

If you're seeing heavy color casts, adjust the printer; cleaning or replacing the ink cartridge may fix the problem. Check out Chapter 10 of this minibook for more about printing Photoshop files.

Chapter 8: Working with Painting and Retouching Tools

In This Chapter

✔ Working in the Swatches panel

✔ Getting to know foreground and background colors

✔ Introducing painting and retouching tools

✔ Using the new content-aware feature

✔ Discovering blending modes

✔ Saving presets for tools

This chapter shows you how to use the painting and retouching tools in Photoshop. If you're unsure whether the painting you're about to create will look good, create a new layer and paint on it. (See Chapter 9 of this minibook to find out how to create and use layers.) That way, you can delete the layer by dragging it to the Trash Can (at the bottom of the Layers panel) if you decide that you don't like what you've done. Don't forget to make the Eraser tool your friend! You can also repair painting or retouching mistakes by Alt+dragging (Windows) or Option+dragging (Mac) with the Eraser tool selected to erase the last version saved or the present history state.

Have fun and be creative! Because Photoshop is pixel based, you can create incredible imagery with the painting tools. Smooth gradations from one color to the next, integrated with blending modes and transparency, can lead from super-artsy to super-realistic effects. In this chapter, you discover fundamental painting concepts, and we show you how to use retouching tools to eliminate wrinkles, blemishes, and scratches. Don't you wish you could do that in real life?

Using the Swatches Panel

Use the Swatches panel to store and retrieve frequently used colors. The Swatches panel lets you quickly select colors and gives you access to many other color options. By using the panel menu, where you see the cursor in Figure 8-1, you can select from a multitude of different color schemes, such as Pantone or Web-safe color sets. These color systems are converted to whatever color mode in which you're working.

Figure 8-1:
Click the panel menu to access additional color options.

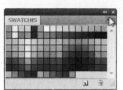

To sample and store a color for later use, follow these steps:

1. **To sample a color from an image, select the Eyedropper tool in the Tools panel and click a color in the image.**

Alternatively, you can use any of the paint tools (the Brush tool, for example) and Alt-click (Windows) or Option-click (Mac).

The color you click becomes the foreground color.

2. **If the Swatches panel isn't already open, choose Window⇨Swatches.**

3. **Store the color in the Swatches panel by clicking the New Swatch button at the bottom of the Swatches panel.**

Anytime you want to use that color again, simply click it in the Swatches panel to make it the foreground color.

Choosing Foreground and Background Colors

At the bottom of the Tools panel reside the foreground and background color swatches. The *foreground color* is the color you apply when using any of the painting tools. The *background color* is the color you see if you erase or delete pixels from the image.

Choose a foreground or background color by clicking the swatch, which opens the Color Picker dialog box, shown in Figure 8-2. To use the Color Picker, you can either enter values in the text fields on the right or slide the hue slider.

Pick the *hue* (color) you want to start with and then click in the color panel to the left to choose the amount of light and saturation (grayness or brightness) you want in the color. Select the Only Web Colors check box to choose one of the 216 colors in the Web-safe color palette. The hexadecimal value used in HTML documents appears in the text field in the lower right corner of the Color Picker.

To quickly save a color, click the Add to Swatches button directly in the Color Picker.

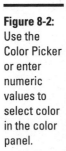
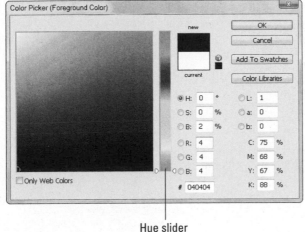

Figure 8-2:
Use the Color Picker or enter numeric values to select color in the color panel.

Hue slider

The Painting and Retouching Tools

Grouped together in the Tools panel are the tools used for painting and retouching. The arrow in the lower right area of a tool icon indicates that the tool has more related hidden tools; simply click and hold the tool icon to see additional painting and retouching tools. In this chapter, we show you how to use the Brush, Clone Stamp, Eraser, Gradient, Healing Brush, History Brush, Patch, Red Eye, and Spot Healing Brush tools. You also discover ways to fill shapes with colors and patterns.

Changing the brush

As you click to select different painting tools, note the Brush menu (second from the left) on the Options bar, as shown in Figure 8-3. Click the arrow to open the Brushes Preset picker. You can use the Master Diameter slider to make the brush size larger or smaller and to change the hardness of the brush.

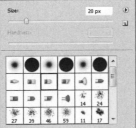

Figure 8-3:
The Brushes Preset picker.

The hardness refers to the "fuzziness" of the edges; a softer brush is more feathered and soft around the edges, whereas a harder edge is more definite (see Figure 8-4).

Figure 8-4:
The lines on the left have a soft edge (left) as compared to the lines on the right, which have a hard-edged brush stroke.

If you don't feel like accessing the Brushes Preset picker every time you want to make a change, press the right bracket (]) several times to make the brush diameter larger or press the left bracket ([) to make the brush diameter smaller. Press Shift+] to make the brush harder or Shift+[to make the brush softer.

Choose Window⇨Brushes to see a list of brush presets, plus more brush options you can use to create custom brushes. You can also choose other brush libraries from the panel menu. When you select an additional library, a dialog box appears, asking whether you want to replace the current brushes with the brushes in the selected library. Click the Append button to keep existing brushes and add the library to the list, or click OK to replace existing brushes.

Access the Brushes Preset picker while you're painting by right-clicking (Windows) or Control-clicking (Mac) anywhere in the image area. Double-click a brush to select it; press Esc to hide the Brushes Preset picker.

The Spot Healing Brush tool and Content-Aware feature

The Spot Healing Brush tool was a great tool to begin with, but now, with the new Content-Aware feature, it's even better. No matter what level of Photoshop user you are, you will appreciate the magic in this tool option.

In its default settings, the Spot Healing Brush tool quickly removes blemishes and other imperfections in images. Click a blemish and watch it paint matching texture, lighting, transparency, and shading to the pixels being healed. The Spot Healing Brush tool doesn't require you to specify a sample spot — it automatically samples from around the retouched area.

Now take this concept a step further by checking the Content-Aware option on the Options bar. The concept is the same, but if you look at Figure 8-5, you can see that painting with the Spot Healing Brush sets into action an incredible number of calculations that attempt to render pixels similar in detail to its surroundings.

Figure 8-5: Using the Spot Healing Brush tool with the Content-Aware option enabled.

Does this work every time? Of course not. Does it work often enough to save you hours of work? Yes!

You can also take advantage of the Content-Aware feature by using the Fill feature. Simply follow these steps:

1. **Select the area to be replaced by the new content.**

2. **Choose Edit⇨Fill and, in the Fill dialog box, select Content-Aware from the Use drop-down menu, shown in Figure 8-6.**

   The content is replaced.

Figure 8-6:
Use the
Content-
Aware
feature
in the Fill
dialog box.

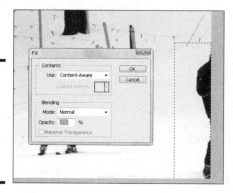

The Healing Brush tool

 You can use the Healing Brush tool for repairs, such as eliminating scratches and dust from scanned images. The difference between the Spot Healing Brush tool and the Healing Brush tool is that a sample spot is required before applying the Healing Brush. Follow these steps to use this tool:

1. **Select the Healing Brush tool in the Tools panel (it's a hidden tool of the Spot Healing Brush tool).**

2. **Find an area in the image that looks good and then Alt-click (Windows) or Option-click (Mac) to sample that area.**

   For example, if you want to eliminate wrinkles on a face, choose a wrinkle-free area of skin near the wrinkle. (Try to choose an area relatively close in skin tone.)

3. **Position the mouse cursor over the area to be repaired and start painting.**

   The Healing Brush tool goes into action, blending and softening to create a realistic repair of the area.

4. **Repeat Steps 2 and 3 as necessary to repair the blemish, wrinkles, or scratches.**

The Patch tool

 Hidden behind the Healing Brush tool in the Tools panel is the Patch tool. Use it to repair larger areas, such as a big scratch or a large area of skin, by following these steps:

1. **Click and hold the Healing Brush tool to select the Patch tool; on the Options bar, select the Destination radio button.**

   You can patch either the source area or the destination — it's up to you. We recommend dragging a good source over the area that needs repaired.

2. **With the Patch tool still selected, drag to create a marquee around the source you want to use as the patch.**

   The source is an unscratched or wrinkle-free area.

3. **After you create the marquee, drag the selected source area to the destination to be repaired.**

   The Patch tool clones the selected source area while you drag it to the destination (the scratched area); when you release the mouse button, the tool blends in the source selection and repairs the scratched area!

 Make the patch look better by choosing Edit➪Fade Patch Selection immediately after you apply the patch. Adjust the opacity until no telltale signs show that you made a change.

The Red Eye tool

 So you finally got the group together and shot the perfect image, but red eye took over! *Red eye* is caused by a reflection of the camera's flash in the retina of your photo's subject or subjects. You see this effect more often when taking pictures in a dark room, because the subject's irises are wide open. If you can, use your camera's red-eye-reduction feature. Or, use a separate flash unit that you can mount on the camera farther from the camera's lens.

You'll love the fact that red eye is extremely easy to fix in Photoshop. Just follow these steps:

1. **Select the Red Eye tool (hidden behind the Spot Healing Brush tool).**

2. **Click and drag to surround the red-eye area.**

   You should see a change immediately, but if you need to make adjustments to the size or the darkness amount, you can change options on the Options bar.

The Brush tool

 Painting with the Brush tool in Photoshop is much like painting in the real world. What you should know are all the nifty keyboard commands you can use to be much more productive when painting. These shortcuts are truly outstanding, so make sure that you try them while you read about them. By the way, the keyboard commands you see in Table 8-1 work on all the painting tools.

Table 8-1	Brush Keyboard Shortcuts	
Task	*Windows*	*Mac*
Choose the Brush tool	B	B
Increase the brush size	]	]
Decrease the brush size	[	[
Harden the brush	Shift+]	Shift+]
Soften the brush	Shift+[	Shift+[
Sample the color	Alt-click	Option-click
Switch the foreground and background colors	X	X
Change the opacity by a given percentage	Type a number between 1 and 100	Type a number between 1 and 100

If you're really into brushes, you have lots of useful options available in the Brushes panel (choose Window⇨Brushes to open it), as shown in Figure 8-7.

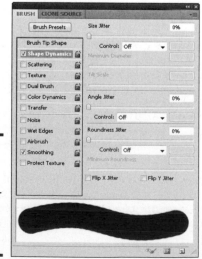

Figure 8-7: Additional options are available for painting in the Brushes panel.

You have several attribute choices, most of which have dynamic controls in the menu options that allow you to vary brush characteristics by tilting or applying more pressure to a stylus pen (if you're using a pressure-sensitive drawing tablet), among other things.

A warning sign indicates that you don't have the appropriate device attached to use the selected feature, such as a pressure-sensitive drawing tablet.

The following options are available in the Brushes panel:

✦ **Brush Tip Shape:** Select from these standard controls for determining brush dimensions and spacing.

✦ **Shape Dynamics:** Change the size of the brush as you paint.

✦ **Scattering:** Scatter the brush strokes and control the brush tip count.

✦ **Texture:** Choose from preexisting patterns or your own.

Create a pattern by selecting an image area with the Rectangular Marquee tool. Choose Edit➪Define Pattern, name the pattern, and then click OK. The pattern is now available in the Brushes panel's Texture choices.

✦ **Dual Brush:** Use two brushes at the same time.

✦ **Color Dynamics:** Change the color as you paint.

✦ **Transfer:** Adjusts the dynamics for the build-up of the paint.

✦ **Noise:** Adds a grainy texture to the brush stroke.

✦ **Wet Edges:** Makes the brush stroke appear to be wet by creating a heavier amount of color on the edges of the brush strokes.

✦ **Airbrush:** Gives airbrush features to the Brush tools. Enable the Airbrush feature by clicking the Airbrush button and adjusting the pressure and flow on the Options bar.

If you click and hold the Brush tool on the Image area, the paint stops spreading. Turn on the Airbrush feature and notice that when you click and hold, the paint keeps spreading, just like using a can of spray paint. You can use the Flow slider on the Options bar to control the pressure.

✦ **Smoothing:** Smoothes the path created with the mouse.

✦ **Protect Texture:** Preserves the texture pattern when applying brush presets.

In addition to the preceding options, you can adjust the jitter of the brush. The *jitter* specifies the randomness of the brush attribute. At 0 percent, an element doesn't change over the course of a stroke; at 100 percent, a stroke totally varies from one attribute to another.

Book IV
Chapter 8

Working with
Painting and
Retouching Tools

After reviewing all the available brush options, you may want to start thinking about how you'll apply the same attributes later. Saving the Brush tool attributes is important as you increase your skill level.

The Clone Stamp tool

The Clone Stamp tool is used for pixel-to-pixel cloning. The Clone Stamp tool is different from the Healing Brush tool in that it does no automatic blending into the target area. You can use the Clone Stamp tool for removing a product name from an image, replacing a telephone wire that's crossing in front of a building, or duplicating an item.

Here's how to use the Clone Stamp tool:

1. **With the Clone Stamp tool selected, position the cursor over the area you want to clone and then Alt-click (Windows) or Option-click (Mac) to define the clone source.**

2. **Position the cursor over the area where you want to paint the cloned pixels and then start painting.**

   Note the cross hair at the original sampled area, as shown in Figure 8-8. While you're painting, the cross hair follows the pixels you're cloning.

Figure 8-8:
A cross hair over the source shows what you're cloning.

When using the Clone Stamp tool for touching up images, you should resample many times so as to not leave a seam where you replaced pixels. A good clone stamper Alt-clicks (Windows) or Option-clicks (Mac) and paints many times over until the retouching is complete.

Choose Window⇨Clone Source to open the Clone Source panel, shown in Figure 8-9. With this handy little panel, you can save multiple clone sources to refer to while working. Even better, you can scale, preview, and rotate your clone source — before you start cloning.

Figure 8-9:
Additional options in the Clone Source panel. In this example the apple rotates 180 degrees while being cloned.

The Clone Source panel can be extremely helpful with difficult retouching projects that involve a little more precision.

Follow these steps to experiment with this fun and interactive panel:

1. **If the Clone Source panel isn't visible, choose Window⇨Clone Source.**

   The Clone Source icons across the top have yet to be defined. The first stamp is selected as a default.

2. **Alt-click (Windows) or Option-click (Mac) in the image area to record the first clone source.**

3. **Click the second Clone Source icon at the top of the Clone Source panel and then Alt-click (Windows) or Option-click (Mac) somewhere else on the page to define a second clone source.**

   Repeat as needed to define more clone sources. You can click the Clone Source icons at any time to retrieve the clone source and start cloning.

4. **Enter any numbers you want in the Offset X and Y, W and H, and Angle text boxes in the center section of the Clone Source panel to set up transformations before you clone.**

5. **Select the Show Overlay check box to see a preview of your clone source.**

   Whatever you plan to do, it's much easier to see a preview *before* you start cloning. If you don't use the Clone Source panel for anything else, use it to see a preview of your clone source before you start painting. If it helps to see the clone source better, select the Invert check box.

   You see an *overlay* (or preview) before cloning begins. This overlay helps you better align your image, which is helpful for precision work. If you want the preview to go away after you start cloning, select the Auto Hide check box.

The History Brush tool

Choose Window⇔History to see the History panel. You could play around for weeks in the History panel, this section gives you only the basic concepts.

At the top of the History panel is a snapshot of the last saved version of the image. Beside the snapshot is an icon noting that it's the present History state, as shown in Figure 8-10.

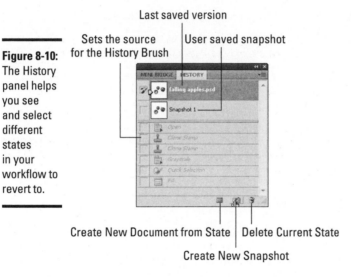

Figure 8-10: The History panel helps you see and select different states in your workflow to revert to.

Last saved version

Sets the source for the History Brush

User saved snapshot

Create New Document from State | Delete Current State

Create New Snapshot

 When you paint with the History Brush tool, it reverts by default back to the way the image looked in the last saved version. You can click the empty square to the left of any state in the History panel (see Figure 8-10) to make it the source for the History Brush tool. Use the History Brush tool to fix errors and add "spunk" to images.

The Eraser tool

 You may not think of the Eraser tool as a painting tool, but it can be! When you drag the image with the Eraser tool, it rubs out pixels to the background color. (Basically, it paints with the background color.) If you're dragging with the Eraser tool on a layer, it rubs out pixels to reveal the layer's transparent background. (You can also think of using the Eraser tool as painting with transparency.)

The Eraser tool uses all the same commands as the Brush tools. You can make an eraser larger or softer or more or less opaque. Even better, follow these steps to use the Eraser tool creatively:

1. **Open any color image and apply a filter.**

   For example, we chose Filter⇨Blur⇨Gaussian Blur. In the Gaussian Blur dialog box that appears, we changed the blur to 5 and then clicked OK to apply the Gaussian Blur filter.

2. **Select the Eraser tool and press 5 to change it to 50 percent opacity.**

   You can also use the Opacity slider on the Options bar.

3. **Hold down the Alt (Windows) or Option (Mac) key to repaint 50 percent of the original image's state before applying the filter.**

4. **Continue painting in the same area to bring the image back to its original state.**

   The original sharpness of the image returns where you painted.

Holding down the Alt (Windows) or Option (Mac) key is the key to erasing the last saved version (or history state). This tool is incredible for fixing mistakes or removing applied filters.

The Gradient tool

Choose the Gradient tool and click and drag across an image area to create a gradient in the direction and length of the mouse motion. A short drag creates a short gradient; a long drag produces a smoother, longer gradient.

From the Options bar, you also can choose the type of gradient you want: Linear, Radial, Angle, Reflected, or Diamond.

As a default, gradients are created using the current foreground and background colors. Click the arrow on the Gradient button on the Options bar to assign a different preset gradient.

To create a gradient, follow these steps:

1. **Choose the Gradient tool and click the Gradient Editor button on the Options bar.**

   The Gradient Editor dialog box appears. At the bottom of the gradient preview, you see two or more *stops,* which is where new colors are inserted into the gradient. They look like little house icons. Use the stops on top of the gradient slider to determine the opacity.

2. **Click a stop and click the color swatch to the right of the word *Color* to open the Color Picker and assign a different color to the stop.**

3. **Click anywhere below the gradient preview to add more color stops.**

4. **Drag a color stop off the Gradient Editor dialog box to delete it.**

5. **Click the top of the gradient preview to assign different stops with varying opacity, as shown in Figure 8-11.**

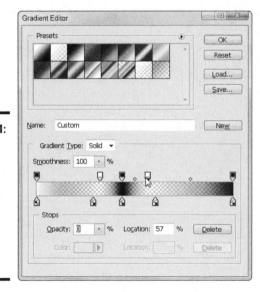

Figure 8-11: Assigning varying amounts of opacity using the stops on top of the gradient slider.

6. **When you're finished editing the gradient, name it and then click the New button.**

   The new gradient is added to the preset gradient choices.

7. **To apply your gradient, drag across a selection or image with the Gradient tool.**

Blending Modes

You can use blending modes to add flair to the traditional opaque paint. Use blending modes to paint highlights or shadows that allow details to show through from the underlying image or to colorize a desaturated image. You access the blending modes for paint tools from the Options bar.

You can't get an accurate idea of how the blending mode works with the paint color and the underlying color until you experiment. (That's what multiple undos are for!) Alternatively, you can copy to a new layer the image you want to experiment with and hide the original layer; see Chapter 9 of this minibook for more about layers.

This list describes the available blending modes:

✦ **Normal:** Paints normally, with no interaction with underlying colors.

✦ **Dissolve:** Gives a random replacement of the pixels, depending on the opacity at any pixel location.

✦ **Behind:** Edits or paints only on the transparent part of a layer.

✦ **Darken:** Replaces only the areas that are lighter than the blend color. Areas darker than the blend color don't change.

✦ **Multiply:** Creates an effect similar to drawing on the page with magic markers. Also looks like colored film that you see on theater lights.

✦ **Color Burn:** Darkens the base color to reflect the blend color. If you're using white, no change occurs.

✦ **Linear Burn:** Looks at the color information in each channel and darkens the base color to reflect the blending color by decreasing the brightness.

✦ **Darker Color:** Compares the total of all channel values for the blend and base color and displays the lower value color.

✦ **Lighten:** Replaces only the areas darker than the blend color. Areas lighter than the blend color don't change.

✦ **Screen:** Multiplies the inverse of the underlying colors. The resulting color is always a lighter color.

✦ **Color Dodge:** Brightens the underlying color to reflect the blend color. If you're using black, there's no change.

✦ **Linear Dodge:** Looks at the color information in each channel and brightens the base color to reflect the blending color by increasing the brightness.

✦ **Lighter Color:** Compares the total of all channel values for the blend and base color and displays the higher-value color.

✦ **Overlay:** Multiplies or screens the colors, depending on the base color.

✦ **Soft Light:** Darkens or lightens colors, depending on the blend color. The effect is similar to shining a diffused spotlight on the artwork.

✦ **Hard Light:** Multiplies or screens colors, depending on the blend color. The effect is similar to shining a harsh spotlight on the artwork.

✦ **Vivid Light:** Burns or dodges colors by increasing or decreasing the contrast.

✦ **Linear Light:** Burns or dodges colors by decreasing or increasing the brightness.

✦ **Pin Light:** Replaces colors, depending on the blend color.

✦ **Hard Mix:** Paints strokes that have no effect with other Hard Mix paint strokes. Use this mode when you want no interaction between the colors.

✦ **Difference:** Subtracts either the blend color from the base color or the base color from the blend color, depending on which one has the greater brightness value. The effect is similar to a color negative.

✦ **Exclusion:** Creates an effect similar to, but with less contrast than, Difference mode.

✦ **Hue:** Applies the hue (color) of the blend object to underlying objects but keeps the underlying shading or luminosity intact.

✦ **Saturation:** Applies the saturation of the blend color but uses the luminance and hue of the base color.

✦ **Color:** Applies the blend object's color to underlying objects but preserves the gray levels in the artwork. This mode is helpful for tinting objects or changing their colors.

✦ **Luminosity:** Creates a resulting color with the hue and saturation of the base color and the luminance of the blend color. This mode is the opposite of Color mode.

Painting with color

This section provides an example of using blending modes to change and add color to an image. An example of using a blending mode is tinting a black-and-white (grayscale) image with color. You can't paint color in Grayscale mode, so follow these steps to add color to a black-and-white image:

1. **Open an image in any color mode and choose Image⇨Mode⇨RGB.**

2. **If the image isn't already a grayscale image, choose Image⇨ Adjustments⇨Desaturate.**

This feature makes it appear as though the image is black-and-white, but you're still in a color mode and can apply color.

3. **Choose a painting tool (the Brush tool, for example) and, from the Swatches panel, choose the first color you want to paint with.**

4. **On the Options bar, select Color from the Mode drop-down list and then use the Opacity slider to change the opacity to 50 percent.**

   You can also just type **5**.

5. **Start painting!**

   Color Blending mode is used to change the color of pixels while keeping intact the underlying grayscale (shading).

Another way to bring attention to a certain item in an RGB image (such as those cute greeting cards that have the single rose in color and everything else in black and white) is to select the item you want to bring attention to. Choose Select➪Modify➪Feather to soften the selection a bit (5 pixels is a good number to enter in the Feather Radius text field). Then choose Select➪Inverse. With everything else selected, choose Image➪Adjustments➪Desaturate. Everything else in the image looks black and white, except for the original item you selected.

Filling selections

If you have a definite shape that doesn't lend itself to being painted, you can fill it with color instead. Make a selection and choose Edit➪Fill to access the Fill dialog box. From the Use drop-down list, you can choose from the following options to fill the selection: Foreground Color, Background Color, Color (to open the Color Picker while in the Fill dialog box), Pattern, History, Black, 50% Gray, or White.

If you want to use an existing or saved pattern from the Brushes panel, you can retrieve a pattern by selecting Pattern in the Fill dialog box as well. Select History from the Use drop-down list to fill with the last version saved or the history state.

If you'd rather use the Paint Bucket tool, which fills based on the tolerance specified on the Options bar, it's hidden in the Gradient tool. To use the Paint Bucket tool to fill with the foreground color, simply click the item you want to fill.

Saving Presets

All Photoshop tools allow you to save presets so that you can retrieve them from a list of presets. The following steps show you an example of saving a Brush tool preset, but the same method can be used for all other tools as well:

**Book IV
Chapter 8**

**Working with
Painting and
Retouching Tools**

1. Choose a brush size, color, softness, or any other characteristic.

2. Click the Tool Preset Picker button on the left side of the Options bar.

3. Click the triangle in the upper right corner to access the fly-out menu and then choose New Tool Preset.

   The New Tool Preset dialog box appears.

4. Type a descriptive name in the Name text field (leave the Include Color check box selected if you want the preset to also remember the present color) and then click OK.

5. Access the preset by clicking the tool's Preset Picker button and choosing it from the tool's Preset Picker list.

Each preset you create is specific to the tool it was created in, so you can have a crop preset and an eraser preset, for example. After you get in the habit of saving presets, you'll wonder how you ever got along without them.

Chapter 9: Using Layers

In This Chapter

✔ **Discovering layers**

✔ **Using text as a layer**

✔ **Implementing layer masks**

✔ **Organizing layers**

✔ **Using Smart Objects**

✔ **Using 3D layers to create 3D objects**

✔ **Merging and flattening a layered image**

*L*ayers are incredibly helpful in production. By using layers, you can make realistic additions to an image that you can remove, edit, and control with blending modes and transparency. Unfortunately, showing you all the features of layers goes beyond the scope of this chapter. This chapter covers basic layer concepts to get you started working with layers in Photoshop. We show you how to create composite images using easy layer features — just enough knowledge to get yourself into a complex mess of layers! Even if you're an experienced Photoshop user, read this chapter to discover all sorts of neat key commands that can help you in your workflow.

If you're a video professional, you can open videos in Photoshop. Photoshop Extended automatically creates a Movie layer, and with the Timeline, you can do pixel editing frame by frame!

You can also make regular layers into 3D files. Though many 3D features are beyond the scope of this book, you can discover enough to be dangerous in the later section "Experimenting with 3D Files."

Have fun with layers and don't worry if you mess up — you can always press F12 to revert the image to the state it was in the last time you saved it.

Creating and Working with Layers

Layers make creating *composite images* (images pieced together from other, individual images) easy because you can separate individual elements of the composite onto their own layers. Much like creating collages by cutting pictures from magazines, you can mask out selections on one image and place them on a layer in another image. When pixel information is on its own layer, you can move it, transform it, correct its color, or apply filters only to that layer, without disturbing pixel information on other layers.

The best way to understand how to create and use layers is to, well, create and use layers. The following steps show you how to create a new, layered image:

1. **Choose File➪New to create a new document.**

   The New dialog box appears.

2. **Select Default Photoshop Size from the Preset Sizes drop-down list, select the Transparent option from the Background Contents area, and then click OK.**

   Because you selected the Transparent option, the image opens with an empty layer instead of a white background layer. The image appears as a checkerboard pattern, which signifies that it's transparent.

   If you don't like to see the default checkerboard pattern where there's transparency, choose Edit➪Preferences➪Transparency and Gamut (Windows) or Photoshop➪Preferences➪Transparency and Gamut (Mac). In the Preferences dialog box that appears, you can change the Grid Size drop-down list to None to remove the checkerboard pattern entirely. If you don't want to remove the transparency grid, you can change the size of the checkerboard pattern or change the color of the checkerboard.

   When you open an existing document (say, a photograph), this image is the background layer.

3. **Create a shape on the new image.**

   For example, we created a black square by using the Rectangular Marquee tool to create a square selection; we then filled the selection with black by double-clicking the Foreground color swatch, selecting black from the Color Picker, and clicking in the selection with the Paint Bucket tool (hidden under the Gradient tool).

   After you select a color, you can also use the key command Alt+Delete (Windows) or Option+Delete (Mac) to fill the selected area with color.

4. **To rename the layer, double-click the layer name (Layer 1) in the Layers panel and type a short, descriptive name.**

   A good practice is to name layers based on what they contain; for this example, we named the layer we created in Step 3 the catchy name *square*.

5. **Create a new layer by Alt-clicking (Windows) or Option-clicking (Mac) the New Layer button at the bottom of the Layers panel.**

   The New Layer dialog box appears.

6. **Give your new layer a descriptive name and then click OK.**

7. **Create a shape on the new layer.**

   In this example, we created a red circle using the Elliptical Marquee tool and filling the selection with red.

   The new shape can overlap the shape on the other layer, as shown in Figure 9-1.

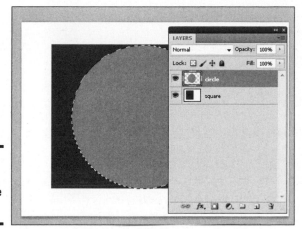

Figure 9-1:
The circle overlaps the square.

Duplicating a layer

Perhaps you want to create a duplicate of a layer for your composite. This technique can be helpful for creating do-it-yourself drop shadows and for adding elements to an image, such as more apples in a bowl of fruit.

 Alt+drag (Windows) or Option+drag (Mac) a layer to the New Layer button at the bottom of the Layers panel to duplicate it. Again, by holding down Alt (Windows) or Option (Mac), you can name the layer while you create it.

Selecting a layer

When you start working with layers, you may move or adjust pixels, only to discover that you accidentally edited pixels on the wrong layer. Select the layer you plan to work on by clicking the layer name in the Layers panel.

 Photoshop CS5 represents a selected layer by simply highlighting the layer in the Layers panel. The indicator paintbrush icon is gone in this version.

Here are some tips to help you select the correct layer:

✦ Select the Move tool and then right-click (Windows) or Control-click (Mac) to see a contextual menu listing all layers that have pixel data at the point you clicked and to choose the layer you want to work with.

✦ Get in the habit of holding down the Ctrl (Windows) or ⌘ (Mac) key while using the Move tool and when selecting layers. This technique temporarily turns on the Auto Select feature, which automatically selects the topmost visible layer that contains the pixel data you clicked.

✦ Press Alt+[(Windows) or Option+[(Mac) to select the next layer down from the selected layer in the stacking order.

✦ Press Alt+] (Windows) or Option+] (Mac) to select the next layer up from the selected layer in the stacking order.

Controlling the visibility of a layer

Hide layers that you don't immediately need by clicking the Eye icon in the Layers panel. To see only one layer, Alt-click (Windows) or Option-click (Mac) the eye icon of the layer you want to keep visible. Alt-click (Windows) or Option-click (Mac) the Eye icon again to show all layers.

Rearranging the stacking order

Layers are like clear pieces of film lying on top of each other. Change the stacking order of the layers in the Layers panel by dragging a layer until you see a black separator line appear, indicating that you're dragging the layer to that location. You can also use these useful commands to help move a layer:

Command	Windows Shortcut	Mac Shortcut
Move selected layer up	Ctrl+]	⌘+]
Move selected layer down	Ctrl+[	⌘+[

Creating a Text Layer

When you create text in Photoshop, the text is created on its own layer. By having the text separate from the rest of the image, applying different styles and blending modes to customize the type, as well as repositioning the text, is simplified.

T. To create a text layer, choose the Type tool and click the image area. You can also click and drag to create a text area. The Options bar, shown in Figure 9-2, gives you the controls to change the font, size, blending mode, and color of the text.

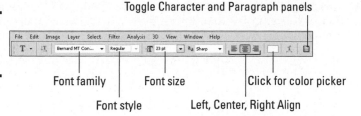

Figure 9-2:
The Text
tool options.

Toggle Character and Paragraph panels

Font family   Font size   Click for color picker

Font style   Left, Center, Right Align

When you're finished typing, you must confirm your text entry by select-ing the check box (on the right of the Options bar) or pressing Ctrl+Enter (Windows) or ⌘+Return (Mac).

Warping text

When you click the Create Warped Text button on the Options bar, the Warp Text dialog box appears. You can use it to apply different types of distortion to your text.

You can still edit text that's been warped. To remove a warp, click the Create Warp Text button again and select None from the Style drop-down list.

Fine-tuning text

For controls such as leading, baseline shift, and paragraph controls, click the Toggle the Character and Paragraph Panels icon near the right end of the Options bar.

Use the keyboard commands in Table 9-1 to fine-tune text in Photoshop. Make sure that you have text selected when you use these shortcuts.

Table 9-1	Helpful Typesetting Key Commands	
Task	Windows	Mac
Increase the font size	Shift+Ctrl+>	Shift+⌘+>
Decrease the font size	Shift+Ctrl+<	Shift++⌘+<
Increase the kerning (the cursor must be between two letters)	Alt+→	Option+→
Decrease the kerning (the cursor must be between two letters)	Alt+←	Option+←
Increase the tracking (on several selected letters)	Alt+→	Option+→
Decrease the tracking (on several selected letters)	Alt+←	Option+←
Increase or decrease the leading (on several selected lines)	Alt+↑ or Alt+↓	Option+↑ or Option+↓

To change the font, drag over the font family name on the Options bar and then press the up-arrow key (↑) to move up in the font list or the down-arrow key (↓) to move down in the font list.

After you're finished editing text, confirm or delete the changes by clicking the buttons on the right end of the Options bar.

If you'd rather use key commands to confirm or delete changes, press the Esc key to cancel text changes; press Ctrl+Enter (Windows) or ⌘+Return (Mac) to commit text changes (or use the Enter key on the numeric keypad).

Using Layer Masks

In this section, we show you how to create a layer mask from a selection or a pen path. A *layer mask* covers areas of the image that you want to make transparent and exposes pixels that you want visible. Masks can be based on a selection you've created with the selection tools, by painting on the mask itself or by using the Pen tool to create a path around the object you want to keep visible.

Creating a layer mask from a selection

You need to have two images open to follow these steps where we show you how to create layer masks from a selection:

1. **When combining images, choose Image⇨Image Size to make sure that the images are approximately the same resolution.**

   Otherwise, you may create some interesting, but disproportional, effects.

2. **Choose Window⇨Arrange⇨Tile to position the images in separate windows.**

3. **Using the Move tool, click one image and drag it to the other image window.**

   A black border appears around the image area when you drop an image into another image window. By dragging and dropping an image, you automatically create a new layer on top of the active layer.

   Hold down the Shift key when dragging one image to another to perfectly center the new image layer in the document window.

4. **Using any selection method, select a part of the image that you want to keep on the newly placed layer and choose Select⇨Modify⇨Feather to soften the selection. (Five pixels should be enough.)**

5. **Click the Layer Mask button at the bottom of the Layers panel.**

A mask is created to the right of the layer, leaving only your selection visible, as shown in Figure 9-3.

6. **If you click the Layer thumbnail in the Layers panel, the mask thumbnail shows corner edges, indicating that it's activated.**

While the layer mask is active, you can paint on the mask.

Figure 9-3:
Click Layer
Mask to
create a
custom
mask from
an active
selection.

7. **Select the Brush tool and paint black while the mask thumbnail is selected to cover areas of the image that you don't want to see; press X to switch to white and paint to expose areas on the image that you do want to see.**

You can even change the opacity while you paint to blend images with each other.

To create a smooth transition from one image to another, drag the Gradient tool across the image while the layer mask is selected in the Layers panel.

Creating a vector mask from a pen path

A *vector mask* masks a selection, but it does so with the precision you can get only from using a path. The following steps show you another, slightly more precise, way to create a layer mask by using a pen path:

1. **Use the Pen tool and click from point to point to make a closed pen path.**

If you already have a path, choose Windows➪Paths and click a path to select it.

See Chapter 5 of this minibook for more about working with the Pen tool.

2. **On the Layers panel, click the Layer Mask button and then click it again, see Figure 9-4.**

Wow — a mask from your pen path! Anything not contained within the path is now masked out. Use the Direct Selection tool to edit the path, if necessary.

Figure 9-4:
Create a
mask from
your pen
path.

If you no longer want a vector mask, drag the thumbnail to the Trash Can in the Layers panel. An Alert dialog box appears, asking whether you want to discard the mask or apply it. Click the Discard button to revert your image to the way it appeared before applying the mask or click the Apply button to apply the masked area.

Organizing Your Layers

As you advance in layer skills, you'll want to keep layers named, neat, and in order. In this section, we show you some tips to help you organize multiple layers.

Activating multiple layers simultaneously

Select multiple layers simultaneously by selecting one layer and then Shift-clicking to select additional layers. The selected layers are highlighted. Selected layers move and transform together, making repositioning and resizing easier than activating each layer independently.

Select multiple layers to keep their relative positions to each other and take advantage of alignment features. When you select two or more layers and choose the Move tool, you can take advantage of alignment features on the Options bar (see Figure 9-5). Select three or more layers for distribution options.

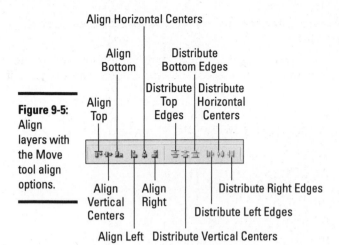

Figure 9-5:
Align
layers with
the Move
tool align
options.

Align Horizontal Centers

Align Bottom

Distribute Bottom Edges

Distribute Top Edges

Distribute Horizontal Centers

Align Top

Align Vertical Centers

Align Right

Distribute Right Edges

Align Left

Distribute Left Edges

Distribute Vertical Centers

Auto-Align Layers tool

Do you ever have multiple shots of a group, one with the guy's eyes shut
and the girl looking the other way? Or maybe you like the smile in one better
than in another. With the auto-alignment feature, you can pull the best parts
of multiple images into one "best" image.

To use this tool, simply have the Move tool active, select multiple layers,
and then click the Auto-Align Layers button to the right of the alignment
tools. The Auto-Align Layer dialog box appears, as shown in Figure 9-6; make
your selection and click OK.

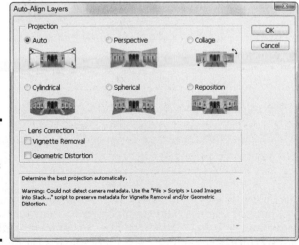

Figure 9-6:
The Auto-
Align Layers
feature can
help create
a better
composite.

Book IV
Chapter 9

Using Layers

Layer groups

After you start using layers, you'll likely use lots of them and your Layers panel will become huge. If you often scroll to navigate from one layer to another, take advantage of *layer groups,* which essentially act as folders that hold layers you choose, as shown in Figure 9-7. Just as with a folder you use for paper, you can add, remove, and shuffle around the layers within a layer group. Use layer groups to organize layers and make the job of duplicating multiple layers easier.

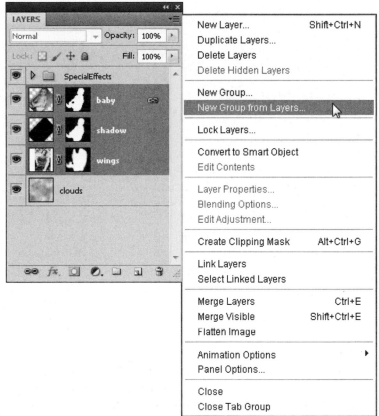

Figure 9-7:
Select the layers that you want to group together and then choose New Group from Layers.

To create a layer group, follow these steps:

1. **After creating several layers, Shift-click to select the layers you want to group together in a set.**

2. **Choose New Group from Layers from the Layers panel menu, name the group, and then click OK.**

   That's it. You've created a layer group from your selected layers.

With the Blending Mode drop-down list in the Layers panel, you can change all layers within a group to a specific blending mode, or you can use the Opacity slider to change the opacity of all layers in a group at one time. *Pass through* in the blending mode indicates that no individual blending modes are changed.

After you create a layer group, you can still reorganize layers within the group or even drag additional layers in or out. You can open and close a layer group with the arrow to the left of the group name.

Duplicating a layer group

After you create a layer group, you may want to copy it. For example, you may want to copy an image, such as a button created from several layers topped off with a text layer. The most efficient way to make a copy of that button is to create a layer group and copy the entire group. To copy an image made up of several layers that aren't in a layer group would require you to individually duplicate each layer — how time-consuming!

To duplicate a layer group, follow these steps:

1. **Select a group from the Layers panel.**

2. **From the panel menu, choose Duplicate Group.**

The Duplicate Group dialog box appears.

3. **For the destination, choose the present document or any open document or create a new document.**

Be sure to give the duplicated set a distinctive name!

4. **Click OK.**

Using Layer Styles

Layer styles are wonderful little extra effects that you can apply to layers to create drop shadows and bevel and emboss effects and to apply color overlays, gradients, patterns and strokes, and more.

Applying a style

To apply a layer style (for example, the drop shadow style, one of the most popular effects) to an image, follow these steps:

1. **Create a layer on any image.**

For example, you can create a text layer to see the effects of the layer styles.

2. **With the layer selected, click and hold the Add a layer Style button at the bottom of the Layers panel; from the menu options, choose Drop Shadow.**

   In the Layer Style dialog box that appears, you can choose to change the blending mode, color, distance spread, and size of a drop shadow. You should see that the style has already applied to your text. Position the cursor on the image area and drag to visually adjust the position of the drop shadow.

3. **When you're happy with the drop shadow, click OK to apply it.**

To apply another effect and change its options, click and hold the Layer Style button in the Layers panel and choose the name of the layer style from the menu that appears — Bevel and Emboss, for example. In the dialog box that appears, change the settings to customize the layer style and click OK to apply it to your image. For example, if you choose Bevel and Emboss from the Layer Styles menu, you can choose from several emboss styles and adjust the depth, size, and softness.

Here are some consistent items you see in the Layer Style dialog box, no matter which effect you choose:

✦ **Contour:** Use contours to control the shape and appearance of an effect. Click the arrow to open the Contour fly-out menu to choose a contour preset or click the contour preview to open the Contour Editor and create your own edge.

✦ **Angle:** Drag the cross hair in the angle circle or enter a value in the Angle text field to control where the light source comes from.

✦ **Global light:** If you aren't smart about lighting effects on multiple objects, global light makes it seem as though you are. Select the Use Global Light check box to keep the angle consistent from one layer style to another.

✦ **Color:** Whenever you see a color box, you can click it to select a color. This color can be for the drop shadow, highlight, or shadow of an emboss, or for a color overlay.

Creating and saving a style

If you come up with a combination of attributes you like, click the New Style button in the upper right area of the Layer Style dialog box. After you name the style, it's stored in the Styles panel. After you click OK, you can retrieve the style at any time by choosing Window⇨Styles. If it helps, click the panel menu button and choose either Small or Large List to change the Styles panel to show only the name of the styles.

After you apply a layer style to a layer, the style is listed in the Layers panel. You can turn off the visibility of the style by turning off the Eye icon or even throw away the layer style by dragging it to the Layers panel's Trash Can.

Thinking about opacity versus fill

In the Layers panel, you have two transparency options — one for opacity and one for fill. Opacity affects the opacity of the entire layer, including effects. Fill, on the other hand, affects only the layer itself, but not layer styles. Figure 9-8 shows what happens when the Bevel and Emboss style is applied to text and the fill is reduced to 0 percent — it looks like the text was embossed on the image. You can do lots of neat stuff with the Layer Fill feature!

Figure 9-8:
A text layer with styles applied and the fill reduced to 0 percent.

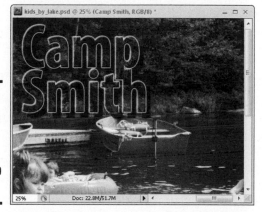

Smart, Really Smart! Smart Objects

Choose File⇨Place and place an image, an illustration, or even a movie into a Photoshop document. You can then see that, as always, a new layer is created and — even better — a Smart Object is created. The double square icon in the lower right corner of the layer thumbnail indicates that this layer is a Smart Object.

What does being a Smart Object mean? It means that you have much more flexibility in the placement of your images. Have you ever placed a logo, only to find out later that you need it to be three times its size? Resizing is no longer an issue, because the Photoshop Smart Object is linked to an embedded original. If the original is vector, you can freely resize the image repeatedly without worrying about poor resolution. Want to change the spelling of the Illustrator logo you placed? Just double-click the Smart Object and the embedded original is opened directly in Adobe Illustrator. Make your changes, save the file, and — *voilà* — the file is automatically updated in the Photoshop file.

What could be better? Smart Filters, of course. You can apply Smart Filters to any Smart Object layer, or even convert a layer to use Smart Filters, by choosing Filters⇨Convert for Smart Filters. After a layer has been converted to a Smart Object, you can choose filters, any filters, and apply them to the layer. If you want to paint out the effects of the filter on the layer, simply paint with black on the Filter Effects thumbnail. Paint with different opacities of black and white to give an artistic feel to the filter effect, as shown in Figure 9-9. You can even turn off filters by turning off the visibility on the Filter Effects thumbnail by clicking the Eye icon to the left of the Filter Effects thumbnail.

Figure 9-9: Cover the filter effects by painting on the Filter Effects thumbnail.

Experimenting with 3D Files

As we mention earlier in this chapter, working with 3D files is beyond the scope of this book, but even a 3D novice can experiment with the new 3D features implemented in Photoshop CS5. Follow these steps to try out some 3D features on your own:

1. **Open an existing Photoshop document.**

To eliminate any confusion, it is best if this document simply has a Background layer and no additional layers.

2. **If you have an image open with multiple layers select a layer that you want to apply 3D perspective.**

3. **Select the Move tool.**

4. **Choose 3D⇨New 3D Postcard from Layer.**

The image looks like it's now on a perspective plane. Also, note that the type layer now has a 3D icon on the layer thumbnail in the Layers panel, as shown in Figure 9-10, indicating that it's now a 3D layer.

3D icon

Figure 9-10:
Creating a
3D layer in
Photoshop
CS5.

5. **Experiment with angle and positioning by clicking and dragging on the 3D layer with the Object Rotate tool and the Camera Rotate tool.**

Notice that these tools have additional options available on the Options bar across the top of your Photoshop document.

Merging and Flattening the Image

Merging layers combines several selected layers into one layer. *Flattening* occurs when you reduce all layers to one background layer. Layers can increase file size, thereby also tying up valuable processing resources. To keep down file size, you may choose to merge some layers or even flatten the entire image to one background layer.

**Book IV
Chapter 9**

Using Layers

Merging

Merging layers is helpful when you no longer need every layer to be independent, such as when you have a separate shadow layer aligned to another layer and don't plan to move it again or when you combine many layers to create a composite and want to consolidate it to one layer.

To merge layers (in a visual and easy way), follow these steps:

1. **Turn on the visibility of only the layers you want merged.**

2. **Choose Merge Visible from the Layers panel menu.**

    That's it. The entire image isn't flattened, but the visible layers are now reduced to one layer.

To merge visible layers on a *target* (selected) layer that you create while keeping the visible layers independent, create a blank layer and select it. Then hold down Alt (Windows) or Option (Mac) when choosing Merge Visible from the panel menu.

Flattening

If you don't have to flatten your image, don't! Flattening an image reduces all layers to one background layer, which is necessary for certain file formats. After you flatten an image, you can't take advantage of blending options or reposition layered items. (Read more about saving files in Chapter 10 of this minibook.)

If you absolutely must flatten layers, keep a copy of the original, unflattened document for additional edits later.

To flatten all layers in an image, choose Layer⇨Flatten Image or choose Flatten Image from the panel menu on the Layers panel.

Chapter 10: Saving Photoshop Images for Print and the Web

In This Chapter

✔ Determining the correct file formats for saving

✔ Preparing images for the Web

✔ Discovering the color table

✔ Saving your settings

A productive workflow depends on you choosing the proper format in which to save your Photoshop files. Without the correct settings, your file may not be visible to other applications, or you may delete valuable components, such as layers or saved selections. This chapter provides you with the necessary information to save the file correctly for both print and the Web. We cover the file format choices before moving on to the proper use of the Save for Web & Devices feature (for saving in the GIF, JPEG, PNG, and WBMP file formats).

Saving files in the correct file format is important not only for file size but also in support of different Photoshop features. If you're unsure about saving in the right format, save a copy of the file, keeping the original in the PSD format (the native Photoshop format). Photoshop alerts you automatically when you choose a format in the Save As or the Save for Web & Devices dialog box that doesn't support Photoshop features. When you choose a format that doesn't support some of the features you've used, such as channels or layers, a yield sign appears when a copy is being made. With the capability of all Adobe applications (and even non-Adobe applications) to read native Photoshop (.psd) files, be wise and keep files in this native file format unless you have a compelling reason not to.

Choosing a File Format for Saving

When you choose File➪Save for the first time (or you choose File➪Save As to save a different version of a file), you see at least 18 different file formats to choose from in the Save As Type drop-down list. We don't cover every format in this chapter (some are specific to proprietary workflows), but we show you which formats are best for the typical workflow you may face.

Wonderful and easy Photoshop PSD

If you're in an Adobe workflow (you're using any Adobe product), you can keep the image in the native Photoshop PSD format. By choosing this format, transparency, layers, channels, and paths are all maintained and left intact when placed in the other applications.

If compatibility with older versions of Photoshop is an issue, choose Edit⇨Preferences⇨File Handling (Windows) or Photoshop⇨Preferences⇨File Handling (Mac). Choose Always from the Maximize PSD and PSB File Compatibility drop-down list. This choice saves a *composite* (flattened) image along with the layers of your document. (The PSB format is used for saving large Photoshop documents, measuring more than 30,000 by 30,000 pixels.)

Leaving the Maximize PSD and PSB File Compatibility drop-down list set to Always creates a larger file. If file size is an issue, leave the drop-down list set to Ask and use the feature only when you need to open the Photoshop file in older versions of Photoshop.

Photoshop EPS

Virtually every desktop application accepts the Encapsulated PostScript (EPS) file format. It's used to transfer PostScript-language artwork between various applications. It supports vector data, duotones, and clipping paths.

When you choose to save in the EPS format, an EPS Options dialog box appears. Leave the defaults alone and click OK.

Alter the settings in the EPS Options dialog box *only* if you're familiar with custom printer calibration or if you need to save your image to a specific screen ruling. Screen rulings (*lpi,* or lines per inch) are usually set in a page layout application, such as Adobe InDesign or QuarkXPress.

Photoshop PDF

If compatibility is an issue, save your file in the Photoshop PDF (Portable Document Format) format. PDF files are supported by more than a dozen platforms when viewers use Acrobat or Adobe Reader. (Adobe Reader is available for free at www.adobe.com.) What a perfect way to send pictures to friends and family! Saving a file in the Photoshop PDF format supports your ability to edit the image when you open the file by choosing File⇨Open in Photoshop.

If you're planning to send a layered file by e-mail, choose Layer⇨Flatten Layers before choosing to save the file as a PDF. This command cuts the file size considerably.

TIFF

The Tagged Image File Format (TIFF) flexible bitmap image format is supported by most image-editing and page-layout applications widely supported by all printers. TIFF supports layers and channels, but has a maximum size of 4GB. We hope your files aren't that large!

DCS

The Photoshop Desktop Color Separation (DCS) 1.0 and 2.0 formats are versions of EPS that enable you to save color separations of CMYK (Cyan, Magenta, Yellow, Black) or multichannel files. Some workflows require this format, but if you've implemented spot color channels in an image, using the DCS file format is required to maintain them.

Choose the DCS 2.0 format unless you receive specific instructions to use the DCS 1.0 format — for example, for reasons of incompatibility in certain workflows.

Saving for the Web and Devices

To access the maximum number of options for the GIF, JPEG, PNG, and WBMP file formats, save your image by choosing File⇨Save for Web & Devices. The Save for Web & Devices dialog box appears, and you can optimize the image as you save it. This procedure may sound like a big deal, but it's just the process of making the image as small as possible while keeping it visually pleasing.

Saving images for the Web is a give-and-take experience. You may sacrifice perfect imagery to make the image small enough that it can be downloaded and viewed quickly by users. Read the upcoming sections on the GIF and JPEG formats to see how to best handle creating Web images.

The following sections describe the differences between GIF, JPEG, PNG, and WBMP. Choose the appropriate format based on the type of image you're saving.

Ensuring that the image size is correct before you save the file for the Web is a good practice. If you need to read up on resizing images, see Chapter 6 of this minibook. Generally speaking, you should resize the image to the right pixel dimensions. Choose Filter⇨Sharpen⇨Unsharp Mask to regain some of the detail that was lost in resizing the image and then save the image for the Web.

GIF

Supposedly, the way you pronounce *GIF* (Graphics Interchange Format) is based on the type of peanut butter you eat. Is it pronounced like the peanut butter brand (Jif) or with a hard *g*, as in *gift?* Most people seem to pronounce it as "gift" (minus the T).

Use the GIF format if you have large areas of solid color, such as a logo like the one shown in Figure 10-1.

Figure 10-1: An image with lots of solid color makes a good GIF.

The GIF format isn't *lossy* (it doesn't lose data when the file is compressed in this format), but it reduces file size by using a limited number of colors in a color table. The lower the number of colors, the smaller the file size. If you've ever worked in Index color mode, you're familiar with this process.

Transparency is supported by the GIF file format. Generally, GIF files don't do a good job on anything that needs smooth transitions from one color to another, because of the format's poor support of *anti-aliasing*, which is the method Photoshop uses to smooth jagged edges. When an image transitions from one color to another, Photoshop produces multiple colors of pixels to create an even blend between the two colors.

Because anti-aliasing needs to create multiple colors for this effect, GIF files generally aren't recommended. In fact, when you reduce the size of a GIF, you're more apt to see *banding* (an artifact that appears as streaks in the image) because the anti-aliasing can't take place with the limited number of colors available in the GIF format.

You can, of course, dramatically increase the number of colors to create a smoother transition, but then you risk creating monster files that take forever to download.

Saving a GIF

When you choose File⇨Save For Web & Devices, you first see the available GIF format options. They may be clearer to you if you have an image open (with lots of solid color in it).

To save a file for the Web as a GIF, follow these steps:

1. Choose File⇨Save for Web & Devices.

The Save for Web & Devices dialog box appears.

2. At the top, click the 2-Up tab.

You see the original image on the left and the optimized image on the right (or top and bottom, depending on the image proportions).

In the lower portion of the display, you see the original file size compared to the optimized file size, as well as the approximate download time. The download time is important. Nobody wants to wait around for a Web page to load; most people don't wait more than ten seconds for an entire Web page to appear, so try to keep an individual image's download time to five seconds or fewer. Remember that waiting for all images on a page to load can add up to a monstrous wait time!

Change the download speed by choosing from the Preview menu (look for the arrow on the upper right side of the Save for Web & Devices dialog box). The Preview menu is labeled in Figure 10-2.

3. Choose GIF 32 No Dither from the Preset drop-down list.

You may see a change already. As you can see in Figure 10-2, Photoshop supplies you with presets to choose from, or you can customize and save your own.

4. Choose whether you want dithering applied to the image by selecting an option from the Specify the Dither Algorithm drop-down list.

This choice is purely personal. Because you may be limiting colors, Photoshop can use dithering to mix the pixels of available colors to simulate missing colors. Many designers choose the No Dither option because dithering can create unnatural color speckles in an image.

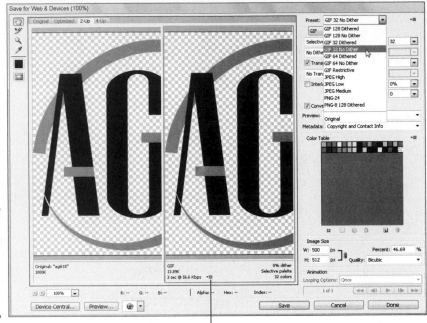

Figure 10-2:
Choose from
presets, or
create your
own custom
settings.

Preview menu

5. **If your image is on a transparent layer and you want to maintain that transparency on a Web page, select the Transparency check box.**

Using the color table in the Save for Web & Devices dialog box

When you save an image in GIF format using the Save for Web & Devices dialog box, you see the color table for the image on the right side of the dialog box. The color table is important because it not only lets you see the colors used in the image but also enables you to customize the color table by using the options at the bottom.

You may want to customize your color table by selecting some colors to be Web safe and locking colors so that they're not bumped off as you reduce the number that's used.

To customize a color table, follow these steps:

1. **If your image has only a few colors that you want to convert to Web-safe colors, choose the Eyedropper tool from the left of the Save for Web & Devices dialog box and click the color in Optimized view.**

The sampled color is highlighted in the color table.

2. **Click the Web Safe button at the bottom of the color table, as shown in Figure 10-3.**

   When you cross over this button, the tooltip Shifts/Unshifts Selected Colors to Web Panel appears.

   A diamond appears, indicating that the color is now Web safe.

3. **Lock colors that you don't want to delete as you reduce the number of colors in the color table.**

   Select a color with the Eyedropper tool, or choose it in the color table and then click the Lock Color button. A white square appears in the lower right corner, indicating that the color is locked.

   If you lock 32 colors and then reduce the color table to 24, some of your locked colors are deleted. If you choose to add colors, those locked colors are the first to return.

Figure 10-3:
Customize colors by using the color table in the Save for Web and Devices window.

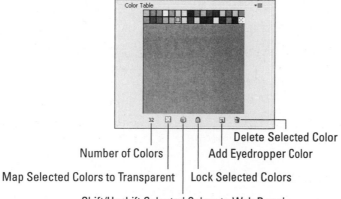

Number of Colors

Map Selected Colors to Transparent

Shift/Unshift Selected Colors to Web Panel

Delete Selected Color

Add Eyedropper Color

Lock Selected Colors

How is the color table created? Based on the color-reduction algorithm method you choose, the Save for Web & Devices feature samples the number of colors you indicate. If keeping colors Web safe is important, select the Restrictive (Web) option for the method; if you want your image to look better on most monitors but not necessarily to be Web safe, choose the Adaptive option.

4. **Use the Colors drop-down menu or enter a number to add or delete colors from the color table.**

5. **If your image uses transparency, select the Transparency check box near the top of the Save for Web & Devices dialog box.**

   Remember that transparency is counted as one of your colors in the color table.

6. **Select the Interlaced check box only if your GIF image is large (25K or larger).**

   Selecting this option causes the image to build in several scans on the Web page — a low-resolution image that pops up quickly and is then refreshed with the higher-resolution image when the download is complete. Interlacing gives the illusion of the download going faster but makes the file size larger, so use it only if necessary.

7. **Click Save.**

   Now the image is ready to be attached to an e-mail message or used in a Web page.

JPEG

JPEG (Joint Photographic Experts Group) is the best format for continuous-tone images — those with smooth transitions from one color to another, as in photographs — like the image shown in Figure 10-4.

The JPEG format is lossy, so you shouldn't save a JPEG and then open it, edit it, and save it again as a JPEG. Because the JPEG compression causes data to be lost, your image will eventually look like it was printed on a paper towel. Save a copy of the file as a JPEG, keeping the original image in PSD format if you need to edit the image later, open the original PSD, make your changes, save the PSD, and then save a copy of the edited file as a JPEG.

The JPEG format does *not* support transparency, but you can cheat the system a little by using matting.

Figure 10-4: Images with smooth transitions from one color to another are good candidates for the JPEG file format.

A good image to save in the JPEG format is a typical photograph or illustration with lots of smooth transitions from one color to the next. To save an image as a JPEG, follow these steps:

1. **Choose File⇨Save for Web & Devices and then click the 2-Up tab to view the original image (left) at the same time as the optimized image (right).**

2. **Choose one of the JPEG preset settings from the Settings drop-down list.**

You can choose Low, Medium, or High or customize a level between the presets by using the Quality slider.

3. **Leave the Optimized check box selected to build the best JPEG at the smallest size.**

The only issue with leaving this check box selected is that some very old browsers don't read the JPEG correctly (not likely an issue for most viewers).

4. **Leave the Embed Color Profile check box deselected unless you're in a color-managed workflow and color accuracy is essential.**

Checking this box dramatically increases the file size, and most people aren't looking for *exact* color matches from an image on the monitor.

5. **If you have to have the file size even smaller, use the Blur slider to bring down some detail.**

It's funny, but one JPEG that has exactly the same pixel dimensions as another may vary in file size because the more detailed an image is, the more information is needed. So, an image of lots of apples will be larger than an image of the same size that has a lot of clear blue sky in it. The Blur feature blurs the image (surprise!), so you may want to use it for only a low source image in Dreamweaver.

6. **(Optional) Choose a matte color from the Matte drop-down list.**

Because JPEG doesn't support transparency, you can flood the transparent area with a color you choose from the Matte drop-down list. Choose the color you're using for the background of your Web page by choosing Other and entering the hexadecimal color in the lower portion of the Color Picker.

7. **Click Save.**

PNG

PNG (Portable Network Graphics) is almost the perfect combination of GIF and JPEG. Unfortunately, PNG isn't yet widely supported. Note that PNG-24 images have file sizes that can be too large to use on the Web.

PNG supports varying levels of transparency and anti-aliasing. This variation means that you can specify an image as being 50 percent transparent and it shows through to the underlying Web page! You have a choice of PNG-8 and PNG-24 in the Save for Web & Devices dialog box. As a file format for optimizing images, PNG-8 doesn't give you any advantage over a regular GIF file.

PNG files are *not* supported by all browsers. In older browsers, a plug-in may be required in order to view your page. Ouch! By choosing PNG, you can shoot yourself in the foot because not all viewers can view the PNG file.

If you're saving a PNG file, you have a choice of PNG-8 or PNG-24. The PNG-8 options are essentially the same as the GIF options; see the "Saving a GIF" section, earlier in this chapter, for details.

PNG-24 saves 24-bit images that support *anti-aliasing* (the smooth transition from one color to another). These images work beautifully for continuous-tone images but are much larger than a JPEG file. The truly awesome feature of a PNG file is that it supports 256 levels of transparency. In other words, you can apply varying amounts of transparency in an image, as shown in Figure 10-5, where the image shows through to the background.

Figure 10-5:
A PNG-24 file with varying amounts of trans-parency.

WBMP

The Wireless BitMap (WBMP) format is optimized for mobile computing, has no compression, is one-bit color (just black and white — no shades), and is one bit deep. WBMP images aren't necessarily pretty, but they're functional (see Figure 10-6). You have dithering controls to show some level of tone value.

If you're creating images for mobile devices, know that WBMP is part of the Wireless Application Protocol, Wireless Application Environment Specification Version 1.1.

Click the Preview in Default Browser button at the bottom of the Save for Web & Devices dialog box to launch your Web browser and display the image as it will appear with its present settings. If you haven't set up a browser, click the down arrow and choose Other from the drop-down list. Browse to locate a browser in which to preview your image.

Want to see how your mobile content will look on specific devices? Click the Device Central button in the lower left corner of the Save for Web & Devices dialog box.

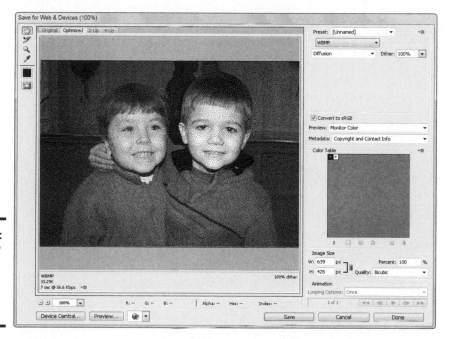

Figure 10-6:
The WBMP
format
supports
black-and-
white only.

Matte

Matting appears as a choice in the GIF, JPEG, and PNG format options. Matting is useful if you don't want ragged edges appearing around your images. Matting looks for pixels that are more than 50 percent transparent and makes them fully transparent; any pixels that are 50 percent or less transparent become fully opaque.

Even though your image might be on a transparent layer, it will have some "iffy" pixels — the ones that aren't sure what they want to be . . . to be transparent or not to be transparent. Choose a matte color to blend in with the transparent iffy pixels by selecting Eyedropper, White, Black, or Other (to open the Color Picker) from the Matte drop-down list in the Save for Web & Devices dialog box.

Saving Settings

Whether you're saving a GIF, JPG, or PNG file, you probably spent some time experimenting with settings to find what works best for your needs. Save selected options to reload later by saving the settings. Do so by clicking the arrow to the right of the Preset drop-down list. Choose Save Settings from the menu that appears and name your settings. Your named, customized settings then appear in the Preset drop-down list.

Book V

Acrobat 9.0

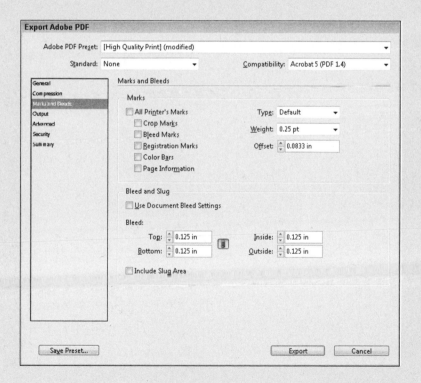

Contents at a Glance

Chapter 1: Discovering Essential Acrobat Information

In This Chapter

✔ **Discovering Acrobat and PDF files**

✔ **Understanding when to use PDF files**

✔ **Becoming familiar with the Acrobat workspace and tools**

A dobe Acrobat 9 provides a variety of tools for sharing and reviewing documents. Adobe Creative Suite applications can create Portable Document Format (PDF) files, and you can also use Acrobat to create PDF files from programs that aren't part of the Creative Suite. After you create a PDF file, you can use Acrobat to enhance the files by adding interactivity, merging PDF documents, adding comments or annotations, or applying security that restricts features, such as printing or editing.

In this chapter, you find out why you may want to create PDF files and acquaint yourself with the Adobe Acrobat tools and workspace. You see how easy it is to navigate through PDF files with the navigational tools, tabs, and viewing options in Acrobat. In the following chapters of this minibook, you explore how to use Acrobat to create PDF files from documents produced in a variety of programs and discover ways to enhance your PDF files with Acrobat.

Working with PDF Files

Adobe Acrobat is used to create, review, and modify PDF files. You can use PDF as a way to share documents created with the Adobe Creative Suite. Because PDF is a common file format, you can use it to share Creative Suite files for review, approval, or final publication. When you use a program in the Creative Suite, such as Illustrator or InDesign, to create a document, others would need the same software to open or edit the files. By converting your documents to PDF, they can easily be shared with others who might not have the same software as you because PDF files can be viewed by users on virtually all types of computers and operating systems.

PDF provides a common file format for viewing files, regardless of what software program was used to create them. Additionally, Acrobat provides extensive tools for reviewing, commenting, and marking files so that you can easily collaborate on a project without modifying the original document, along with tools to make PDF files interactive, merge related documents together, and secure files to restrict viewing or editing.

Because the software to view PDF files is free, you can be assured that those receiving your files don't need to purchase any special software. In fact, the odds are quite good that most users already have some type of free PDF viewing software, such as Adobe Reader.

PDF has become a popular way to share files because it provides a true reproduction of an original document. PDF is used by the Internal Revenue Service to distribute tax forms online. Many financial services firms and insurance companies use PDF because the electronic documents can be secured, and they accurately represent documents that have been approved for distribution. Graphic artists even use PDF files to send books, like the one you're reading now, to the printing plant.

Although PDF files provide a high-quality representation of an original file, they're more than just a picture of a document. PDF files retain the high-quality appearance of text while keeping the text searchable. Logos and illustrations created with Adobe Illustrator retain a high-quality appearance when converted to PDF, and intricate details from bitmap images, such as those edited with Adobe Photoshop, can also be maintained. PDF files allow you to distribute a high-fidelity electronic document. When creating a PDF file, you can choose settings that make the file suitable for high-quality printing or make the file smaller and more suitable for posting to a Web site or sharing as an e-mail attachment.

Although Acrobat is part of the Creative Suite, it's *not* a design tool — rather, it's a tool for distributing documents created in other software programs and enhancing these documents for online distribution. You generally don't use Acrobat to build new documents. Acrobat is a medium for sharing files, not for creating them. With Acrobat, you can

✦ Share documents with users who don't have the same software or fonts that you use.

✦ Review and mark PDF files that others send you. With Adobe Acrobat, you can enable a PDF file to be reviewed by users with the free Adobe Reader software.

✦ Combine documents created in other programs. You can use Acrobat to merge PDF files together into one document, even files that may have been originally created in different programs.

✦ Create a PDF portfolio. You can combine various file formats into a single PDF package and yet retain the files in their original file formats.

✦ Edit Adobe PDF files to make minor changes to text or graphics.

✦ Apply security to PDF files when you don't want them changed or you want to restrict viewing to certain individuals.

✦ Add interactivity to PDF files by enhancing them with sounds, movies, animations, and buttons.

✦ Create interactive forms to collect information electronically, avoiding the need for manual data collection.

We cover these capabilities throughout the rest of this minibook.

Knowing When to Use Adobe PDF Files

So when does it make sense to use Adobe PDF files? Here are some examples:

✦ **When you want to review a document quickly and efficiently:** When documents need to be reviewed or approved, Acrobat really shines. The reviewers don't need to have the Creative Suite software — or whatever you used to create the document. They only need a program to view PDF files, such as the free Adobe Reader or the Apple Preview application. Recipients can then use commenting, markup, and annotation tools to add suggestions and edits to a file. You can even combine comments from multiple reviewers into a single document and manage the review process online or via e-mail.

✦ **When you've created a document that you don't want others to edit:** Your recipients may have the same software you used to build the document, but you can keep them from editing the original file by distributing it as a PDF file. Whether you want to secure a spreadsheet from editing or an InDesign document from modification, Acrobat includes security options that allow you to protect your original content.

✦ **When you've created a presentation that includes files from different programs:** By converting the documents to PDF, you can combine them into a single file. For example, you can merge PowerPoint, Excel, and InDesign files into a single PDF document. Whether you need to protect your brand and identity by keeping documents from being edited or simply want to ease the process of sharing files, PDF makes it easy to share your ideas.

✦ **When you have a sensitive document:** If you have a document containing information that you don't want unauthorized persons viewing or you don't want printed, you can enhance the file with security with the Adobe Acrobat security tools. With the security options, you can require users to enter a password to view the file, or you can limit other features, such as the ability to print or edit the document.

Introducing the Adobe Acrobat Workspace and Tools

To take advantage of all that Acrobat has to offer, you'll want to discover the workspace and tools so you can get around within a PDF file. Acrobat opens with a blank workspace, and most tools and capabilities aren't available until you open a document. You can open a document by clicking the folder icon in the upper-left corner of the Document window or choosing File⇨Open.

When you open a document, you see the Acrobat workspace, which is divided into three areas. The largest portion of the workspace is the *Document window,* which displays the document you have opened. Across the top, the tools are stored in the toolbar well. Along the left side of the window, you find the navigation panels that help you find your way through the document. When you open a PDF document with Acrobat, you can use the toolbars and buttons in the toolbar well to navigate a file and you can use the navigation panel to move through a PDF file. For example, a PDF file may contain multiple pages. You can use the navigational buttons or the Pages panel to move between pages and then use a tool to manipulate the file, such as the commenting tools.

In the toolbar, you find useful information for navigating through your document, including

✦ **Current page and total pages:** To move to a specific page, click in the area showing the current page, type a different page number, and press Enter (Windows) or Return (Mac).

✦ **Previous Page and Next Page buttons:** Use these navigational buttons to skip forward or backward one page at a time.

Changing page magnification

Sometimes you want to see the entire page of a document; other times, you may only need to read the text or examine a small portion of a page. Acrobat provides several preset viewing options to help you with this, and you can also customize the magnification to zoom in on the page.

If things are a bit too small for you to see clearly, increase the magnification used for viewing pages with the Zoom drop-down list in the toolbar. Preset magnification choices are available in this drop-down list. You can also use the minus (–) and plus (+) symbols to the left of the current magnification level to zoom out or in.

The Marquee Zoom tool is the magnifying glass icon located to the left of the minus and plus symbols. You can use the Marquee Zoom tool to identify specific portions of a page that you want to magnify. Select this tool and then click and drag around a portion of the page to increase the magnification. You can also click multiple times on an area with this tool to increase the page magnification, but clicking and dragging a box with the Marquee Zoom tool is generally a much faster way to focus on a portion of a page you want to view. You can change the Marquee Zoom from its default attribute of increasing the magnification to decreasing the zoom by selecting the Marquee Zoom tool and Ctrl-clicking (Windows) or Option-clicking (Mac) in the Document window. The magnifier's plus (+) sign changes to a minus sign (–) to indicate that you're decreasing the document's magnification. It's usually faster to choose a preset zoom percentage though.

To the right of the magnification percentage box are page buttons that you can use to change the page magnification:

✦ **Scrolling Pages:** Use this button to avoid scrolling from left to right when reading a document. The view is changed to fit the document's width in the available space on your display, making it necessary to only scroll up and down on a page. This also sets the page view to display the top or bottom of adjacent pages. When you scroll and reach the bottom of one page, the top of the next page becomes visible.

✦ **One Full Page:** Use this button to fit the current page within the available screen space on your monitor. For smaller documents, such as a business card, the magnification is increased. For larger documents, the magnification is generally decreased unless you have a large monitor. When viewing pages in the Fit Page mode, only one page is displayed at a time. This mode is good for viewing the entire display of a page layout.

Toolbars

The toolbars in Acrobat 9 are customizable, so you can display different toolbars or change the location of existing toolbars to meet your needs.

Customizing the location of toolbars on your screen can make it easier for you to work with PDF files in Acrobat. For example, you may want all the tools for navigating through your documents in one section of the toolbar well. To achieve this, you can rearrange the location of specific toolbars.

Along the left edge of every group of tools is a dotted double line. By clicking and holding onto this edge with your mouse, you can drag any toolbar to a new location on your screen. This new location can be within the same area holding the other toolbars, or anywhere in the Acrobat work area. If you pull a toolbar out of the docking area, the toolbar becomes independent and floating. You can reposition or drag floating toolbars back into the docking area when you're finished working with them. You can also close a floating toolbar by clicking its Close Window button. You can place toolbars along the left or right side of the Acrobat work area — turning either side of the Acrobat workspace into a docking area for toolbars.

Although the flexibility of placing toolbars anywhere you like is useful, it may lead to a chaotic work environment. Instead of leaving toolbars all over your screen, you can have Acrobat clean up the workspace by choosing View⇨Toolbars⇨Reset Toolbars.

Toolbars contain both tools and buttons. For example, you choose the Marquee Zoom tool to change the magnification by clicking or selecting an area of the page. Buttons perform an immediate task, such as printing, saving, or applying security to a PDF document. In general, most of the task buttons are on the top row of the docking area, immediately below the menu bar, and most of the tools are on the bottom row — but you can move these toolbars.

Some tools and task buttons also include additional options that you can access through drop-down lists within the toolbars. Tools and buttons that contain additional choices are noted by the small triangle immediately to the right of the icon. Click this small triangle, and you see a drop-down list providing the additional choices for that tool or button.

Less than half the toolbars are visible in the default Acrobat display. You can add to the tools that are displayed or limit them by clicking the check box next to those you want to display or hide in the More Tools dialog box. Toolbars that have a check mark next to their names are visible, whereas those without a check mark aren't visible.

To display additional tools, choose View⇨Toolbars⇨More Tools. In the More Tools dialog box that appears, select the tools you want displayed in the toolbar and then click OK. The Selecting and Zoom Toolbar section displays the navigation tool choices that can be displayed.

You can choose to show or hide additional toolbars by right-clicking (Windows) or Control-clicking (Mac) in the toolbar well. After right-clicking/Control-clicking, choose the toolbar you want to show or hide from the contextual menu that appears.

Viewing modes

Acrobat provides several viewing modes that control how the document's displayed. For example, you can choose to display the pages of a book or a magazine side-by-side, or view only one page at a time. You can choose which viewing mode is used by choosing View⇨Page Display and selecting the viewing option you want.

The viewing modes are

✦ **Single Page:** This mode displays only the current document page on-screen and doesn't show any adjoining pages. When you scroll to the top or bottom of the current page, other pages aren't visible at the same time as the current page.

✦ **Single Page Continuous:** With this mode, you can see the current document page, and if you scroll to the top (or bottom) of the current page, the adjoining page is also visible. If you reduce your page viewing magnification, many document pages are visible.

✦ **Two-Up (previously known as Facing):** Use this mode to see pages as a *spread,* where you can view both the left and right sides of adjoining pages at the same time. When you have documents with pictures or text that spans a pair of pages, use this option to see the pages presented side-by-side in Acrobat. As with the Single Page mode, other pages that go before or fall after the spread aren't visible — only the one pair of pages is visible on-screen, regardless of the magnification or scrolling.

✦ **Two-Up Continuous (previously known as Continuous-Facing):** If you have a document with many pages containing text or pictures on their adjoining pages, you can use this mode to scroll from one pair of visible pages to the next. When the Two-Up Continuous view is selected, you can see adjoining page spreads. This option is identical to the Two-Up option, but it also shows pages above or below the spread you're presently viewing.

If you have pages where images or text goes across pages, the Two-Up choice is useful. By default, the pages generally display incorrectly. For example, a magazine will display the cover (page 1) and page 2 together, instead of pages 2 and 3. To correct this, choose View⇨Page Display⇨Show Cover Page during Two-Up. Additionally, the default option is for Acrobat to display a space between pages that are displayed together in the Two-Up mode. You can replace the space with a dotted line to divide the adjoining pages by choosing View⇨Page Display⇨Show Gaps between Pages.

You can add viewing modes as menu buttons by choosing View⇨Toolbars⇨ More Tools, as described earlier in the "Toolbars" section of this chapter.

Additional viewing options

Acrobat has two additional options for changing your document display:

✦ **Full Screen mode (View⟶Full Screen Mode):** You can use the Full Screen mode option to hide all menus, toolbars, and other parts of the Acrobat interface. This option is useful if you want to focus on the document being displayed, not the program being used to view it. Use this mode, for example, when you've a converted PowerPoint file to a PDF document and want to deliver the presentation with Acrobat. If you're viewing a document in the Full Screen mode, press the Esc key to return to the regular viewing mode.

When using the Full Screen mode, you can select Edit⟶Preferences and choose Full Screen to define attributes that change the way the file displays. You can set the display to advance automatically from one page to the next at a certain interval, choose from many different page transition types, and define the background color.

You can set a document to automatically open in Full Screen mode by choosing File⟶Properties and choosing this option from the Initial View panel of the Document Properties dialog box.

✦ **Reading mode (View⟶Reading Mode):** The many toolbars and buttons of Acrobat can get in the way of the document you wish to review. Use Reading mode to temporarily hide all the toolbars and buttons, making it easier to focus on the content of the PDF file.

Navigation panels

Acrobat offers a variety of panels that are helpful when navigating through PDF documents. The navigation panels are displayed along the left side of your Document window as small icons. Click an icon to make its panel visible. For example, click the Pages icon to display thumbnail-size representations of each page, as shown in Figure 1-1.

In the Pages panel, click a thumbnail page to display that page in the Document window. You can also choose View⟶Navigation Panels to access these same panels. There are 12 panels: Articles, Attachments, Bookmarks, Comments, Content, Destinations, Layers, Model Tree, Order, Pages, Signatures, and Tags.

Many panels have more advanced uses that are covered in later chapters of this minibook. In this chapter, we provide you with a brief understanding of how you can use the Pages panel to more easily navigate through a PDF document. Follow these steps:

1. **Make sure that the Pages panel is visible by clicking its panel icon.**

2. **In the Pages panel, click any page thumbnail to navigate directly to that page.**

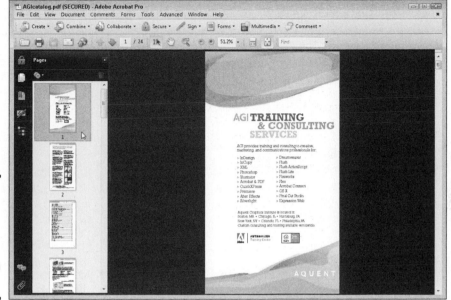

Figure 1-1:
Click the
icons to the
left to see
navigational
panels, such
as Pages.

A dark border appears around the selected page and a red box in the
Pages panel indicates what portion of the page is being viewed.

You can click in the corner of the small red box and drag diagonally
upward to increase the magnification on the section of the page contained within the box. Alternatively, make the box larger by clicking and
dragging down and out to expand the size of the viewing area. Changing
the size of the red box displayed on the page in the Pages panel changes
the focus of the magnification.

Chapter 2: Creating PDF Files

Converting documents to the Portable Document Format (PDF) is a great way to share files when readers don't have the same software as you or when you want to consolidate multiple file types together into a single document. Adobe Acrobat lets you create files from all software programs and scanned documents and even pages from the Web. Although you can also create PDF files from Adobe Creative Suite 5 (CS5) documents, you don't need Acrobat for this because the ability to create PDF files is built into the individual Creative Suite programs, such as Photoshop, Illustrator, and InDesign. In this chapter, you find out how to create Adobe PDF files from a variety of programs.

Creating PDF Files from Microsoft Office

Adobe Acrobat includes tools that make it easy to convert Microsoft Word, Excel, and PowerPoint files to PDF.

These capabilities are much more robust for the Windows versions of these programs, so Macintosh users may discover that not all these options are available.

When you install Acrobat on your computer, it looks for Microsoft Office programs. If Acrobat locates Word, Excel, PowerPoint, or Outlook, it installs an add-in — the PDF Maker — to these programs that helps convert Microsoft Office documents to PDF in a single click.

You can tell whether the PDF Maker add-in has been installed in your Microsoft Office programs by looking for the Acrobat toolbar or the Acrobat tab, depending upon which version of Microsoft Office you use. In Office 2007, the Acrobat tab appears to the right of the View tab. In earlier versions of Microsoft Office, the toolbar appears at the top of the Document window. If the toolbar isn't visible, choose View⇨Toolbars to see whether the Acrobat toolbar is available in the Toolbars submenu. If it remains unavailable, you may need to reinstall Adobe Acrobat to gain access to the PDF Maker tools.

When you convert documents to PDF, the original file remains unchanged, so you have both the original file and a separate PDF document. The original document and the PDF file aren't linked, so changes to the original source file aren't reflected in the PDF file. When you edit the PDF document, the changes don't update in the original file.

PDF conversion options

PDF Maker provides a variety of controls over how PDF files are created from Microsoft Office programs, such as Word and Excel. For example, you can have Acrobat create the file without asking you to confirm the location and name of the file each time you click the Create PDF button, and Acrobat will simply save the file in the same location as the original document. Similarly, you can choose to create PDF files that balance your need for quality and file size.

PDF Maker also provides controls over the type of PDF file you create because some PDF files may need to be of a higher quality for printing and others may need to be smaller to allow for fast electronic distribution. For example, you may want to post a PDF document to a Web site, where you want to make the file small so that it can be downloaded quickly.

When working in Microsoft Word, Excel, or PowerPoint, you can access the PDF Maker controls by clicking the Acrobat tab and then clicking the Preferences button (Office 2007) or by choosing Adobe PDF⇨Change Conversion Settings (earlier versions of Microsoft Office). In the Acrobat PDF Maker dialog box that appears, you can then choose from a variety of settings that control how the PDF file is created. In this section, we focus on the most useful options for Microsoft Office users.

From the Conversion Settings drop-down list in the Acrobat PDF Maker dialog box, you can find these useful options that control how the PDF file is generated:

✦ **Standard:** Choose this option to create PDF files that will be printed on an office laser printer or distributed via e-mail. This setting meets the needs of most users — it provides some compression of graphics, but they remain clear on-screen and look reasonably good when printed. In addition, this setting builds the fonts into the PDF file to maintain an exact representation of the document, regardless of where the file is viewed.

✦ **Smallest File Size:** With this setting, you can control the file size of the PDF documents you create. This setting provides significant compression of images and also reduces resolution, which causes graphics within the files to lose some clarity and perhaps appear jagged.

In addition, fonts aren't embedded in PDF files created with this setting. If the fonts used in the document aren't available on a computer where a PDF created with the Smallest File Size setting is viewed, Acrobat uses a font substitution technology to replicate the size and shape of the fonts used in the document. This feature typically provides a similar appearance to the original document, but it's not always an exact match of the original file.

Because this setting is so lossy, use it only if you need to compress a large file to a small enough size to send as an e-mail attachment. Make certain the recipient has the fonts used in the document installed on his or her computer. Otherwise, Adobe uses font substitution.

✦ **Press Quality:** If you need to provide PDF files to your commercial printer or copy shop, use this setting to create a PDF file that's designed for high-quality print reproduction. Along with including fonts in the PDF file, the graphics aren't significantly compressed, and they maintain a much higher resolution. Overall, these files tend to be larger than similar PDF files created with different settings, but the quality of the PDF file is more important than the file size when you're having the PDF professionally printed.

Several other highly technical options might be useful for you if you have a specialized profession. For example, if you archive items with PDF, the PDF/A options are designed for this. Additionally, the PDF/X options are useful for those submitting advertisements to publications that require the PDF advertisements adhere to the PDF/X standard.

PDF conversion options from Microsoft Word and Excel

Although Microsoft Word and Excel are widespread standards on many corporate computers, they aren't always the best choice for distributing documents. Formatting of Microsoft Word documents and Excel spreadsheets changes depending on the fonts available on users' computer or even the printer with which they print, whereas PDF files can keep the file looking consistent on various computer types. In addition, Microsoft Word and Excel files can be easily edited, and users can also copy and extract information from these files with few limitations, whereas PDF files are more difficult to copy from, and they can be secured with robust security options.

Converting a Word or Excel file to a PDF file overcomes these limitations and is quite straightforward. Choose from two methods:

✦ From inside Microsoft Word or Excel, make sure that the document you want to convert to a PDF file is open and then click the Create PDF button in the main toolbar to convert the document.

✦ With Office 2003 or earlier, choose Adobe PDF⇨Convert to Adobe PDF.

No matter which method you choose, you must specify the location of the PDF file that's created and name the file unless you have changed the PDF Maker preferences.

In Office 2007, click the Preferences button in the Acrobat tab, or with earlier versions of Office, choose Acrobat⇨Change Conversion Settings. In the Adobe PDF Maker dialog box, deselect the Prompt for PDF Filename option so that PDF files are generated in one step, without inputting the PDF filename.

You can add functionality into the PDF documents you create. Click the Preference tab if you're working in Office 2007 or choose Acrobat⇨Change Conversion Settings in earlier versions of Office. In the dialog box that appears, review the following settings:

✦ **Attach Source File:** Causes the original Office document to become embedded within the PDF file as an attachment. When the PDF file is distributed, the original source file is included within the PDF file.

✦ **Create Bookmarks:** Adds interactive bookmarks that make navigating the PDF file easy. Bookmarks are added based on Microsoft Word styles, such as text that's styled as Heading 1. The bookmarks appear in the Bookmarks panel when viewing the PDF.

✦ **Add Links:** Automatically converts Word links, such as Web addresses, into PDF links that you can use when viewing the file in Acrobat or Adobe Reader. Within the PDF Maker preferences dialog box, click the Word tab to access additional link options that can be built into PDF files created from Word.

Converting PowerPoint files to PDF

You can convert your PowerPoint presentations to Adobe PDF documents with the PDF Maker add-in that installs with Adobe Acrobat. PDF versions of PowerPoint presentations can be distributed to avoid concerns about the file being edited or concerns that the recipient may not have the same fonts that you used, causing the presentation to look different on various computers.

From PowerPoint, click the Create PDF button to save the file as a PDF file. Of course, make sure that the presentation you're converting is open before you click the button. In older versions of Office, you can also choose Acrobat⇨Convert to Adobe PDF from PowerPoint's main menu. If you're working with a new file, you must save it before PDF Maker will convert the file.

As with Word and Excel, you can select options relating to the conversion of your PowerPoint documents to PDF. To access the preferences, click the Preference button in the Acrobat tab or in older versions of Office, choose Acrobat⇨Change Conversion Settings. Along with the conversion settings that impact the quality of the resulting PDF file, select two additional options:

✦ **Preserve Slide Transitions:** With this option, you can have the slide transitions that were created in PowerPoint converted into PDF transitions that will be used when the presentation is delivered using Adobe Acrobat's Full Screen mode option.

✦ **Convert Multimedia:** Because Adobe PDF files can contain integrated sound and movie files, you can choose this option to have sounds and movies used in a PowerPoint file converted into the PDF document.

After you create the PDF, you can use Acrobat as the tool for delivering your presentations that have been created using PowerPoint. After you convert the file to PDF, open it in Acrobat and choose View➪Full Screen Mode. You can even distribute the document to users with the free Adobe Reader, and they can use the free Adobe Reader software to view and display the PowerPoint presentation file. Press the Esc key to stop viewing a document in the Full Screen mode. To distribute a document so that it always opens in Full Screen mode, open the document, choose File➪Document Properties, and select the Open in Full Screen Mode check box.

Creating PDF Files from Adobe Creative Suite Applications

You can also convert Photoshop files, Illustrator files, or InDesign documents to the PDF format. In this section, we show you how.

Converting Photoshop and Illustrator files to PDF

Both Adobe Photoshop CS5 and Adobe Illustrator CS5 can save documents directly in the Adobe PDF file format. To do so, simply choose File➪Save or File➪Save As. Then, from the File Type drop-down list, choose Adobe PDF (Illustrator) or Photoshop PDF (Photoshop). In these programs, you can create PDF files without Adobe Acrobat or Acrobat Distiller because they've integrated PDF creation capabilities.

You can use Adobe Reader or Acrobat to view PDF files created from Photoshop or Illustrator. You can also open and edit PDF files using the same program in which they were created.

Converting InDesign documents to PDF

Like Photoshop and Illustrator, the ability to convert InDesign documents to PDF is integrated into the application. With Adobe InDesign, you can choose File➪Export and select Adobe PDF from the File Type drop-down list. InDesign provides a significant number of options for controlling the size and quality of the resulting PDF file. Many of these options are similar to those available for PDF Maker for Microsoft Office.

In the Adobe InDesign Export PDF dialog box, you can choose from the Preset drop-down list at the top of the dialog box. The choices are many, but we list and describe here the most commonly used settings:

✦ **Smallest File Size:** Creates compact Adobe PDF files that are intended for display on the Internet or to be distributed via e-mail. Use this setting to create PDF files that will be viewed primarily on-screen.

✦ **High Quality Print:** Creates Adobe PDF files that are intended for desktop printers and digital copiers.

✦ **Press Quality:** Use this setting to create PDF files that will be delivered to a commercial printer for high-quality, offset print reproduction.

When creating PDF files to be used for high-resolution printing, here are some settings you should use. Select Marks and Bleeds in the list on the left of the Export PDF dialog box, as shown in Figure 2-1, and specify the amount of space items need to extend off the page, referred to a *bleed*. If you're delivering the file to a printing firm, they can provide you with guidance as to the required value. A good rule to follow is to use at least .125 inches if you have any items in your layout that extend to the edge of your document pages and beyond. Specify the value you want by entering the number in the Bleed and Slug section of the Marks and Bleeds tab. If the amount of bleed needs to be the same on all four sides, type the value in the Top text box and then click the link icon to the right of the Top and Bottom Bleed text boxes.

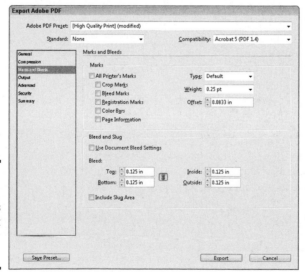

Figure 2-1:
Setting the bleed values in the Export Adobe PDF dialog box.

Converting Other Electronic Documents to PDF

As described earlier in this chapter, creating PDF files from Creative Suite applications and Microsoft Office programs is simple. You can also create PDF files from many other programs. When you installed the Adobe Creative Suite on your computer, you also installed a new printer — the *Adobe PDF printer* — which is used to convert electronic documents to PDF files. The Adobe PDF printer captures all the same information that's normally sent to your printer, and, instead of printing on paper, the information is converted into an Adobe PDF file.

To create a PDF file from any program, choose File⇨Print. In the Print dialog box, select Adobe PDF as the printer and click OK (Windows) or Print (Mac).

To change the type of PDF file that's created, such as a smaller file for Internet Web posting or a higher quality file for delivery to a commercial printer, do this:

✦ **Windows:** Click the Properties button in the Print dialog box to open the Adobe PDF Document Properties dialog box, as shown in Figure 2-2. Here, you can choose the settings you want to use to control the quality and size of the resulting PDF file.

✦ **Mac:** Choose PDF Options from the Copies and Pages drop-down list in the Print dialog box and then select the PDF settings you want to use.

Figure 2-2:
You can change conversion settings when printing to the Adobe PDF printer.

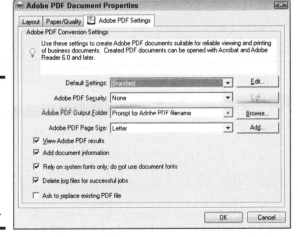

We discuss the PDF conversion settings earlier in this chapter, in the "PDF conversion options" section.

Using the Print menu to control the quality of PDF files created from non-Adobe programs may appear strange, but it's the easiest way for Adobe to capture all the same information that you'd expect to see when you print your files. This provides an easy and standard method for generating PDF files from any program. In fact, you can even use this method for creating PDF files from Adobe Creative Suite programs. It's useful to have this available as an option if you're having difficulty with the Export command. The Print and Export commands use different processes for creating PDF files, so you can use one option if you have difficulty with the other when creating PDF files from Creative Suite programs.

Bookmarks, links, page transitions, and multimedia aren't exported if a PDF is generated with the Print menu option. You must use the Export option to have these items included in PDF files.

Creating PDF Files from Paper Documents and the Web

PDF files don't need to start as electronic publishing files. Adobe Acrobat provides options for converting both paper documents and Internet Web pages into PDF format.

Converting paper documents to PDF

To convert paper documents into PDF, you need a scanner to digitize the information. If you expect to scan a large number of pages into PDF, consider purchasing a scanner with an automatic document feeder. Some scanners can scan both the front and backside of a document at the same time. Scanners, such as the Fujitsu ScanSnap, now fit easily on your desktop and let you convert a large number of paper documents to PDF in a short period of time. Some scanners, such as the ScanSnap, automatically launch Acrobat and convert scanned documents to PDF; others require you to scan the file. If a scanner is already hooked to the computer on which you use Acrobat and doesn't automatically start Acrobat, follow these steps to scan in a paper document and then convert it to PDF format:

1. **From the Acrobat main menu, choose File⇨Create PDF⇨From Scanner.**

Then choose the type of PDF document you wish to create. For pages with text, choose one of the Document options: Black and White for line art or text that contains no shades of gray; Grayscale for documents that contain varying shades of gray; or Color for documents that contain color. For photographs, choose the Image option.

2. **Make sure that your scanner is turned on, put the document to be scanned into the scanner, and then click the Scan button.**

   If necessary, continue to scan multiple pages into a single document. When you're done scanning, the scanned page appears in Acrobat.

   If you have a PDF open and choose Create PDF from Scanner, a window appears, giving you the opportunity to *append* the file (add to the existing file) or create a new PDF file.

   The scanned document opens in Acrobat.

   If the pages need to be rotated, choose Document⇨Rotate Pages.

3. **Choose File⇨Save to save the finished document as a PDF.**

Scanned text is fully searchable if you use one of the Document preset choices because Acrobat uses Optical Character Recognition (OCR) to convert the image to text. If you open a previously scanned file, you can use Acrobat's OCR capability by choosing Document⇨OCR Text Recognition⇨Recognize Text using OCR. This command makes previously scanned text searchable.

Converting Web pages to PDFs

By converting online content to Adobe PDF, you can capture contents from an Internet Web site. Because Web content can change rapidly, you can capture something that may not remain online for a long period of time. You can convert things, such as news stories or business information, from a Web site into PDF. Because PDF files can easily be combined together, you can merge a PDF from a Web site with other PDF files, such as spreadsheets, word-processing documents, and brochures.

If you want to convert only a single page and are using Internet Explorer, click the Convert Web Page to PDF button. This step converts the current Web page to a PDF. If you want to convert more than a single page, follow these steps from within Acrobat (not your Web browser):

1. **From the Acrobat main menu, choose File⇨Create PDF⇨From Web Page.**

   The Create PDF from Web Page dialog box opens.

2. **In the URL text box, enter the URL for the Web site you're converting to PDF.**

3. **To capture additional pages that are linked from the main page you're capturing, click the Capture Multiple Levels button, and then select one of the following:**

   • Select the Stay On Same Path check box if you want only pages from the entered URL converted to PDF.

   • Select the Stay On Same Server check box to download only pages that are on the same server as the entered URL.

Be cautious about selecting the Get Entire Site radio button instead of the Get Only radio button. The Get Entire Site option may take an enormous amount of time and not have any relevance to what you need.

4. **Click the Settings button to open the Web Page Conversion Settings dialog box and see accepted file types and change PDF settings (on the General tab).**

5. **On the Page Layout tab of the Web Page Conversion Settings dialog box, make changes to page size, orientation, and margins if the Web page requires a wider or longer layout. See Figure 2-3.**

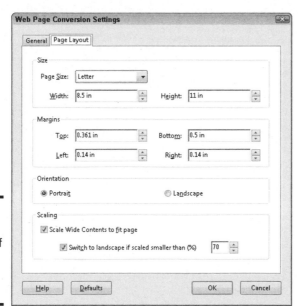

Figure 2-3:
Changing
the layout of
Web pages
converted
to PDF.

6. **When you're done making changes in the Web Page Conversion Settings dialog box, click OK.**

7. **In the Create PDF from Web Page dialog box, click the Create button to generate a PDF.**

   The Downloading Status window opens, showing the rate of download.

When the download is complete, the Web page (for the entered URL) selected appears as a PDF document, with *hyperlinks* (links to other pages within the site) intact. When links on the converted Web page are selected, you can open the linked page either in Acrobat or the Web browser.

Chapter 3: Adding Interactivity to PDF Files

In This Chapter

✔ Adding interactive bookmarks

✔ Creating and editing links

✔ Using buttons for easy navigation

*B*ecause many Adobe PDF documents are viewed online, you need to make the documents easy for readers to navigate. With Acrobat, you can design documents that are easier to navigate than their printed counterparts and that include rich interactive features that simply aren't available with paper documents.

Rather than making readers scroll through a document to find what they want, you can add links within an index or a table of contents, or you can add links to Web sites and e-mail addresses. Acrobat also includes features (known as *bookmarks*) to build your own online table of contents, and you can add buttons that link to specific pages within a PDF document or that cause an action to occur when clicked, such as closing the document. We discuss all these features in this chapter.

Adding Bookmarks to Ease PDF Navigation

One reason for distributing PDF documents is that it's convenient and cost-effective. But if users can't easily find the information they need or they can't effectively understand how the contents of a file are structured, they may become frustrated or they may need to print the document, which defeats the purpose of electronic distribution.

A table of contents in a traditional, printed book doesn't work well with electronic PDF files. It requires you to constantly return to the page containing the table of contents and then navigate to the page containing the data you need. But you can make your documents more user-friendly by adding bookmarks, which are the equivalent of a table of contents that's always available, no matter what page is being viewed in the Document window.

Bookmarks provide a listing of contents that reside within a PDF file or links to relevant external content. Bookmarks sit within a panel, and when you click one, you're taken to a specific destination in the PDF document (or possibly to an external file), much like a hyperlink. You can create bookmarks from existing text, or you can use your own text to describe the content, which is useful if the destination of the bookmark is a figure, chart, or a graphic.

By default, the Bookmarks icon resides along the left side of the Acrobat Document window in the *navigation panel.* Click the Bookmarks icon to make the panel appear; click the Bookmarks icon a second time to hide it. If the icon isn't visible, choose View⇨Navigation Panels⇨Bookmarks to make it appear.

Creating bookmarks that link to a page

By navigating to a page, and to a specific view on a page, you can establish the destination of a bookmark link. With a PDF document open, follow these steps:

1. **If the Bookmark icon isn't visible, choose View⇨Navigation Panels⇨Bookmarks.**

   The Bookmarks panel appears on the left of the Document window.

2. **In the Document window, navigate to the page that you want as the bookmark's destination.**

3. **Set the magnification of the view that you want by using the Marquee Zoom tool to either zoom in or zoom out.**

   The zoom level that you're at when you create the bookmark is the view that viewers see when they click the bookmark.

4. **In the Bookmarks panel, click the Options icon (it shows gears) and from the menu that appears, choose New Bookmark.**

   The new bookmark appears in the Bookmarks panel as Untitled.

5. **Change the name by typing something more descriptive.**

   If you leave the bookmark as Untitled but want to rename it later, you must click the bookmark and then choose Options⇨Rename Bookmark from the menu in the Bookmark panel.

6. **Test your bookmark by scrolling to another page and viewing it in the Document window; then click your saved bookmark in the Bookmark panel.**

   The Document window shows the exact location and zoom that you selected when you created the bookmark.

If you use the Selection tool to highlight text, such as a headline or a caption, that's part of the bookmark destination and then choose Options⇨New Bookmark, the selected text becomes the title of the new bookmark. You can use this shortcut to avoid entering a new name for new bookmark titles. You can also press Ctrl+B (Windows) or ⌘+B (Mac) to quickly create a bookmark.

Creating bookmarks that link to external files

Although bookmarks are most commonly used to link to content within a PDF file, you can also use bookmarks to create links to other documents. To create a link to an external file, follow these steps:

1. **Choose Options⇨New Bookmark in the Bookmarks panel.**

2. **Replace the Untitled bookmark entry that appears in the Bookmarks panel with an appropriate title for the bookmark.**

3. **Choose Options⇨Properties from the Bookmarks panel menu.**

   The Bookmark Properties dialog box appears. With this dialog box, you can change a bookmark so that it links to any type of file. In this example, we use a PDF document, but the bookmark could be a link to another PDF file, a Photoshop file, or even a Microsoft Excel file. Just remember that this bookmark creates a relative link. The linked file must travel with the PDF document in order for the link to work.

4. **In the Bookmark Properties dialog box, click the Actions tab, choose Open a File from the Select Action drop-down list, and then click the Add button.**

   The Select File to Open dialog box appears.

   You can create links to Web sites as well. Choose Open a Web Link to access an Internet Web address.

5. **Click the Browse button, choose a file to which the bookmark will navigate, and then click the Select button.**

Note that the other file isn't attached to the current document. If you distribute a PDF file containing the bookmarks to external files, you must distribute any external files that are referenced along with the source file; otherwise, the links won't work. In addition, the linked files need to be in the same relative location as the original documents — so don't change the name of the linked file or the folder in which it's located.

Using bookmarks

Bookmarks are intuitive to use, which make them an attractive option to add to PDF files. After you click a bookmark, the action associated with it is performed, which typically navigates you to a certain page within the PDF file.

Unfortunately, the Bookmarks panel doesn't open automatically with a document, even when bookmarks are present within a file. To display the Bookmarks panel when a file is opened, follow these steps:

1. **Choose File⇨Properties.**

2. **In the Document Properties dialog box that opens, select the Initial View tab, as shown in Figure 3-1.**

3. **From the Navigation drop-down list, choose Bookmarks Panel and Page and then click OK.**

   After the file is saved and then reopened, the Bookmarks panel is displayed whenever the document is opened.

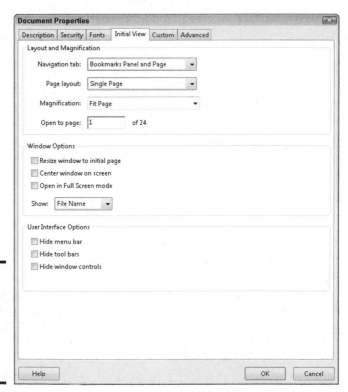

Figure 3-1:
The Documents Properties dialog box in Adobe Acrobat.

Editing bookmarks

You can change the attributes of bookmarks so that they link to other locations by clicking to select a bookmark and then choosing Options⊏̣> Properties in the Bookmarks panel. In the Bookmark Properties dialog box, choose the color and font type of the bookmark on the Appearance tab: To change the bookmark's font style, choose a style from the Style drop-down list; to change the bookmark's color, click the Color box and choose a color from the Color Picker.

On the Actions tab of the Bookmark Properties dialog box, you can delete existing actions (in the Actions section of the Actions tab) by clicking to select an action and then clicking the Delete button. Also, you can add actions by choosing another action from the Add Action section and then clicking the Add button. You can add more than one action to a bookmark.

Adding Interactive Links

When viewing a PDF file electronically, you can add links for e-mail addresses, Web addresses, and references to other pages. Links are attached to a region of a page, which you identify with the Link tool.

To add an interactive link to your PDF document, follow these steps:

1. **Locate an area of a page where you want to add a link and then choose View⊏̣>Toolbars⊏̣>Advanced Editing to display the Advanced Editing toolbar.**

2. **Select the Link tool and then click and drag to select the region that you want to link to.**

   The Create Link dialog box appears.

3. **Choose an action that the link will perform:**

   - *Go to a Page View:* This option is the default, where you can scroll to the page that is the destination of the link.

   - *Open a File:* Alternatively, you can choose to link to another file; click the Browse button to locate the file.

   - *Open a Web Page:* If you choose this option, you're choosing to link to a Web address. In the Address text box, enter the complete address of the Web site to which the link should direct viewers. To create a link to an e-mail address, type **mailto:** followed by an e-mail address. (Note that mailto: is all one word.)

   - *Custom Link:* Use this option to choose from other types of links in the Link Properties dialog box.

4. **Click Next and follow the instructions in the next dialog box before clicking OK.**

The Link tool is relatively simple to use, but you may prefer to create links from text in another way: With the Selection tool, select the text, right-click (Windows) or Control-click (Mac) the selected text, and then choose Create Link from the contextual menu that appears.

You can have links transferred automatically from your original Microsoft Office documents when using PDF Maker.

You can edit links by choosing the Link tool and double-clicking the link to open the Link Properties dialog box. While editing a link, you can change how it's presented in the Appearance tab. Make a link invisible or add a border to the link, such as a blue border that commonly is used to define hyperlinks. On the Actions tab of the Link Properties dialog box, you can add, edit, or delete actions, just as you can with bookmarks (see the preceding section).

Adding Buttons to Simplify Your PDF Files

Along with links and bookmarks, buttons provide another way to make your files more useful when they're viewed online. You can create interactive buttons entirely within Acrobat — designing their appearance and adding text to them. Or you can import buttons created in other Adobe Creative Suite applications, such as Photoshop and Illustrator. For example, you can create buttons that advance the viewer to the next page in a document.

Additional form editing tools are only available on the Windows platform.

Buttons are added by entering the Form Editing mode. Choose Forms⇨Add or Edit Fields to open the Forms Editor. You may have to click OK to have a scan for form fields performed.

To add a button to your PDF document, follow these steps:

1. **Choose View⇨Toolbars⇨Advanced Editing.**

   The Advanced Editing toolbar appears.

2. **Click the OK Button tool and drag where you want the button to appear in the document.**

3. **Type in an appropriate name for your button in the Field Name dialog box that appears.**

4. **Click the Show All Properties button to see the Button Properties dialog box.**

5. **In the General tab, you can enter a name for the button in the Name text box and provide a ToolTip in the ToolTip text box.**

   A *ToolTip* is the text that appears whenever the mouse cursor is positioned over the button.

6. **In the Appearance tab, establish how your button will look by setting the following options:**

   - *Border Color/Fill Color:* Click the square to the right of the appropriate attribute in the Borders and Colors section of the Appearance tab and then choose a color from the Color Picker.

   - *Line Thickness and Style:* These options don't appear unless you change the border color from None (red diagonal line) to another selection.

   - *Font Size/Font:* Change the size and font of the button text by making a selection from the Font Size and the Font drop-down lists.

   - *Text Color:* Change the color of the text by clicking the color square and choosing a color from the Color Picker.

7. **In the Options tab, make these selections:**

   - *Layout:* Use the Layout drop-down list to specify whether you want to use a *label* (text that you enter in Acrobat that appears on the face of the button) or whether you want an *icon* (an imported button graphic that you may have designed in Photoshop or Illustrator).

   - *Behavior:* Choose Push from the Behavior drop-down list to create different appearances for a button so that it changes based upon whether the mouse cursor is positioned over the button. The button appearance can also change when clicked.

   - *State:* To specify the different appearances (see Behavior, discussed in the preceding paragraph), click the State on the left side of the Options tab and then choose the Label or Icon status for each state.

   - *Label:* If you choose to use a label, enter the text for it in the Label text field.

   - *Icon:* If you choose to use an icon, specify the location of the graphic file by clicking the Choose Icon button. You can create button icons in either Photoshop or Illustrator.

8. **In the Actions tab, choose an action from the Select Action drop-down list and then click the Add button.**

   Actions are applied to buttons similar to the way in which they're applied to links and bookmarks:

- To choose actions that are a part of the menu commands, such as printing a document, closing a file, or navigating to the next or preceding page, choose the Execute Menu Item action and then specify the command to be accessed.

- You can also choose the activity that causes the action to occur, known as the *trigger*. The default trigger is *Mouse Up,* which causes the action to occur when the mouse button is depressed and then released. You can choose other actions, such as the mouse cursor merely rolling over the button without the need to click it.

9. **After you make all your changes in the Button Properties dialog box, click Close.**

Chapter 4: Editing and Extracting Text and Graphics

In This Chapter

✔ Manipulating text with the TouchUp tools

✔ Modifying graphics with the TouchUp tools

✔ Pulling text and graphics out of PDFs for use in other documents

You may assume that PDF files are mere pictures of your documents and can't be edited, but nothing is further from the truth. Adobe Acrobat includes a variety of tools for editing both text and graphics. You can use these tools as long as the file hasn't been secured to prohibit editing. We introduce you to these great tools in this chapter. (We discuss security, which allows you to limit access to these tools, in Chapter 6 of this minibook.)

Editing Text

The tools for editing text and graphics are located on the Advanced Editing toolbar (see Figure 4-1).

Figure 4-1:
The Advanced Editing toolbar.

You can add several TouchUp tools to the Advanced Editing toolbar by choosing View⇨Toolbars⇨More Tools and checking the tools you want to add.

For text tools, you have three choices:

✦ **TouchUp Text tool:** Used to manipulate text.

✦ **TouchUp Object tool:** Used to manipulate objects.

✦ **TouchUp Reading Order tool:** Used to correct the reading order or structure of the document.

The TouchUp Reading Order tool isn't used for changing the appearance of the document, so we don't discuss it in this chapter.

Using the TouchUp Text tool to manipulate text

The TouchUp Text tool is used for *touching up,* or manipulating, text. This touchup can include changing actual text characters or the appearance of text. You can change *cat* to read *dog,* or you can change black text to blue, or you can even change the Helvetica font to the Times font.

When you change a PDF file, the original source document isn't modified.

You have a few ways to accomplish text edits:

✦ Choose the TouchUp Text tool, click within the text that you want to change to obtain an insertion point, and then start typing the new text.

✦ Click with the TouchUp tool in your text and press the Backspace or Delete key to delete text.

✦ With the TouchUp tool, drag to highlight text and enter new text to replace the highlighted text.

When changing text — whether you're adding or deleting — Acrobat tries to use the font that was specified in the original document. Sometimes, this font is built into the PDF file, which means that it's *embedded* in the file. Other times, the font may not be available either because it hasn't been embedded or it's been embedded as a *subset* where only some of the characters from the font are included in the PDF file. In these cases, Acrobat may provide the following warning message:

```
All or part of the selection has no available system font. You cannot
add or delete text using the currently selected font.
```

Fortunately, you can change the font if you need to edit the text. However, when you change the font, the text may not retain the same appearance as the original document. In some instances, you may not have the exact same font on your computer as the font used in the PDF document, but you may have a similar font you can use without causing a noticeable change — most people won't notice the difference between Helvetica and Arial or between Times and Times New Roman. Fonts with the same name but from different font designers often look very similar. For example, Adobe Garamond looks similar to ITC Garamond, even though they're two different fonts.

To change the font that's used for a word or a range of words, follow these steps:

1. **With the TouchUp Text tool, drag over the text you wish to select.**

You may see a Loading System Fonts message followed by another Loading Document Fonts message. Depending on the number of fonts installed on your system, it may take a while for this message to disappear.

2. **Right-click (Windows) or Control-click (Mac) the highlighted text and choose Properties from the contextual menu.**

The TouchUp Properties dialog box appears, as shown in Figure 4-2.

Figure 4-2:
The
TouchUp
Properties
dialog box.

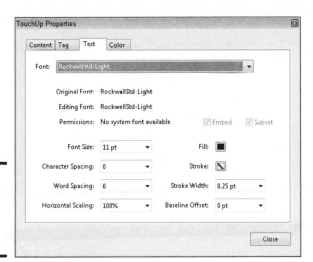

3. **In the Text tab, choose the typeface you want to use from the Font drop-down list and make any other changes you want.**

In this dialog box, you can also change the size by selecting or typing a number into the Font Size drop-down list. In addition, you can modify the color by clicking the Fill color swatch.

4. **When you're satisfied with your changes, click the Close button to apply your changes to the selected text.**

Using the TouchUp Object tool to edit graphics

You can use the TouchUp Object tool to access editing software for modifying graphics. For example, you can use the TouchUp Object tool to select a graphic, bring the graphic into Photoshop, and then save the modified version back into the PDF file. In other words, you can edit the graphics used in PDF documents, even if you don't have access to the original graphic files.

To edit a photographic file from Acrobat in Photoshop, follow these steps:

1. **Select the image with the TouchUp Object tool, right-click (Windows) or Control-click (Mac) on a photographic image with the TouchUp Object tool, and then choose Edit Image from the contextual menu.**

   The image file opens in Adobe Photoshop.

2. **With the many tools of Photoshop, make the necessary changes to the graphic and then choose File⇨Save.**

   When you return to the PDF file in Acrobat, the graphic is updated automatically in the PDF document.

If you have the original graphic file, it remains untouched — only the version used within the PDF file is modified. It isn't necessary to have the original graphic file to perform these steps.

You can also use Acrobat to edit vector objects from within PDF files, such as those created with Adobe Illustrator. Just follow these steps:

1. **Select a piece of vector artwork with the TouchUp Object tool, right-click (Windows) or Control-click (Mac) the vector artwork, and then choose Edit Object from the contextual menu.**

   Note: Acrobat displays Edit Object in the contextual menu if it detects a vector object, and it displays Edit Image if it detects a bitmap image. Acrobat also displays Edit Objects (note the plural) if you have more than one object selected.

   If you're editing a complex illustration, be sure to select all its components by holding down the Ctrl (Windows) or ⌘ (Mac) key while clicking them with the TouchUp Object tool.

   After choosing Edit Object, the object opens for editing in Adobe Illustrator.

2. **Make the necessary changes in Illustrator, choose File⇨Save.**

   The graphic is updated in the PDF document.

If Acrobat doesn't start Photoshop or Illustrator after choosing the Edit Image or Edit Object command, you may need to access preferences by choosing Edit⇨Preferences⇨Touch Up and then specifying which programs should be used for editing images or objects.

You can also use the TouchUp Object tool to edit the position of text or graphic objects on a page, which includes the ability to relocate individual lines of text or to change the position of a graphic on a page. After you select an object with the TouchUp Object tool, you can simply drag it to a new location on the page.

Exporting Text and Graphics

Although editing text and graphics is helpful, you may need to take text or images from a PDF document and use them in another file. Fortunately, Acrobat also includes tools to make this a breeze. Of course, you should always make certain that you have the permission of the owner of a document before reusing content that isn't your original work.

You need the Select & Zoom toolbar for extracting text and graphics, so make sure that it's visible. If it isn't, choose View⇨Toolbars⇨Select & Zoom.

You can export text, images, or charts from Acrobat by copying and pasting, by saving as a specific file type, or by using the Snapshot tool. These methods are discussed in detail in the following sections.

Exporting text with Select, Copy, and Paste

Make sure that the Select & Zoom toolbar is visible (choose View↔
Toolbars↔Select & Zoom) and then follow these steps to select, copy, and
paste text from a PDF file:

1. **With the Select tool, highlight the text you want to export.**

The Select tool is the I-bar/black arrow in the toolbar. When you hold
the arrow over a section of your document, it turns into an I-bar cursor,
which you can drag to select the text you want to copy.

If the Cut, Copy, and Paste commands are unavailable after you've
selected some text, the author of the document may have set the security settings to disallow copying. If you can't select the text, you may be
trying to copy text that is part of an image.

2. **Right-click (Windows) or Control-click (Mac) the selected text and
choose Copy from the contextual menu.**

Being able to extract the text out of a PDF document by selecting and
copying it is useful if you don't have access to the original source document, but you need to use the text from a PDF file.

3. **Open another text-editing program, such as Adobe InDesign or
Microsoft Word.**

You can paste the copied text into a new document or a preexisting file.

4. **Insert your cursor in the document at the appropriate spot and choose
File↔Paste or Edit↔Paste.**

The text is pasted into the document, ready for you to use.

Exporting text with Save As

The File↔Save As command exports all the text in your PDF file. The Save
as Type drop-down list gives you various format options. After choosing an
option and any settings, click the OK button to select the settings and click
the Save button to save the text. The File↔Export command gives you the
same options.

Here are the formats you can use to export text:

✦ **Microsoft Word Document:** Click the Settings button to choose whether
to save the comments or images with your document. If you choose
to save the comments or images, you can select additional formatting
options.

✦ **Rich Text Format:** Click the Settings button to choose whether to save
the comments or images with your document. If you choose to save the
comments or images, you can select additional formatting options.

✦ **Text (Accessible):** Use this format to create a file that can be printed to a Braille printer.

✦ **Text (Plain) (Secondary Settings):** This format creates a plain vanilla file with no formatting. You can save some secondary options in various file encodings. Also, you can select to save the images in your PDF in a separate images folder.

✦ **Encapsulated PostScript, PostScript:** These formats are generally used by commercial printers or IT professionals that need PostScript output.

✦ **Various Adobe PDF options, such as PDF/E for engineering or PDF/A for archiving:** These are used to switch to a specific subset of the PDF file format used for a particular industry or line of work.

✦ **Various graphics formats (JPEG, JPEG2000, PNG, TIFF):** If you choose one of these options, your text will no longer be editable as the entire PDF pages are converted to an image.

Text that's copied from a PDF file is no longer linked to the original document. Edits made to the extracted text aren't reflected within the PDF file, and it's extremely difficult to have the extracted text reinserted into the PDF document. Think of the extraction process as a one-way trip for the text, which can be extracted but not reinserted.

You can also copy text within a table to the Clipboard or open it directly in a spreadsheet program, such as Microsoft Excel, and maintain the table's formatting after it's extracted. Just follow these steps:

1. **Click the Select tool and click and drag to select the text in the table.**

Depending upon how the table was created, you may also be able to position your cursor just outside the edge of the table and then draw a box around a table.

A border appears around the selected table.

2. **Right-click (Windows) or Control click (Mac) and choose Open Table in Spreadsheet from the contextual menu.**

Alternatively, you can save the table directly to a file or copy to the Clipboard to be pasted later: If Acrobat has trouble identifying the text in the table, it may be saved as an image file, which is not editable text.

• *To save the table directly to a file,* choose Save as Table from the contextual menu.

• *To copy the table to the Clipboard so that you can paste it into other documents,* choose Copy as Table from the contextual menu.

The table opens in Excel or whatever spreadsheet program you have installed on your computer.

And that's it. You can now use that table in another program.

Extracting graphics

You can also extract graphics from PDF files, but extracting graphics is very different from editing them. We discuss editing graphics and vector objects earlier in this chapter. When editing graphics, you open the original graphic file at its highest possible quality. Extracting graphics is different because they're removed at the quality of the screen display resolution, which may be of much lower quality than the original, embedded graphics.

With the Select tool, right-click (Windows) or Control-click (Mac) an image, or drag with the Select tool to select a part of the image. Then you can either drag and drop the selection into an open document or choose Copy Image from the contextual menu. The image is now available to be pasted into other applications. The other option in the contextual menu is to Save Image As and save the selected area as a BMP graphics file.

Snapshot tool

You can use the Snapshot tool to select both text and images and create a picture of a certain area within a PDF file. The result is commonly referred to as a *screen grab* of a section within a PDF file. The result is an image, and your text is no longer editable.

To use the Snapshot tool, choose Tools⇨Select & Zoom⇨Snapshot Tool. You then have two options.

✦ After you select the Snapshot tool, click anywhere in the page. The snapshot tool automatically captures everything displayed on the screen.

✦ After you select the Snapshot tool, click and drag a rectangle around an area of the page.

You can include text and images. The area you've selected will be saved to the Clipboard so that you can paste it into another document. The Snapshot tool remains active so that you can keep selecting areas and saving them to the Clipboard. However, the previous selection in your Clipboard is deleted when you make a new selection. So, make certain you've pasted a selection into your other document before you make a new selection.

You have to select another tool to deactivate the Snapshot tool.

Chapter 5: Using Commenting and Annotation Tools

In This Chapter

✏ **Adding comments to PDF files**

✏ **Working with comments**

*O*ne of the fantastic features of Acrobat is the capability to mark up documents electronically with virtual sticky notes, or *comments*. You can mark up text to indicate changes and add annotations and drawing comments to a PDF (Portable Document Format) file. The Acrobat commenting tools don't change the original file, and you can remove the comments at any time, which means you can disable comments for printing or viewing at any time. In this chapter, we describe these great features and show you how to put them to work for you.

Creating Comments with the Comment & Markup Toolbar

You can easily add annotations to PDF files, including stamps, text highlights, callouts, and electronic sticky notes by using the Comment & Markup toolbar, which you can access by clicking the Comment option in the Tasks toolbar. You can then choose Show the Comment & Markup Tools.

You can also access the Comment & Markup toolbar by choosing View➪Toolbars➪Comment & Markup.

The Comment & Markup toolbar, as shown in Figure 5-1, provides several tools for adding comments to PDF documents. It also includes a Show menu to help manage comments and the process of adding comments. We discuss these tools in the following sections.

The Sticky Note tool

Use the Sticky Note tool to add electronic sticky notes to your files. You can click the location where you want the note to appear within a PDF document. An icon, representing the note, appears, along with a window where you can enter text. After entering text in the sticky note, close the window so that the document isn't hidden beneath it.

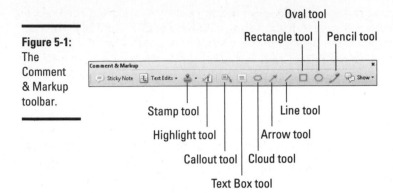

Figure 5-1:
The Comment & Markup toolbar.

You can change the icon and color used to represent the note by right-clicking (Windows) or Control-clicking (Mac) the note and choosing Properties from the contextual menu. In the Properties dialog box that appears, make the changes to the note icon or color and then click Close.

The Text Edits tool

The Text Edits tool is actually six separate text commenting tools. Use these tools to replace selected text, highlight selected text, add a note to selected text, insert text at cursor, underline selected text, and cross out text for deletion.

To use the Text Edits tool, follow these steps:

1. **Choose the Text Edits tool and drag to select text that requires a change or comment.**

2. **Click the arrow to the right of the Text Edits tool to access the drop-down list containing your six choices.**

3. **Choose an option from the list of available editing choices:**

   - *Replace Selected Text:* Replaces the selected text.

   - *Highlight Selected Text:* Highlights the selected text.

   - *Add a Note to Selected Text:* Allows you to add a note to the selected text.

   - *Insert Text at Cursor:* Places a cursor at the end of the selected text.

   - *Underline Selected Text:* Underlines the selected text.

   - *Cross Out Text for Deletion:* Crosses out the selected text.

   Your selected text changes, depending on what you choose from the list.

After selecting the text that requires a comment, you can press the Delete or Backspace key to indicate a text edit to remove the text. Similarly, you can start to type, and Acrobat will create an insertion point. Also, if you right-click (Windows) or Control-click (Mac) after selecting the text, you can select the type of edit or comment you want to insert from the contextual menu.

The Stamp tool

You can use stamps to identify documents or to highlight a certain part of a document. Common stamps include Confidential, Draft, Sign Here, and Approved.

The stamps are grouped into sections. Some stamps automatically add your default username along with the date and time you applied them to the document; these stamps are available under the Dynamic category in the Stamps menu. The more traditional business stamps, such as Confidential, appear under the Standard Business category. You can access each of the different categories by clicking the arrow to the right of the Stamp tool in the Comment & Markup toolbar, as shown in Figure 5-2.

Figure 5-2:
Access the different types of stamp groups.

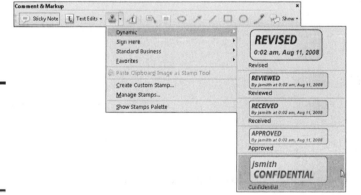

To apply a stamp to your document, follow these steps:

1. **Select the Stamp tool from the Comment & Markup toolbar.**

2. **Click the arrow to the right of the Stamp tool and from the menu, choose the stamp you want to apply to the document.**

3. **Drag within your document at the location where you want the stamp to appear.**

The Highlight Text, Underline Text, and Cross Out Text tools

The Highlight Text, Cross Out Text, and Underline Text tools provide the same functionality and options that are available with the Text Edits tool, but with easier access. If you want to delete the highlighted, crossed-out, or underlined formatting to your text, just click the formatted area and hit the Delete or Backspace key. Your text will remain, but the formatting will disappear.

To highlight text, follow these steps:

1. **Select the Highlight Text tool from the Comment & Markup toolbar.**

2. **Drag over the text that you want highlighted.**

   The text is now highlighted.

To underline text, follow these steps:

1. **Select the Underline Text tool by selecting Tools⇨Comment & Markup Tools⇨Underline Text.**

2. **Drag over the text that you want underlined.**

   The text is now underlined.

To cross out text, follow these steps:

1. **Select the Cross Out Text tool by choosing Tools⇨Comment & Markup Tools⇨Cross Out Text Tool.**

2. **Drag over the text that you want crossed out.**

   The text is now crossed out.

The Attach File tools

With the Attach File tools, you can attach an existing text file, a sound file, or any file copied to the Clipboard from your computer (or computer network) and attach it to the PDF.

Follow these steps for file and sound attachments:

1. **Choose Comments⇨Comment & Markup Tools⇨Attach a File as a Comment.**

   A pushpin icon appears.

2. **Click where you want the attachment noted.**

   The Add Attachment dialog box appears.

3. **In the Add Attachment dialog box, browse to the file that you want to attach and click the Select button.**

   You can attach text, graphic, or sound files.

4. **Select the type of icon to represent the attached file and then click OK.**

   Several types of icons can represent the attached file. You can select a paperclip, a graph, a pushpin, or a tag. Whatever icon you select appears on your document to denote that another file is attached. When you roll over the icon, a little annotation appears telling you the filename.

   With the Record Audio Comment tool, you can share a verbal comment by using a microphone and recording a message directly into the PDF. The sound is added as a comment.

The file(s) that you attach with the Attach File tools becomes embedded within the PDF file. The attached file remains in its original file format, even if the attached file isn't a PDF file. For example, you can attach an Excel spreadsheet to a PDF document.

The drawing tools

There are three shape tools, two line tools, and a pencil in the Comment & Markup toolbar. Use the drawing tools to add lines, ovals, rectangles, and other shapes to your PDF file. These shapes can call attention to specific portions of a document.

To use the Cloud Shape tool, follow these steps:

1. **Select the Cloud Shape tool from the Comment & Markup toolbar.**

2. **Click in your document to begin the shape.**

3. **Click again in another position to set the length of the first part of the cloud and then click again to begin shaping your cloud.**

   Click as often as you like to create your shape.

4. **When you're finished with your shape, double-click to close the cloud shape.**

5. **While the Cloud Shape tool is selected, click the shape you created and drag the corner points to resize, if necessary.**

6. **After creating the cloud shape, right-click (Windows) or Control-click (Mac) the shape and choose Properties from the contextual menu to change the color and thickness of the line values; when you're finished, click OK.**

   You can also use the Style drop-down list in the Properties dialog box to change the appearance of a selected comment. Instead of the cloud edges, you can change them to dotted lines, dashed lines, and so on.

To use the rectangle and oval shapes, follow these steps:

1. **Select either the Rectangle or Oval Shape tool from the Comment & Markup toolbar.**

2. **Click and drag in your document to draw the shape.**

3. **While the drawing tool you chose is selected, click the shape you created and drag the corner points to resize, if necessary.**

4. **After creating the shape, right-click (Windows) or Control-click (Mac) the shape and choose Properties from the contextual menu to change the color and thickness of the line values; when you're finished, click OK.**

   You can also use the Style drop-down list in the Properties dialog box to change the appearance of the shape.

The Text Box tool

When creating notes that you want to prominently display on a document, you can use the Text Box tool.

Follow these steps to add a text box to hold your comments:

1. **Select the Text Box tool from the Comment & Markup toolbar.**

   A text field is placed directly on the document.

2. **Drag to add the comment.**

3. **Right-click (Windows) or Control-click (Mac) and choose Properties from the contextual menu to set the color of the text box that contains the note.**

4. **Make your choices to modify the appearance of the text box and then click OK.**

You can select the text box and move it to another position any time you want. You can resize the text box by dragging an anchor point.

The Callout tool

The Callout tool creates a callout text box that points to a section of your document with an arrow. The callout text box is made up of three parts: the text box, the knee line, and the end point line. You can resize each part individually to customize the callout area of your document.

To use the Callout tool, follow these steps:

1. **Select the Callout tool from the Comment & Markup toolbar.**

2. **Click where you want the arrowhead point to be.**

3. **Drag up or down or to the side to position the text box and begin typing.**

   You can click the text box and then use the anchor points on the line to resize the box.

4. **Right-click (Windows) or Control-click (Mac) and choose Properties from the contextual menu to set the color of the callout text box.**

   You can change the size, color, and font characteristics of the text in the callout **text** box.

5. **Make your choices to modify the appearance of the callout text box and then click OK.**

You can select the callout text box and move it to another position any time you want. You can resize the text box by dragging an anchor point.

The Pencil tool

With the Pencil tool, you can create freeform lines on your documents. These lines can be useful when you're trying to attract attention to a specific portion of a page. Just follow these steps:

1. **Select the Pencil tool from the Comment & Markup toolbar.**

2. **Click and drag to draw on your document.**

3. **Edit the color and thickness of lines created with the Pencil tool by right-clicking (Windows) or Control-clicking (Mac) the line and choosing Properties from the contextual menu.**

   Alternatively, you can press Ctrl+E (Windows) or ⌘+E (Mac) to access the Properties toolbar.

4. **Make your choices and click OK.**

By right-clicking (Windows) or Control-clicking (Mac) the Pencil tool, you can choose the Pencil Eraser tool. Use the Pencil Eraser tool to remove portions of lines that had previously been created with the Pencil tool.

Managing Comments

One of the most powerful features of PDF commenting is the ability to easily manage and share comments and annotations among reviewers. For example, you can determine which comments are displayed at any time, and you can filter the comments by author or by the type of commenting tool used to create the comment. In addition, you can indicate a response to a comment and track the changes that may have been made to a document based upon a comment. Also, you can consolidate comments from multiple reviewers into a single document.

Viewing comments

You can use any of several methods to see a document's list of comments:

✦ Click the Comments tab along the bottom left side of the document window in the Navigation panel.

✦ Choose Comment⇨Show Comments List.

✦ Choose View⇨Navigation Panels⇨Comments.

No matter which method you use, the Comments List window that shows all the comments in the document appears along the bottom of the Document window. You can see the author of each comment and any notes entered by reviewers. By clicking the plus sign to the left of a comment, you can view more information about it, such as what type of comment it is and the date and time it was created.

If you've clicked the plus sign to the left of the comment to expand the view, it changes to a minus sign, which you can then click to return to the consolidated view showing only the author and the initial portions of any text from the note.

To the right of the plus sign is a check box that you can use to indicate that the comment has been reviewed or to indicate that a certain comment needs further attention. Use these check boxes for your own purposes; their status doesn't export with the document if you send the file to others, so they're for your personal use only.

Changing a comment's review status

Acrobat makes it easy to indicate whether a comment has been reviewed, accepted, or has additional comments attached to it.

To change the status of a comment, follow these steps:

1. **Choose Comments⇨Show Comments List to see the entire list of comments and the status of each one.**

   You can also click the Comments tab located on the bottom left side of the screen to display the comments.

2. **In the Comments List, right-click (Windows) or Control-click (Mac) a comment and choose Set Status⇨Review from the contextual menu.**

3. **Select Accepted, Rejected, Cancelled, or Completed, depending on what's appropriate to your situation.**

   The comment you modified appears in the list, showing the new status you assigned to it.

Replying to a comment

You can right-click (Windows) or Control-click (Mac) a comment in the Comments List and choose Reply from the contextual menu to add a follow-up note to the comment. This way, new comments can be tied to existing comments. If your documents go through multiple rounds of review, adding a reply allows a secondary or final reviewer to expand on the comments from an initial reviewer. This also allows an author or designer to clearly respond to the suggestions from an editor.

Collapsing or hiding comments

Because the Comments List can become rather large, you can choose to collapse all comments so that only the page number on which comments appear is displayed in the list. To do so, click the Collapse All button in the upper left of the Comments List window; it has a minus sign next to it. To view all comments, click the Expand All button in the same location; this button has a plus sign next to it.

To hide all the comments within a document, click and hold the Show button on the Commenting toolbar and choose Hide All Comments. You can then click the Show button in the Comments toolbar and choose to show comments based upon

✦ Type of comment, such as note, line, or cross out

✦ Reviewer, such as Bob or Jane

✦ Status, such as accepted or rejected

✦ Checked State, which can be checked or unchecked

Use these filtering options to view only those comments that are relevant to you.

Sharing comments

You can share your comments with other reviewers who have access to the same PDF document by following these steps:

1. **Make sure that the Comments List is visible by clicking the Comments tab on the bottom left of the Document window.**

2. **Select the comment that you want to export by clicking it (Shift+click for multiple selections).**

3. **From the Comments List window, choose Options⇨Export Selected Comments.**

   The Export Comments dialog box appears.

4. **Browse to the location where you want the comments to be saved and give the saved file a new name.**

   You now have a file that includes only the comments' information, and not the entire PDF file.

You can share your file with reviewers who have the same PDF file, and they can choose Options⇨Import Comments in the Comments List window to add the comments into their document. You can use this method to avoid sending entire PDF files to those who already have the document.

Summarizing comments

You can compile a list of all the comments from a PDF file into a new, separate document. To summarize comments, follow these steps:

1. **From the Comments List window, choose Options⇨Summarize Comments.**

   The Summarize Options dialog box appears.

2. **Create a listing of the comments with lines connecting them to their locations on the page by selecting the radio button from the top — Document and Connector Lines on a Single Page.**

   In the Include section, you can choose which comments should be summarized.

3. **Click the Create PDF Comment Summary button.**

   This step creates a new PDF document that simply lists all the comments, as shown in Figure 5-3.

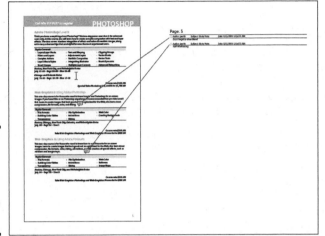

Figure 5-3:
A new PDF
document
is created,
listing all the
comments.

Enabling commenting in Adobe Reader

Acrobat 9.0 Professional makes it easy to include users of the free Adobe Reader in a review process. To include Adobe Reader users in a review, choose Comments⇨Enable for Commenting in Adobe Reader. After saving the file, you can share it with users of Adobe Reader, who can then use commenting and markup tools and save their comments into the file. A user of Adobe Acrobat 9.0 Professional must enable commenting in a PDF file before users of Adobe Reader can add comments to a file.

Chapter 6: Securing Your PDF Files

In This Chapter

✔ **Finding out about security in Acrobat**

✔ **Using passwords**

✔ **Setting limits for editing and printing**

You may think that because you've converted your documents to PDF (Portable Document Format) that they're secure. This isn't quite true because Adobe Acrobat includes tools for changing text and images, as well as extracting them for use in other files. For example, you can use the Select tool (see Chapter 4 of this minibook) to select and copy a passage of text or the Select Object tool to copy or edit graphics.

Applying security provides you with control over who can view, edit, or print the PDF documents you distribute. You can restrict access to certain features, which deters most users from manipulating your files. All Adobe applications recognize and honor security settings applied in Acrobat, but some software ignores Adobe's security settings or can bypass them all together. For this reason, we recommend that you share your most sensitive PDF documents only when you've applied security protection. This way, the only users who can open a file are those who know the password or have the correct certificate, depending upon the type of security applied to the file.

In this chapter, we discuss using security protection to limit access to PDF files and show you how to limit what users can do to the contents of your PDF documents.

Understanding Password Security

By requiring users to enter a password to open and view your PDF files, you limit access to those files so that only certain users can view them. You can also apply security to limit access to certain Acrobat and Adobe Reader features, such as copying text or graphics, editing the file, and printing. Adobe calls this type of security *password security* because it requires a password to either open the document or to change the security that's been applied to the document.

Apply security options to limit the opening or editing of your PDF document, restricting these capabilities to users who have been provided the proper password. This is done by clicking the Secure button on the Tasks toolbar. If the Secure button isn't visible, choose View➪Toolbars➪Tasks.

Click and hold down the Secure button in the Tasks toolbar and choose 2 Encrypt with Password to bring up the Password Security - Settings dialog box.

In the Password Security - Settings dialog box, choose an Acrobat version from the Compatibility drop-down list. The higher the version of Acrobat, the greater the level of security.

Your choice here is based on your needs for security and also the version of Acrobat or Adobe Reader that your audience uses. Lower versions of Acrobat provide more compatibility with the widest number of viewers, as they support much older versions of the free Adobe Reader. In the following list, we explain the compatibility choices before showing you how to enable security in the following sections:

✦ **Acrobat 3 and Later:** If the users who receive your PDF files may have older versions of the software, you can choose Acrobat 3 and Later from the Compatibility drop-down list to ensure that the recipients can view the PDF file you're securing. This option provides compatibility for users who may not have updated their software in many years, but the level of security is limited to 40-bit encryption. Although this amount keeps the average user from gaining access to your files, it won't deter a determined hacker from accessing them and can be easily circumvented by a sophisticated user.

✦ **Acrobat 5 and Later:** When sharing files with users who have access to Adobe Reader or Adobe Acrobat Version 5 or 6, this option provides expanded security, increasing the security level to 128-bit, which makes the resulting PDF files more difficult to access. Along with the enhanced security, you can also secure the files while still allowing access to the file for visually-impaired users. Earlier versions of security don't provide this option, but it's included when you choose either Acrobat 5- or 6-compatible security.

✦ **Acrobat 6 and Later:** Along with the enhanced security offered with Acrobat 5 compatibility, this setting adds the ability to maintain plain text metadata. In short, this option allows for information about the file, such as its author, title, or creation date, to remain visible while the remainder of the file remains secure.

✦ **Acrobat 7 and Later:** This choice includes all security options of Acrobat 6 compatibility and also allows you to encrypt file attachments that are part of a PDF file. It uses the *Advanced Encryption Standard,* which is a very high level of encryption, making it unlikely that an unauthorized user can decrypt the file without the password.

✦ **Acrobat 9 and Later:** Choose this option if your audience is using the latest version of Acrobat and you need more advanced security. The encryption improves to 256-bit AES, making the file much more difficult for even the most determined hacker to access.

Applying Password Security to Your PDF Documents

Selecting the Encrypt with Password option from the Secure button in the Acrobat task bar limits access to the PDF file. Only those who know the password can open the file. Documents are only as secure as the passwords that protect them. To guard against discovery of a password, use passwords that are six or more characters in length and include at least one number or symbol. Avoid using words in the dictionary and short passwords. For example, the password `potato` is less secure than `p0tat0`, which mixes numbers and letters.

To apply password security to a file, follow these steps:

1. **With a PDF file open, click and hold the Secure button on the Security taskbar and choose Encrypt with Password.**

Click OK when the dialog box appears, verifying that you want to apply security to this PDF. The Password Security - Settings dialog box appears, as shown in Figure 6-1.

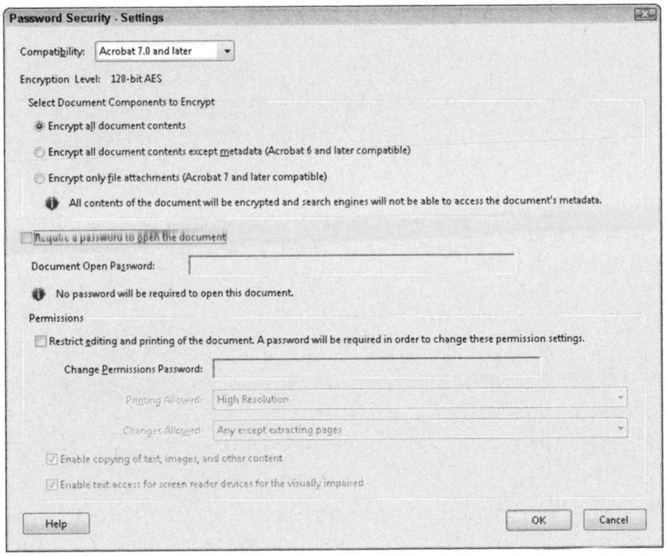

Figure 6-1:
The
Password
Security –
Settings
dialog box.

2. **Choose Acrobat 7 and Later from the Compatibility drop-down list.**

   Although Acrobat 9 and later provides more robust security, few people are using version 9 of Acrobat, making it difficult to distribute the file with this high level of security.

3. **Select the Require a Password to Open the Document check box.**

4. **Enter a password in the Document Open Password text box.**

   You can also add additional security settings, which we outline in the next section. Or you can use this setting as the only security to be applied to the document.

   If password protection is the only security measure you apply to the document, authorized users can access the document by entering a password. Users with the password may also be able to edit or print the document unless you apply additional security measures. We discuss ways to limit the editing and printing of PDF files in the next section.

5. **Click OK.**

6. **Confirm the password, click OK again, and the dialog box closes.**

7. **Save, close, and then reopen the PDF file.**

   A password dialog box appears asking for the password to access the secured file. Every time a user accesses the file, he or she will be required to enter a password.

Limiting Editing and Printing

In addition to restricting viewing of a PDF file, you can also limit editing and printing, restricting users from making changes to your document. This allows users to view a file but not change it.

To limit editing and printing of your PDF document, follow these steps:

1. **With a PDF file open, click and hold the Secure button on the Security taskbar and choose Encrypt with Password.**

   The Password Security – Settings dialog box opens.

2. **In the Permissions area, select the check box labeled Restrict Editing and Printing of the document.**

   You can now specify a password that will be required for readers to edit the file or change the security settings. (See the previous section.)

With this option selected, you can apply a password for access to features, such as printing or editing. This password can be different than the password used to open the document — in fact, you don't even need to use a document open password if you don't want to, but it's a good idea to use both of these passwords for sensitive data. If you apply a document open password without a permissions password, it's easy for an experienced user to bypass the security in the PDF file.

3. **In the Change Permissions Password text box, enter a password.**

   Users that enter this permissions password when opening the document can change the file or the security settings. The permissions password can also be used to open the file and provides more privileges than the open password.

4. **Choose whether users can print the document by selecting from the Printing Allowed drop-down list.**

   The choices include Low Resolution or High Resolution, or you can prohibit printing by choosing None. The settings you choose here apply to anyone who accesses the document and doesn't know the permissions password.

5. **Choose from the Changes Allowed drop-down list (see Figure 6-2) to restrict editing.**

   For the most security, choose None.

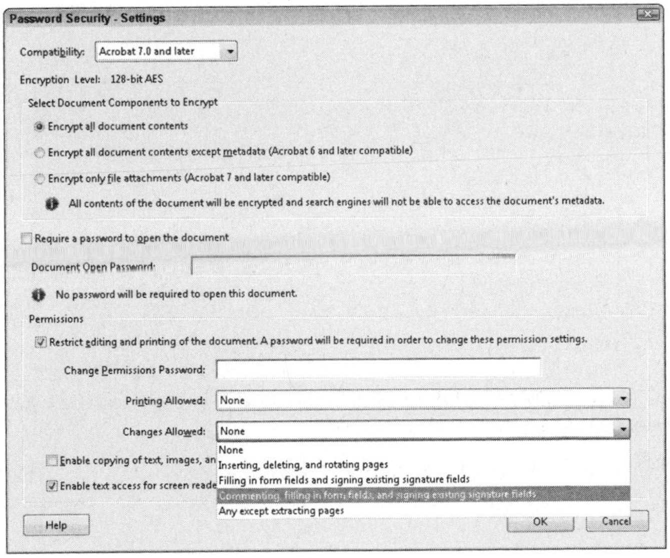

Figure 6-2:
Restrict
what users
can edit.

Password Security - Settings

Compatibility: Acrobat 7.0 and later

Encryption Level: 128-bit AES

Select Document Components to Encrypt

○ Encrypt all document contents

○ Encrypt all document contents except metadata (Acrobat 6 and later compatible)

○ Encrypt only file attachments (Acrobat 7 and later compatible)

All contents of the document will be encrypted and search engines will not be able to access the document's metadata.

☐ Require a password to open the document

Document Open Password:

No password will be required to open this document.

Permissions

☑ Restrict editing and printing of the document. A password will be required in order to change these permission settings.

Change Permissions Password:

Printing Allowed: None

Changes Allowed: None
   None
   Inserting, deleting, and rotating pages
   Filling in form fields and signing existing signature fields
   Commenting, filling in form fields, and signing existing signature fields
   Any except extracting pages

☐ Enable copying of text, images, an

☑ Enable text access for screen reade

Help   OK   Cancel

6. **Select the last two check boxes if desired:**

   - *Enable Copying of Text, Images, and Other Content:* When deselected, this option restricts copying and pasting of text and graphics from a PDF file into other documents. Selecting this option lets users extract text and images from a file by using the simple Copy and Paste commands.

   - *Enable Text Access for Screen Reader Devices for the Visually Impaired:* When you choose Acrobat 5 or Later from the Compatibility drop-down list at the top of the dialog box, you can also select this check box to allow visually impaired users to have the PDF file read aloud to them.

7. **When you're satisfied with the settings, click OK.**

Choosing more advanced security settings, and choosing the latest version of compatibility, runs the risk of your file not being visible to many users that may not have upgraded. Always understand your audience and the software versions they're using before distributing files.

Book VI

Dreamweaver CS5

The 5th Wave   By Rich Tennant

"As a Web site designer I never thought I'd say this, but I don't think your site has enough bells and whistles."

Contents at a Glance

Chapter 1: Getting Familiar with New Features in Dreamweaver

In This Chapter

✔ Previewing pages in BrowserLab

✔ Looking at the improved related documents feature

✔ Fine-tuning styles in real-time with the improved CSS Styles panel

✔ Working with InContext Editing

Dreamweaver CS5 lets you create and manage single pages, such as e-mail newsletters, or groups of pages that are linked to each other, referred to as a *site*. Users can create basic Web sites with simple links from one page to another or advanced Web sites that include custom coding and interaction with people viewing the pages.

As part of the Adobe Creative Suite, Dreamweaver CS5 works seamlessly with several other Adobe applications, such as Photoshop CS5, Illustrator CS5, Bridge, and Device Central. Even if you've never used Dreamweaver, you'll be impressed by its many tools, panels, and powerful features that make building Web pages easy and intuitive.

If you've used other Web-page editing applications such as GoLive or Microsoft Expression Web, moving to Dreamweaver is a smooth transition. Dreamweaver CS5 is an industry standard Web site creation and management tool, with the tools needed to do advanced coding or create data-driven Web sites.

Exploring the Improved CS5 Interface

Dreamweaver CS5 includes a number of subtle but useful enhancements to its workspace, improving on the overhaul in version CS4. The document toolbar has been rethought, including quick access to page-specific options. The workspace also includes some handy new panels for features such as InContext Editing and Adobe Business Catalyst, as shown in Figure 1-1.

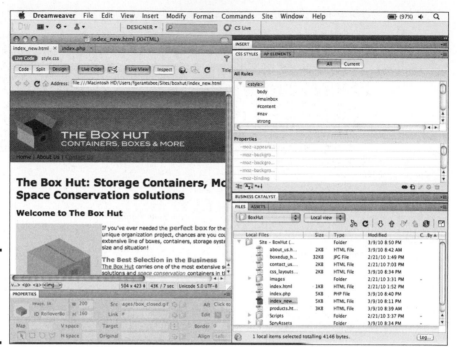

Figure 1-1:
The Dream-
weaver
Designer
workspace.

In the workspace, panels and panel groups appear tabbed, and you can separate them by dragging a tab to another location, just as in other Adobe applications. If you choose View➪Toolbars➪Standard, you can use the Go to Bridge button to navigate and use Adobe Bridge. Using Adobe Bridge with Dreamweaver CS5 is useful because you can search and navigate assets such as text, Flash, and image files. You can then drag and drop them directly on your page. (Read more about adding imagery to a Web page in Chapter 4 of this minibook.)

Previewing Pages in Adobe BrowserLab

One of the biggest challenges of designing for the Web is that you must cater to a variety of browsers and browser versions. Testing pages across these browsers is often a cumbersome task, but Adobe's new BrowserLab service lets you easily preview and compare your work across different browsers for consistency.

The BrowserLab service, free and available at the Adobe Web site at `http://labs.adobe.com/technologies/browserlab`, is just a step away when you're working in Dreamweaver. Choose File➪Preview in Browser to check how your pages appear in different browsers, all in a single glance. (See Figure 1-2.) In addition, you can test pages in browsers on different operating systems, so if you're a Mac user trying to see how your Web site looks in Internet Explorer on a PC, you're covered!

Figure 1-2:
Use Adobe BrowserLab to check out and compare pages in several browser environments at a time.

Improved Related Files Feature

Modern Web sites often rely on more than just markup and style sheets for increased functionality, so it's not uncommon for Web sites of any size to rely on server-side programming languages, such as PHP (shown in Figure 1-3) or ASP.NET. For this reason, a single page can be composed of a number of different files that the server puts together on the fly. Dreamweaver improves on its Related Documents view on the Document toolbar by revealing attached dynamic files, such as server-side includes. You can quickly navigate to and edit these related files as easily as you now do with style sheets and JavaScript files.

You must have a testing server enabled in order to discover and view server-side related files.

It helps to know a bit about the Related Documents feature (introduced in CS4) to appreciate these improvements. Quite often, pages rely on several other files, such as attached style sheets and JavaScript files. The Document toolbar includes a Related Documents section, shown in Figure 1-4, where you can see and jump to other documents used by and attached to your page. Selecting a document on the Related Documents toolbar displays the special Split view, where you can edit the selected file in Code view while continuing to work with the original page in Design view.

Figure 1-3:
Reveal
server-side
includes,
such as the
header, in
the Related
Documents
view.

Figure 1-4:
The Related
Documents
toolbar
lets you
view and
edit other
files that
your page
depends on.

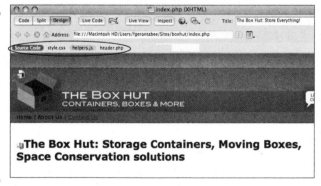

The best part is that you don't have to jump between multiple Document windows; just edit while you watch the changes applied to your document!

Inspecting Your CSS: Live!

In the past, the only time you could modify or work with CSS in Dreamweaver was in Design view or Code view. After you previewed your page in a browser, you had no easy way to tweak styles while viewing the result in real-time. Though some browsers have created add-ons (most notably, the Firebox add-on FireBug) to take care of the task of inspecting and *debugging* page styles, you have no uniform or easy way to handle these tasks during the design and building phase.

Dreamweaver CS5 handles this problem by adding a real-time CSS inspector feature to Live view, as shown in Figure 1-5. You can now see your page as it appears in a browser while tweaking and tuning styles to see the effects in real-time.

Figure 1-5: You can now inspect elements on your page in Live view and modify them in real-time using the CSS Styles panel on the right.

Use the Inspect button on the Document toolbar in Live view to select elements on the page and to see and modify the styles that control their appearance. Make adjustments on the fly to see how those changes will affect the page in a browser.

Using InContext Editing

A common theme of new features in Dreamweaver CS5 is the integration of new Adobe online services such as BrowserLab and Business Catalyst and the useful addition of InContext Editing. InContext Editing provides a central, browser-based method of managing a Web site without having to edit its original files or dive into code. This feature is useful if you're creating Web sites where you want to give a client, or others in your organization, the ability to update and manage content from a browser without needing to edit pages.

The Dreamweaver Insert panel includes the new category InContext Editing, shown in Figure 1-6. This category features tools for adding *editable regions*, or areas on the page that can be modified by using the Adobe InContext Editing service. Pages can be edited directly in the browser by clients and other contributors. This feature lets you collaborate with others on content while preserving the integrity of, and maintaining control over, your page designs.

Figure 1-6:
The new InContext Editing panel features tools for creating editable regions on a page that can be modified in a browser.

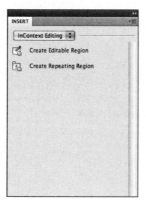

Chapter 2: Introducing Dreamweaver CS5

In This Chapter

✔ **Familiarizing yourself with the workspace**

✔ **Finding out about panels**

✔ **Creating a new Web site**

✔ **Discovering the Property inspector**

✔ **Previewing your page**

✔ **Understanding the Dreamweaver preferences**

Dreamweaver CS5 lets you create and manage Web pages and complete Web sites. In this chapter, you find out how to start a Web site and build pages within it. A *Web site* is simply a group of linked pages that contain text and images and can also contain media, such as Flash movies, sound, and video.

Getting to Know the Workspace

The *workspace* consists of panels, toolbars, and inspectors and puts most all the tools you need within close reach. The Dreamweaver workspace, shown in Figure 2-1, is slightly different from ones you may see in other Adobe applications, but their premise is the same: You can open panels, panel groups, toolbars, and dialog boxes to do the work you need. Whichever document you're editing appears in the Document window, which occupies most of the workspace — and even has its own toolbar.

When Dreamweaver is first launched, you see a Welcome screen. This screen provides the option to open any recent items (if you've created pages already) or to create new HTML, CSS, XML, sites, and many other types of files.

You can customize your workspace with only the panels, toolbars, and arrangement of windows you need or choose from workspace presets included with Dreamweaver.

Document bar

Insert panel

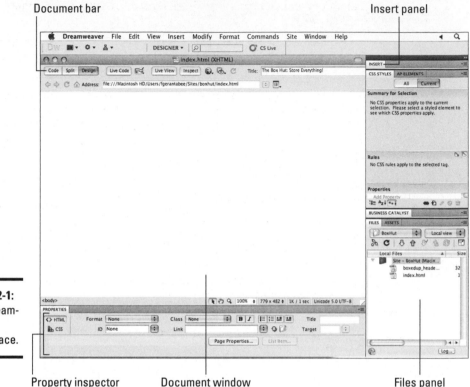

Figure 2-1:
The Dream-
weaver
workspace.

Property inspector   Document window   Files panel

The Insert panel

The Dreamweaver CS5 Insert panel provides you with tools to insert on your page some common Web page elements such as hyperlinks, e-mail links, tables, and images as well as more text formatting options and widgets that enhance your page. Choose Window➪Insert to reveal the panel in the upper-right corner of your workspace.

The Insert panel is divided into eight categories that provide you with different elements to add to your page. You can switch between these categories by using the drop-down list at the top of the panel:

✦ **Common:** Contains the most commonly used objects, such as images and tables.

✦ **Layout:** Contains layout elements — such as tables and CSS elements like the DIV tag — that help you create a Web page layout.

✦ **Forms:** Contains the elements necessary to create a form in your Dreamweaver page.

✦ **Data:** Contains elements related to dynamic content and some Spry data objects.

✦ **Spry:** Contains Spry Framework objects, which are handy widgets used to enhance your Web pages with cool navigation bars, layout panels, and real-time data components.

✦ **InContext Editing:** Creates editable regions for the Adobe InContext editing service, which allows content contributors to update Web site content remotely without the need to edit or disturb the original Web site files.

✦ **Text:** Provides you with text formatting tags.

✦ **Favorites:** Allows you to group and organize the Insert panel buttons you use the most within one common location.

Book VI
Chapter 2

Introducing Dreamweaver CS5

To bring up the Customize Favorite Objects dialog box, simply right-click (Windows) or Control-click (Mac) within the Insert panel and choose Customize Favorites from the contextual menu. The Customize Favorite Objects dialog box, shown in Figure 2-2, appears. Click an object in the Available Objects list and then click the double arrow to add the object to your Favorites category.

Figure 2-2: Customizing the Favorites category in the Insert panel.

The Document toolbar

The Document toolbar, shown in Figure 2-3, contains tools to help you view your document in different modes, such as Code and Design, as well as address such items as the document title and browser compatibility.

✦ **Code View:** Show the code and only the code using this view. Dreamweaver helps you to decipher code by color coding tags, attributes, CSS, and other elements.

✦ **Split View:** Selecting this option splits the Document window between Code and Design views. If you understand a little about code, this view can be extremely helpful because you see both the design and the code simultaneously.

Figure 2-3:
Control your view of the page from the Document toolbar.

+ **Design View:** This option displays your page in Design view in the Document window.

+ **Live Code:** When Live View is enabled, you can view the source code of your document as a user would see it in a browser (via the View Source or Page Source menu options in most browsers). You can't edit page code in this view.

+ **Check Browser Compatibility:** This menu shows options that let you check page integrity, such as accessibility, or whether your CSS rules are compatible across different browsers.

+ **Live View:** Live View renders your page as though it's in a browser — free of borders, guides, and other visual aids. In Live View, you can't edit the previewed content, but you can still jump to Code, Split, or Design view and modify your page content.

+ **Inspect:** The new Inspect button works with Live View to reveal the CSS rules that format elements on your page. When you select an element on the page with Inspect enabled, the CSS Styles panel reveals the properties that format that element, and allows you to disable or modify specific properties and see the results in real time.

+ **Preview/Debug in Browser:** Click this button to preview or debug your document in one of your installed Web browsers, Adobe's BrowserLab, or Device Central.

+ **Visual Aids:** Click this button to select different visual aids (such as borders and guides) to help you see various elements and make designing your pages easier.

+ **Refresh Design View:** Click this button to refresh the document's Design view after you make changes in Code view. Changes you make in Code view don't appear automatically in Design view until you perform certain actions, such as save the file or click this button.

+ **Document Title:** Enter the name of your document in this field.

+ **File Management:** Click this button to display the File Management pop-up menu. Use this menu to check your document in or out (when Check In/Check Out is enabled for your site).

✦ **Previous Page/Next Page/Refresh/Address Bar:** In Live View, these tools work just like they would in a Web browser and enable you to navigate between pages, refresh the page, and see the address of the current page. The address bar also works when Live View is not enabled, revealing the path to the document you're currently working on.

✦ **Related Documents:** Documents used by and attached to your page, such as external CSS and JavaScript files, are listed below (Mac) or above (Windows) the view selection (Code/Split/Design) buttons. You can click any listed document to edit the attached file in Split view without having to switch documents.

Note: XML, JavaScript, CSS, and other code-based file types can only be viewed and edited in Code view; the Design and Split buttons appear dimmed out.

Note: Refreshing also updates code features that are Document Object Model (DOM) dependent, such as the ability to select a code block's opening or closing tags.

✦ **Live View Options:** Click and select options from this menu to control how your document appears and works when Live View is enabled.

Using the panel groups

Dreamweaver provides you with a panel docking area off to the right of the workspace. The panels in Dreamweaver appear grouped and tabbed, and you can easily access the appropriate panel for the job by either clicking the tab of the panel to bring it forward or by selecting the named panel from the Window menu.

Close a panel by either selecting the name of the panel from the Window menu or by tearing the panel out of the group and clicking the Close icon.

Saving your workspace

Just as with the other Creative Suite 4 applications, you can organize your workspace by turning on the visibility of the panels and toolbars that you use regularly and closing the others. You can also save your workspace so that you can recall it at any time:

1. **Choose Window⇨Workspace Layout⇨New Workspace.**

The New Workspace Layout dialog box appears.

2. **Type an appropriate name in the Name text box.**

3. **Click OK to create the new workspace.**

To recall a workspace you've previously saved, you can use one of the following methods:

✦ Select the workspace from the Workspace menu near the top of the screen (above the panel group).

✦ Open the workspace by choosing Window➪Workspace Layout➪*[your workspace name]*.

Dreamweaver CS5 features several new workspaces geared toward different types of users as well as different tasks. You can recall any of these workspaces using either of the ways described in the previous list or by selecting a workspace from the application bar, which appears at the top of your screen, as shown in Figure 2-4.

Figure 2-4:
The
application
toolbar
allows
you easy
access to
your saved
workspaces.

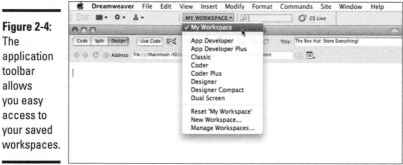

You can hide the application toolbar by choosing Window➪Application Bar.

Creating a Site

Sites are quite important to maintain the links and consistency and the general organization of your Web pages. (See Chapter 3 of this minibook for more on creating sites.) Some good news is that the process of creating a new site has been simplified in Dreamweaver CS5.

To create a site, follow these steps:

1. **Choose Site➪New Site.**

The Site Setup dialog box appears.

This dialog box walks you through the steps to create a new site. In this chapter, you breeze through the steps, but you can find more details about them in Chapter 3 of this minibook.

2. **In the Site Name box, type a name for your new site.**

   For this example, we entered **chapter2**.

3. **The Local Site Folder field shows you where the new site folder will be created. If you want to change it, you can click the Folder icon to select an existing folder. For now, leave the default folder path and click Save.**

   The site appears in the Files panel.

Checking Out the Property Inspector

After you've created a site, you can begin to add new pages as well as assets, such as images, to that site. The Property inspector becomes one of your most useful panels because it provides you with information about any element you've selected in the Document window. This contextual panel, shown in Figure 2-5, displays text attributes when text is selected or image attributes when images are selected, and so on.

Figure 2-5:
The Property inspector shown with text (top) and an image (bottom) selected.

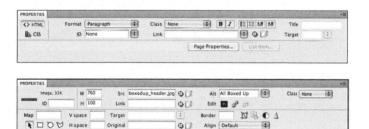

To see this panel in action, you'll create a new page with some elements on it. You may have none of your own pages yet, so you'll use one of the CSS Starter pages that loaded with your Dreamweaver CS5 installation, and follow these steps:

1. **Choose File⇨New to create a new page in Dreamweaver.**

   The New Document dialog box appears.

2. **Choose Blank Page⇨HTML⇨2 Column Fixed Sidebar, and click Create.**

3. **Choose File⇨Save As.**

   The Save As dialog box appears.

4. **Type a name in the Save As text box.**

The location is routed automatically to the site folder you created. See the earlier section "Creating a Site" to see how to create a site.

5. **With your new page open in the Document window, click to select various elements, such as text, a table, or a hyperlink (linked text).**

   With each selection, the Property inspector changes to provide you with specific information about that element (refer to Figure 2-5).

The Property inspector is analogous to the Option bar, which appears at the top of the Illustrator, InDesign, and Photoshop workspaces and the Property inspector in Flash. If you're a former GoLive user, the concept of using the Property inspector is also quite familiar to you because this same feature existed in that application as well.

Previewing Your Page in a Browser or with Live View

Perhaps you've completed your page and you want to investigate how it looks in a browser. You can quickly preview your file by simply clicking the Preview/Debug in Browser button on the Document toolbar and selecting a browser to preview your page, as shown in Figure 2-6. You can also preview your page in Adobe's BrowserLab or Adobe's Device Central (which simulates several different mobile and PDA devices).

Figure 2-6:
The Preview/ Debug in Browser button lets you select from browsers installed on your system.

You can always add browsers from the Preferences panel by choosing Edit⇨Preferences⇨Preview in Browser (Windows) or Dreamweaver⇨ Preferences⇨Preview in Browser (Mac).

Previewing your page using Live View

Dreamweaver CS5's Live View displays your page as you would see it in a browser. This feature is a nice alternative to the Preview in Browser command because you don't ever need to exit Dreamweaver.

To view your page in Live View, follow these steps:

1. **With a page open in the Document window, click the Live View button on the Document toolbar.**

2. **To see the resulting source code of your page, click the Live Code button that appears next to the Live View button.**

   This step is equivalent to using the View Page Source or View Source options available in most every browser. In this mode, you can only view code, not edit it.

3. **To edit your page code, switch to Split view or Code view on the Document toolbar.**

Previewing your page using the new Adobe BrowserLab

Adobe's BrowserLab is a unique service that is accessible from directly within the Dreamweaver environment. You can view and simulate your Web site in a number of different browsers, browser versions, and operating system environments from one single location. You can even preview different environments side-by-side, as shown in Figure 2-7, to see how different browsers render your site.

Figure 2-7:
The Dummies.com site shown in BrowserLab as it will appear in Firefox for Windows XP (left) and Internet Explorer 7 on Windows XP (right).

To preview your site in Adobe BrowserLab, click the Preview/Debug in Browser button on the Document toolbar (refer to Figure 2-6) and choose Preview in Adobe BrowserLab or File⇨Preview In Browser⇨Adobe BrowserLab.

Understanding Dreamweaver Preferences

You can change many preferences in Dreamweaver CS5 for Mac OS X preferences). You see categories, such as Accessibility, AP Elements, and General in the panel on the left, along with subcategories that appear in the panel to the right.

To access general preferences, choose Edit⇨Preferences (Windows) or Dreamweaver⇨Preferences (Mac). The general rule for changing preferences is that if you don't know what it means, don't touch it. But if you want to tweak certain things, this is the place to go.

Preferences are especially helpful to people who hand-code and want to enter their own code hints, highlight colors, or change the font that appears in Code view.

Chapter 3: Creating a Web Site

In this chapter, you see the basic steps for putting a Web site together, from creating your first new, blank site to adding files to Web sites to playing (just a little) with HTML.

Web Site Basics

A *Web site* is a collection of related pages linked to one another, preferably in an organized manner. With the proper planning and a goal in sight, you can easily accomplish the task of creating an outstanding Web site. Figure 3-1 shows the general structure of a Web site. A Web site starts with a main page (or its *home page*), the central link to other pages in the site. The main page is also the page viewers see first when they type your URL in a browser. The main page is typically named `index.html` but may also be `index.htm` or even `default.htm`. Check with your service provider to find the correct name.

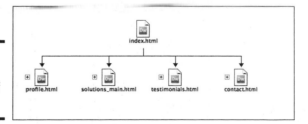

Figure 3-1:
The structure of a Web site.

Pages are linked by *hyperlinks,* or references that take viewers from one point in an HTML document to another or from one document to another. (Read more about hyperlinks and how to create them in Chapter 6 of this minibook.)

You should understand the following terms when you forge through the steps to create a Web site:

✦ **FTP (File Transfer Protocol):** Allows a user on one computer to transfer files to and from another computer over a TCP/IP network. FTP is also the client program the user executes to transfer files. You can use FTP to transfer Web pages, images, and other types of files to a host Web server when you publish your site.

✦ **HTTP (Hypertext Transfer Protocol):** The client-server TCP/IP protocol used on the Internet for the exchange of HTML documents.

✦ **TCP/IP (Transmission Control Protocol/Internet Protocol):** Underlying protocols that make possible communication between computers on the Internet. TCP/IP ensures that information being exchanged goes to the right place, in a form that can be used, and arrives there intact.

✦ **URL (Universal Resource Locator):** A standard for specifying the location of an object, such as a file, on the Internet. You type the URL, such as www.dummies.com, into a Web browser to visit a Web page. A URL is also used in an HTML document (a Web page) to specify the target of a link, which is often another Web page.

Plan your site: How Web sites are organized is important. Typically, the purpose of a Web site is to sell something — a product, a service, or a thought, such as "Vote for me!" Without sound organization, a Web site may fail to sell to its visitors. You'll save an extraordinary amount of time if you just think ahead and plan your site's organization. Think about the topics you want to cover and then organize your site as you would a high school essay project, by planning the topic sentence, subtopics, and other elements. This plan can be a tremendous aid when you start mapping pages to be linked to others.

Starting a New Site

Even if you're creating only one page, be sure to create a site. A site gives you an organized method of keeping together images and other assets and offers additional options for managing those files.

To create a new site, follow these steps:

1. **In Dreamweaver CS5, choose Site⇨New Site.**

You can also choose Dreamweaver Site from the Create New column of the Welcome screen. The Site Setup dialog box appears, as shown in Figure 3-2.

2. **In the Site Name text box, enter a name for the site.**

For example, if your site's focus is on bikes, you might name the site **biking.**

3. **To change the local site folder, click the Folder icon to the right of the Local Site Folder field and select a new location or choose an existing folder.**

The *local site folder* is the path where your new site folder will be created on your computer. It's where your site files and pages will be stored.

4. **Click Save to create your new site.**

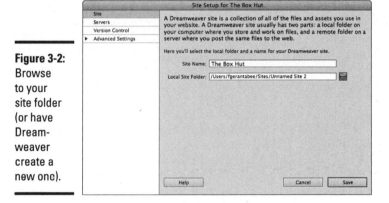

Figure 3-2:
Browse
to your
site folder
(or have
Dream-
weaver
create a
new one).

As soon as you create a site, your site folder is waiting in the Files panel, as shown in Figure 3-3. Think of the Files panel as the control center for all your files, folders, and other assets, such as images, sound, and video that you use to create your Web site.

Figure 3-3:
The Files
panel acts
as a file
browser and
manager.

You can use the Files panel to view files and folders, whether they're related to your Dreamweaver site or not. You can use the Files panel to do typical file operations, such as open and move files.

Creating a New Page for Your Site

After you create a site, you typically build a main page: the index.html or index.htm page. These reserved filenames are recognized by most every Web server as the starting page for a Web site. In addition, default.html and default.htm are also commonly recognized as starting pages. Check with your Web site hosting company or Internet service provider because in some instances your server may require a different name or may prefer one naming convention over another.

The following steps walk you through creating a new page and placing an image on it:

1. **Choose File⇨New.**

The New Page dialog box appears.

You can create many types of new files, from blank pages to more advanced pages that include layouts already created in CSS.

2. **To create a blank page, choose Blank Page⇨HTML⇨<none> and then click Create.**

A blank, untitled HTML page appears.

3. **Choose File⇨Save.**

The Save As dialog box appears.

4. **In the File Name text box, type** index.html**.**

Note that the file is already mapped to your site folder. If you don't see the site's *root* directory (the main folder where all pages and assets are stored), click the Site Root button in the Save As dialog box to locate it.

5. **Click Save.**

Note that when you save a file, it appears in the Files panel.

Adding an Image to Your Page

After you have a blank page, you can add an image to it, including native Photoshop (PSD) files and Fireworks (PNG) images. You can find out more about images in Chapter 4 of this minibook, but in this section you can take a look at how placing images affects the Files panel.

To place an image on a page, follow these steps:

1. **Choose Insert⇨Image.**

   Alternatively, click the Common tab of the Insert panel and click the Insert Image button.

   The Select Image Source dialog box appears.

2. **Navigate to the location of your image and click Choose (Mac) or OK (Windows).**

   If you choose a native Photoshop (PSD) or Fireworks (PNG) file, the Image Preview dialog box appears, allowing you to optimize your image directly in Dreamweaver.

   If you select a Web-ready image, such as GIF, JPG, or PNG and the image is outside your site folder, you see a warning. Dreamweaver alerts you that the image is outside the root folder, which causes issues when you copy pages to a Web server. Click Yes to copy the file to your site's root directory. Assign a new name there or just click Save to keep the same name and duplicate the image file into your site folder.

   The Image Tag Accessibility Attributes dialog box appears.

   All images should have *Alt (alternate) text* — text that appears before the image has downloaded or if the viewer has turned off the option to see images.

3. **Add an appropriate description of the image in the Alternate Text text box.**

   If the image is a logo, the description should include the company name as the Alt text or, if it's a photo or an illustration, describe the image in a few words.

   From an accessibility standpoint, alt text aids screen readers (such as those used by the visually impaired) in identifying image content to users. In addition, Alt text is a valuable tool in providing search engines a way of indexing image content included on your site.

4. **Click OK.**

   The image is added to the page and to the Files panel, as shown in Figure 3-4.

You can edit an image by double-clicking it in the Files panel. You can also use the Property inspector to see details about the image, including its dimensions and file size. You can also modify image properties, including border, hyperlink, and vertical and horizontal padding.

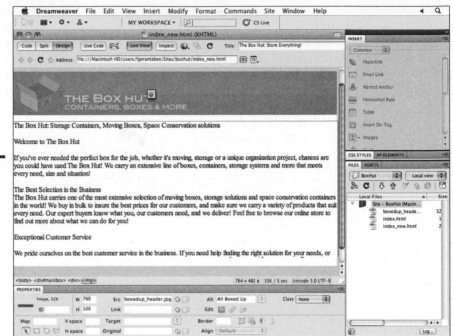

Figure 3-4:
Use the Property inspector to see information about your image and modify image properties.

When you create a larger site with multiple pages linked to each other, you may want to change the view of the Files panel. By clicking the drop-down list (on the top-left side of the Files panel) where your site is located, you can locate folders and other sites you've used recently. By clicking the View drop-down list to the right, you can change the appearance of the Files panel. Refer to Figure 3-4 for an example of how a site appears in Local view.

Open files from the Files panel by double-clicking them.

Naming files

Start the habit of naming files and folders correctly. Follow these rules to make sure that links and pages appear when they're supposed to:

✔ **Use lowercase for all filenames.** Using all lowercase letters in filenames is an easy way to ensure that you have no broken links because you couldn't remember whether you initial-capped a filename. Some Web servers (such as those based on Unix or Mac OS X) are case sensitive. Although a Windows server may be more forgiving of case, you don't want to count on it in the event your files are moved to a different type of server.

✔ **Avoid using spaces in filenames.** If you need to separate words in a filename, use the underscore character instead of a space. For example, rather than use `file new.html`, use `file_new.html` or even `filenew.html`.

✔ **Use only one dot, followed by the extension.** Macintosh users are used to having no naming restrictions, so this rule can be the toughest to adhere to. Don't name your files `finally.done.feb.9.jpg`

B-A-D, for example — it's bad for Internet use. Examples of dot-extensions are `.jpg`, `.gif`, `.png`, `.htm`, `.html`, `.cgi`, `.swf`, and so on.

✔ **Avoid odd characters.** Characters to avoid include dashes (-) or forward slashes (/) at the beginning of the filename. These characters can have other meanings to the Web server and create errors on the site.

Managing Your Web Site Files

You can find out more about uploading your site to a Web server in Chapter 9 of this minibook, but for now, understand that you can go back and open the Site Setup dialog box at any time by choosing Site➪Manage Sites. The Manage Sites dialog box that appears offers options for editing, duplicating, removing, exporting, and importing sites. Click Edit to add an FTP server or change the name of your site as well as add or change any original site settings.

Delving into HTML Basics

The Web page itself is a collection of text, images, links, and possibly media and scripts. The Web page can be as complex or simple as you want — both types are equally effective if created properly. In this section, we show you how to create a page in Dreamweaver and then investigate the HTML that creates it.

To create a blank page, choose File➪New➪Blank Page➪HTML➪<none> and then click Create. A blank, untitled HTML page appears. It has no formatting until you add tables or layers (see Chapter 7 of this minibook). When you type on the page in the document, text appears on the Web page. But there's much more to it than that: Type some text (say, your name) on the page and click the Code button on the Document toolbar.

Dreamweaver works in the background to ensure that your page works in most all recent versions of common Web browsers, such as Firefox, Internet Explorer, and Safari. Lots of code is created to help the Web browser recognize that this is HTML and which version of HTML it uses.

By default, Dreamweaver uses the XHTML 1.0 Transitional standard every time you create a new HTML page. XHTML combines the strictness of XML (Extensible Markup Language) with HTML tags to create a language that works dependably and consistently across Web browsers and new devices (such as cellphones and PDAs) alike.

Select Split view by clicking the Split button on the Document toolbar; this action displays both Design and Code views simultaneously, as shown in Figure 3-5, so that you can see how your changes affect HTML behind the scenes. Select the text; then select the Text option from the Common drop-down list on the Insert panel. Suppose you then choose B (for bold) to bold the selected text. In the code view of your page, you would see that the `<strong>` tag was added before the text and the `</strong>` tag was added after the text.

You can change the orientation and arrangement of the views in Split View. To switch the Design view from the right to the left, choose View➪Design View on Left. To arrange the views vertically, choose View➪Split Vertically. *Note:* You can reverse these options just as easily from the same options on the View menu.

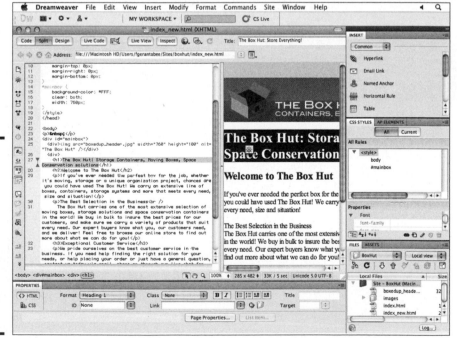

Figure 3-5:
Working in Split view helps you see how your page elements are created and formatted with HTML tags.

HTML code, though easy, is just like any other language, in that you must figure out the *syntax* (the proper sequence and formation of the code) and vocabulary (memorize lots of tags). You don't have to have gobs of tape on your glasses to build good, clean Web pages, but you do have to review the following HTML basics.

If you're an experienced user, you know that by copying and pasting code, you can figure out a lot about HTML code. If you're a new user, copying and pasting code can help you understand the code that others have implemented on their pages and perhaps give you some ideas. Working in Split view also helps you understand how the items you add from the toolbars and panels translate into code.

In general, HTML tags are composed of three parts:

✦ **Tag:** The main part of the HTML information — for example, `<strong>` for strong or bold, `<font>` for the font tag, or `<table>` for an HTML table. A tag is always constructed of a keyword enclosed in a set of brackets, such as `<p>`, or `<blockquote>`.

Because most tags come in pairs, you must enter an opening tag (`<p>`) and a closing tag (`</p>`). In XHTML 1.0 Transitional (the standard used for all new pages created in Dreamweaver), all tags must be closed. You can either close a tag or create a self-closing tag by including the slash before the closing bracket: `<br/>`.

For example, if you make text bold by adding the tag `<strong>`, tell the text where to stop applying boldface by inserting a closing tag `</strong>`. Otherwise, the text continues to appear bold throughout the remainder of the page.

✦ **Attribute:** Gives you a way to further fine-tune the appearance of a specific HTML tag. An attribute is always added to an opening tag and can take different values to control attributes such as the link color, size, and destination. For example, `align` is an attribute of the `<p>` (paragraph) tag that specifies how text inside of the paragraph should align. You may also see that many HTML tags share the same attributes.

Here's an example of a paragraph (`<p>`) tag with an attribute added:

```
<p align="center">This is centered text</p>
```

✦ **Value:** The color, size, and link destination, for example, specified in an attribute. For example, you can specify a hexadecimal number as the value for a color attribute. An example of a value for the `bgcolor` attribute of the `<body>` tag (which controls overall page appearance) could be `"red"` or `"#CC0000"`.

One last thing: *Nesting* is the order in which tags appear. If a `<strong>` tag is applied, it looks like this: `<strong>This text is bold</strong>`. Add an italic tag and you see `<strong><em>This text is bold and italic.</em></strong>`. Notice the in-to-out placement of the tags: You work your way from the inside to the outside when closing tags.

Chapter 4: Working with Images

In This Chapter

- ✔ **Making images work for the Web**
- ✔ **Touring the Property inspector**
- ✔ **Inserting Photoshop files and working with Smart Objects**
- ✔ **Aligning images and adding space around them**
- ✔ **Creating backgrounds from images**
- ✔ **Creating a rollover**
- ✔ **Inserting a Flash movie on a page**

*P*lacing images that are interesting and informative is one of the most exciting parts of building a Web page. In this chapter, you see how to insert and optimize native Photoshop (PSD) files directly in Dreamweaver and how to take care of basic needs such as resizing, cropping, and positioning an image. You also find out how to create interesting backgrounds and create easy rollovers.

If you plan to follow any steps in this chapter, create a site or have a practice site already open. Images are much-needed linked assets on your page — you don't want to lose track of them in your filing system. If you don't know how to create a site, read Chapter 3 of this minibook.

Creating Images for the Web

Placing images isn't difficult, but you must consider the formats they're saved in and their file sizes. (See Book IV, Chapter 10 for details on selecting the correct format and using the Save for Web & Devices feature in Photoshop.)

Putting images on a Web page requires planning to make sure that sizes are exactly what you want. You also need to make sure that you don't prevent a page from loading quickly by having too many images.

If you look in the lower right corner of the Document window, you see the page file size and its approximate download time. In Figure 4-1, the page file size is 33k (kilobytes), and the download time is 5 seconds, based on the assumed connection speed of 56K (kilobits) per second. You can change the download speed by choosing Edit⇨Preferences (Windows) or Dreamweaver⇨Preferences (Mac), selecting the Status Bar category, and clicking the Connection Speed drop-down list.

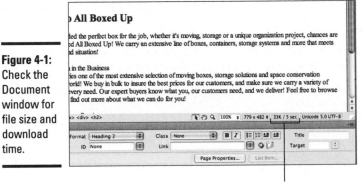

Figure 4-1: Check the Document window for file size and download time.

File size and download time

TIP

The jury is always out when you want to know how fast a page should download, but fewer than 15 seconds is a good target. Unless you have truly compelling content, you'll probably lose viewers if they have to wait any longer. If your page requires more time, consider distributing its content across several pages.

Putting Images on a Page

Putting images on a Web page in Dreamweaver is easier than ever, mostly because of its integration with other Adobe products. You can use menu items, copy and paste, and even drag and drop images on your Dreamweaver page. In the following sections, you not only find out how to place images but also receive some helpful general tips related to putting graphics on the Web.

Inserting an image

If you're preparing images ahead of time, save or move the optimized images into your site folder. You can select an image from anywhere in your directory — it just adds the extra step of copying the image into your site folder.

After you open a page, you can insert an image by following these steps:

1. **Click somewhere on the page to position the cursor wherever you want to place the image.**

2. **Locate the Common category from the drop-down list at the top of the Insert panel and click the Insert Image button or choose Insert⇨Image.**

   If Image isn't the default for your Insert Image button, click and hold the arrow to the right of the button and choose Image from the drop-down list.

   The Select Image Source dialog box appears.

3. **Navigate to the spot where your image is located and click OK (Windows) or Choose (Mac) to place the selected image.**

   If your images are in your site folder, you can click the Site Root button in the Select Image Source dialog box to navigate there quickly. If an image isn't in your site folder, an alert box asks whether you want to copy the file there now.

4. **If you're prompted to copy the image to your site's root folder, click Yes. When the Copy File As dialog box opens, verify that the name is correct and click Save.**

   The Image Tag Accessibility Attributes dialog box requests that you enter alt text. (For more on alt text, see the nearby sidebar, "Gotta have that alt text.")

5. **Type a word or three that best describes your image (such as** Our Family Photo**) in the Alt text field and click OK.**

   The image is placed.

**Book VI
Chapter 4**

Working with Images

Gotta have that alt text

You've probably seen the term *alt text* a gazillion times: It's the text that appears before an image does while a Web page is loading. Alt text also appears as a tooltip when you hover the mouse cursor over an image in a Web page in certain browsers.

Alt text is helpful because it tells viewers something about an image before it appears, but it's also necessary for viewers who turn off the option to view graphics, such as in certain e-mail applications, or folks using Web-reading programs, like those for the visually impaired. U.S. federal regulations require alt tags for any work completed for federal agencies, and the tags are helpful for people with slow Internet connections.

In addition, alt text is a valuable tool for indexing image content for search engines: Search engines such as Google, MSN, and Yahoo! all use alt text as a key method of indexing images for their respective image search listings.

To assign or change alt text to an image that has been placed already, type some descriptive copy in the Alt text field in the Property inspector.

Dragging and dropping an image

In addition to inserting images from the Insert panel or application menus, you can drag and place images directly from the Files panel to the page. If you're dragging an image, the cursor follows it while you move it around the document; release the mouse button when the cursor marks the correct spot where you'd like to drop the image.

If you're taking advantage of the Adobe Bridge workflow, you can leave Bridge running and drag images as you need them directly from the Bridge window into your Dreamweaver page. You can access Bridge by choosing File➪Browse in Bridge.

If the image is a native Photoshop (PSD) or Fireworks (PNG) file, the Image Preview dialog box appears, giving you the opportunity to optimize the image before placing it.

You can also drag and drop an optimized image from your desktop or other folders into a Dreamweaver page. If an image is not in your site folder, you have the opportunity to copy that image to your site folder when it's placed.

Getting to Know the Property Inspector

Many of the tools you use when working with images are located in the Property inspector (see Figure 4-2).

Figure 4-2:
The Property inspector's image-editing options.

You can choose from these properties when an image is selected:

✦ **Editing the original:** If you want to make a quick change, it shouldn't have to involve a lot of directory navigation on your operating system. To edit your original image file, select it and click the Edit in Photoshop button on the Property inspector. The image is launched in Photoshop, where you can make changes and save the image again.

You can select the default image editing application for different image file types by choosing Preferences⇨Files Types/Editors. Photoshop CS5 is the primary editor for almost every image type by default.

✦ **Optimizing an image:** You can optimize images directly from the Dreamweaver page, but this method doesn't provide quite the same abilities as when you place a native Photoshop or Fireworks file, because the image you're selecting has already been optimized. It may already be a GIF or JPEG file — and yes, you can reduce the number of colors in the GIF or convert a JPEG to a GIF, but you can't increase color levels or quality on these images, because they're not linked to the original image file.

✦ **Cropping an image:** This feature is sure to become a favorite because you can make cropping decisions right on your Dreamweaver page. Simply click the Crop tool, acknowledge the warning message that you're editing the image, and then click and drag the handles to the size you want. Press the Enter key and you're done!

✦ **Resampling an image:** You may have heard that you shouldn't resize an image placed on a Dreamweaver page because if you were making the image larger, it would become pixilated, and if you were making the image smaller, you were wasting lots of bandwidth downloading the file. Fortunately, you can now use the Resample button on the Property inspector after you resize the image. Just keep in mind that making the image larger still causes some quality issues, so you should reduce the file size before clicking the Resample button. If you need to make an image considerably larger, find the original and optimize it to the proper size.

To resize an image, you can either click and drag out the lower right handle of the image or type a pixel value in the W (Width) and H (Height) text fields in the Property inspector.

✦ **Brightness and contrast:** If high quality is important to you, open your original image in Photoshop and make tonal corrections with professional digital imaging tools. If volume and quickly getting lots of images and pages posted are important, take advantage of the Brightness and Contrast controls built into Adobe Dreamweaver. Simply click the Brightness and Contrast button in the Property inspector, acknowledge the Dreamweaver dialog box, and adjust the sliders to create the best image.

✦ **Sharpen:** Add crispness to images by applying the Sharpness controls available in Dreamweaver. As with some of the other image editing features in Dreamweaver, you're better off using the Unsharp mask filter in Photoshop; in a pinch, this feature is a quick and useful tool to take advantage of. To use the Sharpening feature, click the Sharpen button, acknowledge the warning that you're changing the image, and use the slider to sharpen the image.

Placing Photoshop Files

If you've created artwork or prepared images in Photoshop, you can place original PSD files directly in your pages. The Image Preview window lets you save Photoshop files into Web-ready image formats such as GIF, JPEG, and PNG and scale and crop artwork before it's placed on the page.

Photoshop Smart Objects

The ability to work with Photoshop files is useful for most designers who depend on Photoshop as part of their workflow. When you place Photoshop files on a page, Dreamweaver creates a *Smart Object,* an image that maintains a connection to the original Photoshop file from which it was created.

The image displays an icon that lets you know whether the original file was updated, and you can apply the changes in the original file to the image in one click.

To place a Photoshop file in your page, follow these steps:

1. **Click wherever you want to place the new image and then click the Image object in the Insert panel's Common category.**

2. **When the Select Image Source dialog box appears, browse and select a Photoshop PSD file and then click Choose/OK to select the image.**

3. **The Image Preview dialog box appears, where you can optimize, crop, scale, and save your image in the Web-friendly GIF, JPEG, or PNG format, as shown in Figure 4-3.**

4. **On the Options tab, select from the Format drop-down list the file format you want to save your image in, and choose from the Quality drop-down list the quality settings that best suit your image.**

   You can use the Saved Settings drop-down list at the top of the dialog box to choose an image-quality preset.

5. **(Optional) Click the File tab to switch to the File options, and then enter settings to scale your image or use the Crop tool at the bottom of the preview window to crop your image.**

6. **Click OK to save the image.**

7. **When the Save Web Image dialog box appears, navigate to your site's root folder and click OK to save the image in the appropriate folder (for instance, your default images folder).**

   If the Image Tab Accessibility Attributes dialog box appears, type a short description of the image in the alternate text field and click OK to place the image.

The new image is placed and a small icon appears in its upper left corner. This Smart Object indicator shows two green arrows, indicating that the image is up-to-date.

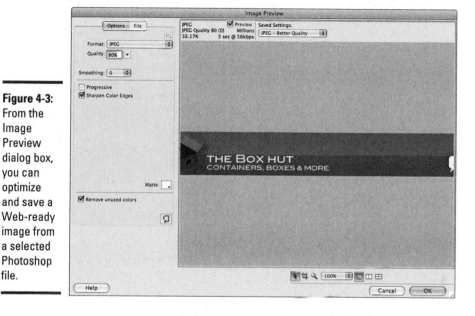

Figure 4-3: From the Image Preview dialog box, you can optimize and save a Web-ready image from a selected Photoshop file.

Select the image you placed in the preceding step list and locate the Original text field in the Property inspector — this field displays the location of the original Photoshop file. To edit the image, you can simply click the Edit in Photoshop button on the right side of the Property inspector to open the source file in Photoshop.

Updating Photoshop Smart Objects

If you make changes to the original Photoshop file, the image you placed in the page displays a red-and-green arrow icon to let you know that it isn't up-to-date.

 To update a Smart Object when you see its indicator, shown in Figure 4-4, select the image and click the Update from Original button on the Property inspector to apply the new changes to the placed image.

Figure 4-4:
The original
has been
modified.

Moving the original PSD file connected to a page image displays an alert icon on the image and disables the link between the two. Keep original PSD files in a set location and be sure to revise the location of your source file by selecting the image and updating the original in the Property inspector.

Aligning an Image

Images and their adjacent text sit on the same baseline as a default, forcing text to run in one line to the right of the image. To control the wrapping of the text around the image, change the alignment of the image by selecting the image and then choosing an option from the Align drop-down list in the Property inspector.

The Align drop-down list provides these options:

✦ **Default:** Baseline alignment is used (described in the second bullet).

✦ **Baseline (Default):** The bottom of the image aligns with the baseline of the current line of text.

✦ **Top:** The image aligns with the top of the tallest item in the line of text.

✦ **Middle:** The baseline of the current line of text aligns with the middle of the image.

✦ **Bottom:** The bottom of the image aligns with the baseline of the current line of text.

✦ **Text Top:** The image aligns with the top of the tallest text in the line, usually (but not always) the same as ALIGN=top.

✦ **Absolute Middle:** The middle of the current line aligns with the middle of the image.

✦ **Absolute Bottom:** The bottom of the image aligns with the bottom of the current line of text.

✦ **Left:** The image aligns to the left, and text flushes to the right of the image.

✦ **Right:** The image aligns to the right, and text flushes to the left of the image.

Adding Space around the Image

You may want to add space around an image to keep the text from butting up to it. To create a space around an image, enter values into the H Space and V Space text fields in the Property inspector.

If you want to add space to only one side of the image, CSS (Cascading Style Sheets) provides the ability to add margins to only one side of an image. See Chapter 5 of this minibook for more information on using CSS to format text and page elements.

In addition, you can open the image in Photoshop and choose Image➪ Canvas Size. In the Canvas Size dialog box that appears, click the middle-left square in the Anchor section and add a value in pixels to the total image size. Click the middle-right square to add the size to the left side of the image.

Using an Image As a Background

Creating backgrounds for Web pages is fun and can be pursued in more ways than most people would imagine. You can create a repeating pattern with a single small image, create a watermark, or use a large image to fill an entire background. As a default, an HTML background repeats the selected image until it fills the screen. In conjunction with CSS properties, you can control or eliminate repeating behavior and even set precise positioning for a single background image.

If you're filling a background with a pattern, be sure to create a pattern image that has no discernable edges. (In Photoshop, choose Filter➪Texture➪Texturizer to see some good choices in the Texturizer dialog box.)

To use to your advantage the default, repeated tiling for a background image, follow these steps:

1. **In Photoshop, choose File➪New to create a new image.**

2. **In the New dialog box that appears, create an image that's much wider than it is high, choose RGB, choose 72 dpi, and then click OK.**

   For example, enter **1000** in the Width text field and **20** in the Height text field.

3. **Select a foreground and background color to create a blend; then use the Gradient tool to Shift+drag from the top to the bottom of the image area to create a gradient fill.**

4. **Choose File⇨Save for Web, save the image as a JPEG file in your site's Web content folder, and then close the image.**

   See Book IV, Chapter 10 for more about the Save for Web & Devices feature.

5. **In Dreamweaver, choose Modify⇨Page Properties or click the Page Properties button in the Property inspector to place the image as a background image in your Web page.**

   If the Page Properties button isn't visible, click the page — be sure not to select another element, such as an image.

6. **In the Page Properties dialog box that appears, click the Browse button to the right of the background image, navigate to the location of your saved background image, and then click Choose/OK; click OK in the Page Properties dialog box.**

   The image appears in the background, repeating and creating a cool background gradient across the page!

Depending on the size and resolution of a user's monitor, your background image may be forced to repeat. Repeating a background image can yield some creative results, as shown in Figure 4-5.

Figure 4-5:
An image set as a background repeats horizontally and vertically by default.

In certain cases, you may not see your background until you click the Preview/Debug in Browser button and preview the page in your default browser.

Creating Rollovers

In Dreamweaver, you can insert image objects, including image placeholders, *rollover* images (images that change when a viewer rolls the mouse over the image), navigation bars, and Fireworks HTML. You access these image objects by choosing Insert⇨Image Objects.

To create a rollover image, follow these steps:

1. **Create the images to be used as the rollover.**

   You can generate these images in Fireworks, Illustrator, Photoshop, or any other application capable of saving images optimized for the Web.

 2. **Place the cursor on the page wherever you want the rollover to appear and choose Insert⇨Image Objects⇨Rollover Image or click the Rollover Image button in the Insert panel.**

   The Insert Rollover Image dialog box, shown in Figure 4-6, appears.

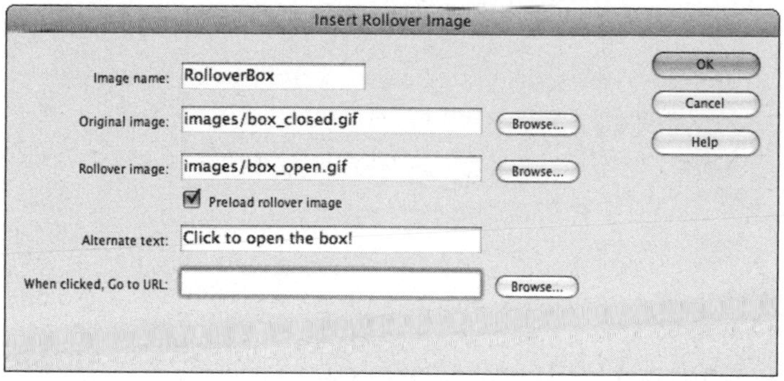

Figure 4-6:
The Insert
Rollover
Image
dialog box.

3. **Type an image name without spaces in the Image Name text field.**

   This name is used in the script creating the rollover.

4. **Click the Browse buttons to the right of the Original Image and Rollover Image text fields to locate the image that you want to appear as a default on the page and the image that appears only when someone hovers the mouse over the image.**

   Figure 4-7 shows an example of original and rollover images.

Figure 4-7:
Rollovers
are made
easy in
Dream-
weaver.

5. **Leave the Preload Rollover Image check box selected.**

   This option downloads the rollover image when the page is downloaded to avoid delays in rollovers.

6. **Type appropriately descriptive alt text in the Alt text field.**

7. **In the When Clicked, Go to URL text field, tell Dreamweaver where viewers are directed when they click your rollover image.**

   You can either click the Browse button to locate another page in your site or enter a URL. *Note:* If you are linking to a different Web site, you need to include the `http://` prefix at the beginning of the URL.

8. **Click OK.**

   The rollover image is created on the page.

9. **To preview the new rollover image, choose File⇨Preview in Browser or click the Live View button on the Document toolbar.**

If you don't yet have a real link to use for a button or hyperlink, you can enter a pound sign (#) to create a dead link. The link or button appears clickable but doesn't go anywhere when clicked. This option is better than hitting the space bar to create an empty space as a link, as that will display a Page Not Found error when clicked.

Inserting Media Content

Dreamweaver makes it easy to enhance Web pages by allowing you to insert interactive content such as Flash (SWF), Flash Video (FLV), and Shockwave files.

Follow these steps to place a Flash file on your Dreamweaver page:

1. **Put the cursor on the page wherever you want to insert the Flash file.**

2. **Choose Insert⇨Media⇨SWF.**

   The Select File dialog box appears.

3. **Navigate to the SWF file that you want to place and click OK (Windows) or Choose (Mac) to select the file.**

4. **In the Object Tag Accessibility Attributes dialog box, type a descriptive title for the movie in the Title field and click OK.**

   The Flash file is placed on the page.

5. **On the Property inspector, click the Play button to preview your new Flash movie.**

   You can also adjust settings for your movie, as shown in Figure 4-8.

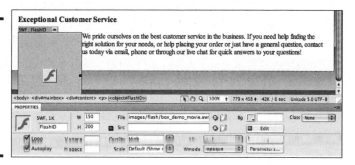

Figure 4-8: Use the Property inspector to adjust and preview Flash movies

Chapter 5: Putting Text on the Page

Adding text to a Web page requires more than just typing on the page. You must carefully plan your Web pages so that search engines (and viewers) can easily find relevant content on your Web site. In this chapter, you read about the fundamentals of text formatting for Web pages, from the basic principles of choosing a font size and font family to spell checking text and implementing Cascading Style Sheets (CSS).

Because you can assign type properties quickly and update several instances in a few easy steps with CSS, it's viewed as the most efficient and preferred method of applying text attributes on a Web page. When you create text for the body of your page, include keywords that provide descriptions of your site's content. This strategy makes your page more relevant to search engines and viewers.

As a default, Dreamweaver formats all text on your page with CSS, which is the standard for formatting and styling text. In Dreamweaver CS3 and earlier, you still had the option to enable and use archaic <font> tags to format text if you so chose; this option has been removed from the CS5 preferences. Now you can format with font tags only by manually inserting <font> tags by choosing Insert➪Tag or by hand-coding methods. By default, when you format text directly from the Property inspector, CSS styles are always created to save and apply the formatting you choose.

Adding Text

To add text to your Web page, simply click the page wherever you want the text to appear; an insertion point appears where you can start typing. You can add text right to the page, in a CSS layer, or in the cell of a table.

Formatting text

Formatting text in Dreamweaver can be as simple as formatting text in any word processing application or even applications such as Illustrator and InDesign. By using the Property inspector, you can easily apply basic font attributes, such as color, typeface, size, and alignment options. Clicking the Text category of the Insert panel gives you several different HTML text tags to apply to selected text (see Figure 5-1).

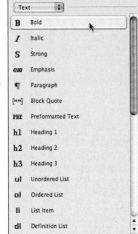

Figure 5-1:
You can
use the Text
category of
the Insert
panel
to apply
basic text
formatting.

Most options in the Text category are apparent, but here's a breakdown of some text tags that may be unfamiliar to you. To use these tags, simply select the text that you want the tag to be applied to and then click the tag on the Insert panel. Here's a description of a few options on this panel:

✦ **Strong:** Choosing this option bolds the selected text.

✦ **Emphasis:** Choose this option to indicate emphasis; it looks like italic.

Dreamweaver favors the accessibility friendly `<strong>` and `<em>` tags over `<b>` and `<i>`, though both bold and italicize text, respectively, `<strong>` and `<em>`, are used in almost all cases, even when you click the B and I buttons.

✦ **h1/h2/h3:** These heading tags create three heading levels; h1 is the largest.

✦ **UL (Unordered List):** This setting creates a bulleted list from the selected text.

✦ **OL (Ordered List):** Use this option to create an ordered (numbered) list from the selected text.

✦ **DL (Definition List):** The definition list creates a structured, non-bulleted list best suited for term and definition style formatting.

When you press the Enter or Return key, a `<p>` tag is created automatically in the HTML source code. This tag may create more space than you like between lines and create new list items. Pressing Shift+Enter (Windows) or Shift+Return (Mac) creates a `<br>` tag, which is essentially a line break or soft return. See Figure 5-2.

Using the Property inspector to style text

Use the Property inspector, shown in Figure 5-3, to apply HTML tags and build CSS classes to format text color, face, size, and other characteristics. The Property inspector is divided into two views: HTML and CSS. You can toggle them by using the buttons on the left side of the panel.

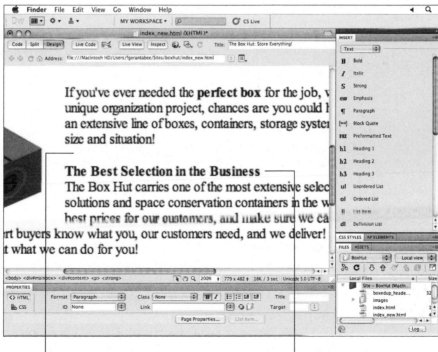

Figure 5-2: A new paragraph break and a soft return or line break.

Hard return

Soft return

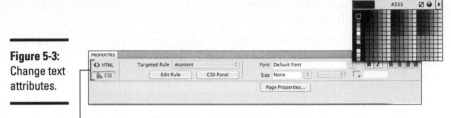

Figure 5-3:
Change text
attributes.

Click to toggle between HTML and CSS properties

Here's what all the buttons on the Property inspector mean:

✦ **Format (HTML):** Use the Format drop-down list to apply HTML tags that
format an entire paragraph, including heading tags (Heading 1 through
Heading 6) that are generally applied to headers and titles, the paragraph tag, and the preformatted text tag. You can easily fine-tune each
of these tags' attributes (color, size, and font family, for example) later
by using CSS.

Note that Heading 1 is the largest format size (on average, about equivalent to 24-point text), and Heading 6 is the smallest. It makes sense if you
think about how these tags were originally used to create technical documents and outlines on the Internet, where text contained in Heading 1
should be treated as more important than text in Heading 2 or Heading 3.

The last choice in the Format drop-down list is Preformatted. Sometimes
you want the browser to display text exactly the way you composed it —
with indents, line breaks, and extra spaces. You can line up text this way
if you choose Preformatted; it's not pretty, but for down-and-dirty lists
and columns, it can work well.

✦ **ID (HTML):** This setting applies a CSS ID style to an element. IDs are a
specific type of CSS rule (or *selector*) that are used to store formatting
information unique to a single item on the page (for instance, positioning information for a container).

✦ **Class (HTML):** This drop-down list applies an existing class style to a
selection on the page. Class styles can be created with the Property
inspector (discussed later in this chapter) or directly from the CSS
styles panel.

✦ **Link (HTML):** Type a hyperlink (such as `http://www.wiley.com`) or
click the folder icon to browse and link to another page within your Web
site. The selected text becomes linked (preview your page in a browser
or enable Live View to see it work).

✦ **Target (HTML):** Choose where the linked target will appear. (Read about targets in Chapter 6 of this minibook.)

✦ **Bold (HTML/CSS):** Bold selected text.

✦ **Italic (HTML/CSS):** Italicize selected text.

✦ **Alignment (CSS):** You can click the alignment buttons on the toolbar to apply left, center, and right alignment. To revert to the default left alignment, click the selected alignment button again.

✦ **Unordered List (HTML):** Automatically insert bullets in front of listed items. As you advance in the use of Cascading Style Sheets, you can apply many more attributes to lists, including customizing the bullets.

✦ **Ordered List (HTML):** Automatically numbers each additional line of text every time you press the Enter (Windows) or Return (Mac) key. To force the text to another line without adding automatic numbering, press Shift+Enter (Windows) or Shift+Return (Mac).

✦ **Text Outdent (HTML):** Undo pressing the Indent with the Text Outdent button. This option removes the `<blockquote>` tag that the Text Indent button creates.

✦ **Text Indent (HTML):** Use this option to indent text. Simply put the cursor in the paragraph of text that you want to indent and press the Text Indent button. A `<blockquote>` tag is applied. You can apply this tag multiple times to a paragraph to indent it even further.

✦ **Targeted Rule (CSS):** Modify an existing CSS rule or create a new one. This drop-down list makes it clear whether you are creating a new rule or modifying an existing one in the Property inspector.

✦ **Edit Rule / CSS Panel buttons (CSS):** For the rule shown in the Targeted Rule drop-down list, you can either edit the properties and values for that rule in the CSS Rule Definition dialog box or view it in the CSS Styles panel on the right, respectively.

✦ **Font (CSS):** Use this drop-down list to select a font family. The *font* is the typeface you choose for displaying text. The lack of typeface selection isn't a restriction in Dreamweaver, but rather in Web design as a whole. Keep in mind that what font the viewer sees on your Web page is based on the availability of the fonts on that user's computer. For this reason, font sets are limited to basic system fonts that are installed on most every computer, regardless of operating system.

The viewer may not have fonts that you load in your font sets, so try to stick to such common typefaces as the ones already included in the existing Dreamweaver font sets.

Assigning and editing fonts

When a viewer opens a page referencing a font set, the text is displayed using the first available font in the font family. If the first font face on the list isn't available, the next font face is referenced, continuing down the list in the font family until a font in the font set is found on the viewer's computer. If you choose Edit Font List from the Font drop-down list, the Edit Font List dialog box appears (see the figure).

Click the existing font lists to see which fonts are included in each set. You can add new fonts to the sets by clicking the double arrow pointing from the Available Fonts panel into the Chosen Fonts panel. Delete a font from an existing font list by clicking the font in the Chosen Fonts panel and clicking the double arrow pointing toward the Available Fonts panel. You can even create an entirely new list yourself by clicking the plus sign (+) in the upper left corner of the Edit Font List dialog box.

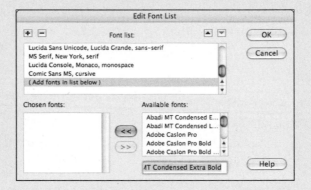

- ✦ **Size (CSS):** Using the Font Size drop-down list, you can apply a fixed font size from 9 to 36 (pixels) or enter a value by entering it directly. You can use the relative sizes shown (x-small and small, for example), which resize the font relatively larger or smaller according to the user's browser font size preferences. If you don't change the font size, it defaults to 12 pixels (px). By default, the unit of measurement is set to pixels, but you can use the neighboring drop-down list to set other units of measurement, including points, picas, ems, and more.

  Keep in mind that the user can set browser preferences to override the size settings you've chosen.

- ✦ **Color (CSS):** Assign a color to your selection by clicking the swatch icon and selecting a swatch from the panel that appears. Colors are represented in HTML and CSS by *hexadecimal codes,* 6-character codes that represent the RGB (Red, Green, Blue) values which form that color. This code is shown at the top of the Swatches panel whenever you select a color.

Spell-checking your text

You can spell-check only the file you have open or multiple files by choosing Commands⇨Check Spelling. From the Check Spelling dialog box, shown in Figure 5-4, you can choose to add words to your personal dictionary, ignore words, or change the spelling of words.

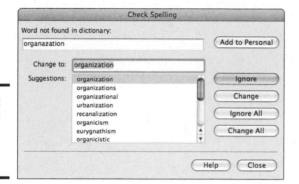

Figure 5-4: Make sure that your spelling is correct.

Understanding Cascading Style Sheets

Using *Cascading Style Sheets* (CSS) is a standard method for styling text and other elements on Web pages. The powerful style sheet design tool allows you to assign properties to type and other page elements quickly and update all instances in a few easy steps. The reason for the name Cascading Style Sheets is because certain *cascading rules* apply when several styles (and style sheets) are used at the same time.

If you apply many different styles to a page, whether they're internally built on the page or linked to external style sheets, you may have conflicts. Conflicts occur when two (or more) styles assign different properties to the same element. For example, if you specify in an internal style sheet that any bolded element is blue but an external style sheet instructs the browser to display any bolded element as red, which style wins? The blue instruction from the internal style sheet wins. If conflicts occur in external style sheets, you can set the order of importance by using the up and down arrows. By default, the Web page's style sheet overrides the browser's default values.

Style sheets are consistent across most modern browser versions, but some older browsers may not provide consistent (if any) support for CSS. Always preview pages in multiple browsers or use the Check Browser Compatibility button (located under the Check Browser Compatibility list on the Document toolbar) to test CSS properties you've used against a variety of browsers and versions.

We definitely offer the quick-and-dirty course on CSS, but if you're interested in finding out more, check out *HTML, XHTML, and CSS All-in-One For Dummies* by Andy Harris.

Dreamweaver CS5 uses Cascading Styles Sheets (CSS) exclusively to format text and no longer provides direct support for <font> tags. You can still add <font> tags if you absolutely need to by choosing Insert⊏>Tag.

Dreamweaver offers CSS starter pages that have CSS layouts available and that include CSS hints visible only in Code view (see Figure 5-5). Find the CSS starter pages by choosing File⊏>New⊏>Blank Page⊏>HTML Template.

Figure 5-5:
Helpful CSS tips are built into the CSS starter pages.

Using CSS for text

Using Cascading Style Sheets in Dreamweaver is extremely intuitive; simply create a blank HTML page, add and select some text, and begin styling your selection directly in the Property inspector CSS view by selecting properties for color, size, typeface, and more.

Assigning formatting to a selection opens the New CSS Rule Dialog box, allowing you to save choices you've made into a new CSS rule (or *style*). You can choose a name, selector type, and location for the new rule.

Several types of selectors determine which style properties should be applied and where. When Dreamweaver finds a selector, it applies the properties and values you've chosen. You make formatting choices once and reapply them repeatedly in a single click!

(You can find out how to take advantage of advanced properties for creating layouts in Chapter 8 of this minibook.)

Creating a new tag style

Creating a tag (or an *element*) selector is a simple and safe route for new users to understand CSS because you can work with existing HTML tags, such as P, H1, and H2. Using existing element tags on your page, you can choose to apply automatic formatting wherever certain HTML tags are used. For instance, you can make anything inside a `<strong>` tag automatically italic, 20 pixels, and red.

To create a tag style with the Property inspector, follow these steps:

1. **Open an HTML page that contains text.**

2. **On the Property inspector, click the HTML button on the left side of the panel to display the Property inspector in HTML view.**

3. **Select a line of text and bold it using the B button located in the Property inspector.**

4. **Switch to CSS view of the Property inspector by clicking the CSS button on the far left side of that panel.**

   The goal is to assign definitive style information to the tag that bolds text, so any bold text on the page also appears red.

5. **Leave the bolded text selected, and in the Property Inspector select <New CSS Rule> from the Targeted Rule drop-down list.**

6. **With the text still selected, use the color selector on the right side of the Property inspector (located below the B and I buttons) to select a red color to apply to the selected, bold text.**

   The New CSS Rule dialog box appears, as shown in Figure 5-6.

7. **From the Selector Type drop-down list, choose Tag (Redefines an HTML Element); choose Strong from the Selector Name drop-down list; choose (This Document Only) from the Rule Definition drop-down list.**

   The selector type determines how the formatting will be applied to elements on the page. Tag styles change the appearance of any element formatted with a specific HTML tag.

New CSS Rule

Selector Type:

Choose a contextual selector type for your CSS rule.

Tag (redefines an HTML element)

OK

Cancel

Selector Name:

Choose or enter a name for your selector.

strong

This selector name will apply your rule to
all <strong> elements.

Less Specific   More Specific

Rule Definition:

Choose where your rule will be defined.

(This document only)

Help

Figure 5-6:
The CSS
Rule dialog
box.

8. Click OK to create the new tag style and close the panel.

Now, every time you apply the <strong> tag to make bold text (using the
B button or other shortcuts), that bold text also appears red. You've
created a tag style that determines how bold text appears any time it
appears in a document.

You can further refine this new tag style by selecting any bold text and continuing to modify text properties from the Property inspector, as shown in
Figure 5-7.

If you'd like to edit and fine-tune the rule you've created, you can click the
Edit Rule button below the Targeted Rule drop-down list to open the CSS
Rule Definition dialog box. This dialog box opens by default to the Type category, where you can modify type related properties. Some common type
properties you'll see in this category are as follows:

✦ **Font family:** Notice that you can apply a font family by using the Font
drop-down list. This method is preferred for assigning a font family.

✦ **Font size:** Enter a text size and then, with the Unit drop-down list to the
right of the size, enter it in pixels, points, inches, centimeters, and other
units of measurement. By specifying a size and unit of measurement
here — 12 pixels, for example — you can ensure that the text appears as
relatively the same size on both the Windows and Macintosh platforms.

✦ **Line height:** By assigning a size in any unit, you can define the space
between lines of text. For example, if the type size is 12, the line height
of 24 pixels is essentially the same as double spacing. If you come from
the typesetting or design world, it works much like leading.

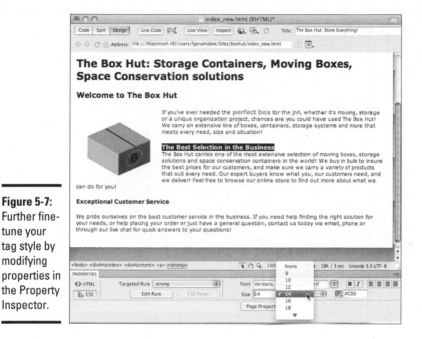

Figure 5-7:
Further fine-tune your tag style by modifying properties in the Property Inspector.

✦ **Font decoration:** Hmm, if you want it, get it here! Blinking isn't a good idea: It's just plain B-A-D and also not compatible on all browsers. Try to use underlines to make key text stand out, or use underlines to create a line underneath paragraph or page headers.

Don't like underlines under links? Create a tag style for the <a> tag (this HTML tag is the one used to create a link) and select None in the Decoration drop-down list.

✦ **Font-Weight:** Make text lighter or heavier with this drop-down list. Just so you know, a value of 700 is the typical boldness of bold text; any heavier is bolder than bold.

✦ **Font-Variant:** Use this drop-down list to choose small caps.

You may be wondering why Normal is a choice in the Style drop-down list. It's because you may have defined small caps, for example, as the variant for all instances of the <strong> tag but then decided that on one page you want to override that attribute. By creating a style defined in the document only with Normal selected in variant, you can override the style (small caps) definition on the external style sheet.

✦ **Font transform:** Choose from Capitalize, Uppercase, Lowercase, or None.

✦ **Color:** Assign a color to your selector by clicking the arrow in the lower right corner of the Color definition swatch or type a number in the Color text box.

Block level versus inline

You may find that when you assign certain properties, you see varying results because some properties you select affect only block-level elements as compared to inline elements. *Block-level* elements apply to elements that take up their own horizontal space on a page, such as an entire paragraph or an ordered or unordered list. If you create a P element style and change the line spacing, the space takes effect within the block-level element.

An *inline element* is one that applies formatting to tags or items that fall within the flow with text, such as the `<strong>` tag. If you choose to apply line spacing to the b element, the leading in paragraphs that contain the `<strong>` tag aren't affected.

You'll eventually figure out which properties work with which tags. Just keep this point in mind so that you're not dumbfounded when some properties don't work as expected!

When you're finished fine-tuning your tag style, click Apply at the bottom of the dialog box to see your changes. You can also click OK to apply your changes and exit the dialog box.

Creating a new class style

For more styling control over pages, you can create *class selectors,* which are named styles for body, text, headlines, subheads, and other elements. Unlike with tag selectors, you can choose just about any name for a class and apply its style selectively to items if and when you want.

If you choose properties that work on a variety of elements, you can get a lot of mileage from a single class style in many places throughout your page. Essentially, class styles are like creating your own character or paragraph styles, if you're familiar with that feature from common page-layout applications, such as InDesign.

This time, you can also make your new rule available to more than one page in your site by defining a new external style sheet. This method saves your rules in an external file that can be attached to several pages at a time.

Follow these steps to create a class style from the CSS Styles panel:

1. **Locate the CSS panel, off to the right, and click the New CSS Rule button at the bottom or choose Format⇨CSS Styles⇨New.**

   The New CSS Rule dialog box appears (refer to Figure 5-6).

2. **From the Selector Type drop-down list, choose Class (Can Apply to Any HTML Element).**

3. **In the Selector Name text box, enter a name for your new class.**

   You can enter any name you want, but make sure that it has no spaces and is descriptive of how you'll use it. `Reallycoolstyle` is a bad name; `headlinestyle` is a better name. Dreamweaver inserts the period at the front of the style name because it's a necessary naming convention.

4. **From the Rule Definition drop-down list at the bottom, choose (New Stylesheet File).**

5. **Click OK.**

   The Save Style Sheet File As dialog box appears. Locate your site folder (or if you haven't defined a site, a folder where you'll keep all relevant information, such as image files and pages for your site).

6. **Enter a name for the style sheet.**

   Enter an appropriate name, such as **main.css** or **basic.css** if it's the main set of styles you're creating for your Web site. (Dreamweaver will add the mandatory `.css` extension at the end of the filename.)

7. **Leave the URL as is and the Relative To drop-down list set to Document.**

8. **Click Save.**

   You've created a new `.css` file, or an external stylesheet. The CSS Rule Definition dialog box appears.

   In this dialog box, you can create the set of attributes that you want included in the CSS definition for the style you're creating. As you might notice, this dialog box is the same one you work with when you edit an existing CSS style (see the previous section). The difference with the tag and class styles lies only in the fact that you must apply a class style to an element using the Property inspector (via the Class or Style drop-down lists).

9. **Apply a font, size, style, line height (leading), and any other attributes that you couldn't apply to text using straight HTML coding.**

10. **After you select attributes for your class style, click OK to close the dialog box and return to your page.**

Now you can apply the CSS class style to some text. When applying a class style, you can choose to apply it to only some text or to an entire paragraph of text. Follow these steps to apply a class style to an entire paragraph:

1. **Place the cursor in a paragraph of text or click and drag to select a line of text.**

2. **If the Property inspector isn't visible, choose Window⇨Properties. Click the HTML button on the left side of the Property inspector to toggle to HTML view.**

3. **From the Class drop-down list in the Property inspector, select a new style, as shown in Figure 5-8.**

   The new style is applied to the selection.

Figure 5-8:
Apply a class style to a selected piece of text by using the Class drop-down list.

Chapter 6: Linking It Together

*L*inks are a major and necessary component of any Web site. You must incorporate links on your Web site; this way, viewers can easily navigate your site to see the information they're seeking. In this chapter, we show you how to add links easily and effectively in Dreamweaver.

The Basics of Linking

Links, or *hyperlinks*, are navigational aids; viewers click links to go to other Web pages, to a downloadable resource file, to an e-mail address, or a specific spot on a Web page (known as an *anchor*). As you create the first link from one of your Web pages to another, you've essentially created a Web site — it may be a small site, but it's a start. While you're still in the small site stage, here are a couple of recommendations to keep in mind as you add more pages and create more links, making your site even bigger:

✦ Two kinds of links exist:

- *Internal links* connect viewers to other parts of your Web site.

- *External links* connect viewers to other pages or content outside your site.

We show you how to create both kinds of links in this chapter.

✦ Before you start working with any pages to be linked, make sure that you've created a Dreamweaver site (see Chapter 3 of this minibook for details); the site helps you locate local files to link to, and later you can check and validate links between pages in your site.

Creating Internal Links

Internal links, an essential part of any user-friendly site, help viewers easily and quickly navigate to other pages on your Web site.

If you need to change filenames after they've been linked somewhere, do so *only* within the Files panel in Dreamweaver. Otherwise, you end up with broken links. Take a look at the "Resolving Link Errors" section, later in this chapter, to find out how to change the names of linked files without breaking the links.

You can create a link from text or an image (such as a button graphic). The following sections outline several methods you can use for creating links.

Using the Hyperlink dialog box to create a link

To create a hyperlink with text as the link, you can use the Hyperlink command:

1. **Select some text, make sure that the Common category of the Insert panel is forward, and click the Hyperlink button.**

   The Hyperlink dialog box appears with your selected text already entered in the Text field, as shown in Figure 6-1. (You can also choose Insert⇨Hyperlink.)

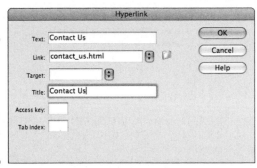

Figure 6-1: Create a link from selected text with the Hyperlink button.

2. **You can either enter a URL (or location of a file) or click the Browse folder icon to the right of the Link drop-down list and browse to the file you want to link to.**

You can also enter an external link here; see how to link to external locations a little later, in the "Linking to Pages and Files Outside Your Web Site" section.

3a. **If you want the page to appear in the same Document window, essentially replacing the existing page, leave the Target drop-down list blank or choose _self.**

3b. **If you want to force the link to create its own Document window, choose _blank.**

4. **Click OK to create your link.**

Using the Property inspector to create a link

You can also link text and images from the Property inspector HTML view.

1. **Select on your page the element you want to link up.**

2. **With your text or image selected, click the HTML button on the left side of the Property inspector to switch to HTML view and then type the link location into the Link text box.**

3. **To locate the destination file, click the folder icon (Browse) to the right of the Point to File button.**

The Select File dialog box opens.

4. **Navigate to the folder containing the file you want to link to, select it, and click OK (Windows) or Choose (Mac).**

Creating hyperlinks with Point to File

If you're in a hurry and want a more visual way of linking up your pages, you'll love this quick method for creating hyperlinks:

1. **Select the text you want to use as a link on your page.**

2. **In the Property inspector, find the Point to File icon next to the Link field; click and drag the icon and pull it toward the Files panel — an arrow follows your movement.**

3. **Move the arrow pointer over the file in the Files panel that you want to link to and release the mouse button (see Figure 6-2).**

Voilà! The connection is made, the filename appears in the Hyperlink text box, and the selection is now hyperlinked to your selected file.

Figure 6-2:
Creating a
hyperlink
from the
Property
inspector.

Creating Anchors

Anchors are a link to a specific section of a page, on either the same page
as the link or another page entirely. Anchors are especially handy for long
pages that have a lot of text. You've probably seen and used anchors, for
example, when clicking a Back to Top button or when navigating within a
page using a table of contents. Anchors are extremely helpful to viewers and
should be implemented whenever possible.

To create an anchor in Dreamweaver, follow these steps:

1. **Insert the cursor in a location on the page that you want to link to.**

   The anchor may be placed before a line of text or on its own line.

2. **Click the Named Anchor button in the Common category of the Insert
   panel.**

   The Named Anchor dialog box, shown in Figure 6-3, appears.

   You can avoid clicking the Anchor button by using the keyboard shortcut Ctrl+Alt+A (Windows) or ⌘+Option+A (Mac).

3. **Type a short name that's relevant to the content or location on the
   page (for example,** *TopOfPage* **or** *headline***).**

In Figure 6-3, you see that the text *TopOfPage* was entered because this anchor returns the viewer to the top of the page. Anchors are case sensitive, so keep this in mind when deciding on a name.

4. **Click OK.**

   The new anchor appears in your page, as shown in Figure 6-3.

Figure 6-3: Top: Create a simple anchor name in the Named Anchor dialog box. Bottom: The completed anchor.

You've created the anchor but have no links directed to it yet. You can define an anchor as a link manually or by using the Point to File tool, as described in the following two sections.

Linking to an anchor manually

Here's one reason why a short, appropriate name is useful for anchors: You may end up having to type it! By manually linking to an anchor, you can link within the page you're working on or direct the link to an anchor on a completely different page.

You can manually define an anchor as a link by following these steps:

1. **Select the text that will become the link.**

2. **If the Property inspector isn't open, choose Window⇨Properties.**

3. **Select the text that you want to link to your new named anchor and click the Hyperlink button located on the Insert panel.**

4. **In the Hyperlink dialog box, locate the Link field and click the drop-down list directly next to it.**

   Your named anchor appears as a selection, as shown in Figure 6-4.

5. **Select your anchor to apply it and then click OK.**

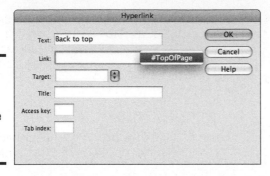

Figure 6-4:
Select the anchor name in the Hyperlink dialog box.

You can also link to a page and add an anchor reference to it from the Property inspector. For example, if you want to link to this spot from another page, you select an element on that page and in the Link text box (in HTML view) type the name of the page, a pound sign (#), and the name of the anchor — for example, **birds.html#canary**. This action directs the browser to the birds page and then to the canary anchor within that page.

Frequently, you see anchors separated by the pipe sign (|). You can create this type character by pressing Shift+\. The backslash key is directly above the Enter (Windows) or Return (Mac) key.

Linking to anchors with Point to File

You can use the same cool Point to File icon you used earlier to create hyperlinks for creating anchors. The Point to File icon in the Property inspector can also target anchors you've created on your page. Follow these steps:

1. **Select the text you want to use as a link on your page.**

 2. **In the Property inspector, find the Point to File icon located next to the Link field, click and drag over the icon, and release the arrow directly over an anchor icon on your page.**

The text is now linked to the anchor, and the anchor's name appears in the Property inspector's Link text field preceded by a pound sign (such as #canary).

Linking to Pages and Files Outside Your Web Site

You can link to pages anywhere, in your site or out. An *internal link* (sometimes referred to as a *relative URL*) is one within your site. The link to another page in your site may appear as contact.html in the Link text box in the Property inspector. But if you're directing people to a contact page posted on another site, you have a link that looks more like this: `http://www.aquent.com/contact`. By typing the `http://` and the address of the external link (sometimes referred to as an *absolute URL*) in the Property inspector, you're essentially directing the browser to a site on the Internet that's away from your site.

You must include the `http://` prefix in front of a Web address. Omitting this prefix results in a Page Not Found error in your browser because it may interpret `www.aquent.com`, for example, as a local filename rather than as an outside Web address.

Linking to E-Mail

Linking to an e-mail address opens on the viewer's computer a new mail message that's already addressed to the e-mail address you specify in the link (as long as the viewer has set up an e-mail program on her machine, of course).

Linking to an e-mail address is easy and extremely helpful if you want to give users an easy way to contact someone through your Web site. To create an e-mail link, follow these steps:

1. **Select the element that will be the link to an e-mail.**

The element can be either text or an image.

2. **In the Property inspector, locate the Link text box, type** mailto:*<address>*, **and then press Enter or Return.**

For example, type **mailto:info@agitraining.com** and press the Enter or Return key. The `mailto:` directive tells the browser that the link is to an e-mail address so that the default e-mail application on the user's computer opens with a new, preaddressed message.

Linking to a PDF File

To link to a PDF file instead of a Web page, you link to the name and location of the PDF file. If you link to a PDF file and the Acrobat PDF plug-in is loaded in the viewer's browser, the PDF is opened in the browser window. If the viewer doesn't have the Acrobat plug-in (free from `www.adobe.com`), the browser prompts the viewer to save the file to his computer. You can then view this file later on using Adobe's Acrobat Reader or another compatible program, if available.

Resolving Link Errors

Page names can change, and pages can be deleted (intentionally or not), so you should periodically check for broken links. You can ensure that links are working correctly in several ways. The most cumbersome, to preview a page and click every link, would take a long time and wouldn't be much fun. To check local links more efficiently and quickly, follow these steps:

1. **Choose Site➪Check Links Sitewide.**

The Results panel appears, with the Link Checker tab active.

Any broken links appear, including page, scripts, and images, as shown in Figure 6-5.

Figure 6-5: Check to make sure that no links are broken.

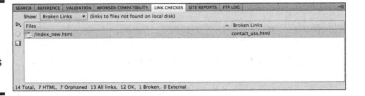

2. **Use the Show drop-down list in the top-left corner to sort the link results by broken link, external link, or orphaned file.**

To focus only on broken links, leave Broken Links selected.

If you don't have broken links — congratulations! If you do, you can fix them directly in the Results panel. The page that has the broken link is listed in the Files column on the left. The broken link appears under the Broken Link column on the right.

3. **Click the name of the broken link and correct the filename, if it's a problem, or click the Browse folder icon to locate the correct location or file.**

4. **Click OK (Windows) or Choose (Mac).**

The broken link is repaired.

Orphaned files are pages or images that are not in use or linked to from any place within your site. Although having orphaned files isn't necessarily a problem, to ensure that you don't have important files that are orphaned, select Orphaned Files from the Show menu under the Link Checker section of the Results panel.

Chapter 7: Creating Tables

In This Chapter

✔ Creating tables

✔ Manipulating rows, columns, and cells

✔ Selecting tables and cells

✔ Changing the colors of tables or cells

✔ Adding and importing content

✔ Setting alignment for table cells

Tables are useful for presenting data such as schedules and pricing and can be helpful when you're arranging elements in a tabular format.

In this chapter, you find out how to create a table and make changes that alter the look of the table. Tables are also used as an alternative method of creating page layouts.

Working with Tables

When you think of a *table,* think of a grid that has multiple cells in it, much like a spreadsheet. Tables are used in HTML pages so that elements can be contained and positioned within specific cells. You can change the colors of cells in tables, divide or *span* the cells (combine them with other cells), and apply borders to them.

In some cases, you don't see the table itself because you can place content into row and column form without showing the table; in this case, it's just a formatting tool. When you create a table, you can determine how many rows and columns it contains. You can also choose to span rows and columns to create unique tables, as shown in Figure 7-1.

To create a table in Dreamweaver, follow these steps:

1. **Put the cursor where you want the table to appear, make sure that the Common tab on the Insert panel is visible, and then click the Table button.**

   Alternatively, you can choose Insert⇨Table. Whichever method you use, the Table dialog box appears, as shown in Figure 7-2.

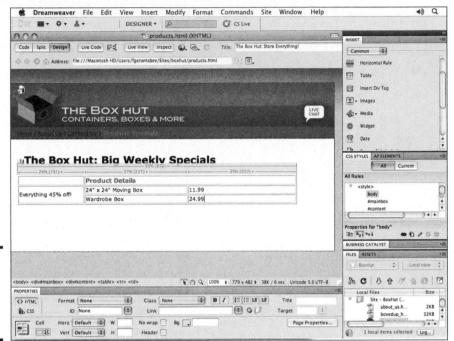

Figure 7-1: A table with rows and columns merged.

Figure 7-2: Set table specifica- tions in the Table dialog box.

2. **Enter or select the attributes of the table you want to create:**

   • *Rows:* In the Rows text box, enter the number of rows you want in the table. Rows stack vertically and can be added or deleted after you create the table.

- *Columns:* In the Columns text box, enter the number of columns you want in the table. Columns are created horizontally across a table and can be added or deleted after you create it.

- *Table Width:* Enter a width measurement in the Table Width text box and then select a measurement (Pixels or Percent) from the drop-down list to the right. Table width is an important attribute because it sets the default size for the table. If you leave this setting at 100 percent, the table occupies 100 percent of your Web page, dynamically expanding and reducing its size when the page is resized. You can change the width to a different percentage, such as 50 percent, to have the table occupy half the width of your Web page, or enter a pixel value to ensure that the table always stays the same size.

- *Border Thickness:* Enter (in pixels) the thickness you want for the width of the border surrounding the cells and outside the table. If you want to see no table formatting, type **0** in the Border Thickness text box. ***Note:*** In Design view, you still see a dashed table border — it's only a visual aid. You see true borders when you view the page in a browser or in Live view.

- *Cell Padding:* Enter a number in the Cell Padding text box if you want to use padding to create a margin around all content inside the cell.

- *Cell Spacing:* Enter a number in the Cell Spacing text box if you want to change the spacing to push cells apart.

- *Header:* Select the type of header you want to include in your table (or select None if you want no headers). Including headers is important, especially if you're creating a table containing data to assist viewers in associating the header with the data. Screen readers rely on headers to help visually impaired users navigate the table without getting lost.

- *Accessibility:* You can provide additional information to help visually impaired users understand the contents of your table. Add a caption that's relevant to your table in the Caption text box. In the Summary area, include several lines of text to provide more information about the purpose of the table.

3. **Click OK.**

    Your table is created.

When working with tables, try to take advantage of the Expanded table feature in Dreamweaver. (Find the Expanded button in the Layout section of the Insert panel.) Expanded view adds cell padding and spacing in a table and increases the size of the border to make selection easier. For an accurate preview, return to Standard view (click the Standard button in the Layout section of the Insert panel) after you finish editing.

Editing your table's attributes

Even if you've already created a table, you can go back and edit its attributes by selecting the table and entering changes in the Property inspector, as shown in Figure 7-3.

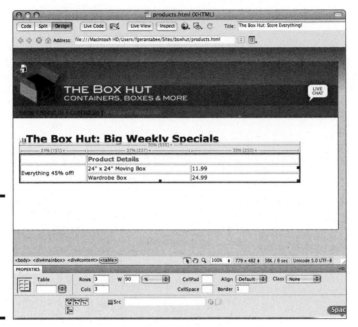

Figure 7-3:
Make changes to your table with the Property inspector.

If the Property inspector isn't expanded (refer to Figure 7-3), click the arrow in the lower right corner of the inspector. The inspector then expands, offering additional options.

When a table is selected, you can use the handles that appear in the lower right corner as well as the bottom and left sides to resize the table manually.

Adding and deleting rows and columns

You can use the Property inspector to add or delete rows and columns as fast as your client's (or boss's) needs require, but the Modify menu gives you a little more control over which rows and columns are deleted and where new ones are added.

To add a row, follow these steps:

1. **Insert the cursor in a cell in the row that you want to add a new row above or below.**

2. **Choose Insert⇨Table Objects⇨Insert Row Above or Insert Row Below.**

Alternatively, press Ctrl+M (Windows) or ⌘+M (Mac).

The new row appears.

To add more rows to the bottom of the table, place the cursor in the last current row and press the Tab key.

Follow these steps to delete a row:

1. **Insert the cursor in a cell of the row you want to delete.**

2. **Choose Modify⇨Table⇨Delete Row.**

Alternatively, press Ctrl+Shift+M (Windows) or Shift+⌘+M (Mac).

The row is deleted.

To add a column, follow these steps:

1. **Insert the cursor in a cell.**

Insert the cursor in the cell in the column that you want a new column added to the left or right of.

2. **Choose Insert⇨Table Objects⇨Insert Column to the Left or Insert Column to the Right.**

The new column appears.

Follow these steps to delete a column:

1. **Insert the cursor in a cell of the column you want to delete.**

2. **Choose Modify⇨Table⇨Delete Column.**

Alternatively, press Ctrl+Shift+– (minus) (Windows) or Shift+ ⌘+– (minus) (Mac).

The column is deleted.

Spanning or merging cells

Often, you need to span or merge cells. You can combine cells with other cells horizontally or vertically. By merging cells, you can create more interesting and useful tables. Figure 7-4 contains a table with one large, merged cell across the top.

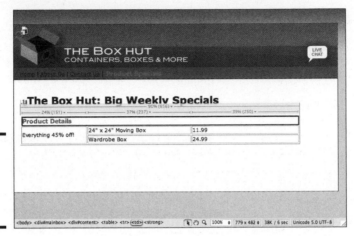

Figure 7-4:
The top
row's cells
have been
merged.

Follow these steps to merge cells in a row or column:

1. **Click within a cell and then drag across to select neighboring cells in the row or drag down to select neighboring cells in the column.**

2. **Choose Modify⇨Table⇨Merge Cells.**

   The cells are merged.

To split a merged cell back into separate cells, follow these steps:

1. **Put the cursor in the merged cell or column.**

2. **Choose Modify⇨Table⇨Split Cell.**

   The Split Cell dialog box appears, as shown in Figure 7-5.

Figure 7-5:
Split cells
as easily as
you merge
them.

3. **Choose whether you want to split into rows or columns by selecting either the Rows or Columns radio button.**

4. **Enter the number of rows or columns you want to create by splitting the cell in the Number of Rows/Columns text box.**

5. **Click OK.**

   The merged cell is now split into the number of cells you specified.

Selecting a Table and a Cell

You can use several methods to select a cell or the whole table. After a cell or table is selected, you can change all sorts of attributes for the selected cell or table, including the color, size, and format of its contents.

To select a table or cell, follow these steps:

1. **In Design view, select the Layout category from the Insert panel and select Expanded to put your table in Expanded view.**

You can more easily select and make changes in this view. (Remember to click the Standard button to see a more realistic preview of your table.)

2. **Select a cell by Ctrl-clicking (Windows) or ⌘-clicking (Mac) it.**

The tag selector is an incredible tool to use to select any tag element, though it's especially helpful when selecting individual components of a table or a nested table. The tag selector is in the lower left corner of the Document window, as shown in Figure 7-6.

**Book VI
Chapter 7**

Creating Tables

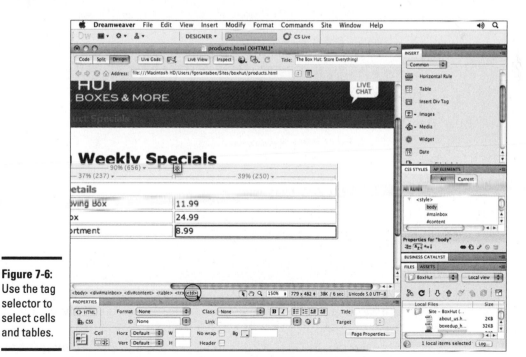

Figure 7-6:
Use the tag selector to select cells and tables.

To use the tag selector, just put the cursor inside a cell. The tag selector shows the tags that apply to the insertion point's location. Then select <td> to select the cell that holds the cursor, <tr> to select the entire row, or <table> to select the entire table.

The table tag is <table> (it's a difficult one to remember, right?), and each row is in a <tr> (table row) tag. Each cell is in a <td> (table data) tag. Tables created with headers also make use of the <th> (table header) tag.

Changing the Color of Table Cells

You can change colors of a single cell, multiple cells, or an entire row in Dreamweaver. You can use either standard HTML attributes or use CSS rules to apply color to any portion of a table, but the easiest way is to use the Property inspector to assign a background color.

To change the color of cell or multiple cells in a table, follow these steps:

1. **Ctrl-click (Windows) or ⌘-click (Mac) anywhere within a cell to select that cell.**

   You can continue to add cells to your selection by keeping the key pressed and clicking more cells.

2. **In the Property inspector, make sure that HTML view is selected (click the HTML tab on the left edge of the panel) and locate the Bg Color Picker.**

3. **Assign color to cells by following one of these methods:**

   - Click the swatch to the right of *Bg* and select a color from the Color Picker that appears. Remember that you can choose from additional color models by clicking the palette menu in the upper right corner of the Color Picker.

   - If you know the hexadecimal number of your color, you can type it in the text field next to the Bg color swatch.

   - Select a color from any element you can see onscreen by clicking the color fill box to the right of *Bg* and then moving the Eyedropper tool over any color on your screen that you want the cell color to pick up. Click when the color appears in the Color Picker preview window.

4. **The color is applied as a background to the selected cells.**

In addition to using the Property inspector, you can include background color settings in a new CSS rule and apply them to an entire table, cell, or row with the Property inspector.

You can use CSS to add a color to a cell or table by following these steps:

1. **Create a CSS Class rule from either the Property inspector or the CSS Styles panel (as discussed in Chapter 5 of this minibook).**

2. **Under the Background category in the CSS Rule Definition dialog box, assign a color to the Background color property and then click OK.**

3. **Select the table or cell you want to apply the new Class style to.**

4. **Assign the class by using the Class drop-down list in the Property inspector.**

Adding and Importing Content

Adding content to a table is easy: Insert the cursor into the cell and type directly into a cell for text or click Image in the Common section of the Insert panel to insert an image in a cell. You can also cut, copy, and paste content from documents and other Web pages directly into table cells.

Importing CSV and tab-delimited files

If you already have spreadsheet-style data in text form, you don't have to retype it into a Dreamweaver table. Dreamweaver has an incredibly easy feature you can use to bring in tabular data as a formatted table: Import Tabular Data.

CSV (comma-separated values) and tab-delimited files are plain text files that can be generated from a number of popular programs, such as Microsoft Excel. You can use these files to save spreadsheet data in a way that lets it be exchanged with other applications such as Dreamweaver.

In CSV files, columns are noted by commas between values, and each line return indicates a new row. In tab-delimited files, a tab between values indicates a new column and a line return forces a new row.

To import tabular data, follow these steps:

1. **Using Microsoft Excel or a similar program, create a spreadsheet of data, and save it as `.csv` (Comma-Separated Values). You can save this wherever you'd like, as long as you can easily locate it.**

2. **Return to Dreamweaver, and open a page where you'd like to add a table.**

3. **Put the cursor on the page where you want the table to be created.**

4. **Choose File➪Import➪Tabular Data.**

   The Import Tabular Data dialog box appears.

5. **Use the Browse button to browse to the location of a CSV (.csv) file or a tab-delimited (.txt) plain-text file.**

6. **Verify or select the delimiter that your file uses.**

   Typically, the *delimiter* (where a new column will be created) is a comma or tab; however, you can also instruct Dreamweaver to create a new column from other delimiters, such as Comma, Semicolon, Colon, or other options, by using the Delimited drop-down list.

7. **Determine the table width.**

   You can choose to have the table automatically sized to fit the data by leaving the Fit to Data radio button selected, or you can enter a number in the Set To text box to set a percentage or pixel value.

8. **Enter numbers in the Padding, Spacing, and Border text boxes and specify top-row formatting in the Format Top Row drop-down list at the bottom of the dialog box.**

9. **When you're finished with these settings, click OK.**

   Your table is created!

You can export table data from Dreamweaver just as easily as you can import it, by selecting a table and choosing File➪Export➪Table. When the Export Table dialog box appears, choose an element to be the delimiter and choose the type of line break. Click Export, determine where you want to save the file, and click Save.

Setting alignment for table cells

As a default, all elements center vertically inside a cell and are flush left. Change these settings on a cell-by-cell basis by selecting a cell or cells and then changing the Horz (horizontal) and Vert (vertical) alignment in the Property inspector.

Make sure the Property inspector is fully expanded to see the Horz and Vert drop-down lists.

If you select every cell in a row, you also have the opportunity to change the alignment of an entire row. In the Property inspector, you find a horizontal alignment drop-down list that changes the alignment of an entire row or selected cell. Choose from Left (default), Center, or Right. Note that any changes you make in the individual cell alignment override the row alignment.

You can also change the vertical alignment in the Property inspector when you have a row selected. Click the Vert drop-down list and choose Default, Top, Middle Bottom, or Baseline.

To select an entire row at once, position the cursor on the left side of the row you want to select. When the black arrow appears, simply click. You can also use this method of selecting an entire column by positioning the cursor on top of the column you want to select until the black arrow appears.

**Book VI
Chapter 7**

Creating Tables

Chapter 8: Creating CSS Layouts

In This Chapter

✔ Getting started with CSS pages

✔ Modifying layouts

✔ Positioning content with the AP Div tool

✔ Using behaviors with DIV tags

Creating a page layout sometimes requires more precision than tables or standard HTML tags are capable of. More designers are moving to the flexible and preferred method of Cascading Style Sheets (CSS) positioning to create innovative layouts without boundaries. Dreamweaver provides you with an extensive gallery of CSS-based layouts to get started, or you can build your own using the Insert panel's Layout tools, including the Insert DIV and AP Div objects.

Using CSS Starter Pages

Dreamweaver provides you with a library of sample pages with CSS-based layouts as an alternative to starting from scratch. These CSS sample pages feature useful and common layout ideas, and because they're created with CSS positioning, they're highly flexible. You can modify them directly from the CSS Styles panel or the Property inspector. Just add your content and go!

Follow these steps to create a new document from a CSS sample page:

1. **Choose File⇨New.**

The New Document panel appears.

2. **Choose Blank Page from the left, select a layout from the Layout column on the right (for example, the 2 Column Liquid, Left Sidebar, Header and Footer layout), and click Create.**

A new, untitled page opens, based on the layout you chose.

3. **Choose File⇨Save to name and save the document.**

4. **Replace the placeholder text in each column with your own content.**

Modifying a New Layout

A CSS layout, as its name indicates, is controlled completely by style sheet rules, so you can modify the look and feel of the page directly from the CSS Styles panel and the Property inspector. Each column, box, and space on your new page is positioned and sized using CSS rules and properties, all of which you can adjust from either the Property inspector (on the CSS Styles panel) or the CSS Rule Definition panel.

You can modify the layout by following these steps:

1. **If the CSS Styles panel isn't already open, choose Window⇨CSS Styles to open it.**

2. **Select the All tab to display the style sheet and its rules.**

The internal style sheet is shown as <style> at the top. Click the arrow to its left to expand it and show all the rules it contains. ***Note:*** Layouts using an attached (external) style sheet display the style sheet name (such as styles.css) instead of the <style> tag.

3. **Select the** body **rule.**

This tag-based style controls the general formatting of the entire page (everything inside the <body> tag).

4. **Click the field next to the background rule to edit it; rather than keep the #4E5869 (medium gray) setting, type a hexadecimal color (such as #CC0000 for red) to change the page's background color.**

5. **Click the swatch next to the color rule to open the Swatches panel; pick a new default type color for the text on your page.**

6. **At the top of the CSS Styles panel, select another style (for example, the** .twoColElstHdr #container **style) to view its properties.**

The .twoColHybLtHdr #container ID style controls the size and appearance of the main layout container on the page.

7. **In the Property inspector, edit the properties to change the appearance of the style.**

For example, you can change the width of the rule by entering a new number in the Width Rule text box. If you enter **95%**, for example, you make the entire layout wider.

Each column and section that comprises your layout is controlled by one of the ID styles listed in the CSS Styles panel. Most every ID style features a width property you can use to change the size of different areas on the page.

Continue to modify different styles listed in the CSS Styles panel and see how they affect different elements on your page. Try changing the type color, font family, and other properties, such as padding and background color.

To figure out exactly which ID controls which column or section, click within the page area and look at the tag selector at the bottom of the Document window. The last <div> tag at the end of the chain shows you which container you're in and its corresponding ID in the CSS Styles panel (for example, <div#mainBox>).

Creating AP Divs

Dreamweaver uses CSS-positioned virtual containers, or *boxes,* created by the DIV tag to freely position content on a page. The *DIV* tag is a basic tag used to create areas for content on your page. You can create DIV tags from several places in Dreamweaver, including the Layout section of the Insert panel. Each DIV tag can have a unique ID style assigned to it to control its position, appearance, and size. The process of placing content often requires two steps: creating the DIV tag and then creating its corresponding style.

Dreamweaver makes this task easy with the AP Div tool, which enables you to draw boxes freely on the page and place content inside.

AP Div is short for *absolute-positioned* DIV; an item with an *absolute* position is fixed at a specific location on the page. When you draw an AP Div, its position is commonly set using the *top* and *left* CSS properties, with the top-left corner of the page as its reference point.

If you have used much earlier versions of Dreamweaver, you may remember Dreamweaver layers. The AP Div object replaced the Layer object as of version CS3, and the AP Elements panel now replaces the Layers panel.

C33 treats every element on a page as a box that holds content; this approach is referred to as the *CSS Box model.* Although CSS can consider a box to be most any containing element on a page (such as a table or a list), DIV tags are most commonly used to create virtual boxes that you can use to position text, images, and even other boxes.

Each box can have its own width, height, position (via the top and left properties), border, margins, and padding; each one is set using CSS rules.

To create AP Divs, follow these steps:

1. **On the Insert panel, select the Layout category.**

2. **Select the Draw AP Div tool.**

The cursor appears as a cross hair when you move it back over the page.

3. **Click anywhere on the page and drag to draw a new AP Div, as shown at the top in Figure 8-1; release the mouse button.**

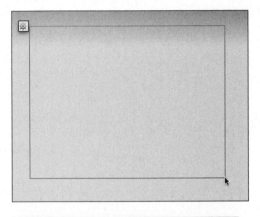

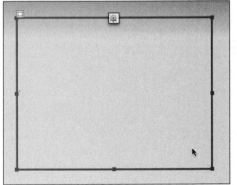

Figure 8-1:
Click and
drag the
page with
the Draw AP
Div tool to
create
a box.

4. **Move the mouse pointer over the edge of the box until it changes to a hand; click once and handles appear on all sides (refer to the bottom of Figure 8-1).**

5. **Click and drag any of these handles to resize the box vertically or horizontally.**

6. **To move the box, click and drag it by the tab that sits on its top-left edge and place the box where you want it on the page.**

   Take a look at the Property inspector, and you see the name as well as many DIV properties listed.

7. **If the CSS Styles panel isn't open, choose Window⇨CSS Styles to open it; under the All panel, click to the left of the style sheet (`<style>`) to expand it.**

You see a new #apDiv1 ID style that's attached to the new AP Div you created. For each new DIV created, Dreamweaver assigns apDiv with a corresponding number in order of creation.

8. **Click inside the new box to type, paste, or insert new content.**

When you draw an AP Div on the page, two things occur: Dreamweaver inserts a tag to create the box and creates an ID selector that stores the DIV's position, width, height, and other properties. After you create an AP Div, you can type, paste, or insert content directly inside it. You can also assign a class rule to any DIV from the Property inspector — most often for handling content formatting, leaving the ID selector to control positioning and dimensions.

Each AP Div you draw is listed automatically in the AP Elements panel (choose Window⇨AP Elements to display it), as shown in Figure 8-2. The AP Elements panel can help you select, hide, and show any AP Divs on the page. This panel is handy when you have lots of AP Divs on the page and want to navigate among them accurately. Most of all, because you can modify the properties for any AP Div from its corresponding ID style, the panel helps you figure out which ID style belongs to an AP Div.

**Book VI
Chapter 8**

**Creating CSS
Layouts**

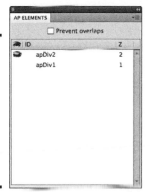

Figure 8-2:
Use the AP Elements panel to select, hide, and rearrange AP Divs in your page.

The AP Elements panel is often grouped with the CSS Styles panel, just in case you're looking for it.

To modify a box (AP Div), follow these steps:

1. **Choose Window⇨AP Elements to open the AP Elements panel.**

2. **In the panel (refer to Figure 8-2), locate and select apDiv2 to highlight it on the page.**

   The Property inspector displays its size and position in addition to other properties.

3. **Using the text boxes in the Property inspector, change the box width by entering a number into the W field and change the box height by entering a number in the H field.**

4. **Click the swatch next to Bg Color and choose a color from the pop-up Swatches panel to set a background color for the box.**

   For additional properties, such as border or padding, add them in the CSS Styles panel.

5. **If the CSS Styles panel isn't already visible, open it by choosing Window↷CSS Styles.**

6. **Double-click the** #apDiv2 ID **style that controls the box.**

   The CSS Rule Definition dialog box appears, as shown in Figure 8-3.

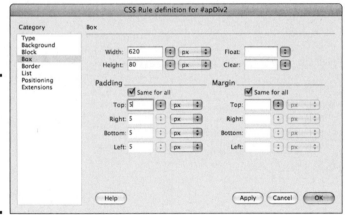

Figure 8-3: Add CSS properties across a variety of categories to build rules.

7. **Select the Border category from the left to change the border.**

8. **In the Style column, use the Top drop-down list to set a border style (such as Solid) to all four sides.**

   Use the Top drop-down list under the Width category to select a border thickness (for example, medium) for all four sides. Use the topmost Color Picker under the Color column to assign a border color to all four sides.

   To assign different values to any or all sides for style, width, or color, deselect the Same for All check box under their respective columns.

9. **In the Box category on the left, under Padding, set the padding for all four sides of the box to the thickness you want (for example, enter 5 px in the text boxes).**

10. **Click OK to exit the panel and apply the changes.**

    You see how the CSS properties you applied affect the `apDiv2` box on the page.

To hide a box shown under the AP Elements panel, click the column to the left of its name (under the Eye icon) until a closed Eye icon appears. To make the box reappear, click the Eye icon until the box opens again.

You may notice the Prevent Overlaps check box, deselected by default, at the top of the AP Elements panel. Because AP Divs can easily overlap each other, selecting this check box overrides that behavior by forcing boxes next to each other and preventing the creation of new boxes on top of each other.

Creating Relatively Positioned DIVs

The precision and to-the-pixel positioning of AP Divs can be quite liberating for designers, especially those who like the flexibility of print-based layouts. However, on certain occasions, you may want boxes to flow inline with other content on the page. AP Divs literally float above other elements, so shifting other page content has no effect on their position.

For more traditional inline behavior, you can create DIVs that use *relative positioning,* which allows an element to be shifted along with content surrounding it, making for a more liquid layout. This type of positioning is important for nested content or any situation where items should fall in line with other page content. For this task, use the Insert Div Tag tool, which can be found within the Insert panel's Common and Layout categories.

Follow these steps to create a relatively positioned DIV:

1. **Click within your page to position the cursor within an existing AP Div and then click the Insert Div Tag tool under the Insert panel's Common and Layout categories.**

2. **When the Insert Div Tag dialog box appears, fine-tune the location of your new DIV by selecting a location from the Insert drop-down list, shown in Figure 8-4.**

    (For example, choose After Start of Tag to place it within an existing DIV tag in your page.)

You can also use the Insert Div Tag dialog box's drop-down list to place the DIV before, after, or inside existing elements on the page. Leave the Insert drop-down list set to At Insertion Point to leave the box where you drew it or choose another location where you want the DIV created.

Figure 8-4:
Choose a
specific
location to
create and
place the
new DIV.

3. **If you have an existing class selector you want to apply, choose it from the Class drop-down list; otherwise, leave it blank.**

4. **Assign an ID selector to the DIV to control its appearance by selecting from the ID drop-down list.**

   If one isn't available, enter a new name and click the New CSS Rule button to create one.

5. **When the New CSS Rule dialog box appears, be sure that your new selector is set to ID and that the name has a pound sign (#) in front of it. Click OK.**

6. **When the CSS Rule Definition dialog box appears, click and select Positioning from the Category list on the left to view CSS positioning properties.**

7. **In the Positioning area, select Relative from the Position menu, enter a width and height value in the Width and Height text boxes, and then click OK.**

8. **Click OK to close the Insert Div Tag dialog box.**

   A new, relatively positioned DIV appears with placeholder text, as shown in Figure 8-5.

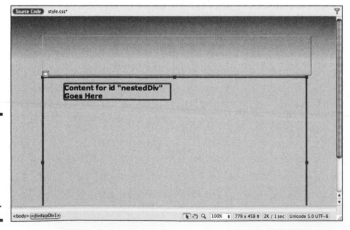

Figure 8-5:
You can
create a
new DIV
within
another DIV.

Using Behaviors with Boxes

To add cool effects and serious interactivity, you can use the built-in Dreamweaver *behaviors,* a collection of ready-to-use scripts that you can apply to boxes, form elements, text, and images on a page. Used with boxes (AP Divs), behaviors can enhance them with special effects or mouse interaction (such as clicks and rollovers) to make the page more exciting.

The Behaviors panel features a whole new set of effects, such as Fade/Appear, Shrink, Highlight, Slide, and more — all of which you can apply to the AP Divs you create.

You can add behaviors by following these steps:

1. **Choose Window⇨Behaviors to open the Behaviors panel.**

2. **Select a box by using the AP Elements panel or select a box directly on the stage.**

3. **In the Behaviors panel, click the plus sign.**

   The menu of available behaviors appears.

4. **From the menu, choose the behavior you want to apply.**

   For example, to apply a fade effect, choose Effects⇨Appear/Fade, as shown in Figure 8-6.

   The Appear/Fade dialog box opens.

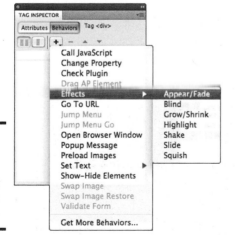

Figure 8-6: Add a cool Appear/Fade effect to a DIV on your page.

5. **Make sure the effect is set to Fade and select the Toggle Effect check box to make sure the box reappears when it's clicked a second time. Then click OK.**

The behavior is added to the list. The phrase onClick to its left indicates that this action occurs when the box is clicked.

6. **Choose File⇨Save to save the page.**

To see the effect in action, preview the page in a browser.

7. **Choose File⇨Preview in Browser and pick a browser to launch the page.**

When you test the page, clicking the box makes it disappear or reappear — lots of fun for you and highly interactive for users!

If your browser is restricting the Web page from running scripts or ActiveX controls, click the message at the top of the browser window and select Allow Blocked Content to properly test the new behaviors.

When effects behaviors are used, Dreamweaver needs to copy to your local site several files that make the effects possible.

Chapter 9: Publishing Your Web Site

In This Chapter

✔ **Checking for broken links and missing files**

✔ **Running your site reports**

✔ **Checking browser compatibility**

✔ **Publishing to a Web server**

✔ **Making site improvements**

*W*hen you're ready to launch your Web site, you can take lots of steps to ensure that it looks good and works well. Dreamweaver tools and reports streamline the process of testing and fixing any problems so that you can present visitors with a favorable first impression.

Clean Up after Yourself!

The first step toward getting your Web site ready for the world is making sure that everything works and all files are in order. Dreamweaver is packed full of tools that let you know exactly what's broken and what can be done better and how your site will perform across a spectrum of different browsers.

One key benefit of a Dreamweaver site is its ability to see relationships between various pages and files and detect any broken links or missing images before you publish your Web site for public viewing. Choose Site⇨Check Links Sitewide to comb your entire site to find broken links or missing or *orphaned* (unlinked) files.

To use the Check Links Sitewide feature, follow these steps:

1. **Choose Window⇨Files to open the Files panel.**

   You can also use the F8 shortcut key (Windows or Mac).

2. **Open the Files panel menu (it's in the upper right corner) and choose Site⇨Check Links Sitewide.**

   The Link Checker panel appears and displays any results. Each listing shows the broken link and the name of the page that contains it to the left, as shown in Figure 9-1.

Figure 9-1:
The Link
Checker
lists the
filename
and the
broken link.

SEARCH	REFERENCE	VALIDATION	BROWSER COMPATIBILITY	LINK CHECKER	SITE REPORTS	FTP LOG	

Show: Broken Links ▾ (links to files not found on local disk)

Files		Broken Links
/about_us.html		contacts.html

15 Total, 8 HTML, 7 Orphaned 19 All links, 18 OK, 1 Broken, 0 External

3. **To open and edit the page to correct the link, double-click the file-name that's shown.**

   You can then edit the broken link directly from the Link Checker panel without opening the file. Click the broken link that's displayed, and a folder icon appears next to it, on the right.

4. **Double-click the folder to open the Select File dialog box and choose an available file to correct the link or relink it to a different file.**

5. **Click OK (Windows) or Choose (Mac).**

If you want to change a link that appears across several pages, open the Files panel menu and choose Site⇨Change Links Sitewide. When the panel appears, you're asked which file the original link points to and you can specify a new file to link to instead. *Warning:* Your answer changes all links to that file sitewide, so don't use this command if you want to change that link on only certain pages.

Running Site Reports

The Dreamweaver site reports provide a detailed look at potential issues lurking within your site as well as assistance in cleaning out redundant or empty tags from your pages.

Reports are in two categories:

✦ **Workflow:** Shows you where your files have been, and when, and are useful if you're using functions, such as the Check In/Check Out feature to share work with others.

✦ **HTML:** Points out design and accessibility issues, such as missing ALT tags for images, improperly nested tags, or empty tags that you can clean up.

You can run a site report by following these steps:

1. Choose Site⇨Reports.

The Reports dialog box appears, as shown in Figure 9-2.

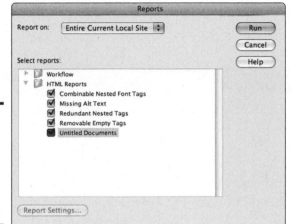

Figure 9-2:
Use the
Reports
dialog box
to choose
reports you
want to run.

2. Choose each report you want to see by selecting the check box next to the report name.

As shown in Figure 9-2, we chose all reports in the HTML Reports category.

3. At the top of the Reports dialog box, use the drop-down list to select what aspect of the Web site you would like to run the reports on.

You can choose the Current Document, Entire Current Local Site, Selected Files in Site or a specific folder of your choice. If you are unsure, choose the Entire Current Local Site option.

4. Click the Run button to run the selected reports.

The Results panel appears and displays the results of each report.

Each report result displays the file and line number and a description of the problem.

5. To address a problem that's shown, double-click the filename to open the page.

The page opens for editing, and the section in which the problem occurs appears highlighted in Split view.

Checking CSS Compatibility

If you're using CSS for formatting and layout throughout your site, make sure that your page appears properly across all popular browsers, such as Internet Explorer, Firefox, Chrome, and Safari. Over the years, different browsers adopted CSS at different levels and paces, requiring designers to test pages in a variety of browsers and versions.

To eliminate this time-consuming task, Dreamweaver provides the Browser Compatibility Check, which works hand in hand with the Adobe Web site to discover and report any CSS-related display issues that may occur in selected browsers and versions. The Browser Compatibility Check checks CSS compatibility by default in these browsers: Firefox 1–3; Internet Explorer (Windows) 6.0–8.0; Internet Explorer (Macintosh) 5.2; Netscape Navigator 7.0–8.0; Opera 7.0–9.0; and Safari 1.0–3.0.

For any problem that the Browser Compatibility Check discovers, the Results panel displays a description of the problem along with a direct link to the CSS Advisor section of the Adobe Web site. The CSS Advisor reports on known browser-display issues and possible solutions for fixing them.

Follow these steps to test a page with the Browser Compatibility Check:

1. **Open a page for editing by choosing File⇨Open or by selecting it from the Files panel.**

2. **In the Document window (next to the Live Code button), click and hold the Check Browser Compatibility button and then choose Check Browser Compatibility from the menu that appears, as shown in Figure 9-3.**

Figure 9-3: Use the Check Browser Compatibility button to check the CSS in your page.

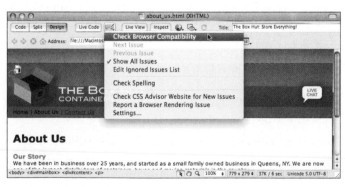

The Results panel appears, with the Browser Compatibility tab forward. Any results are displayed on this tab.

3. **To view details and possible solutions for any results that may appear, select the result (see Figure 9-4).**

Figure 9-4:
The Browser
Compatibility
Check
displays any
problems.

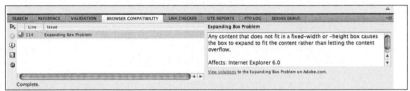

The description, as well as a link to the Adobe Web site, appears on the right side of the panel.

Possible compatibility issues are listed along with the filename, line number, and description of the problem.

4. **Click the link below the detail panel to jump to the Adobe Web site for solutions.**

Getting Connected

When you're ready to publish your site for the world to see, set up a remote server in your site definition so that you can connect and copy files to your Web-hosting account or dedicated server.

Typical remote server information consists of an ID and a password, an FTP (File Transfer Protocol) or network address, and the name of the specific directory where your files need to go. This information is available from the company your hosting service was purchased from or from your network administrator.

To set up a remote connection, follow these steps:

1. **Choose Site⊅Manage Sites.**

   The Manage Sites panel appears.

2. **Select your site from the list and click the Edit button.**

3. **When the Site Setup dialog box appears, select the Servers category on the left.**

   Here you can add connection information to a Web server where you can store and publish your Web site.

Servers, more often referred to as "Web hosting accounts" can be purchased from Web hosting providers. Your Web hosting account is essentially a folder on a remote computer, where you can store your files and point your users so they can view your site from any computer or device. There are thousands of hosting providers (such as GoDaddy, FatCow, 1 and 1) from which you can purchase these services.

4. **Below the listing of servers (which is likely empty right now), click the Add new Server button.** This opens a dialog box where you can enter your connection information.

5. **Enter a name for your connection in the Server Name text field.**

6. **Under the Connect Using drop-down list, select the type of connection you're going to create.**

   In most cases this is FTP, but check with your IT Administrator if you're unsure. If you're connecting to a Web hosting account, FTP is the most common way in which you'll connect.

7. **Enter your FTP address, Username, and Password in their respective text fields (as shown in Figure 9-5).**

   This information is provided to you when you set up a Web hosting account. If you are unsure of this information, contact your Web hosting provider or IT Administrator.

8. **Enter your Root Directory in the appropriate text field.**

   This is the name or location of the folder where your web site files will be kept on the remote server. If you are unsure of this information, leave it blank.

9. **Enter your Web URL in the text field shown.**

   This is the actual Web address where users will find your Web site (for example, http://www.mycoolwebsite.com).

Figure 9-5:
Enter your connection information when adding a new server.

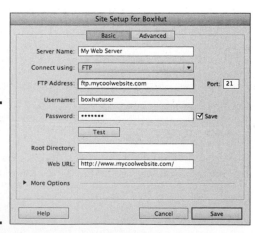

10. **Click the Test button to test your connection.**

If the connection is made successfully, Dreamweaver will let you know. If not, you may need to double-check the information you entered and try again.

If you experience difficulty connecting to your remote server or the connection is taking unusually long, select the Use Passive FTP checkbox under the More Options section at the bottom. (You'll need to expand this by clicking the arrow next to More Options.) Passive FTP can also be a workaround if you're trying to connect from behind a firewall.

11. **If your settings are correct, click Save to create the Server connection.**

12. **Click Save again to exit the Site Setup dialog box.**

Your Web site — live!

After your connection is up and running, you're ready to upload files and present your Web site to the world. Files can be transferred to and from your remote Web server by using the built-in FTP functionality of the Files panel. It displays files in your local directory and the remote server, and between them, you can put, get, or synchronize site files.

Follow these steps to upload your Web site to a remote Web server:

1. **Choose Window⇨Files to open the Files panel.**

2. **Click the Expand to Show Local and Remote Sites icon.**

The panel expands so that you see both the local site and the remote site to which you want to copy (upload) the files.

3. **Make sure that the correct site definition is selected in the Show drop-down list in the upper left corner of the panel.**

Your local files appear on the right.

4. **To connect to and display files on the remote Web server, click the Connect button at the top of the panel.**

When the connection is made, all files (if any) are displayed on the left side of the panel.

5. **To copy files, select and drag them from the local files on the right to the remote files on the left, as shown in Figure 9-6.**

Alternatively, select the files you want to copy on the right and click the Put button at the top of the Files panel.

You can put all of the files within your site on your Web server at once by selecting the root folder at the top of the local files panel and clicking the Put button.

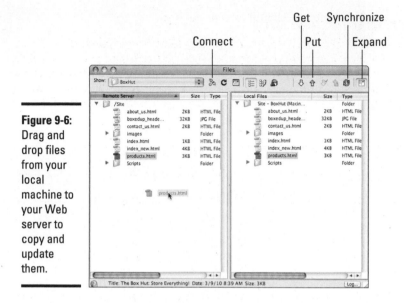

Figure 9-6:
Drag and
drop files
from your
local
machine to
your Web
server to
copy and
update
them.

6. **After you copy all files to the remote Web server, test your site by opening a browser and typing the Web site's URL.**

   The URL is a full address, such as www.mywebsite.com, or an IP address, such as http://192.1.1.1.

   If you notice broken images or files, return to Dreamweaver to double-check whether all files were copied to the server and then run the Link Checker by choosing Site⇨Check Links Sitewide.

To retrieve files from a remote Web server, follow these steps:

1. **Select the files you want to retrieve from the remote files on the left side of the Files panel.**

2. **Click the Get button (which appears as a green, downward pointing arrow) at the top of the panel or drag the files to the local root folder on the right.**

To return the Files panel to its original position on the right side of the work-space, click the Expand button in the upper right corner of the panel to dese-lect it. The Files panel minimizes and docks back with the panel group on the right.

Synchronizing your site

The handy Dreamweaver site synchronization feature compares files between your local and remote sites to ensure that both are using the same, and most recent, versions of your site files. This check is essential if there's a chance that files on the remote server may be more up-to-date or if you're unsure which files have been updated since the last time you worked on a Web site.

Follow these steps to synchronize your local and remote directories:

1. **If the Files panel isn't already visible, choose Window⇨Files to open it.**

2. **Select the site you want to synchronize in the Show drop-down list in the upper left corner of the panel.**

Your local files appear on the right.

3. **Click the Connect button at the top of the panel to connect to the remote server.**

If you're not viewing your Files panel in Expanded view, choose Remote Server from the drop-down list at the top to display your remote files.

4. **Click the Synchronize button at the top of the Files panel.**

The Synchronize Files dialog box appears.

5. **From the Synchronize drop-down list, choose whether you want to synchronize the whole local site or only files selected in the Files panel (if any).**

6. **From the Direction drop-down list, choose whether you want newer files put to the remote server, retrieved from the remote sever, or both.**

7. **To clean up unused or old files on the remote server, select the Delete Remote Files Not on Local Drive check box.**

8. **Click the Preview button to begin the process.**

This step may take a while, depending on the number of files in your site.

The Synchronize Files dialog box appears and displays all changes that will be made between the local and remote folders.

9. **Select, change, or delete any actions as necessary.**

10. **Click OK to have Dreamweaver complete the synchronization process.**

Be careful when using the Delete Remote Files Not on Local Drive option; some files on the remote server are installed by the Web hosting company and are necessary for the operation of your site.

Improving Your Site

Remember that a site is like a living organism: It continues to grow and will still need care after it's live. As you add to your site, find new and innovative ways to present information to site visitors; after all, it's all about giving them what they came looking for.

To improve your site and keep visitors coming back, try these tips:

✦ **Solicit feedback from focus groups or colleagues in different fields.** Let them tell you the best and worst features of your site, and then use this feedback to assist in design, layout, and content decisions.

✦ **Use Web statistics to your advantage.** Use these statistics, often provided for free by Web hosting companies, to see where users are spending the most time and where they leave your site.

✦ **Provide a feedback form.** Site visitors can then comment on the service and information they receive, with the opportunity to provide comments and suggestions.

✦ **Always keep your content fresh.** Stale information and features can deter return visits and ruin first impressions.

✦ **Respond immediately to problems that surface.** Don't ignore or put off broken links, images, or misspellings.

Book VII

Flash Professional CS5

The 5th Wave   By Rich Tennant

"See? I created a little felon figure that runs around our Web site hiding behind banner ads. On the last page, our logo puts him in a nonlethal choke hold and brings him back to the home page."

Contents at a Glance

Chapter 1: Getting Started in Flash CS5

In This Chapter

✔ Creating, saving, and opening documents

✔ Getting familiar with the workspace and tools

✔ Creating and saving workspaces

✔ Introducing Flash Player 10

✔ Understanding layers

✔ Importing and exporting files

✔ Understanding the publishing process

*W*elcome to the world of Flash, one of today's hottest applications for creating eye-catching motion graphics featuring sound, video, and visual effects. In this minibook, you explore the whole process, from basic graphics creation and animation to complex effects and user interaction.

Flash can create full Web sites, complex games, and highly functional, rich Internet applications. One or more of the sites you visit each day is likely to use Flash.

Creating Your First Flash Document

You can start creating a new, blank Flash document and set up your workspace in one of two ways:

✦ From the start page, choose Flash File (ActionScript 3.0) under the Create New column.

✦ Choose File➪New➪Flash File (ActionScript 3.0).

Your new document is created and the workspace appears. Before you get to work, specify some important settings, such as width and height, for your file by using the Document Properties dialog box.

To open the Document Properties dialog box, choose Modify⇨Document and set these options:

+ **Frame Rate:** Because Flash files behave like movies, the frame rate is an important setting that affects the performance and playback speed of your movie. The default setting of 24 frames per second (fps) should work well.

+ **Dimensions:** The width and height you specify determine the size of your stage and in turn, the visible area of your finished movie. For now, leave the default setting of 550 pixels wide by 400 pixels high.

+ **Background Color:** Click the swatch to pick a background color for your stage from the Web-safe color palette. This setting also determines the background color of any Web pages created by Flash when you publish your movie to the Web.

+ **Ruler Units:** Select from this drop-down list the unit of measurement used for all measurement values in your document, including document size, width and height values, and ruler increments when rules are visible in the workspace.

When you're done fine-tuning your document's properties, click OK.

Getting Familiar with the Workspace

On the Flash workspace, shown in Figure 1-1, you create your Flash movies. The most prominent item you'll notice is at the top of your screen: The *stage* is where the action happens — where you draw, build, or import graphics, create text, and construct layouts.

The gray area surrounding the stage is the *pasteboard*. Items placed on it aren't visible in your finished movie because they're outside the bounds of the stage. However, it helps to think of this area as *backstage* — where text, artwork, and images can make their entrances or exits or be placed until they're ready to appear in your movie.

The Tools panel

What CS5 application would be complete without a fancy toolbar? Flash has a comprehensive set of tools for just about any drawing task you need to wrap your hands around. Table 1-1 gives you a rundown and description of the tools you'll find. The Tools panel has been redesigned to make your work area flow more smoothly. A double arrow at the top lets you toggle between expanded and icon views to maximize your work area.

Pasteboard

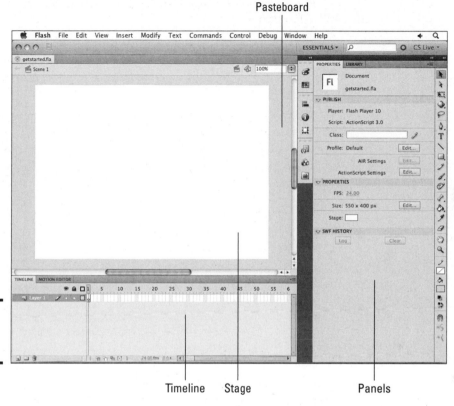

Figure 1-1:
The Flash
workspace.

Timeline   Stage   Panels

Table 1-1		The Tools Panel
Button	*Tool Name/Keyboard Command*	*What You Can Do with It*
	Selection (V)	Select and move objects on the stage and work area
	Subselection (A)	Select and move specific points on a path or a shape
	Free Transform (Q)	Change an object's dimensions, rotation, or proportions
	Gradient Transform (F)	Change the size, intensity, and direction of a gradient fill
	3D Rotation (W)	Translate 2D artwork into the 3D plane and rotate it around an x, y, and z axis

(continued)

Table 1-1 *(continued)*

Button	Tool Name/Keyboard Command	What You Can Do with It
	3D Translation (G)	Click and drag artwork along the x, y, or z axis to illustrate depth and distance
	Lasso (L)	Create freehand selections around one or more points
	Pen (P)	Create accurate, point-by-point straight and curved paths
	Add Anchor Point (=)	Add anchor points along an existing path
	Delete Anchor Point (-)	Remove anchor points from an existing path
	Convert Anchor Point (C)	Change the curve orientation of an existing point
	Text (T)	Create text on the stage
	Line (N)	Draw straight lines
	Shape Tools (R, O)	Create rectangular, oval, or multisided shapes on the stage
	Primitive Tools (R, O)	Create rounded rectangles and multiradiused ovals that can be modified
	Pencil (Y)	Draw freehand paths
	Brush (B)	Draw broad, freehand fill areas
	Spray Brush (B)	Create a spattered, airbrush-like painting with symbols from the library

Button	Tool Name/Keyboard Command	What You Can Do with It
	Deco (U)	Create animated or non-animated flower- and-leaf style fills or symmetrical artwork with symbols
	Bone (M)	Join shapes or symbols with virtual "bones" for creating posable inverse kinematics (IK) objects
	Bind (M)	Edit connections between objects created using the Bone tool
	Paint Bucket (K)	Apply or modify the fill color of an area
	Ink Bottle (S)	Apply or modify the stroke color and style of a shape or path
	Eyedropper (I)	Sample the color property from an object
	Eraser (E)	Erase parts of a fill or path
	Hand (H)	Reposition the stage and work area within the workspace
	Zoom (Z)	Zoom in or out of a selected area of the stage

**Book VII
Chapter 1**

**Getting Started in
Flash CS5**

The Timeline

Below the stage sits the *Timeline,* where you bring your artwork to life through animation. The Timeline is composed of frames, each one representing a point in time moving from left to right. The Timeline is further broken out into *layers;* new documents automatically contain one new layer labeled Layer 1. Each layer on the Timeline is composed of frames that span horizontally from left to right, each one representing a point in time, just like frames in a movie reel (see Figure 1-2).

The Motion Editor

The Motion Editor lets you see and modify all properties of an animation in a graph-style format. All properties that can be animated are displayed in rows, each of which contains a value line that can be manipulated to change the behavior of a selected tween. You can also add complex forces, such as gravity and inertia, and even add to or subtract from your tween without using the Timeline or stage.

Keyframe   Timeline ruler

Figure 1-2:
The
Timeline
contains
frames and
layers.

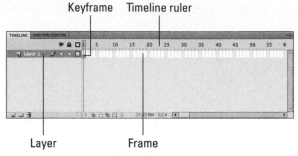

Layer   Frame

The Property inspector

Sitting at the right side of your workspace, the Property inspector lets you get (and set) attributes, such as height and width, for a selected item on the stage or work area (see Figure 1-3). The contextual Property Inspector displays adjustable options for any item you select on the stage, such as width and height for a selected shape or fill and stroke color. When you don't have any objects on the stage selected, the Property inspector will display global document properties such as frame rate.

Figure 1-3:
The
Property
inspector
shows
options for
selected
graphics,
frames, or
tools.

To modify a document's properties, such as frame rate and dimensions, at any time, either use the Property inspector when no items on the stage are selected or choose Modify➪Document.

Panels (right side)

The numerous panels included in Flash give you total control over most aspects of your movie, from creating and managing colors to exploring the structure of your project and adding code to frames.

The default (Essentials) workspace launches with the Property inspector and Library panel in full view, as well as a minimized group of eight panels that include

+ Color
+ Swatches
+ Align
+ Info
+ Transform
+ Code Snippets
+ Components
+ Motion Presets

Get familiar with panel behaviors and features so that you can manage their appearance and make organizing your workspace a snap.

Taking a look at the panel group

The panel group sits on the right side of the workspace and features multiple grouped panels. Panels can be added to or removed from the panel group on the right.

You can't freely reposition the panel group in the workspace. However, you can resize or collapse it to icon view with the double arrows found in its upper-right corner.

You can remove and float panels from the panel group. Simply click and drag a panel away from the group by its title tab. To add a panel to the group, drag it into the panel group on the right.

Managing individual panels

You can position each panel individually anywhere in the workspace by dragging it by its title tab. You can find additional appearance options under each panel's menu, accessible from the icon in its upper-right corner (see

Figure 1-4). This panel menu also provides another way of reaching that panel's primary tasks.

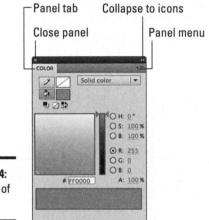

Figure 1-4:
Anatomy of
a panel.

To group panels, simply drag one on top of the other; after they're grouped, you can move and minimize several panels as one unit. This technique is handy for keeping commonly used or related panels together.

You can save panel groups and panel positions as part of custom workspaces. (See the later section "Creating and Saving Workspaces.")

Panels can always be toggled on or off from the Window menu. If you don't see a panel you need or have accidentally closed one, look for it on the Window menu. Many panels have shortcut keys; if you use a panel often, use its shortcut key combination for easy access.

Creating and Saving Workspaces

One of the most useful additions in recent versions of Flash is its ability to save your *workspaces,* or the appearance and layout of workspace items such as the toolbar, Timeline, Property inspector, and panels.

Saving workspaces is essential if you're sharing a computer workstation with other people and want to recall your favorite panels and setup instantly. However, a workspace can also be useful for maintaining different views for different projects, even if you're the only person working on your computer.

To create and save your workspace layout, follow these steps:

1. **Open and position any panels you want to make available, including the Tools panel, Timeline, Motion Editor, and Property inspector.**

   You can toggle panels on or off from the Window menu.

2. **Choose Window⇨Workspace⇨New Workspace.**

3. **Enter a new name for your workspace and click OK.**

To recall a workspace, choose Window⇨Workspace⇨*Your Workspace Name* or select a workspace from the Workspace selector in the upper-right corner of your screen. The current workspace rebuilds and appears exactly as you saved it.

You can view all saved workspaces at any time by choosing Window⇨Workspace⇨Manage Workspaces. From this dialog box, you can also choose to delete or rename existing workspaces.

You can't modify, delete, or rename default workspaces, such as Default, Classic, and Designer.

Saving and Opening Documents

Always save a document after you make significant changes or additions to it, and always save (though it isn't necessary) a new document immediately after you create it. To save a document, choose File⇨Save. Enter a name for the file and choose a location on your hard drive to save it. You can save Flash work files in .fla format or the new .xfl file format.

To open an existing document, choose File⇨Open and locate the Flash file on your hard drive. Flash files are saved using the .fla extension, and published Flash movies are saved using the .swf extension.

You may need at some point to save a copy of your document under a new name, to either create an alternative version or perhaps make it compatible with an older version of Flash. Flash CS5 can save .fla files in CS4 format to make it compatible with the previous version of Flash.

Flash CS4 can't open .xfl or Flash CS5–format .fla files. To share a file with someone using Flash CS4, choose File⇨Save As⇨Flash CS4 Document (*.fla).

To save a copy of your document under a new name, choose File⇨Save As. Choose a location on your hard drive and enter a new filename. The drop-down list at the bottom of the Save As dialog box lets you choose in which version of Flash to save the file. For example, you can save files one version earlier into Flash CS4 format.

FLA vs. XFL File Format

If you used previous versions of Flash, you probably noticed that Flash CS5 features a new file format: .xfl. Thus new, uncompressed file format results in a project folder containing a number of .xml files and any original assets (such as images and audio files) that you may have imported into your project's library. Because of this *open* file format, resources in your project can be exchanged with and opened in other applications. The XFL file format opens up the possibility of Flash files eventually being editable in other applications.

The traditional FLA file format combines all your project's vital information and resource files into a single file, making it more portable but less likely to exchange with other applications. You don't have direct access to assets you've imported into your project; for most purposes, however, the standard FLA file format is suitable, especially if Flash CS5 Professional is your sole editor for Flash applications.

Saving a document in an older version of Flash may make some newer features unavailable. Avoid saving files in an older file format unless you absolutely need to make them available to an older version of Flash.

Getting to Know Flash Player 10

Flash Player is at the heart of Flash technology. The player, which you can find as a plug-in to Web browsers or as a standalone application, runs and plays completed Flash movies, known as SWF (ShockWave Flash) files.

Beyond simple playback, Flash Player is also responsible for deciphering and carrying out instructions written in *ActionScript,* the powerful, built-in Flash scripting language. ActionScript, discussed in Chapter 7 in this minibook, gives your Flash movies many more capabilities, including playback control, real-time user interaction, and complex effects.

Users must have Flash Player installed in order to view movies. If you don't have it installed, you can get the free download from the Adobe Web site at www.adobe.com. Fortunately, the Flash Player is installed on over 90 percent of Internet-enabled PCs on average worldwide.

Talking about Layers

If you've worked with other programs that use layers (such as Photoshop or Illustrator), the concept is much the same as using layers to arrange and stack artwork in these applications. If you're new to *layers,* think of them as clear pieces of film stacked on top of each other. Each layer can contain its own artwork and animations.

In Flash, you use layers to stack artwork and animations on the stage, allowing them to exist together visually but to be edited or moved independently from one another. You can reorder layers to position artwork in front of or behind artwork on other layers.

 To create a new layer, click the New Layer icon at the bottom of the Timeline. The layer is automatically assigned a name; you can rename any layer by double-clicking its name and typing a new name.

To delete a layer, follow these steps:

1. **In the Timeline window below the stage, select the layer you want to delete.**

Hold down the Shift key to select multiple layers. You can then click the Trash icon to delete all selected layers at one time.

 2. **Click the Delete Layer icon below the Timeline.**

The beauty of working with layers is that you can easily change the stacking order and appearance of artwork and animations distributed across those layers. To reorder layers, simply select a layer by clicking its label on the Timeline and then click and drag the layer up or down in the stacking order and release it to its new position (see Figure 1-5). Layers at the top of the list appear in front of other objects in lower layers; in contrast, layers at the bottom of the list appear below or behind items on higher layers.

Figure 1-5:
Shuffling
layers is
easy —
just drag.

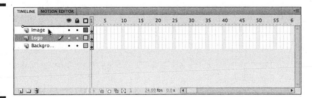

Two additional aspects of managing layers include toggling a layer and its contents to be visible or invisible and locking layers to prevent their contents from being accidentally moved or modified.

 To toggle a layer's visibility on or off, click any layer in the column below the Eye icon. To toggle all layers on or off, click the Eye icon at the top of the column.

 To prevent layer contents from being modified, click any layer in the column below the Padlock icon. To unlock it, click the Padlock icon again. To lock or unlock all layers, click the Padlock icon at the top of the column.

Locking layers ensures that you don't accidentally move or delete the art-work it contains. Make a habit of locking layers whenever you aren't working with them.

Layer visibility affects only what you see inside the authoring environment and has no effect on the finished SWF file. Layers whose visibility is toggled off in your document still appear when published. You can, however, over-ride this behavior in your document's publish settings, discussed in Chapter 9 of this minibook.

Importing Files

Sometimes you need to use assets — such as artwork or photo files created in Adobe Photoshop or Illustrator, MP3 sound files, and even video files — that weren't created in Flash. Here are some of the file formats you can import into your Flash movie:

✦ Images: EPS, GIF, JPEG, PNG, TIFF

✦ Flash SWF

✦ Layered artwork files: AI (Adobe Illustrator) and PSD (Photoshop)

✦ Audio files: AIFF, MP3, and WAV

✦ Video files: DV, F4V, FLV, MOV, MPEG, QuickTime

You can import these types of files directly to the stage for immediate use or to your document's library (see Chapter 3 of this minibook) for storage until you're ready to place them on the stage.

Follow these steps to import files to the stage:

1. **Choose File⇨Import⇨Import to Stage.**

2. **Select from your hard drive the file or files you want to import.**

Imported items are placed on the stage on the selected layer and frame.

Follow these steps to import files directly to the library:

1. **Choose File⇨Import⇨Import to Library.**

2. **Select the files from your hard drive that you want to import and click the Open button.**

Imported files don't appear on the stage but are available in the Library panel for later use.

FLA and SWF files

The life of a Flash project involves at least two different types of files: your authoring (FLA or XFL) file, in which all your work is created, and the final product, your compressed movie or SWF file.

FLA and XFL are used only during the authoring process. When you're ready to distribute your finished movie, publish a SWF file that can be displayed by Flash Player.

These SWF files can be created from either the Publish or Export menu options and are compressed movie files (typically smaller than their FLA and XFL counterparts) that contain all the graphics and information necessary to display your movie.

Flash Player can't read FLA or XFL files, and SWF files can't be deconstructed into usable FLA files. Changes to your Flash movie are always made in the original FLA or XFL file and must be exported to a new SWF file again if you want to view them in Flash Player.

To select multiple files for import, hold down the Shift key when prompted to select files from your hard drive. You can bring several files to the stage or library in one step.

Exporting Files from Flash

In contrast to the Import menu, the Export menu is used to generate files from your current document *out* of Flash, most often to create a compressed SWF file (movie) for final delivery. Additionally, the menu can be used to generate static (such as JPEG or GIF) images from specific frames in your movie.

Publishing Your Movie

The final step in preparing your movie to be posted on the Web, distributed on CD-ROM, or used as a desktop application is the publishing process, which includes these important tasks:

✦ **For Web publishing:** Export the final SWF file that's playable by Flash Player and create all additional files (such as Web pages) necessary to display your movie.

✦ **For desktop publishing:** Create an AIR application that's viewable in the AIR runtime.

✦ **For the desktop or a CD/DVD-ROM:** Create self-contained .app or .exe files.

The File menu's publish settings and options handle the setup and publication of your movie so that you can show the world your new creation.

Flash can create all these file types at publish-time:

✦ **HTML:** To display movies on the Web, you need to contain them within a Web page or HTML file. Flash takes care of creating this page for you.

✦ **JPG, GIF, or PNG:** You can create static images from the first frame of your Flash movie in these Web-friendly image formats. These are useful for a number of purposes, including previews or stand-ins when the Flash plug-in is not available.

✦ **Projector:** If you want to distribute your movie as a standalone file, you can create a Mac or PC compatible *projector* that includes Flash Player. Projectors are good in situations where you want to distribute a movie offline and not require your users to download the Flash player.

✦ **SWF:** This is the most common format in which you'll publish your Flash movies. SWF files are playable in the Flash player/plug-in, and are compressed, ready-to-view versions of your original file.

Chapter 9 of this minibook explores publishing in more detail.

Chapter 2: Drawing in Flash CS5

In This Chapter

✔ **Creating shapes and lines**

✔ **Editing and selecting shapes**

✔ **Tweaking and splicing shapes and lines**

✔ **Transforming shapes and artwork**

✔ **Creating and modifying text**

✔ **Working with colors and gradients**

✔ **Using the Brush tool**

Many great creations start with the most basic shapes and build from there. In this chapter, you discover the secrets of drawing shapes and lines and working with colors in Flash.

Drawing Shapes and Lines

To get your creation started, become familiar with the Shape and Line tools on the Tools panel and use them as the starting point for everything from basic buttons to complex illustrations.

When you're ready to create more complex artwork beyond the capabilities offered by the Shape and Line tools, the Pen and Pencil tools are standing by. These tools work quite differently, and for that reason should be chosen based on the kind of artwork you want to create.

The following sections show you how to get started creating basic shapes and lines.

Drawing basic shapes with the shape tools

 On the Tools panel, locate the Rectangle tool; also notice a small arrow in the lower-right corner of the icon, which means that more tools are hidden underneath. Click and hold the Rectangle tool to reveal the Oval and Polystar tools; select the shape tool you want to use.

Before you draw the shape, set some colors for it by using the two swatches at the bottom of the Tools panel. The Fill color swatch (indicated by the paint bucket icon) lets you specify a color to fill your shape. The Stroke Color swatch (indicated by the pencil icon) controls the outline color.

Flash lets you choose colors from the Swatches panel. You can add your own colors to this panel, but for now, choose one of the available colors for your shape's fill and stroke.

Click and drag on the stage to create a shape. Notice that shapes are drawn by default from the left corner outward. You can draw shapes from the center (which is sometimes easier) by holding down the Option (Mac) or Alt (Windows) key while drawing the shape.

To constrain a shape proportionally, hold down the Shift key while drawing or resizing.

Merging shapes

If you overlap two or more shapes in Flash, they automatically *merge,* or become one complete shape. You can take advantage of this behavior by using an overlapping shape to knock out another, or you can make more complex shapes by combining simpler ones.

You may also find that overlapping strokes results in divided fill areas, which can be a desirable effect. Experiment by drawing and overlapping shapes and using the Selection tool to select parts of the resulting object.

Creating perfect lines with the Line tool

The Line tool makes constructing perfect, straight lines quick and easy. To create a straight line, choose the Line tool from the Tools panel, click and drag on your stage where you want the line to start, and release the mouse button where you want the line to end.

To modify your line's color or appearance, select it with the Selection tool and use the Property inspector to change the stroke color and size. You also find a Style drop-down list, which lets you choose among straight, dotted, dashed, and artistic stroke styles.

To create perfectly vertical or horizontal lines, hold down the Shift key while using the Line tool. You can also create diagonal lines in 45-degree increments by using this same method.

Creating lines and curves with the Pen tool

Using the Pen tool may be a bit different from tools you're used to, unless, of course, you've used the Pen tool in applications such as Illustrator or Photoshop. The Pen tool isn't a freehand drawing tool; rather, you use it to create *paths,* or outlines, composed by connecting anchor points. When you click and create new points, lines are automatically drawn to connect those points. You can then either bend those lines into precise curves or leave them straight.

The best way to understand the Pen tool is to practice working with it. Visualize a shape you want to draw (for example, a leaf), and try to create it with the Pen tool.

To get started, follow these steps:

1. **Select the Pen tool from the Tools panel.**

2. **Use the Color swatch on the bottom of the Tools panel to set a stroke color.**

3. **Click to set the first point on the stage and then construct a line by clicking again to set a second point where you want the line to end.**

4. **Click to set a new point and before releasing the mouse button, drag to the left or right to bend the new line into a curve.**

    The more you drag in a particular direction, the more extreme the curve you create.

5. **Continue creating new points and experimenting with different curves.**

6. **Move your mouse pointer over the first point you created (a loop appears above the icon) and click to close the path and complete the shape.**

Book VII
Chapter 2

Drawing in
Flash CS5

The Pen tool attempts to continue a curve in the same direction even after a new point is set. To reset the last point drawn back to a straight line, hold down the Option (Mac) or Alt (Windows) key and click the last point created before setting a new one.

Drawing freehand with the Pencil tool

The precise nature of the Pen tool is great for certain situations, but if you prefer the intuitive feel of freehand drawing or want to create more natural or rough artwork, consider using the Pencil tool.

An attractive feature of the Pencil tool is that it has three different modes to choose from. Each mode provides a different level of *smoothing,* so even if your hand isn't the steadiest, the Pencil tool compensates by automatically smoothing out lines or curves while you create them.

 Select the Pencil tool and choose the appropriate smoothing mode using the selector in the lower-right corner of the Tools panel:

✦ **Straighten:** Forces lines to the nearest straight line; perfect for drawing or tracing straight edges or boxy outlines.

✦ **Smooth:** Smoothes out lines or curves to the next closest perfect curve.

✦ **Ink:** Provides less smoothing and keeps lines and curves as natural as possible.

The mode you select depends completely on what type of shapes and lines you're trying to draw. If your shape is more diverse than one mode can handle, you can switch modes from line to line as needed.

Selecting and Editing Shapes

After you create a shape, you can select and move it by using the Selection tool at the top of the Tools panel. Flash shapes are easy to edit because you can select the stroke and fill independently to separate one from the other.

To select and move the stroke or fill only, follow these steps:

1. **Select the Selection tool from the Tools panel.**

2. **Click either your shape's stroke or fill once to activate it.**

To select the entire shape, double-click the fill of your shape or use the Selection tool to drag around it on the stage (see Figure 2-1).

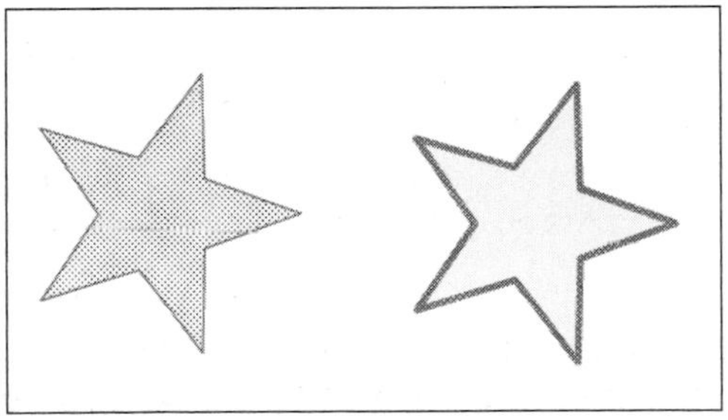

Figure 2-1:
Fill (left)
or stroke
(right)?

3. **Click and drag the selected stroke or fill or use the arrow keys to separate it from the rest of the shape.**

Modifying fill and stroke colors

You can choose your fill and stroke colors ahead of time before you start drawing, but if you change your mind, modifying colors is easy to do.

You can modify either the fill or stroke colors of a preexisting shape in these three ways:

✦ Select the entire shape and change its fill and stroke colors from the swatches in the Property inspector (see Figure 2-2).

Figure 2-2:
Use the Property inspector to change the shape's fill or stroke color.

✦ Select the entire shape and change the fill and/or stroke colors by using the Fill and Stroke swatches on the Tools panel.

✦ Specify colors on the Tools panel and use the Ink Bottle tool by clicking the stroke or use the Paint Bucket tool by clicking the fill.

To apply a fill color to your shape, select it on the stage and choose a color from the Fill swatch at the bottom of the Tools panel. Grab the Paint Bucket tool and click inside the shape. To apply a stroke color, select a color from the Stroke swatch at the bottom of the Tools panel and select the Ink Bottle tool. Click the edge of your shape once to set a stroke with the selected color.

You can also set Fill or Stroke colors from the Fill and Stroke section of the Property inspector when the Ink Bottle or Paint Bucket tools are selected.

To remove a fill or stroke completely, select a shape and select None from either the Fill or Stroke color swatch.

Merge versus Object Drawing mode

Being able to freely tear apart shapes can be quite flexible and useful, though some people prefer to work with shapes as single objects (similar to Illustrator CS5). For this reason, Object Drawing mode was created; this optional mode automatically combines the stroke and fill of a shape into a single object, which you can move and resize as a whole. A shape drawn in

Object Drawing mode has a bounding box around it; the stroke and fill are moved together as one object.

 You can enable Object Drawing mode when any drawing or shape tool is selected, as shown in Figure 2-3, by clicking the Object Drawing mode button at the bottom of the Tools panel. Try drawing a shape on the stage — notice that the shape appears with a bounding box around it and that the stroke and fill can no longer be individually selected and separated.

Figure 2-3:
A shape drawn in Object Drawing mode.

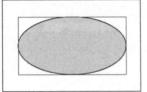

To convert a shape drawn in Object Drawing mode to its raw form, select the shape and choose Modify⇨Break Apart or double-click the shape to edit it within the Drawing Object itself.

 Unlike shapes drawn in Standard mode, drawing objects can't be merged; break apart any drawing objects first or choose Modify⇨Combine Objects⇨ Union to merge them.

Splicing and Tweaking Shapes and Lines

You can easily dissect mergeable shapes (not drawing objects) by selecting only certain portions with the Selection or Lasso tools, as shown in Figure 2-4. Try drawing a marquee around only half the shape with the Selection or Subselection arrow; notice that only half the shape or line becomes selected and you can then separate it.

Figure 2-4:
To reshape, grab an edge or a corner.

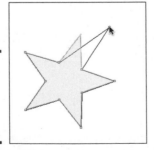

Tweaking a shape with the Selection and Subselection tools

If you need to tweak the shape beyond its original form, you can use Selection or Subselection tools to tweak, distort, and reshape. To tweak or reshape with the Selection tool, move it outside and close to an edge or corner of your shape; notice that a small curved or angled line icon appears next to your pointer. Click and drag to bend, reshape, or distort the outline of your shape, as shown in Figure 2-5.

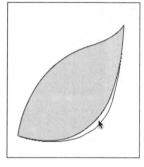 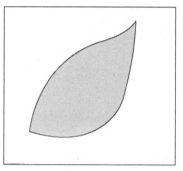

Figure 2-5: To modify a curve with the Selection tool, drag an edge.

You can use the Selection tool to bend straight edges into curves. Try it on a line or straight edge from a rectangle and you'll see that you can easily pull the line into a curve!

To tweak or reshape with the Subselection tool, click the outside edge or stroke of a shape to activate its path. Each point is represented by a hollow box. Click any point to activate it; click and drag it or move it using the arrow keys to reshape (see Figure 2-6).

Figure 2-6: Use the Subselection tool to modify specific points.

Editing a shape with the Lasso tool

When you need to create a selection with more precision than the Selection tool allows (for example, around an odd shape or a tricky area), use the Lasso tool. The Lasso tool draws freehand selections around specific areas of your artwork. To draw a selection with the Lasso tool, select it from the Tools panel and click and drag to draw a selection around the target area, as shown in Figure 2-7. Be sure to close the selection by overlapping the starting and ending points.

Figure 2-7: Select areas with the Lasso tool; close the path for best results.

You can perform partial selections only with *raw* (broken apart) shapes and lines. Artwork drawn in Object Drawing mode needs to be broken apart first (choose Modify⇨Break Apart) or modified in Edit mode. To enter a drawing object's Edit mode, double-click it with the Selection tool.

Modifying artwork created by using the Pen and Pencil tools

Interestingly enough, although the Pen and Pencil tools behave in completely different ways, both ultimately create the same element: a path. A path can be filled (if closed) or modified on a point-by-point basis, or you can apply a stroke to it.

To fine-tune a path, choose the Subselection tool (the white arrow) from the Tools panel. Click the path; it becomes highlighted and the points show up as hollow boxes. You can now select any individual point and selectively drag it or move it with the arrow keys to reshape the path.

To adjust a curve by using the Subselection tool, highlight the point adjacent to the curve you want to modify. A handle appears; you can grab and move this handle to adjust the curve.

To add or subtract points, click and hold down on the Pen tool to select the Add Anchor Point or Subtract Anchor Point tools. Click exactly on the path where you want to add an anchor point or click a point directly to remove it.

Transforming Artwork and Shapes

After you have some drawing done, you may want to adjust the width, height, or rotation of your artwork. Depending on the level of precision you're looking for, you can do this in two ways: manually by using the Transform tool or by dialing in exact values on the Transform panel.

Using the Free Transform tool

 Select a shape or some artwork on your stage and then choose the Free Transform tool from the Tools panel. A bounding box with handles at all four sides and corners appears, as shown in Figure 2-8. You can drag any of the side handles to resize the width and height.

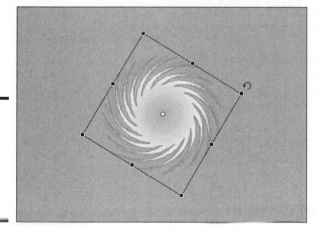

Figure 2-8:
Using the Free Transform tool to rotate and resize.

To rotate your artwork, hover over any corner handle until you see the rotation icon (a circular arrow) and then click and drag to rotate the artwork freely.

To resize your art proportionally, hold down the Shift key while dragging a handle. If you hold down the Shift key while in Rotation mode, it limits your movements to precise 45-degree increments.

Using the Transform panel

For those times when you need to dial in exact transformation values, you can use the Transform panel (shown in Figure 2-9); choose Window⇨ Transform to open it. The Transform panel displays text boxes you can use to enter exact transformation values for width and height or a specific rotation angle in degrees.

Figure 2-9: Enter precise amounts of scaling, rotation, and skewing.

Follow these steps to transform artwork by using the Transform panel:

1. **Select the object you want to transform on the stage and open the Transform panel by choosing Window⇨Transform.**

2. **To increase the size of the artwork, enter width and height percentage values higher than 100 percent; to decrease the size, enter values less than 100 percent. To keep the sizes proportional, select the Constrain Values check box.**

3. **To rotate your artwork, select the Rotate radio button, click the number to activate the text box, type a value higher than 0 degrees, and press Enter.**

   Rotation is performed clockwise; to rotate counterclockwise, enter a negative number.

Skewing your artwork

Skewing transforms your artwork on a 3D plane and can add interesting perspective to shapes. You can perform skewing from the Transform panel by selecting the Skew option button and entering values for horizontal and vertical skew amounts.

Give it a try: Select your shape, type some skew values, and press Enter to see the transformation applied. If you're not happy, don't fret; simply click the Remove Transform button in the lower-right corner of the Transform panel to restore your normal settings.

Working with Type

If you're looking to display important information in your Flash movie or you simply want to add creative text elements to your design, the flexible Text tool in Flash can create attractive type for design elements, buttons, titles, and informational text areas.

TLF versus classic text

Flash CS5 features several new typesetting improvements in the new TLF (Text Layout Framework) text engine, bringing to the table many abilities already found in applications such as Illustrator and InDesign.

Here are the new Flash TLF text features:

✦ Vertical and Vertical Left-to-Right orientation

✦ Multicolumn text areas

✦ Threaded text across several type areas

Though TLF text is the default when you work with the Text tool, you still have the option to set text areas as *classic* text, providing support for older movies and projects.

Follow these steps to create basic type on the stage:

1. **In a new or existing file, add a new layer to the timeline by choosing Insert⇨Timeline⇨Layer.**

2. **Choose the Text tool from the Tools panel.**

3. **Click anywhere on the stage to create a text box and then enter some text.**

4. **Click and drag within the text box to select all the text you just entered, as shown in Figure 2-10.**

5. **Fine-tune the appearance of your text by selecting character, color, size, and other options in the Character section of the Property inspector.**

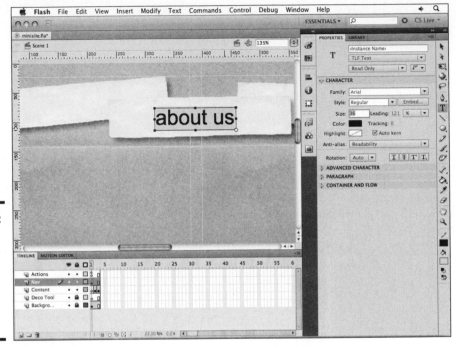

Figure 2-10:
Use the
Property
inspector
to modify
typeface,
style, size,
and color.

Creating multicolumn and threaded text

Like many existing Adobe applications, Flash now lets you split single text areas into multiple columns as well as "thread" text across several individual text boxes at once. This capability is especially handy if the amount of text in a box is too large for that area alone; using threaded text, you can make text that originates in one box "flow" into a different box elsewhere in your movie.

To create multicolumn text, follow these steps:

1. **In a new or existing file, add a new layer to the timeline by choosing Insert➪Timeline➪Layer.**

2. **Select the Text tool from the Tools panel. Make sure that the text drop-down list at the top of the Property Inspector (below the <Instance Name> field) is set to TLF Text.**

3. **Click and drag on the stage to create a text box that has a fixed width and height.**

   The text box appears with a bounding box and handles on all four sides and corners, as shown in Figure 2-11.

4. **To adjust the size of the box, hover over a handle on any corner or side until a double arrow appears. Click and drag the handle to resize the box.**

In port   Bounding box

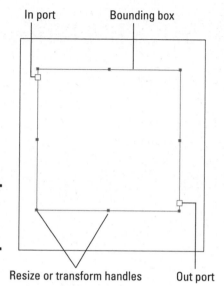

Figure 2-11:
Anatomy of
a text box.

Resize or transform handles   Out port

5. Click within the box and either type or paste some text into the box.

For best results, enter enough text until you eventually see a red plus sign appear on the out port (refer to Figure 2-11) of the box.

Typing too much text in a fixed-size text box creates an *overrun*, indicated by a red plus sign in the out port of the text box.

6. With the Text tool still active, locate the Container and Flow options in the Property inspector.

You should see a Columns option, already set to 1.

7. Click and drag over the 1 to set it to 2, or double-click the 1 and enter 2 instead.

This step creates two columns in the text box and reformats your text appropriately, as shown in Figure 2-12.

Next, you add a second text box and thread it to the first so that any text that overruns the first box automatically appears in the second.

8. On the same layer and with the Text tool selected, click the stage to deselect the first text box and then click and drag to draw a second text box somewhere next to it.

9. Use the bounding box handles to adjust the size of this new box on the stage.

10. Click the first text box on the stage to make it active, and click the out port directly (where the red plus sign appears).

The icon changes <icon> to indicate that you're carrying overrun text from that box.

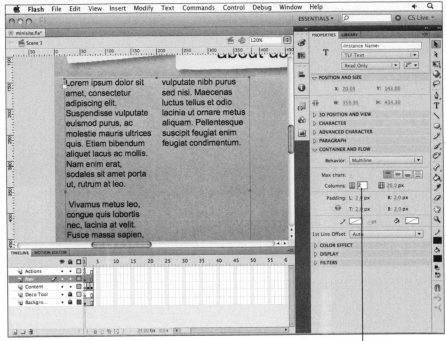

Figure 2-12:
Set multiple columns for a text box in the Property inspector's Container and Flow section.

Set the number of columns for the text box.

11. Hover over the new box you created, and click it to make it active.

A line appears between the two boxes, and the overrun text from the first box continues into the second, as shown in Figure 2-13. The two boxes are now threaded.

Figure 2-13:
Two text areas threaded together on the stage.

Transforming type

You can transform type just like shapes and artwork by using either the Transform tool or the Transform panel. Regardless of any transformations your type undergoes, it remains editable.

To transform a line of type, make sure that it's active by first selecting it using the Selection or Text tools. To transform, choose the Transform tool or open the Transform panel.

Distorting and modifying character shapes

You can distort and modify type outlines just like any other shape or path. However, type is created on a special type path so that it can be edited at any point. You need to break your type characters off a path first in order to tweak any of their outlines.

To modify or distort type outlines, follow these steps:

1. **Select the type you want to modify and choose Modify➪Break Apart.**

2. **If your type is longer than a single character, repeat Step 1 until the bounding box disappears from around the characters, and you see the stippled fill pattern within each character.**

3. **Use the Selection or Subselection tool to modify the outlines (as we demonstrate with shapes earlier in this chapter).**

4. **(Optional) Use the Ink Bottle tool to apply a stroke to the type.**

If you're familiar with Adobe Illustrator, think of Break Apart as the Flash equivalent of the Create Outlines command.

Creating Colors and Gradients

You've undoubtedly (or not) seen and made use of the built-in color swatches in Flash, but suppose that you want to use colors that are *not* included in the Swatches panel. Here's where the Color panel comes into play. From this panel, you can mix and create your own color swatches, make gradients, and even apply transparency effects to existing colors on the stage.

You may have already seen the Swatches panel in action, if you used it to select fill and stroke colors from the Tools panel and Property inspector. The Swatches panel exists on its own free-floating panel as well, which you can open by choosing Window➪Swatches.

The 256 colors on this panel represent the Web-safe color spectrum, which is optimized to ensure that all users, even those with monitors using lower color depth settings, can enjoy your creations.

You can add colors to the Swatches panel from the Color panel, which means that you have access to your own, custom colors from anywhere the Swatches panel appears.

Creating and adding colors from the Color panel

The Color panel features two ways to select a precise color: the color wheel on the right or the sliders on the left. You can combine the two methods to hone in on just the right shade. After you choose the color you want, you can easily add it as a swatch to the Swatches panel by choosing Add Swatch from the panel menu, as shown in Figure 2-14.

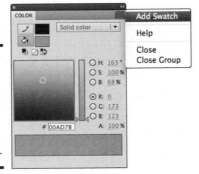

Figure 2-14: Select a custom color by using the sliders or color wheel.

To apply a color choice automatically to the stroke or fill swatches, click either the Fill or Stroke color swatch in the upper-left corner of the Color panel. Any changes made using the color wheel or sliders are applied automatically to the selected swatch.

To select a color on the color wheel, click and drag the cross hair inside the color wheel until you find the right hue (for example, greens). Use the slider to the right to select the exact shade of that color.

To select a color with the sliders, first select either the RGB (Red, Green, Blue) or HSB (Hue, Saturation, Brightness) sliders from the Color panel's panel menu. Move the sliders to find the exact color you want. You can fine-tune this color further with the color wheel and slider.

To save your new color as a swatch, find the color you want and choose Add Swatch from the panel menu. Your new color appears as a new swatch on the Swatches panel, and you can select the color anywhere that the Swatches panel appears.

Creating gradients

Gradients are blends between two or more colors that you can use to fill any area or shape, just like a solid color. If you look at the Swatches panel, you see some gradient presets you can use right away. You can also use the Color panel to create your own gradients and add them to the Swatches panel.

Follow these steps to create a gradient:

1. **Open the Color panel by choosing Window⇨Color and choose Linear Gradient from the Color Type drop-down list.**

Linear is one of two gradient types you can create.

2. **Double-click one of the horizontal sliders that appears above the gradient ramp at the bottom to see the Swatches panel; pick a color to apply to that slider.**

To add more colors to your gradient, click anywhere on the gradient ramp to add a slider. You can then double-click this slider to set the color.

3. **Adjust the color blends of the gradient by moving the sliders closer together or farther apart.**

To remove colors or sliders, click the slider you want to remove and drag it off the panel to the left or right.

4. **Choose Add Swatch from the panel menu to save your new gradient.**

The gradient swatch is added to the Swatches panel alongside the existing gradients.

In addition to being able to create *linear gradients,* which blend colors evenly in a straight line, you can create *radial gradients,* a special type of gradient shape where colors blend from the center outward in a circular motion. To set a gradient as a radial gradient, choose Radial from the Type drop-down list on the Color panel.

Both gradient types are created and added to the Swatches panel in the exact same manner, as described in the preceding step list.

Applying and transforming gradients

After you create a gradient, you can use it to fill a shape the same way you set a solid fill color. After you apply a gradient to a shape on the stage, you can use the Gradient tool to modify the gradient's direction, size, and intensity.

To modify a Linear gradient fill, follow these steps:

1. **Click and hold down your mouse pointer on the Free Transform tool to select the Gradient Transform tool. Select a shape with a gradient fill.**

   A bounding box appears.

2. **Use the bounding box's center point to move the transition point of the gradient.**

3. **Use the handle on the right side to modify the intensity of the gradient.**

4. **Change the direction of the gradient by using the rotating arrow icon in the upper-right corner of the selection area.**

If you're working with a radial gradient, notice that the Gradient Transform tool behaves slightly differently. An extra round handle appears and lets you scale the gradient, and the rotating-arrow icon (which rotates the gradient area) is located in the lower-right corner. Experiment with both linear and radial gradients to see their differences.

Working with the Brush Tool

Tools, such as the Pen and Pencil, offer you different ways of creating stroked paths. In contrast, the Brush tool paints with fills. Much like a good old-fashioned paintbrush, this tool can create thick, broad strokes with solid colors or gradients for excellent artistic effects.

The Brush tool features several different brush sizes and tips as well as five modes for controlling how (and where) the Brush tool works its magic.

Follow these steps to use the Brush tool:

1. **With the Brush tool selected, choose a brush size and tip shape from the bottom of the Tools panel.**

2. **Choose a fill color from the Fill color swatch on the Tools panel, Property inspector, or Color panel.**

3. **Freely paint on the stage to see the Brush tool in action.**

The different Brush modes change where and how the tool works against different objects on the stage. A good way to see these modes in action is to draw a shape on the stage and make sure that the shape has both a stroke and fill set. Experiment by changing modes and trying to paint over the shape. In Figure 2-15, the selected object was painted over with the Brush tool in Paint Selection mode. This mode affects only the area of the selected shape.

Figure 2-15:
Painting
in Paint
Selection
mode
affects only
the selected
shape.

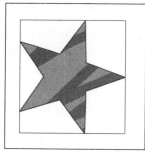

Because the strokes left behind by the Brush tool are simply filled shapes, you can apply a stroke to this tool, change its fill color, or use it to create interesting shapes that you can tweak by using the same methods we demonstrate in the earlier section "Transforming Artwork and Shapes."

To apply an outline to a painted area, set a color by using the Stroke color swatch on the Tools panel, select the Ink Bottle tool, and click the outer edge of the fill. You can now use the Property inspector to change the width, color, and style of the stroke as well.

Chapter 3: Symbols and Animation

In This Chapter

✔ Understanding symbols and the library

✔ Creating and editing symbols

✔ Using the Spray Brush and Deco tools

✔ Working with frames and keyframes in the Timeline

✔ Creating animations with tweens

✔ Understanding frame-by-frame animation

✔ Working with the frame rate

*O*nce you're familiar with the Flash drawing tools, explore the topic that Flash is best known for: animation. In this chapter, you bring your creations to life with movement, interactivity, and sounds. Flash CS5 introduces significant new changes to the way animation is created on the Timeline, which is exciting for new and experienced users alike.

First, you explore some central concepts in Flash: symbols and the library. Because the symbol is an essential part of creating animation in Flash, you discover how to create and modify symbols before diving into your first animation tasks.

Visiting the Library

Each Flash document contains a *library*, a repository of reusable graphics, animations, buttons, sounds, video, and even fonts. As you build your Flash movie, you can add to your library any piece of artwork you've created on the stage, where the artwork is stored as a *symbol*, as shown in Figure 3-1. Your library is managed from the Library panel, which is visible in the default workspace. If you don't see your Library panel, choose Window⇨Library to open it.

What makes symbols powerful is that you can reuse them as many times as necessary. Simply drag and drop a copy (an *instance*) from the Library panel onto the stage anywhere in your movie. Most importantly, each instance remains linked to the original in your library. Any changes made to the original (or *master*) automatically update any instances of the same symbol used throughout the movie.

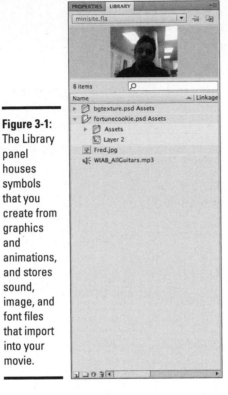

Figure 3-1:
The Library panel houses symbols that you create from graphics and animations, and stores sound, image, and font files that import into your movie.

Symbols are broken down into three main categories: graphics, buttons, and movie clips. You can find out more about button and movie clip symbols in Chapters 6 and 7 of this minibook.

Creating and Modifying Graphic Symbols

Certain types of animation in Flash require the use of symbols, so you should become familiar with the most basic symbol type: *graphics*. You can convert any object on the stage into a graphic symbol, allowing you to take advantage of additional features that are unique to symbols. You can also create empty graphic symbols from the Library panel or by choosing Insert➪New Symbol and adding content to them afterward.

Follow these steps to create a graphic symbol:

1. **Choose Insert⇨New Symbol or choose New Symbol from the Panel menu in the upper right corner of the Library panel.**

    The Create New Symbol dialog box appears.

2. **Assign a name to the symbol, choose Graphic from the Type drop-down list, and click OK.**

    You see a blank slate on the stage, where you can add to your symbol.

3. **Within the new symbol, use your drawing or type tools to create some interesting artwork.**

4. **Choose Scene 1 from the navigation bar above the stage to exit the symbol and return to the main Timeline.**

    You see your new symbol listed in the Library panel. *Note:* The symbol will not appear on the stage until you place it from the Library (discussed later in this chapter).

Follow these steps to create a graphic symbol from existing artwork on the stage:

1. **Create some interesting artwork using the drawing tools.**

2. **Using the Selection tool, select the new artwork on the stage.**

3. **Choose Modify⇨Convert to Symbol.**

    The Convert to Symbol dialog box appears.

4. **Enter a name for the symbol, choose Graphic from the Type drop-down list, and click OK.**

    Your new symbol is now listed in the Library panel.

Whenever you convert existing graphics to a symbol, the graphics remain on the stage, enclosed inside a blue bounding box (see Figure 3-2). The Property inspector confirms that the selection is now a graphic symbol (indicated by the icon).

Don't confuse symbols with drawing objects: Both display artwork inside a bounding box, but drawing objects don't have the same abilities as symbols, nor are they stored automatically in your library. Use the Property inspector to determine whether an object is a symbol or a drawing object if you're unsure — a distinctive icon and description appear for each one at the top of the Property inspector.

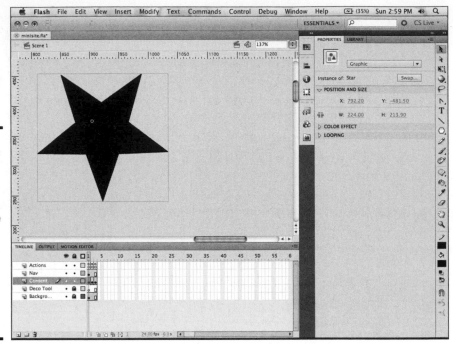

Figure 3-2: A symbol appears enclosed in a bounding box, and the Property inspector (right) shows the symbol's name and type.

Adding symbols to the stage

If you need to reuse a symbol after you add it to your library, you can simply drag a copy from the Library panel and drop it on the stage (see Figure 3-3). Each copy of a symbol is referred to as an *instance* in Flash. Although all instances of a symbol remain linked back to the original in the Library, you have the flexibility to scale, transform, and rotate each instance individually.

Follow these steps to add symbols to the stage:

1. **Locate in your library a symbol that you want to add to the stage.**

2. **Drag a copy from the Library panel to the stage; repeat this step a few times so that you have several instances on the stage.**

3. **Select each instance individually and experiment with different scaling, transforming, and rotating for each one.**

Modifying symbols

After you create symbols, you can modify them from within the library or directly on the stage. Changes made to a symbol are applied to all instances of that symbol throughout the movie.

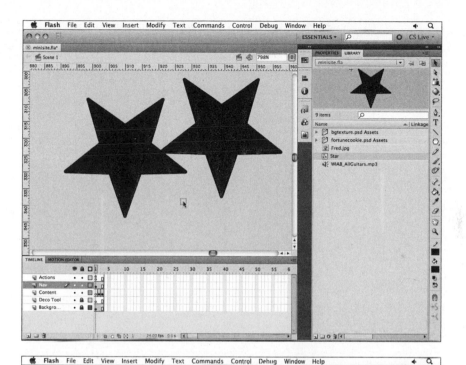

Figure 3-3:
Drag and
drop a
symbol
from your
library to
the stage to
add as many
instances as
you want.

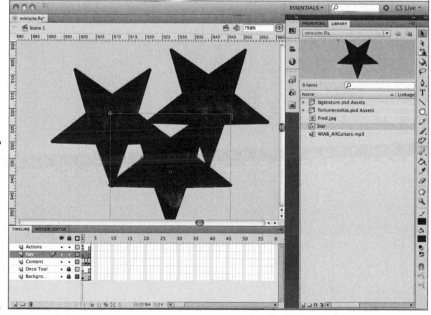

To edit a symbol from within the library, follow these steps:

1. Select a symbol in the Library panel and choose Edit from the panel menu, or double-click any symbol in the Library panel.

To see the true effect of editing the master symbol, use a symbol you dragged previously to the stage.

The symbol appears on the stage in Edit mode.

2. Make some changes in color, shape, or size.

3. Exit the symbol by selecting Scene 1 from the navigation bar above the stage to return to the main Timeline.

Instances of this symbol on the stage reflect the changes you've made to the symbol in the library.

Editing a symbol in place on the stage can be more intuitive, and you may want to modify it to work better with other artwork on the stage. You can directly edit a symbol from any of its instances on the stage (as shown in Figure 3-4), but keep in mind that regardless of which instance you edit, all instances are affected.

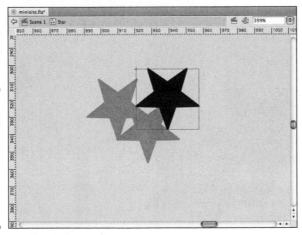

Figure 3-4:
Double-click a symbol instance to edit the symbol in place on the stage.

To edit a symbol in place, follow these steps:

1. Select and double-click any symbol instance on the stage.

You're now in the symbol's Edit mode, but you can still see other objects on the stage in the background. Flash dims objects in the background so that you can see your changes in context.

2. Make changes and exit the symbol's Edit mode by selecting Scene 1 on the navigation bar above the stage.

A closer look at the Library panel

The Library panel is the main storage location for all your symbols, and much like any library, it has essential organizational tools that make managing your symbols easy.

The most basic and common functions are made easy by using several icons found along the bottom of the panel, as shown in the sidebar figure:

- **Panel menu:** All panels have panel menus, which offer additional options or modify the view of the panel itself. The Library panel's panel menu carries out additional symbol and library-related tasks.

- **Pin Library:** Clicking this icon ensures that the current library stays active even when you switch between other open documents. Normal behavior *(unpinned)* is for library views to switch automatically when moving between open documents.

- **New Library Panel:** Click this icon to create a duplicate Library panel in case you want multiple, distinctive views of your current library. You can also open a new Library panel to view libraries from other documents that are open in your workspace.

- **Search:** The text box and magnifying glass under the preview panel can help you search for symbols by name in the Library, which is especially helpful for large libraries. Simply type a full or partial name, and the panel displays matches, if any exist.

- **New Symbol:** Create a new symbol, identical to the command found by choosing Insert⇨New Symbol.

- **New Folder:** Create folders you can sort your symbols into for easy categorization. You can create folders within folders for even finer sorting capabilities.

- **Properties:** If a symbol is highlighted in your library, clicking the Properties icon opens the Symbol Properties window. From there, you can redefine the symbol's name, type, or registration point.

- **Trash Can:** Yes, you guessed it — this symbol deletes *(trashes)* the highlighted symbol in the library. *Be careful:* No warning is given before the deed is done. However, you can choose Edit⇨Undo to reverse this action, if necessary.

Panel menu

New Library

Pin Library   Search

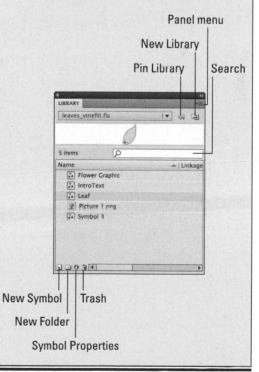

New Symbol | Trash

New Folder

Symbol Properties

Book VII
Chapter 3

Symbols and
Animation

Sorting symbols

Symbols in a library can be sorted using any of the column headers at the top of the symbol list. You may be able to see only the Name and Linkage columns at first glance, but if you use the horizontal scroll bar at the bottom of the panel, you can see additional columns labeled Use Count, Date Modified, and Type.

To sort by any column, click the column name. If the arrow next to the column name is pointing up, the sort is descending, with the highest value at the bottom. If the arrow is pointing down, the sort is ascending, with the highest value at the top.

Organizing symbols with folders

As with any workspace, folders can help sort an otherwise large and unwieldy group of items. You can create folders within the Library panel to sort symbols, imported images, sounds, and other assets as you see fit.

You have a number of ways to group symbols into a folder:

1. **At the bottom of the Library panel, click the New Folder icon to create a new folder.**

2. **Inside the Library panel, click to select a symbol to move into a folder.**

   Shift-click to select several symbols at a time.

3. **Drag the selected symbols into the new folder.**

Or, follow these steps instead:

1. **In the Library panel, click to select the symbol(s) you want to group into a folder.**

   Shift-click to select several symbols at a time.

2. **Right-click or Control+Click (Mac) and choose Move To from the contextual menu that appears, as shown on the left in Figure 3-5.**

3. **When the Move to Folder dialog box appears, select New Folder and enter a name for the new folder in the text field.**

4. **Click Select to create a folder and group selected symbols into it.**

You can also sort symbols into folders as you create them. The Convert to Symbol and New Symbol dialog boxes provide an option to sort new symbols into existing folders or to create new ones as you go.

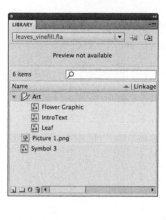

Figure 3-5:
Keep your
library
organized
by grouping
symbols into
folders.

Duplicating symbols

You may want to create a variation of one of your symbols that goes beyond what you can do on an instance-by-instance basis. A good example is two birds that are similar in appearance but one has different-shaped wings or a different base color. This instance is a good case for duplicating an existing symbol so that any changes can be made to the copy and treated as a new symbol.

To duplicate a symbol, select from the Library panel the symbol you want to copy and choose Duplicate from the panel menu in the upper-right corner of the panel. You're given a chance to name the new version of the symbol when the Duplicate Symbol dialog box appears.

You can rename any symbol directly from the Library panel. Select the symbol and choose Rename from the panel menu.

Painting with Symbols

Flash CS5 features two unique tools that enable you to get truly creative with symbols: Spray Brush and Deco. These tools can use symbols from your library, allowing you to paint random textures or fill areas with complex patterns. You can even easily draw symmetrical artwork with the Deco tool's included Symmetry Brush mode or use some of its included presets to create a variety of interesting patterns and graphics on the stage.

**Book VII
Chapter 3**

**Symbols and
Animation**

The Spray Brush tool

The Spray Brush tool paints with instances of a single symbol from your library. You can use the Property inspector to dial in settings for scaling, rotation, and brush angle.

Follow these steps to paint with the Spray Brush tool:

1. **Click the New Layer button, found below the Timeline, to create a new, empty layer to paint on.**

2. **Select the Spray Brush tool from the Tools panel (click and hold the Brush tool to find the Spray Brush tool).**

The Property inspector displays options for the Spray Brush tool.

3. **In the Property inspector, click the Edit button in the Symbol options area.**

The Select Symbol dialog box appears, prompting you to select a symbol from your library.

4. **Choose a symbol and click OK to close the dialog box.**

5. **In the Symbol options area, use the Scale Width and Scale Height sliders to reduce or increase the scaling for each instance painted on the stage.**

6. **In the Brush options area, enter values for the width and height of the brush, and the brush angle, if you want.**

7. **Click and drag on the stage to begin painting.**

The Spray Brush paints with the symbol you selected using the settings you chose in the Property inspector, as shown in Figure 3-6. You control the size, scatter, and scaling.

The Spray Brush tool creates groups from all the paint droplets it leaves behind. You can break apart these groups by choosing Modify⇨Break Apart, or edit its contents by double-clicking the group on the stage.

The Deco tool

The Deco tool features 13 distinctive modes you can use to create interesting textures, patterns, and symmetrical drawings from symbols in your library or from preset patterns. In the following steps, we show you how to experiment with the Deco tool's drawing modes using symbols from your library. First, we show you how to use the Vine Fill:

1. **Open or create a new Flash document, and add at least two graphic symbols to your library using the methods described earlier in this chapter.**

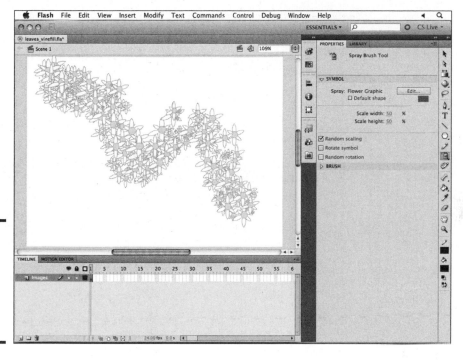

Figure 3-6:
The Spray Brush paints with symbols from your library.

2. **Select the Deco tool from the Tools panel.**

   The Property inspector changes to reflect the current drawing effect, set to Vine Fill.

   Vine Fill mode creates a vine-style pattern between two symbols, using one as the *leaf* (that decorates the vine path) and one as the *flower* (that appears at the end of each *vine*).

3. **In the Leaf section of the Property inspector, click the Edit button to select a symbol from your library to serve as the leaf.**

4. **From the dialog box that appears, choose a symbol from your library and click OK to set that symbol.**

5. **In the Flower section of the Property inspector, click the Edit button to select a symbol from your library to serve as the flower.**

6. **From the dialog box that appears, select a symbol from your library and click OK to set that symbol.**

7. **In the Advanced Options section of the Property inspector, click the color swatch and choose the vine color that will interconnect the two symbols you've chosen when the pattern is created.**

8. **Click the New Layer button below the timeline to create a new, empty layer to paint on.**

9. **Click the stage, and the Deco tool begins to draw a new vine pattern using the symbols you've chosen.**

   The Deco tool draws a vine and caps the vine with the flower symbol you chose. Continue to click and release to draw new vines.

To give the Grid Fill drawing effect a try, follow these steps:

1. **Click the New Layer button below the timeline to create a new, empty layer to use with the Grid Fill.**

2. **If the Deco tool isn't active, select Deco tool from the Tools panel.**

3. **Change the drawing effect from Vine Fill to Grid Fill using the drop-down list at the top of the Property inspector.**

   Grid Fill creates a uniform grid-style pattern within a selected area. You can use Grid Fill to fill either a specific shape on the stage or the entire stage itself.

4. **Click the Tile 1 Edit button to select a fill symbol.**

5. **When the Select Symbol dialog box appears, choose a symbol from your library to use as a pattern and click OK.**

6. **In the Property inspector, click and drag over the Horizontal Spacing and Vertical Spacing values to specify a distance in pixels between each row and column.**

7. **(Optional) Use the Pattern Scale slider to reduce or increase the size of the symbol used to create the pattern.**

8. **Click the stage with the Deco tool, and the stage fills up with a grid pattern using the symbol and settings you chose, as shown in Figure 3-7.**

Figure 3-7:
Fill shapes or the stage itself with Vine and Grid Fills using the Deco tool and symbols from your library.

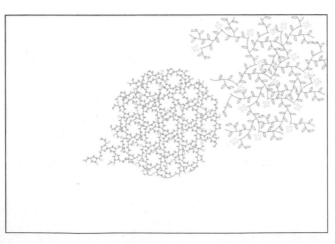

The last drawing effect we show you how to use is the Symmetry Brush, which lets you draw cool symmetrical artwork with symbols. Follow these steps to use the Symmetry Brush:

1. **Click the New Layer button to insert a new layer on the timeline.**

2. **If the Deco tool isn't active, select it from the Tools panel.**

3. **In the Property inspector, select the Symmetry Brush from the Drawing Effect drop-down list.**

4. **To the right of *Module,* click the Edit button.**

5. **From the Select Symbol dialog box that appears, select a symbol from your library to use with the Symmetry Brush and then click OK.**

6. **On the stage, click and drag to begin drawing with the Symmetry Brush.**

   The symbol you chose is duplicated in a rotating pattern around the brush point. Release the mouse button to stop drawing.

   The new pattern displays two handles — one to adjust pattern size and one to adjust the distance between each symbol.

7. **Move the cursor over the top of the vertical handle until you see a black arrow; click and drag to readjust the size of the pattern.**

8. **Move the cursor over the end of the horizontal handle until you see a black arrow; click and drag clockwise or counterclockwise to reduce or increase the distance between symbol instances, respectively.**

If you look at the advanced options for the Symmetry Brush (at the bottom of the Property inspector), you see quite a few other interesting modes that let you reflect symbols or reconfigure them into a grid. Experiment with them and try different symbols from your library for contrast.

Understanding Frames and Keyframes

The *Timeline,* located below the stage, is where your animation is created. Be sure to take a detailed look at the components that make the Timeline tick: frames, keyframes, and the playhead.

The Timeline is composed of a series of consecutive *frames* (see Figure 3-8), each of which represents a point in time (much like a historical timeline). When Flash Player plays your movie, the playhead moves from left to right across the Timeline. The *playhead* is represented by a red, vertical line in the Timeline window. The numbers above the Timeline represent specific frame numbers.

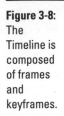

Figure 3-8:
The
Timeline is
composed
of frames
and
keyframes.

Frame number

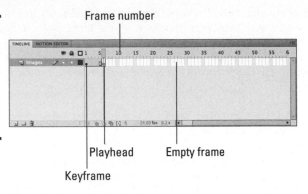

Playhead

Empty frame

Keyframe

Think of historical milestones represented at specific points on a timeline with prominent markers. On a Flash timeline, significant events (such as the beginning and end of an animation sequence) are represented as *keyframes*.

Every time you want to place a graphic, an animation, or a sound, first create a keyframe at the specific point on the Timeline where you want it to occur. When you create a new document, a single keyframe is automatically created on Frame 1. Keyframes look like standard frames, except with a hollow or black circle inside.

Add more keyframes as necessary to create animations or have graphics appear and disappear at specific points along the Timeline. Each layer can have its own keyframes.

Creating Animation with Motion and Shape Tweens

When you understand the basics of the Timeline, as we describe in the preceding section, you're ready to create your first animation. The good news is that Flash does a lot of the hard work for you.

Flash can automatically create animation sequences from nothing more than a starting point and an ending point, figuring out everything else between them. This method of creating animation is known as *tweening*. Motion and shape tweens are the two types of tweens you work with on the Flash timeline.

Creating a motion tween

A *motion tween* is a type of Flash-generated animation that requires the use of symbols and is best for creating movement, size, and rotation changes, fades, and color effects. All you need to do is tell Flash where to change the appearance of a symbol instance, and it fills in the blanks in between key changes in the symbol's appearance to create an animation sequence.

Only one object at a time can be tweened on a layer. If you want to tween several objects simultaneously, each object needs to live on its own layer and have its own tween applied.

To create a motion tween, follow these steps:

1. **Drag a symbol from your library to the stage to a new layer.**

    The symbol is added to Frame 1. For example, we positioned the symbol in the upper right corner of the stage, which is where the motion will begin.

2. **Right-click the first frame of the layer your symbol is on and choose Create Motion Tween from the contextual menu that appears.**

    A shaded span of frames — a *tween span* — appears on the Timeline, and the layer is converted to a *tween layer*. A tween layer, as the name suggests, is a layer that contains one or more motion tweens. Tween layers become dedicated to animation, and cannot hold other items that are not-related to that animation.

    To create animation, you can move the playhead to different points along the tween span and make changes to your object's appearance or position.

3. **Drag the playhead to a new frame and then reposition your symbol.**

    For this example, we dragged it to Frame 15 and repositioned the symbol in the middle of the stage, slightly toward the bottom.

    A new keyframe (which appears as a bullet point) has been created automatically at this frame to mark the change.

4. **Drag the playhead to another frame and move the symbol instance to another location on the stage, as shown in Figure 3-9.**

    For this example, we dragged it to Frame 24 and repositioned the symbol in the upper left corner of the stage.

    In addition to another keyframe, a motion path is created on the stage to show the path of animation the symbol will take.

5. **Press Enter or Return to play the Timeline and preview your animation.**

    For the motion tween we created, the symbol moves from right to left.

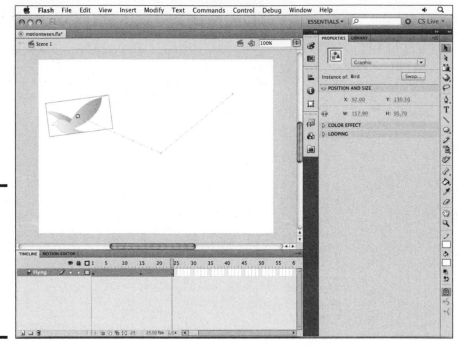

Figure 3-9:
A motion path is created to show the trajectory of your tweened object.

 To see all frames of your animation at one time, select the Onion Skin option underneath the Timeline. This option lets you select and show several frames at once so that you see the frames that the Flash tween created for you.

You're just scratching the surface of what Flash can do. Feel free to experiment further with different symbols and positions and to alter the length of your animations by placing starting and ending keyframes closer together or farther apart.

Resizing tween spans

If you want a tween to play out longer or shorter or have more time for additional keyframes and motion, you can expand the number of frames in a tween span. By default, the length of each new tween span is based on the frame rate. A frame rate of 24 frames per second (fps) creates a 24-frame tween span every time, a frame rate of 30 fps creates a 30-frame tween span, and so on.

To expand or trim a tween span, follow these steps:

1. **Locate and select a tween span on the Timeline and select the last frame in the span.**

2. **Move the cursor over the last frame of the span until a double-arrow icon appears.**

3. **Click and drag left or right to trim or lengthen the span, respectively.**

If you resize a tween span after animation already has been created, existing keyframes shift from their original positions on the Timeline, which causes certain animations to begin or end at different times than you originally intended.

Using the Motion Editor panel

The Motion Editor panel gives you precise control over each aspect of a motion tween. The Motion Editor displays the various properties of a motion tween (such as position, scale, and transparency) in a graph-style format that you can use to edit or add to animations. You can use the Motion Editor only on motion tween spans, not to modify shape tweens or *classic* tweens (motion tweens created in Flash CS3 or earlier).

The Motion Editor can be found behind the Timeline panel at the bottom of the default workspace.

Follow these steps to modify a motion tween with the Motion Editor:

1. **Click the Motion Editor tab (you can find it behind the Timeline panel) to bring forward the Motion Editor panel.**

2. **Select a tweened object on the stage; you can click either the object or the motion path to select the tween.**

   The Motion Editor displays each property as a row with a graph line running through it, as shown in Figure 3-10. The graph line represents the changes in a property value (such as scaling percentage) throughout the course of a tween span.

Figure 3-10:
Editing
properties
with
precision in
the Motion
Editor panel.

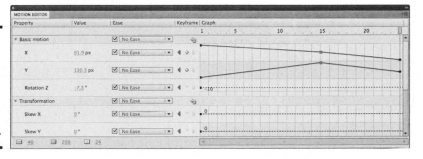

3. **Locate a property that your tween is using, such as Alpha, X, or Y, and click the row's title to expand it.**

   Along each line, you find points, or *keyframes,* that mark changes in the value of that property at different times.

4. **Select a keyframe and drag it up or down to change the value of the current property.**

5. **Move the pointer over a different portion of the line. While holding down the Ctrl key (Windows) or the ⌘ key (Mac), click directly on the line to create a new point (or keyframe).**

   Drag this point up or down to change the property's value at this position.

6. **Press the Enter or Return key to play back the Timeline and see how your modifications have affected the current tween.**

Creating a shape tween

You can easily see how Flash can open up new worlds for creating quick, sleek animation without much effort. After experimenting with motion tweens (see the preceding sections), you may find working with symbols a bit limiting, especially if your goal is to modify the shape of an object from start to finish, such as morphing a star into a circle. In this case, you should take advantage of *shape tweens.*

For the most part, shape tweens are created in quite a similar manner to motion tweens. However, unlike motion tweens, shape tweens must use raw shapes instead of symbols.

In addition to morphing between distinctively different shapes, shape tweens can morph color. As with motion tweens, you can tween only one shape at a time on a single layer. If you want to create multiple shape tweens simultaneously, isolate each one on its own layer.

Follow these steps to create a shape tween:

1. **Create a new Flash document. At the bottom of the workspace, click the Timeline panel's tab to bring it forward.**

2. **On an empty layer, draw a shape (for example, a star or polygon with the Polystar tool) on Frame 1.**

   You can include a stroke and a fill, because the shape tween can handle both.

3. **Click on Frame 25 and choose Insert⇨Timeline⇨Blank Keyframe.**

Rather than choose the motion tween, we choose a blank keyframe because we don't want a copy of the shape drawn on Frame 1 to be carried over to the new keyframe.

4. **Draw a distinctively different shape on the new, blank keyframe on Frame 25.**

5. **Select Frame 1 and choose Insert⇨Shape Tween.**

   You see an arrow and a green shaded area appear between the starting and ending keyframes, indicating that you've successfully created a shape tween.

6. **Turn on the Onion Skin Outlines option below the Timeline (see Figure 3-11) to see the frames that Flash has created for you.**

7. **If necessary, use the sliders that appear on the timeline ruler to show Onion Skin Outlines across the entire range of frames from beginning to end.**

8. **Press Enter or Return to play back your animation.**

   The original shape transforms into the final shape.

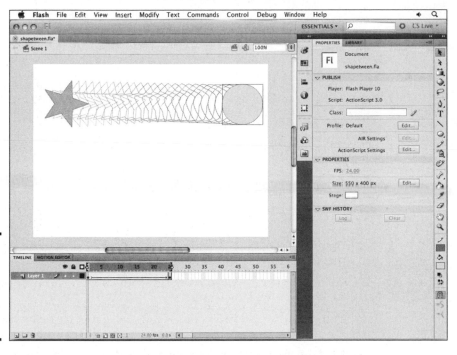

Figure 3-11:
A shape tween with Onion Skin Outlines (for visual aids).

Try using these steps to create a tween between two type characters. Create the letters using the Text tool. Break the characters into their raw forms before creating a shape tween by choosing Modify⇨Break Apart.

Tweened versus Frame-by-Frame Animation

If you come from a traditional animation background, you may want to create animation the old-fashioned way: frame by frame. Flash easily supports this method, but you should decide which method you want to use based on the type of animation you want to create.

Both methods have advantages: Although motion and shape tweens give you the power to create sleek animations quickly and easily, you may find that they're limited. Frame-by-frame animation is significantly more time-consuming and complex to create but can afford some detail and flexibility that you can't otherwise achieve.

To create a frame-by-frame animation, follow these steps:

1. **Create a new Flash document to work in.**

2. **Create a blank keyframe for each frame you want to include in your animation. You can do this easily by clicking a frame and using the F7 shortcut key.**

   Frames don't have to be consecutive; you can leave space between keyframes to control the time that elapses between each one.

3. **Draw (or insert) a graphic for each state of your animation on the appropriate keyframes.**

4. **Play back your animation by pressing the Enter or Return key.**

In Chapter 4 of this minibook, you explore advanced animation techniques using the IK and Armature features in Flash — they let you create sophisticated animation with the ease of tweens and the complexity of frame-by-frame animation.

If your goal is simply to move an object from one location to another, to create fades, or to transform size and rotation, it makes sense to use motion tweens and let Flash do the thinking for you. If you're trying to create highly complex animations that tweens can't handle (for example, a person running), you may want to try the more traditional frame-by-frame approach.

In some cases, you can break artwork into individual moving parts (like wheels on a bicycle) across several layers to achieve effects similar to frame-by-frame by using motion tweens. You can explore these effects in Chapter 4 of this minibook.

Understanding Frame Rate

The *frame rate,* which plays an important part in the performance and appearance of Flash movies, dictates how many frames are played back per second by Flash Player, in turn affecting the speed and smoothness of your animations.

You can modify the frame rate in one of these three ways:

+ **Choose Modify⇨Document.**

+ **With nothing on the stage selected, use the Property inspector.** You see your document properties.

+ **Click and drag over the frame rate value displayed at the bottom of the Timeline panel.**

The frame rate is based completely on the result you're trying to achieve. Although the default frame rate in Flash is 24 frames per second (fps), you may also want to consider a rate of 30 fps. It's consistent with broadcast and digital video frame rates and should provide a good starting point for smooth, consistent animation. To keep this topic in perspective, remember that a film projector (like the one at your local movie theater) runs at 24 fps.

If you want to increase the overall speed and smoothness of an animation, you can try increasing the frame rate gradually until you find one that's right for you. Flash can support frame rates of as much as 120 fps.

Changing the frame rate affects the playback of your entire movie. If you're trying to adjust the speed of a specific animation, consider modifying the tween itself.

**Book VII
Chapter 3**

Symbols and
Animation

Chapter 4: Applying Advanced Animation

In This Chapter

✓ Creating zoom and fade effects

✓ Creating a custom motion path

✓ Creating fade-outs and fade-ins

✓ Copying and pasting motion

✓ Creating Motion Presets

✓ Creating gravity and inertia effects with easing

✓ Morphing graphics with shape tweens

✓ Animating poses with the IK and Armature tools

✓ Masking artwork and animation

✓ Previewing a movie

*W*ith motion and shape tweens, creative animation possibilities are limited only by your imagination. You no doubt want to explore what's possible, and in this chapter, you get started with some popular animation effects, such as fades and transformations. In addition, we show you how to use new features, such as Inverse Kinematics (IK), which give you new and unprecedented abilities to create sophisticated animation with less effort.

Creating Transformations

Some of the most common effects — such as zoom, flip, lean, and spin — are all different types of *transformations,* or changes to a symbol's dimensions, rotation, or skew. You can perform transformations on a symbol from the Tools panel, Transform panel, or Modify menu and combine transformations for many animation possibilities.

Follow these steps to create a zoom-in effect:

1. **On the first frame of a new layer, use one of the Shape tools to create an interesting shape on the stage.**

2. **With the shape selected, choose Modify⇨Convert to Symbol.**

   The Convert to Symbol dialog box appears.

3. **Enter a name for the symbol in the Name text box, (for example, type** Zoom Shape**), choose Graphic from the Type drop-down list, and click OK.**

   The symbol is added to your library and is ready to be used as part of a motion tween.

4. **Select the first keyframe; right-click and choose Create Motion Tween from the contextual menu that appears.**

   A new tween span is created on the layer. If you're working with the default frame rate of 24 fps, the tween span should be exactly 24 frames long, as shown in Figure 4-1.

5. **Click the frame ruler above the Timeline at Frame 24 to reposition the playhead at this point.**

6. **Choose Window⇨Transform to open the Transform panel. From the panel, enter** 300% **in the Scale Width and Scale Height text boxes.**

   The new keyframe that's created automatically at Frame 24 within the tween span marks the change in scaling you've just made.

7. **Press Enter or Return to play your movie.**

   The instance slowly increases in scale, creating the illusion that you're zooming in closer to the object.

The zoom-out effect is identical to the animation you just created — but in reverse. Rather than start with the smaller symbol instance, you start with the larger one and gradually pull away by tweening into the smaller one. Rather than create a new animation, you can copy and reverse the existing one by using a few handy shortcuts from the Timeline menu, which appears when you right-click (Windows) or Control-click (Mac) a frame.

To continue the existing tween and reverse the zoom effect, follow these steps:

1. **On the same layer as the existing tween, right-click Frame 48 and choose Insert Frame to add frames and extend the current "zoom-in" tween.**

   Inserting frames after a motion tween span is an effective way of extending that tween without shifting existing keyframes.

2. **Select the next empty frame on the same layer.**

   If your tween span is 24 frames long, it's Frame 25.

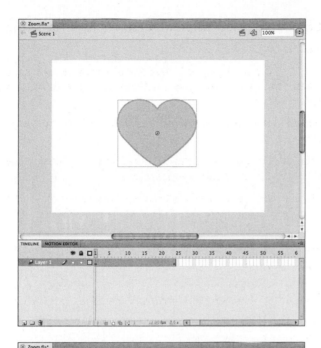

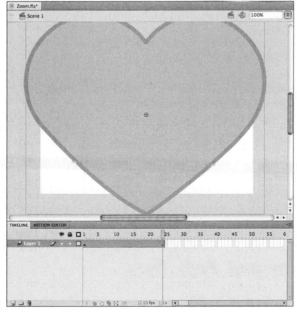

Figure 4-1:
Create a
motion
tween span
for your new
symbol and
increase
its scale
over the
course of 24
frames.

3. **Right-click and choose Paste Frames from the contextual menu that appears.**

   A copy of the tween span is pasted back-to-back with the existing one.

4. **Right-click the new tween span and choose Reverse Keyframes from the contextual menu that appears.**

5. **Click Frame 1 and then press Enter or Return to play back your animation.**

   The zoom-in effect plays, followed immediately by the exact reverse (zoom-out).

Joining Motion

The beauty of the new tween engine is that you no longer need to create several tweens or keyframes to have lots of different motion changes. You can create several different movements, transformations, and color effects sequentially within a single tween span.

You may, on occasion, end up with two or more tween spans back-to-back, especially if you copy and paste tween spans, as described in the previous section. You can, however, easily join tweens into a single span for easier editing and tweaking.

Follow these steps to join multiple tween spans:

1. **While holding down the Shift key, click and select two or more consecutive tween spans on a single layer.**

2. **Right-click (Windows) or Control-click (Mac) any selected tween and then choose Join Motions from the contextual menu that appears.**

   The tween spans are joined as one. You can now edit the tween span as a whole directly on the Timeline or by using the Motion Editor.

You can undo joined motion by choosing Split Motion from the Timeline's contextual menu.

Creating Fade-Ins and Fade-Outs

Fade effects are quite popular because they can add a cinematic feel and smooth transitions between images, text, and graphics. You can see fades used in familiar media such as photo slide shows or film, where images or scenes fade from one to another.

In Flash, a fade is a type of basic color transformation that you can apply to any symbol by modifying its transparency, or *alpha*.

To create a fade-in, follow these steps:

1. **Create a new Flash document. Select the Type tool and create some text on the stage.**

Use no more than two words with a font size of 24 points. You can set the type size and style from the Property inspector's Character options when the Type tool is active, so make sure that the panel is visible by choosing Window⇨Properties.

2. **Select the type with the Selection tool and convert it to a graphic symbol by choosing Modify⇨Convert to Symbol.**

This step adds the type to the library as a symbol and makes it available for tweening.

3. **Right-click (Windows) or Control-click (Mac) the first keyframe of the current layer and choose Create Motion Tween from the contextual menu that appears.**

A new tween span is created, and the playhead moves ahead to the end of the tween span.

4. **Grab the playhead and drag it back to Frame 1. Using the Selection tool, click the new symbol once to select it.**

5. **In the Property inspector's Color Effects section, choose Alpha from the Style drop-down list.**

6. **Use the slider or text box to set the alpha of the symbol instance to 0 percent.**

The symbol becomes fully transparent and seems to disappear. (Don't worry: It's still there.)

7. **Click Frame 24 in the Timeline; with the Selection tool, select the symbol.**

8. **In the Property inspector, choose Alpha from the Style drop-down list and then use the slider or text box to set the alpha to 100 percent.**

9. **Press Enter or Return to play the movie.**

The text appears to fade in from nowhere to the stage.

Much like the zoom-out effect, the fade-out is simply the reverse of a fade-in. You can use the Timeline menu's Reverse Frames command to turn a fade-in into a fade-out. Follow these steps:

1. **Select the tween span that contains your fade-in.**

2. **Right-click (Windows) or Control-click (Mac) anywhere on the selected frames to open the contextual menu and then choose Reverse Keyframes.**

   This action reverses the animation so that the symbol starts out fully opaque.

3. **Press Enter or Return to play the movie.**

   The text you created fades out on the stage.

Try duplicating and then reversing the fade-in tween to have the text fade in and then out.

Copying and Pasting Motion

A recent addition to Flash is its capability to copy the behavior of a motion tween that you then paste into a completely different symbol instance. This technique is handy if you need to have multiple objects follow exactly the same animation behavior, such as birds of different colors and sizes all following the same flight pattern.

To copy and paste motion, you need an existing tween to copy *from* and then a symbol instance on a different layer to copy *to*. The following steps show you how to copy animation behavior from one tween that you can paste and apply to a different symbol afterward:

1. **Select an existing tween span on the Timeline, right-click (Windows) or Control-click (Mac), and then choose Copy Motion from the contextual menu that appears.**

2. **On a new layer, place an instance of a symbol from your library.**

   It can be the same symbol you've already tweened or a completely different symbol.

3. **Right-click (Windows) or Control-click (Mac) the first keyframe of the new layer and choose Paste Motion from the contextual menu that appears.**

   A new tween span is created.

4. **Press Enter or Return to play your movie.**

   The new symbol instance animates in the same way as the original object from which its motion was copied.

You can work with two instances of the same symbol, but the beauty of this feature is that you can copy and paste animation between completely nonrelated symbol instances. You can also paste motion between symbol instances that have drastically different size, color, and rotation properties.

Creating and Using Motion Presets

In the earlier section "Copying and Pasting Motion," you see the power of duplicating animation behavior across a number of symbols. However, what happens if you want to reuse animation behavior across several movies, even at a different time?

Motion Presets take to a new level the concept of reusing animation behavior, by allowing you to take a "snapshot" of an animation's behavior and save it as a handy preset that can be applied anywhere and at any time for any project. As with Copy and Paste Motion, Motion Presets store *behavior*, not specific symbols.

Motion Presets are especially useful if you've taken the time to design a particularly complex animation sequence, such as a bouncing ball complete with eases and loss of inertia, and want to use it within another project later. You can use the Motion Presets panel to save, manage, and apply Motion Presets.

Motion Presets are saved within the application, not the project file, so you can access all your created presets from within any project.

Creating a Motion Preset

To create a Motion Preset, follow these steps:

1. **Open the Motion Presets panel by choosing Window⟶Motion Presets**

2. **Select on your Timeline the Motion Tween span you want to save as a preset.**

   You can generally select the entire span by clicking it once directly in the Timeline panel.

3. **In the lower left corner of the Motion Presets, click the Save Selection As Preset icon.**

4. **When the Save Preset As dialog box appears, enter a preset name in the text field, as shown in Figure 4-2, and then click OK.**

   The new preset appears in your Motion Presets panel.

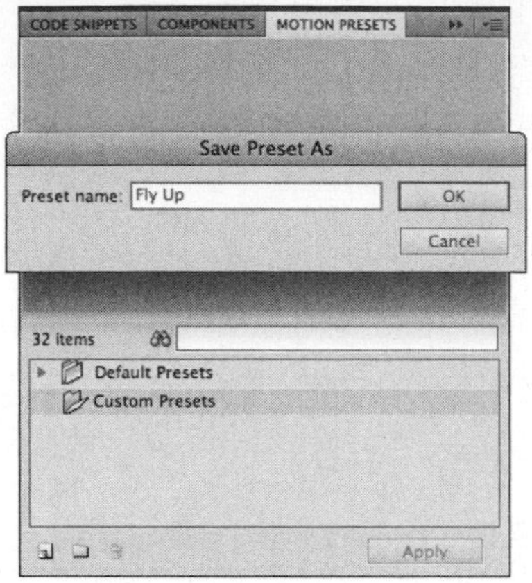

Figure 4-2:
Select
a tween
span on the
Timeline
and create a
new motion
preset.

Applying a Motion Preset

Once you've created a Motion Preset, you can apply the animation behavior stored in that preset to any symbols on the stage. To apply a Motion Preset, follow these steps:

1. **Click to select on the Timeline a layer containing a symbol instance that you want to apply a motion preset to.**

For the best result, make sure that the layer has no other animation on it and that it contains a single instance of a symbol.

2. **If the Motion Presets panel isn't already visible in your workspace, open it by choosing Window➪Motion Presets.**

3. **Locate the Motion Preset you want to apply.**

If you have none of your own presets, you can choose from a number of precreated presets in the Default Presets folder.

4. **Click to select the preset you want to apply, and click the Apply button in the lower right corner of the Motion Presets panel, as shown in Figure 4-3.**

Your selected layer and symbol now have a new animation applied.

5. **Press Enter (Windows) or Return (Mac) to preview the animation on the Timeline.**

Though you should target an existing symbol instance on the stage with Motion Presets, if you attempt to apply a Motion Preset to nonsymbol graphics, Flash converts the selected graphics to a symbol on the fly.

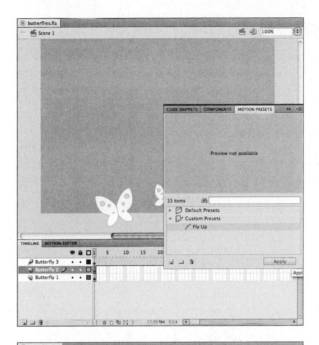

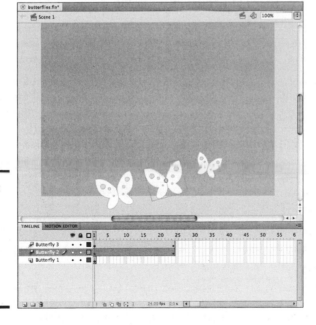

Figure 4-3:
Select a
symbol on
the stage
and apply
a Motion
Preset to
animate it.

Animating along a Path with Motion Guides

The motion tweens described earlier in this chapter involve simple animation from one location to another. For some tweens, you'll want to have your symbol follow a more elaborate path of motion, such as a race car following a track. In these cases, you can give your tween a specific path to follow by creating a custom motion path.

Starting in Flash CS4, experienced Flash users may have noticed the absence of the Add Motion Guide button below the Timeline. Because the animation engine has been completely revised, the process of creating motion guides no longer requires a separate layer. You can now modify or replace the motion paths that are created automatically with each new tween span.

Motion guides are especially useful when you work with a shape that has an obvious orientation (or direction, such as the nose of a car or an airplane). For this reason, make sure to use a symbol with an obvious orientation (such as a triangle) as your tweened object in these steps:

1. **Create a new Flash document, and create some interesting graphics on the stage.**

2. **Using the Selection tool, select the graphics you created and press the F8 shortcut key to convert the graphic to a symbol.**

3. **When the Convert to Symbol dialog box appears, choose Graphic from the Type drop-down list and enter a name for the symbol in the Name text box.**

4. **Create another new layer on the Timeline, select the Pencil tool in the Tools panel, and select a stroke color from the Property inspector on the right.**

   Make sure that Object Drawing mode is turned off. This button appears at the bottom of the Tools panel when the Pencil tool is selected.

5. **Draw a path on the stage with the Pencil tool, as shown in Figure 4-4.**

6. **Switch to the Selection tool and double-click the path you just created.**

7. **Choose Edit⇨Cut to remove the path from the stage temporarily.**

8. **Right-click (Windows) or Control-click (Mac) Frame 1 of the layer that contains your symbol and choose Create Motion Tween from the contextual menu that appears.**

   A new tween span is created for your triangle symbol.

9. **Choose Edit⇨Paste in Place to paste the path you created earlier.**

   Flash automatically converts the path to a motion path, and your symbol snaps to the path, as shown in Figure 4-5.

Figure 4-4:
Use the
Pencil tool
to create a
unique path
for your
symbol to
follow.

Logo and illustration courtesy of Jambone Creative (www.jambonecreative.com).

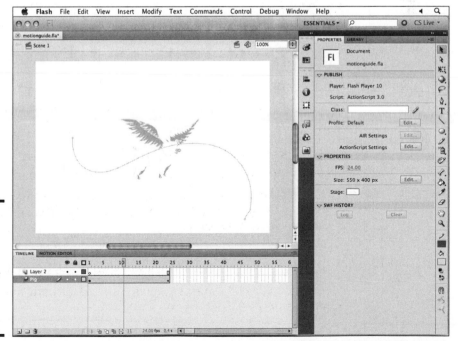

Figure 4-5:
Pasting a
complete
path to a
tween layer
converts it
to a motion
path.

Logo and illustration courtesy of Jambone Creative (www.jambonecreative.com).

**Book VII
Chapter 4**

**Applying Advanced
Animation**

Snap to it: The importance of snapping

Snapping, which is an essential part of your workflow, can often make positioning items on the stage much easier and more accurate. Snapping is similar to turning on a magnet: When you drag an object, it jumps to the closest guide, path, or object that it finds on the stage, depending on which type of snapping you've enabled. Snapping is useful for lining up objects uniformly, for positioning artwork on a ruler guide, and especially for positioning a symbol at the beginning or end of a motion guide path.

By default, snapping is enabled for alignment, guides, and objects. Additionally, you can choose View⇨Snapping⇨Snap to Grid (when working with a grid) or View⇨Snapping⇨Snap to Pixels, which ensures that objects are positioned to the nearest whole pixel on the stage.

You can find snapping options by choosing View⇨Snapping, and you can fine-tune snapping behavior by choosing View⇨Snapping⇨Edit Snapping.

10. **Press Enter or Return to play your movie.**

The symbol follows the path you created. Next, you can tweak the tween so that the symbol follows the exact orientation of the path.

11. **Select Frame 1 of your tween span; in the Property inspector, locate and select the Orient to Path check box (it's located under the Rotation options).**

12. **Press Enter or Return again to play your movie and you'll see that the symbol now changes rotation to match the direction of the path.**

Starting off your symbol on the right foot often helps produce better results when using Orient to Path. If the symbol orientation isn't what you expect, try rotating the symbol in the right direction at both the beginning and ending frames of the tween span.

Watch out for paths that overlap themselves — the results may not be what you expect.

Creating Inertia and Gravity with Easing

When objects take motion in real life, several factors affect their speed as they move. Picture a ball bouncing on a sidewalk: When the ball hits the ground and bounces, it loses speed as it moves upward because gravity pulls it back toward the ground. When the ball changes direction and moves back downward, increased gravity makes it pick up speed as it nears the ground again.

You can reproduce the two most recognizable forces, inertia and gravity, by using a special tween option: *Ease.* The new animation engine makes lots of easing behaviors available, including Bounce, Spring, Ease In (speed up), Ease Out (slow down), and more. You can assign easing to any tween span with the Motion Editor.

To create an easing behavior, follow these steps:

1. **Create a new Flash document. Select the Oval tool and create a perfect circle at the bottom of the stage.**

   Hold down the Shift key to constrain the circle while you draw it.

2. **With the new circle selected, press the F8 keyboard shortcut; when the Convert to Symbol dialog box appears, choose Graphic from the Type drop-down list and enter a name for the symbol in the Name text box.**

   In this example, we named the circle Ball.

3. **Right-click (Windows) or Control-click (Mac) the first frame of the layer and choose Create Motion Tween from the contextual menu that appears.**

   A new tween span is created, and the playhead advances to the last frame of the tween span.

4. **Using the Selection tool, select and move the symbol straight to the top of the stage while preserving its horizontal position.**

   Drag the symbol slowly toward the top of the stage to keep it from shifting left or right. The Snap to Objects behavior keeps the symbol aligned with its original horizontal position until you release it.

5. **Press Enter or Return to preview the animation.**

   The ball should now move from the bottom to the top of the stage.

6. **Click directly on the tween span on the Timeline to select it and then click the Motion Editor's panel tab to bring it forward.**

   You see the various properties of your tween represented on the Motion Editor panel.

7. **Scroll to the bottom of the Motion Editor, locate the Eases row, and change the Simple (slow) value from** 0 **to** 100, **as shown in Figure 4-6.**

   You can click and drag over the value to change it, or double-click and enter a value by hand.

   You see that the default Simple (slow) ease is already listed. You can add other types of eases to use later, but for now the default works fine.

   Changing the value creates an *ease out,* which slows the animation as it comes to completion.

8. **Scroll to the top of the Motion Editor and locate the Basic Motion row; directly to the right, choose Simple (slow) from the drop-down list.**

   This step applies the ease to the motion properties of your tween.

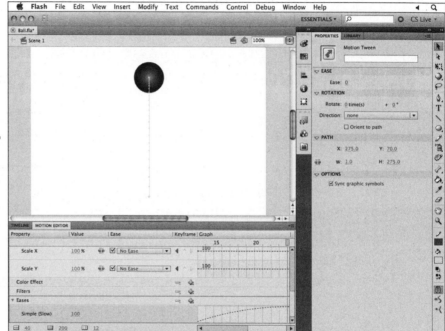

Figure 4-6: Apply an ease to your tween from the Motion Editor; the ease slows down the ball when it reaches the top of the stage.

9. **Press Enter or Return to play back and preview your animation.**

   The animation slows down gradually as it reaches completion.

You can see how easing affects the speed of the tween as it progresses, and now a simple animation becomes much more lifelike. However, what goes up must come down, so the following steps walk you through making the Ball return to the ground:

1. **Click the Timeline tab and then click directly on the layer anywhere within the tween span to select the entire motion tween.**

2. **Right-click (Windows) or Control-click (Mac) the selected frames to open the contextual menu and then choose Copy Frames.**

3. **On the same layer, select the next empty frame immediately after the tween span ends.**

4. **To paste the tween you copied in Step 2, make sure that the frame is selected, right-click (Windows) or Control-click (Mac), and choose Paste Frames from the contextual menu that appears.**

5. **Click the newly pasted tween span to select it.**

6. **To flip the tween backward, right-click (Windows) or Control-click (Mac) the selected frames and choose Reverse Keyframes from the contextual menu that appears.**

7. **Press Enter or Return to preview your animation.**

   The ball goes up and then down, and conveniently the animation is not only reversed but is also easing.

Fine-Tuning Shape Tweens with Shape Hinting

Chapter 3 of this minibook explores the possibilities of morphing shape and color with shape tweens. Flash does a great job of recalculating shapes during a tween, but sometimes you need to give it a little help, especially when two shapes have common features. Flash may overthink things and perform more shape morphing than it has to. In these cases, you can use *shape hints* — sets of matched markers that can tell Flash that two points on two different shapes are related. You can attach shape hints to the outlines of shapes on the starting and ending frames of a shape tween to let Flash know which common points exist between the two.

Two good examples of related shapes are the letters *F* and *T*. The two letters have many common angles. A shape tween between the two is a great way to make use of shape hints.

Before you get started, create a new document. Select the Type tool and, using the Property inspector, set the font style to Arial Black (or its equivalent) and set the font size to 200. Then follow these steps:

1. **On the first frame of a new layer, type F in the middle of the stage.**

2. **Select the letter with the Selection tool and choose Modify➪Break Apart to break down the type to its raw outlines.**

3. **On Frame 20 of the same layer, create a new, blank keyframe by using the F7 keyboard shortcut.**

4. **Type T on the new keyframe and position it in the same place as the *F* on the first frame.**

   You can use the Property inspector to match the X and Y positions, if necessary.

5. **Break apart the *T* by choosing Modify⇨Break Apart.**

6. **Create a shape tween by right-clicking (Windows) or Control-clicking (Mac) the first frame and choosing Create Shape Tween from the contextual menu that appears.**

   An arrow and green shaded area appear, indicating that the tween was created successfully.

7. **Press Enter or Return to preview your movie.**

   The *F* morphs into the *T*.

Even though the shape tween was successful, the outcome may not have been what you expected. Chances are good that the *F* seems to get mashed up (instead of completing a smooth transition) before being completely reconstructed into the *T* because Flash can't see the common angles between the two shapes (even though you can). That's where shape hints come in: You can add them to suggest common points to Flash and smooth out the tween.

Before you get started, make sure that Snap to Objects is enabled by choosing View⇨Snapping⇨Snap to Objects. Then follow these steps:

1. **Select Frame 1 of your shape tween and choose View⇨Show Shape Hints to turn on shape hinting.**

2. **Choose Modify⇨Shape⇨Add Shape Hint to create a new shape hint on the stage.**

   A red button, labeled with the letter *a,* appears.

3. **Repeat Step 2 to add another shape hint.**

   This time, the shape hint appears labeled with the letter *b*.

   Sometimes, shape hints stack on top of each other; move one to reveal the others underneath if only one is visible.

4. **Position the two shape hints on the outline of the *F*.**

   To do so, move shape hint (b) over just a bit so that you can see shape hint (a). Then move (a) and snap it to the lower left corner of the *F*. Position the second shape hint (b) in the upper left corner of the *F*.

5. **Select Frame 20.**

   You see the companions to the shape hints you created, waiting to be positioned.

6. **Position shape hints (a) and (b).**

   This step matches the lower left and upper left corners of the *T* to the ones in *F*, as shown in Figure 4-7. The buttons turn green to indicate a successful match.

If you can't get the hints to snap perfectly to the edge (the hints will appear red), make sure snapping is enabled by choosing View⇨ Snapping⇨Snap to Objects.

Figure 4-7: Keeping matching corners in place during the shape tween.

7. **Press Enter or Return to preview your animation.**

   If you watch carefully, you see that the shape hints are keeping those two corners anchored while the rest of the shape transforms, creating a smoother transition.

Note: Much like motion guides, shape hints do their work without appearing in your final, published movie.

Add Shape Hints with the shortcut key combination Shift+Ctrl+H (Windows) or Shift+⌘+H (Mac).

You can also add some remaining hints to finalize your tween by following these steps:

1. **Select Frame 1 of your shape tween and make sure that shape hints are still visible by choosing View⇨Show Shape Hints.**

   If they're already enabled, you see a check mark.

2. **Create one new shape hint with the keyboard shortcut Shift+Ctrl+H (Windows) or Shift+⌘+H (Mac).**

   The shape hint is automatically labeled with the letter *c.*

3. **Position the (c) shape hint on the *F,* as shown in Figure 4-8, in the upper right corner.**

4. **Select Frame 20 and you see the companion to the new shape hint waiting to be placed.**

5. **Position the shape hint on the *T* to match the angle you marked on the *F.***

6. **Press Enter or Return to play your animation.**

   You see that the shape hints have provided a much smoother transition from what you started with.

Figure 4-8:
Position
the new
shape hint
as shown on
both letters.

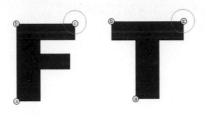

Shape hints have their own contextual menu that appears when you right-click (Windows) or Control-click (Mac) any shape hint on the first frame of a shape tween. To clear a selected shape hint, choose Remove Shape Hint or choose Remove All Hints to clear all hints on the stage and start over.

Though it often isn't necessary to add more than a handful of shape hints, you may be wondering: How many shape hints are allowed? The answer is 26 — the exact amount of letters in the alphabet. After Flash runs out of letters to label shape hints, it doesn't allow you to create more.

Creating Inverse Kinematics Poses and Animation

A significant feature for designers and animators is the Flash support for Inverse Kinematics (IK), a principle relied on in 3D and computer animation and modeling. *Inverse Kinematics* determines how jointed or connected objects position themselves relative to one another when moved.

For example, when animating a human arm, if the forearm changes position, it ultimately affects the position of the connected hand and upper arm. These principles help create life-like animation and interaction.

Flash features two tools, Bone and Bind, that you use to connect objects and edit those connections. Connected objects can be posed, and changes between those poses can ultimately be animated. You can create IK relationships between symbol instances or shapes.

To create and connect IK container objects, follow these steps:

1. **Create a new Flash document and place two symbol instances on a new layer.**

They can be instances of the same symbol or of two different symbols.

2. **Select the Bone tool from the Tools panel, move the pointer over the first object until a plus sign appears, drag until the cursor is over the second object, and release the mouse button, as shown in Figure 4-9.**

Figure 4-9:
Drag the
Bone tool to
draw virtual
bones that
connect two
shapes or
symbols.

This step draws a virtual bone between the two shapes, connecting them.

You've now converted the two symbol instances to IK container objects, and the layer has been converted to an Armature layer.

3. **Choose the Selection tool and drag either of the connected symbols to see how the connected objects will behave.**

   The second symbol changes its position based on the position of the first.

You can add more objects to the chain. Although you can't add objects randomly to an Armature layer, you can connect existing IK container objects to artwork on other layers to add them to the chain.

Follow these steps to add objects to an existing armature layer:

1. **Create a new layer on the Timeline and drag a symbol instance to it from the Library panel.**

   Position the symbol where you want it relative to the existing IK container objects on the stage.

2. **Choose the Selection tool and select in the existing Armature layer the object you want to connect the new symbol to.**

3. **Choose the Bone tool, locate the *joint* (or connection point) on the selected IK container object, and click and drag from that point to the new symbol.**

   A new bone is drawn to connect the two objects, and the symbol is removed from its original layer and added to the Armature layer.

4. **Choose the Selection tool and drag the new symbol around to see how its motion affects the other objects in the chain.**

Creating animation with poses

After you create a series of connected IK objects, you can put them into motion with poses. *Poses* capture different positions of your IK objects, and Flash can animate from pose to pose to create sophisticated animation sequences.

After an Armature layer is created, poses can be inserted (much like keyframes) to note different points along the Timeline where a new pose will be created.

To create and animate poses, follow these steps:

1. **Click and select an empty frame on an existing Armature layer (for example, Frame 15).**

2. **Right-click (Windows) or Control-click (Mac) the selected frame and choose Insert Pose from the contextual menu that appears, as shown in Figure 4-10.**

A new keyframe is created, where you can pose the IK objects again.

Much like a keyframe, a pose lets you change the position of IK objects at a specific point on the Timeline.

Figure 4-10:
Right-click any frame on an Armature layer to insert a pose.

3. **Choose the Selection tool and reposition the connected objects on the Armature layer to create a unique pose, as shown in Figure 4-11.**

Figure 4-11: Change the position of any of your IK objects when you insert a pose.

4. **Press Enter or Return to play back the Timeline.**

   Flash creates an animation to transition from one pose to the next.

Adding easing to Armature layers

Just as with motion tweens, you can mimic the forces of gravity and inertia using easing with IK animations. Although the Motion Editor isn't available for posed animation, you can easily add easing behavior from the Property inspector to give your IK animation a more realistic look and feel.

Follow these steps to add easing to an Armature layer:

1. **Click and select the first frame of an existing IK Armature layer on the Timeline.**

2. **Locate the Ease options on the right side of the Property inspector — the default value is set to zero (no ease) — and then click and drag to change the value to 100 (Ease Out).**

3. **(Optional) Select another type of ease from the Type drop-down list.**

4. Press Enter or Return to view the animation.

You see the easing change the behavior of your animation.

Using Mask Layers

The concept of masking involves using a shape (or shapes) to hide or reveal portions of a piece of artwork — much like viewing the outside through a small window in your house. The window's size limits what you can see when you're inside. Flash features a special type of layer, known as a *mask*, and its contents are used to selectively reveal (or hide) artwork or animation on another layer.

If you've worked with layer and selection masks in other Adobe applications such as Photoshop and Illustrator, the concept of masks should already be familiar to you. The technique for creating masks in Flash is a bit different, but the core concepts of masking are the same.

You can convert any layer into a mask by using the Layer contextual menu, launched by right-clicking (Windows) or Control-clicking (Mac) the layer's name area. Artwork on a mask layer isn't visible; the content of a mask layer always represents the *visible* area of the layer underneath.

Animated text is a great candidate for masking. The following steps walk you through creating a tween to which you add a mask layer for added effect. Before you get started, create a new document and select the Type tool. Choose a fill color and then use the Property inspector to set the typeface to Arial Black (or similar) and the font size to 40. Then follow these steps:

1. On a new layer, select the Text tool and type a few words on the layer.

For this example, we typed **FLASH ROCKS** in capital letters.

2. Switch to the Selection tool and select the text. Choose Modify⇨ Convert to Symbol or press the F8 keyboard shortcut to convert the text to a new graphic symbol.

3. In the Convert to Symbol dialog box, choose Graphic from the Type drop-down list and enter a name for the symbol in the Name text box.

4. Place the text off the stage to the left so that it's sitting in the pasteboard area.

You animate the text to bring it across the stage, entering from one side and exiting on the other.

5. To create a new tween span, right-click (Windows) or Control-click (Mac) the layer that contains your text and choose Create Motion Tween from the contextual menu that appears.

An instance of the text is created there as well.

6. **Move the pointer over the last frame of the new tween span until you see the double arrows. Click and drag to extend the tween span to Frame 40.**

7. **On Frame 40, select the text and drag it all the way to the right side of the stage.**

   A keyframe is created at Frame 40, and it creates a tween that moves the text from left to right across the stage.

8. **Insert a new layer above the tween layer and name it** Mask; **create a shape to use as your mask on this layer. Make sure that the shape is at least as tall as the text symbol you created.**

   For example, we used the Polystar tool to create a star in the center of the stage. The Star option for the Polystar tool is available in the Property inspector, under Options.

9. **Right-click (Windows) or Control-click (Mac) the new layer name and choose Mask from the contextual menu that appears.**

   The new layer is converted to a mask layer, and the tween layer appears indented underneath, as shown in Figure 4-12. Both layers are locked automatically.

10. **Press Enter or Return to play your movie.**

    The text animates, appearing through the shape (a star, in this example), much like you're viewing the animation through a window.

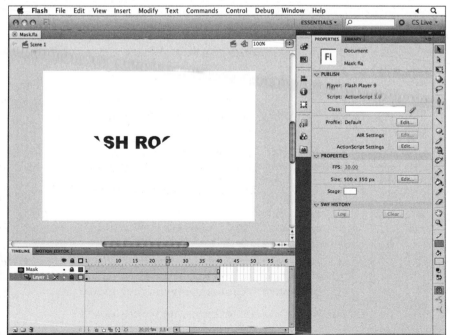

Figure 4-12: The text animation reveals itself partially behind the star shape you created.

For the masking layer to take effect, both the mask layer and the layer being masked must be locked. To edit the contents of either layer, unlock the layers by clicking and removing the padlock icons on each layer.

Mask layers can contain just about anything a standard layer can, including tweens. Try creating a motion tween on your mask layer and see what happens!

Previewing Your Movie

Previewing a movie in Flash Player to check its speed and size is a good idea, and it gives you an accurate depiction of how your animation will look and perform in Flash Player. In certain cases, such as when working with movie clips (discussed in detail in Chapter 6 of this minibook), previewing your movie is necessary to see a complete picture of your work.

To view a movie in Preview mode, choose File➪Publish Preview➪Flash or use the keyboard shortcut Ctrl+Enter (Windows) or ⌘+Return (Mac).

This step creates a .swf file from your current authoring file and displays it immediately in Flash Player. Previewing is a helpful way to see how your movie will appear to users and can highlight any potential snags.

Ultimately, the final viewing environment for most Flash movies is on the Web in a browser, such as Internet Explorer, Safari, or Firefox. Part of what Flash creates for you at publish time is not only a finished .swf but also an HTML (HyperText Markup Language) page to contain your movie. To see how your movie looks as viewed in a browser, choose File➪Publish Preview➪Default (HTML). Your default system browser launches and presents your movie in a Web page, just as users will see it.

Chapter 5: Importing Graphics and Sounds

In This Chapter

✔ Importing bitmap images and vector artwork

✔ Importing Illustrator and Photoshop files

✔ Editing bitmaps in Photoshop

✔ Converting bitmap images to symbols

✔ Adding sounds to a movie

You may decide to enhance your Flash movies with the addition of photos or graphics created in other applications, such as Photoshop CS5 and Illustrator CS5. Flash natively supports Photoshop and Illustrator file format imports as well as many popular image formats. Combine this feature with the ability to import and use .mp3 and other popular sound formats, and you can truly make your Flash movies an immersive multimedia experience.

Bitmap versus Vector Artwork

In computer based design, you need to be aware of two graphic types: bitmap and vector. The drawing environment in Flash natively creates vector graphics, but you can use both bitmap and vector graphics in a Flash movie.

Vector graphics refer to scalable artwork consisting of points, paths, and fills that the computer creates based on mathematical formulas. Though you may see a plain red rectangle, Flash sees an equation that creates the points, paths, and fill color necessary to create that rectangle. Changing the rectangle's size, position, or color is a matter of simply recalculating the formula and redrawing the shape. As a result, vector graphics maintain crisp quality even when scaled far beyond their original size. Flash (like its cousin Illustrator CS5) can natively create detailed vector illustrations and typography that you can easily scale or modify.

Bitmap graphics are created much like the picture on your TV set. If you've ever looked closely at a television screen, you've seen that the picture is created from lots of multicolored, tightly arranged dots. The same is true of bitmap graphics, which are created from many pixels of varying colors on your computer screen. The detail of the image can vary based on how many *pixels,* or dots, are used per inch to create the image. This amount is referred to as *dots per inch,* or *dpi.* Because of the immense range of colors and detail that a bitmap image can re-create, it's the format of choice for digital photographs and photo art. Flash doesn't natively create bitmap graphics but easily imports a variety of popular image formats and natively supports Photoshop (.psd) files.

Bitmap images are created with a certain amount of pixel data; rescaling the image means either eliminating that data or trying to create information where it didn't exist before. For this reason, bitmaps are far more limited than vectors in terms of scalability and can lose quality quickly if scaled too far beyond their original size, as shown in Figure 5-1. In that figure, both stars are zoomed at 400 percent. The bitmap image begins to pixelate as you zoom in, revealing the pixels that create it.

Figure 5-1:
A star created with vector graphics (left) and the same star as a bitmap (right).

Importing Other File Formats

Your choice of file formats is based on which applications you commonly work with. Flash supports many popular file formats and industry standard Photoshop and Illustrator file formats, giving you lots of flexibility. Flash doesn't generate bitmap artwork, though, so you may ask yourself which format you should use to save photos, graphics, and type created in other applications before you import them into Flash.

Flash supports and imports a number of file formats, including:

✦ Illustrator (`.ai`)

✦ Photoshop (`.psd`)

✦ Encapsulated PostScript (`.eps`)

✦ Flash SWF (`.swf`)

✦ JPEG

✦ GIF

✦ PNG

Flash, like many Web-centric applications, works at a screen resolution of 72 dpi. Images at higher (or lower) resolutions are conformed to screen resolution upon import, and their sizes on the Flash stage may be different from what you expect.

Vector graphics, such as illustrations and typography, can be created in applications such as Adobe Illustrator CS5. Artwork that contains layers should be saved natively in Illustrator (`.ai`) format because Flash can import and re-create those layers exactly as they were in the original document without a loss of quality. You work with the Adobe Illustrator Import panel to view and distribute imported layers in the "Importing Photoshop and Illustrator Files" section, later in this chapter.

Bitmap graphics, such as photos, can be saved and imported in a variety of formats. If you're working with a layered Photoshop document, you can import the `.psd` document directly into Flash by using the Photoshop Import panel. As with the Illustrator Import panel, you can view and choose how to distribute layers into Flash. Layer effects, such as drop shadows, are maintained and, where possible, converted into their Flash equivalents.

Other popular formats include JPEG, GIF, and PNG:

✦ **JPEG** (Joint Photographic Experts Group) can reproduce the wide range of color and detail necessary to reproduce photographs while keeping file size reasonable. For that reason, it's the best choice for photocentric documents (see Figure 5-2).

✦ **GIF** (Graphics Interchange Format; see Figure 5-3), a lightweight format with a limited color gamut (range) of 256 colors, is a good choice for reproducing crisp type, logos, and titling. GIF also supports transparency, so it's a good choice when the graphics you need to import must be placed discretely against varying backgrounds.

✦ The **PNG** (Portable Network Graphics) format has capabilities that cross over between those of JPEGs and GIFs. PNG also supports transparency and opacity. Between the two PNG types (PNG-8 and PNG-24), you can reproduce both simple graphics and photos with depth and accuracy.

Figure 5-2:
JPEG files have the color depth necessary to reproduce detailed photos.

Figure 5-3:
GIFs are useful for logos and type.

Ultimately, your choice of format depends on which type of graphics you're working with and how they work in context with the rest of your Flash movie.

Importing Bitmap Images

When you need to make use of a photo or graphic file, such as JPEG, GIF, or PNG, import it into Flash by choosing File⇨Import.

Imported bitmaps are added to your library as *assets*. Assets aren't to be mistaken for symbols, which you can duplicate and manage from the library. Assets are simply non-Flash items that you import, store, and use throughout your movie. Although bitmap assets can be converted to symbols, they're not automatically converted on import; you still need to add them as symbols (see Chapter 3 of this minibook).

To import a bitmap image, follow these steps:

1. **In a new Flash document, choose File⇨Import⇨Import to Stage.**

The Import dialog box appears, asking you to find a file on your local computer.

To import an image (or images) to the library for later use, such as a series of photos that will be used in a photo gallery, choose File⇨Import⇨Import to Library. This command places the chosen images directly in the library so that you can use them when you're ready.

2. **Locate on your hard drive a bitmap file such as JPEG or GIF, select it, and click Open (Windows) or Import (Mac).**

The file is imported and placed on your stage on the active layer.

3. **Locate and open the Library panel (choose Window⇨Library), and you see that the bitmap has also been placed in your library.**

If you try to import an image to the stage and the active layer is locked, the Import to Stage option is unavailable (grayed out). In that case, choose a different, unlocked layer or unlock the active layer.

Editing Bitmaps in Adobe Photoshop CS5

You can jump directly into Adobe Photoshop CS5 to edit any bitmap on the stage or in the library. In addition, changes you perform and save automatically update the bitmap back in your Flash CS5 project.

To edit a bitmap in Adobe Photoshop CS5, follow these steps:

1. **Select a bitmap image either on the stage or in the Library panel.**

Note: The image must be an original bitmap asset, not a symbol containing a bitmap.

2. **Right-click (Windows) or Control-click (Mac) to open the bitmap's contextual menu, shown on the left in Figure 5-4.**

3. **Choose the Edit with Adobe Photoshop CS5 menu option.**

The bitmap opens in Adobe Photoshop CS5 (refer to the right side of Figure 5-4).

4. **Make any changes you want to your file, such as cropping, color correcting, or resizing.**

5. **Choose File⇨Save to save the changes to your file.**

Many file options such as Save As or Save for Web create copies of the original file and therefore don't update the source file in your Flash project.

Figure 5-4:
Right-click any bitmap on the stage or in your library to edit in Photoshop CS5 (left) and then modify it in Photoshop CS5 (right) and save it to update your movie.

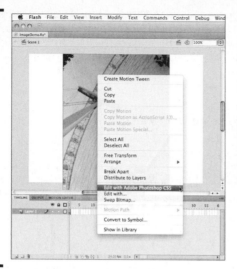

6. **Return to Flash CS5.**

   Your original file is updated in the library and on the stage (see Figure 5-5).

Figure 5-5:
Changes to an image in Photoshop CS5 are updated in your Flash project.

Editing an imported bitmap may change the original source from which it was imported, especially if the original file is in the same file path location as it was when it was imported into Flash. If Flash can't locate the original source file, it generates a temporary file and only the library copy is updated.

Converting Bitmap Images to Symbols

When a bitmap image is on the stage or in the library, it can be converted to a symbol just like any other graphic on the stage. The process is the same, and the image inherits the same abilities that graphic symbols do, including tween ability, tint, transparency, and management from a master symbol in the library.

Follow these steps to convert a bitmap image to a symbol:

1. **Choose an imported bitmap image from the library and drag the image to the stage.**

   If you already have a bitmap on the stage, select it with the Selection tool.

2. **Choose Modify⇨Convert to Symbol.**

   The Convert to Symbol dialog box appears.

3. **Enter a name in the Name text box, choose Graphic from the Type drop-down list, and set the registration point using the grid.**

   You can also convert bitmaps to buttons or movie clips by choosing Button or Movie Clip from the Type drop-down list.

4. **Click OK to complete the conversion.**

   The bitmap image appears as a new graphic symbol in your library. You can now drag several instances to the stage and then tween and transform it.

Symbols created from imported bitmaps create dependencies and continue to reference the original raw bitmaps in the library. Deleting raw bitmap assets from the library causes them to disappear from any symbols that use them.

Modifying tint and transparency

After you convert a bitmap image to a symbol, you can apply the same transparency and color effects available to graphic symbols. To create these effects, you use the Color drop-down list on the Property inspector, so make sure that the Property inspector is visible (choose Window➪Properties) before you get started.

Follow these steps to apply a color tint:

1. **Drag a symbol from the Library panel to the stage that uses an imported image.**

2. **Locate the Color Effect section of the Property inspector on the right; from the Style drop-down list, select Tint.**

   A percentage slider and color swatch appear.

3. **Click the swatch to choose a color from the Swatches panel and then use the percentage slider to adjust the amount of color that's applied (see Figure 5-6).**

Figure 5-6: Applying a 50 percent color tint creates an interesting color overlay effect.

Note: Flash remembers color settings, such as Tint and Alpha percentages between uses (refer to Figure 5-6). If you set an object to 50 percent alpha, the next time you select Alpha for a symbol, Flash automatically applies the same 50 percent setting again (which you can easily change with the slider).

Applying motion tweens

Any bitmap that's been converted to a symbol can have motion tweens applied in exactly the same way as you would with any other symbol.

When you're working with symbols created from images, you open up creative options, such as cinematic fades, moving slide shows, and unique presentation ideas.

To create a motion tween with a bitmap image, follow these steps:

1. **Drag an instance of a bitmap-based symbol to the stage from the Library panel on a new, empty layer. Position the symbol on the one side of the stage.**

   For this example, we placed a symbol on the left side of the stage. The instance should be on Frame 1 of the new layer.

2. **Right-click (Windows) or Control-click (Mac) the first keyframe of the new layer and select Create Motion Tween from the contextual menu that appears.**

   The playhead advances to the end of a new tween span. (At the default frame rate, it's Frame 24.)

3. **Position the symbol on the other side of the stage. Select the symbol once more and drag the playhead back to the beginning of the tween span at Frame 1.**

   We moved the symbol to the right side of the stage.

4. **Using the Selection tool, click the symbol once to select it.**

5. **Locate the Style drop-down list in the Color Effect section on the Property inspector, choose Alpha, and set the percentage to 0.**

   The symbol is set to full transparency and disappears.

6. **To make sure the symbol returns to full opacity later, drag the playhead back to Frame 24 and use the Alpha slider in the Property inspector to return the symbol's opacity to 100%.**

7. **Press Enter or Return to play the animation.**

   The image (symbol) appears to slide and fade in from the left side of the stage, as shown in Onion Skin view in Figure 5-7.

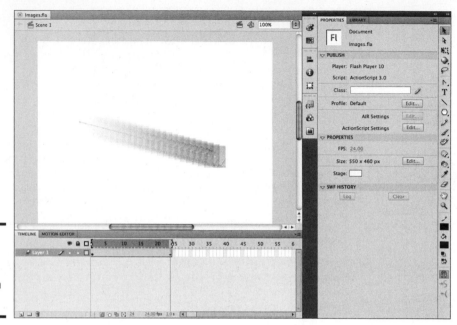

Figure 5-7:
The image fades and flies in from the left.

Creating Bitmap Fills

As an alternative to solid colors or gradients, bitmap images can be used as fills for shapes, illustrations, and even type. Bitmap fills can create cool effects and let you add interesting photographic textures to enhance your artwork.

You can create bitmap fills from existing bitmaps that have already been imported into your library, or you can use the Color panel to import a bitmap whenever you need to create a new bitmap fill.

Follow these steps to create a bitmap fill:

1. **Create a new Flash document.**

2. **Create a shape on the stage and then set a fill and stroke color with the swatches at the bottom of the Tools panel.**

To use a bitmap fill on type, you first have to break apart the type by choosing Modify➪Break Apart. Type is created and edited on a type path, so you need to break it off the path and down to its raw form (points and paths).

3. **Select the shape with the Selection tool and choose Window➪Color to launch the Color panel, as shown in Figure 5-8.**

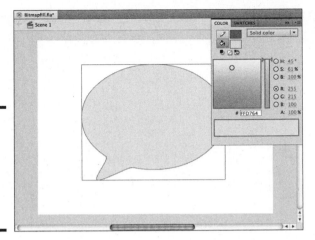

Figure 5-8:
Create an
interesting
shape with
the shape
or drawing
tools.

4. **Make the fill color active by clicking the Paint Bucket icon on the Color panel.**

5. **Choose Bitmap Fill from the drop-down list in the upper-right corner of the panel.**

   If you have no bitmaps in your library, choose a bitmap file from the Import to Library dialog box that appears.

   Or, if you have bitmaps already in your library, a thumbnail preview of each one appears at the bottom of the Color panel. Click the one you want to fill the shape with.

   The shape is now filled with the bitmap you chose (see Figure 5-9).

**Book VII
Chapter 5**

**Importing Graphics
and Sounds**

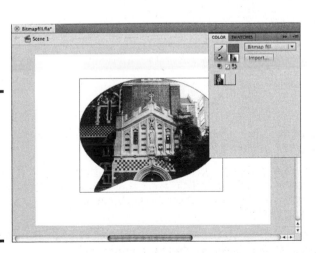

Figure 5-9:
The
imported
bitmap
image
fills the
shape like
a picture
frame.

After you apply a bitmap fill, you may want to adjust the positioning and size of the bitmap within the fill area. Use the Gradient Transform tool (located underneath the Transform tool). Gradients and bitmap fills, although quite different, both have a visible orientation point that you can adjust.

 To position a bitmap fill, select the Gradient Transform tool and select a shape that uses a bitmap fill. When the circular bounding box appears, drag its center point to reposition the bitmap, or use the outside handles to rotate, scale, and skew the bitmap.

Importing Photoshop and Illustrator Files

Flash offers the seamless import of Photoshop and Illustrator files with the Illustrator and Photoshop Import panels. Graphics created in these applications can be imported with ease and the highest quality possible, which is great news if Photoshop and Illustrator are already essential parts of your creative workflow.

Using the Import panels, you can view, select, and convert Photoshop layers to symbols or keyframes or distribute them to Flash layers while maintaining common layer effects, such as drop shadows and blurs. The ability to select individual layers means that you can use specific elements from .psd and .ai files without the need to bring in lots of unnecessary art from complex files.

Importing Photoshop (.psd) files

Whether you need a simple photograph or complex compiled artwork, the Photoshop Import options make it easy to import any .psd file while keeping individual layers editable, even with type and layer styles. You can distribute Photoshop layers to Flash layers, sequence them as keyframes, or individually convert layer contents to symbols that are added to the library.

Flash even supports Photoshop layer comps, so you can choose from and import any layer comp in your .psd file.

Before you begin, locate a Photoshop file that you want to import into Flash. A great example is a file that combines layers and type and the basic use of Photoshop layer styles, such as drop shadows.

To import a Photoshop file, follow these steps:

1. **Choose File⇨Import⇨Import to Stage.**

2. **When the Import dialog box appears, choose a Photoshop file from your hard drive and click Open (Windows) or Choose (Mac).**

The Import to Library dialog box appears (as shown in Figure 5-10) with full Photoshop file import options and a full view of all layers in your file.

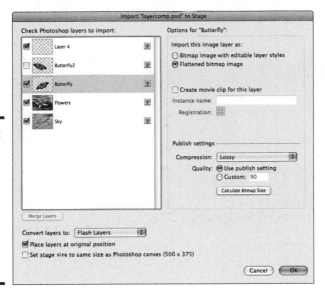

Figure 5-10:
You can choose layers to import and even convert individual layers into symbols.

3. **With the check boxes next to each layer, select the layers you want to import into Flash.**

Now you can set options for how to import the contents of each layer.

4. **Highlight a layer you've chosen to import.**

You can choose from several options that appear on the right side of the panel. (See the nearby sidebar, "The Photoshop Import Options panel," for a detailed explanation of each option.)

5. **Click OK to import the file.**

The artwork you selected appears on the stage.

Because you can selectively import layers and merge layers directly from the Import panel, consider using .psd files instead of importing flattened artwork (such as JPEG or GIF files). This panel allows you to extract specific elements and maintain transparency from Photoshop layers.

The Photoshop Import Options panel

The Photoshop Import Options panel gives you a detailed choice of what is imported, and how, from .psd files. You can send bitmap artwork directly to the library as assets or movie clips; type and vector layers can be converted or kept as editable paths or type layers.

Here's a detailed look at what you see in this panel:

- **Select Photoshop Layer Comp:** If your document contains layer comps, you can select one from this drop-down list. The layers and positioning that make up the selected comp become active in Layer view.

- **Layers view:** All layers in the .psd file appear listed on the left side of the Import to Library panel, and you can choose which layers to import by selecting the check boxes to the left. Highlighting a layer displays its import options on the right.

- **Merge Layers button:** When more than one layer is highlighted, you can choose to merge the layers on import into a single layer, which has no effect on the original .psd file.

- **Convert Layers to Flash Layers or Convert Layers to Keyframes:** Selecting the Flash Layers option maintains the layer structure (as well as layer groups) and distributes layer contents exactly as they are in your .psd file. Selecting the Keyframes option distributes layer contents across a sequence of keyframes on the Timeline.

- **Place Layers at Original Position:** This check box (selected by default) positions layer contents exactly as they are in the original .psd.

- **Set Stage to Same Size As Photoshop Canvas:** Selecting this option resizes your movie to match the original size of the .psd file.

- **Import This Image Layer As:** The two options shown convert the layer contents to either a bitmap image with editable Flash filter effects (converted from Photoshop layer styles) or a flattened bitmap image, which merges any applied layer styles along with the bitmap image.

- **Editable Paths and Layer Styles (Shape Layers Only):** You can keep shape layers and vector artwork editable in Flash by selecting this option, which places artwork on the stage as drawing objects.

- **Editable Text (Type Layers Only):** Selecting this option keeps imported text layers editable, re-creating Photoshop type layers as Flash type layers.

- **Vector Outlines (Type Layers Only):** Selecting this option converts type layers into raw vector graphics (drawing objects). Type is no longer editable, but its outline can be manipulated with tools, such as the Subselection tool and Pen tool.

- **Create Movie Clip for This Layer:** Selecting this option converts the layer contents to a new movie clip symbol that's also added to the library. You have the option of setting a registration point as well as an instance name. (See Chapter 7 of this minibook for more on instance names.)

✔ **Publish settings:** For each layer, you can set individual compression and quality settings or choose to use the document's publish settings instead. A handy Calculate Bitmap Size button lets you see how your selected compression and quality settings affect the resulting file size of the imported content.

Importing Illustrator (.ai) files

Because Illustrator and Flash both natively create vector artwork, you can import graphics created in Illustrator into Flash for placement or editing with tools, such as the Pen tool and Subselection tool.

Importing .ai files is nearly identical to importing .psd files, with a full layer view and lots of options for converting and distributing artwork and type from Illustrator layers. Before you begin, select an Illustrator file to use. The flexibility of the Illustrator Import panel can best be explored with files that make use of type and graphics.

To import an Illustrator file, follow these steps:

1. **In a new Flash document, choose File⇨Import⇨Import to Stage; choose an Illustrator file from your hard drive and choose Open (Windows) or Import (Mac).**

   The Import to Stage dialog box appears with a full view of all layers in your Illustrator document.

2. **Select the check boxes for the layers you want to import into your document.**

3. **Highlight each layer you've chosen for import to set options for each one, as shown in Figure 5-11.**

   You can import each layer and individual path as either a bitmap or an editable path. You can import groups as bitmaps or movie clips.

4. **Click OK to import the artwork to the Flash stage.**

   Check out the stage and the Library panel to see how your artwork was placed in Flash (see Figure 5-12).

Look for the Incompatibility Report button at the bottom of the layer view in the Import panel. This button can indicate potential problems that can prevent the artwork from importing properly into Flash. If you see the Incompatibility Report button, click it and read the warnings to address any pending issues before import.

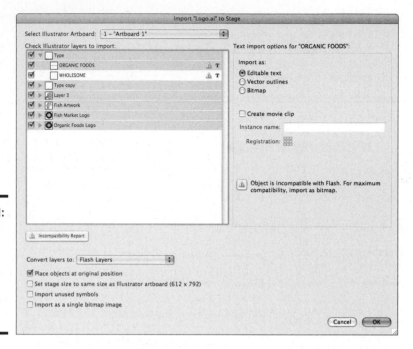

Figure 5-11:
You can bring Illustrator type paths into Flash as editable text.

Figure 5-12:
A finished import, with all Illustrator layers converted to Flash layers.

A view of the Illustrator Import Options panel

The Illustrator Import Options panel gives you a detailed choice of elements to import from `.ai` files. You can convert grouped artwork, compound paths, and type layers to movie clips or bitmaps or keep them as editable paths or type layers.

Layer view: All layers in the `.ai` file appear in this panel, and you can choose which layers to import by selecting the check boxes to the left. Highlighting a layer displays its import options on the right.

Incompatibility Report button: When this button is active, potential issues in your Illustrator file may need to be resolved for a clean, successful import. Click this button and review the report to resolve any problems before completing the import.

Convert Layers to Flash Layers or Convert Layers to Keyframes: Selecting the Flash Layers option maintains the layer structure (as well as layer groups) and distributes layer contents exactly as they are in your `.ai` file. Selecting the Keyframes option distributes layer contents across a sequence of keyframes on the Timeline.

Place Layers at Original Position: This check box (selected by default) positions layer contents exactly as they appear in the original Illustrator file.

Set Stage to Same Size as Illustrator Canvas: Selecting this option resizes movie dimensions to match the original size of the `.ai` file.

Import Unused Symbols: Illustrator CS5 files can contain their own symbol libraries, which work in a similar manner to Flash symbols. Symbols that exist in an imported `.ai` file but that aren't being used on the canvas are added to the Flash library when you select this check box.

Note: You can choose to import an Illustrator document's entire symbol library without importing any visible artwork from its canvas.

Import As a Single Bitmap Image: Selecting this option flattens and rasterizes the entire Illustrator document and places it as a bitmap image on the stage as well as a bitmap asset in your Flash document's library.

Import as

- *Bitmap Image:* Selecting this option *rasterizes* (converts vector to bitmap) the selected artwork and imports it to the stage and library as a bitmap. Any vector artwork or type loses its editability.

- *Editable Path (Individual Paths Only):* Selecting this option places vector paths in Illustrator as drawing objects that you can further modify on the Flash stage.

- *Editable Text (Type Layers Only):* Selecting this option keeps imported text layers editable, re-creating Illustrator type paths as Flash type layers.

- *Vector Outlines (Type Layers Only):* This converts type to vector outlines, which will no longer be editable as a type layer in Flash.

Create Movie Clip for This Layer: Selecting this option converts the layer contents to a new movie clip symbol, which is also added to the library. You have the option of setting a registration point as well as an instance name. (See Chapter 6 of this minibook for more on instance names.) This option and Convert to Bitmap are the only available options for entire Illustrator layers and grouped artwork.

A Note about Illustrator Symbol Libraries

In recent versions of Adobe Creative Suite, the relationship between Illustrator and Flash has been significantly improved. Now, Illustrator symbols offer support for most Flash symbol properties, allowing you to easily develop symbol libraries in Illustrator and import them directly into Flash projects. This includes the ability to set registration points (new in CS5), 9-slice scaling options, and symbol types, all of which are carried over seamlessly into Flash.

If you're importing an Illustrator file that uses symbols on the artboard, those symbols are automatically added to your Library. However, if a document contains a symbol library but not all symbols are in use on the artboard, be sure to check the Import Unused Symbols option in the Illustrator Import Options panel so that all symbols from the document's library are added to your Flash project's library.

Importing Sounds

The best multimedia creations use not only visuals and motion but also sound and music, so your Flash movies should, too. Flash fully supports the import, placement, and control of sounds in lots of different formats, so you can easily bring in loops, sound effect files, and even music from your .mp3 collection.

You can enhance your movie with background music or narrative, and sound effects can make using buttons and menus more intuitive. Flash can stream longer sounds (such as soundtracks or long-form narration) to minimize loading time so that users get right to the good stuff.

Flash imports the following audio file formats:

+ AIFF
+ MP3
+ Windows WAV

Note: Additional file formats are available with the optional QuickTime plug-in installed.

Follow these steps to import a sound into your library:

1. **Create a new Flash document and choose File⇨Import⇨Import to Library.**
2. **Browse and choose an** .mp3, .wav, **or** .aiff **file from your hard drive and click Open (Windows) or Choose (Mac).**

3. **Choose Window⇨Library to launch the Library panel.**

    The sound appears in the library with a speaker icon, as shown in Figure 5-13.

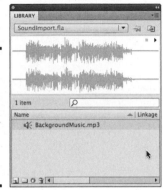

Figure 5-13: Imported sounds appear next to a speaker icon in your Library panel.

4. **Select the sound and check out the Preview window.**

    A waveform preview of your sound appears, and you can listen to the sound by using the Stop and Play buttons in the upper right corner of the panel.

If you need audio files to work with, many Web sites, such as Flash Kit and FlashSound, provide low-cost or free sound effects and loops in Flash-friendly formats. Adobe also has a listing of sound effects sites at www. adobe.com/cfusion/knowledgebase/index.cfm?id=tn_14274.

Placing sounds on the Timeline

After you have your favorite sounds into your Flash document, you can place them on keyframes along the Timeline to have them play at specific points in your movie.

You can assign sounds with the Property inspector, which displays the Sound section when a keyframe is selected. Sounds can be combined across different layers and used inside buttons to create sound effects for controls and navigation menus.

To place a sound on the Timeline, follow these steps:

1. **On a new layer, create a blank keyframe along the Timeline and launch the Property inspector (if it's not already visible).**

2. **On the right side of the Property inspector, locate the Sound section and select a sound from the Name drop-down list.**

This drop-down list shows all sounds in your library (see Figure 5-14). The sound is now placed on your Timeline.

Figure 5-14:
Place
sounds on
a keyframe
from the
Sound
section in
the Property
inspector.

3. **Press Enter or Return to play your movie.**

   The sound plays when the playhead reaches the keyframe.

After you place a sound on your Timeline, you can use additional options in the Property inspector to control looping, repeating, and playback performance. The most common options to experiment with are the Repeat and Loop options, which control the number of times (if any) a sound should repeat when it's played.

To repeat the sound, follow these steps:

1. **Select the keyframe where you already have a sound placed and locate the Sound options in the Property inspector.**

2. **Locate the Repeat drop-down list and enter the number of times you want the sound to repeat in the text box to the right.**

   By default, the sound repeats at least once, but if you enter **2**, for example, your sound repeats twice.

3. **Press Enter or Return to play your movie.**

   The sound you placed plays and then repeats the number of times you entered in Step 2.

To *loop* the sound (repeat it endlessly), follow these steps:

1. **Select the keyframe and, with the Sound options, click the arrow beside Repeat and choose Loop from the drop-down list.**

   The sound is now set to loop continuously until the movie is shut down or another action turns it off.

2. **Choose File⇨Publish Preview⇨Flash to preview your movie.**

   The sound plays and then continues to repeat until you close the preview.

Editing sounds

One hidden treasure in Flash is the Edit Envelope dialog box, which performs trims and volume effects and lets you dial in volume and pan settings for each sound placed in your movie. Although nothing quite replaces well-recorded and edited source files, you can do last-minute, nondestructive edits so that your sounds complement the rest of your movie.

To edit a sound, select a keyframe that has a sound placed on it or add a sound to a new keyframe, and then follow these steps:

1. **Select the keyframe on which the sound is placed.**

2. **In the Property inspector, locate and click the Edit Sound Envelope button (the pencil icon to the right of the Effect drop-down list) in the Sound section.**

   The Edit Envelope dialog box appears with a waveform preview. The center time ruler has two sliders on the far left and far right.

3. **Move these sliders to edit the in and out points of the sound or to trim unnecessary silence, as shown in Figure 5-15.**

   The lines above each waveform represent the volume envelope.

4. **Click the lines above each waveform and drag them up or down to adjust the overall volume of the sound or to add handles and vary the volume at different points during the sound.**

   The higher the line or handle, the louder the sound.

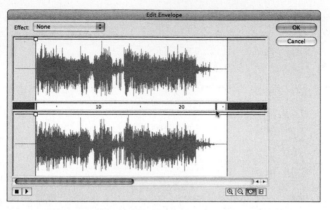

Figure 5-15: Eliminate silence by sliding the starting trim point to the right and the ending trim point to the left.

5. **Use the Effect drop-down list in the upper left corner to choose from several preset volume and pan effects to enhance your sound.**

6. **When you're done, click OK and then press Enter or Return to play your movie and hear the changes made to the sound.**

Chapter 6: Lights, Camera, Movie Clips!

In This Chapter

- Exploring movie clip uses and advantages
- Creating and updating movie clips
- Previewing movie clip animation
- Transforming and tweening movie clip instances
- Modifying movie clips
- Using the 3D Translation and 3D Rotation tools

Complicated machines, such as automobiles, are made from many smaller machines and moving parts. To build an automobile any other way just isn't possible. Along those lines, you may find that some animations are too elaborate to create on the main timeline alone. You can break them down into smaller animations that can be brought together as part of a larger animation.

You'll find that your movie may need to reuse several identical animations. (Think about the four spinning wheels on a car.) In these cases, you have movie clips.

Introducing Movie Clips

The powerful and versatile *movie clip* symbol type can include entire, independent animations yet be placed and maintained in your movie just as easily as graphic symbols. The movie clip is one of three symbol types in Flash, and just like graphic symbols (see Chapter 3 of this minibook), they can be easily duplicated and maintained from a single master symbol in the library.

Movie clips are unique in that each one contains its own timeline that looks and works just like the main one. This timeline is completely self-contained, so animations in movie clips don't depend on or rely on the length of an animation contained within the main Timeline. Movie clips can almost be thought of as movies within a movie. Movie clips behave just like other symbols, so several instances of the same movie clip can be dragged to the main stage to easily duplicate animations. If you need to change an animation that appears several times throughout a movie, you need to modify only the original movie clip in the library that contains it.

Movie clips have all the same features as graphic symbols: You can easily drag multiple instances to the stage, and each instance can have its own scaling, tint, alpha, and rotation applied.

Because a movie clip can contain independent animations, it's a useful way to break down complex animations into smaller, more manageable pieces. Trying to coordinate too many animations across the main Timeline may be not only quite difficult but also in some cases impossible, depending on what you're trying to create.

Movie clips can also be nested inside other movie clips, giving you virtually unlimited levels of depth and complexity.

The frame rate, a global setting for your movie, sets the rate for all movie clips as well as for the main Timeline. To speed up or slow down individual movie clip animations, consider modifying the length of any included tweens before adjusting the overall frame rate.

In conjunction with Flash Player 10, movie clips provide 3D support, allowing you to rotate and position in the 3D realm the 2D artwork contained in movie clip symbols. In addition, all 3D properties can be animated, opening the door for stunning camera, rotation, and depth effects.

Flash CS5 includes the 3D Rotation and 3D Translation tools, which let you transform movie clip instances along the x, y, and z axes. You can animate 3D properties as part of a standard motion tween and modify them from the Motion Editor panel. We explore these tools in detail later in this chapter.

Creating and Placing Movie Clips

Movie clips are created as new, empty symbols as well as from existing content on the stage. If you create a movie clip from scratch, you can add animation and graphics later by editing the symbol.

Follow these steps to create a movie clip from existing graphics:

1. **Create some interesting graphics on the stage by using the drawing tools.**

2. **Select the new artwork and choose Modify➪Convert to Symbol.**

   The Convert to Symbol dialog box appears (see Figure 6-1).

Figure 6-1:
Enter a
name for
your movie
clip.

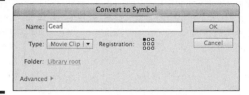

3. **Enter a name for your new movie clip in the Name text box, choose Movie Clip from the Type drop-down list, select a Folder (if it's other than the main Library root), and click OK.**

   The artwork now appears as a movie clip on the stage.

4. **Choose Window⇨Library to check out your new symbol in the library with a special Movie Clip icon next to it, as shown in Figure 6-2.**

Figure 6-2:
Add artwork
to your
library as a
movie clip
symbol.

Nonanimated graphics converted to movie clips behave the same as graphic symbols, so you can place, tween, and modify instances on the stage. The difference, however, is that you can always add animated content later to the movie clip by editing it and creating tweens on its own Timeline.

In most cases, you take full advantage of movie clips by adding animation in a new movie clip symbol. To do so, you can start with a new, empty movie clip symbol and add the animated content afterward.

To create a new movie clip symbol and add animation, follow these steps:

1. **Choose Insert⇨New Symbol.**

   The Create New Symbol dialog box appears (refer to Figure 6-1).

2. **Enter a name for the movie clip in the Name text box, select Movie Clip from the Type drop-down list, choose a folder (if it's other than the Library root) to sort the new symbol into, and click OK to create the new symbol.**

**Book VII
Chapter 6**

**Lights, Camera,
Movie Clips!**

You see a new Timeline, shown in Figure 6-3, and the symbol is ready for you to add animation. This timeline works just like the main one: You can add and reorder layers and create tweens. You still need to convert any artwork to graphic symbols before creating motion tweens.

Figure 6-3: The timeline of your new movie clip symbol can contain tweens, just like the main Timeline.

3. **Create a new graphic on Frame 1 of the existing layer 1, select the graphic, choose Modify⇨Convert to Symbol, and choose Graphic from the Type drop-down list.**

4. **Right-click Frame 1 and choose Create Motion Tween to create a new tween span on the layer; click and drag the last frame of the tween span to shorten it to 24 frames (only if the span is greater than 24 frames).**

5. **On Frame 24, change the position or rotation of your symbol to set it in motion.**

6. **Press Enter or Return to preview the new Movieclip Timeline and make sure your animation plays back properly.**

7. **Click the Scene 1 link above the stage to return to the main Timeline.**

8. **Locate your new movie clip symbol in the Library panel and drag two instances of it to the stage, as shown in Figure 6-4.**

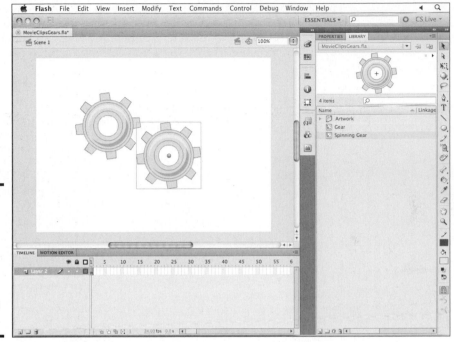

Figure 6-4:
Drag two
instances
of the new
movie clip
from the
Library
panel to the
main stage.

If you press Enter or Return to watch your movie clip play on the stage,
you'll probably be a little disappointed. Don't worry: To see your movie clip
in action, you just need to preview the movie in Flash Player.

Previewing Movie Clip Animation

Movie clips contain their own timelines, and pressing Enter or Return starts
the main Timeline, not the movie clip Timeline. To view movie clip animation, preview your movie in Flash Player using one of two methods:

✦ **Test Movie** mode exports a compressed (.swf) Flash movie and immediately launches it in Flash Player. Test Movie is used to give you a quick
   look at how the finished movie will appear to users as you build. Test
   the new movie clip by choosing Control➪Test Movie.

   You can preview your movie in Test Movie mode by using the shortcut
   key combination Ctrl+Enter (Windows) or ⌘+Return (Mac).

✦ **Publish Preview** works similarly to Test Movie but exports the .swf
   (compressed Flash movie) using the final delivery settings you've
   already created by using File➪Publish Settings. Publish Preview can
   also display your movie in an HTML (Web) page in your system's default
   browser. To preview a movie in Publish Preview, choose File➪Publish
   Preview➪HTML or File➪Publish Preview➪Flash.

Chapter 9 of this minibook covers publish settings for your movie, but you should know how these seemingly identical methods differ. Both methods let you accurately preview movie clip animation while you create it in your movie.

Modifying Movie Clip Instances

You can modify each movie clip instance with its own size, transformation, and color settings. This type of flexibility lets you get lots of mileage from a single movie clip symbol before having to create a new version or variation of your symbol in the Library panel. Just like graphic symbols, these transformations don't affect the master symbol or other instances on the stage.

Although all instances of a movie clip share a timeline with its master symbol in the library, each individual instance can be stopped, started, and controlled individually using ActionScript. For more on how to control movie clip instances with ActionScript, see Chapter 7 of this minibook.

To transform any instance of a movie clip, you can use the Transform tool, the Transform panel, or the Transform submenu (choose Modify⇨Transform). Try dragging two more instances of your new movie clip on the stage and applying different transformations to each one.

To apply a transformation to a movie clip instance, choose the Transform tool from the Tools panel and select an instance on the stage. Use the handles to resize, distort, and skew the instance or select an instance on the stage with the Selection tool and use the Transform panel (open it by choosing Window⇨Transform) to type exact amounts for horizontal and vertical scale, rotation, and skew.

Use the Style drop-down list in the Color Effect section of the Property inspector with any selected movie clip instance to apply unique tints and alpha (transparency) effects and to change brightness. To apply a color effect to a movie clip instance, select an instance on the stage and choose an effect from the Style drop-down list. Use the option controls to dial in the exact amount and type of color effect you need.

Combining Movie Clips

To create a new animation from several smaller ones, you can create a new movie clip from other movie clip instances on the stage. This technique allows you to group several movie clips and drag them as one instance to the stage. Unlike with a group, however, you gain all the advantages of working with symbols, including the ability to duplicate, maintain, and tween the combined movie clips as one unit.

The practice of including one movie clip inside another is sometimes referred to as *nesting.* Although movie clips can include other movie clips, graphic symbols, and buttons, graphic symbols shouldn't include movie clip instances. Movie clips should always be included in other movie clips so that their animation plays back properly.

Follow these steps to create a new movie clip from other movie clips on the stage:

1. **Select two or more movie clip instances on the stage.**

These can be instances of different movie clip symbols in your library or of the same symbol.

2. **Choose Modify➪Convert to Symbol.**

The Convert to Symbol dialog box appears, as shown in Figure 6-5.

Book VII
Chapter 6

Lights, Camera, Movie Clips!

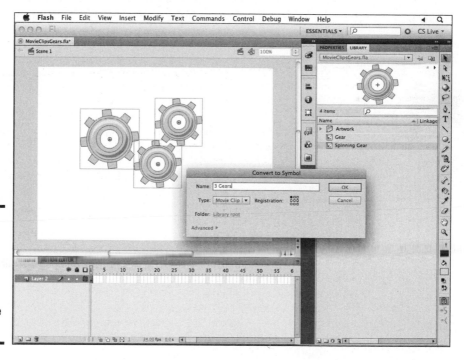

Figure 6-5:
You can combine multiple movie clip instances into a single movie clip.

3. **Enter a name for your new symbol in the Name text box, choose the movie clip from the Type drop-down list, and set the registration point by clicking a point on the grid shown to the right. Click OK to create the new symbol.**

The *registration point* sets the location from which a symbol's position is determined on the stage. This point can be any of the four corners or four sides or the center of the symbol.

The symbol instances appear on the stage as a single movie clip, and a new movie clip appears in your library.

You can now drag and drop several instances of the new movie clip to the stage. Experiment by adding a few instances to the stage and applying different transformations or color effects to each one. Preview your movie by choosing Control⇨Test Movie. You see that the movie clips now are treated as one item, but still animate and behave as they did when they were separate instances on the stage.

When you nest movie clips, you create *dependencies* between those symbols in your library. Movie clips that include other movie clip symbols do so by reference; the included movie clip symbols aren't duplicated but are connected to the movie clip that includes them.

Movie clips become dependent on any other symbols they're created from. The smaller symbols remain in the library and are referenced by the movie clip that includes them, which means that you can't remove included movie clips without destroying the symbols that they're part of. For this reason, be sure not to trash any symbols in your Library panel until you're sure that they're not being used in your movie *or* by another movie clip symbol.

 A helpful way to see which symbols are in use is to choose Select Unused Items from the Library panel's panel menu. This command highlights symbols in your Library panel that aren't being used anywhere on the stage or by other symbols in the library. If a movie clip isn't used on the stage but is included in another symbol, it isn't highlighted, indicating that it's "in use."

Rendering and Animating Movie Clips in the 3D Realm

The extensive drawing and animation capabilities of Flash can be greatly enhanced by the 3D Translation and 3D Rotation tools. You can use each of these tools to rotate and position 2D content in any movie clip instance around or along x, y, and z axes.

Combined with the powerful Flash animation engine, you can animate these properties as part of a motion tween to add cool depth, camera panning, and perspective effects to your movies.

Using the 3D Rotation tool

 This 3D Rotation tool can be used on any movie clip instance to rotate and transform the symbol around x, y, and z axes.

To render a movie clip instance in 3D, follow these steps:

1. **Place a movie clip instance on a new layer on the timeline by dragging the clip from the Library panel.**

2. **Select the 3D Rotation tool from the Tools panel and click the new movie clip instance to select it.**

   Color-coded circular handles appear, each one corresponding to an axis along which the movie clip can be rotated.

3. **Rotate your movie clip (see Figure 6-6):**

   - Click and drag the green line that crosses your movie clip horizontally directly on the line to spin the clip around the y (vertical) axis.

   - Click and drag the red line that crosses your movie clip vertically to rotate the clip around the x (horizontal) axis.

   - Click and drag the blue circle that surrounds your movie clip to rotate it around the z axis (depth).

   - Click and drag the outermost red circle in any direction to rotate multiple axes at one time.

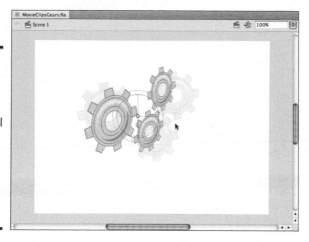

Figure 6-6: Use the handles in the 3D Rotation tool to rotate a movie clip around the x, y, and z axes, or all at one time.

Book VII Chapter 6

Lights, Camera, Movie Clips!

To reset all transformations performed with the 3D Rotation tool, select the movie clip and hold down Ctrl+Shift+Z (Windows) or ⌘+Shift+Z (Mac).

Using the 3D Translation tool

In contrast to the 3D Rotation tool, which rotates movie clips *around* an axis, the 3D Translation tool slides a movie clip *along* a specific axis to change its perceived distance and depth relative to other objects on the stage.

Think of this concept as having three train tracks moving left and right, up and down, or forward and backward that your movie clip can ride along.

To use the 3D Translation tool to move a movie clip in three dimensions, follow these steps:

1. **Using the Selection tool, place a movie clip by dragging it from the Library panel or click to select an existing movie clip instance on the stage.**

2. **Choose the 3D Translation tool from the Tools panel, which you can find under the 3D Rotation tool.**

   Three guides appear and correspond to the x, y, and z axes. You can slide your movie clip along any of these three guides by clicking and dragging the appropriate guide, as shown in Figure 6-7:

   - *To slide a movie clip from left to right along the x axis,* click and drag the arrow connected to the red horizontal guide line.

   - *To slide a movie clip up or down along the y axis,* click and drag the arrow connected to the green vertical guide line.

   - *To change the perceived distance of a movie clip on the stage,* click and drag the blue center point to slide it along the z axis.

Figure 6-7:
To change the perceived depth and distance, slide and position a movie clip along the x, y, and z axes.

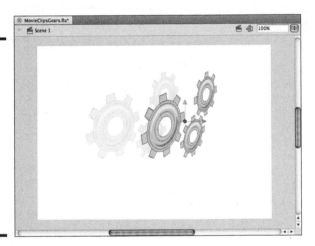

3D Translation and 3D Rotation transformations can be combined on the same movie clip for interesting perspective effects.

Tweening 3D properties

After you have a feel for how the 3D Rotation and 3D Translation tools transform movie clips, you can incorporate these effects into a motion tween to create stunning effects just as easily as you would with position and transparency.

Follow these steps to create a tween with 3D properties:

1. **Place a single movie clip instance on a new layer on the Timeline by dragging it from the Library panel.**

2. **Right-click (Windows) or Control-click (Mac) the first frame of the new layer and choose Create Motion Tween from the contextual menu that appears.**

   A new tween span is created, and the playhead jumps to the end of the span.

3. **Select the 3D Rotation tool and click the movie clip to make it active; circular handles appear around the instance.**

4. **Click and drag the axes to rotate the movie clip until you set an angle and a position.**

5. **Press the Enter or Return key to play back your timeline, and your movie clip tweens from its original 2D position to the 3D settings you applied, as shown in Figure 6-8.**

6. **Repeat Steps 3 through 5 with the 3D Translation tool to see your movie clip slide in three dimensions.**

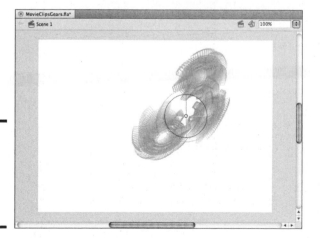

Figure 6-8:
A 3D
tween in
Onion Skin
Outlines
mode.

Chapter 7: Controlling Your Movie with ActionScript

In This Chapter

✓ Introducing ActionScript

✓ Adding actions to the timeline

✓ Creating button controls

✓ Applying code snippets

✓ Enabling buttons with ActionScript

*W*hether you're creating a Web site, presentation, or game, a truly interactive experience is one in which users can control the action. If you want to take your movies to the next level, ActionScript can help. The built-in Flash scripting language has come a long way and can help you do anything from control movie playback to create complex games.

This chapter introduces you to ActionScript and shows you how to use it to create interactive elements, such as clickable buttons, in your movies.

Getting to Know ActionScript

ActionScript is a powerful scripting language that you can incorporate into your movies to control playback, navigation, and imported media, such as images, video, and audio. ActionScript is written as a series of commands (or *statements*) that are placed on the timeline, buttons, movie clip, and external files using the Actions panel and the new Code Snippets panel. Think of ActionScript as a set of instructions you can give your movie to tell it how to behave and add abilities.

ActionScript is often used for timeline control so that animations can be told when and where to stop, loop, play, or jump to other points along a timeline. You can also make truly interactive movies by adding ActionScript to buttons on the stage so that users can control the animation, too.

The new Code Snippets panel

An excellent new addition for designers and code newbies is the new Flash CS5 Code Snippets panel, shown in Figure 7-1. If you have never written ActionScript, the learning curve can be a bit daunting, and sometimes you just need to get the job done. The Code Snippets panel contains dozens of useful pieces of code that you can easily apply in a single click. Whether you want to navigate the timeline, play sounds, or control video in your movie, a code snippet can help.

If you press the Enter or Return key to watch a movie clip play on the stage, you'll probably be a little disappointed. Don't worry: To see a movie clip in action, you just need to preview the movie in Flash Player.

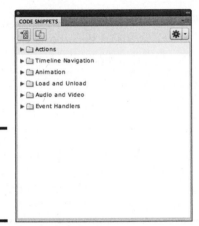

Figure 7-1:
The new
Code
Snippets
panel.

The Actions panel

If you're comfortable writing code by hand, you can use the Actions panel to write your own code statements throughout your movie. The Actions panel, shown in Figure 7-2, acts as a wizard, reference book, and script editor all in one. You can also add actions from the Actions panel using a categorized tray or drop-down list or type them directly into the script editor. A handy Script Assist mode (see the next section) is available so that you can add and modify actions without having to type the code by hand. (We highly recommend the Script Assist mode for new users.)

To launch the Actions panel, choose Window➪Actions or use the F9 (Windows) or Option+F9 (Mac) shortcut key combination.

To place an action on a frame, select the frame on the timeline and launch the Actions panel.

Script Assist mode

For users new to ActionScript, an alternative to using the Code Snippets panel or tackling hands-on coding is *Script Assist* mode. This mode acts as a wizard within the Actions panel to let you use a series of menus, buttons, and text boxes to build scripts without having to get into the nuts and bolts of writing code by hand. Script Assist mode helps prevent time-consuming errors so that you spend more time being creative and less time trouble-shooting.

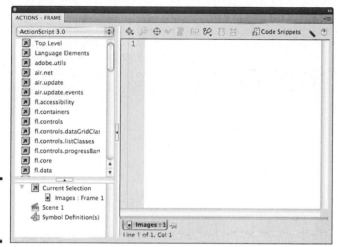

Figure 7-2:
The Actions panel.

 To enable Script Assist mode, click the Script Assist icon in the upper-right corner of the Actions panel.

Previewing ActionScript

ActionScript is understood and processed within Flash Player, so most scripted movies need to be tested by choosing Control➪Test Movie.

In some cases, you can also enable simple actions in the authoring environment so that you can see your work in progress while still working from the timeline.

ActionScript 3.0 versus ActionScript 2.0

Since its introduction in Flash Player 9, ActionScript version 3.0 has brought many major changes and improvements to the way ActionScript performs and to the way it's created within movies.

Previous versions of ActionScript (1.0+, 2.0) are still in use among some Flash projects, so you still have options for creating or saving movies with older ActionScript version settings, if necessary.

If you have worked with older versions of ActionScript, you should be aware of some key differences:

+ ActionScript 3.0 can only be placed on keyframes in the timeline or external (.as) files. You cannot place ActionScript 3 statements directly on symbol instances.

+ ActionScript 3.0 is stricter about a number of coding practices. Actions that Flash Player would normally "let slide" in ActionScript 2 may cause errors in ActionScript 3.

+ ActionScript 3.0 projects can be published only to Flash Player 9 or later. This consideration is important if your project or company limits the use of Flash Player to version 8 or earlier.

If you're a first-time coder or have never worked with scripting or programming languages, some concepts in ActionScript 3.0 may present a significant learning curve.

In the interest of keeping with best practices and taking advantage of the latest tools in Flash CS5, this chapter covers only ActionScript 3.0.

Specifying the correct publish settings

When you choose to create a new Flash file, you can select an ActionScript 2.0 or 3.0 version file. If you're adding ActionScript to an existing Flash file, you should verify and adjust the ActionScript version in your Publish Settings to match the version you've chosen to work in.

ActionScript versions are matched to specific versions of Flash Player, and 3.0 scripts don't work in a version 2.0 movie (and vice versa).

To verify and select the appropriate ActionScript version, choose File⇨ Publish Settings; click the Flash tab and choose ActionScript Version 2.0 or ActionScript Version 3.0 from the Script drop-down list.

The Flash Player and ActionScript version shows in the Property inspector panel when no tools or objects are selected.

Creating ActionScript with the Actions Panel

The Code Snippets panel is a helpful way to get up and running, but when you're ready to venture out on your own, you'll find that coding using the Actions Panel's Code Editor window may give you more flexibility for certain tasks.

All ActionScript code is added to keyframes on the timeline, and here you'll add some common ActionScript statements within the Code Editor (see the top of Figure 7-3) and with the assistance of the Actions Panel's Script Assist mode (see the bottom of Figure 7-3).

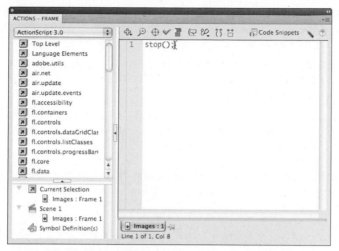

Figure 7-3:
The Actions Panel lets you create code by freely typing in the Code Editor window (top) or building scripts by using the Script Assist mode (bottom).

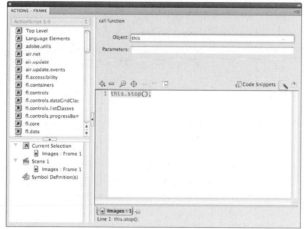

Adding a stop ( )

The `stop()` statement does exactly what it sounds like: It stops the timeline at whatever frames it's placed on. A common use of `stop()` is to keep a movie from looping, which is the default behavior for Flash Player.

Follow these steps to create a `stop` action in your movie:

1. **On a new layer, create a motion or shape tween from frames 1 through 24 and press Enter or Return to play back and preview the animation.**

   For more information on creating tweens, see Chapter 3 of this minibook.

2. **Click the New Layer button below the timeline to create a new layer and name it Actions. If necessary, drag the layer upward so that it's the topmost layer in the stack.**

   This dedicated layer is where you add ActionScript to control your new motion tween.

3. **Add a keyframe on frame 24 of the new Actions layer with the F6 shortcut key.**

4. **Select the keyframe and choose Window⇨Actions to launch the Actions panel.**

5. **In the Actions panel, locate the Script Assist button and click it.**

   The top panel expands, and you're now working in Script Assist mode.

   You can add ActionScript to keyframes with existing content, but it's always a good practice to separate scripts from visual elements on the stage by creating a dedicated layer for your ActionScript.

6. **Click the plus sign at the top of the Actions panel and choose flash. display⇨MovieClip⇨Methods⇨Stop.**

7. **Specify in the Object text box the name of the object you want to control. Because you're stopping the current (main) timeline, enter the word this in place of the not_set_yet text in the Object text box, as shown at the top of Figure 7-4.**

   The actions panel reads

   ```
   import flash.display.MovieClip;
   this.stop();
   ```

   Take a look at your timeline (refer to the bottom of Figure 7-4), and you'll notice that a lowercase *a* now appears inside the keyframe, which indicates that there is ActionScript on the keyframe. These scripts run when the playhead passes that keyframe.

8. **Choose Control⇨Test Movie to preview your movie.**

   The animation plays until frame 24 and then stops.

Using goto: gotoAndPlay ( ) and gotoAndStop ( )

To loop a movie or to send the playhead to a different point on the timeline, you can tell your movie to jump forward or backward to a specific frame with one of two variations of the goto statement: gotoAndPlay() and gotoAndStop().

Each of these two statements requires a frame name or number so that Flash Player knows where to send the playhead. When placed on a frame, these actions send the playhead forward or backward to the specified frame and stop, or they resume playback from that point.

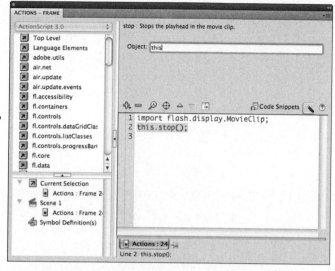

Figure 7-4:
The Actions panel view, showing a `stop()` action (top); a lowercase *a* indicates that ActionScript has been added to frame 24 of the Actions layer (bottom).

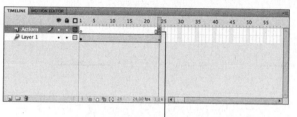

Indicates ActionScript on the keyframe

To use `gotoAndStop`, follow these steps:

1. **On the Actions layer, select and create a new keyframe at frame 23.**

2. **Choose Window⇨Actions to open the Actions panel.**

3. **Click the plus sign and choose flash.display⇨MovieClip⇨Methods⇨ gotoAndStop.**

4. **In the Object field, target the current timeline by typing this in the Object text box. Enter 1 in the Frame text box and make sure the Scene text box is empty.**

   The statements should now read

   ```
   import flash.display.MovieClip;
   this.gotoAndStop(1);
   ```

5. **Choose Control⇨Test Movie to preview your movie.**

   The tween plays and jumps to the first frame, where it stops.

Follow these steps to use `gotoAndPlay()`:

1. **Create a new keyframe at frame 22 on the Actions layer and launch the Actions panel with the new keyframe selected.**

2. **Click the plus sign and choose flash.display⇨MovieClip⇨Methods⇨ gotoAndPlay.**

   In the Object text box, have the timeline refer to itself by typing **this**.

3. **Enter 5 in the Frame text box and make sure the Scene text box is empty (see Figure 7-5).**

   The actions should now read

   ```
   import flash.display.MovieClip;
   this.gotoAndPlay(5);
   ```

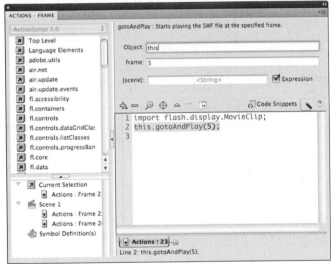

Figure 7-5: The gotoAnd Play() action, placed in ActionScript 3.0.

4. **Choose Control⇨Test Movie to preview your movie.**

   The animation plays until frame 22 and loops between frames 5 and 22.

Using frame labels

Many statements (like the goto statements described in the preceding section) reference exact frame numbers to navigate the timeline. If you happen to change the placement of something on your timeline (such as the start or end of an animation), frame numbers may become inaccurate. For cases like these, you can assign names directly to keyframes on the timeline that you can call directly from ActionScript.

Frame labels are familiar names you can assign to any keyframe (such as `start`, `end`, or `big_finale`). You can then tell ActionScript to jump to these frames by name as an alternative to using a frame number. If the location of the named frame changes, scripts still function as long as the label name is the same. When you move a keyframe, the label you assign to it moves with it.

Here's how to modify a button to use a frame label instead of a frame number:

1. **Create a new layer on the timeline and assign it the name** Labels.

This name is arbitrary, but it's always a good idea to name layers as intuitively as possible.

2. **Select frame 1 of your new layer.**

3. **Enter** *top* **in the text box shown in the Label area of the Property inspector (see Figure 7-6).**

For example, we assigned this keyframe the label name `top`.

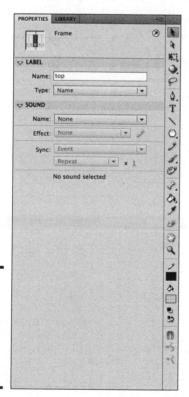

Figure 7-6:
Assign any
keyframe a
label name
with the
Property
inspector.

4. **Select frame 22 of your Actions layer and choose Window⇨Actions to open the Actions panel (if it's not already open).**

   If you haven't already, follow the steps in the previous section, "Using goto," to add a `gotoAndPlay()` statement.

5. **Locate the line that reads `gotoAndPlay(5)`. Replace 5 with the name of the new frame label (top) in double quotes, as shown in Figure 7-7.**

   The code now reads

   ```
   gotoAndPlay ("top");
   ```

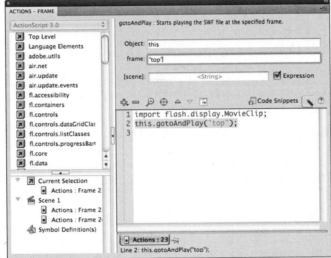

Figure 7-7: Replace the frame number with the frame label you assigned.

6. **Choose Control⇨Test Movie to preview your changes.**

   Click the Rewind button and you see the animation jump to frame 5 and stop just as it did earlier. This time, however, the code uses a frame label instead of an absolute frame number.

   Now, no matter where you move the keyframe, the script follows automatically as long as the frame label remains the same.

Creating Button Symbols

In everyday life, buttons give you control over your world, whether it's switching on a light or your TV at home or navigating Web pages and e-mail messages online. To make your movies better, you can use buttons to give users control over the action with timeline control and navigation.

In Flash, *buttons* are special symbol types built to respond to mouse or keyboard interaction such as clicks, rollovers, and specific key presses. When paired with ActionScript, buttons can be used for just about any navigation or control task. Buttons are created in the same way as other symbol types, and you can easily drag instances to the stage from your library to create more buttons.

Buttons truly come to life after ActionScript is added, but you must understand how to create proper buttons before wiring them up.

Creating a new button

As with graphical symbols, you can create buttons from existing content on the stage or as new empty symbols to which you can add content later.

Follow these steps to create a new button symbol from existing content:

1. **On a new layer in your document, create a new, solid shape on the stage that you want to use as a button and select the shape with the Selection tool.**

2. **Choose Modify⇨Convert to Symbol.**

   The Convert to Symbol dialog box appears.

3. **Enter a name for your new button in the Name text box and choose Button from the Type drop-down list.**

4. **Click OK to create the button.**

Choose Window⇨Library to launch the Library panel, and you see the new symbol with the special button icon next to it.

Understanding button states

Take a look inside your button by double-clicking it on the stage or in the Library panel; its unique timeline contains four specially marked frames: Up, Over, Down, and Hit. Each frame represents a button *state,* or the appearance of a button, as it interacts with a mouse in different ways.

Each frame, or state, can contain unique artwork so that your button can change appearance as it's clicked, pressed, or released. You can even add layers inside your button to stack artwork for more creative flexibility. This list describes the states and what they represent:

✦ **Up:** The appearance of your button when it's not pressed or rolled over. This state is the one you see most of the time as the button sits on the stage.

✦ **Over:** The appearance of the button when the mouse pointer rolls over it. Adding unique content to this frame creates the rollover effect that many people know and love from using Web buttons.

✦ **Down:** The appearance of the button when it's clicked and the mouse button is held down.

✦ **Hit:** Contents aren't visible, but this state sets the *hot spot,* or clickable area, of your button. If the Hit frame is empty, it uses the shape on the last available state by default. You can create a more specific clickable area if you want to give users more or less area to work with or you want to simplify usability for odd-shaped buttons.

Use a filled shape in the Hit frame so that the user has no problem interacting with your button.

Adding content to button states

You can add content to each frame of your button to make it complete:

1. **If it's not already open, edit your new button by double-clicking it on the stage or in the Library panel.**

   You should have some content on the Up state from when you created the button. Now you can define content for remaining states as well.

2. **Select the Over frame on the button's timeline and add a new keyframe with the F6 shortcut key.**

3. **Use the Selection tool or Property inspector or another drawing tool to modify the artwork on the Over frame (see Figure 7-8).**

4. **Select the Down frame and insert a new keyframe by using the F6 shortcut key.**

5. **Modify or add content to the Down frame.**

   This step determines how the button appears when the user clicks and holds down the mouse button.

6. **Select the Hit frame and create a new keyframe by pressing the F6 shortcut key.**

7. **Use existing artwork that's copied to this keyframe or one of the shape tools to fill this frame with a large, filled Hit area.**

8. **Exit the button by clicking Scene 1 above the stage.**

9. **Choose Control⇨Test Movie to preview your movie.**

   Rollover and click your new button to see the different states in action.

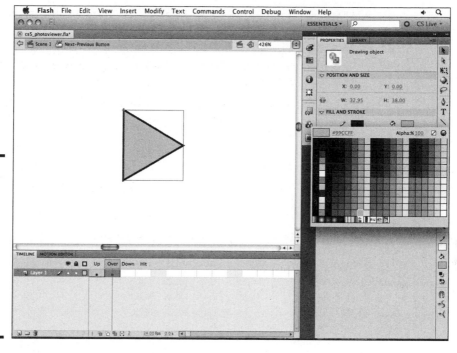

Figure 7-8:
Modified
content
for the
Over frame
appears
when the
user rolls
the mouse
over the
button.

**Book VII
Chapter 7**

Controlling Your
Movie with
ActionScript

Enabling simple buttons

Although choosing Control⇔Test Movie to preview your work is the best way to preview buttons, you may want to see how certain elements of your movie behave in real time on the stage. To see buttons in action on the stage as you build your movie, you can choose Control⇔Enable Simple Buttons. You then see buttons as they would appear and respond to a user in Flash Player.

Buttons can't be selected or modified on the stage with Enable Simple Buttons mode active; you must disable Enable Simple Buttons to apply actions or transformations or to edit the button in place.

Modifying button instances

Individual button instances can have unique transformations and color effects applied, just like graphic symbol instances. In addition, each button can have a unique ActionScript applied to it, so you can use several instances of a single button symbol to create an entire menu or control bar.

Here's how to add and modify additional instances of your button on the stage:

1. **Choose Window⇨Library to make sure that the Library panel is visible.**

2. **Drag two more instances of your button symbol to the same layer as your existing button instance.**

   If necessary, position the buttons so that they're spread apart from each other.

3. **Select one of the button instances and choose Window⇨Properties.**

   The Property inspector opens.

4. **Choose Tint from the Style drop-down list in the Color Effect section.**

5. **Select a color and set the tint percentage to 100 percent.**

   The button becomes tinted with the chosen color.

6. **Select a different button instance, choose the Transform tool from the Tools panel, and use the Transform tool to resize or rotate the selected button.**

Preview buttons by choosing Control⇨Test Movie or Control⇨Enable Simple Buttons.

Putting It All Together: Creating a Simple Photo Viewer

After you've created buttons and gotten a taste of adding ActionScript to the timeline, you put it all together by "wiring up" a photo viewer on the main timeline with ActionScript. The Code Snippets panel does most of the heavy lifting here, but your understanding of the Actions panel and modifying statements will prove quite handy.

For this photo viewer example, create a new Flash file by following these steps:

1. **Import five unique photos or graphics to your Library.**

   For more information on importing images, refer to Chapter 5 of this minibook.

2. **Create a button symbol that can represent both Forward and Backward buttons.**

   For instance, create a right-pointing arrow that can be flipped over.

3. **On the main timeline, create a new layer and add four keyframes back to back (totaling five); on each of those keyframes, place a unique image or graphic from your Library so that you have five images on consecutive keyframes.**

4. Create a new layer and add two button instances to it.

One button should represent a Previous button on the left side of the stage; the other one, a Next button on the right side of the stage.

5. Create a new layer and use the Text tool to create a piece of type that reads "Made with Adobe Flash CS5" on the stage. Place it in the lower-right corner of the stage.

For more information on creating text on the stage, refer to Chapter 2 of this minibook.

Your photo viewer should look similar to the one in Figure 7-9.

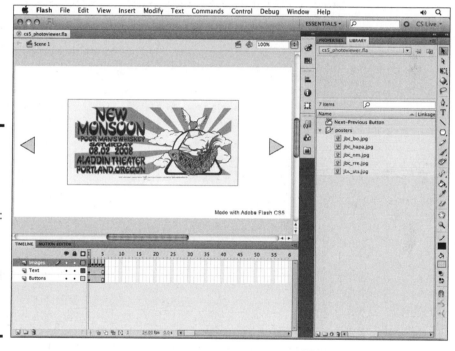

Figure 7-9:
Set up
your photo
viewer
movie as
shown here:
one layer
for the five
photos and
images, one
for buttons,
and one for
text.

**Book VII
Chapter 7**

Controlling Your
Movie with
ActionScript

Applying Code Snippets

The addition of the new Code Snippets panel brings ActionScript within reach for many more Flash users, and provides precreated code fragments for most every common need.

For designers and developers who are experienced in writing their own ActionScript code, the Code Snippets panel can be a valuable tool for creating and managing your own, custom fragments of code that are applied in one click to save typing time.

In the following section, you can explore how to use the Code Snippets panel to carry out common scripting tasks and bring your photo viewer movie to life.

Stopping the main timeline

If you followed the photo viewer example in the following section, and attempt to preview that movie now, you'll notice that the timeline runs on its own, causing it to rapidly flip through the images you've placed on the main timeline (five of them, if you're following along from the previous section).

Because the idea was to create a photo viewer, a user should be able to determine when the next photo is viewed, so you need to stop the timeline at each photo to give her a chance to view it.

To stop the timeline at specific points, follow these steps:

1. **Preview your movie by choosing Control⇨Test Movie (Windows) or Command⇨Test Movie (Mac).**

    Notice that the timeline plays through continuously. The stop actions you add soon will fix this problem.

2. **Close Flash Player and return to your Flash document.**

3. **In the Timeline panel, drag the playhead to the beginning of the timeline (Frame 1).**

4. **Choose Window⇨Code Snippets to open the Code Snippets panel, or expand it from its icon view in the panel group on the right (see Figure 7-10).**

    You can undock the Code Snippets panel for easier access by dragging the panel out of its group on the right-hand side.

5. **Locate and expand the Timeline Navigation folder in the Code Snippets panel.**

6. **Double-click the snippet labeled Stop at This Frame.**

    A new layer (named Actions) is added to the timeline, and a stop action is added at Frame 1.

⎗ Code Snippets

    Every time a code snippet is added, the Actions panel opens to show you the code that was created. A quick and easy way to return to the Code Snippets panel is to use the Code Snippets button at the top of the Actions panel.

Figure 7-10:
Expand
the Code
Snippets
panel
from the
collapsed
panel
group in
the default
(Essentials)
workspace.

7. Repeat Step 6 for Frames 2, 3, 4 and 5, respectively, so that you have a stop on each of the five frames.

When you complete this step, your movie should resemble Figure 7-11.

8. Preview your movie by choosing Control⇨Test Movie (PC) or Command⇨Test Movie (Mac).

This time, you remain stopped at frame 1.

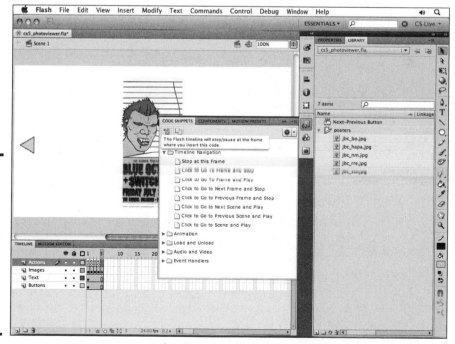

Figure 7-11:
Use the
Code
Snippets
panel to
stop the
timeline at
each of the
five frames
of your
movie.

Poster images designed by and courtesy of Jambone Creative (www.jambonecreative.com)

About instance names

Every time you need to add ActionScript to control a button (or a movie clip), you first need to create an instance name for the button. An *instance name* is a unique ID that tells ActionScript which object on the stage to control or work with. The Code Snippets panel automatically assigns an instance name to a selected button or movie clip when you apply a snippet. You can also add your own instance name by selecting the symbol instance and entering an instance name in the Property inspector.

Instance names can be assigned to buttons, movie clips, and certain text fields. Each instance name needs to be unique, even across several instances of the same symbol.

Creating the previous and next buttons

After your timeline is under control, you need to give users the ability to move back and forth between the images you've placed across the timeline.

As suggested by the movie setup described earlier in the "Putting It All Together" section, you should have a layer on the main timeline with two button instances — one that represents the Previous button and another that represents the Next button.

You can use two instances of the same button symbol or instances of two unique symbols in the library. Follow these steps to create the buttons:

1. **Drag the playhead to Frame 1.**

   The code you add for your buttons must be added at the beginning of the movie.

2. **Click and select a button to use for the Previous button on the stage.**

3. **If the Code Snippets panel isn't already visible, choose Window⇨Code Snippets to open it, or expand it from its icon view in the panel group on the right.**

4. **In the Code Snippets panel, click to expand the Timeline Navigation category.**

5. **Locate and double-click the Click to Go to Previous Frame and Stop code snippet.**

   This step adds some new ActionScript to the existing Actions layer, which is tied to your selected button.

6. **A prompt lets you know that Flash will create an instance name for the new button automatically; click OK.**

7. **Click to select the button you'll use for the Next button on the stage.**

8. **Within the Code Snippets panel, you should already have expanded the Timeline Navigation category. Locate and double-click the Click to Go to Next Frame and Stop code snippet.**

   This step adds code to the Actions layer, as shown in Figure 7-12.

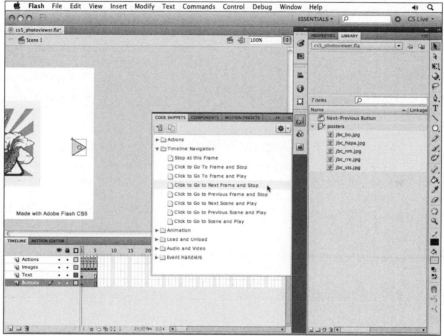

Book VII Chapter 7

Controlling Your Movie with ActionScript

Figure 7-12: On Frame 1 of the timeline, use the Code Snippets panel to add the code that makes your button advance the slide show.

9. **Save your movie by choosing File⇨Save. Next, you test it to see your new code in action.**

10. **Choose Control⇨Test Movie.**

   When your movie launches in Flash Player, click the Next button a couple of times to advance through your images. Click the Previous button to navigate backward.

Linking to a Web site or Web page

Users move around the Web by using buttons or hyperlinks to navigate to Web pages within a site or to other Web sites.

You can easily link to a Web site or Web page within Flash movies by using a button or piece of text and a bit of code help from the Code Snippets panel. For your photo viewer, you link the text you placed on the stage to the Adobe Web site to let users know just how cool Flash is!

To create a clickable link to a Web site or Web page, follow these steps:

1. **Drag the playhead to Frame 1 on the timeline.**

   As with buttons, you add code for a text box at the beginning of the timeline.

2. **Use the Selection tool to click and select the text box you created on the stage when you set up your movie.**

3. **If the Code Snippets panel isn't already visible, choose Window⇨Code Snippets to open it, or expand it from its icon view in the panel group on the right.**

4. **In the Code Snippets panel, click to expand the Actions category.**

5. **Locate and double-click the Click to Go to Web Page code snippet, shown in Figure 7-13.**

   This step adds some new ActionScript to the existing Actions layer, which is tied to your selected button.

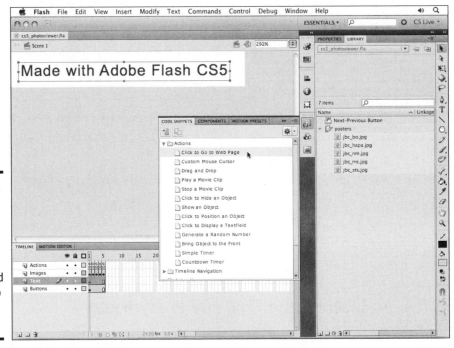

Figure 7-13: Use the Code Snippets panel to open a browser and go to a Web page when clicked.

You see a prompt that lets you know Flash will create an instance name for your text field automatically; click OK.

6. **When the Actions panel opens to show you the new code that has been created, as shown in Figure 7-14, take a moment to review it.**

Notice that the Adobe Web site (www.adobe.com) has automatically been inserted as the default. Keep in mind, however, that you can edit this Web address to make your text link to any site you want.

Figure 7-14:
You can modify the Web address placed by the Code Snippets panel in the Actions panel. The Adobe Web site address is used by default as a placeholder.

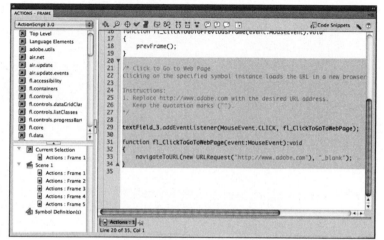

Book VII
Chapter 7

Controlling Your
Movie with
ActionScript

7. **Save your movie and choose Control➪Test Movie to preview it.**

Click the text field. Your default system browser opens to the Adobe Web site.

Chapter 8: Getting Into the (Work)Flow

In This Chapter

✓ Creating and managing workspace layouts

✓ Setting up grids and guides

✓ Using snap options and the Align panel

✓ Using animation helpers

✓ Creating custom keyboard shortcuts

✓ Using the Movie Explorer panel

Sometimes the difference between a good project and a great project is having a seamless workflow. Visual aids, such as guides and grids, alignment aids, and proper placement of tools and panels are essential parts of creating better movies in less time. The Flash workspace is highly customizable so that you can work in the most efficient way possible and spend more time being creative. Flash CS5 includes a new, easy-to-use interface as well as some helpful workspace presets for most every type of user.

Using Workspace Layouts

Your Flash workspace consists of all the panels and tools you rely on, so why not take some time to customize it? You can save the position and appearance of these essential components by creating custom workspace layouts.

Workspace layouts take a snapshot of the appearance and position of panels you're using so that you can recall that same configuration at any time. You can save as many workspace layouts as you want for different projects or different designers who may share the same computer with you.

Choose Window⇨Workspace to recall, save, reset, or manage your workspace layouts.

 Flash CS5 comes with several layout presets: Animator, Classic, Debug, Designer, Developer, Essentials, and Small Screen. You can select and use these layouts as a starting point for a new workspace layout or to reset the workspace. The default layouts *can't* be deleted or overwritten (even by saving a layout under the same name).

Creating new layouts

Before creating a new workspace layout, open any panels you need, close any panels you don't use often, and position and size them exactly how you think is best. All panels can be toggled on or off from the Window menu. Grouping options for each panel are available under their respective panel menus, or you can drag and drop panels on top of one another to group them.

To create a new workspace layout, follow these steps:

1. **Position all panels and toolbars as you want to see them.**

2. **Group any panels or resize individual panels and groups.**

   You can also collapse any panels or groups to Icon mode to maximize the screen area.

3. **Choose Window⇨Workspace⇨New Workspace.**

   A dialog box appears, prompting you to name the new layout.

4. **Enter a name for the new layout in the Name text box and click OK.**

   The new workspace is created.

5. **Choose Window⇨Workspace.**

   You see the new workspace as an available selection.

Managing layouts

After you create workspace layouts, you can rename, delete, or update them as needed. Deleting layouts you no longer use is good practice so that you can keep the list manageable. Also rename layouts to indicate when they were created (for example, MyLayoutFeb2010). You can manage layouts by using the Manage panel.

To delete a layout, choose Window⇨Workspace⇨Manage Workspaces. Select the layout you want to delete and click the Delete button. Click OK to close the Manage Workspaces dialog box. *Note:* You can't undo this action, but a dialog box gives you the same warning and a chance to change your mind.

To rename a layout, choose Window⇨Workspace⇨Manage Workspaces. Select the layout you want to rename and click the Rename button. Enter the new name in the Name text box, click OK, and then click OK again to close the dialog box.

To update (or overwrite) an existing layout, recall the layout by choosing it from the Workspace menu. Make any adjustments to your workspace and choose Window⇨Workspace⇨New Workspace. When prompted, assign it the name of the layout you're trying to update. A warning alerts you that you're about to replace an existing layout by the same name; click OK to overwrite the layout with the new changes.

To condense right-side panels to Icon view, collapse the entire panel group by using the double arrows in the upper right corner of the screen. To hide the labels and view the icons alone, hover over the edge of the panel group until you see the double arrows. Click and drag the panel to resize it to be as narrow as possible.

Fine-Tuning with Grids and Guides

Having lots of visual aides at your fingertips is indispensable when you need to line up, arrange, or measure objects on the stage with absolute accuracy. You'll want some designs to take advantage of the place-it-anywhere flexibility that Flash provides, but other designs demand more precise control over placement and sizing. In these cases, you can take advantage of the large array of Flash visual aids and helpers, many of which you can enable and set from the View menu.

These visual aids don't appear in any way in your final movie; they're strictly for your benefit during the design and building process.

Enabling rulers and guides

The Flash built-in rulers appear on the top and left edges of the stage and are used to position and measure objects on the stage. You also use the rulers to create vertical and horizontal guides by dragging them off the ruler bars. Ruler units are in pixels by default, but you can choose Modify⇨Document to change to other measurement units, such as inches, centimeters, or millimeters.

The top ruler represents the *X,* or horizontal axis, and the left ruler represents the *Y,* or vertical axis. The upper left corner of the stage represents absolute 0 for both X and Y, with X increasing as you move right and Y increasing as you move down.

To set up and use rulers and guides, follow these steps:

1. **In a new document, choose View⇨Rulers.**

The rulers appear on the top and left edges of your stage.

2. **Click and drag anywhere on the stage.**

Markers on both rulers follow to indicate your X and Y positions and the width of your selection area. Now you can create guides that you can use to position artwork on the stage.

3. **Click the top ruler bar and drag down.**

   You're carrying a guide with you while you drag.

4. **Watch the ruler on the left and drop the guide where you want it (see Figure 8-1).**

   Use the left ruler for reference so that you know exactly how far down you're placing the new guide — for example, at 120 pixels.

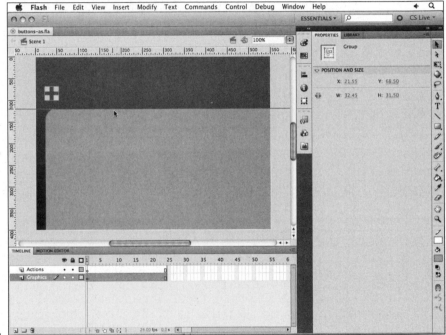

Figure 8-1:
To create a new, horizontal guide, click and drag from the top ruler and release a guide on the stage.

5. **Click and drag on the top ruler again to place another guide.**

   Position this one slightly above the one you previously created — for example, place it at 100 pixels.

6. **Use the Type tool to create a single line of type on the stage, as shown in Figure 8-2.**

   Use a large enough font that you can easily see and drag the new text.

7. **Choose the Selection tool; grab the text with it and drag until the bottom of the text snaps in place on the lower guide you've created.**

**Book VII
Chapter 8**

Getting Into the
(Work)Flow

Figure 8-2:
Create a
line of type
and position
it with the
help of
guides.

Your text snaps easily to the new guides because of a built-in mechanism —
snapping. Think of snapping as turning on a magnetic force that allows
objects to adhere to each other or to visual helpers (such as guides) to
make positioning easier. By default, Snap Align, Snap to Guides, and Snap to
Objects are enabled (choose View➪Snapping). You can also enable Snap to
Pixels and Snap to Grid.

Enabling the grid

If you've ever drawn on graph paper, you know how fun it can be to follow
the lines and create perfect shapes and drawings. As with good old graph
paper, you can enable and use the Flash grid to draw and position objects
and create precise layouts by just following the lines. As with guides, you
can snap type, drawing objects, and symbols to gridlines. You can also draw
along gridlines to easily measure and match shapes.

To enable the grid, choose View➪Grid➪Show Grid (see Figure 8-3). To take
full advantage of the grid, choose View➪Snapping➪Snap to Grid to make it
magnetic.

Figure 8-3:
You can
position
objects and
draw on top
of the grid.

Follow these steps to draw and position objects with the grid:

1. **Choose View➪Grid➪Show Grid to make sure the grid is enabled and choose View➪Snapping➪Snap to Grid to turn on snapping for the grid.**

2. **Grab the Rectangle tool, choose a stroke color, and set the fill color to None.**

3. **Draw a rectangle with the gridlines as a guide.**

The shape snaps to the nearest gridline while you draw.

4. **Use the Selection tool to click and drag the new shape and snap it into place.**

When you move objects along the grid, they snap by their registration point to the gridlines. You can use the gridlines to snap objects (including type) to the exact position you want, as shown in Figure 8-4.

To customize the appearance of your grid, choose View➪Grid➪Edit Grid. From this dialog box, you can specify the grid's size and color and the snapping accuracy.

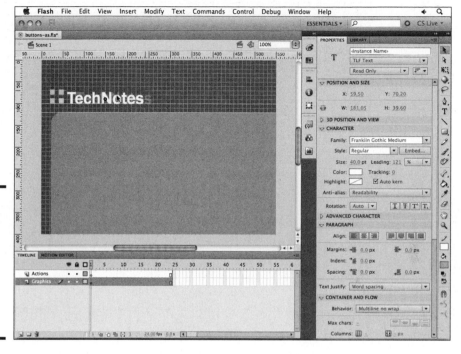

Figure 8-4:
With
snapping
enabled,
objects
snap to the
grid while
you move
them.

Aligning Artwork

If you need to line up or space out several graphics on the stage, you can use the handy Align panel to assist you. The Align panel lets you line up, distribute, or space two or more objects relative to each other or the stage.

To experiment with the Align options, create a new layer, draw a shape on the stage, and place it on the bottom below any graphics you already have on the stage. Then follow these steps to align and distribute two or more graphics:

1. **Select a graphic on the stage and duplicate it two to three times by choosing Edit⇨Copy and then choosing Edit⇨Paste.**

2. **Loosely position the graphics across the stage from left to right.**

3. **Select all the new copies you created with the Selection tool and launch the Align panel by choosing Window⇨Align.**

    The first row contains all the Align buttons, broken down into two groups: vertical and horizontal.

4. **Locate the Align to Stage check box at the bottom of the Align panel and uncheck it.**

   You can see in the next section what effect this step has.

5. **Click the Align Vertical Center button to align the selected graphics horizontally by their top edge.**

   The graphics reposition themselves so that they're all flush by the top edge. Align selected graphics horizontally with each other with the buttons under the Align row. The second row contains buttons that evenly distribute graphics vertically or horizontally by their center, top, or bottom edges.

6. **Click the middle button of the second group (Distribute Horizontal Center) to distribute graphics based on their center points, as shown in Figure 8-5.**

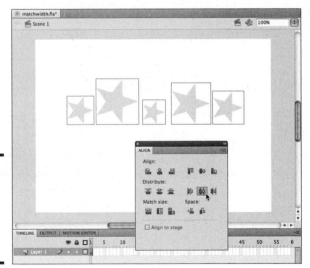

Figure 8-5: Distribute graphics horizontally across the stage.

Distributing to the stage

The Align to Stage check box (located on the bottom of the Align panel) can be selected so that any distribution uses the stage as a point of reference. The distribute options are useful if you want to distribute objects across the full width of the stage regardless of their distance from each other.

To distribute objects across the stage, follow these steps:

1. **Leave selected the graphics you just distributed on the stage. If they aren't selected, use the Selection tool to reselect them by dragging a selection area around them on the stage.**

2. **Locate and select the Align to Stage check box on the Align panel.**

3. **Click any horizontal distribution button in the Distribute row.**

   The graphics redistribute and spread across the full width of the stage, as shown in Figure 8-6.

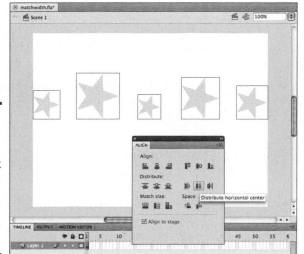

Figure 8-6: Selecting the Align to Stage check box spreads graphics across the full width of the stage.

Using Match Size options

If you need to resize two or more objects on the stage so that they're all the same width and height, you can take advantage of the Match Size options in the Align panel. Match Size options can conform two objects to the same width or height, or both.

To match two objects in size, follow these steps:

1. **Select two or more different-size graphics, symbols, or drawing objects on the stage.**

2. **Choose Window➪Align to launch the Align panel (if it's not already open).**

3. **If it's selected, deselect the Align to Stage check box at the bottom of the Align panel.**

4. **Locate the Match Size button group on the bottom of the panel and click the last button of the three (Match Width and Height).**

   The objects resize to the same width and height, as shown in Figure 8-7.

   Note: You can also match only width or height by clicking either the first or second buttons of the group, respectively.

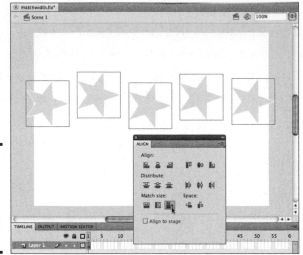

Figure 8-7:
Match the
width and
height of
two or more
graphics.

With the Stage button enabled, Match Size resizes any selected objects to the full width and height of your stage. Using this feature is an easy way to create a full-size background or to stretch a graphic to fit the entire stage.

When you use Match Size, the largest of the selected objects always dictates the resizing. All other objects are resized to match the largest selected object.

Experimenting with Animation Helpers

Sitting discretely below the Timeline are some highly useful icons that can be a big help while you're developing and fine-tuning animations. The Onion Skin, Onion Skin Outlines, and Edit Multiple Frames options let you view, move, and manipulate entire animations at a time to save time and guarantee better results.

When creating animation, you can enable onion skinning to view several frames at a time. With tweened animation, onion skinning can reveal all frames created between the starting and ending keyframes to help you make adjustments and see them in action. You can choose between two types of onion skinning, depending on whether you want to view frames as outlines or full-color previews.

Before you get started, create a new motion tween or open a document with an existing tween that you can use for this example.

To enable onion skinning, follow these steps:

1. Select the Onion Skin icon underneath the Timeline.

A set of brackets appears above the Timeline.

2. Adjust the brackets so that all frames in your tween are selected.

You see a full preview of all frames generated by your tween.

You can't select the frames shown in between, but you can move the instances on the starting and ending keyframe. Select the symbol instance on the starting keyframe of your tween and move it. The onion skin reveals how the frames in between change when you shift starting or ending instances.

As an alternative to seeing frames in your tween in full color, you can preview them as outlines by using the Onion Skin Outlines option (see Figure 8-8). This option works exactly like the Onion Skin option but shows selected frames using a wire-frame-style outline view. The Onion Skin Outlines option can be a better choice if the full-color preview looks cluttered.

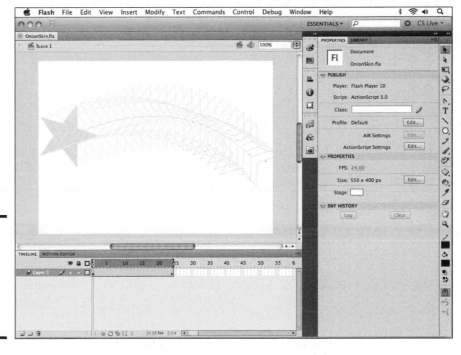

Figure 8-8:
An animation shown in Onion Skin Outlines mode.

Using Keyboard Shortcuts

Part of creating a smooth and fast work environment is having your favorite commands, panels, and tools at your fingertips. Most Flash menu items and panels are equipped with shortcut key combinations that provide easy access without having to comb through several menus. If you need your own, custom keyboard shortcuts, Flash lets you create and save keyboard shortcut sets that you can fully customize to speed your workflow.

To view the default keyboard shortcuts and create your own, choose Edit⇨Keyboard Shortcuts (Windows) or Flash⇨Keyboard Shortcuts (Mac).

You can map almost any available tool, command, or panel to a keyboard shortcut. You can choose to memorize existing keyboard shortcuts for commonly used items or create custom keyboard shortcuts that are more intuitive for you.

To create a new keyboard shortcut, follow these steps:

1. **Choose Edit⇨Keyboard Shortcuts (Windows) or Flash⇨Keyboard Shortcuts (Mac).**

   The Keyboard Shortcuts dialog box launches (see Figure 8-9).

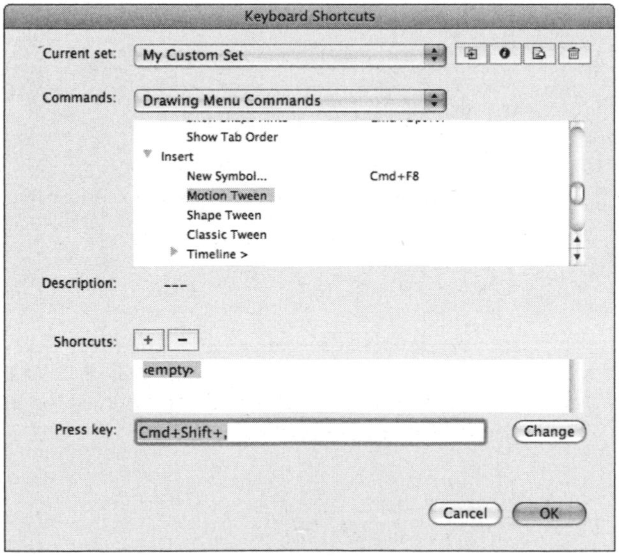

Figure 8-9: Drill down through the menus to select the command you want to create a shortcut for.

2. **Scroll down and click the plus sign (Windows) or triangle (Mac) to the left of where it reads *Control.***

You see all menu items on the Control menu and any keyboard shortcuts assigned to them.

3. **Locate and select the menu command you want to create a shortcut for (refer to Figure 8-9).**

For this example, we selected Insert⇨Motion Tween.

The default set can't be modified, so you need to duplicate the default set and make changes to the new copy.

4. **Click the Duplicate Set icon at the top of the dialog box and type** My Custom Set **in the Name text box when prompted; click OK to create the new set.**

5. **With the current menu item selected, locate and click the plus sign beside *Shortcuts* to add a new shortcut for the menu item.**

The word <empty> appears, ready for you to enter a keyboard shortcut.

6. **Hold down Ctrl+Shift (Windows) or ⌘+Shift (Mac) plus the key you want to assign as the keyboard shortcut (for example, Ctrl+Shift+M or ⌘+Shift+M).**

Use a letter or a number for a keyboard shortcut. You can also use the Shift, Ctrl, and Alt keys (Windows) or Shift, ⌘, and Option keys (Mac) in combination with a letter or a number to create keyboard shortcuts.

You may receive a warning if the keyboard shortcut you've selected is already in use. Make sure the shortcut isn't assigned to a crucial menu command before you decide to overwrite it.

The Shortcuts text box fills in the keyboard shortcut as you hold it. Note that if the keyboard shortcut already exists, a warning appears.

7. **To confirm the shortcut, click the Change button.**

8. **Click OK to close the dialog box and save the shortcut to your new set.**

At any time, you can return to your custom set in the Keyboard Shortcuts dialog box to add new shortcuts or modify existing ones. If at any point you want to switch sets, return to the Keyboard Shortcuts dialog box and select a different set from the Current Set menu.

Working with the Movie Explorer

As a Flash project grows and becomes more complex, moving around the document can be a bit of a guessing game. As you add movie clips, ActionScript, media files, and other elements, the project's inner workings can overwhelm even the most organized designer.

**Book VII
Chapter 8**

Getting Into the
(Work)Flow

For these cases, the Movie Explorer panel (see Figure 8-10) offers an at-a-glance view of your movie. From this panel, you see exactly what's being used and where, and you can navigate directly to any item on the list. You can filter the panel to show only the types of items you want, whether it's ActionScript, movie clips, sounds, or type, by clicking and selecting the icon buttons at the top of the panel. To launch Movie Explorer, choose Window➪Movie Explorer.

Figure 8-10: The Movie Explorer panel.

Chapter 9: Publishing and Final Delivery

In This Chapter

✔ **Getting ready to publish**

✔ **Picking a publish format**

✔ **Previewing your work**

✔ **Publishing for Web delivery**

✔ **Choosing settings for your movie**

✔ **Publishing Adobe AIR applications for the desktop**

✔ **Creating custom publish profiles**

*T*o show your creations to the world, publish the final movie with the Publish command. Before publishing, you can use the Publish Settings option to specify important settings for your final movie, including quality and version settings as well as your choice of file formats. Different options let you publish for the Web, CD-ROM, and even mobile phones. We cover all these options in this chapter.

Getting Familiar with the Publish Process

The `.fla` or `.xfl` files you use to build your movie are intended only for the Flash authoring environment. When you're ready to deliver a final product, create a final `.swf` (compressed movie) file that Flash Player can display in a Web browser.

Flash Player is responsible for displaying your movie in Web pages and mobile phones and on CD-ROM (when packaged as a projector). Adobe AIR (Adobe Integrated Runtime) provides an environment where movies can be run as desktop applications.

The Publish command, activated when you choose File➪Publish, creates your final `.swf` file (often pronounced "swiff") as well as additional files, such as `.html` (Web) pages that you need to display your movie in different environments. When the Publish process is complete, you can then upload completed files to the Web, copy them to CD-ROM, or package them for mobile phone delivery.

Before publishing your final movie, use the Publish Settings dialog box to tell Flash exactly which files you want to generate and which settings to use for each file type. You can specify settings for every file format you choose as well as quality settings for sounds and images used in your movie. The file types you choose depend on your movie's final destination, whether it's the Web, your desktop, a CD-ROM, a mobile device, or a standalone, kiosk-style presentation.

Selecting Your Formats

Depending on where and how you plan to distribute your movie, you can have Flash create a variety of different formats at publish time. Although the most common deployment for Flash is a SWF file and a companion HTML (HyperText Markup Language) file for the Web, it can generate files that can be used for CD-ROMs and mobile phones as well.

To choose file formats, choose File➪Publish Settings and open the Publish Settings dialog box (see Figure 9-1). On the Formats tab, select the check box next to each format you want to create. Enter the file path in the text box or click the folder icon to browse to the destination (optional) for each file you create. By default, all files use the same name and are published to the same location as the original .fla file.

Take a look at the different file formats you can publish and where they're used:

✦ **Flash (.swf):** SWF is the most common file type you publish; it's the one Flash Player and its plug-in use. Think about Flash Player as a movie projector and the SWF file as a movie reel you load on it. When publishing for the Web, this file type is the one to choose, most often accompanied by an HTML (Web) page that contains it.

✦ **HTML (.html):** An HTML file, or a Web page, is used as a container for your Flash movie when the target venue is the Web. HTML files also provide an extra level of abilities, such as checking for the Flash plug-in or enabling additional runtime parameters, such as looping.

✦ **GIF Image (.gif), JPEG Image (.jpg), and PNG Image (.png):** These selections create static images from your movie in the Web-friendly GIF, JPEG, and PNG formats (depending on which check boxes you selected). You can use these images as placeholders (in case the user doesn't have Flash Player or its plug-in) or as elements you can use if you're creating a non-Flash version of your site.

Keep in mind, however, that images are generated only from the first frame of your movie, so exporting an image from it may not yield much if your movie starts out blank or with minimal content.

Figure 9-1:
Choose from
the Formats
tab the files
you want
to create
during the
publish
process.

Publish Settings

Current profile: Default

Formats | Flash | HTML

Type: File:

☑ Flash (.swf)   minisite.swf

☑ HTML (.html)   minisite.html

☐ GIF Image (.gif)   minisite.gif

☐ JPEG Image (.jpg)   minisite.jpg

☐ PNG Image (.png)   minisite.png

☐ Windows Projector (.exe)   minisite.exe

☐ Macintosh Projector   minisite.app

Use Default Names

Publish | Cancel | OK

✦ **Windows Projector (.exe) or Macintosh Projector:** A *projector* is a
package that includes your movie and Flash Player all in one. Projectors
are commonly used for delivery on non-Web formats, such as CD-ROM,
but you can use them for any situation where you want standalone distribution, such as over e-mail or an intranet. Because the projector contains Flash Player, a user doesn't need to install a program to view your
movie. Projectors are created as EXE files for Windows or APP files for
the Mac. If you're delivering to users on both platforms, publish a projector for each one.

A projector can't be viewed in a Web browser, so it isn't a viable choice
if you're trying to work around requiring users to have Flash Player or
its plug-in.

Previewing Your Settings

Before you publish, always use Publish Preview to test the settings you created in the Publish Settings dialog box. Like the Test Movie command, Publish Preview can immediately create and display a SWF file in Flash Player for immediate viewing, but that's where the similarity ends.

Publish Preview creates a preview for any file formats you choose in the Publish Settings dialog box, including Web pages, images, and projectors. The preview lets you see how these files will look before you complete your final publish task and gives you a chance to adjust your publish settings for the best results possible.

To preview any selected publish formats, choose File⇔Publish Preview and select the format you want to preview. The default is a SWF file with an accompanying HTML page.

Publish Preview shows how the final movie will look in an HTML page. To preview an HTML and an embedded SWF file, choose File⇔Publish Preview⇔HTML.

Press the Publish Preview shortcut key combination Ctrl+F12 (Windows) or ⌘+F12 (Mac) to create a preview from the default selection (HTML page and SWF file) at any time.

If HTML or SWF aren't among your selected publish formats, the Publish Preview defaults to the next format you selected after choosing Publish Settings⇔Format.

When previewing a movie with either the Test Movie or Publish Preview (Flash option only) command, you can use the Bandwidth Profiler. This graph, shown in Figure 9-2, appears at the top of the preview window and shows the total file size of your movie, as well as where and how data is loaded as the movie plays. This step can be important in gauging whether the file size may be too much to users to download or whether you should distribute data-intensive items (such as sound files or images) more effectively across the Timeline.

The bars across the graph appear at frames where data is loaded, and the height of the bar indicates how much data was loaded when the playhead reached that frame.

To view your movie with the Bandwidth Profiler, choose File⇨Publish Preview⇨Flash. When the movie appears in Flash Player, choose View⇨ Bandwidth Profiler.

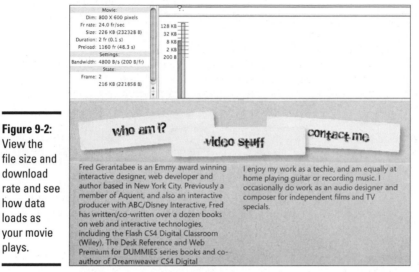

Figure 9-2:
View the file size and download rate and see how data loads as your movie plays.

Publishing for the Web

If your movie's final destination is the Web, select the two necessary file formats in the Publish Settings dialog box: Select the HTML (`.html`) and Flash (`.swf`) check boxes. The HTML file (or Web page) acts as a container for your SWF file, displaying it in the browser and placing it against a matching background. This HTML file also contains code that sets additional options in your movie at runtime (such as instructions to loop automatically).

Playback of the actual SWF file is handled by Flash Player, which works as a plug-in for all major Web browsers.

When you publish your final movie and HTML file, you upload both files to your Web-hosting account or company server or wherever your movie needs to go to make it available for public viewing.

To publish the necessary files for the Web viewing, choose File⇨Publish Settings and select the HTML (`.html`) and Flash (`.swf`) check boxes on the Formats tab. Click the Publish button to create the final files that you'll upload to your Web server of choice.

Uploading your files to the Web with FTP

File Transfer Protocol (FTP) is the method used to connect and transfer files between your local computer and a remote Web server and is the most common way of posting finished files to the Web for the public to see.

FTP connections occur between your computer and a server that opens the connection to receive the files. Servers often are maintained by a hosting company that provides you with an account and a space for your Web site files. You may also be posting your work to a network machine or a dedicated server maintained by your company. Flash doesn't have FTP capabilities, but there are many FTP clients available that you can install on your computer vary in price and features.

Adobe Dreamweaver CS5 includes full FTP functionality and can create and store connections to several different servers or hosting accounts. If you want a more basic (and free) option, you can connect to a Web server via FTP directly from Windows Explorer or choose the Go➪Connect to Server option in the Finder on Macintosh OS X. Alternatively, browsers such as Firefox support cool, free add-ons such as FireFTP. In most applications, copying files to and from the server is as simple as dragging and dropping from one window to another.

Remember: To connect to a server, you need to purchase or have access to a Web-hosting account, network computer, or dedicated server. Most FTP connections require a user ID and password; check with your server administrator or hosting company to find information for your specific account.

Publishing for CD-ROM

Flash's ability to include full-featured video, audio, and graphics has made it quite a popular choice for creating CD-ROM based presentations, e-brochures, learning materials, and interactive application installers. When packaging for a CD-ROM, consider that a SWF file alone may not be enough, especially because users might not have a standalone version of Flash Player installed on their computers.

For this reason, you can package movies for CD-ROM as projectors. (See the section "Selecting Your Formats," earlier in this chapter, for more on projectors.)

To create standalone projectors for Windows or Mac, select the Windows Projector (.exe) or Macintosh Projector check boxes on the Formats tab of the Publish Settings dialog box. Projectors are created when you publish, along with other formats you've chosen. These projectors can then be copied to and distributed on a CD or a DVD.

Choosing the Right Settings

After you pick the file types you want to publish, you can specify settings for each selected format in the Publish Settings dialog box. Take time to familiarize yourself with the available options and experiment with different settings until your finished movie is just right.

Flash stores publish settings as part of your document, so you need to set them only once for each Flash movie. Be sure to save your movie after you choose your publish settings so that your settings are available the next time you open the document.

Choosing settings for Flash (.swf) files

SWF files are compressed movies used by Flash Player for display on the Web or directly on a user's computer. When you choose to publish a SWF file, you have the opportunity to specify settings that determine version, security, and quality.

Flash settings are available on the Flash tab in the Publish Settings dialog box (see Figure 9-3). (First make sure that you select the Flash [.swf] check box on the Formats tab.)

The following list takes a look at some of the settings you'll work with and how each one affects the performance and quality of your Flash movie:

+ **Player:** This drop-down list controls which version of Flash Player your movie is created for. In most cases, you want to select the latest version, Flash Player 10, so that you can take advantage of the player's latest features. In some cases, you may need to publish your movie to be compatible with a previous version of Flash Player; here, you can specify versions as far back as Flash Player 1. You can also publish your movies for Adobe AIR, as well as *Flash Lite,* a version of Flash player developed for mobile devices.

+ **Script:** What you choose in this drop-down list is completely dependent on which version of ActionScript (if any) you're working with. Because each version contains differences in both features and structure (particularly between ActionScript 3.0 and previous versions), publish in the version you've used throughout your movie. If your movie doesn't use any ActionScript, leave the default setting for the Flash Player version you choose.

Chapter 7 of this minibook discusses ActionScript and the differences between Versions 2.0 and 3.0.

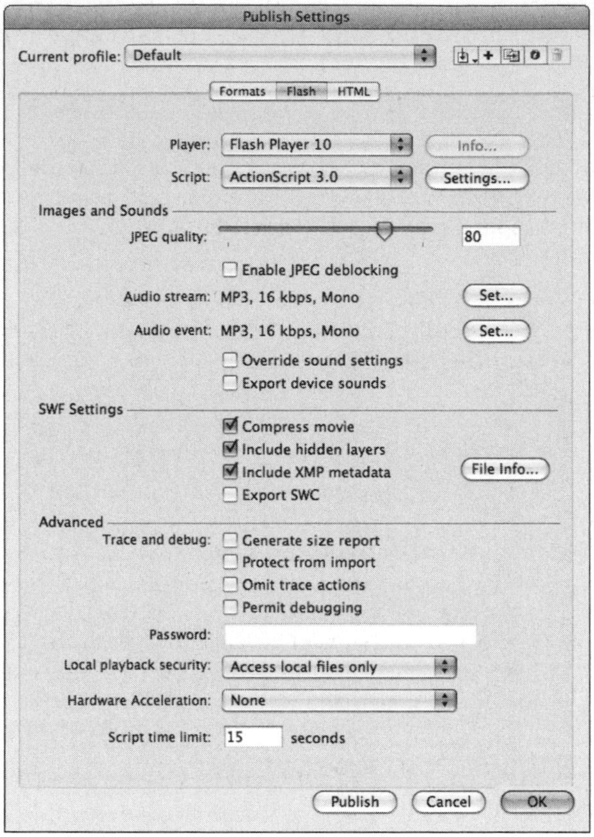

Figure 9-3:
The Flash tab is available when Flash (.swf) is a selected publish format.

✦ **JPEG Quality:** Flash performs a certain amount of compression on bitmap graphics in your movie (such as imported photos) to reduce file size and increase performance. Use this slider to determine the amount of compression applied and, in turn, the resulting file size and quality of your movie. The higher the quality, the less compression applied and the larger the resulting file size.

✦ **Audio Stream and Audio Event:** If your movie includes sound, you can set its quality in your final SWF file by clicking the Set button beside either Audio Streams or Audio Events. By default, sound is converted to 16 kbps, Mono and MP3 format, but you can change both compression and quality settings as needed. Keep in mind that, like the JPEG quality settings, higher-quality settings for sound likely increases the overall file size of your movie.

Chapter 5 of this minibook discusses stream and event sounds.

✦ **SWF Settings area:** In previous versions of Flash, hidden layers were published by default to your final movie. This behavior can be toggled off by selecting the Include Hidden Layers check box to ensure that layers that are turned off in your FLA file don't show in the resulting SWF file.

The Compress Movie check box, which is selected by default, compresses your SWF file to reduce the file size and, in turn, the download time. Leave this check box selected, especially if your file is ActionScript or text intensive.

Because the Include Hidden Layers check box is selected by default, any layers that are turned off on the Timeline appear in your final movie. Be sure to deselect this option if you want to ensure that hidden content isn't included.

✦ **Advanced area:** The Flash authoring software can't open or decompile SWF files for editing, but it can import them as frame-by-frame movies into a FLA document. This strategy opens the door for artwork and graphic resources to be extracted, perhaps against your will. Selecting the Protect from Import check box prevents SWF files from being imported into the Flash authoring environment. The Password text box below the check boxes becomes active when the Protect from Import check box is selected so that you can assign a password to allow only certain parties (a colleague or client, for example) to import the SWF file if they need to.

Choosing settings for HTML files

For presenting Flash movies on the Web, you'll need to publish an HTML file that contains your SWF file. This HTML file not only displays your movie but also includes all code necessary to control dimensions, appearance, and run-time options (such as telling your movie to loop). The HTML file features the same background color as your movie so that it matches seamlessly when viewed in a browser.

Select the HTML (`.html`) check box in the Formats tab of the Publish Settings dialog box and then click the HTML tab. On the HTML tab, you can choose from the following options for your published HTML file:

✦ **Template:** This setting generates an HTML file based on different possible environments, such as standard browsers, Pocket PCs, or additional options for full-screen support.

For any selected template, an `AC_RunActiveContent.js` file is created. Copy this file to your Web server with any other generated files. This file is a workaround for recent changes to Internet Explorer's handling of active content.

✦ **Detect Flash Player Version check box:** This option adds code in your HTML file to display alternative content if the user doesn't have Flash Player installed. You can customize this content in any HTML editor. The default content provides a link for the user to download and install the latest version of Flash Player.

✦ **Dimensions:** The code in your HTML file specifies a size for your Flash movie, which, by default, matches your movie's dimensions. You can override this setting and force your movie to a different size in either pixels or percentage by typing values in the Width and Height text boxes.

✦ **Playback:** Check boxes in this area set runtime options for your Flash movie. By default, Flash Player is directed to loop movies and to make the contextual menu available to the user. You can disable either of these features, force the movie to pause at the start, or use *device fonts* (fonts from the user's machine instead of embedded fonts).

✦ **Quality:** Control the overall display quality of your movie by selecting a Low, Medium, or High quality setting from the drop-down list.

✦ **Window Mode:** This drop-down list lets you choose how Flash appears in the context of your Web page. You can set Flash movies to be opaque or transparent to reveal the background of the page.

✦ **HTML Alignment:** Select a left, right, top, or bottom alignment of your movie as determined by the HTML code using the provided drop-down list.

✦ **Scale:** This drop-down list lets you choose whether the HTML page scales the Flash movie to a size other than its default size.

✦ **Flash alignment:** This option controls the positioning of your Flash movie within the page. Use the drop-down lists to select vertical or horizontal alignment values, or both.

Publishing your movie

After you select the correct settings for the file formats and files you want to create, you can publish your movie in one of two ways:

✦ At the bottom of the Publish Settings panel, click the Publish button.

✦ Choose File➪Publish.

In most cases, you'll publish a SWF and companion HTML file so you can view your movie in a Web browser, as shown in Figure 9-4.

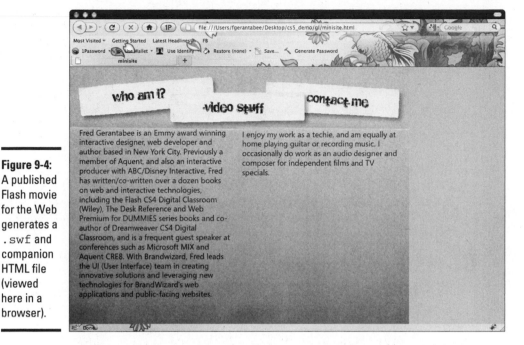

Figure 9-4:
A published
Flash movie
for the Web
generates a
`.swf` and
companion
HTML file
(viewed
here in a
browser).

Publishing Desktop Applications with Adobe AIR

The Adobe AIR (Adobe Integrated Runtime) platform gives designers and
developers a way to use their existing skills to create cross-platform desktop
applications.

Users can download the AIR runtime for free and install it to manage and
play AIR applications directly from their desktops. The best news for designers and developers is that AIR applications can be created from standard
FLA files in Flash by making a few simple changes to your publish settings.

AIR applications have several advantages over the use of standard Flash projectors; AIR applications can work with the operating system, files, and other
applications without the restrictions faced by projectors in the past.

Because AIR applications publish in their own unique format, it's not necessary to create installers for both Windows and Mac; an AIR application
installs and runs on both operating systems!

Many features unique to AIR applications are beyond the scope of this minibook, so this section covers only the basics of publishing AIR applications
from any Flash movie.

Publishing an AIR application

Before you get started, download and install the Adobe AIR runtime from the Adobe Web site at www.adobe.com/products/air. The following steps are based on the Adobe AIR 2 Beta 2 installer, which was the newest available version at the time of this writing.

Follow these steps to publish your movie as an AIR application:

1. **Open a document in Flash CS5 that you want to publish as an AIR application.**

2. **Choose File⇨Publish Settings and select the Flash tab at the top to view Flash movie (.swf) publish settings.**

   If the Flash tab isn't available, make sure that Flash (.swf) is selected on the Formats tab.

3. **Locate the Player drop-down menu and select Adobe AIR 2 as the player type, as shown in Figure 9-5.**

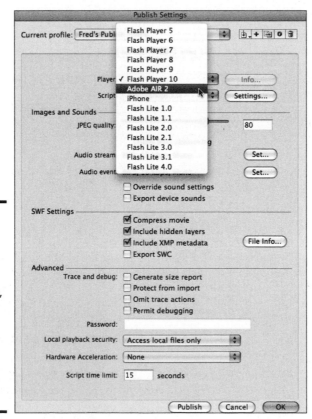

Figure 9-5:
To publish your Flash movie as an AIR application, choose AIR 2.0 as the player type in the Publish Settings dialog box.

4. **Click the Settings button directly next to the Player drop-down menu.**

The AIR 2 Application & Installer settings dialog box opens, as shown in Figure 9-6.

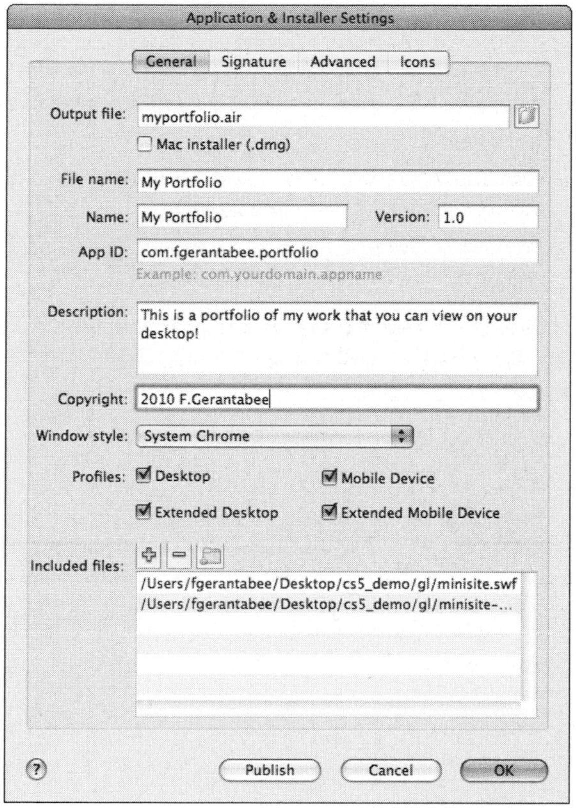

Figure 9-6:
The AIR Application & Installer Settings dialog box.

Book VII Chapter 9

Publishing and Final Delivery

A number of options and settings are available:

- *Output file:* Choose a filename and location for your published AIR application. The Mac Installer (.dmg)/Windows Installer (.exe) check box provides an alternative installation file type for the Mac and Windows platforms. If you're unsure which one to use, leave this option deselected.

- *File name:* The name of your file as displayed by the AIR application installer.

- *App Name:* Your application displays this name (Super Picture Viewer, for example) when it's installed and when it's running on your desktop.

- *Version:* This option indicates which version of an application is installed or running. Attach a version number so that users can distinguish between installations as you create updated releases of your application.

- *App ID:* This identifier is often used to distinguish one company's applications from another, or even several applications from the same publisher. A common naming scheme is the "reverse DNS" scheme, such as `com.mycompany.mycoolapp`. If your company is at `coolwidgets.com` and your app is The Picture Widget, for example, your app ID might be `com.coolwidgets.picturewidget`.

- *Description:* In this area, you can provide a description of your application — for example, "The Picture Widget lets you view and organize your mobile phone snapshots quickly and easily."

- *Copyright:* Enter your copyright information here (for example, 2010 CoolWidgets.com).

- *Window Style:* This setting determines how your application is "framed" within the operating system environment. You can use the default system windows (System Chrome); your own, custom frame, or even no frame (Custom Chrome — opaque or transparent).

- *Included Files:* This panel shows all files to be packaged and included in the AIR application, typically a `.swf` file and an application manifest (`.xml`) file. If your application depends on other files (such as external audio or video files), you can add them here as necessary.

5. **Enter or modify the AIR 2 Settings and then click the Publish button.**

   A dialog box appears, prompting you to choose a digital certificate for signing your application.

6. **Click the Create button on the far right side, and in the dialog box that opens, fill in the information necessary to create your own, self-signed certificate.**

   For more information on digital certificates, see the later sidebar named "What is a digital certificate?"

7. **Enter information for the publisher name, organization unit, organization name, country, and password, and then click Browse to choose a save location, as shown in Figure 9-7.**

8. **Click OK to create and save your certificate.**

   This step returns you to the digital signature dialog box, where your new certificate is already selected.

9. **Reenter the password you chose when you created your certificate and click Publish.**

   A dialog box notifies you that your AIR file has been created.

10. **Click OK to exit the Application & Installer Settings dialog box and then click OK to close the Publish Settings dialog box.**

Publisher name:	Fred Gerantabee
Organization unit:	Author
Organization name:	John Wiley & Sons
Country:	US
Password:	••••••
Confirm password:	••••••
Type:	1024-RSA
Save as:	/Users/fgerantabee/Desktop/mycert.p12

Cancel   OK

Installing and running your new AIR application

Before giving your new desktop application a test run, make sure that you've installed the latest version of the Adobe AIR Runtime from www.adobe.com/products/air.

Any user who needs to run your application needs to also install the Adobe AIR Runtime using the same URL shown above. The good news is that many users already have AIR installed, and if not, it's a fast, free download from the Adobe Web site.

To install and run the AIR application, locate and double-click the .air file you published. The Adobe AIR Runtime launches, and a dialog box prompts you to install the new application, as shown in Figure 9-8. Click Install. Your application is now installed!

What is a digital certificate?

A *digital certificate* is a verification of the publisher's authenticity (that's you!). You can create a digital certificate yourself, or Flash creates a temporary (AIRI) file until you do. A certificate is only necessary to publish a working AIR application.

Because an AIR application (much like any other desktop application) has access to many aspects of the user's computer, a certificate is necessary for AIR to trust an application before installing it. Though you can create your own certificate for publishing purposes, you can also obtain a certificate from globally trusted third-party providers such as ChosenSecurity, GlobalSign, Thawte, or VeriSign if you intend to distribute your application commercially.

Creating Publish Profiles

If you want to use the same publish settings across multiple movies, you can capture your settings as a profile that you can recall and use in other documents.

To create a new publish profile, follow these steps:

1. **Choose File⇨Publish Settings to open the Publish Settings dialog box (refer to Figure 9-1).**

2. **Select some formats and choose settings as described, in the earlier section "Choosing the Right Settings."**

3. **Locate the Create New Profile icon in the upper right corner of the dialog box and click it.**

   The Create New Profile dialog box appears, prompting you to assign the new profile a name.

4. **Enter the profile name in the Profile name text box and click OK.**

   The profile is created and is an available option under the Current Profile drop-down list at the top of the Publish Settings dialog box.

To make your profile available to other documents, export it:

1. **Choose File⇨Publish Settings to open the Publish Settings dialog box.**

2. **Choose Export from the Import/Export icon at the top of the Publish Settings dialog box.**

   You're prompted to name and save your profile (stored as a separate .xml file). Although you can save the file anywhere, keep it in the Flash application's Publish Profiles folder, which is the default location.

3. **Assign the XML file a name by typing it in the File Name (Windows)/ Save As (Mac) text box, choose a Save location, and click Save.**

To import a profile from another document, follow these steps:

1. **Choose File➪Publish Settings to open the Publish Settings dialog box.**

2. **Choose Import from the Import/Export icon at the top of the dialog box.**

   The Import Profile dialog box appears, as shown in Figure 9-9.

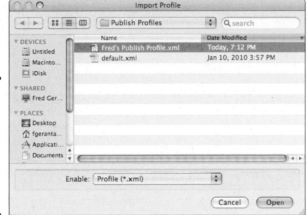

Figure 9-9: Import profiles you've exported to locations on your hard drive.

3. **Locate the XML file you created when you exported the profile and click Open.**

   The profile is now available under the Current Profiles drop-down list at the top of the Publish Settings dialog box.

Additional resources

One outstanding element of working with Flash is the community that supports it. Countless Web sites are dedicated to Flash tutorials, training videos, sample files, free resources (such as fonts and sounds), and forums to discuss and assist developers of all levels with a variety of Flash help topics.

(continued)

(continued)

We don't have room to list them all, but here's a short list of established and highly visited sites that can get you started. (**Note:** This list isn't complete, nor is it an endorsement of any specific Web site. These Web sites have been shown to be reputable and highly useful resources for Flash developers. You're encouraged to be a part of the Flash community by using and contributing to these and other online resources to further your own knowledge.)

ActionScript.org:

www.actionscript.org

Adobe Flash Exchange and Support Center:

www.adobe.com/cfusion/exchange/index.cfm

Adobe XMP metadata information:

www.adobe.com/products/xmp/overview.html

Colin Moock: www.moock.org

FFiles.com: www.ffiles.com

FlashKit: www.flashkit.com

Flash Magazine:

www.flashmagazine.com

Fonts for Flash:

www.fontsforflash.com

Kirupa.com: www.kirupa.com

Moluv.com: www.moluv.coma

Chapter 10: Working with Flash Catalyst CS5

*W*ould you like to create Flash Web sites or desktop applications the easy way? Flash Catalyst CS5 can make that easy. You can start by creating your design in Photoshop or Illustrator and importing the resulting file into Catalyst. Then, you can do the following:

✦ Create buttons that change while the user hovers the mouse cursor over them or clicks them (just like buttons in Flash).

✦ Add buttons, sliders, and other user interface components that link to other locations or perform other marvelous tricks.

✦ Add animation, such as moving components on and off the screen.

✦ Develop an entire site with multiple pages.

✦ Easily add animated transitions, such as resizing, rotating, or moving objects, or fading objects or pages in and out.

In larger projects that might require programming code (such as desktop applications or database-driven Web sites), Catalyst makes it easy for the designer and the developer to interact smoothly. The developer can use the information from Flash Catalyst directly in Adobe *Flash Builder,* a program for adding ActionScript. The designer can then incorporate changes made in Builder back into Flash Catalyst files.

Discovering Flash Catalyst

While Catalyst empowers you as a designer to create a working Web site using your Photoshop or Illustrator files, it also allows designers of large desktop applications to create prototypes of their applications within Flash Catalyst. In this chapter, we assume that you are a Web site designer and not an applications prototyper.

In Figure 10-1, you see Catalyst with an example of a Web site designed in Photoshop and transformed into an interactive Web site. You can find the original site at www.tellnshow.com.

If you're an artist working in Adobe Fireworks, you can also interact with Catalyst using files that are saved in the FXG format. (Choose Commands➪Export to FXG from the Fireworks menu.) However, these files do not currently support layers. If you want to use Fireworks files in Catalyst, perhaps the easiest thing to do is to export them into Photoshop format to preserve layers before importing into Catalyst.

The Catalyst screen consists of the following, as shown in Figure 10-1:

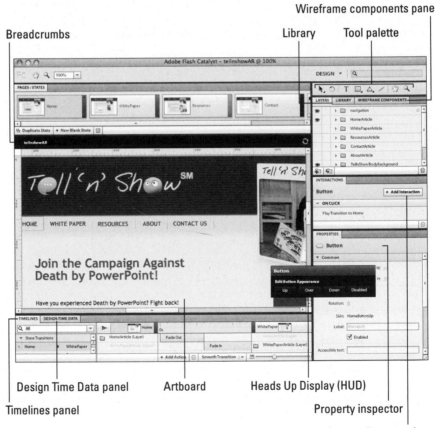

Figure 10-1: Exploring the power of Flash Catalyst.

Thanks to Ellen Finkelstein for permission to use her Web site as an example in the chapters on Catalyst. You can find this HTML site at www.tellnshow.com.

- ✦ **Artboard:** Like the Stage in Flash: where you do your main designing.

- ✦ **Heads-up Display (HUD):** Use this dark floating panel to easily convert objects. It changes based on what you select.

- ✦ **Tools palette:** Container for selection tools, basic shapes, zoom, text, and a rotation tool.

- ✦ **Layers panel:** Rearrange, view, and lock layers, as well as add and delete layers. It sits below the Tools palette, along with Wireframe Components and Library.

- ✦ **Library panel (hidden in Figure 10-1):** For objects that you plan to use more than once, or objects that you import, such as images or SWF files.

- ✦ **Wireframe Components panel (hidden in Figure 10-1):** A selection of user-interface components you can add to your website.

- ✦ **Interactions panel:** Where you define what action to take for button clicks and other interactions.

- ✦ **Properties panel:** Set properties for selected objects.

- ✦ **Breadcrumbs:** Navigate back from working with button states (or states of other components) to the main Artboard. Figure 10-1 shows only one breadcrumb item.

- ✦ **Timelines panel:** Specify movement of objects, rotation, changes in opacity, resizing, and more.

- ✦ **Design-Time Data panel (hidden in Figure 10-1):** For applications requiring data, you can add sample data using this panel.

Preparing Your Artwork

Careful preparation of your design in Photoshop or Illustrator is key to getting good results in Catalyst — and not tearing your hair out in frustration! You may have to work a little differently than you're used to so that Catalyst understands the design file.

Creating unique objects

For Catalyst to recognize buttons and other objects, all the artwork that's going to become a button or other component needs to be a unique object that is selectable. (Of course, you can use multiple objects, such as a rectangle and text.)

This is important in Photoshop or Illustrator, where it's easy to ignore this principle. If you create a series of buttons, for example, by adding some text and some dividers over a background, then when you bring the file into Flash Catalyst, you have no unique objects to select. So, be sure that each button can be selected individually or as a group of objects making up that button.

Organizing your layers

If you create your layers in Photoshop or Illustrator the same way that you plan to work with them in Catalyst, you'll have a much easier time creating your project. The idea is to be able to toggle on the visibility of layers to reveal every page in the Web site. Figure 10-2 shows a set of layers in Photoshop that illustrate this principle. We recommend the following:

✦ Create a folder for each page of your Web site; and within each folder, place layers with the unique design for each page.

✦ Create a folder as your top layer, which contains your navigation buttons and anything that doesn't change from page to page, such as your logo. You may want to call this folder something descriptive, such as *Navigation*.

✦ Assign your background layer a color that appears if you fade out or fade in a page. (Some of it may also appear if your pages don't fully cover the background.)

Figure 10-2:
Creating a
logical layer
structure in
Photoshop.

Always label each layer as descriptively as possible, especially if you're planning to work with a developer using Flash Builder. The developer may need to use the names of the layers in the code.

Adding the looks for button states

You can create the different looks for your button states (or states of other components) in several ways:

✦ Stack your button states on individual layers in Photoshop or Illustrator and label the layers carefully to explain what they are. Then you can turn off the visibility of the layers to define the different states in Catalyst, as we describe later in this chapter.

✦ Add button states in Catalyst (rather than adding the looks in Photoshop or Illustrator), using glows, drop shadows, resizing, or more in Catalyst, which we describe later in this chapter.

✦ Export a button state from Photoshop or Illustrator as a PNG, JPG, or GIF file, and import it into the new state in Catalyst. We also discuss this method later in this chapter.

Importing Your File into Catalyst

Flash Catalyst allows you to import files in Photoshop format or Illustrator format. When importing from Photoshop, for example, all the layers import intact. The layers of the Photoshop file are in the Layers panel.

You can use Catalyst without importing any file, but its real power for a Web designer lies in its ability to add interactivity to Photoshop or Illustrator files.

To import your file, follow these steps:

1. **Do one of the following:**

- Open Catalyst. In the Welcome Screen under Create New Project from Design File, choose either From Adobe Illustrator AI File or From Adobe Photoshop PSD File.

- From within Catalyst, choose File➪New Project from Design Comp, choose an Adobe Photoshop (psd) or Adobe Illustrator (ai) file, and then click Open.

2. **Browse to find your PSD or AI file, select it, and click Open.**

The Photoshop (or Illustrator) Import Options dialog box appears, as shown in Figure 10-3.

3. **To select specific layers to import, click the Advanced button, specify the layers that you want, and then click OK.**

   You may have some layers that you created for temporary use that you don't want to end up in the final Web site file.

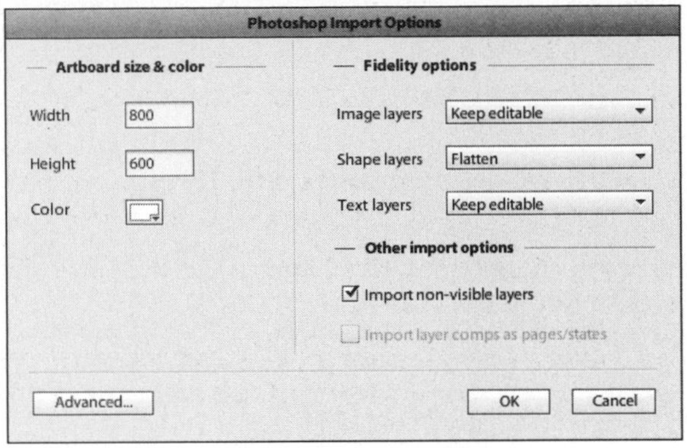

Figure 10-3:
The Import
Options
dialog
box gives
you some
choices.

4. **(Optional) Choose a background color for the Artboard.**

   You might have already assigned a background color in your design file.

5. **(Optional) In the Fidelity Options section, change how you import layers by choosing from the Image Layers, Shape Layers, or Text Layers drop-down lists.**

   You can't edit flattened content, such as text. By default, shape layers are flattened so that you can more easily work with them in Catalyst.

6. **Be sure that the Import Non-Visible Layers check box is selected.**

   That way, even if some of your layers are hidden, you import them anyway.

7. **Click OK.**

   A progress bar might appear while Catalyst imports your file.

8. **If you see a message telling you that the file contains a large number of bitmap graphics and/or vector paths (with instructions for optimizing the graphics), click Continue.**

9. **If the Import Issues dialog box appears with messages, such as a list of empty layers that weren't imported or missing fonts, click OK.**

   If you're missing fonts, you may need to install them or use different fonts in the imported file.

Behind the dialog box, your Photoshop file or Illustrator file appears in a Catalyst window.

Defining Pages in Catalyst

After importing your file, the first step is to define pages. After all, most Web sites have more than one page! If you created your layers correctly, defining new pages in Flash Catalyst is simple. Just follow these steps:

1. **Click the Duplicate State button above the Artboard for as many new pages as you want to create.**

   New pages appear in the Pages/States panel, named Page1, Page2, and so on.

2. **For each page, double-click its name, and then type a new name that matches the name of the Web page (no spaces allowed).**

3. **Select the first page and click the Eye icon in the Layers panel for each layer that you want to hide.**

   Hide all layers that you don't want to appear on the first page. The Eye icon disappears for each layer that you hide. The first page appears on the Artboard.

4. **Repeat Step 3 for each page.**

   Each page should appear when you click that page in the Pages/States panel, as shown in Figure 10-4. Here you see the second page, WhitePaper, displayed.

**Book VII
Chapter 10**

**Working with
Flash Catalyst CS5**

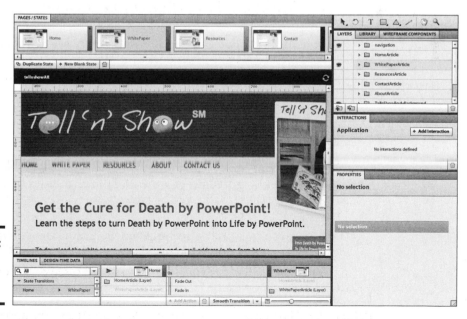

Figure 10-4:
Hide layers
to define
pages.

Working with Buttons

When your layers and pages are set up, it's time to start creating buttons, which are the nuts and bolts of your user interface. First, you convert your artwork into buttons, and then you assign different looks for the different states of the buttons. Catalyst offers so many ways to enhance the design of your buttons through adding filters, animation, or different artwork for their different states — and all without programming.

Converting artwork to buttons

Before you can get fancy with how your button looks when it gets clicked, you first need to convert your artwork into a button. To create a button using Flash Catalyst, follow these steps:

1. **Using the Select tool, press and hold the Shift key, and then click each item in the button (such as the text, the background, and so on) to select all the parts of the button, as shown in Figure 10-5.**

The Heads-up Display (HUD) appears, if it's not already visible.

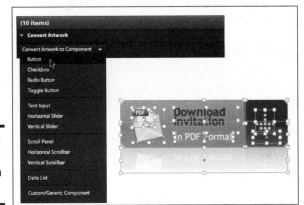

Figure 10-5:
Converting artwork to a button.

2. **In the HUD, from the Convert Artwork to Component drop-down list, choose Button.**

This names the button *Button1* and copies it into the Library. Catalyst switches to Component Editing mode, allowing you to apply different looks to different states of the button, which we describe in the following section.

3. **To rename your button, click the Library tab, expand the Custom Components pane, right-click *Button1*, and choose Rename. Then type your new name into the text box that appears.**

Button names cannot contain spaces or hyphens.

Now that your artwork is a button, you can assign the looks for the different states in the following section.

Defining button states

You can create the artwork for the different states of your buttons in Flash Catalyst, or in Photoshop or Illustrator. Catalyst has several filters that you can use to easily add drop shadows or glows to objects. You can use these filters for the different states, or you might want to change the size or color of the button.

To define the states of a button, follow these steps:

1. **Select the button and choose Modify⇨Edit Component.**

   You are now in Component Editing mode, as shown in Figure 10-6. The four states of the button appear in the Pages/States panel.

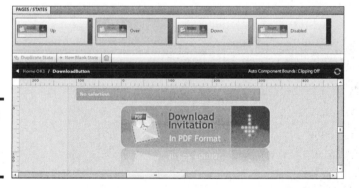

Figure 10-6: Adding states to a button.

Book VII Chapter 10

Working with Flash Catalyst CS5

2. **Click any state in the Pages/States panel that you want to edit.**

3. **Edit the button in the Artboard.**

   In the following sections, see instructions for various ways to edit your button, such as adding a filter or resizing a button for a different state.

4. **Exit Component Editing mode by choosing Modify⇨Exit Editing.**

Adding a filter to a different state of a button

To add an inner or outer glow, a drop shadow, an inner shadow, a bevel, or a blur to create a new state for a button, follow these steps:

1. **Select the button and choose Modify➪Edit Component.**

   The four states of the button (Up, Over, Down, and Disabled) appear in the Pages/States panel.

2. **In the Pages/States panel, click the State that you want to edit.**

3. **Click the button again to select it. In the Properties panel, expand the Filters pane (if it's not already open).**

4. **Click the Add Filter button and choose a filter.**

   Filter controls appear in the pane, as shown in Figure 10-7. You might need to scroll down to see them all.

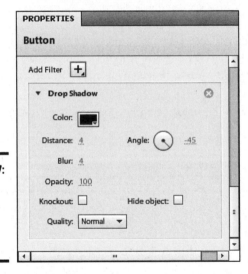

Figure 10-7: Filter controls for adding a drop shadow.

5. **Adjust the look of the filter, using the filter controls that appear in the pane.**

   Each filter is different. For example, the Inner Glow filter lets you specify a color, blur, opacity, strength, *knockout* (hides the fill), and quality.

6. **Test your new button state by clicking the Play button at the top of the Timelines panel, or by choosing File➪Run Project.**

   If you choose File➪Run Project, your Web site opens in your default browser. Check out your new button state with the filter.

7. **Exit the Component Editing mode by choosing Modify➪Exit Editing or clicking your project name in the Breadcrumbs section above the Artboard.**

Resize the button in a different state

Resizing a button so that it grows when the mouse passes over it is an effective way to bring attention to the button. This can be done with animation so that the button does not jump to a new size, but grows instead. To resize the button that grows using animation, follow these steps:

1. **Select the button and choose Modify⇨Edit Component.**

2. **Click the state that you want to edit in the Pages/States panel.**

3. **Click all or part of the button and drag a resizing handle on the button to resize it.**

   In the Timelines panel, a Resize bar appears. If your button has more than one part, you may also see a Move bar, if resizing one part of the button also moved another part.

4. **In the Timelines panel, to adjust the timing of the animation, click and drag the Resize bar's small semicircular thumbtab that appears to the right, as shown in Figure 10-8. Do the same for the Move bar, if you have one.**

   We dragged our Resize bar and Move bar to play the resizing animation for half a second.

Figure 10-8:
Adding
animation
when
resizing
objects
between
states.

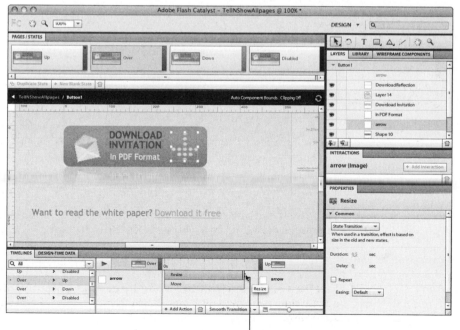

Semicircular thumbtab

5. **In the State Transitions list of the Timelines panel, notice which state transition is highlighted. Then choose the opposite from the list and drag the tab of the Resize bar on the Timelines panel for the same distance you did in Step 4 and do the same for the Move bar.**

   This sets the animation to resize back to its original state.

   If you animate the Up > Over states, be sure to select the Over > Up state as well so that it animates back to its normal size when the mouse is off the button.

6. **Test your new button state by clicking the Play button at the top of the Timelines panel, or by choosing File⇨Run Project.**

   If you choose File⇨Run Project, your Web site opens in a browser window. Check out your new button state with the animation.

7. **Exit the Component Editing mode by choosing Modify⇨Exit Editing.**

Importing a new image for a different state

If you created images for each button state in Photoshop or Illustrator, you can import them into Catalyst as long as they are in one of the following formats: PNG, GIF, or JPG. To import an image, follow these steps:

1. **Select the button and choose Modify⇨Edit Component.**

   The four states of the button (Up, Over, Down, and Disabled) appear in the Pages/States panel.

2. **In the Pages/States panel, click the state that you want to edit.**

3. **In the Artboard, delete the button or part of the button.**

4. **Choose File⇨Import⇨Image.**

5. **Select the image file and click Open.**

   The new image replaces the button for the state you selected.

6. **Test your new button state by clicking the Play button at the top of the Timelines panel, or by choosing File⇨Run Project.**

   If you choose File⇨Run Project, your Web site opens in a browser window. Check out your new button state with the animation.

7. **Exit the Component Editing mode; choose Modify⇨Exit Editing.**

Hiding buttons to reveal other button states

You can set up your Photoshop or Illustrator file that you import to include button states that are stacked in layers, similar to how you stack your pages in layers. If you do that, then when you convert your artwork to a button, using the HUD, be sure to select all the different states on the different layers before you convert it. Then select your button, choose Modify⇨Edit Component, and choose a state in the Pages/States panel. You can show the artwork for that state by clicking the Eye in the layers panel, and hide the other layers that you don't want to show.

Assigning Interactions to Components

You can make pretty buttons by defining states, but they won't do anything useful. To get your buttons to do something, you need to add interactions. *Interactions* define a response to a user action. The most typical interaction occurs when you click a button and find yourself on a different Web page.

Before you can add an interaction to a button, you need to make sure that it's really a button. See the section, "Converting artwork to buttons" earlier in this chapter for details.

To add an interaction to a button, follow these steps:

1. **Select the button.**

2. **In the Interactions panel, click the Add Interaction button to open the panel shown in Figure 10-9.**

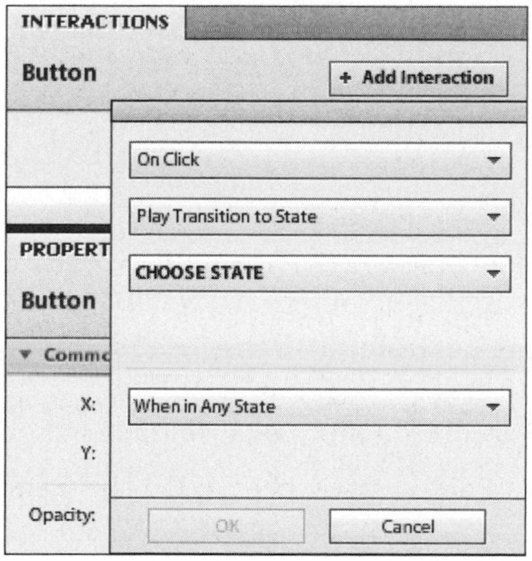

INTERACTIONS

Button   + Add Interaction

PROPERT

Figure 10-9:
Add
interactivity
to buttons to
make them
work for
their pay.

Button

▼ Comm

X:

Y:

Opacity:

On Click ▼

Play Transition to State ▼

CHOOSE STATE ▼

When in Any State ▼

OK   Cancel

3. **From the top drop-down list, choose which action initiates the response.**

The most common choice is On Click, which means that the user has to click the button.

4. **From the second drop-down list, choose the response.**

   To add a link to another page inside your Catalyst project, choose Play Transition to State. (We discuss transitions in the next section.) To add a link to an outside Web page, choose Go to URL, which requires an absolute URL (one with `http://` in it). Other options are to play, pause, or stop a video; or play simple animation that you create in the Catalyst Timelines panel.

   Typically, when you pass the cursor over a link on a Web site, the cursor changes to a hand. If you want your button to display the hand icon, with the button selected, expand the Appearance item in the Properties panel, scroll down, and select the Hand Cursor check box. You need to do this for every button on every page.

5. **Enter the necessary information for the response.**

   If you choose Go to URL, a text box opens, where you need to enter an absolute URL. If you choose Play Transition to State, skip to Step 7.

6. **If you choose Go to URL, in the new drop-down list that appears, choose how you want the link to open.**

   The most common options are Open in Current Window or Open in New Window.

7. **From the Choose State drop-down list, choose the state.**

   If you choose Go to URL in Step 4, choose Any State. If you choose Play Transition to State, choose the page you want to link to.

8. **Click OK.**

9. **Test your button by choosing File⇨Run Project (or by pressing Ctrl+Enter on Windows/⌘+Return on a Mac).**

   When your temporary browser page opens, click the button and see what happens!

Figure 10-10 shows an image that we turned into a button. With a Go to URL interaction, the button links to an Adobe PDF file. Clicking the button opens the PDF file, which users can then save or print.

To edit an interaction, select the button and double-click the interaction listed in the Interactions panel. To delete an interaction, select it in the Interactions panel and click the Trash button.

Continue adding interactions to buttons until all your internal and external links work. Congratulations! You have a Web site!

Figure 10-10:
The image
is a button
to download
the
Invitation,
which is a
PDF file.

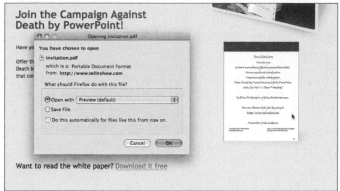

Adding Animation

When you think of animation, you probably think of Flash, and you're right. Catalyst offers a limited number of animations — *transitions* — related to user interface components, pages, and states. And that might be all you need for your Web site. For example, you can move, resize, or rotate a button. You can also fade a page during the transition to another page. In this section, we show you how to add simple animation in Catalyst.

You create transitions in the Timelines panel, as shown in Figure 10-11. When you work in the Timelines panel, you might want to expand it, which you can do by dragging its top border upward.

Filter drop-down list   Available objects after transition

Play transition button   Length of transition

Figure 10-11:
Use the
Timelines
panel for
subtle
transition
effects.

Available transitions   Available objects before transition   Transition effect   Timing slider

The Timelines panel in Catalyst is quite different from the Timeline in Flash. You won't find any frames, so you can't create keyframes. Instead, you simply specify the length of a transition in seconds.

Assigning beginning and ending states

Although the word *states* properly applies to button variations, Catalyst sometimes uses the word to mean *pages*. On the left side of the Timelines panel is a list of state transitions. In the default view, the list contains every possible pairing of pages. In Component Editing mode, which we discuss in the "Defining button states" section earlier in this chapter, the list contains button states.

To define a transition, follow these steps:

1. **If you want to create a page transition, choose the two pages that you want to work with from the State Transitions list.**

   If you want to create a button transition, double-click the button and choose the two button states you want to work with.

   You can use the Filter drop-down list above the first column to filter the State Transitions list; for example, you can show only transitions that include the Home page.

   In Figure 10-11, we are creating a page transition, and choose Home⇨ WhitePaper.

2. **In the second column of the Timelines panel, select the objects that you want to animate, or select the objects from the Artboard.**

   For a page transition, the second column lists all available objects on the pages. At the top, you can choose the entire page to select everything on the page, which is ideal for a simple page fade. Select specific objects to apply the transition only to those objects.

   For a button transition, select the button from the Artboard. Applying certain transitions to an inappropriate object can provide odd results. For example, as shown in Figure 10-12, we rotated the text as a transition from the WhitePaper page to the Home page. Each click rotates 90 degrees. After two clicks, the text is upside-down!

3. **If the transition that you want isn't listed in the third column, click Add Action at the bottom of that column and then choose the transition you want.**

   We're opting for Fade. We explain the available transitions in more detail in the next section.

4. **In the third column of the Timelines panel, pass the cursor over the transition's horizontal block to display the semicircular thumb tab. Then drag to change the time of the transition, as shown in Figure 10-13.**

Figure 10-12:
Button transitions can result in odd results.

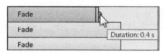

Figure 10-13:
Change the speed of the transition by dragging on the thumb.

Drag to the right to lengthen the time of the transition (make the effect slower) or to the left to shorten it (make the effect faster). Alternatively, you can drag the slider at the bottom of the fourth column to adjust the timing or use the Properties panel to enter a duration.

Make the transition long enough to notice but not so long that your viewers get bored! For example, 1/10th of a second might be too quick, whereas a whole second would seem to drag out forever.

You can test the animation in the Timelines panel. Just click the Play button at the top of the second column. For example, if you added a fade between pages, when you click to go from the first page to the second page, you'll see the fade effect.

To delete a transition, select the transition in the third column of the Timelines panel, and click the Trash can (Delete) button.

Defining the transition

In the previous section, we explain the steps for adding transitions. Here, we delve a little deeper into the available transitions and how to configure them. In all cases, you work in the Timelines panel. To add a transition to a component, such as a button, first double-click the component to enter Component Editing mode.

Adding a Fade transition

When you add a Fade transition, your objects fade in or out as you change states. For example, an entire page can fade out when you click a button to go to another page on the side. The fade usually lasts only about half a second, so it just provides a soft transition between pages. You can fade individual objects, including buttons, as well.

In many cases, after you select the state transition in the Timelines panel's first column, the Fade transition automatically appears in the third column. (If you don't see it, choose it from the Add Actions pop-up list at the bottom of the third column.) Just drag the semicircular thumbtab to adjust the length of the fade. We found that half a second was a good length. Click the Play button (refer to Figure 10-11) to view the transition.

For more controls, go to the Properties panel, where you can set the opacity, duration, delay, and easing. Easing effects control how the transition starts and ends.

Rotating an object

You can rotate an object while moving from one page to another. Why would you do that? We showed you some funny results with this effect in Figure 10-12. However, if you also include a fade out and the timing of the rotation is shorter than the fade out, you'll see the object rotating before the new page appears. Think of it as a whirling, disappearing act. You can also rotate a button when you hover over or click it.

To add a rotation transition, click Add Action and choose Rotate from the pop-up list. In the Properties panel, you can set the angle, duration, and delay. You can also choose an *easing* effect, which determines how the rotation starts and ends.

Rotating an object in 3D

The Rotate transition rotates in 2D, but the Rotate 3D transition adds a new dimension to your transitions. To add a rotation transition, click Add Action and choose Rotate 3D from the pop-up list. In the Properties panel, you can set the From and To angles in three directions, the duration, and a delay.

Moving an object

You can move an object during a transition. As we described for rotation, if you add the Move effect to a page transition, you won't see the movement until you return to the page unless you also have a fade transition. On the other hand, it could be pretty funny to move the object without a fade so that when viewers return to the page, the object has mysteriously moved! (Well, if that's your kind of humor.)

To add a Move transition, click Add Action and choose Move from the pop-up list. In the Properties panel, you can set the X (horizontal) and Y (vertical) distance of the move, the duration, delay, and easing effects.

Resizing an object

Resizing an object is just like rotating it. Select the object, choose Resize from the Add Action pop-up menu, and set its properties. You specify the new size in pixels.

Adding a sound effect

Why be silent? You can add a sound effect and make noise! After selecting an object, follow these steps:

1. **Click the Add Action pop-up menu and choose Sound Effect.**
2. **In the Select a Visual Asset dialog box (Catalyst thinks sounds are visual?), click the Import button.**
3. **In the Open dialog box, choose an MP3 file, and click Open.**
4. **Expand the Media item and choose the MP3 file you selected.**
5. **Click OK.**

In the Properties panel, you can adjust the duration, set a delay, and choose to repeat the sound. (Please don't!)

Setting object properties

You can set some specific properties that apply to certain types of objects. After selecting an object, choose Set Property from the Add Action pop-up menu. In the Properties panel, choose one of the following from the Property drop-down list:

✦ **Text:** For a component that includes text, such as a check box's label, you can specify text, which animates a change in the text content. This option isn't available for all objects.

✦ **Alpha:** Click to the right to display a text box, where you can enter an Alpha value. *Alpha* is equivalent to opacity. A setting of 25% dims an object so that it's only 25% opaque. You could use this setting to make a button appear unavailable.

✦ **Enabled:** Choose True or False. This setting is available only for components that you converted to buttons. By selecting False, you deactivate the button.

Book VIII

Fireworks CS5

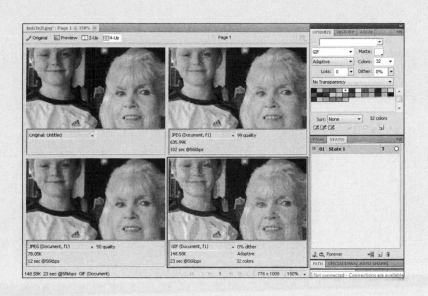

Contents at a Glance

Chapter 1: Introducing Fireworks CS5

In This Chapter

✔ **Understanding when you should use Fireworks**

✔ **Discovering the workspace**

✔ **Finding out about the tools**

✔ **Looking into the views**

✔ **Using the basic selection tools**

Adobe Fireworks is an incredible application with specific solutions to meet online designers' needs. When you use Fireworks, you have the freedom to create test Web sites, experiment with advanced scripting features, and come up with compelling graphics that look good and work well on Web pages.

In this chapter, you encounter the software and its workspace. You also discover how to use selection tools so that you can start to manipulate graphics in Fireworks right away.

Why Use Fireworks?

Considering all the applications included in the Creative Suite, why do you need one more? The reason is mostly because after CS2 (and the removal of ImageReady), the Creative Suite provided no easy way to create interesting Web graphics. Sure, you can save images for online use in Photoshop and Illustrator using the Save for Web & Devices feature, but what about rollovers, easy image maps, and interactive wireframes? (A *wireframe* is essentially a mock-up or rough draft created to demonstrate or test a Web site before it is in its final form. In Web design, wireframes are basic visual guides used to suggest the layout and placement of fundamental design elements.)

In Fireworks, you can work intuitively by taking advantage of its logical interface, which provides panels and features that relate to the Web and that offer you the easiest way to *optimize* (make Web-ready) graphics.

Jumping Right into the Interface

So what's the big deal about Fireworks being built specifically for Web graphics? Well, first of all, you're working strictly with pixels — no messy *dpi* (dots per inch) or *lpi* (lines per inch), which are typical printing terms.

Figure 1-1 shows the dialog box that appears when you choose File⇨Open to open a vector graphic from Illustrator. The dialog box offers conversion choices but emphasizes pixel dimensions.

Figure 1-1:
Pixel dimensions play an important role in Fireworks.

When you're working with Web images, you should know the approximate width, in pixels, of your final page. Typical Web pages range from 650 to 1,000 pixels wide, but most designers stick with a page built to span approximately 800 pixels. When you create images, you must think about how they will fit within the context of the total page. An image 600 pixels wide would fill most of a page, whereas an image that's 1,200 pixels wide would force the viewer to scroll to see the entire image.

After launching Fireworks CS5, you notice right away that its workspace is similar to the workspaces in the other CS5 applications. Adobe has done a good job of organizing each application so that the learning curve is quick and integration is easy.

You shouldn't be surprised to find a toolbox to the left of the workspace and panels to the right. The tools even look much like the tools you may already be familiar with from working in other CS5 applications.

Using the tools

The Tools panel is sorted into six categories: Select, Bitmap, Vector, Web, Colors, and View. Table 1-1 lists the tools by category and the keys you can easily press to access them.

Table 1-1		Fireworks Tools	
Icon	*Tool Name*	*What You Can Do with It*	*Keyboard Shortcut*
Selection			
	Pointer	Select paths and objects	V or 0
	Subselection	Adjust paths, much as you do with the Direct Select tool in Illustrator and Photoshop	A or 1
	Scale	Scale objects or selections	Q
	Crop	Crop images	C
Bitmap			
	Marquee	Make rectangular selections	M
	Lasso	Make freeform selections	L
	Magic Wand	Select similar colors	W
	Brush	Paint on image	B (toggle with Pencil)
	Pencil	Draw bitmap paths	B (toggle with Brush)
	Eraser	Erase bitmap data	E

(continued)

Table 1-1 *(continued)*

Icon	Tool Name	What You Can Do with It	Keyboard Shortcut
	Blur	Blur image	R
	Rubber Stamp	Clone image data	S
Vector			
	Line	Create vector lines	N
	Pen	Create Bézier paths	P
	Rectangle	Create vector shapes	U
	Type	Create text	T
	Freeform	Create freeform paths	O
	Knife	Cut paths	Y
Web			
	Rectangle Hotspot	Create image map hotspots	J
	Slice	Create slices for tables or CSS	K
	Hide Slices and Hotspots	Hide slices and image map hotspots	2
	Show Slices and Hotspots	Display slices and image map hotspots	2
Color			
	Eyedropper	Sample color	I
	Paint Bucket	Fill color	G

Icon	Tool Name	What You Can Do with It	Keyboard Shortcut
View			
🖐	Hand	Pan the artboard	
🔍	Zoom	Zoom in and out of artboard	X

As you select each tool, notice that the Properties panel displays additional options. (If your Properties panel isn't visible, choose Window➪Properties.)

Understanding the views

The tabs at the top of an image give you the opportunity to view it in four ways:

✦ **Original** displays your image as it appears before being optimized for the Web.

✦ **Preview** displays the image as it will appear when it's saved for the Web, based on your current settings. (You can find out more about those settings in Chapter 5 of this minibook.)

✦ **2-Up** offers the opportunity to see an image in two windows, with different settings applied in each one. Most users tend to compare the original and optimized images in this view (see Figure 1-2).

Views

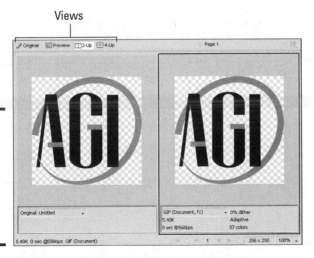

Figure 1-2: Compare the original (left) and optimized (right) images in 2-Up view.

✦ **4-Up** is for people who are never quite sure which is the best way to optimize an image. You don't necessarily need to compare different formats when you use this view; you can experiment with different options for one format, such as pushing the limit with the amount of colors you want to keep in a GIF file, as shown in Figure 1-3.

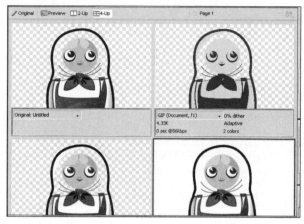

Figure 1-3: In 4-Up view, you can experiment with ways to optimize an image.

Investigating the panels

Not unlike the other CS5 applications, Fireworks lets you detach panels from the docking area on the right side of the workspace. Because this procedure is so similar to the methods you use to dock and undock panels in other CS5 applications, we don't bore you with the details here.

If you can't locate a panel, choose its name from the Window menu.

Working with Basic Selection Tools

You can work in Fireworks using the same selection tools for both vector and bitmap images.

Making a selection in a bitmap image

If you're familiar with Photoshop selection techniques, you'll have no problem using the same tools in Fireworks. Here's the lowdown on making selections with the Marquee and Lasso tools:

✦ **Marquee:** To make a selection with the Marquee tool, simply select it from the Tools panel, and then click and drag to surround the area you want to select. You can add to the selection by holding down the Shift key and dragging another marquee region, or deselect a portion of the active selection by holding down the Alt (Windows) or Option (Mac) key while dragging with the Marquee tool.

 ✦ **Lasso:** To use the Lasso tool, select it from the Tools panel and click and drag to create a path that then becomes your selection. As mentioned in the Marquee bullet, you can add to the selection by holding down the Shift key and creating another selection region, or subtract from the selection by holding down the Alt (Windows) or Option (Mac) key while dragging a selection region with the Lasso tool.

 You can use both the Marquee and Lasso tools interchangeably when making a selection.

 By making a selection with the Marquee tool or Lasso tool and then clicking and dragging with the Pointer tool, you can move one part of an image to another, as shown in Figure 1-4. If you make no selection before you drag, everything on the existing layer is moved.

Figure 1-4:
Drag a
selection to
move it.

Switch to the Subselection tool and notice that if you have an existing selection, the pointer changes to a double arrow, indicating that you will *clone* (copy) the selection when you click and drag it.

Making a selection in a vector image

By using the same tools you use to select bitmap images, you can adjust vector paths. Use the Pointer tool to move an entire vector shape, as shown in Figure 1-5.

Use the Subselection tool to move the individual points on the path.

Figure 1-5:
The Pointer tool lets you move a vector shape.

Tatyana

Chapter 2: Free to Create

In This Chapter

✔ Understanding layers in Fireworks

✔ Finding the difference between vector and bitmap images

✔ Using the bitmap and vector drawing tools

✔ Discovering masking

You can easily import graphics into Fireworks from the other Creative Suite 5 applications or create your own graphics. Fireworks comes with a full set of tools for creating both bitmap and vector images. This chapter briefly discusses bitmap and vector graphics; you can find out more by reading Book I, Chapter 6.

Knowing What Happens in Layers

Create a new document by choosing File⇨New. If the Layers panel isn't visible, choose Window⇨Layers. By default, the Layers panel contains two layers: Web Layer and Layer 1.

Web Layer is reserved for Web objects, such as hotspots, slices, and other interactive objects. You can't delete, duplicate, or rename objects in this layer. You find out more about the Web Layer in Chapter 6 of this minibook.

Layer 1 is also a default layer. Everything that you create or import, whether it's a bitmap or a vector graphic, lands here, essentially becoming a sub-layer of Layer 1.

You can rename both main layers and sublayers. You can also reposition, delete, and duplicate them by using the tools at the bottom of the Layers panel (see Figure 2-1).

Figure 2-1:
The Layers panel always includes Web Layer and Layer 1.

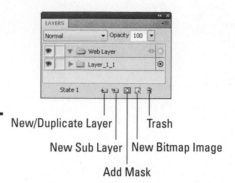

New/Duplicate Layer   Trash

New Sub Layer | New Bitmap Image

Add Mask

Understanding this layer organization and how it relates to drawing in Fireworks is important. When you use bitmap tools to paint and create pixels, everything falls on one layer, much as you would expect. But when you start creating vector shapes, every new shape lands on a new layer. This arrangement makes it easier for you to move the shapes independently but can be confusing to new Fireworks users.

Choosing Vector or Bitmap Graphics

If you didn't read enough about vector versus bitmap graphics before starting this minibook, you get even more information in this section.

Fireworks lets you work in a painterly fashion with the bitmap tools. These tools work like the brush and retouching tools in Photoshop, in that they are pixel based. You can use the bitmap tools to create smoother transitions and more realistic contours and shapes.

Why not use bitmap images for all your artwork? One drawback is that bitmap images tend to have a little larger file sizes than vector images. Also, bitmap images aren't scalable, as vector graphics are. Sometimes, it's fairly clear when to use a bitmap instead of a vector image; see Figure 2-2 for an example.

Most designers use bitmap images for more realistic artwork, such as photo-realistic renderings, and vector images for more graphical artwork, such as stylized buttons and logos.

No matter whether you use bitmap or vector drawing tools to create a graphic, it's a bitmap image when it's *optimized* (saved for the Web). Even if you use vector drawing tools in Fireworks, you see the graphic broken into pixels in the preview windows.

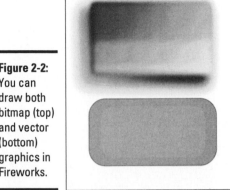

Figure 2-2:
You can draw both bitmap (top) and vector (bottom) graphics in Fireworks.

Creating with Bitmap Tools

The first set of tools we investigate in this chapter are the bitmap tools: Blur, Brush, Eraser, Lasso, Magic Wand, Marquee, Pencil, and Rubber Stamp. We cover these tools briefly, focusing on the differences between using them in Fireworks and in other bitmap applications, such as Photoshop. If you don't see the Tools panel, choose Window⇨Tools.

Selecting pixels

The selection tools let you grab hold of pixels. You use the Marquee tool, for example, to select a section of pixels that you want to move, clone, or change in some way. To experiment with the Marquee tool, follow these steps:

1. **Choose File⇨New to create a new Fireworks document.**

The New dialog box appears.

2. **Type 500 in both the Width and Height text boxes; leave Canvas set to White; then click OK.**

A new, blank document opens.

3. **Use the Marquee tool to click and drag in the workspace from top left to bottom right to create a rectangular marquee.**

4. **Choose File⇨Swatches to open the Swatches panel.**

5. **Click any color you want to use for the fill of your selection.**

6. **Click the Paint Bucket tool (in the Colors section of the Tools panel) and then click inside the selection marquee to fill it with your selected color.**

You've successfully created a bitmap graphic in Fireworks. In the next section, you use other bitmap tools to make changes in this artwork.

Moving pixels

In this section, you use the Marquee tool to move the pixels to another location. If you're a Photoshop user, notice that the Marquee tool works just like the selection tools in Photoshop.

To move the graphic you just selected, follow these steps:

1. **With the Marquee tool, click and drag over the bottom of your bitmap rectangle.**

2. **Select the Pointer tool and then drag the marquee down, as shown in Figure 2-3.**

Figure 2-3:
Move a
selection
with the
Pointer tool.

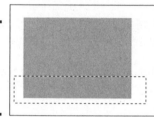 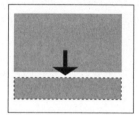

Changing the way pixels appear

If you've followed along, you know how to select and move pixels and you're ready to change the way selected pixels appear. To do that, follow these steps:

1. **Choose Select⇨Deselect or use the keyboard shortcut Ctrl+D (Windows) or ⌘+D (Mac), to make sure you have no active selections.**

2. **Hold down the Marquee tool to select the hidden Oval tool.**

3. **While holding down the Alt (Windows) or Option (Mac) key, click and drag from the center of the rectangle you created (see the top of Figure 2-4).**

Many shortcuts you use in Illustrator and Photoshop also work in Fireworks — but not all. Finding compatible shortcuts is sort of hit-or-miss when you're in the beginning stage with Fireworks. For details, choose Help⇨Fireworks Help and select Preferences and Keyboard Shortcuts from the list of topics on the left side of the Help window.

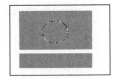

Figure 2-4:
Making a
feathered,
oval
selection.

4. To *feather* (soften) the edges of the selection, choose Feather from the Edge drop-down list in the Properties panel and set a feathering value (10 pixels is the default) in the combo box to the right of the Edge drop-down list (refer to the middle of Figure 2-4).

5. Press Ctrl+X (Windows) or Command+X (Mac) to delete your feather selection.

   The bottom of Figure 2-4 shows the result.

Using additional bitmap tools

Many bitmap tools are available for you to use in Fireworks, and here are some of these additional tools:

✦ **Brush:** The Brush tool lets you paint just like you would in Photoshop, and you can mix it up with the selection tools to create interesting artwork.

   Options for the Brush tool — such as size, softness, and transparency — are located in the Properties panel at the bottom of the workspace. Unfortunately, not all the great brush shortcuts in Photoshop work in Fireworks, so you may have to access the Properties panel in Fireworks more often than you may be used to.

**Book VIII
Chapter 2**

Free to Create

✦ **Editing tools:** Because you're working with pixels, you can edit those pixels rather easily. Choose a tool:

- *Pencil:* Use the Pencil tool to add detail.
- *Blur:* The Blur tool softens edges.
- *Eraser:* The Eraser tool eliminates pixels.

✦ **Rubber Stamp:** The Rubber Stamp tool is similar to the one in Photoshop, and you use it the same way. Simply Alt-click (Windows) or Option-click (Mac) a bitmap source that you want to clone; then release the Alt or Option key and start painting somewhere else in the image area. The source is re-created or cloned as you paint with the Rubber Stamp tool.

If you make a mistake, you can undo multiple steps in Fireworks by pressing Ctrl+Z (Windows) or ⌘+Z (Mac) repeatedly. If you want to redo a step (essentially undoing an undo), press Ctrl+Y (Windows) or ⌘+Y (Mac).

Creating with Vector Tools

The Vector tools in Fireworks are similar to the ones you may be used to in Illustrator or Photoshop. What you should notice right off the bat in Fireworks is that every time you create a new vector shape with one of the vector tools (such as Line, Pen, Shape, or Type), Fireworks creates a new sublayer automatically. This arrangement lets you move the shapes freely and independently.

Before repositioning or making other transformations in vector images, confirm which sublayer is active by looking for the highlighted sublayer in the Layers panel. Otherwise, you may unexpectedly move the wrong image.

Using shape tools

To use a shape tool, simply click it and drag it in the workspace. A shape is created, and a new sublayer is added automatically in the Layers panel.

In addition to the basic shape tools, Fireworks has more shapes that are useful for designing buttons, icons, and other Web graphics. To find these shapes, click and hold the Rectangle tool in the Tools panel. Hidden shape tools appear such as stars, arrows, and beveled rectangles.

After you create a shape using a shape tool, you can edit it by using the Pointer and Subselection tools:

✦ **Pointer:** If you need to reposition the shape, select the Pointer tool, and click and drag it to a new location. You can also grab the highlighted anchor points to resize the shape.

✦ **Subselection:** If you need to make more defined shape changes (such as changing the corner radius, bevel, or overall shape of the vector graphic), switch to the Subselection tool. It works much like the Select and Direct Select tools in Illustrator and Photoshop.

Creating a path

The most popular vector tool in most applications is the Pen tool. Using this tool in a freeform manner, you can create any shape you want (including the type you need to make a button look like it has a reflection, for example) or create your own, custom graphics.

Fireworks offers three types of path tools, shown in Figure 2-5:

✦ **The Pen tool** works much like other Pen tools. You create a path by clicking from one location to another (creating anchor points) or by clicking and dragging to create curved sections of paths.

✦ **The Vector Path tool** lets you click and drag in a painterly fashion to create a path.

✦ **The Redraw Path tool** lets you reshape a path (by dragging it over an existing path) while maintaining the original stroke information.

Figure 2-5:
These three tools help you create paths in Fireworks.

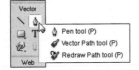

Changing an existing path

If you have a hard time using the Pen tool or want to make freeform adjustments, you can get truly excellent results by using the Freeform tool.

To use the Freeform tool with an existing path active (select it with the Pointer tool), follow these steps:

1. **Click the Freeform tool to select it; then click and drag in the workspace to change the way the path looks.**

You can bend the path in different smooth directions.

2. In the Properties panel, set options to specify the width of the change.

Another tool hidden in the Freeform tool is the Reshape Area tool, which is handy for reshaping existing paths (see Figure 2-6). This tool lets you set a reshape size area in the Properties panel and then edit selected paths by clicking and dragging over them.

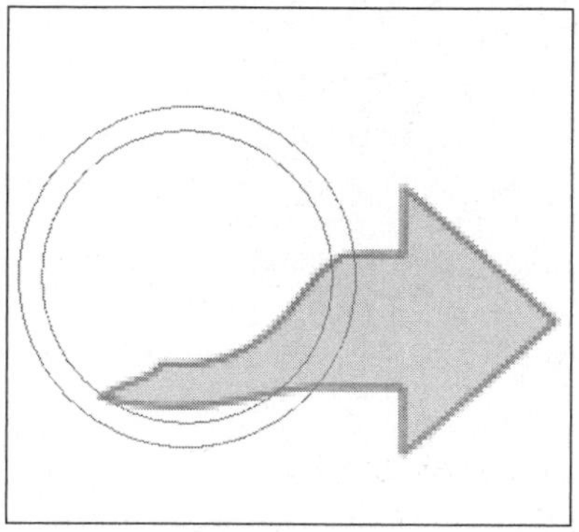

Figure 2-6:
Change existing paths with the Reshape Area tool.

The additional path-scrubber tools let you edit paths that have pressure-sensitive strokes. In fact if you do not have paths created using a pressure-sensitive device, you cannot use these tools.

Working with type

Feel free to scale your text to your heart's delight; text is vector! To create text in an image area, simply select the Text tool, click to set the insertion point, and then start typing. Use the Properties panel to change the font and size as well as other text attributes. Chapter 4 in this minibook discusses text and its formatting capabilities.

Masking: Going Beyond Tape

You can mask in Fireworks, but you don't use quite the same method as you use in Illustrator, InDesign, or Photoshop. The result is essentially the same, however.

A *mask* lets you choose which part of a graphic is exposed and which part is covered (by the mask). See Figure 2-7 for an example of two vector graphics that have been masked with a gradient fill to fade the transparency from 100 percent to none.

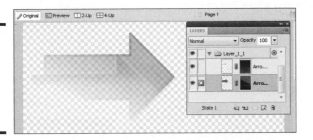

Figure 2-7: Two vector shapes with masks applied to them.

To apply a gradient mask, follow these steps:

1. **Create a vector shape (such as an arrow).**

2. **In the Layers panel, choose Add Mask from the panel menu.**

A blank mask appears to the right of the vector shape's sublayer, as shown in Figure 2-8.

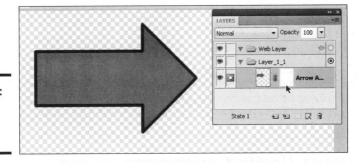

Figure 2-8: Adding a mask to a sublayer.

3. **With the new mask active, click and hold the Paint Bucket tool to select the hidden Gradient tool.**

4. **With the Gradient tool, click and drag across the shape to make the gradient on the mask and create the transparency effect on the vector shape.**

Notice that where the gradient is darker, the image is less visible, and where the gradient is lighter, the vector shape is more visible, as shown in Figure 2-9.

Figure 2-9: The arrow shows through more where the gradient is lighter.

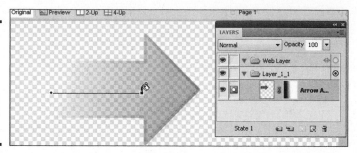

You can experiment with this effect on other shapes. Also, you can try clicking and dragging the gradient until you get the depth and direction you want.

A gradient tends to work better as a mask if you use its default colors: black and white.

Chapter 3: Livening Up Your Artwork with Color

In This Chapter

✔ Defining colors for the Web

✔ Finding and applying colors to graphics

✔ Creating your own colors in Fireworks

✔ Using gradient fills

*L*ike most other Creative Suite applications, Fireworks lets you define an object's fill and stroke. You can use some unique tools for that selection, as well as some hidden features that work slightly differently from the ones you may be used to.

In this chapter, you find out how to apply a fill or stroke color to your artwork, and you discover the basic steps for working with gradient fills.

Choosing Web Colors

Colors appear differently on a monitor from the way they do when you view them offscreen, but this issue isn't as serious now as it was in the past. Years ago, you had to base your color selections on the lowest common denominator. Most viewers now have monitors that can display thousands, if not millions, of colors.

When you're choosing a color for the Web, don't fret over the exactness of a color viewed on different monitors unless precision is critical. Critical color can apply to your company logo or to fabrics that viewers might be comparing onscreen.

In Fireworks, you can choose colors from several panels, with each panel offering a different model from which to create them. Even though you're working in RGB (Red, Green, Blue), you can still enter CMYK (Cyan, Magenta, Yellow, Key or Black) or HSB (Hue, Saturation, Brightness) values.

Finding Colors in Fireworks

Perhaps you want to create a simple shape with a fill, which seems easy, but if you're unfamiliar with Fireworks, you may need a little direction to get this task done.

You can find most Fireworks color functions in the Colors section of the Tools panel. This section features an Eyedropper tool for sampling color, as well as color boxes that help you easily stroke and fill both bitmap and vector graphics.

You can set additional attributes for color in the Properties panel, including textures you can apply from the Texture drop-down list.

Applying Colors to Vector Objects

To create and color a vector object, follow these steps:

1. **Choose File⇨New to create a new blank document.**

2. **Create a path or a shape with the bitmap or vector drawing tools and leave that object selected.**

3. **To apply a fill color, click the Fill Color box located in the Colors section of the Tools panel and then click the color you want to apply from the pop-up Swatches panel (see Figure 3-1).**

4. **To apply a stroke color, click the Stroke Color box in the Tools panel and then click the color you want to apply from the pop-up Swatches panel.**

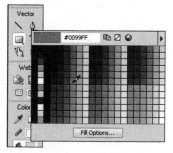

Figure 3-1: Take advantage of the Fill Color options.

Adding Colors to Fireworks

Assigning a fill or stroke color to graphics is relatively simple. But what if the color you want to use isn't in the default Swatches panel? In that case, you need to create a color and add it to the panel. You can accomplish this task in several ways. In the following sections, we cover using the Eyedropper tool and the Color Palette panel.

Adding a color with the Eyedropper tool

The Eyedropper tool is useful when you have a color to sample. Just select the tool, click any color (in your working document or in any other open Fireworks document), and then choose Window⇨Swatches. When the Swatches panel pops up, as shown in Figure 3-2, click an empty area, and your sample color is added.

Figure 3-2:
Select
a color
with the
Eyedropper
tool and
then
click the
Swatches
panel to
save the
color.

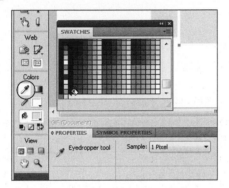

 To remove a color from the Swatches panel, position the mouse pointer over the color you want to delete and press Ctrl+Alt (Windows) or ⌘+Option (Mac). When the scissors pointer appears, click the mouse; the color is deleted.

Adding a color with the Color Palette panel

The color palette is a dynamic and fun way to set color. Each of its three tabs offers the opportunity to choose a stroke or fill color and a different method of selecting that color.

You can open the Color palette by choosing Windows⇨Others⇨Color Palette.

The three color palette tabs are

✦ **Selector:** The Selector tab (see Figure 3-3) lets you pick a color in any of four color models: HLS (hue, lightness, saturation), HSV, CMYK, and RGB. Click the large color panel and then enter color values by using the sliders or text boxes at the bottom. To adjust the tonal value, use the slider to the right of the large color panel.

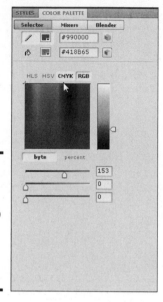

Figure 3-3:
The color palette's Selector tab gives you a choice of four color models.

✦ **Mixers:** The Mixers tab (see Figure 3-4) lets you assign multiple colors by using the color wheel. You can also create a tint build at the bottom of the window so that you can build combinations of colors. In addition, you can export the colors as a bitmap or a table using the Export buttons on the left side of the Mixer tab, which makes it easy to reference them later.

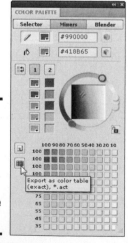

Figure 3-4:
On the Mixers tab, create colors with the color wheel or the tint builder.

✦ **Blender:** The Blender tab (see Figure 3-5) lets you select two colors and then view and choose combinations of those colors.

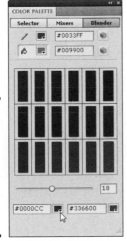

Figure 3-5:
Blend two colors using the Blender tab in the Color Palette panel.

To blend colors, enter two color values in the text boxes at the bottom of the Blender tab and then use the slider to view various combinations of the two selected colors.

Creating Gradients

You can add some dimension to a graphic by filling it with a gradient. To create a gradient in Fireworks, follow these steps:

1. **Create a shape that you want to fill with a gradient.**

2. **With the shape selected, click and hold the Paint Bucket tool in the Colors section of the Tools panel and then select the hidden Gradient tool, as shown in Figure 3-6.**

Figure 3-6:
Select the Gradient tool.

3. **Click the Fill Color box in the Tools panel to assign colors to the gradient.**

   The Fill Options window appears, as shown in Figure 3-7.

Figure 3-7: Assign the gradient colors.

4. **To assign colors to the gradient, simply click the existing color stops and choose a color from the pop-up palette.**

5. **Click anywhere on the gradient ramp to add a stop, and edit the color.**

   If you don't want to create your own gradient, click the Preset drop-down list to choose among existing gradients, as shown in Figure 3-8.

Figure 3-8: Pick a preset gradient from this drop-down list.

Chapter 4: Creating Text in Fireworks

In This Chapter

- ✔ Creating and formatting text
- ✔ Setting a text attribute
- ✔ Working on spacing, alignment, and orientation
- ✔ Applying effects
- ✔ Styling text
- ✔ Checking your spelling
- ✔ Setting text on a path
- ✔ Outlining your text

You definitely don't want to attempt to create a brochure in Fireworks, but you can take advantage of its excellent capabilities to format your on-screen text. Whether you're working with paragraphs or single lines of text, you have lots of options for applying fonts, styles, and interesting effects. In this chapter, you find out where to find the features you need to make your words look just the way you like them.

Creating Text

You can create text in either of two ways:

- ✦ Select the Type tool, click in the image area, and begin typing.
- ✦ Copy (or cut) text from another application, select the Type tool, and paste it on the artboard.

In a hurry? You can select text from one application and then click and drag it into the Fireworks workspace.

Setting Text Attributes

Text can create mood and feeling, so you have to make sure your message has the right font and style. You can apply text attributes by using one of two main methods: the Type menu or the Properties panel. In this chapter, you use the Properties panel (see Figure 4-1), because it provides an easier method of locating text attributes. If the Properties panel isn't visible at the bottom of the Fireworks workspace, choose Window⇨Properties.

Figure 4-1:
Choose font, size, and other attributes.

Whether you use the Type menu or Properties panel, you can set text attributes from the Properties panel either before or after you enter text.

The same rule applies in Fireworks as in all other applications: You have to select it to affect it. Before you apply any attributes, use the Pointer or Text tool to select the text you want to format.

To set text attributes with the Properties panel, follow these steps:

1. **Select the text you want to format.**

2. **Choose a font from the Font drop-down list and then choose a style from the Style drop-down list.**

If you don't see your favorite font in bold, you can take advantage of the Bold button to create faux bold text. (It isn't the true bold font, but it's close). The same trick works with the Italic button.

3. **To assign color, click the color selector box to the right of the Size drop-down list and then choose a color from the pop-up Swatches panel.**

Fine-Tuning Spacing, Alignment, and Orientation

Unfortunately, the Fireworks text controls leave much to be desired, compared with the other Creative Suite applications. But if you want to fine-tune your text, you might consider adjusting the spacing between characters or lines.

Sliders are available in the Properties panel for adjusting the *kerning* (spacing between two characters), *tracking* (spacing between multiple letters), and *leading* (spacing between lines of text). Select the text you want to format, adjust the slider as shown in Figure 4-2, and then click off the slider to confirm the change.

Set Text Orientation

Figure 4-2:
Adjust
kerning,
tracking,
and leading.

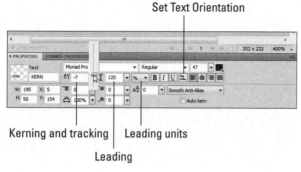

Kerning and tracking | Leading units

Leading

Kerning and tracking are controlled using the same Kerning tool. To kern between two letters, insert the cursor between the two letters before making a change. To adjust tracking, select multiple letters before making a change.

To align selected text, click the Left, Center, Right, or Justified alignment button in the Properties panel.

You can also change the orientation of selected text by clicking the Set Text Orientation button (refer to Figure 4-2).

Adding Effects

Spunk up your text by adding Live Effects from Photoshop. You can add drop shadows or 3D effects or even make your text look like wood!

To add effects to your text, follow these steps:

1. **With the Pointer tool, select some text and then click the Add Filters button in the Properties panel, shown in Figure 4-3.**

**Book VIII
Chapter 4**

**Creating Text in
Fireworks**

Figure 4-3:
Click the
Filters
button
to apply
additional
effects.

2. **Select Photoshop Live Effects from the pop-up window that appears.**

The Photoshop Live Effects dialog box appears (see Figure 4-4).

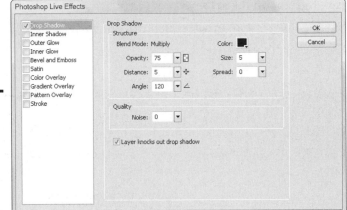

Figure 4-4:
Set text effects in the Photoshop Live Effects dialog box.

3. **In the list on the left side of the dialog box, select the effect you want to apply.**

4. **Set the related options on the right side of the dialog box and click OK.**

The effects are applied to your text, as shown in Figure 4-5.

Figure 4-5:
Create interesting text effects.

Don't apply all these effects to your text at the same time. You've heard it before, but we have to say it again: Just because you *can* do something doesn't mean that you always *should*.

Giving Your Text Some Style

You can choose among an array of interesting default styles to apply to both objects and text. You can also create your own styles — an extremely helpful capability when text needs to be consistent throughout an entire Web site.

Styles are applied to the entire text area.

Applying an existing style

To apply an existing text style, follow these steps:

1. **Create some text by typing, cutting, copying, and pasting or by dragging the text on the artboard.**

2. **Use the Pointer tool to select the text you want to affect.**

3. **Choose Window⇨Styles.**

   The Styles panel appears (see Figure 4-6).

4. **From the drop-down list, choose a category of style that you want to apply.**

   In Figure 4-6, the Chrome Styles category was selected.

5. **Click the style preview that you want to apply to your selected text.**

Figure 4-6:
Click a style to apply interesting attributes to your selection.

New Style

Creating your own style

Save yourself time by applying all the text attributes you need to make your text look just right.

To create a custom style, follow these steps:

1. **Select some text and apply all the formatting and effects you want to use, following the procedures described earlier in this chapter.**

2. **Choose Window⇨Styles to display the Styles panel.**

3. **From the Style Category drop-down list, choose a category for saving the style.**

4. **Click the New Style button in the lower right corner of the Styles panel (refer to Figure 4-6).**

   The New Style dialog box appears.

5. **Type an appropriate name for the style in the Name text box.**

6. **Select the attributes you want to save and click OK.**

   You have a saved style that you can apply to selected text at any time.

Spell-Checking Your Text

Checking your spelling is simple, right? It certainly is simple in Fireworks, so you have no excuse for typographical errors.

To check the spelling of your text in Fireworks, follow these steps:

1. **Choose Text⇨Spelling Setup.**

   The Spelling Setup dialog box appears.

2. **Choose the language that you want to use for the spelling check.**

3. **Set any other options you want to use and click OK.**

4. **Choose Text⇨Check Spelling.**

   The Check Spelling dialog box appears with the first questionable spelling highlighted.

If you want to add unique words in your document to the spell-checking dictionary, click the Add to Personal button in the upper right corner of the Check Spelling dialog box.

Attaching Text to a Path

Add some excitement by attaching text to a path. In Figure 4-7, the text is attached to a curvy path, but you can just as easily create angled text or text that follows a circle.

Follow these steps to attach text to a path:

1. **Select the text that you want to attach to the path.**

2. **Create a path with the Pen, Line, or Shape tool.**

   See Book III, Chapter 5 for additional details on creating a path using the Pen tool.

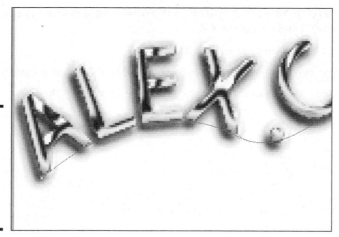

Figure 4-7:
You can make text curve by attaching the text to a path.

3. **Using the Pointer tool, select the text area and then Shift-click the path.**

   Both the text and the path are selected.

4. **Choose Text⇨Attach to Path.**

   If you want the text to run inside a shape, such as a circle, choose Text⇨Attach in Path.

To change the orientation of the attached text on the path, choose Text⇨ Orientation and then choose an orientation option from the submenu. In Figure 4-8, the orientation has been changed to Skew Vertical.

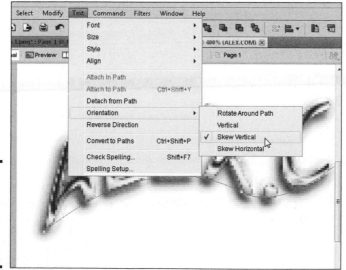

Figure 4-8:
You can change the text orientation on the path.

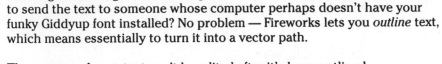

Outlining Text

Creating interesting text with unique fonts can be fun. But what if you need to send the text to someone whose computer perhaps doesn't have your funky Giddyup font installed? No problem — Fireworks lets you *outline* text, which means essentially to turn it into a vector path.

The content of your text can't be edited after it's been outlined.

To outline your text, follow these steps:

1. Create some text with the attributes you want, including the font.

The size doesn't have to be exact, however; you can rescale even after outlining the text.

2. With the Pointer tool, select the text area.

You can't outline individual letters or words within a text area.

3. Choose Text⇨Convert to Paths.

The text is outlined.

To edit the new vector path, switch to the Subselection tool and click an individual letter, as shown in Figure 4-9.

You can ungroup your text by selecting it then choosing Modify⇨UnGroup.

Figure 4-9:
Turn your text into vector paths.

Chapter 5: Getting Images
In and Out of Fireworks

In This Chapter

✔ **Importing images**

✔ **Editing images**

✔ **Optimizing and exporting images**

C reating images for your Web site is most likely what you'll use Fireworks for most often. In this chapter, you find out how to work with images from various sources, discover the importance of optimizing, and see how to export your images.

Getting Images into Fireworks

Besides making your own graphics and illustrations, you can use four main methods for getting images into Fireworks:

✦ **Open:** Fireworks isn't picky. As long as you open images (vector or raster) by choosing File⇨Open, you can open pretty much anything in Fireworks.

When you open a native Adobe Illustrator or Photoshop file, expect to see a dialog box, like you see in Figure 5-1. This particular dialog box appears when you open a Vector image from Adobe Illustrator. As you can see, you have to make some decisions as to what size the file should be, which artboards should be imported, and how you want to handle layers and groups.

When importing a Photoshop file, your choices are relatively the same, as shown in Figure 5-2. The integration between Fireworks and Photoshop is excellent; you can keep layers intact and continue your editing process in Fireworks.

✦ **Import:** By choosing File⇨Import, you can place an image directly in an existing image. The imported image is placed as a sublayer in the selected layer, as shown in Figure 5-3. Note that to complete your import, you need to click on the image area.

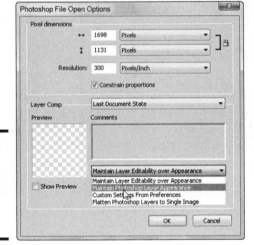

Figure 5-1: Importing a native Illustrator file into Fireworks.

Figure 5-2: Importing a native Photoshop file into Fireworks.

Figure 5-3: Choose the Import menu item to add an additional image as a layer in Fireworks.

✦ **Drag and drop:** You can drag and drop an image from other applications, such as Adobe Illustrator and Adobe Photoshop, right into the Fireworks workspace.

To drag and drop between Adobe applications on the Windows platform, you must drag your selection down to the application's tab on the taskbar and wait for the application to come forward. Then you can drag into the work area.

✦ **Browse:** Just as you can in the rest of the Creative Suite applications, you can take advantage of Adobe Bridge to preview, search, and organize images before opening them in Fireworks. Because images typically open in Photoshop by default, you right-click the image and choose Open with Adobe Fireworks CS5 from the contextual menu.

To open a file in Bridge, you must click the Browse in Bridge button on the Application bar in Fireworks, as shown in Figure 5-4.

Figure 5-4:
Click this button to open Adobe Bridge.

Editing Images

After you have an image open in Fireworks, you can start editing it. The editing features in Fireworks are similar to those in Photoshop but aren't as extensive. You can do many basic tasks in Fireworks — crop, paint, and even curve adjustments — but we suggest that you perform most of your in-depth retouching in Photoshop.

This section introduces five basic image-editing tasks that you typically perform when creating Web graphics. We also discuss the Image Editing panel, which lets you choose among multiple editing tools.

Scaling

Making images the right size is important. If an image is too large, you waste valuable download time; if it's too small, the image looks pixelized and out of focus. We cover three scaling methods in the following sections.

Proportional scaling

To scale an image in Fireworks proportionally (keeping the same width and height ratio), follow these steps:

1. **Select the layers you want to scale.**

If you have multiple layers, you can hold down the Ctrl (Windows) or ⌘ (Mac) key and click the layers in the Layers panel to add them to the selection.

2. **Select the Scale tool in the Select section of the Tools panel.**

Anchor points surround your selection.

3. **To make an image smaller, click and drag a corner anchor point toward the center; to make an image larger, click a corner anchor point and drag outward.**

Typically, you don't scale a bitmap image to a dramatically larger size, because it may become pixelized. The rule of thumb is to *not* make raster images more than 20 percent larger. This rule, of course, doesn't apply to vector objects.

Nonproportional scaling

If you *don't* want to scale proportionally, follow these steps:

1. **Select the layers you want to scale.**

2. **Select the Pointer tool in the Select section of the Tools panel.**

3. **To resize an image, click and drag a corner anchor point without using the Shift key.**

Numeric scaling

If you need to constrain scaling to an exact amount, you're better off using the Image Editing panel. Follow these steps to perform numeric scaling:

1. **Select the layers you want to scale.**

2. **Choose Window⇨Others⇨Image Editing.**

The Image Editing panel appears.

3. **Click Transform Commands and choose Numeric Transform from the drop-down list.**

The Numeric Transform dialog box appears, as shown in Figure 5-5.

4. **In the Width and Height text boxes, type the percentage by which you want to scale and click OK.**

Figure 5-5:
You can scale numerically by using the Image Editing panel.

Cropping

If you don't need part of an image, get rid of it. Unwanted image data is a bad thing for Web graphics because it takes up valuable time when downloading. Follow these steps to eliminate unwanted image areas:

1. **Select the Crop tool from the Select area of the Tools panel or from the Image Editing panel.**

   Refer to the preceding section, "Numeric scaling," to see how to open the Image Editing panel.

2. **Click and drag to select the area you want to keep when the crop is complete.**

3. **Press the Enter or Return key.**

   The image is cropped to the selected area, and the Crop tool is deselected.

If you're working with a wireframe of a larger Web page design, you may want to export only a small portion — for example, to export just the navigational tools, not the rest of the page. To crop only when exporting, follow these steps:

1. **Click and hold the Crop tool to select the Export Area tool.**

2. **Click and drag to select the area you want to keep when the image is exported.**

3. **Double-click in the middle of the cropped area.**

   The Image Preview window appears, offering you the opportunity to set export settings for this section of your image.

4. **Choose your export settings.**

**Book VIII
Chapter 5**

**Getting Images
In and Out of
Fireworks**

You can choose preset GIF and JPEG settings from the Saved Settings drop-down list in the upper right area of the Image Preview dialog box or use the Options, File, and Animation tabs on the left to set up custom export options.

5. **Click Export.**

The selected area is exported to a location you choose and you return to your image, which is still intact.

Painting

Fireworks has many of the same painting capabilities as Photoshop, but the method in which you use them can be quite different at times.

When you select the Brush tool from the Bitmap section of the Tools panel, for example, you make decisions about the size of the brush, paint color, and blending mode from the Properties panel (see Figure 5-6) rather than from the Options panel, as in Photoshop.

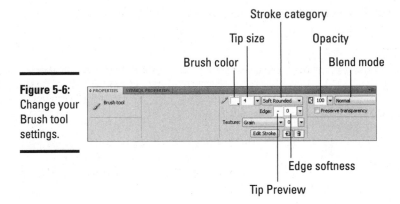

Figure 5-6:
Change your
Brush tool
settings.

Cloning

The Rubber Stamp tool works much like the Clone Stamp tool in Photoshop. Follow these steps to clone (copy) pixels in Fireworks:

1. **Select the Rubber Stamp tool in the Bitmap section of the Tools panel.**

2. **Hold down the Alt (Windows) or Option (Mac) key and click the part of the image you want to clone.**

In Figure 5-7, the crosshair on the boy's left shoulder indicates the pixels that are being cloned.

Figure 5-7:
Select pixels for cloning and start painting.

3. **Position the mouse pointer over the area where you want the cloned pixels to appear and start painting.**

   The cloned pixels appear in the image area (see the left side of Figure 5-6).

As you paint, follow the marker for the source; it moves simultaneously with the mouse pointer. You can use the Properties panel to change brush attributes.

Filtering

Filters offer you many opportunities to edit your images. You can choose to blur an image or adjust its colors by using the Curves or Hue Adjustment layer. To access your filters, you can choose them from the Filters menu or choose Window⇨Others⇨Image Editing.

If you want to apply additional filters that you can change later or even delete, click the Add Filters button in the Properties panel and choose Photoshop Live Effects from the drop-down list. The Photoshop Live Effects dialog box appears (see Figure 5-8).

Figure 5-8:
Use Photoshop Live Effects to create non-destructive changes to your artwork.

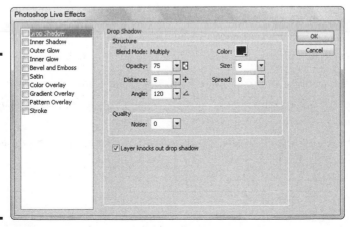

In the following example, you use the Hue/Saturation filter to add a color tint to an image. Follow these steps:

1. **Open an image and select it with the Pointer tool.**

2. **Click the Add Filter button in the Properties panel.**

3. **Choose Adjust Color and then Hue/Saturation.**

   The Hue/Saturation dialog box appears (see Figure 5-9).

Figure 5-9:
Applying
a color
tint with
the Hue/
Saturation
filter.

4. **Check the Colorize check box to apply a color tint.**

5. **Adjust the Hue slider until you find a color you want and click OK.**

If you want to edit or delete a filter, follow these steps:

1. **Double-click on the listed filter to edit it.**

   The Hue/Saturation Filter panel opens, where you can make changes to the filter.

2. **Delete a filter by selecting it from the filter list and clicking the minus icon (–) located on top of the filter list.**

Red eye, be gone!

Red eye is a typical result of using a camera with a built-in flash, but you can fix this problem easily. Click and hold the Rubber Stamp tool to select the Red Eye tool; then simply click and drag a marquee around each red-eye occurrence.

Optimizing Images for the Web

Now that you have created and edited your image, you're ready to prepare it for the Web. You must consider two major factors in Web graphics: speed of download and appearance. Having the best of both worlds is difficult, however; usually, you opt to give up some appearance for better speed. This process is *optimization*.

Previewing Web settings

Fireworks helps you with the optimization process from the beginning. By using the 2-Up preview in the upper left section of the image window, you can easily compare your optimized image with the original, based on your settings in the Optimize panel.

You can even use the preview windows to compare two to four Web formats and see which one looks best but has the most reasonable file size. Each preview window includes important information, such as file size.

If you want to go crazy, you can compare four settings by clicking 4-Up (see Figure 5-10). Using the preview windows, you can quickly change various settings — such as format, number of colors, and quality — and see the effect immediately, without previewing the image on the Web.

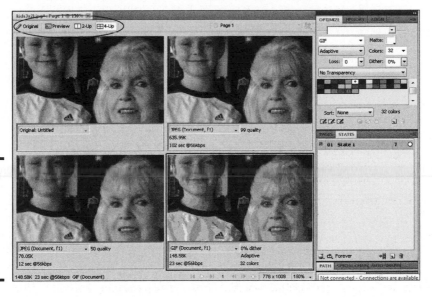

Figure 5-10: Compare four Web image formats by choosing 4-Up view.

Book VIII Chapter 5

Getting Images In and Out of Fireworks

Working with the Optimize panel

Now that you know how to compare images, where do you make the necessary optimization changes? In the Optimize panel, of course (see Figure 5-11). For a more thorough description of each file format, including its benefits and drawbacks, see Book IV, Chapter 10, which covers Web optimization in Photoshop CS5.

Figure 5-11: Use the Optimize panel to find the best quality at the smallest file size.

When you understand the Web-format settings, you can click the preview image you want to optimize; choose Window⇨Optimize to open the Optimize panel; and apply settings that provide the best, most size-efficient image. If you aren't sure what to pick, choose a default setting from the Saved settings drop-down menu. Typically, line art and vector graphics (created with solid colors) are best to save as GIF files, whereas photographs or images with gradient tints should be saved as JPG files. After choosing the optimal settings, you can export the image, as the following section explains.

Exporting for the Web

You can export individual images or entire Web pages by using the Export feature of Fireworks.

To export a Fireworks document, follow these steps:

1. **Choose File⇨Export.**

The Export dialog box opens, as shown in Figure 5-12.

2. **Navigate to an appropriate location to save your file.**

If you intend to use this image on a Web site, the best practice is to save it in the folder you typically use for Web images.

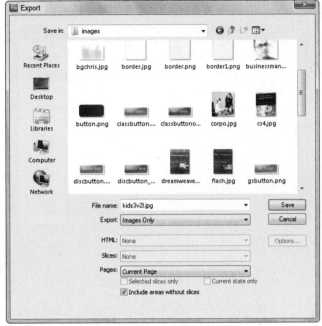

Export

Figure 5-12:
After your
document is
optimized,
you can
export it for
Web use.

3. **Type a name in the File Name text box.**

4. **Choose Images Only from the Export drop-down list and click Save.**

In Chapter 6 in this minibook, you discover how to export entire pages with sliced images.

Chapter 6: Hotspots, Slices, and CSS Layouts

In This Chapter

✔ Getting familiar with Fireworks layers

✔ Hyperlinking with hotspots and image maps

✔ Creating slices

✔ Exporting images and HTML as tables or CSS

A simple method for organizing content and making a Web site dynamic is the faithful hyperlink. You can link to another location from a button, some text, or even a move of the mouse pointer. By using layers in Fireworks, you can make those links dynamic and visually interesting.

In this chapter, you find out how Fireworks uses layers and then create navigational links by using the Slice feature.

Understanding Layers

Even though you may be an Adobe Photoshop or Illustrator user, the Layers panel in Fireworks may be somewhat of a mystery because it works a little differently from the way you might expect. (Read on to find out how to take advantage of Fireworks layers.) To see the Layers panel, choose Window⇨Layers.

Navigating the Layers panel

Figure 6-1 shows the two main components of the Layers panel:

✦ **The Web Layer** serves as a repository for anything code related, such as links and slices. In Figure 6-1, you see the links in the Web Layer section.

✦ **The default Layer 1** includes sublayers that are created automatically for every object you add to the Fireworks canvas.

Figure 6-1:
The Layers panel in Fireworks.

New/Duplicate Layer   Trash

New Sublayer   New Bitmap Image

Add Mask

Note that if you open an image from Photoshop that already has a Background layer, it carries through into Fireworks (refer to Figure 6-1).

Working with the Layers panel

Here are just some of the things you can do in the Layers panel to organize your artwork better:

✦ **Hide and show layers:** Click the Visibility (Eye) icon to hide or show a layer or sublayer.

✦ **Send objects forward and backward:** Drag individual layers and sublayers to arrange objects on those layers in front of or behind each other.

✦ **Rename layers:** By double-clicking the layer or sublayer name, you can rename the layer, which can be a huge help later when you're trying to find a specific object.

✦ **Organize layers:** Create appropriately named layers to house related sublayers, thereby gaining the ability to move, copy, or delete multiple layers at the same time.

✦ **Keep Web components separate:** Use the Web Layer to keep track of hotspots and slices as well as control the visibility of those items.

Creating Hotspots

Fireworks gives you lots of ways to take advantage of hyperlinks. In this section, you see how to create a *hotspot* — essentially, a simple link from text or a graphic to a URL (Universal Resource Locator) on the Web. In Chapter 7 of this minibook, you find out how to create buttons that interact with the user.

Defining a hotspot

To link text or a graphic to a Web URL, you must first define it as a hotspot. You can define a hotspot by using either of two methods:

✦ Select the Hotspot tool in the Web section of the Tools panel and click and drag over the part of the image you want to create as the linked part of the image, as shown in Figure 6-2. Click and hold down the Rectangle Hotspot tool to see that you have a choice of creating a rectangular, circular, or polygon hotspot.

Figure 6-2:
Click and drag over an area with the Hot spot tool to incorporate a hyperlink into your Fireworks document.

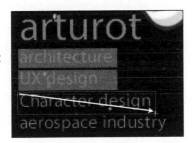

✦ Select the item (text or graphics), right-click (Windows) or Control-click (Mac) the selected item, and choose Insert Hotspot from the contextual menu.

Linking a hotspot

After you define a hotspot, you can define the location (typically, a Web page) that you want the hotspot to link to. Follow these steps:

1. **Choose Window⇨URL.**

The URL panel appears (see Figure 6-3).

Figure 6-3:
Assign a link
to a hotspot.

2. **Type a URL address that you want the viewer to go to after selecting this region.**

   In Figure 6-3, a link to a fictitious external Web site (`http://www.uxbyarturot.com`) is referenced. Note that you can add your URL to a library for later use by clicking the plus sign to the right of the URL text box.

   When you reference pages beyond your Web site *(external links),* you must start the link with `http://`.

3. **Choose Window⇨Layers to display the Layers panel, if it isn't already open.**

   The hotspot you created appears as a separate sublayer of the Web Layer.

4. **Double-click the name of this sublayer and give it a more appropriate name, as shown in Figure 6-4.**

In the next section, you discover options for working with multiple hotspots.

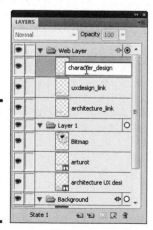

Figure 6-4:
A new
hotspot
layer
appears
under the
Web layer.

Working with Image Maps

When you create a graphic and add multiple hotspots to it, it becomes an *image map*. In Figure 6-5, the image map was created with the Polygon Hotspot tool.

Figure 6-5:
Use an image map to define clickable regions in an image.

Creating an image map

To create an image map of your own, follow these steps:

1. **Open a graphic file that you want to assign multiple hotspots to.**

2. **Click and hold the Rectangle Hot Spot tool in the Web section of the Tools panel and choose one of the three hidden hotspot tools: Rectangle, Circle, or Polygon.**

3. **If you chose the Rectangle or Circle tool in Step 2, simply click and drag to define the hotspot. To create a region with the Polygon tool, simply click and release from point to point to create a custom region.**

TIP

If you didn't get the shapes just right, don't fret. You can use the Pointer and Subselection tools to move and resize the hotspots.

Linking an image map

After you create an image map, you can define hotspots on it and link those hotspots to URLs. For directions on both procedures, refer to the "Creating Hotspots" section, earlier in this chapter.

Here are some types of links other than URLs that you can use:

✦ **E-mail address:** Type **mailto:*youremail address*** in the URL text box to create a link that opens a message window, with your address already entered and ready to go!

✦ **Link to another page in your Fireworks document:** Many people like to create prototypes of their Web sites in Fireworks and demonstrate the link from one page to another. You can use the Pages panel to add a page to your document and then use the Link drop-down menu, shown in Figure 6-6, to link from one page to another.

To export multiple pages from Fireworks, choose File➪Export and then select All Pages from the Pages drop-down menu. You can test your links by opening the newly created HTML file in a browser.

Figure 6-6:
Link from one Fireworks page to another.

✦ **Non-HTML files on the server:** You can type **2010/catalog.pdf**, for example, to instruct the browser to open a PDF file named `catalog` that's inside the `2010` folder.

Repeat the process of defining hotspots and assigning URLs as many times as you like.

Testing and exporting an image map

After you've created and linked an image map, you're ready to test and export it for use on your Web page. Follow these steps:

1. **Test your image map by choosing File⇨Preview in Browser.**

2. **If you're happy with the results, close the browser window and return to Fireworks to export your file.**

3. **Choose File⇨Export.**

The Export dialog box appears.

4. **Type a name in the Name text box.**

5. **Choose HTML and Images from the Export drop-down list.**

6. **Choose Export HTML File from the HTML drop-down list.**

7. **Choose None from the Slices drop-down list and click Save.**

8. **If you have created multiple pages in your Fireworks file, don't forget to choose All Pages from the Pages drop-down menu, as shown in Figure 6-7.**

Figure 6-7:
Export
multiple
pages from
Fireworks
using the
All Pages
option.

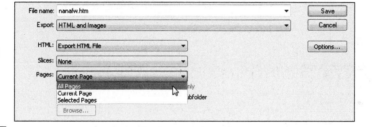

9. **When you're finished, click Save.**

That's it! Now you can choose File⇨Open in your browser and locate the HTML file to test your finished project or choose File⇨Open in a Web-editing program (such as Adobe Dreamweaver) to modify the HTML file.

In Figure 6-8, you see the completed file in a Web browser, along with the associated code that was created in Fireworks.

Figure 6-8:
The finished
image map,
as viewed
in a Web
browser
(top) and the
HTML code
created
for the
image map
(bottom).

```
 1  <!DOCTYPE html PUBLIC "-//W3C//DTD XHTML 1.0 Transitional//EN"
 2  "http://www.w3.org/TR/xhtml1/DTD/xhtml1-transitional.dtd">
 3  <!-- saved from url=(0014)about:internet -->
 4  <html xmlns="http://www.w3.org/1999/xhtml">
 5  <head>
 6  <title>Astronaut.png</title>
 7  <meta http-equiv="Content-Type" content="text/html; charset=utf-8" />
 8  <!--Fireworks CS5 Dreamweaver CS5 target.  Created Fri Mar 05 11:34:49 GMT-0600
    (Central Standard Time) 2010-->
 9  </head>
10  <body bgcolor="#ffffff">
11  <img name="Astronaut" src="images/Astronaut.png" width="237" height="335"
    border="0" id="Astronaut" usemap="#m_Astronaut" alt="" /><map name="m_Astronaut"
    id="m_Astronaut">
12  <area shape="rect" coords="17,284,172,305" href="http://www.uxbyarturot.com"
    alt="" />
13  <area shape="rect" coords="17,263,112,284" href="javascript:;" alt="" />
14  <area shape="rect" coords="17,243,112,263" href="javascript:;" alt="" />
15  </map>
16  </body>
17  </html>
18
```

Slicing Up Your Art

Slicing is a technique for breaking large files into smaller packets so that
they download faster on the Web. It's also a method for attaching URLs to
different regions of an image, like image maps. Unlike image maps, however,
slices are created in a grid pattern.

You can even use slices to optimize different parts of an image with separate
settings. Perhaps you can get away with having one section of an image be of
lower quality than another section.

A perfect candidate for sliced artwork is a navigation bar, such as the one
shown in Figure 6-9. Each tab is an individual slice that, when clicked in a
Web browser, takes the viewer to a different location.

Figure 6-9:
Use slices
for navbars.

| Home | About | Contact | Downloads |

Creating the basic image

First, you create the basic image — a rectangle, for this example. Follow these steps:

1. **Choose File⇨New to open the New Document dialog box.**

2. **Type** 500 **in the Width text box and** 200 **in the Height text box; then click OK.**

   The new, blank document opens. (Notice that it's larger than the image you're creating; you see how to modify it later in these steps.)

3. **Select the Rectangle tool in the Vector section of the Tools panel and click and drag to create a rectangle.**

   For this example, any size is fine.

4. **With the rectangle selected, click Fill Color in the Colors section of the Tools panel and choose a color.**

   For this example, we chose a light color (yellow).

5. **Choose Window⇨Info to open the Info panel.**

6. **Enter** 300 **in the W (Width) text box and** 50 **in the H (Height) text box, or use the Width and Height text boxes in the Properties panel to set this size.**

   The rectangle is resized.

7. **With the Pointer tool, click anywhere in the canvas outside the rectangle to deselect the rectangle.**

8. **Right-click (Windows) or Control-click (Mac) and choose Modify Canvas⇨Fit Canvas from the contextual menu (see Figure 6-10).**

   The canvas adjusts to the size of the rectangle (see Figure 6-11).

When you have no objects selected, you may also click the Fit Canvas button in the Properties panel.

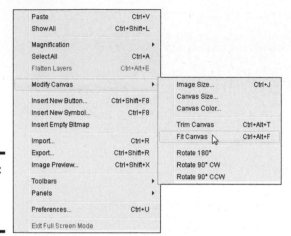

Figure 6-10:
Choose the Fit Canvas command.

Figure 6-11:
The canvas adjusts to fit your object.

Adding text

You can add some text areas to the navbar. Follow these steps:

1. **Select the Text tool in the Vector section of the Tools panel.**

2. **Click Fill Color in the Colors section of the Tools panel and choose a color.**

   For this example, we chose a dark color (black).

3. **Set the font and font size in the Properties panel.**

   For this exercise, we changed the font to Arial and used the Font Size slider to change the size to 25.

4. **Click the left half of the rectangle to position the insertion point wherever you want the text to begin, and type the text.**

   For this example, we typed **Home**, as shown in Figure 6-12.

5. **Click twice to the right of the text area to deselect the active text area and create a new one.**

   You can hold down the Alt+Shift (Windows) or Option+Shift (Mac) keys and drag the initial text box to the right to clone and align a new text box.

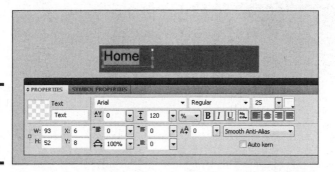

Figure 6-12:
Adding
text to the
navbar.

6. **Type a word or two for your next navigation tab.**

   For example, we typed **About**.

7. **Use the Pointer tool to reposition the text.**

Doing the actual slicing and dicing

After you've prepared a simple but efficient navbar, use the Slice tool to create a couple of slices and then export them. Follow these steps:

1. **Select the Slice tool in the Web section of the Tools panel; then click and drag from the upper left corner of the Home section of the rectangle toward the lower right corner, as shown in Figure 6-13.**

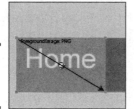

Figure 6-13:
Creating a
slice.

For this example, your drag doesn't have to be exact.

If you're going for perfection, choose View➪Rulers to display the rulers. When the rulers are visible, you can click and drag guides out of them.

When you have an active slice, the Properties panel changes to offer you various slice options.

2. **Change the format by making a choice from the Slice Export Settings drop-down list.**

   Choose the GIF format if the artwork has lots of solid color, or choose JPEG for images with lots of gradation of color.

3. **Enter a link in the Link text box.**

   For example, type **http://www.agitraining.com**.

4. **Enter a brief description of the link in the Alt text box.**

   Alt text is the text that appears while a page is downloading. It also appears in place of the graphic if a viewer has turned off the graphics display in his Web browser.

   For example, type **Training** in the Alt text box, as shown in Figure 6-14.

Figure 6-14:
Enter the
URL and alt
text.

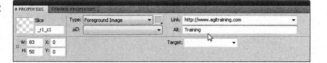

5. **With the Slice tool, click and drag to surround the second half of the navbar.**

6. **Type** http://www.adobe.com **into the Link text box and type** Adobe, Inc. **into the Alt text box.**

That is slicing in simple form. You can make the process as complicated as you want by creating entire sliced pages (because search engines like to search for text content) to navbars with many links and destinations.

In the next section, you find out how to get your navbar out of Fireworks and on a Web page.

Exporting Slices

You can export finished slices for use on a Web page.

Exporting slices as tables

To export sliced artwork as tables (for these steps, your test navbar), follow these steps:

1. **Choose File⇨Export.**

   The Export dialog box appears.

2. **Browse to the folder where you store your Web files and make sure that you pick a file connected with the Web site you're creating your images for.**

3. **In the File Name text box, enter a name.**

   For this example, we typed **navbar.htm**.

4. **Choose Export HTML and Images from the Export drop-down list.**

5. **Choose Export Slices from the Slices drop-down list and click Save.**

Now that you've exported the HTML code and the image, you can open the image in a Web-editing program such as Dreamweaver and add elements or simply copy and paste it into an existing page or template. Find out more about Dreamweaver in Book VI.

Changing the export format from table to CSS

If you want more control of your slices, you can change the code that Fireworks creates upon output.

In Figure 6-15, the selection for CSS and Images creates CSS (Cascading Style Sheets) rather than an HTML table when exported.

Typically, creating a layout of a page using CSS code is beneficial because the information is more accessible and flexible for the user.

Figure 6-15:
You can choose to export slices as CSS.

Chapter 7: Using Buttons and Symbols

In This Chapter

✔ Understanding states

✔ Creating rollover buttons

✔ Converting graphics to symbols

*B*efore you jump into creating buttons and animations, you need to understand states and how they work in Fireworks. States let you organize layers in such a way that you can create several versions of your artwork; these states can be used for rollovers or animations.

Using States in Fireworks

You may want to use states for two reasons:

✦ **Animation:** You can build and edit animated GIFs with states like the one you see in Figure 7-1. One step of the animation goes into each frame. The states (sometimes referred to as *frames*) are played one after another to create the appearance of motion — an effect a little like those cool flip books you may have found in boxes of caramel corn. By using layers, you can specify which items are animated and which items remain static.

Figure 7-1: In this example, the astronaut fades to 0 percent opacity over three states.

✦ **Rollovers:** You can also use states to produce rollovers. By slicing an image (discussed in Chapter 6 of this minibook), you can trigger the different versions (or states) that appear when the user's mouse pointer crosses over the artwork.

Making a Rollover Button

You can create interactive buttons in Fireworks to make rollovers, swap images, and react to other interactions with viewers. For all these effects, use the States panel.

In this section, you find out how to use states to create a *rollover* button — a button that changes when a mouse pointer passes over it.

Creating the basic art

First, you need to create the basic art for the button. (For this example, the button is a rounded rectangle, but you can substitute another shape.) Follow these steps:

1. **Click and hold the Rectangle tool in the Vector section of the Tools panel and then select Rounded Rectangle from the list of hidden tools.**

2. **Click and drag in the workspace to create a shape.**

   Any size is fine for this example.

3. **Choose Window⇨Styles to open the Styles panel.**

4. **Choose a style from the drop-down list.**

   In Figure 7-2, we selected Plastic Styles.

   This basic button is what the viewer initially sees on your Web page.

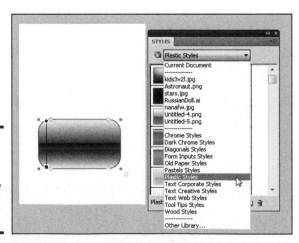

Figure 7-2:
Using the Styles panel, apply any style to the shape.

Adding rollover behavior

In this section, you add rollover behavior to the button and create the version of the button artwork that viewers will see when their mouse pointers pass over it. Follow these steps:

1. **Select the rounded rectangle shape you created in the preceding section and then right-click to select Insert Rectangular Slice.**

    The shape is highlighted, as shown in Figure 7-3, indicating that a hotspot has been created.

Figure 7-3:
Right-click
to add a
rectangular
slice to a
selected
object.

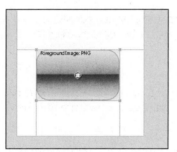

2. **Right-click (Windows) or Control-click (Mac) the center of the slice and choose Add Simple Rollover Behavior from the contextual menu, as shown in Figure 7-4.**

Figure 7-4:
Choose
Add Simple
Rollover
Behavior to
make your
button a
rollover.

3. **Choose Window➪States to open the States panel.**

4. **From the States panel menu, choose Duplicate State, as shown in Figure 7-5.**

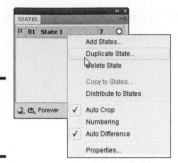

Figure 7-5:
Choose to
duplicate a
state.

The Duplicate State dialog box appears. Keep the settings at the default of State 1 being inserted after the current state, as shown on the left in Figure 7-6.

Figure 7-6:
Duplicate
your original
state before
making
changes
that will
occur on
rollover.

5. **Click OK.**

   A State 2 row appears in the States panel, as shown on the right in Figure 7-6.

6. **If it makes it easier to see your objects, click the Hide Slices and Hotspots tool in the Web section of the Tools panel to hide the slice, as shown in Figure 7-7.**

Figure 7-7:
Hide slices
so that you
can see
your image.

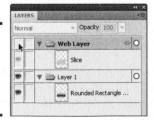

7. **With the Pointer tool, select the original shape you created.**

8. **Choose Window⇨Styles to open the Styles panel.**

9. **Choose a new style from the drop-down list.**

   This step creates the version of the button that appears when viewers pass their mouse pointers over the button.

10. **Save the file.**

Testing and exporting the button

The rollover you created is not quite a standalone piece of artwork; unlike a `.jpg`, `.gif`, or `.png` file, the rollover needs supporting HTML, and JavaScript code in order to make it work. In order to collect all the parts to make your rollover work, you will Export the rollover out of Fireworks. Follow these steps:

1. **If the eye icon is turned off on the left side of the Web layer in the Layers panel, turn it on now.**

   Your slices and hotspots are now visible.

2. **Choose File⇨Preview in Browser to test your button.**

3. **If you're happy with the effect and want to use the button on a Web page, choose File⇨Export to open the Export dialog box.**

4. **Name the file.**

   Remember that you need to follow standard Web-based naming conventions.

5. **Choose HTML and Images from the Export drop-down list.**

6. **Make sure that Export HTML File is selected in the HTML drop-down list and that Export Slices is selected in the Slices drop-down list, and then click Save.**

Discovering Fireworks Symbols

When you make Web graphics, you may discover that you repeatedly create the same button or the same background image. To stay consistent and save lots of time, you can turn artwork into a symbol or use some of the precreated symbols in the Common Library panel.

Symbols are simply elements you can store in the Common Library or Document Library panel. Use the Common Library to store symbols that you can access across Fireworks; the Document Library is for symbols to be accessed only within the associated document.

**Book VIII
Chapter 7**

**Using Buttons
and Symbols**

Fireworks has three types of symbols: graphic, animation, and button. In this section, you find out how to use and modify symbols.

Symbol instances refer to the placement of the symbols on the artboard. Symbol instances are dynamically linked back to the original symbol used to create them.

If you convert artwork to a symbol, the new symbol object is linked dynamically to all instances of that symbol on the artboard. If you change the symbol object, all instances are updated automatically.

Working with a precreated symbol

To use a precreated symbol in Fireworks, follow these steps:

1. **Choose Window⇨Common Library to open the Common Library panel.**

   The precreated symbols in this library are organized in categories, such as Animations, Buttons, and Flex Components.

2. **Double-click the category you want to use.**

3. **Select a symbol to see a preview in the preview pane at the top of the Common Library panel.**

4. **When you find a symbol you want to use, drag it out to the artboard.**

   The symbol instance is placed on the artboard (see Figure 7-8).

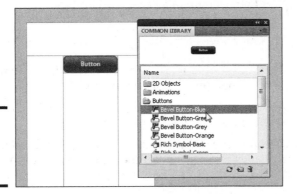

Figure 7-8:
Creating
a symbol
instance.

If you're creating a navigation bar with four buttons, for example, repeat Step 4 three times.

Converting artwork to a symbol

If you find yourself in the position of repeatedly creating the same button, animation, or graphic, follow these steps to convert that artwork to a symbol:

1. **With the Pointer tool, select the artwork you want to convert.**

2. **Choose Modify⇨Symbol⇨Convert to Symbol.**

   The Convert to Symbol dialog box opens.

3. **Type a name for the symbol in the Name text box.**

4. **Select the symbol type: Graphic, Animation, or Button.**

5. **To scale the symbol without distorting it, check the Enable 9-Slice Scaling Guides check box (see Figure 7-9).**

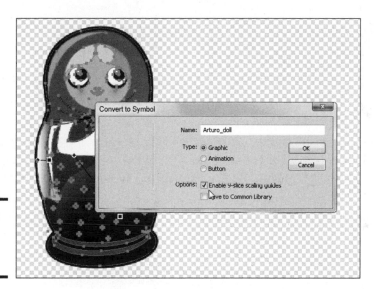

Figure 7-9:
Setting symbol options.

6. **To store the symbol so that it can be used in multiple documents, check the Save to Common Library check box.**

7. **Click OK to close the Convert to Symbol dialog box. Then click Save to save the symbol in the Custom Symbols folder.**

   The saved symbol can now be found by choosing Window⇨Common Library. Double-click the Custom Symbols folder to locate any symbols created and saved to the Common Library.

Adobe Illustrator has many symbols you can borrow from its symbol libraries. Simply drag a symbol from the Illustrator Symbols panel onto the artboard and then copy and paste the symbol into Fireworks. All components, such as vector shapes, are maintained. Find out more about Illustrator symbols in Book III, Chapter 11.

**Book VIII
Chapter 7**

Using Buttons and Symbols

Scaling with 9-slice

A helpful feature of Fireworks is *9-slice scaling,* which lets you determine what part of a symbol will be scaled. This feature can be extremely helpful when you're working with buttons that have rounded corners or other elements you don't want to scale. To use this feature, simply check the Enable 9-Slice Scaling Guides check box in the Convert to Symbol dialog box.

Editing a symbol

You can edit a symbol object or just one instance of it. You might want to edit the symbol object if you decide to change the color of all your buttons to orange at the same time, but you have to edit each symbol instance individually if you want each button to have a different word on it.

To edit a symbol object or instance, right-click on it and choose Symbol⇨ Edit Symbol, or choose Modify⇨Symbol⇨Edit Symbol. You are then entered into the Symbol editing mode. Here you can use your tools to reposition, recolor, retype, or make any other modifications that you'd make to any other graphic in Fireworks.

Exit the editing mode by clicking the arrow in the breadcrumbs bar in the upper-left of the workspace, as shown in Figure 7-10.

Figure 7-10:
Exit the
Symbol
editing
mode by
clicking on
the arrow.

If you no longer want an object to be a symbol, choose Modify⇨Symbol⇨ Break Apart.

Editing a symbol without breaking the link

At times, you may want to change an instance but maintain its link to the symbol object. Perhaps you're creating a cool graphic effect of butterflies and want to change one butterfly's position and opacity, as shown in Figure 7-11.

Figure 7-11:
Edit properties of symbol instances without breaking the link to the original symbol.

You can use the Properties panel to modify the following instance properties without affecting the symbol object or other symbol instances:

✦ Blending mode

✦ Opacity

✦ Filters

✦ Width and height

✦ X and y coordinates

Editing a symbol component

At times, you need to break apart a symbol so that you can edit its components, perhaps to change their colors. To edit individual components of a symbol, follow these steps:

1. **Select the symbol instance you want to modify.**

2. **Choose Modify⇨Symbol⇨Break Apart.**

The symbol instance is no longer linked to the symbol object.

3. **With the Subselection tool, select the components of the artwork that you want to edit.**

They're now ready for you to make any changes that you would make to regular (nonsymbol) objects on the artboard.

When you modify the original symbol object, this instance is no longer affected.

Chapter 8: Don't Just Sit There — Animate!

In This Chapter

✓ **Creating and editing animations**

✓ **Adjusting your playback**

✓ **Working with tweening**

✓ **Animating with masks**

✓ **Exporting animations for the Web**

*A*nimations, used in moderation, can liven up a page. You can make simple animations to create effects of light and movement — or go to the max with dancing babies. The subtle approach probably is better because most folks are more intrigued by interesting content than by distracting animations. Still, you find animations being used every day, especially in rotating banner ads.

The animations you produce in Fireworks aren't quite the same as those in Flash. Fireworks animations typically are smaller and are saved in the GIF format, which doesn't require a plug-in to view. You create them by using the States panel, which we cover in detail in Chapter 7 of this book.

In this chapter, you use the States panel to create multiple versions of your artwork that play one after another to create an animation.

The terms *states* and *frames* can be used interchangeably (though we generally prefer the term *states*).

As you create images for animation, experiment to find out how many colors you can include without increasing the file size dramatically. If you're working with size restrictions (as many advertising sites require), you may have to make the image files smaller by deleting states or adjusting color. Creating animations is a give-and-take process, in which you're trying to get the best effects from the smallest files.

Getting Started with Animation

Creating images is a simple process in Fireworks. Creating images for animations is also simple but slightly different, in that the images are created from several states that play one after another to create the illusion of movement. In the first two sections of this chapter, you create a simple manual animation of a bouncing ball. Later in the chapter, you find out how to automate the process.

Creating an animation

To create an image for animation, follow these steps:

1. **Create or open the object you want to animate.**

   For this example, create a circle with the Ellipse tool.

2. **With the Pointer tool, select the circle.**

3. **Choose Window⇨States.**

   The States panel appears, listing one state (see Figure 8-1).

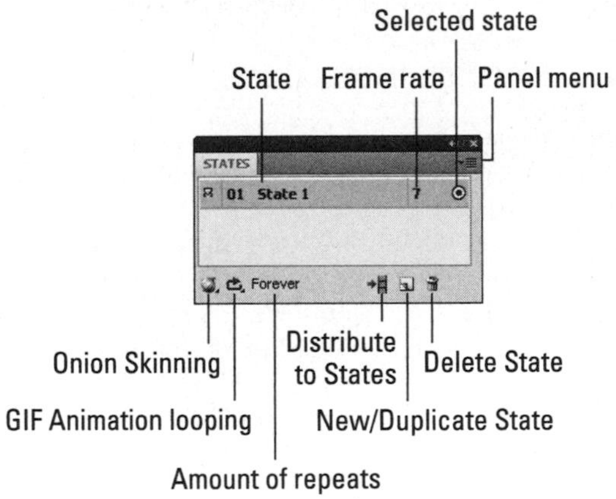

Figure 8-1:
The States panel.

4. **From the panel menu in the upper right corner, choose Duplicate State.**

   The Duplicate State dialog box appears.

5. **Use the Number slider to add three new states, as shown in Figure 8-2.**

6. **In the Insert New States section, select the After Current State radio button and then click OK.**

   Because all the states are identical, you see no change. The objects are positioned on top of one another.

Figure 8-2:
Duplicating
states to
create an
animation.

Onion skinning

Onion skinning can be a huge help when you're trying to create a good flow for an animation. Onion skinning gives you the opportunity to edit the selected state but view (in a dimmed view) the states that come before and after the selected state, as shown in Figure 8-3.

Figure 8-3:
Keep track
of states
with onion
skinning.

To use onion skinning in an animation, follow these steps:

1. **Select the State 2 row in the States panel.**

2. **Click the Onion Skinning button in the lower left corner of the panel (refer to Figure 8-1).**

   A drop-down list appears.

3. **Select Show All States to show one state before and one after the selected state.**

Making the animation move

Creating the actual animation certainly isn't rocket science, but you need to pay attention to the state you select before making your move.

To put your animation in motion, follow these steps:

1. **Select State 2 in the States panel to view the state 2 circle.**
2. **Using the Pointer tool, drag the circle slightly up and to the right.**
3. **Select State 3 to view the state 3 circle.**
4. **Drag the circle below and to the right of the state 2 circle.**
5. **Select State 4 to view the state 4 circle.**
6. **Drag the circle above and to the right of the state 3 circle.**

   You should see a flow that — in a primitive way — represents a bouncing ball (see Figure 8-4).

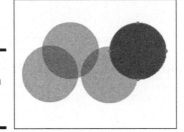

Figure 8-4: Creating an animation manually.

Testing the animation

You can test an animation directly in the Fireworks artboard or on the Web.

Testing in Fireworks

Fireworks provides several playback controls on the right side of the artboard window, as shown in Figure 8-5.

To use these controls to test an animation in Fireworks, follow these steps:

1. **Click the Play button to start the animation.**

   Notice that the Play button changes to the Stop button.
2. **After playing the animation, click the Stop button to stop the animation.**

In the "Adjusting Playback" section, later in this chapter, you find out how to control the speed of each state (or frame) and discover where to turn *looping* (repeat) off and on.

Adding an object to multiple states

Perhaps you created the perfect animation but then discovered that you forgot to include an element. You can copy or create the missing object in one state and then add it to all the other states. Follow these steps:

1. **Select the state in which you want the new object to appear.**

   Make sure that you click on the state's name (in the States panel) to select it.

2. **Copy and paste the artwork for the new object to the selected state or create the new object in that state.**

3. **Make sure that the new artwork is selected, right-click (Windows) or Control-click (Mac) the selected state in the States**

panel, and choose Copy to States from the contextual menu.

The Copy to States dialog box appears.

4. **Select the All States radio button (see the following figure) and click OK.**

The selected object is included in all the states.

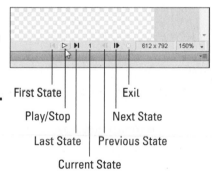

Figure 8-5:
Test the animation in Fireworks with the playback controls.

First State — Exit
Play/Stop — Next State
Last State — Previous State
Current State

Testing on the Web

The Preview in Browser feature gives you a more accurate idea of how your animation will appear to the viewer. This procedure is so easy that no steps are necessary: Choose File⇨Preview in Browser and select the browser in which you want to preview the animation. If the animation does not work in your browser, make sure that you have GIF selected as the Export File Format in the Optimize panel in Fireworks.

Adjusting Playback

You can speed or slow an entire animation or control the speed of each slide individually. Controlling the timing of individual states can be helpful in an advertising animation, for example, if you want to keep one state visible longer than the others. You can also loop an animation. This section describes both types of changes.

Changing the frame rate

The *frame rate* is the speed at which your animation will play. To change the frame rate, follow these steps:

1. **Select the states for which you want to set the frame rate.**

2. **Choose Properties from the panel menu in the upper right corner of the States panel.**

   The State Delay pop-up appears, as shown in Figure 8-6.

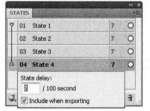

Figure 8-6:
Change the
frame rate.

3. **In the text box, enter a value (in 100ths of a second) to make the animation go faster or slower.**

   The lower the value you enter, the faster the animation plays. Make sure that the Include When Exporting check box is selected. Click anywhere on the artboard to close the window.

4. **(Optional) To test the results of your frame rate change, click the Play button in the lower-right side of the artboard window.**

Want to display one state longer than the others? Select only that particular state and then change its frame rate to be slower than the other states' frame rates.

Playing it again: Looping

You can choose to loop an animation into eternity or just a certain number of times. To do this, follow these steps:

1. **Click the GIF Animation Looping button in the lower left corner of the States panel (refer to Figure 8-1).**

   A menu drops down.

2. **Choose the number of times you want the animation to loop (see Figure 8-7).**

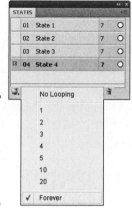

Figure 8-7: Set the loop for the animation in the States panel.

3. **Save and close the animation.**

You've completed a manual animation. In the next section, you find out how to create an animation in which Fireworks creates the states for you automatically.

Tweening in Fireworks

Tweening is the process of creating a state between two others, usually as a start or stop point for the animation. Use tweening to simulate an object moving, like a ball bouncing, or fading an image in or out of an animation.

Creating a symbol

To use the tweening feature in Fireworks, you must have a symbol — for this example, an arrow. To create this symbol, follow these steps:

1. **Choose File⇨New and create a new document large enough to contain your animation.**

   For this example, create a document that measures 500 pixels by 500 pixels.

2. **Click and hold the Rectangle tool and select the Arrow tool from the Vector section of the Tools panel.**

3. **In the upper left corner of the canvas, click and drag to create a small arrow.**

4. **Choose Modify⇨Symbol⇨Convert to Symbol.**

   The Convert to Symbol dialog box appears.

5. **Type an appropriate name (such as Arrow) for the symbol in the Name text box, select the Graphic radio button, and click OK.**

   Fireworks converts your arrow graphic to a symbol.

Cloning the symbol

After you create a symbol, you need to clone the symbol to create start and end points for the animation. Follow these steps:

1. **Select the arrow symbol on the canvas.**

2. **Holding down the Alt (Windows) or Option (Mac) key, drag the arrow to the lower right corner of the canvas.**

   As shown in Figure 8-8, by holding down the Alt or Option key while you drag, you're cloning the arrow.

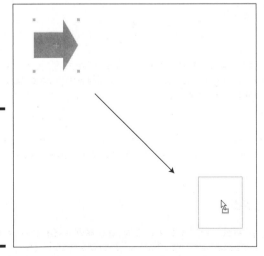

Figure 8-8:
Create a
start and
end point
for the
animation
by cloning
the symbol.

3. **Choose the Scale tool in the Select section of the Tools panel and make the cloned arrow (in the lower right corner) larger than the original.**

4. **Using the Pointer tool, position both arrow symbols on the canvas the way you want them.**

   These symbols are the start and end points for your animation, so place them where you want the animation to begin and end.

Tweening the symbols

When you have two instances of the symbol on the artboard, you're ready to tween the symbols to create an animation. Follow these steps:

1. **Use the Pointer tool to select one of the arrow symbols and then Shift-click the other to select both at the same time.**

2. **Choose Modify⇨Symbol⇨Tween Instances.**

   The Tween Instances dialog box appears.

3. **Enter a value in the Steps text box.**

   For this example, enter **5** (see Figure 8-9) to create five new states (or frames) for transforming the small arrow into the large arrow.

Figure 8-9:
Set the number of states.

4. **If you want the symbols to appear one at a time, you want those states to be distributed to separate states in the States panel, so select the Distribute to States check box.**

5. **Click OK.**

6. **Test your animation by clicking the Play button in the lower right section of the Fireworks workspace and then save the file.**

Animating with Masks

If you're a Photoshop user, you're probably familiar with masks. Masks let you choose the viewable area of an image. The process is much like cutting a hole in a piece of paper and then placing an image under it. The hole in the paper shows only the area of the image below that you want to expose; the rest of the paper masks (covers) the parts of the image that you don't want to expose.

You can take this masking feature a step further in Fireworks by animating a mask. In this section, you create a simple object and mask and then animate the mask.

Creating an image and a mask

To create the image and mask for your animation, follow these steps:

1. **Create a new document that measures 500 pixels by 500 pixels.**

2. **With the Star tool (hidden in the Rectangle tool), create lots of stars close together.**

   Use any colors and sizes you want for the stars. This step creates multiple layers.

3. **Choose Window⇨Layers to open the Layers panel.**

4. **Click the top layer listed in the Layers panel and then Shift-click the bottom layer to select all the layers you created.**

5. **From the panel menu in the Layers panel, choose Flatten Selection.**

   The layers are flattened into one bitmap layer.

6. **Select the Marquee tool in the Bitmap section of the Tools panel, make a narrow rectangular selection through the middle of the stars, and then click the Add Mask button at the bottom of the Layers panel (see Figure 8-10).**

   Fireworks creates a mask based on the image area you selected.

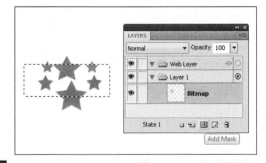

Figure 8-10: Select an area for masking (top) and the mask based on the selection (bottom).

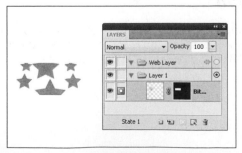

Animating the mask

In this section, you animate the mask but not the stars. Follow these steps:

1. **In the Layers panel, click the chain icon that appears between the stars layer and the mask, as shown in Figure 8-11.**

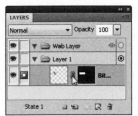

Figure 8-11: Click the chain to unlock it from the image.

This chain lets you move the layer and mask independently.

2. **In the Layers panel, click the mask to select it.**

3. **From the panel menu in the States panel, choose Duplicate State.**

The Duplicate State dialog box appears.

4. **Select the After Current State radio button and click OK.**

State 2 appears.

5. **With the Pointer tool, select the mask and then drag the mask down slightly on the canvas.**

The stars stay in place; only the mask moves.

6. **Repeat Steps 3–5 at least once.**

7. **Test your animation by clicking the Play button in the lower right section of the Fireworks workspace.**

You can come up with some creative animations by using this technique, perhaps using a logo or other text as a mask.

Exporting an Animation

You created it, you tested it, you previewed it, and now you want to use it. To make an animation work, all you have to do is choose the GIF format in the Optimize panel. (GIF is the Web format that supports animation.) No HTML is needed.

To export an animation, follow these steps:

1. **Choose File⇨Export.**

   The Export dialog box appears.

2. **Choose Images Only from the Export drop-down list.**

3. **Name the file.**

4. **Put the file in your site location by navigating to the correct folder and clicking Export.**

Index

976 Adobe Creative Suite 5 Design Premium All-in-One For Dummies